The Monograph and its Chapters

This is one of five volumes that make up the Monograph on the Planning and Design of Tall Buildings. For reference purposes the broad outline of the material contained in the five volumes is as follows:

PC PLANNING AND ENVIRONMENTAL CRITERIA FOR TALL BUILDING

1. Philosophy of Tall Buildings
2. History of Tall Buildings
3. Social Effects of the Environment
4. Sociopolitical Influences
5. Economics
6. Architecture
7. Interference and Environmental Effects
8. Urban Planning
9. External Transportation
10. Parking
11. Operation, Maintenance, and Ownership
12. Energy Conservation
13. Motion Perception and Tolerance
14. Project Management
15. Application of Systems Methodology

SC TALL BUILDING SYSTEMS AND CONCEPTS

1. Structural Systems
2. Mechanical and Service Systems
3. Electrical Systems
4. Vertical and Horizontal Transportation
5. Cladding
6. Partitions, Walls, and Ceilings
7. Foundation Systems
8. Construction Systems

CL TALL BUILDING CRITERIA AND LOADING

1. Gravity Loads and Temperature Effects
2. Earthquake Loading and Response
3. Wind Loading and Wind Effects
4. Fire
5. Accidental Loading
6. Quality Criteria
7. Structural Safety and Probabilistic Methods

SB STRUCTURAL DESIGN OF TALL STEEL BUILDINGS

1. Commentary on Structrual Steel Design
2. Elastic Analysis and Design
3. Plastic Analysis and Design
4. Stability
5. Stiffness
6. Fatigue and Fracture
7. Connections
8. Load and Resistance Factor Design (Limit States Design)
9. Mixed Construction

CB STRUCTURAL DESIGN OF TALL CONCRETE AND MASONRY BUILDINGS

1. Characteristics of Concrete and Masonry Tall Buildings
2. Design Criteria and Safety Provisions
3. Concrete Framing Systems for Tall Buildings
4. Optimization of Tall Concrete Buildings
5. Elastic Analysis
6. Nonlinear Behavior and Analysis
7. Model Analysis
8. Stability
9. Stiffness, Deflections, and Cracking
10. Creep, Shrinkage, and Temperature Effects
11. Design of Cast-in-place Concrete
12. Design of Structures with Precast Concrete Elements
13. Design of Masonry Structures

This Monograph is a major focus of the Council on Tall Buildings and Urban Habitat. The objective is to document the state of art relative to the planning and design of tall buildings and to indicate possible future advances and areas of further research. Please inform the Headquarters of any significant omissions or of additions that should be made.

The opinions expressed are those of the committees and do not necessarily reflect those of the publisher, the professional society sponsors, or the U.S. National Science Foundation which partially supported the work that led to this Monograph.

Published by
American Society of Civil Engineers
345 East 47th Street
New York, N. Y. 10017

Council Headquarters
Fritz Engineering Laboratory–13
Lehigh University
Bethlehem, Pennsylvania 18015

Tall Building
Systems and Concepts

Library of Congress Catalog card number: 80-65692
ISBN 0-87262-239-8

Printed in the United States of America

Monograph on

Planning and Design of Tall Buildings

Volume SC

Tall Building
Systems and Concepts

Group Coordinators

Fazlur R. Khan
John Rankine

Group Editors

Walter P. Moore, Jr.
Howard D. Eberhart
Henry J. Cowan

Group Secretary

Lynn S. Beedle

Council on Tall Buildings and Urban Habitat

Steering Group

F. R. Khan*	Chairman	Skidmore, Owings & Merrill	Chicago
T. Naka*	Vice-Chairman	University of Tokyo	Tokyo
D. Sfintesco*	Past Chairman	C.T.I.C.M.	Paris
L. S. Beedle*	Director	Lehigh University	Bethlehem
G. W. Schulz*	Secretary	Universität Innsbruck	Innsbruck
L. W. Lu	Research Advisor	Lehigh University	Bethlehem
W. H. Arch	Redpath Dorman Long Ltd.		Bedford
R. T. Baum	Jaros, Baum & Bolles		New York
S. Chamecki	UNESCO		Paris
F. L. Codella	Tower International		Cleveland
C. M. Correa	Architect		Bombay
H. J. Cowan	University of Sydney		Sydney
B. M. Dornblatt*	B. M. Dornblatt and Associates, Inc.		New Orleans
P. Dubas	Swiss Federal Institute of Technology		Zurich
J. F. Fitzgerald	Schal Associates, Inc.		Chicago
G. F. Fox	Howard, Needles, Tammen, & Bergendoff		New York
Y. Friedman*	Architect		Paris
B. Frommes	IFHP		Luxembourg
J. M. Garrelts	Columbia University		New York
M. P. Gaus	National Science Foundation		Washington
J. A. Gilligan	United States Steel Corporation		Pittsburgh
I. V. Gramolin	GOSSTROY		Moscow
T. R. Higgins	Consulting Engineer		New York
B. G. Johnston	University of Arizona		Tucson
T. C. Kavanagh	Iffland Kavanagh Waterbury		Hastings-on-Hudson
H. R. Lane	H. R. Lane AIA Assoc. Architects		Los Angeles
I. Martin	Capacete-Martin & Assoc.		San Juan
C. Massonnet	Université de Liège		Liège
W. A. Milek	American Institute of Steel Construction		New York
A. Moharram	Arab Consulting Engineers		Cairo
R. Y. Okamoto	Department of City Planning		San Francisco
L. Ouyang	Ouyang and Associates, Architects		Hong Kong
M. Paparoni*	Equisticaca Consultores Associates		Caracas
E. O. Pfrang	National Bureau of Standards		Washington
E. A. Picardi	Oxford Development Group, Ltd.		Edmonton
J. Rankine	Rankine & Hill Engineering Consultants		Sydney
R. C. Reese	Consulting Engineer		Toledo
L. E. Robertson	Skilling, Helle, Christiansen, Robertson		New York
W. A. Rutes	Holiday Inns, Inc.		Memphis
G. Sebestyén	Hungarian Institute for Building Science		Budapest
P. H. Sedway	Sedway/Cooke		San Francisco
R. Thoma	Hentrich, Petschnigg & Partners		Düsseldorf
B. Thürlimann	Swiss Federal Institute of Technology		Zurich
E. K. Timby	Howard, Needles, Tammen & Bergendoff		New York
A. W. Turchick	American Society of Civil Engineers		New York
I. M. Viest	Bethlehem Steel Corporation		Bethlehem
W. Voss	Henn & Voss		Braunschweig
G. Wästlund	Kungliga Tekniska Hogskolan		Stockholm

*Member of Executive Committee

Editorial Committee

L. S. Beedle (Ch.), D. Sfintesco, F. R. Khan, L. W. Lu, G. W. Schulz, R. Kowalczyk, M. P. Gaus, J. I. Moyer

Group PC: T. C. Kavanagh, R. Y. Okamoto, Y. Friedman, R. Thoma, R. C. Herrenkohl, W. Henn, C. Norberg-Schulz

Group SC: F. R. Khan, J. Rankine, W. P. Moore, H. D. Eberhart, H. J. Cowan, L. S. Beedle

Group CL: L. E. Robertson, T. Naka, R. J. Mainstone, E. H. Gaylord, L. W. Lu

Group SB: T. R. Higgins, P. Dubas, C. N. Gaylord, M. Watabe, L. W. Lu

Group CB: R. C. Reese, I. Martin, B. Thürlimann, G. Wästlund, J. G. MacGregor, I. Lyse, T. Huang

Chairman, Vice-Chairman, and Editors of each committee (identified in each chapter), affiliates representing sponsors, and selected national representatives.

Professional Society Sponsors

International Association for Bridge and Structural Engineering (IABSE)
American Society of Civil Engineers (ASCE)
American Institute of Architects (AIA)
American Planning Association (APA)
International Federation for Housing and Planning (IFHP)
International Union of Architects (UIA)

Foreword

This is one volume of a multivolume Monograph bringing together current knowledge about tall buildings themselves and about their interactions with the urban environment. Topics covered in the Monograph include structural and service systems, foundation, loadings and structural safety, structural design methods, architecture and urban planning, related cultural, social, and political factors, and the management and operation of buildings in use.

The entire Monograph consists of 52 chapters arranged in the following five volumes:

> Volume PC: Planning and Environmental Criteria for Tall Buildings
> Volume SC: Tall Building Systems and Concepts
> Volume CL: Tall Building Criteria and Loading
> Volume SB: Structural Design of Tall Steel Buildings
> Volume CB: Structural Design of Tall Concrete and Masonry Buildings

This particular volume (SC) deals with the structural, mechanical, and electrical systems of the tall building, and with its foundation, its construction, its cladding, and with its internal subdivision.

Volume SC concentrates on the systems; and in the case of loading and structural design, it provides the concepts that are the basis for much of the material contained in Volumes CL, SB, and CB. On the other hand, the system considerations, as well as the design concepts with regard to the mechanical, electrical, service, and vertical transportation aspects are self-contained within this particular volume. The work rests on the premises and understanding of the planning and environmental criteria that are contained in Volume PC; and there is frequent reference thereto.

The Monograph as a whole should be of value to all those with major responsibilities for planning and deign practice. In addition to its function to communicate to knowledgeable persons the state-of-the-art and the most advanced knowledge in the field, the text on a given topic may well be most useful to those in *other* disciplines. The Council has seen considerable benefit accrue from the mix of professions, and this is no less true in the Monograph itself. In keeping with this, and to afford such benefit to all appropriate professionals, every effort has been made to pro-. vide a comprehensive glossary for each volume.

In the same vein, where more than one point of view is appropriate, those views are set forth. Since there are several instances in which there is no final answer, there are numerous points of controversy; and such controversy has not been avoided.

Tall Buildings

What is a tall building? The important criterion is whether or not the design is influenced by some aspect of "tallness." A tall building is *not* defined by its height or number of stories. A suggested definition, then, might be "a building in which 'tallness' strongly influences planning, design, and use"; or "a building whose height creates different conditions in the design, construction, and use from those that exist in 'common' buildings of a certain region and period."

As a consequence, there is some variation among chapters on this matter of tallness. Each one has proceeded on the basis that "tall" constitutes whatever creates the "tall building problem" for that particular subject. Topics are not included in the Monograph simply because they pertain to buildings in general. If, on the other hand, a topic is particularly important for a tall building, then the objective has been to treat that topic even if it is also a problem for all buildings

A "building" is a structure that is designed essentially for residential, commercial, or industrial purposes. other categories include institutional, public assembly, and multiple-use structures. An essential characteristic of a building is that it has floors. Structures designed for entertainment, such as towers, monuments, and "space needles," generally are excluded from consideration.

The Council

This Monograph has been prepared by the various topical and advisory committees of the Council on Tall Buildings and Urban Habitat. The Council is an activity sponsored by engineering, architectural, and planning professionals throughout the world, and was established to study and report on all aspects of the planning, design, construction, and operation of tall buildings.

The Professional Society sponsors are the International Association for Bridge and Structural Engineering (IABSE), the American Society of Civil Engineers (ASCE), the American Institute of Architects (AIA), the American Planning Association (APA), the International Federation for Housing and Planning (IFHP), and the International Union of Architects (UIA). The particular contribution of several of these are described further in the Foreword of Volume CL.

The Council does not take an advocacy role for tall buildings. Rather, its premise is that in those situations in which they are viable, it seeks to encourage the use of the latest knowledge in their implementation.

Direct contributions to the Monograph have come from many countries and many people. One further notable characteristic is that much of the material has been prepared by practicing designers. Members of design and industrial firms account for nearly two-thirds of the 175-member editorial team. The wide mix of disciplines has also been notable—right from the initial planning phase to the final reviews of the written contributions. To this the Monograph owes its unusually broad perspective.

In addition to the editorial committee, more than 800 individuals supplied specific contributions. All told, about 1300 committee members from 78 countries had opportunity to review at least one chapter.

The idea of developing a Monograph was part of the original concept when the Council was formed ten years ago as the "Joint Committee on Tall Buildings." In 1968 there developed an awareness of the significant amount of research information—and design approaches as well—that were not documented in a form that was useful in advanced design work. There was a need for a comprehensive examination of all aspects of the topic, and the Monograph was envisioned as the mechanism for disseminating as much of the results of that study as practicable. The urgency of meeting that need stemmed from the exploding urban population creating increasing demand for tall buildings, the requirement for economy of construction, and the evident neglect of human factors in urban design at the expense of livability and quality of life.

The major steps that were then followed by the Council in the production of the Monograph are described in the Foreword of Volume CB. In the early days both the Critical Path Method (CPM) and the Program Evaluation and Review Technique (PERT) approaches were tried. With respect to forcing a careful development of all the steps involved, the effort was most successful. But as a method of assuring that deadlines were met, it did not work—largely because a project such as this depends so much upon volunteer effort. In such a case the best deadline still remains a conference or meeting.

High-Rise Building Data Base

Where are the tall buildings in the world? What are their heights? Of what material are they built? How are they used? What has been the record of their skyward climb? This is the subject of the "High-Rise Building Data Base" that is included as an appendix to this volume. It consists of a tabular presentation of the answers to the above questions, covering the tallest buildings in each country as well as the tall buildings in the major cities of the world.

The data are only as up-to-date (and as accurate) as our advisors could provide from each city. In some parts of the world tall building construction is very active. In other parts it is slow or nonexistent. Consequently, in those cases where the reader has information available that is not included, the data should be forwarded to Headquarters for incorporation in the computer data base and for later publication.

The following classifications of the use of high-rise buildings have been adopted:

1. Commercial: office, store and shops, bank, public utility.
2. Residential: apartment (rental and condominium), hotel, dormitory, hostel.
3. Industrial: warehouse, manufacture ("flatted factory"), material processing.
4. Institutional: school, hospital (health care facility), laboratory, library, museum, correctional institution, court of law, religious edifice.
5. Public Assembly: theater, hall and auditorium (meeting rooms), restaurant, observation.
6. Special Purpose: transport interface (air, rail, bus, ship), garage (parking deck), mausoleum.
7. Multiple Use (megastructures that are various combinations of the above).

Units, Symbols, and References

With regard to the units, it will be evident to the reader that complete uniformity in the text was not achieved. The general guideline was to use SI units first, followed by American units in parentheses and metric when necessary. A conversion table for units is supplied at the end of the volume. Because of the extensive amount of new artwork that otherwise would have been involved (and the consequent delay), many previously existing drawings and tables remain with their original units. However, enough conversions are given throughout to enable a proper interpretation.

A list of symbols appears at the end of the volume. Because of variations among chapters the chapter number is identified with each citation.

The spelling was agreed at the outset to be "American" English. An early decision relating to the method of citing and arranging the references and bibliographical material was made. The following format is suggested for those who wish to refer to a chapter, to a volume, or to the Monograph as a whole in their own publications:

To refer to a chapter:

Council on Tall Buildings, Committee 2C, 1980
ELECTRICAL SYSTEMS, Chapter SC-3, Vol. SC of Monograph on Planning and Design of Tall Buildings, ASCE, New York.

To refer to a particular volume:

Council on Tall Buildings, Group SC, 1980
TALL BUILDING SYSTEMS AND CONCEPTS, Volume SC of Monograph on Planning and Design of Tall Buildings, ASCE, New York.

To refer to the entire Monograph:

Council on Tall Buildings, 1978–1981
PLANNING AND DESIGN OF TALL BUILDINGS, a Monograph in 5 volumes, ASCE, New York.

The Monograph has been, from the start, the prime focus of the Council's activity, and it is intended that its periodic revision and the implementation of its ideas and recommendations should be a continuing activity on both national and international levels. Readers who find that some topic is inadequately treated or calls for further thought are invited to bring that fact to our attention. Perhaps they also can draw our attention to publications or recent research results that have been overlooked. It is planned that periodically a "Monograph Update" containing new information about tall buildings and the urban habitat will be collected and disseminated. Every reader is urged, therefore, to submit any new material for inclusion in future revisions and addenda. Each committee will then have an opportunity to update its material.

As one of the Committee leaders said, "We never can reach the 'perfect' Monograph. A Monograph as it is at this moment, published as soon as possible, is much better than the perfect Monograph never published at all."

Acknowledgment

This work would not have been possible but for the financial support of our major sponsor, the National Science Foundation, which supported the program out of which the Monograph developed. The understanding and support of Dr. Michael Gaus of NSF has been most appreciated. In addition, the following individuals and organizations have become sponsors during the most recent years: Gerald D. Hines Interests; Jaros, Baum and Bolles; Kozai Club; Prof. Ahmad Moharram; Skidmore, Owings and Merrill; and Skilling, Helle, Christiansen, Robertson.

Acknowledgment is next due the staff at the Fritz Engineering Laboratory with whom it has been my pleasure to be associated. Special mention is due Dr. Le-Wu Lu who has been codirector of the project from which this effort has evolved. Other staff members involved were: Professor George Driscoll, Nuray Aydinoglu (Research Associate), Jack Gera (Draftsman), Richard Sopko (Photographer), Mary Snyder (Secretary), Barbara Bryan (Administrative Assistant), Perry Green (Research Assistant), Pat McHugh (Research Assistant), and Suzanne Gimson, Edward Beedle, Mark Follet, and Barry Anderson (Student Assistants).

Special acknowledgment is due Jamie Moyer, who since 1975 has served as the associate responsible for all processing and production phases of the Monograph effort at Lehigh. She performed outstanding service not only to us on the headquarters staff but to each member of the editorial committee.

We are indebted to David Dresia, Paul Parisi, Richard Torrens, and Irving Amron (ASCE) for guidance and direction during the publication phases of the work. Janet Davis served notably as editorial consultant to ASCE. Her attention to editorial detail was remarkable.

Next, tribute is due the Chairmen and Vice-Chairmen who provided leadership to the committee. To the Committee Editors fell the major burden of writing, editing, adjusting, and rewriting. Their contributions have been most significant. All of these are identified on the title page of the respective chapters.

The true "authors" of the Monograph were sometimes the committee editors, but in most cases they were the contributors and reporters whose papers formed the essential first drafts—the starting point. These are identified in the acknowledgment page that follows the title page for each chapter.

The coordinating and editing effort on the volume as a whole has been the work of the Group Coordinators, Fazlur R. Khan and John Rankine, and the Group Editors, Walter P. Moore, Jr., Howard D. Eberhart, and Henry J. Cowan. "Jack" Cowan applied his skills not only from his experience in Australia as educator in both structural engineering and architecture, but also from his extensive experience as an author in his own right. Howard Eberhart similarly contributed from his wide-ranging experience at the University of California, Berkeley. Walter Moore, as a practicing engineer in Houston, Texas, brought to the effort his considerable experience in the design of tall buildings, especially in that unique city. The Council is equally indebted to John Rankine whose wide design experience in Australia and other parts of the world has made him well qualified in his role as a group leader.

The Council has been most fortunate to have the leadership of Fazlur R. Khan, who has been responsible for the structural design of some of the world's tallest buildings and of many innovations in approach. Not only that, his grasp of the interaction between engineering, architecture, and planning has played no small role in the development of this volume and in the progress the Council has made over the years. He currently serves as Chairman of the Council.

The Council acknowledges, with sincere gratitude, the contributions of all of these leaders.

Lehigh University
Bethlehem, Pennsylvania
1980

Lynn S. Beedle
Editor-in-Chief

Preface

Skyscrapers first appeared in a number of urban centers in the United States nearly 100 years ago. Since that time, steady advances have been made in the application of technical principles to the construction of tall buildings. The period of the 1930s made its mark with the construction of the 102-story Empire State Building in New York. After World War II the population explosion, in combination with rapid urbanization, provided the impetus for the development of new and improved systems and concepts for tall buildings.

Although tall buildings are a relatively recent development, it is certainly true that monuments and edifices of considerable height were built in much earlier times. The pyramids of Giza in Egypt, the Mayan temples in Tikal, Guatemala, the Kutab Minar in India are but a few examples of man's desire to reach for the sky. Tall buildings are first of all tall structures and as such have interested the structural engineer. Dr. Leo Finzi at the 1973 Italian National Conference on Tall Buildings underlined this special interest when he said, "For the structural engineer, the tall building has a fascination in itself because the design of the structure raises, and in a way that cannot be denied, all the more up-to-date and difficult problems concerned with conceiving, calculating, making and erecting these structures." Building tall buildings and towers has fascinated mankind from the beginning of civilization. In August, 1973, at the National Conference on the Planning and Design of Tall Buildings in Tokyo, Japan, Professor Yasumi Yoshitake began his talk with a biblical passage in Genesis about the Tower of Babel. "Come," they said, "let us build ourselves a city and a tower with its top in the heavens, and let us make a name for ourselves, lest we be scattered abroad upon the face of the whole earth." He further states that this story "seems to reveal the innate human desire for a tall structure . . . (but) also implies the dream and the fear which architects and architectural engineers in Japan now have at the coming of the age of tall buildings."

The practicality of the tall building requires the consideration of many other technological and planning factors beyond those essential to the character of the structure itself. It should be recalled that the first system which allowed the structural engineer to develop the modern skyscraper was the invention by Elisha Otis in the 1850s of the first safe vertical transportation system. That breakthrough set the stage for other planning and technological systems to be brought to bear to meet the challenges of buildings of even greater height. Vertical transportation is an essential part of the tall building; but as buildings get taller, special considerations need to be given in many other areas. The internal environment, the fire safety needs, and other emergency requirements for tall buildings require the compatible development of their own system. Even the architectural elements, which for a short building are left entirely to traditional architectural detailing, need to be carefully analyzed in terms of such factors as building movement and the long-term effects of deflection, so that all doors, partitions, windows, and exterior cladding will perform satisfactorily through seasonal changes over a long period of time.

Whereas the structural system remains dominant, there is an increasing awareness that the success of the tall building architecturally, functionally, and economically very much depends on the innovative development of compatible systems of all elements of the building, including, for example, fire fighting, communicating, heating, ventilating, air conditioning, plumbing, partitions, walls, and cladding. In fact, all systems should go hand in hand in the total design process for a tall building. Indeed there have been occasions on which the important service systems have had to be fitted into a building only after its structure was designed and finalized. Speaking as a building services engineer, Mr. R. Banbam at the Regional Conference on Tall Buildings in Bangkok, Thailand, commented that "Regrettably, in Asia, all too often he (the building services engineer) is required to design systems around an architectural plan and a structural system which have been developed to a point where modifications cannot be made to either." This statement truly represents the thrust and purpose of this volume on Systems and Concepts.

The need to work as a team in the early formulation of the building design is a necessity all over the world. Every professional working on the complex problems involved in the tall building needs to realize the impact that his concepts will have on other members of the team. Building systems are not independent, but rather they are interrelated beginning with the foundation systems and ending with the construction systems. As such, even in this age of specialization, everyone needs to understand and appreciate this interrelationship of systems from the very beginning of the project.

This volume tends to treat the various systems independently by chapters; but because of their interdependence, they are grouped together in this one volume. They represent the current state-of-the-art of tall buildings systems around the world and should serve to stimulate the imagination of the reader to develop even more advanced systems. The search for better, newer, and more efficient systems and concepts will continue throught the coming years, and we hope that this volume of the Monograph will act as important source material for the present design of tall buildings, and that it will be a foundation for future innovation.

Fazlur R. Khan
John Rankine
Walter P. Moore, Jr.
Howard D. Eberhart
Henry J. Cowan

1980

Contents

SC-3   Electrical Systems

SC-4   Vertical and Horizontal Transportation

SC-5 Cladding

SC-6 Partitions, Walls, and Ceilings

SC-7 Foundation Systems

SC-8 Construction Systems

Tall Building
Systems and Concepts

Chapter SC-1

Structural Systems

Prepared by Committee 3 (Structural Systems) of the Council on Tall Buildings and Urban Habitat as part of the Monograph on the Planning and Design of Tall Buildings.

John V. Christiansen   Chairman
Fritz Reinitzhuber   Vice-Chairman
Walter P. Moore, Jr.   Editor

AUTHOR ACKNOWLEDGMENT

Special acknowledgment is due those individuals whose contributions and papers formed the substantial first drafts of the various sections of this chapter. First are the state-of-art reporters from the 1972 International Conference whose material was published in the Lehigh Proceedings. For the indicated sections, these individuals are:

L. W. Lu, Section 1.1
U. Yuceoglu, Section 1.1
Yu. D. Bychenkov, Section 1.2
J. V. Christiansen, Sections 1.2, 1.3
R. O. Disque, Sections 1.2, 1.3
T. Hisatoku, Section 1.2
G. F. König, Sections 1.2, 1.3
J. Kozák, Section 1.2
N. G. Matkov, Section 1.2

F. Nishikawa, Section 1.2
H. Sontag, Section 1.2
H. P. Vasiliev, Section 1.2
M. Kavyrchine, Section 1.3
A. F. Nassetta, Section 1.3
L. E. Robertson, Sections 1.3, 1.4
A. G. Sokolov, Section 1.3
A. H. Yorkdale, Section 1.3
H. Bandel, Section 1.4

In addition to the state-of-art reporters, valuable discussions were presented at the 1972 International Conference by the following people:

R. Dziewolski, Section 1.2
W. P. Moore, Jr., Sections 1.2, 1.3
F. K. Reinitzhuber, Sections 1.2, 1.3
H. Bandel, Sections 1.3, 1.4

R. A. Sofronie, Section 1.4
R. J. Brungraber
J. Nasser

CONTRIBUTORS

The following is a complete list of those who have submitted written material for possible use in the chapter, whether or not that material was used in the final version. The Committee Chairman and Editor were given quite complete latitude. Frequently length limitations precluded the inclusion of much valuable material. The Bibliography contains all contributions. The contributors are: H. Bandel, J. F. Brotchie, R. J. Brungraber, Yu. D. Bychenkov, J. V. Christiansen, R. O. Disque, R. Dziewolski, I. Erenyi, T. Hisatoku, M. Kavyrchine, G. F. König, J. Kozák, R. E. Lewis, L. W. Lu, K. G. Martin, N. G. Matkov, W. P. Moore, Jr., J. Nasser, A. F. Nassetta, F. Nishikawa, Z. Pawlowski, P. Pun, F. K. Reinitzhuber, L. E. Robertson, R. A. Sofronie, A. G. Sokolov, H. Sontag, A. P. Vasiliev, A. H. Yorkdale, U. Yuceoglu.

COMMITTEE MEMBERS

L. G. Aycardi, H. Bandel, N. G. Bondre, G. E. Brandow, J. F. Brotchie, R. J. Brungraber, Yu. D. Bychenkov, P. W. Chen, J. V. Christiansen, P. Cizek, J. H. Daniels, J. De Bremaeker, F. De Miranda, D. Dicke, R. O. Disque, R. Dziewolski, I. Erenyi, D. G. Eyre, D. Fournier, H. Gallegos, C. N. Gaylord, G. B. Godfrey, R. J. Hansen, R. D. Hanson, S. H. Hardin, T. Hisatoku, L. Y. Huang, J. W. Kamerling, M. Kavyrchine, G. F. König, J. Kozák, G. Lacombe, R. E. Lewis, M. A. Macias-Rendon, J. Mason, N. G. Matkov, G. G. Mayor, A. C. Megerdichian, W. P. Moore, Jr., J. Munoz-Duque, J. Nasser, A. F. Nassetta, F. Nishikawa, A. Ostapenko, Z. Pawlowski, T. Perzynski, E. A. Picardi, M. V. Posokhin, P. Pun, W. Quasebarth, G. Rahulan, F. K. Reinitzhuber, L. E. Robertson, B. Rubanenko, D. Sfintesco, R. A. Sofronie, A. G. Sokolov, H. Sontag, E. Suzuki, R. S. Taboloff, A. R. Toakley, G. Van Resbeck, A. P. Vasiliev, E. P. Wiesinger, R. N. Wright, M. S. Yolles, A. H. Yorkdale, S. Zaczek.

SC-1 Structural Systems

1.1 INTRODUCTION

In general, the structural system of a building is a three-dimensional complex assemblage of various combinations of interconnected structural elements. These may be discrete members or they may be continuous assemblages. The primary function of the structural system is to carry effectively and safely all the loads acting on the building, and eventually to transmit them to the foundation. A structural system is therefore expected to:

1. Carry dynamic and static vertical loads.

2. Carry horizontal loads due to wind and earthquake effects.

3. Resist stresses caused by temperature and shrinkage effects.

4. Resist external or internal blast and impact loads.

5. Resist and help damp vibrations and fatigue effects.

In addition, a structural system is usually subject to the following constraints:

1. It should conform with the architectural requirements and those of the user or owner, or both.

2. It interacts with and facilitates an appropriate solution to the service systems, such as heating, ventilating, and air conditioning, horizontal and vertical transport, and other electrical and mechanical systems.

3. It facilitates simple and fast erection of the building.

4. It is resistant to fire.

5. It enables the building, the foundation, and the ground to interact properly.

6. It is economical.

In the process of selecting the most suitable structural system for a tall building, several factors have to be considered and optimized in addition to the height of the

3

building. For this complicated process, no simple clear-cut method is available. The design team must use every available means—imagination, ingenuity, previous experience, and relevant literature—to arrive at the best possible solution in each particular case.

In various types of structural systems, whether they are steel, concrete, or composite systems, there are several subsystems or components common to all. These can be grouped in the following way:

1. Floor systems.

2. Vertical load resisting systems.

3. Horizontal load resisting systems.

4. Structural joints. (This subject is covered in Chapter SB-7 for steel structures, Chapter CB-5 for concrete structures, and Chapter SB-9 for mixed structures.)

5. Energy dissipation systems (for buildings subjected to substantial dynamic loading).

The most frequently used tall building structural systems for steel and concrete structural frames based on their tallness criteria are given as examples in Figs. 1.1 and 1.2 (Khan, 1974). These along with other systems will be considered in the later sections of this chapter.

In principle, in any structural system, all of the load-resisting systems and components should be equally active and ideally should work together under all types and combinations of design loads. In other words, the parts of the structural system that primarily resist horizontal loads should be able to contribute to the resistance to vertical loads as well. This is, in fact, the case in some structural systems, and many individual components such as floor systems are common to (or merged together with) either or both horizontal load resisting frames and vertical load resisting frames. Even if the two framing systems are discrete and sufficiently separate, one must always consider them as being interrelated. Consequently, their possible interactions should be taken into account. We will, however, attempt to isolate them and treat each separately in order to facilitate the discussion.

The most efficient structural system is the one that manages to combine all the structural subsystems or components into a completely integrated system in which most of the elements take part in resisting the loads. However, this ideal case is unlikely to be fully achieved in practice, due to constraints such as efficiency and ease of assembly and construction, manufacturing of joints, economic considerations, and other requirements.

In this chapter, the following structural systems and their subsystems will be discussed from a broad viewpoint: (1) Framing systems to resist gravity and vertical loads (including floor systems); (2) framing systems to resist horizontal loads; and (3) energy dissipation systems.

1.2 FRAMING SYSTEMS TO RESIST GRAVITY LOADS

It is extremely difficult to apply accurately a classification system that succeeds in isolating criteria for tall buildings. Many methods have been tried, among them the following groupings:

1. Number of stories or building height.

2. Building usage or type.

3. Building materials (steel versus concrete).

4. Building structural system.

This certainly in no way exhausts the possibilities that have been proposed at one time or another, but it does indicate the difficulties. Nevertheless it was concluded that a reasonable method could be arrived at based upon the type of structural system used to resist the loads.

Every building, whether it is tall or short, must have a structural system capable of carrying all kinds of loads—vertical, horizontal, temperature, etc. In principle, the entire resisting system of the building should be equally active under all types of loading. In other words, the structure resisting horizontal loads should be able to

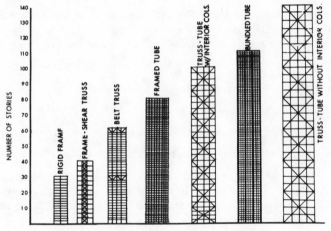

Fig. 1.1 Types of steel structure *(Khan, 1974)*

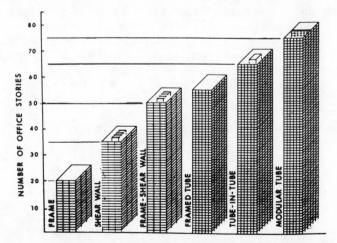

Fig. 1.2 Concrete structural systems for office buildings *(Khan, 1974)*

resist vertical loads as well, and many individual elements are common to both types of systems. In short, one must always remember the possible interaction of structural systems even though we will attempt to isolate them in this chapter.

Although the combination of systems to resist all types of loads concurrently is normal, this section of the chapter considers only the resistance to gravity loads. The framing systems chosen to resist gravity loads may be divided into: (1) The horizontal framing system or the floor structure; and (2) the vertical framing system or the columns, bearing walls, and hangers.

1   Horizontal Framing Systems—Floor Structures

Floor structures are responsible for a high percentage of the cost of tall buildings. Although such floor structures do not differ substantially from those found in low-rise buildings, there are certain aspects and properties that must be borne in mind:

1. Dead weight of the floor. For tall buildings it is certainly reasonable to reduce the weight of the floors, permitting a reduction in the size of the supporting structures (columns, foundation) and the use of larger spans.

2. Capacity of the floor to handle loads during the erection process.

3. Suitability for the accommodation of ducts and piping.

4. Fire resistance properties.

5. Suitability for continuous construction regardless of the season of the year.

6. Elimination of extensive temporary shoring procedures.

Today there are tendencies to use larger floor spans in tall buildings, particularly in steel structures. This is primarily due to the desire to create greater space flexibility in the use of the floor. In addition it makes it possible to accommodate a greater variety of tenant floor plans.

The floor structures can be built using elements of steel and reinforced concrete in various combinations. (However, in these days of industrial unrest, it is undesirable that a floor system should contain a major element that can only be obtained from a single source, if a change to an alternative element would involve considerable expense and redesign.) Structural systems, of course, are influenced by the material used, but in all cases they are a combination of slabs, joists and girders, and secondary beams (in the case of larger spacing of floor beams). The characteristic element for the whole floor structure is the floor slab, whose thickness and reinforcement is dependent upon the span, the loading and the support conditions.

In categorizing types of floor slabs, the following structural systems may be distinguished: (1) Two-way systems; (2) one-way systems; and (3) beam and slab systems.

Two-way systems include:

1. Flat plates supported by columns [Fig. 1.3(a)]. The vertical loads are transmitted to the column from all directions.

2. Flat slab supported by columns with capitals or drop panels, or both [Fig. 1.3(b)]. This system is similar to the flat plate except it maintains a thicker

section over the columns to accommodate the higher shears and moments found at that location.

3. Slab of constant thickness [Fig. 1.4(a)]. This type of slab spans in two directions between girders or bearing walls. The boundary conditions may provide simple supports or continuous supports in one or two directions. Torsional restraints may be found in the supporting elements.

4. Slab with waffles [Fig. 1.4(b)]. This slab has a waffle pattern in the middle part of its span to reduce the dead weight of the system.

5. Two-way joists (ribbed slab) [Fig. 1.4(c)]. This system and the conditions for its use are similar to slabs with waffles.

One-way systems include:

1. Slabs of constant thickness [Fig. 1.5(a)]. These slabs span in one direction

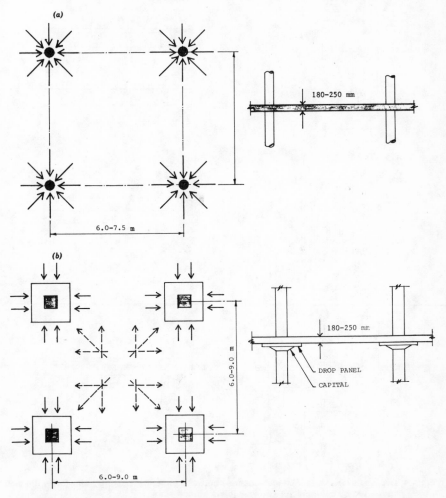

Fig. 1.3 Flat slabs: (a) Point supports (columns); (b) Supported by columns with capital

with spans of 3 m to 8 m (10 ft to 25 ft). The support conditions vary from simple to continuous.

2. Closely spaced joists [Fig. 1.5(b)]. The joists have the capacity of transverse distribution of loads and are, from the statical point of view, similar to the one-way slab of constant thickness.

Beam and slab systems are shown in Fig. 1.6. This type of slab is supported by beams (or secondary beams) which are closely spaced at about 1 m to 4 m (3 ft to 14 ft). The slab can be simply supported or continuous, and may be composite with the joists. These systems are most typical with floor structures made of steel.

Integration of mechanical and electrical services often plays a significant role in

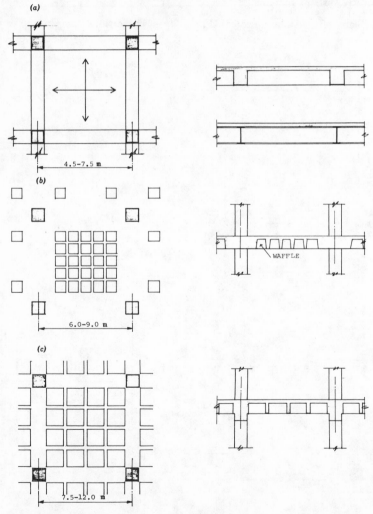

Fig. 1.4 Two-way systems: (a) Flat slab spanned between girders or bearing walls; (b) Waffle slab supported by columns; (c) Two-way joists (ribbed slab)

the choice of the proper floor system. The accommodation of ductwork, pipes, and wiring in the floor structure usually takes place in one of the following three ways (Fig. 1.7):

1. Lattice floor joists and girders. Piping and wiring pass through the latticed webs (typical for large spans and steel structures).

2. Floor joists of small depth spanning one-way or beam and slab system with a smaller spacing crossing the main direction of the piping and wiring. The deeper girders may eventually be pierced by openings.

3. Integral floor slab structures of minimum depth where the piping and wiring are suspended and covered by a soffit (typical for small spans and reinforced concrete structures).

Floor Structures in Concrete.   The possibilities for the various uses of concrete in floor structures are summarized in Fig. 1.8. In determining the advantages and disadvantages of concrete, many factors must be considered. These include the dead load, heat and sound insulation, damping of vibrations, fire resistance, durability, modulus of elasticity, quality, production, economies, and speed of erection.

Slabs of uniform thickness.   As previously stated, these slabs may be part of either a one-way or a two-way system. Characteristics are as follows.

Description.   Thickness: 100 mm to 250 mm (4 in. to 10 in.). Span: 3 m to 8 m (10 ft to 25 ft).

Advantages.   Minimum story heights; minimum structural depth; smooth soffit; adaptable to an irregular support layout; flexibility of installation; good heat and sound insulation; and good damping characteristics.

Disadvantages.   Heavy system (requires larger foundation, vertical supports, etc.); relatively short span capability; relatively large deflection.

Applications.   Hotels and apartments—less often in office buildings. Examples are:

1. The Lake Point Tower, 70-story apartment building in Chicago, USA.

2. The Concordia, high-rise 48-story apartment building in Cologne, Germany.

3. A multitude of 30-story to 50-story apartment buildings in Chicago and New York, USA.

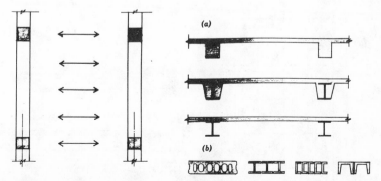

Fig. 1.5 One-way systems: (a) One-way slab of constant thickness; (b) Joists with transverse distribution capacity

4. Hotel in Hradec Králové, Czechoslovakia.

5. Apartment building in Puerto Cabello, Venezuela.

6. Office building Gebruder Sulzer in Wintertur, Switzerland.

Concrete joist structure.

Description. This is a system of a thin slab cast integrally with relatively narrow and closely spaced ribs which may be arranged in a one-way pattern (commonly called pan joists when it is poured in place), or a two-way pattern (referred to as a waffle slab). The one-way system is suitable for prefabrication using precast elements. Waffle slabs are formed by pans (steel, wood, plastic, asbestocement, ferrocement, cardboard, etc.). Due to the forming costs, this system can be relatively expensive at times.

In Great Britain, 300-mm, 400-mm, and 500-mm (12-in., 16-in., and 20-in.) depth waffle slabs are used with spans varying from 6 m to 16 m (20 ft to 52 ft) (Fig. 1.9), and with 200-mm, 300-mm, 400-mm, and 500-mm depths for one-way construction with spans ranging from 4.5 m to 13.5 m (15 ft to 45 ft). In the United States, the depths range from 150 mm to 610 mm (6 in. to 24 in.) for poured-in-place systems, and from 510 mm to 1 m (20 in. to 40 in.) for precast systems, with spans in the range of 8 m to 14 m (26 ft to 46 ft) being common. Spans may be increased by as much as 50% if the joists are post-tensioned.

Advantages. It is a medium to long span system. It readily allows for small perforations to handle piping, ductwork, and other mechanical-electrical systems (Fig. 1.10). It is a relatively lightweight concrete system, yet it has stiffness and may be used as a component in the lateral load resistance system.

Disadvantages. It is not particularly suitable when layouts of supports are

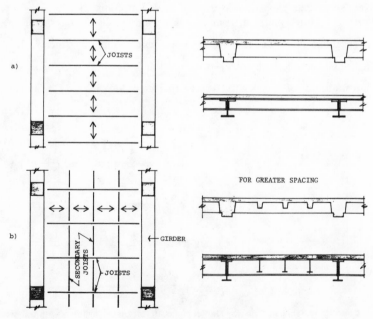

Fig. 1.6 Beam and slab systems

irregular. It is not readily adaptable to irregular bay sizes and shapes. The finished soffit is not usually suitable for exposed architectural application, and it is sometimes difficult to frame large openings.

Applications.   Office buildings and commercial structures. Examples are:

1. Office building BASF in Ludwigshafen, Germany.

2. One Shell Plaza Building in Houston, USA.

3. The CBS Building, New York, USA.

One Shell Plaza, Houston, Texas *(Courtesy: Ezra Stoller)*

4. Canadian Stock Exchange Tower in Montreal, Canada.

5. Standard Bank Centre in Johannesburg, South Africa.

Beam and slab system.

Description. The beam and slab system in concrete consists of a 100-mm to 180-mm (4-in. to 7-in.) slab supported by beams spaced generally from 3 m to 8 m (10 ft to 25 ft) on center. It is desirable to have the beam depth not much less than 1/15 to 1/20 of the span. The problem of depth may be overcome in several ways. In apartment buildings, the beams may be placed along the partition lines and the beam soffits may be placed at the door lintels. The beam depth may be reduced by post-tensioning. The beam and slab may form a composite system with precast elements.

Advantages. It is a long span system. It is readily adapted to large openings, such as those required for stairs, elevators, and mechanical shafts. It is adaptable to any size and shape of building and any plan layout. It is a relatively lightweight concrete system. Precast elements may be used (pre- or post-tensioning).

Disadvantages. It is a deep structural system. Nonstandard wooden forms usually have to be used.

Applications. In office and commercial buildings and in apartment buildings. Examples are:

1. Lonza office building in Basel, Switzerland.

2. Telefunken office building in Berlin, Germany.

3. City Hall, Toronto, Canada.

4. Australia Square Tower Building, in Sydney, Australia.

5. RVHP office building in Moscow, USSR.

Floor Structures in Steel. The one characteristic element of the whole floor structure is the floor slab. The materials used for floor slabs are: (1) Ceramic; (2) reinforced concrete, either cast-in-place or precast; and (3) metal deck with a concrete cover layer.

Concrete is an important component in all floor systems. The concrete has a load-carrying function (at least a load-distribution function). Also, it is required for acoustical reasons and for fire separation between the stories.

The composite structural behavior between the floor slab and the steel girders when achieved can improve the economy and stiffness of the structural system. A composite system is most effective for longer spans and for higher applied loads.

Ceramic slabs. The application of ceramic slabs is an older structural system used mainly in combination with masonry walls. There are many kinds of ceramic slabs in use. In Fig. 1.11, the bottom flange of the steel joist is covered with concrete to support lightweight concrete molded bricks. All elements are made monolithic by concrete cast in place. The spacing of joists is relatively small, amounting to about 610 mm (2 ft). In the final stage, this system is similar to the one-way system.

Fig. 1.12 represents a solution with hollow ceramic plates supported by means of ceramic heels on the bottom flanges of steel joists. The spacing of joists varies from 0.90 m to 1.20 m (3 ft to 4 ft). The ceramic plates support a lightweight fill, which is topped and stiffened by a concrete layer.

These systems are simple, and they do not require heavy construction equipment. Due to the large mass they are acoustically satisfactory. They are seldom used in tall buildings because of the larger dead load, the higher labor costs created by the necessity of plastering, and the impossibility of accommodating wiring, ductwork, and piping.

Reinforced concrete slabs cast in place.   Concrete slabs are cast in place on the upper flanges of joists or girders by means of removable formwork. The thickness of the slab depends on the span and the loading, and varies from about 1/30 to 1/15 of the span. The slab usually has a constant thickness (Fig. 1.13), but it may be stiffened over the flanges (Fig. 1.14), or it may be taken to the bottom flanges to achieve a composite behavior as well as provide for corrosion and fire protection (Fig. 1.15). Various technologies of construction have been developed.

Toronto City Hall, Toronto, Canada *(Joint Committee, 1973)*

For example, the concrete can be transported by pump or it can be transported in containers around the site. Sometimes reinforcement can be a grid or mesh or in the form of permanent steel formwork. Also, the composite action between the steel and concrete can be achieved by means of studs or straps welded to the upper flange of the steel girders.

Advantages.   Using these slabs, it is simple to take into account the various irregularities, such as horizontal openings, columns, irregular floor plans, and variable spacing of girders. It is easy to achieve composite behavior between the slab and girder. This results in a high stiffness for the floor structure in both the vertical and horizontal directions. Also, there is a lower percentage of reinforcement used due to the continuous spans.

Disadvantages.   However, use of these slabs results in increased demand for labor

Australia Square, Sydney, Australia *(Courtesy: Ness Abdullah, Civil and Civic Pty., Ltd.)*

on the site for formwork, laying of reinforcement, casting of concrete, and formwork stripping. It is a wet process requiring long periods for setting and hardening of the concrete; it is dependent upon the weather; and it creates some problems in coordinating the steel erection with the concreting operation.

Precast concrete slabs. These slabs can be laid on steel floor beams. The spacing of the beams varies from 1.2 m to 9 m (4 ft to 30 ft), and must be chosen with regard to the type of precast slab being used. The longitudinal joints are usually placed above the steel girder so that the slab behaves like a simple beam. In principle, two kinds of precast slabs may be used.

One kind is the "catalog" precast slab. These slabs are mass produced and suitable for other applications. For instance, they can be laid on concrete beams or on masonry or concrete walls. It is difficult to achieve composite action with these slabs.

In contrast, the other kind, typical precast slabs, can be used for composite construction. The size of the slab is chosen especially for a particular job with regard to the necessity of reducing the number of joints, meeting the requirements of the manufacturer, and satisfying the transportation and erection conditions. The cross section of the special slabs can be solid, or they may be hollow or ribbed in order to reduce the dead weight.

The composite action may be achieved by means of shear connectors; that is, by studs welded on the steel girder flanges which transfer the horizontal shear when the concrete fill is hardened (Figs. 1.16, 1.17). It can also be achieved with high tensile bolts (Fig. 1.18).

Advantages. The prefabricated slabs correspond to the prefabricated steel structure, thus reducing the amount of labor on site enormously. The simultaneous erection of concrete elements and the steel skeleton reduces the total erection time, and dependence on the weather.

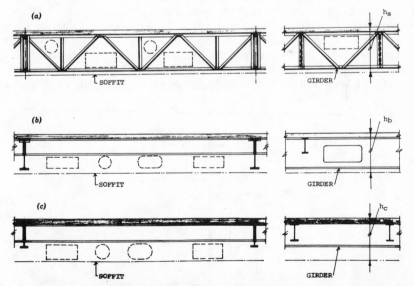

Fig. 1.7 Ductwork, piping, and wiring in floor structures: (a) Latticed structures; (b) Plate girders with holes; (c) Ductwork, piping, and wiring suspended under floor structure

Disadvantages. When floor plans are irregular, different spacing and many different kinds of slabs may be needed. It is usually impossible to achieve composite behavior between steel and concrete when "catalog" slabs are used. The precast slabs are suitable generally for regular column layout without many openings or mechanical installations. They have often been used in multistory parking garages.

Concrete on metal deck. There are three main groups of metal decks:

1. Folded sheet plate with rougher cross-sectional patterns, manufactured to meet particular structural needs [thickness 1 mm to 2.5 mm (1/25 in. to 1/10 in.), depth 40 mm to 80 mm (1-5/8 in. to 3-3/16 in.)]. This sheeting spans up to 6 m (20 ft) [Fig. 1.19(a)].

2. Corrugated steel sheets with finer cross sections, mostly manufactured by well-known companies [thickness 0.6 mm to 1.5 mm (2/100 in. to 6/100 in.), depth 40 mm to 80 mm (1-5/8 in. to 3-3/16 in.)]. These metal decks span from 1 m to 4 m (3 ft to 13 ft) [Figs. 1.19(b) through (g) and 1.20].

3. Flat sheets with reinforcing ribs in their span (Figs. 1.21, 1.22 and 1.23).

The load-carrying capacity of the corrugated sheets is influenced by the depth of the cross section, the thickness of the metal, and the continuity. The steel sheeting or decking can perform various functions. It can be the load-carrying element, or it can act in conjunction with the concrete topping to give a composite structure, or the steel sheet can be used as a nonrecoverable form. Some reinforcement is always needed to cover the negative moments above the supports and the effects of temperature and volume changes, and for fire safety reasons. The sheet is connected to the floor beams by means of tack welds, gunned pins, or welded studs. Welded studs permit composite behavior between steel and concrete.

Advantages. (1) Larger delivery range of steel structural elements and simplified coordination of erection; (2) instantaneous working platform and the protection of work beneath; and (3) lower labor use and a fast erection rate.

Disadvantages: (1) Higher costs associated with the materials; (2) surface finish is required; and (3) fireproofing on underside of metal deck is sometimes required to achieve fire rating. This type of construction is used in all types of tall buildings.

The type of floor joists used in a particular system is affected by many factors, such as load, span, stiffness requirements, structural height, piping and wiring, and

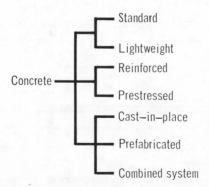

Fig. 1.8 Types of concrete used in floor systems

fire safety, as well as construction and erection problems. The following types of
floor beams and joists are commonly used:

Rolled joists.   These are rather simple from the point of view of production,
and for this reason they often are preferred. However, larger apertures are not
possible and larger spans require higher quality of steel.

Welded I section (plate girders).   These are used where rolled sections are not
sufficient and where higher floor depth is available. The size is usually chosen
according to the statical requirements. Larger apertures in webs should be
reinforced or thicker webs should be used (Fig. 1.24). Welded I sections manufactured on highly mechanized production lines are used with increasing frequency.

Latticed girders.   These are preferred when joints do not require plates and the
latticed bars are of simple cross section (tubes) (Fig. 1.25). These are suitable for
large spans, with larger structural depth and numerous ducts.

Vierendeel girders with combined frame and latticed girders.   These are
used when rectangular openings are required and greater structural depths are

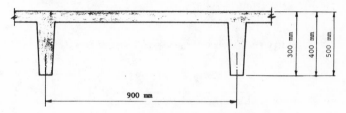

Fig. 1.9 Waffle slab, cross section

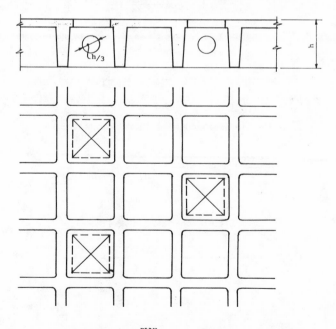

PLAN

Fig. 1.10 Zones for holes

permitted. This is a more expensive floor joist because of the bending moments in the chords and verticals (Figs. 1.26 and 1.27).

Castellated beams. These are used when fabrication technology of the area is sufficiently advanced. In this system, the beam webs are cut in a hexagonal pattern and rewelded. The resulting beam is now deeper and left with holes to accommodate ducts and wiring. It is not necessary that the two pieces of beam which are rewelded to form the castellated girder be of the same size or material. This has a tremendous advantage when the beams are designed to be composite with the floor (Fig. 1.28).

Stub girder. This system is used in order to reduce material weight and

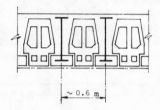

Fig. 1.11 Floor joists with lightweight concrete form pieces

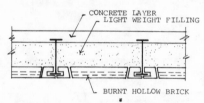

Fig. 1.12 Concrete slab with ceramic plates supported by steel beams

Fig. 1.13 Constant thickness slab on steel beams

Fig. 1.14 Haunched slab on steel beams

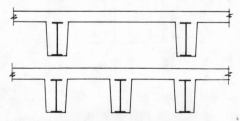

Fig. 1.15 Encased slab-and-beam system

integrate the structural and mechanical systems. The system is fabricated by welding short pieces of floor beams on top of a shallow heavier girder. The length of the stub is on the order of 1.5 m to 2 m (5 ft to 7 ft), and the distance between stubs is about the same. The entire stub girder can be made composite with the concrete

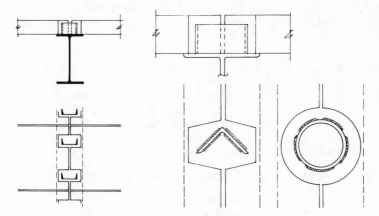

Fig. 1.16 Various kinds of welded shear connectors

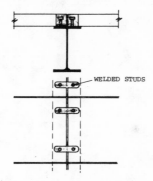

WELDED STUDS

Fig. 1.17 Welded studs

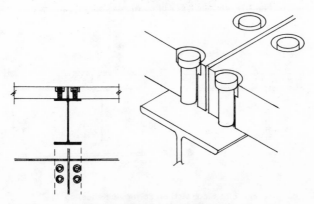

Fig. 1.18 High tensile friction bolts

floor slab. This results in a stiff girder, continuous secondary floor beams, and openings through which ducts can pass (Fig. 1.29).

Staggered truss.   This system is used whenever fixed partitions are found, such as those in apartment houses and hotels. While this is really not a floor beam or joist but instead a full story height truss, it is still an important system used to support gravity loads in tall buildings. The truss allows for column-free space and longer spans, with floors spanning between both the top chords and the bottom chords of the staggered trusses.

2   Vertical Framing Systems

This part of this chapter will pertain only to those elements supporting floor structures. These elements function primarily when vertical loads are applied. However, buildings with central cores, shear-wall systems or rigid frame systems, are able to resist both vertical and horizontal loads with vertical framing systems. Resistance to horizontal loads is discussed elsewhere in this chapter.

Columns.   Columns are linear, vertical elements arranged to carry the loads

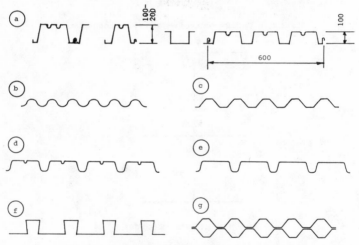

Fig. 1.19 Various types of corrugated sheet plates

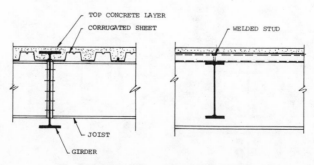

Fig. 1.20 Floor slab on corrugated sheeting

imposed by the floor system. Their cross-sectional area is determined by the material used, the column spacing, the number of stories, and by the loads (both dead load and live load). The materials used for columns are: (1) Steel; (2) reinforced concrete (normally and spirally reinforced); (3) composite (steel and reinforced concrete); and (4) hollow steel cross sections filled with reinforced concrete.

Steel columns may vary in shape (Fig. 1.30) but the rolled wide flange shape is most frequently used. In high-rise buildings, the steel column sizes may be held relatively constant in size in order to achieve the maximum uniformity of layout and detail. Changes in loading can be handled by reducing the thickness of plates or by

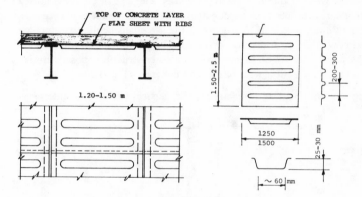

Fig. 1.21 Flat sheet with ribs

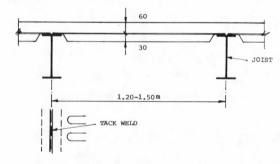

Fig. 1.22 Flat sheet laid on upper flanges of joists

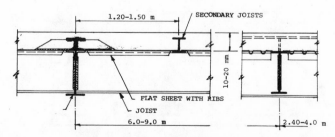

Fig. 1.23 Flat sheet supported on bottom flanges

changing the grade of steel. Joints are provided every two to three stories, accompanied by changes in cross-sectional areas.

Reinforced concrete columns may be of any reasonable shape (Fig. 1.31). They may be long and thin to fit within the partitions. In high-rise structures, the column sizes may be held constant in order to achieve uniformity in layout and maximum opportunity for reuse of forms, or they may be reduced in size in the upper stories to reduce dead load and material quantities. On the lower floors, concrete columns tend to become large in tall buildings, and there they may become cumbersome. To reduce the size of columns, spiral reinforcement of circular cross section may be used. This type of reinforcement greatly increases the ultimate bearing capacity and greatly improves the ductility of the columns. The size of columns must be chosen with great care, because high percentages of reinforcement cause severe problems in connections and joints. The alternative is the use of steel columns which can be used compositely with a reinforced concrete skin (Fig. 1.32). This solution is also suitable from the point of view of fire safety. The other structural possibility is to fill the closed steel cross section with reinforced concrete (Fig. 1.33).

Bearing Walls.   Bearing walls are planar, vertical elements distinguished by their

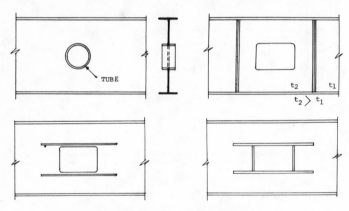

Fig. 1.24 Opening in full-web girder

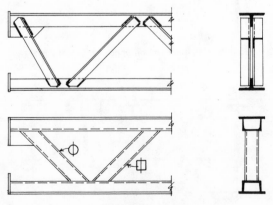

Fig. 1.25 Latticed girders

relative thinness and substantial length. They usually have few openings, and they develop relatively low compressive stresses, so that a nominal percentage of reinforcement is sufficient. If the stress level is large enough to require substantial vertical reinforcement, then the wall is called a wall column. Usually these bearing walls double as supports for floor slabs and as partitions. Sometimes the concrete walls can behave just like the staggered steel trusses discussed earlier. The materials used for bearing walls are as follows (Fig. 1.34): (1) Steel; (2) reinforced concrete; and (3) masonry (brick or concrete masonry—both reinforced and nonreinforced).

Hangers (Tension Supports).   Hangers are slender vertical members, stressed in tension, which carry the floor loads. They can be suspended from heavy cantilevers supported by one or more of the building cores. The hangers are almost always made of steel, and they may be of any appropriate shape, such as flat bars, pipes, I beams, or stranded steel cables. Attention should be paid to the elastic and plastic strains under constant axial forces (particularly in the case of cables). When choosing the size of steel hangers, attention must be paid to the construction technology. For example, the hanger may be placed in compression during erection.

However, the hangers might be prestressed concrete members. Tension supports are the ideal slender member. If the tension rods are embedded in concrete and the pretensioned steel is not extended too much by loads, then it is safe to assume that the concrete serves as protection against corrosion.

Transfer Girders.   The transfer girder is a horizontal framing member commonly used in tall buildings. In many high-rise buildings it is desirable to change the arrangement of the columns in the lower floors. Hence, the transfer girder is used to pick up the typical floor columns and transfer the load to fewer but larger columns below. The transfer girder is usually very large, sometimes being a full story in depth.

Suspended Systems.   In suspended systems, the hangers are supported by a massive structure at the top of the building. The statical system of the top structure can vary (a massive grid of one-story height, a system with oblique tension bars, etc.). However, there is a great advantage in the elimination of supports on the ground floor. This is helpful when tall buildings are located in the city centers occupying small sites where a harmonious joining with small buildings is desirable.

Summary.   It is well to recall that this section has only attempted to discuss structural systems as they behave under vertical loads. The effect of horizontal loads naturally has an effect on the final choice of proper structural systems for tall buildings and the behavior of these structural systems under applied horizontal loads as well as combined loadings is discussed in the next section of this chapter.

1.3   FRAMING SYSTEMS TO RESIST HORIZONTAL LOADS

An important characteristic of tallness in a building is the relative importance of the lateral load-resisting and lateral stabilizing systems. The normal lateral loads are those due to wind and earthquake. The columns of tall buildings must be stabilized or laterally supported by a lateral bracing system, and the lateral bracing system must resist deformations associated with the out-of-straightness and plumb of structural members and the deformation associated with lateral forces (P-Δ effect).

For low-rise and medium-rise structures, the analysis and design with respect to lateral forces has generally been merely a process of checking the vertical load-resistant system for its ability to resist lateral forces. However, for tall

Torres Colon, Madrid, Spain—example of tension supported structure *(Photo: Lynn S. Beedle)*

Torres Colon, Madrid, Spain—completed structure *(Courtesy: Antonio Lamela)*

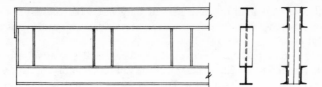

Fig. 1.26 Framed girder

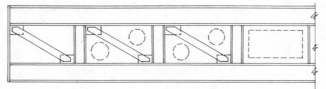

Fig. 1.27 Latticed-framed girder

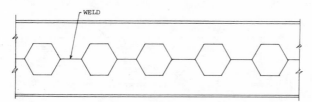

Fig. 1.28 Castellated beam

Federal Reserve Bank, Minneapolis, Minnesota. Architect: Gunnar Birkerts & Associates
(Courtesy: Leslie E. Robertson)

structures the vertical load-resisting system may not have the capacity to resist lateral forces, or even if it does, the design for lateral forces may add substantially to the structural cost.

Fig. 1.35 is a plot that has been used to illustrate the relative structural cost factors with respect to building height. Note that the floor cost increases only slightly with height, that the column cost increases linearly with the number of stories, and the cost of the lateral-resistant system tends to increase at an accelerating rate with height. For economic reasons and for considerations of structural strength and stiffness, it is essential that the lateral force resistant system be carefully considered in the design.

In a broad sense there are three fundamental types of lateral resisting elements:

1. Moment resistant frames.

2. Braced frames.

3. Shear walls.

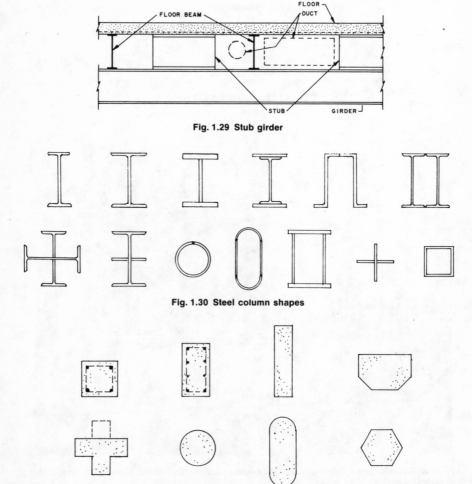

Fig. 1.29 Stub girder

Fig. 1.30 Steel column shapes

Fig. 1.31 Reinforced concrete column shapes

The three fundamental elements are generally in vertical planes and may be placed in one or more of three general locations: (1) Exterior (perimeter); (2) interior;and (3) core (see Fig. 1.36). Obviously, most building structures include several of these elements. However, for convenience of discussion, each one will be examined separately.

1 Moment Resistant Frames

Moment resistant frames consist of linear, horizontal members (beams) in plane with and connected to linear, vertical members (columns) with rigid or semirigid joints. A moment resistant frame is identified by the prominence of its flexibility due to the flexure of the individual beams and columns and the rotation at their joints. The strength and stiffness of the frame are proportional to the column and beam size, and inversely proportional to the story height and column spacing.

Fig. 1.32 Encased columns

Fig. 1.33 Steel (closed cross section) filled with reinforced concrete

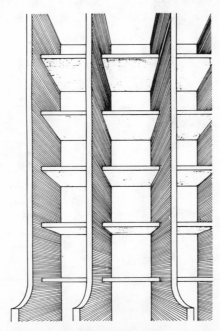

Fig. 1.34 Bearing walls

Location. A moment resisting frame may be internal, that is, in planes within the building, or external, in the plane of the exterior walls or facade (Fig. 1.36). However, internally located frames have some disadvantages which limit their usefulness in tall buildings. The floor space requirements of most buildings limit the number of interior columns available for frames. Also, the floor beams are generally of long span and limited depth.

Exterior located frames do not necessarily have these disadvantages. It is often possible and even desirable to provide closely spaced columns and deep spandrel beams.

Concrete Moment Resistant Frames. Concrete moment resistant frames may be either cast-in-place or precast, or a combination of cast-in-place and precast.

Cast-in-place frames. Three types are in general use: (1) Beam and column frame; (2) flat slab and column frame; and (3) slab and bearing wall frame (Fig. 1.37).

Cast-in-place construction for moment resistant frames has the advantage of inherently providing monolithic joints. The column and beam reinforcement may be extended continuous through the joint, thus providing the necessary joint strength. A system often used in medium-rise to high-rise apartment buildings utilizes a portion of the flat slab floor as a shallow beam continuous with the columns.

Precast frames. Precast frames may be constructed of individual columns and beams. In this case it is necessary to make a strong moment resisting connection of beam to column. This has been done by welding or otherwise connecting the bars and casting or dry packing the joints. Beam and column units have also been cast together as a unit and connected at or near the midpoint of the beam span. This has the advantage of making the field connection at a point of minimum moment. In many cases, the midpoint of the beam span is a location of zero moment and the connection need only be made to develop shear. The problems of transportation on the highway and erecting panels usually limit the width of the panels (and the column spacing) to approximately 4 m (13 ft). Precast beams, columns, and column

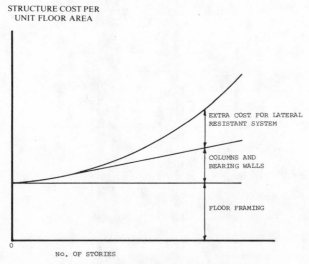

Fig. 1.35 Tall building cost relationships

beam units may be cast on the jobsite or manufactured in plants or factories and shipped to the jobsite. Maximum economic advantage is usually gained by using a large number of identical or standard components. Precast elements of the frame may be conventionally reinforced or they may be prestressed. If prestressed, the individual components are usually pretensioned. Post-tensioning of beams and columns may be provided continuous through the joint, thus eliminating or reducing the requirement for the welding of bars and the casting or dry packing of the joints.

Steel Moment Resistant Frames.   Many rolled and fabricated steel shapes have been used for the columns and beams of steel moment resistant frames, although the wide flange shape has proved to be most common. Wide flange shapes, channel shapes, box shapes, plates, and trusses have all been used. In the past, the connections of beams to columns has been accomplished by the use of riveting, bolting, or welding, but today most connections are either high-tensile bolted or welded.

Steel moment resistant frames may be constructed of individual beams and columns with connections made at beam ends. These connections are required to

Latino Americana Tower, Mexico City, Mexico—example of steel moment-resistant frame *(Courtesy: W. E. Edwards, Bethlehem Steel Co.)*

develop the full moment capacity of the beam. Fig. 1.38 shows how these connections have commonly been made.

Frames have been constructed of one or more columns of one or more stories in height with spandrel beam stubs welded to the column (Fig. 1.39). This allows the connection to be made at a point of minimum moment, and often these connections can be simple bolted shear connections, thus eliminating the requirement for field welding. The beam to column connection may be shop welded. Since shipping and erection requirements limit the width of a panel to approximately 4 m (13 ft), the use of this system is usually limited to a frame with closely spaced columns. The column with beam stubs system is self-bracing in its own plane, an advantage during erection.

Composite Moment Resistant Frames.   Composite frames may consist of steel beams rigidly connected to concrete columns or concrete beams rigidly connected to steel columns. However, the term composite has normally been applied to frames where the beams or columns, or both, as individual members, are of composite concrete and steel construction.

Composite columns.   Composite columns may consist of either: (1) Concrete encased structural steel shapes; or (2) concrete filled tubular steel sections (Fig. 1.40).

Concrete encased steel columns are common. The concrete encasement has often been considered only fire and corrosion protection for the steel. However, in recent years, lateral and sometimes longitudinal reinforcement has been added to the concrete encasement, and the resultant strength of the steel and concrete interacting has been used for structural purposes. A steel shape encased in concrete may be thought of as reinforcement for the concrete.

Concrete filled tubular steel columns have enjoyed some popularity as single columns. The confined concrete fill increases the axial load capacity but has little effect on the flexural capacity. For that reason, it is unlikely that these columns would be a good choice for a moment resisting frame.

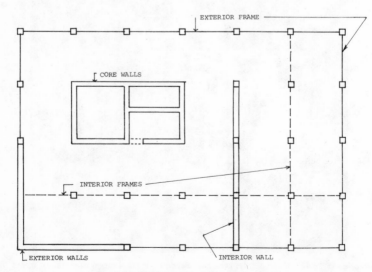

Fig. 1.36 Building plan—structural elements

Composite beams.   Composite beams may be either: (1) Steel beams encased in concrete; or (2) steel beams connected to the floor slab with shear connectors (Fig. 1.41).

Concrete encasement has been used to provide fire and corrosion protection. The encased steel section may have a closed web or an open web. Where the steel section has a closed web, the concrete encasement contributes something to the strength of the beam. Where an open web steel section is used, the strength and stiffness of the beam may be calculated on the basis that it is a concrete beam reinforced with steel shapes. The primary disadvantage of the encased steel beam is that substantial weight is added to the beam without a comparable increase in strength or stiffness.

An often used type of composite beam is the steel beam with shear connectors embedded in the concrete floor slab. All buildings have some concrete cast on their floors. Therefore, with the addition of shear connectors fastened to the top flange,

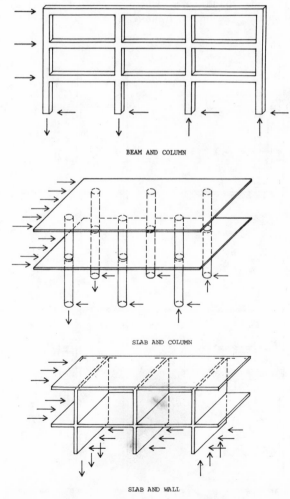

BEAM AND COLUMN

SLAB AND COLUMN

SLAB AND WALL

Fig. 1.37 Moment resistant frames

the strength and stiffness of the steel beam may be substantially increased. Concrete encasement of the beam-column joint connection, especially with the addition of hoop reinforcement, may substantially increase the joint strength and stiffness.

2 Braced Frames

A braced frame consists of a beam and column framework infilled with diagonal bracing. It is a system composed entirely of linear members, and is identified by its flexibility due to the shortening and lengthening of the horizontal floor members and the diagonal bracing members. This system has had wide application in structural steel buildings. The braced frame may be used internally in walls or partitions, where it creates a special problem in the fitting of the partitition in and around the diagonal members. If used externally, it creates an unusual facade and unusually shaped windows, which are often not considered desirable. Its primary use has been in and around cores, where it can be placed in unseen and nonarchitectural spaces. The braced frame is a very stiff and efficient structural

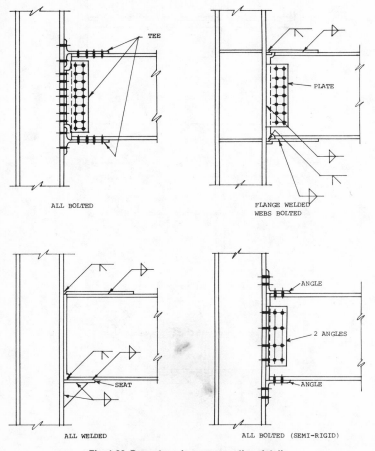

Fig. 1.38 Beam to column connection details

system, since it does not involve the flexural deformation of members. Fig. 1.42 shows a number of different types of bracing systems that have been used:

1. Single diagonal bracing.

2. Double diagonal bracing.

3. K bracing, either vertical or horizontal.

4. Lattice bracing.

5. Knee bracing.

Knee bracing produces a structure somewhere between a full braced frame and full moment resistant frame. The beams and columns of the knee-braced structure are flexurally deformed.

Concrete Braced Frames.   Concrete braced frames have received little use in structures, because of the difficulty of making the end connections of the diagonal members, and the obvious superiority of the concrete shear wall. Braced frame construction in cast-in-place concrete has been used in several special applications.

Lattice bracing has been used in precast concrete exterior facade construction. If the lattice members are closely spaced, a precast panel of a sufficient number of members may be cast to minimize the number of field connections.

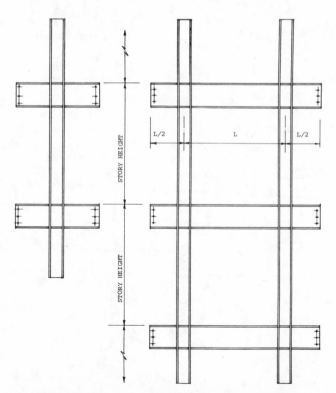

Fig. 1.39 Steel moment resistant frames—panel construction

Steel Braced Frames.   Steel is especially advantageous for use in braced frame construction due to the ease with which end connections may be made. However, its use is limited to areas where there is an ample availability of steel sections. End connections may be of either a welded or bolted type. Steel diagonal framing members are generally slender and may be readily incorporated into partitions, walls, and mechanical spaces. While certain standard arrangements of diagonal bracing are commonly used, any configuration of triangulated bracing may be used to achieve an efficient braced frame. The bracing may be arranged to fit around

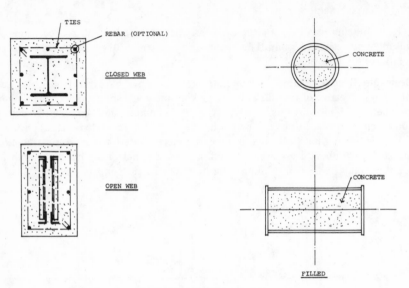

Fig. 1.40 Composite columns

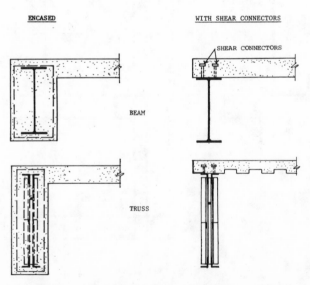

Fig. 1.41 Composite floor members

door and window openings, mechanical openings, and the like. Many complicated but efficient bracing systems have been worked out to brace the cores of high-rise buildings. The earliest steel skeleton high-rise buildings incorporated some kind of braced frame construction.

Composite Braced Frames. Composite braced frames may be of two general types: (1) Steel diagonal bracing may be added to a concrete frame or, much less likely, concrete diagonal bracing may be added to a steel frame; and (2) composite steel and concrete linear members may be used as elements of the frame. The flexibility of a braced frame includes the deformation of the columns and beams as well as diagonal braces that are a part of the frame. If a steel column is encased in concrete, a reduction in deflection of the braced frame may be achieved. If concrete is cast around the beam, or if the beam is made composite with the floor slab, the reduced deformation of the beam will reduce the deflection of the braced frame. Both the concrete encasement of columns and composite floor beams have been commonly used in recent years.

3 Shear Walls

Shear walls may be defined as planar vertical elements distinguished by their relative thinness and substantial length. Shear walls are further identified as having few openings or penetrations, such that they have little or no flexibility due to the

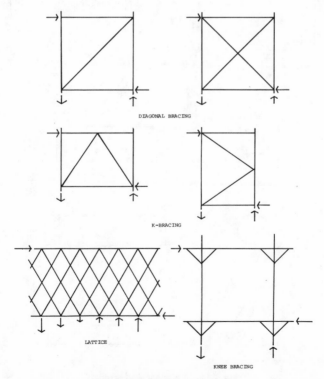

Fig. 1.42 Braced frame types

flexure of individual pieces of the wall. Their flexibility is generally limited to the sum of over-all shear deformation and overturning flexural deformation. If two or more shear wall elements are connected together with relatively rigid members they are called coupled shear walls. Shear walls may be solid or penetrated with a limited number of openings. The shear wall may or may not carry substantial gravity loads. The shear wall may be a single bearing wall, a wall connecting two or more columns, or a panel wall filling the openings of a beam column frame (Fig. 1.43).

Location. Shear walls may be incorporated into a tall building design in a number of locations. They may be internal walls, exterior or facade walls, or core walls. In office and commercial buildings, clear open spaces are required. Most partitions are temporary or movable, and it is difficult to provide internal shear walls. On the other hand, efficient building planning usually gathers together certain utilitarian functions of the building into a relatively compact core or cores. This core may

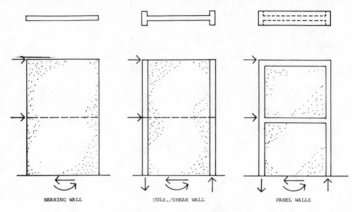

BEARING WALL   COLS./SHEAR WALL   PANEL WALLS

Fig. 1.43 Shear wall types

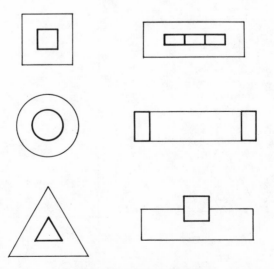

Fig. 1.44 Core shear wall layouts

include elevators, stairs, mechanical rooms and shafts, smoke shafts, toilets, janitor closets, and the necessary interior columns. An attempt is always made to minimize the core size in order to increase the floor efficiency. Nevertheless, in most buildings these cores cover 20% to 25% of the floor area, and they occur as a continuous vertical shaft for the full height of the building. This core, then, offers an excellent opportunity for providing shear walls. Care must be taken to account for the various door openings and for penetrations for mechanical work. Fig. 1.44 indicates schematically some core wall arrangements that have been successfully used.

While it is difficult to place interior shear walls in office buildings, it is often possible to develop locations for exterior or facade shear walls. These walls may be exterior walls of a core, or they may be walls located such that the requirements for window openings are minimal, so that the general integrity of the shear wall may be maintained. In some office and commercial structures the requirement for windows has been reduced to a point where a continuous exterior facade wall may be utilized as a shear wall. Often a bearing and shear wall will have regular penetrations such that its structural action is intermediate between a shear wall and a moment resisting frame. Some "tube" and "shell wall" systems fall in this category.

For high-rise housing projects, such as apartments and hotels, the utility core requirements are substantially less than those for office buildings. For this reason, it is often difficult to develop sufficient strength and stiffness in the core walls. However, the generally fixed arrangement of partitioning in such buildings often allows for the opportunity of providing internal shear walls. These walls serve as partition walls between apartments or rooms and help reduce sound transmission.

Concrete Shear Walls.   Concrete as a material is particularly suitable for shear wall construction, because it is economical and has great shear strength. The necessary openings for doors, windows, and utilities may be provided. Concrete shear walls may also be bearing walls, thereby eliminating or minimizing the requirements for columns and piers. Concrete shear walls may be cast-in-place or precast.

Cast-in-place shear walls.   By proper treatment of construction joints and doweling of reinforcing steel, it is possible to develop monolithic joints which may develop the full shear strength of the concrete. Where feasible, the use and reuse of panel forms and the use of the slip form techniques make possible economy of formwork.

Precast shear walls.   Flat panels suitable for shear walls may be economically cast, transported, and erected. The connections of the panels may be achieved by lapping of reinforcing steel and casting in place pilasters or columns, or by welding reinforcing bars or inserts and grouting or dry packing the joints.

In large panel buildings, a widely used technique consists of achieving vertical castellated shear joints. The edges of the panels have trapezoidal-shaped keys. Reinforcement is provided by projecting steel loops between the keys and the steel bars at each floor level. The joints are then filled with concrete. This type of joint has been tested in many laboratories and seems to be quite efficient.

A ductile behavior was reported in several tests where the adhesion between precast panels and the cast-in-place concrete was destroyed. However, if the adhesion exists, the behavior at failure is rather brittle.

In some cases, precast walls are made of infilled panels within a concrete frame or steel frame structure. Where precast panels infill a steel frame, the panels may be connected to the steel frame by welding steel inserts in the wall to the steel beams and columns of the frame.

The relative lack of ductility of reinforced concrete shear walls has limited their use in high-rise structures in earthquake zones. Several special techniques and wall details have been utilized to overcome this limitation. Since the nonductile failure mode of shear walls is generally that of shear or diagonal tension, or both, very conservative shear stress levels have been used for design purposes. Shear walls have been "slitted" as shown in Fig. 1.45. The initial rigidity of the slitted wall is comparable with a monolithic wall and thus is useful to resist frequent minor earthquakes and windstorms. At the time of the rare destructive earthquake, cracks in the wall are distributed finely with no major diagonal cracks, and the rebar yields in flexure. Thus a smooth deterioration of stiffness can be accomplished, and although there is a reduction of both strength and stiffness of the wall, there is a substantial increase in its ductility. This system has found application in a number of buildings in Japan.

Steel Shear Walls.   Steel plate has been used as a shear wall, as a panel infill to a

Pirelli Building, Milan, Italy. Reinforced concrete building with two pairs of coupled internal shear walls and two end cores. Concrete floor framing concentrates as much load as possible on shear walls and end cores. (Courtesy: Pirelli S.P.A.—Press Department)

steel frame. The steel plate must be stiffened vertically and horizontally at regular intervals by added steel members to prevent diagonal compressive buckling of the plate under lateral load stress. Angles, split wide flange sections, and similar type members, bolted or welded to the plate, have been used as stiffeners. The steel plate panel may be either welded or bolted to the surrounding frame (Fig. 1.46). If properly stiffened and proportioned, the steel plate shear wall may be advantageous for seismic design. A wall can be proportioned so that the first yield is shear yield of the shear wall plate.

Masonry Shear Walls.   Masonry is an ancient building material. The earliest shear walls were masonry and they generally served as both bearing and shear walls. Today, unit masonry is still the wall material most universally available throughout the world. Bearing and shear walls of masonry may be built without sophisticated equipment and materials, and with labor of limited skills. Masonry units are usually of clay or concrete and bonded together with a portland cement paste mortar. The masonry units suitable for use in high-rise buildings are generally manufactured under quality control conditions. Myriad sizes and shapes are available and have been used. Although remarkably tall buildings have been built of unreinforced masonry, most engineers believe that unit masonry structures of substantial height should be reinforced. Therefore, those masonry units most suitable for high-rise buildings are those which provide holes or cavities suitable for the passage and grouting in of reinforcement. Three general types of unit masonry walls are common: (1) Solid masonry (generally unreinforced); (2) hollow unit masonry (reinforced); and (3) grouted cavity masonry (reinforced). They are shown in Fig. 1.47.

Solid masonry walls.   Solid masonry walls have been used in structures for

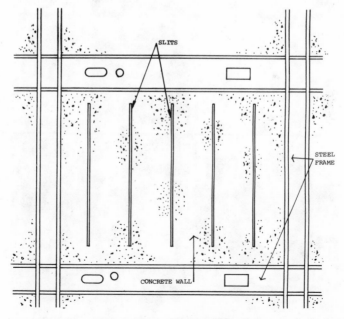

Fig. 1.45 Slitted concrete shear walls

many thousands of years. In ancient times walls of very great thickness were constructed, and, of course, these walls were unreinforced. These walls served both as bearing walls and shear walls and, being unreinforced, they depended entirely upon the stability resulting from the vertical axial stress caused by their own weight and the weight of the contributory floors and roofs. In modern times, it has been considered uneconomical and undesirable to build very thick and heavy walls. Therefore the use of solid unreinforced masonry has been limited to relatively low buildings. However, in certain areas not subject to seismic disturbance, unreinforced masonry walls up to 15 and 20 stories have been constructed.

Hollow unit masonry.   Hollow unit masonry is generally laid up to provide for continuous vertical cells of sufficient size that vertical reinforcing bars may be placed and the surrounding space grouted. Horizontal reinforcement may be provided either by strip reinforcement in the horizontal mortar joints, or by using special hollow units (bond beam or lintel units) that provide an open top, horizontal,

U.S. Steel Building, Pittsburgh, Pennsylvania—triangular shape with braced core *(Courtesy: Harrison & Abramovitz & Abbe)*

continuous channel which may be reinforced and grouted. With proper reinforcement and grouting, reinforced hollow unit masonry has been used in high-rise buildings.

Grouted cavity masonry. Grouted cavity masonry consists of two outer rows (wythes) of solid masonry units laid up to provide a cavity space between them. Horizontal and vertical bar reinforcement is placed in the cavity and the cavity is grouted solid. The grout in the cavity bonds to the reinforcing steel and bonds to the unit masonry, thus producing a monolithic, composite, full-thickness wall.

The major advantage of the use of masonry for shear and bearing walls is architectural. The various types of brick, tile, and concrete masonry units may be desirable as a final architectural finish. The structural wall can then serve as both the architectural and structural system. The masonry shear wall cannot be designed to develop the strength of a reinforced concrete or steel plate shear wall. Its use is generally limited to moderately tall and short-span buildings, such as apartments and other building types where the floor spans are short and a great number of walls may be provided.

4   Combination Systems

This section has discussed various horizontal load resistant elements as separate, distinct systems. This has perhaps been valuable for study purposes. However, in real practice, the structural design process is not necessarily one of selecting this or that system. Rather, like most design processes, it is a creative process where a design is developed in response to a wide range of imposed conditions and restraints. The structural designer must be responsive to practical (construction and cost), utilitarian (use), and esthetic considerations in addition to his normal

Peachtree Center Plaza Hotel, Atlanta, Georgia *(Courtesy: John Portman)*

structural engineering discipline. The best response to these conditions, as well as the best designs, can rarely be pigeonholed into rigid categories, such as those previously listed. Lateral load resistant systems often contain frames, walls, and bracing interacting together.

"Tube" Structures. A tube structure may be defined as a three-dimensional space structure composed of three, four, or possibly more frames, braced frames, or shear walls, joined at or near their edges to form a vertical tubelike structural system capable of resisting lateral forces in any direction by cantilevering from the foundation (Fig. 1.48). Tube structures usually have relatively small shear flexibility, so that the shear lag around the intersecting corners is minimized, and the entire tube participates in the overturning resistance.

    Location. Tubes may be developed around internally located service cores containing elevators, stairs, mechanical rooms and shafts, smoke shafts, toilets, janitor closets, etc. Tubes may also be developed around the exterior perimeter or facade of a building. In both locations the tube structure may generally be extended from the foundations for the full height of the building.

Standard Oil (Indiana) Building, Chicago, Illinois—construction as of 4/5/72 (73 stories)
(Courtesy: E. Alfred Picardi)

Configuration types.

1. Framed tubes. Tubes may consist of moment resistant frames, provided that the columns are closely spaced in order to reduce beam and column flexural deformation to a minimum. When the exterior columns are closely spaced [1 m to 3 m (3 ft to 10 ft) on center], it is possible to develop the entire perimeter of the tube structure as a lateral load resistant system. This system has been called the "boxed frame" or the "framed tube." It has been found that with closely spaced columns and deep spandrel beams, the shear lag around the corner is minimized, and the building walls at right angles to the direction of the applied lateral force contribute greatly to the over-all overturning strength and stiffness of the entire structure.

2. Braced tube. The braced tube is a three-dimensional diagonal braced or trussed system. It is inherently a very stiff system since it involves only axial deformation of members and no flexural deformation.

3. Shear wall tubes. Three, four, or more shear walls may be joined at their edges to form a true tubular structure. In order to be effective as a tube the shear walls must have minimum penetrations for doors, windows, and mechanical work. Shear wall tubes are generally stiffer than frames or braced tubes.

Sears Tower, Chicago, Illinois—example of bundled tube *(Courtesy: Ezra Stoller)*

Range of applicability and use. The limitation on permissible openings usually rules out the use of the shear wall tube in the exterior perimeter wall. However, most high-rise buildings have service cores which may occupy as much as 20% to 25% of the building area and may have horizontal dimensions up to one-half of the building dimension. These cores may be suitable for the development of one or more shear wall tubes. However, because of the limited horizontal dimension, core shear wall tubes have generally not been used as the sole lateral force resisting system for buildings over 20 to 25 stories in height.

Since the tube is thought of as a box beam cantilevering from the foundation, the greater the plan dimension of the tube the greater the stiffness of the structural system with respect to lateral forces. For very tall buildings, say over 20 to 25 stories, the tube must be placed in the exterior wall to achieve sufficient stiffness. It is often possible in high-rise office or apartment buildings to develop a tube structure in the exterior wall, either by using the closely spaced columns or by diagonally bracing the exterior facade.

Multiple Tube Systems.

Tube in tube. For very tall slender buildings, it is necessary to develop as much lateral strength and stiffness as possible. For tall buildings, this has led to the use of core shear walls interacting together with exterior moment resisting frames. This has been called a "tube in tube" scheme. The excellent overturning resistant ability of

Examples in Chicago of three structural systems: John Hancock (braced tube), Sears Tower (bundled tube), and Standard Oil (tubular system) *(Courtesy: Rita P. Krider & Engineering News Record)*

the facade frame is combined with the shear resistant capacity of the core shear walls to achieve a highly efficient structural system (Fig. 1.49).

Bundled tube. The bundled tube system consists of a number of vertical tubular elements fitted together and sharing common side frames. By bundling tubes, the over-all building dimension is increased, and hence the lateral stiffness and stability (Fig. 1.50). Tubes may be terminated at various levels in the building, thus producing variable floor areas. The tube termination levels may correspond to elevator termination levels.

Core Interaction Structures.   Quite often it is impossible, or considered undesirable, to have the exterior columns closely spaced. A structural system has been used on several projects that connects the core tube to the exterior columns at one or more locations in the building where beams or cross-bracing do not interfere, such as at the mechanical floors or at the roof level. The basic principle involved is that of utilizing the core to fully develop horizontal shears, but to provide for vertical shear transfer from the core to the exterior columns, thus developing the total overturning capacity of the full building dimension. Fig. 1.51 illustrates the principle in both steel and concrete.

In addition to increasing the lateral strength and stiffness of the building, the rigid connection of core to exterior columns also reduces problems associated with differential temperature expansion and contraction of the exterior exposed columns and the internal, temperature controlled core, as well as differential shortening.

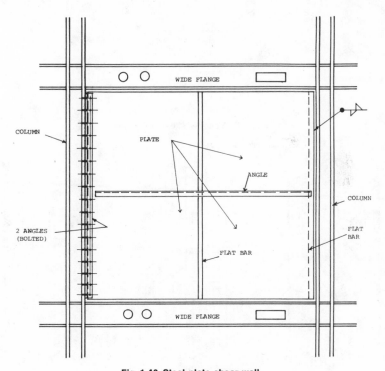

Fig. 1.46 Steel plate shear wall

5 New Structural Concepts

For high-rise buildings up to the height at which buildings have presently been constructed [460 m (1500 ft)], the structural systems now in use will most likely prove adequate and economical. However, the next generation of tall buildings may very well go over 460 m in height. With increasing height, the extraordinary forces of nature (wind, earthquake, fire, and blast), will tend more and more to dominate the structural system, and new structural and associated architectural, mechanical, and electrical concepts will be required. For the human occupants of these supertall buildings to be satisfied tenants, the movement of the building when subjected to the various environmental effects will have to be controlled within certain limits. The general strength and stiffness requirements of today will still have to be met.

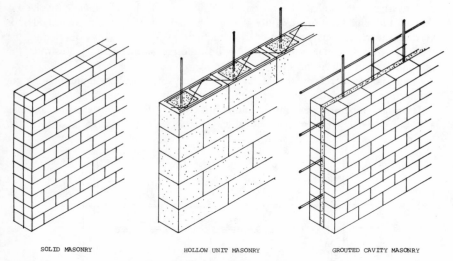

SOLID MASONRY   HOLLOW UNIT MASONRY   GROUTED CAVITY MASONRY

Fig. 1.47 Masonry shear wall types

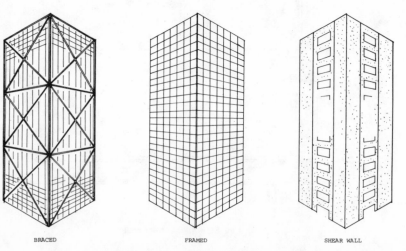

BRACED   FRAMED   SHEAR WALL

Fig. 1.48 Tube structural systems

Also, in these super highrise buildings, the interior spaces will still have to be readily accessible to elevators, stairs, and utilities, and in most cases, to the outside world by access to windows. These human requirements have a tendency to reduce the plan dimension of a tall building to something like 60 m (200 ft). If plan dimensions are limited and the heights increase, it becomes apparent that, unless there is some dramatic increase in the damping or ductility that can be achieved to dissipate wind or earthquake-induced energy, it is unlikely that a tall building will be able to perform satisfactorily if the height-to-width ratio exceeds approximately 7 to 1. The World Trade Center in New York City, which has a height-to-width ratio of 7 to 1, was a borderline case from the standpoint of performance, and it was found

World Trade Center, New York (Courtesy: The Port Authority of New York and New Jersey)

necessary to use 20 000 viscoelastic dampers to reduce dynamic excitation from the wind to tolerable levels. Energy dissipation systems are discussed in more detail in the next section of this chapter. Without a substantial increase in energy dissipation, it would seem that the effective plan dimension (the vertical cantilever beam depth) will have to be increased if taller buildings are to be constructed. Three concepts which might be acceptable to our present space and human requirements can be discussed: (1) The single megastructure or multiuse structure; (2) the cellular structure; and (3) bridged structures.

Megastructures.   With the increased urbanization of the world, it is probable that more types of human activities will be incorporated in the tall buildings of the future. To the present business and private living activities may well be added institutional, merchandising, manufacturing and storage, and parking activities. Since the latter activities require large areas with minimal perimeter facade for views and access, it may be possible to increase the over-all building dimension where structurally required at or near the base, while tapering the building up to a relatively slender top more suitable for living and office use (Fig. 1.52). A suggestion of the megastructure concept may be seen in the John Hancock Building in Chicago, a 100-story, braced, tubular frame building of tapered shape which houses several different human activities.

New York Harbor. "The tallest building in the world" was the description from 1913 to 1930 of the Woolworth Building—seen here in 1974 nestled between the towers of the World Trade Center *(Courtesy: New York Convention & Visitors Bureau)*

Cellular Structures.   It is possible to increase the over-all building dimension and the exterior perimeter without increasing the floor area by planning the structure with a hollow, open center. Many potential plan shapes are possible (Fig. 1.53). The hollow center may be completely open, or it may contain some or all of the utility functions such as stairs, elevators, mechanical and electrical shafts, and toilet rooms. It is most desirable for the floor system to clear span from the outer to the inner wall. All the previously listed structural systems may be appropriate. Exterior wall tubular construction could be used. An exterior and interior wall tube (tube in tube) may be used with or without coupling between the two tubes. Bundled tube construction might be used. The interior tube may be coupled to the exterior wall tube, much in the same way as an interior core wall may interact with an exterior frame. A suggestion of this type of cellular structure is the Sumitomo Building in Tokyo, Japan.

Bridged Structures.   The effective overturning resistance may be increased by using two or more slender shaft buildings linked together at one or more levels by bridges. The concept of bridging may fit in well with some concepts for the future

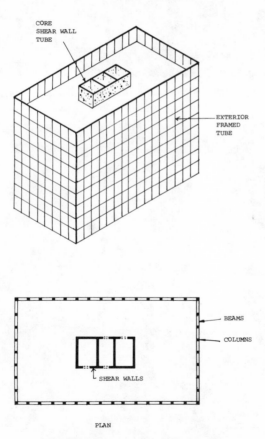

Fig. 1.49 Tube in tube system

John Hancock Center, Chicago, Illinois *(Courtesy: Ezra Stoller)*

Shinjuku Sumitomo Building (second from left), Tokyo, Japan *(Courtesy: Kiyoshi Muto)*

development of cities. Future cities may have several different levels for service access, vehicular circulation, pedestrian circulation, and public areas for park and recreation (Fig. 1.54). The links may be stiff, tubular structures, connected to the tubular structure of the vertical building shafts. If the towers have a core perimeter tube, the links could be dimensioned one or more stories high with a plan dimension equal to the core dimension. If the towers are of exterior tubular construction, then the width of the links could be equal to the full width of the buildings. The links may also be slender bridges suspended and laterally stayed by prestressed steel cables (Fig. 1.55). These bridges may be of very light weight although still suitable for pedestrian or light vehicle traffic. The actions of lateral forces are distributed to

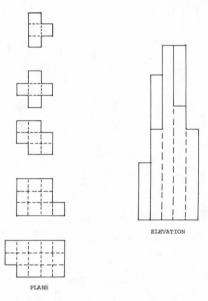

ELEVATION

PLANS

Fig. 1.50 Bundled multiple tube structure

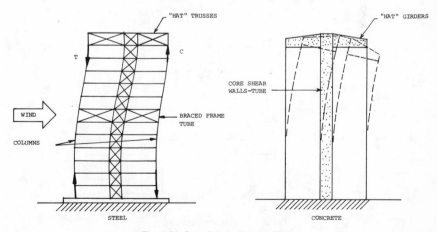

Fig. 1.51 Core interaction systems

all linked buildings proportional to their stiffnesses. The bridge structures may also act as energy dissipators. The vertical tower buildings could be constructed in either steel or concrete by conventional construction methods. The bridge links could be

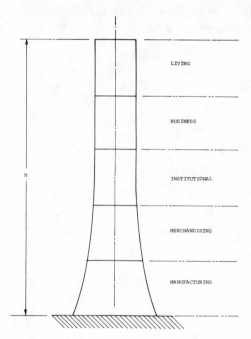

Fig. 1.52 Megastructure

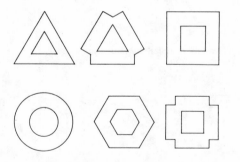

POSSIBLE PLAN SHAPES (HOLLOW TUBULAR BUILDINGS)

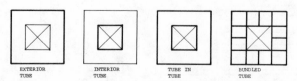

Fig. 1.53 Cellular structures

erected by any one of the methods now commonly used for bridge construction. The cantilever method now used in bridge construction would appear to be most promising.

1.4 ENERGY DISSIPATION SYSTEMS

All the energy that is induced in structures by wind, blast, earthquakes, or machinery is finally dissipated by damping forces. The damping limits and progressively reduces the deformations and accelerations of the induced vibrations. The natural energy dissipation of structural materials can be helped and essentially increased by artificial means. This opens new ways to design structures and make them more economical. In this section, various ways to achieve this are indicated.

1 Natural Damping of Structural Materials

Structural damping is caused by the internal friction within the particles of building materials. The damping forces are proportional to strain and deformations. A large amount of energy is also dissipated in a minute slippage at the connections of members, which is best illustrated by the relatively high damping of bolted structures compared to all welded steel structures. The increased friction of the particles in cracked concrete is also well known, and is preferable to crack-free post-tensioned concrete.

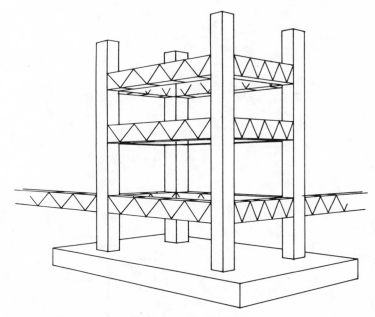

Fig. 1.54 Bridged structures

2 Plasticity of Structural Materials

Due to the plasticity of materials, especially steel, energy is absorbed inelastically. The energy absorption by ductility is not limited to steel alone, but also occurs in combined materials, like reinforced concrete. The confining of the concrete by reinforcement increases its ductility and capacity to absorb energy. Recognition of these facts has led to specific ductile detailing of structures in steel and concrete, especially in ranges of high moments at joint and connection points.

3 Highly Absorbent Structural Systems

Redundant Systems. The capacity of a total structural system to absorb energy is largely influenced by its redundancy. This means that many redundant members participate in resisting loads, and that overstressed portions of a structure can, after deformation, be relieved by neighboring members.

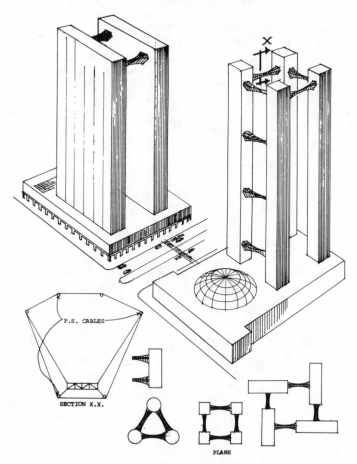

Fig. 1.55 Bridged structures

Combined Systems.   In the case of the use of combined structural systems, for instance frames and shear walls, it is important for the total energy absorption that each system comes into action before any other experiences cause failure.

Bridged Systems.   Increased energy dissipation (and thereby reduced deformations and accelerations) can be achieved by bridging structural systems such as tall buildings, as investigated by Sofronie (1974, 1976) (Fig. 1.56).

Besides compacting the stiffnesses of the various buildings to resist lateral forces, and possibly changing the free-standing cantilever of a tall building to a guided cantilever, the coupling of buildings restricts, orients, and filters vibrations. Special devices provided in their linkage to dissipate energy could be most effective.

4   Artificially Increased Damping

Provision of Viscous Damping by Coating, Joints, or Bearings.   Artificial viscous damping can be effective in reducing the amplitude of vibrations in buildings and building elements, bridges, machines, and plates. This is realized by absorbing energy in viscous coating, joints, or bearing pads. Special design formulas are derived by Brotchie et al. (1972).

Use of Dynamic Vibration Absorbers.   Damped and undamped vibration absorbers are used to a large extent in any kind of machinery. However, the use of a large viscously damped vibration absorber has been, until now, considered for only a few tall buildings. During the design of the Jefferson Memorial Arch in St. Louis,

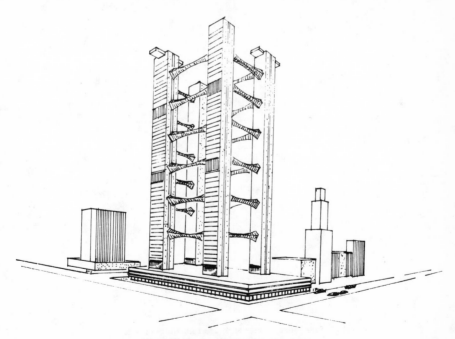

Fig. 1.56 Energy dissipating structure

such a device was considered. Finally, for the Centre Point Tower in Sydney, Australia, the mass of a pressurized water tank was used as a vibration absorber. The tank is cable-suspended and damped by radially arranged dashpots. Tower mass, water tank, suspension and damping are tuned for maximum effects (Fig. 1.57).

Use of Coulomb Friction Joints. The natural Coulomb friction between steel plates or between steel and asbestos braking materials can be effectively used in friction joints. Depending on movements and face pressure, large amounts of energy can be dissipated to heat in order again to damp the structure and reduce wind or earthquake-induced deformations and accelerations. The joints can be provided in wind trussing of tall buildings, in cable connections of guyed towers, or externally attached to existing buildings (Figs. 1.58 and 1.59).

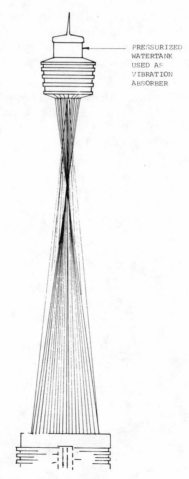

PRESSURIZED
WATERTANK
USED AS
VIBRATION
ABSORBER

Fig. 1.57 Pressurized water tank used as vibration absorber

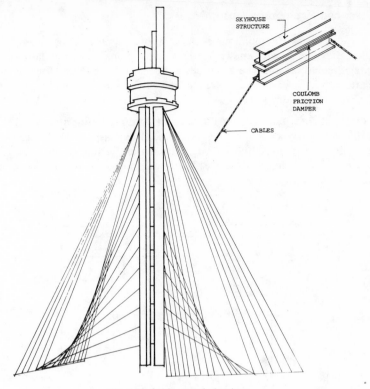

Fig. 1.58 Cable guyed structure

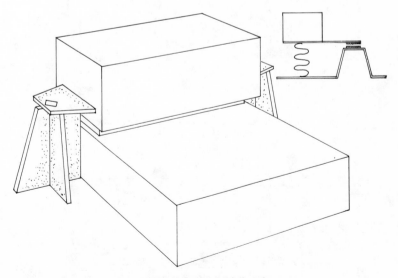

Fig. 1.59 Use of Coulomb friction damper

5   Advanced Foundation Design

The use of special foundations such as spring supports, shock absorbers, and vibration dampers is well known in the design of machine foundations. Similar advantages could certainly be achieved in the design of building foundations, and some attempts have been made to reduce the energy input caused by earthquake in the structure of buildings.

Reduction of Energy Input by Flexible or Sliding Foundations. The shock absorbing soft-story concept has been advanced by Caspe (1970) (Fig. 1.60). The isolation device prevents the foundation from transferring the full effects of the ground vibration in the substructure. The foundation, however, is able to resist all probable wind loading.

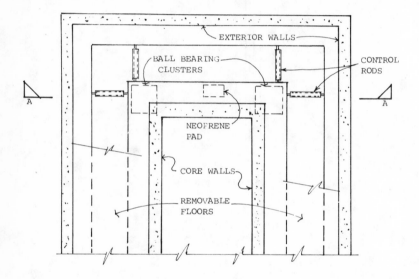

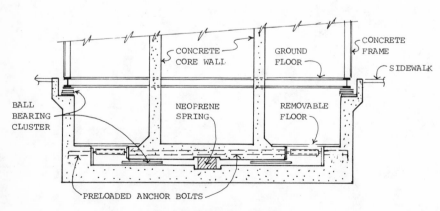

Fig. 1.60 Foundation isolation

6 Aerodynamic Provisions

It is obvious, but not frequently considered, that energy induced in structures can be dissipated by aerodynamic damping. It is also of importance that some aerodynamic shapes essentially reduce the energy induced in buildings by wind.

1.5 CONDENSED REFERENCES/BIBLIOGRAPHY

The following is a condensed bibliography for this chapter. Not only does it include all articles referred to or cited in the text, but it also contains bibliography for further reading. The full citations will be found at the end of the Volume. What is given here should be sufficient information to lead the reader to the correct article: the author, date, and title. In case of multiple authors, only the first named is listed.

AIA 1970, *Building Systems—Why Concrete?*
Abdallah 1973, *The MLC Center, Sydney*
Acier Stahl Steel 1971, *New Hotels In Amsterdam*
Acier Stahl Steel 1972, *Radison Hotel South, Minneapolis, Minnesota*

Bandel 1973a, *Structural Systems for Very Tall Buildings*
Bandel 1973b, *Composite Core and Columns*
Brainov 1975, *The Problem Tall Buildings—Architecture, Structures, Industrialization*
Brotchie 1972, *An Optimization Approach to Viscous Damping of Structures*
Bruna 1973, *Structures of Tall Buildings Using Precast Concrete Skeleton*
Brungraber 1973, *The Use of Lightweight Alloys in Tall Buildings*
Building Materials 1973, *Framing with Steel and Concrete Multibuild System*
Building Materials 1974, *Diamond-Shaped Tower Dons a Special Cladding*
Building Materials 1975, *New Type Sandwich Panels Make Up a Building's Face*
Building Practice 1971, *Concrete Materials—What Does the Future Hold?*
Building With Steel 1972, *Frames for Tall Buildings*
Byrd 1973, *Woolwich Tower Blocks Begin to Suffer After Ten Years Stress*

Caspe 1970, *Earthquake Isolation of Multistory Concrete Structures*
Castiglioni 1971, *Isolation of Multistorey Buildings from Ground-Borne Vibrations*
Christiansen 1973, *Cast in Place, Reinforced Concrete Systems*
Colaco 1974, *Pennzoil Place—A New Slant in Structural Systems*
Concrete 1970, *Strengthening Tower Blocks of Large Panel Construction*
Constructional Review 1973, *No. 1, York Street, Sydney*
Constructional Review 1974a, *MLC Project, Sydney*
Constructional Review 1974b, *T & G Building, Melbourne*
Constructional Review 1974c, *444 St. Kilda Road, Melbourne*
Constructional Review 1974d, *390 St. Kilda Road, Melbourne*
Constructional Review 1975, *Town Hall House*
Contract Journal 1971, *Highrise Hospital Goes Lightweight*

Disque 1973, *Mass Produced Steel Systems*
Dori 1969, *Structural Steelwork of Office Buildings, Rome*
Dziewolski 1973, *Prestressed Composite Structures and Space Structures*

Engineering 1966, *Building High*

Fintel 1968, *Staggered Wall Beams for Multistory Buildings*
Fintel 1971, *Response of Buildings to Lateral Forces*
Finzi 1968, *Light-Gage Floor Systems Provided to Include Utilities, Proposals and Experiments*
Finzi 1973, *The Structural Design of Tall Steel Buildings*
Fleming 1974, *Lateral Truss Systems in Highrise Buildings*
Fowler 1973, *BHP House, Melbourne*

Garnet 1973, *The AMP Center, Sydney*
Giangreco 1969, *Trends in Design of Steel Constructions in Seismic Area*
Giangreco 1971, *Present Trends in the Aseismic Design of Metal Constructions*

Goschy 1975, *Structural Systems*
Grainger 1971, *Whitgift Centre, Croydon*
Gunnar Birkerts and Associates 1973, *Suspended Bank Building: Federal Reserve Bank*

Hisatoku 1973, *Mixed and Composite Concrete and Steel Systems*

Ito 1971, *Structural System Composed of Steel Frame and Shear Walls*
Iyengar 1973, *Structural Systems for Two Ultra High-Rise Structures*

Jendele 1971, *High Buildings with a Concrete Bearing System in Czechoslovakia*
Jendele 1973, *Structural Systems of Tall Reinforced Concrete Buildings*
Johnson 1975, *Composite Structures of Steel and Concrete*
Jossa 1975, *Introduction to the Study of Tall Buildings*

Kajitani 1973, *Nippon Steel Building at Urban Renewal of Tokiwabashi District*
Kavrychine 1973, *Reinforced, Precast and Prestressed Concrete*
Khan 1969, *Tall Steel Structures, The Latest Trends*
Khan 1971, *Lightweight Concrete for Total Design of One Shell Plaza*
Khan 1973, *Newer Structural Systems and Their Effect on the Changing Scale of Cities*
Khan 1973, *Analysis and Design of Framed Tube Structures for Tall Concrete Buildings*
Khan 1974, *A Crisis in Design—The New Role of the Structural Engineer*
Khan 1975, *Tall Building—Recent Developments in Structural Systems and Architectural*
König 1973, *Cast-in-Place Reinforced Concrete Systems*
König 1975, *Tall Reinforced Concrete Buildings*
Kostem 1970, *The Stresses in Folded Plate Roof Traverses*
Kostem 1973, *Optimum Shaped Pneumatic Roofs*
Kozak 1973a, *Structural Systems of Tall Buildings in Steel or Combined Steel and Concrete*
Kozak 1973b, *Structural Systems of Tall Buildings with Core Structures*

Lewicki 1972, *Structural Design of Tall Concrete Buildings*
Lewicki 1975, *Analysis of Work of Secondary Structural System in Building Corner*
Liauw 1974, *Evolution of New Structural Systems for Tall Buildings*
Lubinski 1972, *Statical and Structural Systems of Tall Steel Buildings*

Manu 1975, *Reticular Tall Buildings in the Prahova District*
Mazzolani 1974, *Development of Structural Schemes in the Field of Tall Buildings:*
Mazzolani 1971, *Static of Framed Space Systems with Walls Variously Shaped*
McMillan 1975, *African Eagle Life Centre—A High-Rise Precast Load Bearing Facade*
Miller 1972, *Model Analysis of the Qantas Centre*
Miller 1973, *Qantas Center, Sydney, Design and Construction Planning*
Moore 1973, *Summary—Part I: Structural Systems*
Mukand 1973, *Economy in the Design of Tall Buildings—Structural*
Mukherjee 1974, *Integrated Frame-Wall Systems in Tall Buildings*
Munoz 1973, *Behavior of Tubular Structures*
Murray 1975, *Design to Prevent Floor Vibrations*
Muto 1971, *Fluttering Design of Keio Plaza Hotel*

Naka 1973, *Steel Reinforced Concrete-Structural System and Design Specification*
Nakagawa 1974, *Design and Experiment on Osaka Ohbayashi Building*
Narita 1974, *The Structural Design of Kaijo Building*
Nasser 1973, *Use of Thin Shells for Tall Buildings*
Nassetta 1973, *Structural Steel Tiered Building Frames*
Nejman 1973, *Homeostase in Tall Buildings*
Nelson 1968, *The Use of Viscoelastic Material to Damp Vibrations in Buildings*
New Civil Engineer 1974a, *Half Flexible, Half Rigid Approach for Frankfurt's Giant New Building*
New Civil Engineer 1974b, *Nat-West Banks on Clover-Leaf Cantilevers*
Ng 1974, *Structural Systems of Some of the Tall Buildings in Singapore and Kuala Lumpur*
Nisbet 1973, *Whickham Tower Block: The Design and Construction of a 30-Storey Block of Flats*
Noggaret 1973, *Havas Building at Neuilly: A Sculptured Building in Exposed Steel*

Ohta 1974, *Research and Development of a HPC Tall Building System*
Orme 1970, *System Built Flats on a Deep Buried Quarry*
Osborne 1975, *Precast Panels for Centre Rising Sixty Levels*

Pagano 1963, *Structures*
Pagano 1966a, *Experimental Full-Scale Investigation on Elastic-Plastic Instability*
Pagano 1966b, *Experimental Full-Scale Investigation on Elastic-Plastic Instability*

Pagano 1966c, *Experimental Full-Scale Investigation on Elastic-Plastic Instability*
Pancewicz 1972, *Review of Basic Problems in Tall Steel Buildings*
Paparoni 1973, *Central Park Towers, A System of Segmental Tubes*
Parmar 1974, *Tunas Building—Structural Design of a Slender Building*
Pawlowski 1976, *Trends in Suspended Building Construction*
Peyton 1973, *Collins Place Project, Melbourne*
Peyton 1974, *Collins-Wales Project—A 500 Ft. Tower in Simple Hybrid Construction*
Picardi 1973, *Structural System—Standard Oil of Indiana Building*
Pozzi 1975, *Planning of Structures and its Relationship with Construction Methods*
Pun 1974, *A Pre-Fabricated Building System Developed for Multi-Story Industrial Buildings*

Ramesh 1973, *Tall Buildings with Shear-Wall Systems—A Status Report*
Reinitzhuber 1973, *Summary Report—Part 2: Structural Systems*
Robertson 1973, *Theme Report: Structural Systems*
Roret 1973, *Tall Buildings in Steel*

Sabnis 1972, *Use of Paper Honeycombed Panels in Housing Construction*
Schmidt 1966, *High Rise Buildings of Reinforced Concrete—What are the Limitations?*
Skinner 1972, *The Connaught Centre, Hong Kong*
Smith 1973, *The Bank of New Zealand, Concept and Design*
Sofronie 1973, *Tall Buildings Elastically Coupled*
Sofronie 1974, *On the Bridging of Tall Buildings*
Sofronie 1975, *On the Dynamics of Bridged Structures*
Sofronie 1976, *On the Dynamics of Bridged Structures*
Sokolov 1973, *Weight Analysis of Braced Frames for Prismatic Tall Buildings*
Sontag 1970, *Steel Multi-Storey Garages*
Sontag 1973, *Precast Composite Flooring*
Steinmann 1973, *Tall Buildings in Concrete*
Sung 1974, *A Transfer Bowl for a 20-Storey Tower Block*

Takenami 1974, *Hotel New Otani Tower Project*
Taranath 1975, *Optimum Belt Truss Locations for High-Rise Structures*
Taylor 1973, *Park Tower, Melbourne, 30 Story Apartment Building*
The Building Centre of Israel Quarterly 1971, *Systems Building—Methods, Materials, Management*
Thompson 1973, *OCBC Centre, Singapore*
Thomson 1971, *Head Office for Hearts of Oak Benefit Society (London)*
Tombazis 1975, *Kifissia—Apartment Project, Part II*
Tomii 1973, *Concrete Filled Steel Tube Structures*

Vasiliev 1973, *Prefabricated Reinforced Concrete Multi-story Frame Buildings in the U.S.S.R.*
Vorlicek 1976, *Statistical Design of Tolerances of Assembled Structures*

Wargon 1973, *Centerpoint, Sydney*
Wells 1974, *Structural Systems of Three Sydney High Rise Buildings*
Wittman 1976, *On the Damping of Slender Reinforced Concrete Structures*

Yano 1973, *Design of the Shinguku-Sumitomo Building*
Yano 1974, *Effect of Cyclic Loading on Buildings*
Yorkdale 1973, *Masonry Building Systems*

Zakic 1965, *Results of the Lateral Load Test of the Prestressed Concrete Structure*
Zavelani 1974, *Space Frame Design with Optimal Choice of Standard Components*
Zunz 1971, *Standard Bank Centre, Johannesburg*

Tall Building
Systems and Concepts

Chapter SC-2

Mechanical and Service Systems

Prepared by Committee 2B (Mechanical and Service Systems) of the Council on Tall Buildings and Urban Habitat as part of the Monograph on the Planning and Design of Tall Buildings.

Richard T. Baum Committee Chairman
Rudiger Thoma Vice-Chairman
Richard E. Masters Editor

AUTHOR ACKNOWLEDGMENT

The essential first draft of this chapter is the work of R. E. Masters. Its starting point was the collection of state-of-art reports from the 1972 International Conference, held at Lehigh University, prepared by:

R. T. Baum
S. L. Daryanani
G. R. Jerus
F. Reuter
R. Thoma.

CONTRIBUTORS

The following is a complete list of those who have submitted written material for possible use in the chapter, whether or not that material was used in the final version. The Committee Chairman and Editor were given quite complete latitude. Frequently length limitations precluded the inclusion of much valuable material. The Bibliography contains all contributions. The contributors are: R. T. Baum, R. V. Benazzi, P. R. Crabtree, S. L. Daryanani, G. R. Jerus, D. O. Lloyd, G. H. Marais, R. E. Masters, J. H. McGuire, G. T. Murray, F. Reuter, G. T. Tamura, R. Thoma.

COMMITTEE MEMBERS

P. A. Anderson, R. T. Baum, W. Correalle, S. L. Daryanani, M. N. Dastur, E. H. Hesselberg, U. Inouye, G. R. Jerus, W. Kamler, R. E. Masters, G. C. Mathur, G. Rahulan, F. Reuter, P. Richardson, F. S. Rohatyn, B. Rubanenko, C. E. Schaffner, J. E. Snell, G. R. Strakosch, J. Strunk, T. Y. Sun, R. Thoma, R. G. Werden.

SC-2   Mechanical and Service Systems

Part 1—Heating, Ventilating, and Air Conditioning

2.1 GENERAL OVERVIEW

Since the introduction of the tall building, the various systems that have been developed to satisfy the heating, ventilating, and air conditioning (HVAC) needs of tall buildings have grown in number, as well as complexity. Today, to the still growing technology of HVAC systems, new dimensions have been added: (1) The need for an urgent response to the dwindling supply and rising costs of fossil fuels; and (2) responsive answers to the growing challenge to provide safer buildings in which to live and work. This chapter will deal with HVAC systems as they relate to the tall building. It must be understood that, at best, the thrust will be aimed at pointing out, in general terms, an approach to the various design problems associated with tall buildings and, therefore, is not designed to provide an exhaustive statement on the subject.

2.2 CONCEPTUAL DETERMINATIONS

All concepts developed for a building should address objectives. Therefore, all design effort must be directed toward satisfying stated or implied goals. The HVAC components of a building must fit the over-all objectives of the building as squarely as any other components and, in this sense, must be thought of as an integrated part rather than as an appendage to be placed into or onto the building after the architectural design has been fixed. When one considers the great cost of the mechanical trades (HVAC, electrical, plumbing, fire protection), representing 20% to 50% of the total building cost, a clearer perception of the importance of integrated design solutions is possible. Generally, all HVAC systems should be responsive, but not necessarily limited, to the following considerations:

1. Initial or budget cost.

2. Initial and future occupancy requirements.

3. Architectural and structural restraints and objectives.

4. Internal and external environmental requirements.

5. Seismic requirements (when applicable).

6. Energy consumption and energy source depletion.

7. Annual operating cost.

8. Smoke and fire management.

2.3 LOAD DETERMINATION

The design of any system requires a determination of the heating, ventilating, and cooling loads. The American Society of Heating, Refrigerating and Air-Conditioning Engineers (ASHRAE), headquartered at the United Engineering Center, 345 East 47 Street, New York, New York 10017, USA, can be considered as the most important reference source for heating, ventilating, and air conditioning design in the United States. ASHRAE's Handbook of Fundamentals (1972) and its Handbook and Product Directory represent the authoritative references on the subject (ASHRAE, 1974; 1975; 1976). Particular attention should also be given to ASHRAE's latest Energy Conservation Standard, namely ASHRAE Standard 90-75 (1975c) and companion Standards 55-74 (1974b) and 62-73 (1973a). In this discussion, ventilation will not be treated as a separate entity, but rather as a factor to be considered in the determination of both heating and cooling requirements. The following parameters, generally, should be considered in the determination of heating and cooling loads.

Heating.

1. Transmission losses (slabs on grade, foundations, doors, windows, walls, skylights, roofs, piping and ductwork).

2. Process loads (domestic hot water, kitchen appliances, laundry appliances, hospital equipment, humidification, equipment winterization—such as cooling towers, for example—snow melting, reheat).

3. Infiltration loads (exterior walls, window sash, doors).

4. Ventilation loads (fresh air for occupied areas, fresh air replacement to support kitchen exhaust, garage exhaust, toilet exhaust, various exhaust systems and emergency fresh air to support various 100% outside air pressurization cycles, as during a fire emergency).

Cooling.

1. Sensible heat gains (electrical, people, transmission gains through walls,

windows, roofs, and distribution systems; direct and indirect solar gains through all exterior surfaces; outside air—fresh air makeup and infiltration).

2. Latent heat gains (outside air and people).

3. Miscellaneous: Allowances must also be made, where applicable, for heat gains related to food serving and preparation, computer facilities, and special processes.

2.4 SUBSYSTEM ANALYSIS

Perhaps the most difficult of all tasks to be performed by the designer is to evaluate and select the proper subsystem. At best, one can only highlight and identify certain of the elements that enter into the various judgment equations that are developed in any building. At the outset of the chapter, the requirements to which the HVAC systems must be responsive were listed. It follows that the various

The National Mutual Life Association Building, Sydney, Australia *(Courtesy: G. A. Day, Australian Institute of Steel Construction; Photo by John B. Collins & Associates Pty. Ltd.)*

subsystems must also be goal-oriented. Upon the completion of load calculations, every subsystem must stand the test of every goal of the building, and they may be many in number. For example, the various energy sources available to the building, after identification, should be examined with respect to cost, reliability, impact on environment, and impact on the various major items of heating, ventilating and air conditioning equipment. Potential usage of nondepletable resources and waste heat should be closely evaluated.

All possible heating and cooling plants, related to the energy source, should be tested as to their economic and environmental impact. Further, their possible locations within the building will also affect structural costs, architecture, construction time, and suitability in relation to occupancy requirements. Not uncommonly, the latter requirements have been the primary factor in the determination of below-grade locations for central heating and refrigerating plants, regardless of higher first costs, in certain cases. Similarly, certain initial occupancy requirements have dictated the placement, as well as the number, of air handling systems within the building. Factors to consider, therefore, for heating and cooling plants include:

1. Weight, space requirements, and impact on structure.

2. Ease of operation and maintenance.

3. Part load and full load characteristics and functions.

4. Types of heating media.

5. Types of energy sources.

6. Reliability.

7. Life cycle costs.

8. Potential use of waste heat as heating source.

Generally, air handling systems for tall buildings fall into two major categories —those which are of a central station variety (serving more than one floor), and those of a local type (serving, usually, the floor upon which the equipment is located). Local and central distribution systems may be either factory assembled or built in place. Draw-through systems or blow-through arrangements are also possible. Generally, the blow-through arrangement requires more space and, in cold climates, will give fewer problems related to stratification of outside air with respect to recirculated air. The advisability of using either a blow-through or draw-through arrangement, or, for that matter, a built-up as opposed to a factory assembled system, can only be determined after a thorough examination of space conditions, cost, local labor practices, and quality objectives.

Air and water systems must also take into account airborne and structure-borne noise and vibration problems. Generally, the services of a qualified acoustics and vibration specialist are recommended to assist in the selection of proper vibration and sound attenuation devices and arrangements.

Consideration should also be given to comparing low velocity with medium and high velocity air distribution. There are no hard and fast rules as to which is the proper solution for all buildings. Obviously, the lower velocity systems require more space and, in most cases, lighter construction. They do succeed in reducing resistance to flow, and consequently use less power to move quantities of air from and to desired locations. On the other hand, medium and high velocity distribution systems permit distribution through smaller conduits and make it possible to distribute air in less space. Higher velocities, however, generate friction losses (resulting in higher power requirements), and need more difficult acoustical and vibration solutions.

The designer is constantly being called upon to minimize the amount of space, both in plan and cube, that HVAC systems require. It is a good objective but must be dealt with very carefully. It is of little use to plan minimal space allocation for such equipment and subsystems, and consequently to experience costly maintenance, difficult operation, and inflexibility with respect to possible future demands on such subsystems.

Tall buildings generally contain multiple types of occupancies and require multiple air handling units, either because of occupancy or because of their height. In order to operate these complex mechanical and electrical systems effectively from both energy and manpower conservation viewpoints, the incorporation of a central automation control system is often desirable. The system may include the

Collins Place seen from Exhibition Street and Flinders Lane, Melbourne, Australia; ANZ Tower on the left with Collins Tower and the Great Space *(Courtesy: G. A. Day, Australian Institute of Steel Construction)*

following functions: (1) On-off control and monitor of all mechanical-electrical equipment; (2) remote control point adjustments; (3) logging and alarm; (4) occupancy and lighting control; (5) energy demand limiting and load shedding; (6) energy consumption recording; (7) intercommunication; and (8) integration of fire alarm and security systems.

Just a few considerations have been mentioned, and one can be certain that there are as many more that the designer can identify. In the final analysis, no fixed rules can be listed, nor can a foolproof solution be offered.

2.5 OCCUPANCY LIMITATIONS

1 Hours of Operation

The design of the various systems should be responsive to the requirements of the occupancy. Some buildings operate uniformly with respect to hours of operation; some do not. The various distribution systems should be arranged so as to serve areas efficiently during all modes of operation. Systems, therefore, should be designed to account for both full and partial occupancies. It is clear that the techniques utilized in arranging for distribution systems to serve full occupancy requirements should be different from those serving partially occupied floors. Many techniques can be developed to meet such requirements. Dedicated systems, for example, can be developed for those special areas which historically operate at hours different from the normal occupancy. Alternatively, isolation valves (for water system) and automatic isolation dampers (for air system) can be utilized in many cases to accomplish the same purpose. In any event, the objective should be to operate only the equipment necessary to satisfy those spaces which are in occupancy at any given time.

2 Special Requirements

At the outset of any design, all known and probable special requirements should be identified and accounted for. Provisions should be examined for present and future conference areas, kitchens, computer facilities, special security areas, special wastes, special fume exhausts, special overtime operation, and special temperature and humidity areas. Anticipation of special requirements, particularly those related to future needs, requires good judgment and, in many cases, must rely upon past experience for proper determination.

3 Security

The degree to which systems provide building security often varies with the specific requirements of the users. Banking operations, for example, may require locks that affect egress paths. They, in turn, must be interfaced with fail-safe devices triggered by HVAC smoke detectors, power failures, or sprinkler systems, to mention a few, in such a way that life safety is given priority over security. The HVAC designer must therefore coordinate his design with the security systems of the building.

2.6 FIRE MANAGEMENT

Fire management in high-rise buildings is being subjected to major reexamination by both governmental and private design professionals. One result of this scrutiny has been the design of integrated systems for proper response to fire and smoke within the modern high-rise structure. A second result has been the development and issuance of new fire protection codes and standards throughout the nation. This changing of local building codes and national standards is a continuing process, with revisions being developed by many municipal, state, and Federal agencies. Chapter CL-4 deals extensively with the subject of fire in high-rise buildings.

It should be noted that, while there is no uniformity in the fire management requirements of these codes, there does appear to be some consistency in the over-all approach. All of the newer codes address themselves to the general questions critical to proper systemic approaches. The elements and techniques that must be reviewed and that form the basis of any fire management system are as follows:

1. Means must be included in the building to assure early detection of a fire so as to minimize its impact on both life and property.

Bank of New South Wales, Melbourne, Australia *(Courtesy: G. A. Day, Australian Institute of Steel Construction; Photo by Irvine Green Pty. Ltd.)*

2. Any fire safety approach includes a requirement for containment of any fire by compartmentation of the building and a means of early extinguishment so as to limit the size of a fire. An automatic suppression system (sprinklers, Halon, carbon dioxide) also will serve to reduce the magnitude of smoke generation and warrants inclusion in any over-all system that is incorporated in the design.

3. The need to prevent the dispersion of smoke and other products of combustion that can have a lethal effect on people and cause property damage requires proper use of ventilating and air conditioning supply and return fans. This need is recognized and addressed in a total solution.

4. A communication system is necessary not only to permit proper instructions to building occupants in the event of a fire emergency, but also to permit those people responsible for proper fire response to communicate with one another. This would involve not only internal two-way voice communication, but also early notification of the fire department.

5. The elevatoring system in the building must be removed from the control of the building occupants and placed at the disposal of the fire emergency personnel. This always will involve the elevators serving the area of the fire, and also may involve the elevators serving other portions of the building as well. The means for this altered control are included in the over-all system of fire response.

6. Management must include not only fire resistant values of walls, floors, shafts, and structure, but also of the fuel loading of the contents of the building (both furnishings and equipment) to minimize combustibility and potential smoke generation.

7. A fire safety organization and fire response plan must be developed for the building to permit proper internal occupant response in the event of a fire, posting of all areas of safe refuge that should be used by occupants in an emergency, and regularly called fire drills to assure proper understanding of what is to be done in the event of an actual conflagration.

Before considering the specifics of some of the elements mentioned, it is important to define the high-rise building from the standpoint of fire. This definition will enable us to understand some of the unique problems of the high-rise building with regard to fire safety. The General Services Administration of the United States government sponsored the International Conference on Fire Safety in High-Rise Buildings at Warrenton, Virginia in 1971. This conference arrived at a working definition of a high-rise building. It stated:

A high-rise building is one in which emergency evacuation is not practical and in which fires must be fought internally because of height. (GSA, 1971)

The usual characteristics of such a building are: (1) It is beyond the reach of fire department aerial equipment; (2) it poses a potential for significant stack effect; and (3) it requires unreasonable evacuation time. Figs. 2.1, 2.2, and 2.3 are illustrative.

To properly appreciate any fire management approach that has been suggested for the high-rise building, it is crucial that the difficulty of evacuating a building under a fire emergency is understood. During the normal work day, when people desire to leave the building, they use the vertical transportation system, which consists of elevators and possibly escalators to get them to the street level. During a fire, the elevators will not be available, since they will have been returned automatically to their terminal floor and will be under control of the fire department. Further, the elevator system is not capable of handling the mass of people who would be attempting an exodus under emergency circumstances, and are not designed with the capacity to permit rapid evacuation under emergency conditions.

If the occupants of the building cannot be evacuated vertically, they must be trained to move horizontally to areas of refuge that have been established within the building. Typically, these would be stairwells or other designated fire safe areas. From these areas, people can be removed from the building on a controlled basis by the fire department.

It is wise to recognize that the establishment of these areas and procedures, and their suggested use, contradicts every human instinct, which is to evacuate a burning building as quickly as possible.

Fig. 2.1 Stack effect *(Courtesy: Rolf Jensen)*

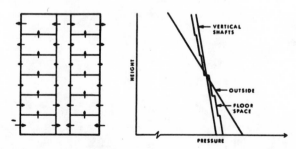

Fig. 2.2 Stack action *(Tamura and McGuire, 1973; Courtesy: National Research Council of Canada, Division of Building Research)*

A further point not to be overlooked is the inherent conflict between the use of stairwells as areas of refuge and the security system in the building. Quite frequently, as part of a building security system, the stairwell doors are locked from the inside to prevent exit from the stairs on any floor other than the main lobby. These are not proper restrictions under fire conditions for either the occupants or firefighters who must be afforded reentry paths from stairwells to any floor in the building. Accordingly, means should be provided to automatically open the secured doors if any of the building fire detection devices are actuated.

The fire protection and detection system that is to be included in a particular building is subject to many influencing factors. Most noteworthy, of course, is the applicable building code. There is considerable variation in both the components of the system that will be required by, and the control action that will be taken by, the building equipment in the event of a fire alarm. The variation in required control action is particularly critical when codes are reviewed for specific operation of the supply and return fan and the use of air for purposes of pressurization and smoke removal from fire zones.

Among the many features of the systems that must be designed for proper and complete life safety of the occupants in a properly engineered high-rise building are: (1) Fully automatic fire standpipe and sprinkler system; (2) an automatic gas or chemical suppression system in areas where water should not be used; (3) smoke detection system; (4) smokeproof or smoke-free egress system; (5) emergency electric power system; (6) automatic elevator recall system; and (7) communication and alarm system.

In high-rise buildings, providing methods to extinguish fires presents numerous problems. The type of building occupancy, the location of egresses, the type of furnishings and materials, along with the location of the building and fire department facilities, directly affect the design of fire extinguishing systems. For example, the requirements for pumping and the amount of water stored in a building should be different within the New York City limits when compared with those required for a rural location in New York State or Kuwait. The city fire department should be equipped with adequate pumping equipment and should have an unlimited source of water in the city mains, while the rural community would probably not be prepared to cope with a single high-rise building within its bounds.

Fig. 2.3 Unreasonable evacuation time (Courtesy: Rolf Jensen)

There are separate purposes behind the installation of fire standpipe systems and sprinkler systems. Standpipe systems are generally required in buildings over seven stories or 25 m (75 ft) in height, as this is the maximum practical distance for firefighters to couple hose together from a street level pumper up the stairway. It is also the maximum practical distance from which a fire can be fought externally from extension ladders and snorkel exterior equipment. Beyond 25 m (75 ft), the firefighter must generally fight the fire from within the building. When fighting fires, time is of the essence, and extinguishing a fire in its incipient stage is far easier than extinguishing a conflagration. To facilitate water supply, it is preferable to extend a pipe riser up the stairwell so the firefighters need only couple a hose to the valve provided on this line at every floor. Generally, the hose is connected in the stairwell one floor below the fire. This permits the use of the hose immediately adjacent to the stair and door, and also provides a line for the firemen to follow as an escape guide route in the event there is dense smoke.

Hence, the standpipe system is used to fight fires. On the other hand, a sprinkler system provides the best means of protection from spontaneous combustion or other fires, as this type of system automatically extinguishes a fire, or at least holds a fire in check until trained firefighters arrive.

The amount of water supplied to a standpipe system should be related to the number of fire hose streams used simultaneously. In New York City, for example, where high-rise experience is significant, the most streams of full bore equivalent, 1.6×10^{-2} m^3/sec (250 gpm), that were brought into play at one time have been three, or 4.7×10^{-2} m^3/sec (750 gpm). However, acceptable methods of providing water for a standpipe system in New York City do not comply with NFPA Pamphlet No. 14 (1969) illustrated in Fig. 2.4. It is regrettable that the experience learned in cities having high-rise buildings was not taken into consideration by the committee that wrote the standard. This standard has been adopted in many areas by reference, because the standard has the backing of a national organization which supposedly had the expertise that the smaller cities did not.

A comparison of certain items in each code highlights the differences between the national standard and New York City Code. The NFPA standard shows a system in which water from the low zone is pumped into the high zone through a series type system. This method presents problems in pump selection because a suction pressure of more than 1.4×10^6 N/m^2 (200 psi) could be transmitted to the high zone pump, since the low zone could extend 85 m (275 ft) and the pressure required at the highest hose valve in the low zone is 4.5×10^5 N/m^2 (65 psi). The NFPA standard refers to the use of approved pumps, and the pumps that are required for such duty have not been tested at suction pressures of this magnitude.

Further, under the piggyback system of pumping, the loss of one pump means the loss of water supply to the upper zone. This in itself is not critical if a fire department has been equipped with superpumps and the time to respond to an alarm is of short magnitude. If the piggyback system were used in the Empire State Building (photo in Vol. SB, Fig. 1.7) or the New York World Trade Center (photo in Chapter SC-4), the suction pressure on a pump installed at or below street level to supply water to the topmost floors would be in excess of 2.8×10^6 N/m^2 (400 psi). Suction pressures in excess of 2.8×10^6 (400 psi) are not desirable.

Another burdensome requirement in the standard is the pumping capacity that must be provided. This is a problem in many ways as the amount of water that can be drawn from some city mains is well below the NFPA suggested flow rate. Most of the water supplied by an automatic fire pump into the system is for first aid hose streams used by building occupants which require a lower demand than 1.6×10^{-2} m³/sec (250 gpm) per stream and, when greater quantities are required, fire truck pumpers generally provide added capacities through the siamese connections of the system.

This leads to the next problem in the system shown in the standard, namely, the siamese connections for fire department use. When two siamese are provided adjacent to each other, how does the firefighter select the proper one? True, they could be marked "19th Floor and Above" and "18th Floor and Below," but such identification could result in connections to the wrong zone or a time delay before the connection is made to the proper zone. In interconnected systems with a cross-connection between zones, the siamese can supply the entire building, which is an advantage. However, the fittings used in the lower zone must be capable of withstanding the maximum pressure of the system. With high pressure fittings, there is no need to waste money or space to provide the express risers indicated in the NFPA standard.

Another consideration is related to the capacity of storage tanks. In New York, it is a requirement to store 13 m³ (3500 U.S. gal) for a single riser system and 19 m³ (5000 U.S. gal) for a multiriser system. Combined standpipe and sprinkler storage is also permitted and the amount required is predicated on providing a 30-minute supply in the remote 1500 sq-ft area at the hydraulic design of not less than 0.1 gal

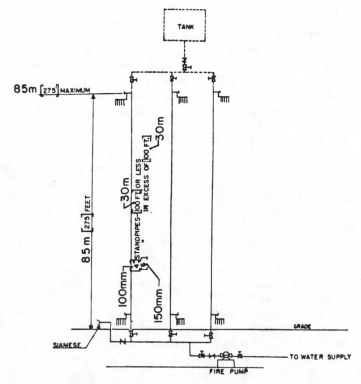

Fig. 2.4 (a) High-rise standpipe system: Typical single-zone system *(NFPA, 1978)*

per sq ft. The design density is usually exceeded due to the actual pressure at the sprinkler head.

The risers should be located within a stair enclosure, and a 65-mm (2-1/2-in.) hose valve for firemen's use should be located on this riser at every floor. An auxiliary hose station should be located just outside the stairwell and should be for use by untrained or partially trained personnel; therefore, the nozzle on this rack should be of an adjustable stream type with a hose of the 40-mm (1-1/2-in.) size. By using a nozzle of this type, the operation can be performed by one person. Before the advent of the adjustable nozzle, the whipping of the hose with an open nozzle caused injuries to many untrained persons. Also, the auxiliary hose can be used without opening the stairwell door. The maximum pressures on a system should be limited or controlled so that the fire hose nozzle can be held and the stream directed at the fire without difficulty.

Risers should be located so that not more than 30 m (100 ft) of hose is used at any one location because of the high pressure drop through hoses at fire stream flows. It should also be remembered that there should be some leeway in hose lengths, because it is necessary to get the hose nozzle in the room before the effective stream distance can be used. The experienced firefighter may be able to ricochet the stream

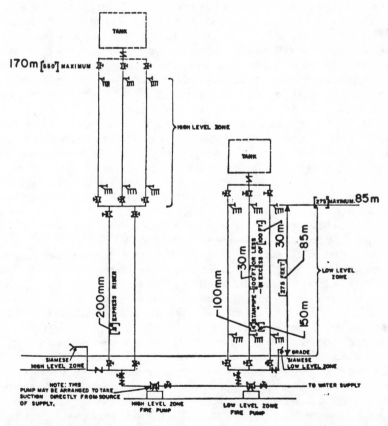

Fig. 2.4 (b) High-rise standpipe system: Typical two-zone system *(NFPA, 1978)*

off a door or wall and direct it toward the fire, but the average person would not think of doing this.

When using fire hose, it is necessary to see the flame and the source of the fire to extinguish it quickly; thus, it is necessary for the trained person to ventilate at the proper time and in the proper direction. In general, sprinklers should be considered for all buildings so the fire can be held in check in its incipient stage. If sprinklers are provided, the water must be available at all times and the source must be dependable.

Due to the increase in the number of high-rise buildings, many communities have adopted fire regulations relative to high-rise buildings. Their primary objective, thus far, has been office type occupancies; however, it is well to remember that the problems in office buildings also exist in other types of high-rise occupancies. The general trend has been to adopt regulations making sprinklers or compartmental-ization (or both) mandatory. Providing sprinkler protection permits more flexibility in subdividing floors, permits more utilization of the open space concept, and provides an automatic suppression system. In order to reduce the initial installation costs, building officials are permitting hydraulically designed systems which permit reduction in pipe sizes without compromising proper water density ratios. A ratio of 6.8×10^{-5} m³/sec-m² (0.1 U.S. gal per min per sq ft) of protected area, for light hazard occupancies, will provide adequate coverage. Under this water-to-area ratio, a sprinkler head could cover an area up to 21 m² (225 sq ft) and, therefore, in combination with hydraulic design, results in economical installations.

The amount of stored water for sprinkler systems should not be arbitrary but based upon the length of time required for the trained firefighters to arrive at the scene in response to the automatic alarm. It should also be dependent on the fire loading and fire areas, and the pipe sizes should be adequate to supply the water in sufficient quantities for the required period of time.

For the purpose of monitoring system performance, water flow devices should be installed in the horizontal sprinkler piping on every floor level. This will pinpoint the exact location of water flow from any system activated; it will cause the air supply and return systems to perform their desired control functions; and it will signal the elevator recall system into its emergency mode. Water flow devices also should be installed in the vertical fire standpipe distribution system for additional system monitoring. All control valves in the fire protection system should be equipped with electric tamper switches that will indicate to building operating personnel and the local fire department an immediate signal of any unauthorized operation. In the ultimate system, all flow and tamper switch alarms would be recorded on an alarm teletype or control panel located in the central fire control center, which would be manned at all times. Alarms also would be provided for the fire pumps to indicate operation, power failure, and abnormal pressure.

Control of the mechanical ventilation systems in the building involves not only proper control of the fans, but also usage of floor dampers located in both the supply and return ducts at each floor. These dampers have the capability of being opened or closed so as to cause supply air to be supplied or not supplied to the floor, and to cause return air to be exhausted or not exhausted from a particular floor.

When there is a fire in a high-rise building, the tendency of smoke to migrate from the fire area to other building sections is directly related to the outdoor air temperature, the building height, and the stack effect created by those parameters (Fig. 2.5). This is especially true if the supply and return fans are not being used in a way that minimizes this tendency. In addition, if the fans are operating with some degree of recirculation of the return air that is carried back to the central mechanical equipment room, the smoke entrained in the return air to that equipment room will be distributed by the supply system into sections of the building not affected by the fire.

It thus becomes necessary to use these fans to thwart the stack effect problem and to keep smoke from spreading from the fire area to occupied building sections not in the actual fire zone. The exact method of control should be reviewed with the local fire authorities, since their criteria vary from city to city. A method of fan control that seems to make sense would have the supply fan go to 100% outside air (using no return air), have the return fan go to 100% spill (exhausting all return air out of the building), and modify the floor dampers to pressurize the fire within its known location while removing the smoke being generated from the fire zone. This would mean closing the damper in the supply duct to the fire area and opening the damper in the return (exhaust) duct from the same area. In areas adjacent to the fire region, the supply fan would inject 100% fresh air, and the return air (exhaust) ducts would be closed. [See Figs. 2.6(a) and (b).] The result of these actions would be to effectively pressurize areas above and below the fire zone, as well as the stairwell and elevator shafts, and remove as many products of combustion from the building as possible, without contamination of areas adjacent to the fire.

The mechanism for causing the fans and duct dampers to operate in this fashion would be the sprinkler system or a system of smoke detectors (or both) that should be installed throughout the building. Smoke detectors should be installed as required by NFPA No. 90A (1976a), as a minimum. It is recommended that, rather than limiting their installation at the suction of each return fan, they be installed at the ducted return air connections to the return air shafts on each floor. This will permit proper floor damper and fan control through smoke detector alarm signals received at the central fire control center.

In addition, NFPA No. 90A (1976a) requires smoke detection to be provided downstream of the air filters in each supply air system, to shut down those fans in the event of a filter fire or smoke being brought into the building from outside. Manual override switches should be provided at the central fire control center to permit the fire department to modify the fan operation and the resultant building pressurization system.

Movement of smoke through a high-rise building can do more damage to the occupants, both psychologically and physically, than the fire itself. Therefore, the nature of the stairwells and other locations that are used for refuge is extremely

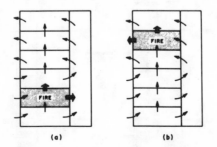

(a)   (b)

Fig. 2.5 Smoke migration patterns *(ASHRAE, 1976)*

important. These areas must be kept smoke-free by either turning on supply air systems or providing dedicated stair pressurizing systems so that any air movement would be out of the stairs and onto the fire floor, rather than the other way around. Smoke balconies, vented to atmosphere, on every floor are probably the safest means of assuring smoke-free areas of refuge.

Having located and protected these areas of refuge from smoke contamination, their use as staging areas for controlled removal of personnel should be reviewed. Assuming they pass all tests, the master fire response plan can and should be developed to serve as the document that will be used by the building fire marshals for proper comprehension of what paths of egress will be used in a fire emergency.

An emergency generator system should be included to furnish power to various building subsystems in the event of a primary power failure due to the failure of either electric utilities or building components. The control systems for generator starting and load transfer should be completely automatic. While this emergency generator should be included as part of the over-all life safety system in the building, it also should be reviewed for integration with the fire management system.

For example, as a minimum, the emergency power should provide general

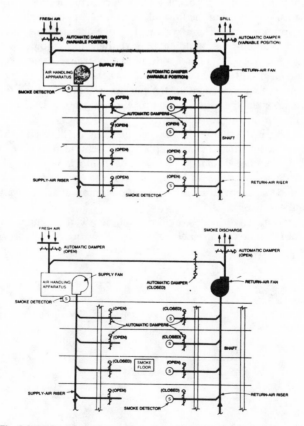

Fig. 2.6 (a) Fan operation, normal mode; (b) Fan operation, fire mode

illumination for safe egress from the building's general office spaces, public corridors, and lobbies, as well as all stairs, exits, and elevator cabs. The system also should permit selective operation of elevators in each bank with means to transfer to each cab selectively so that all elevators may be lowered to their lowest terminal floor. Finally, the system should be integrated with the fire pumps, the alarm system, and the central fire control station and its communication system so that, in the event of simultaneous power failure and fire emergency in the building, it is still possible to respond to the fire emergency.

The means for causing the elevators to return to their terminal floor is the activation of any alarm device included in the total system (smoke detector, sprinkler, or manual pull box alarm). In addition, it is prudent to include in each elevator lobby or vestibule on each floor a smoke detector mounted directly above the elevator button to recall the elevator serving that floor to its lowest floor.

The proper use of the elevators requires the cooperation of the elevator manufacturer and the fire control people. It recognizes that elevator use in the building must be controlled by those who know what to do in the event of fire. It permits the elevators to be used not only for building evacuation, but also for the quickest possible movement of the firefighting personnel to the area within the building where they can do the most good in controlling the fire.

The inclusion of a central fire control station is mandatory. Its location, in general, will be determined by review with the local fire authorities. The best location is on the ground floor at the elevator system terminus. The station will include means of determining fire conditions in the building (either through sprinkler, fire standpipe, or smoke alarm), as well as local fire pull boxes and special telephones. In addition, it should include a two-way communication network with means of giving instruction through loudspeakers at each floor, in stairwells or other areas of refuge, in elevator cabs and elevator machine rooms, and in the mechanical equipment rooms that contain the building fan systems. The communication network should be capable of being indexed so that conversations can be directed to particular areas without causing other locations to overhear them. Whether prerecorded taped messages should be used in an emergency is questionable. Such a feature has been included in some total systems.

In addition to the building communications network, the central fire control station should offer the capability of speaking with the local fire department station. It should permit elevator control, or access to the area of elevator control, so that the cabs can be captured and operated by the fire department. Finally, it should have panels indicating alarm points, operating condition of building equipment, and the means to alter the operating mode of that equipment. The original change in the control of the building environmental and electrical equipment can be made automatically at the central fire control station, or local control points for fans, floors, or elevators. The purpose of the central fire control station is to permit a single location within the building to be the rendezvous and control point for the fire department and building personnel. It is the brain and the heart of the ultimate fire response achieved by the building. Its organization, both internally and in terms of possible functions, should be carefully reviewed and analyzed by the designer of the over-all system.

The purpose of this section has been to examine and develop an efficient method of managing the total resources of a building to contain a fire and facilitate the evacuation of people from a high-rise building. While the alternative solutions are limited only by the imagination of the designers of the system, it should be noted that early and continuing review of applicable codes, as well as regular discussions with the local fire authorities, are both necessary and wise. The fire authorities are familiar with the peculiarities of the situation and, ultimately, can and should control the total system in any building under their jurisdiction.

In recent years, due to the growing awareness of much needed investigation and research on the entire subject of smoke and fire control, much effort has been devoted toward designing solutions to meet this problem. Representative papers illustrate the point (ASHRAE, 1973b, 1975b).

2.7 HYDROSTATIC CONSIDERATIONS

Static and dynamic pressures of various piping systems weigh heavily in the design of HVAC work. A proper balance has to be made between the advantages and disadvantages of more systems as opposed to fewer systems with increased operating and static forces. There are many factors that affect a proper decision. First and foremost must be considered the safety of the system. Utilizing fewer systems with attendant higher working pressures may not prove advisable from several standpoints. Higher working pressures require, in many cases, specially built equipment. While the initial deliveries may be assured, replacement parts for such specialized equipment may prove almost impossible to obtain, and therefore such selections are not prudent. Fewer systems may not necessarily mean reduced cost, either in operation or first cost. The difference in purchase price of certain pieces of equipment varies almost geometrically with increased operating pressures and must be, in each case, tested economically during the design process. Equipment of higher working pressure could require much more time to produce than lower pressure equipment and, consequently, could have an adverse effect on the time needed to build the installation. Other considerations, such as maintenance, stress corrosion (usually associated with higher pressure operation), space economy, and impact on structure, must be weighed before final determinations are made.

2.8 PIPING CONSIDERATIONS

1 Expansion and Contraction

The full range of movement of all piping during the construction as well as operating periods must be anticipated and accounted for. Of particular importance is the determination of those movements which must be supported by the building structure.

2 Access

All expansion joints, major guides and anchors should be available for inspection and maintenance. Wherever possible, the use of expansion joints of all types (slip, ball, bellows, etc.) should be avoided. In those cases, however, where such joints are absolutely necessary, their locations should be within mechanical equipment areas remote from occupied zones. This is particularly true of expansion joints serving steam systems. Considerable care should be taken in positioning guides and anchors for all such joints.

3   Seismic Restraints

In areas subject to earth tremors and quakes, seismic restraints should be designed to safeguard against piping and equipment collapse. Close coordination with the structural engineer is required, with respect to anticipated forces, as well as seismic restraint attachments to the structure. Present thinking with respect to such restraints is to safeguard against piping and equipment causing injury to occupants. We may, for reasons of fire safety in the future, see requirements placed upon seismic designs to assure that critical systems, such as sprinkler systems, be kept operational during such emergencies.

4   Fire Stopping

Piping passing through sleeved openings should be protected. The spaces between the piping and the sleeves should be kept to an absolute minimum, and such voids should be packed with an approved fire resistant material, usually equivalent to mineral wool or asbestos rope. Piping passing through more than one floor, if more than minimal in penetration area, should be enclosed in shafts with enclosing walls having a proper fire resistant rating. The hourly rating will vary with various jurisdictions, and also may vary within a jurisdiction in sprinklered buildings as compared with unsprinklered buildings.

5   Loading

Loads, both static and dynamic, of all piping systems must be designed into the basic structural framing system. Too often, piping loads are considered after the structure has been designed and, in other cases, sometimes overlooked. Prudent design requires that all major piping requirements be identified, positioned, and structurally accounted for.

2.9   STACK EFFECT CONSIDERATIONS

The stack (or chimney) effect of each building should be accounted for in the design of the HVAC systems. This phenomenon will vary with the height of the building and will vary also with differences in the temperatures of the building with respect to outside air temperatures. A few factors are listed for consideration:

1. The most effective entryway of a building utilizes revolving doors. While vestibules can be utilized, their effectiveness in offsetting stack effect problems is greatly diminished whenever inner and outer vestibule doors are simultaneously opened. This can easily occur during busy periods of people movement in an out of the building.

2. Elevator lobbies are particularly vulnerable to the stack action. Consideration should be given to compartmentizing such lobbies by creating vestibuled elevator lobbies on each floor of the building.

3. Pressurization, resulting from supplying more air than is exhausted or returned, is also used to minimize such effects. The degree to which pressurization is employed will vary with both building height and temperature extremes, but, in general, will not exceed 5%. That is to say, at least 95% of all air supplied will be balanced by return air and exhaust air. During a fire mode, as was described in Section 2.6, pressurization techniques assist in the control of smoke movement from areas of danger to areas of refuge.

Part 2—Plumbing and Fire Protection

High-rise building has proliferated due to the population explosion and the growth of business, coupled with the high cost of land. With this trend to develop available land to the utmost, urban property has been developed to increase the per

Fig. 2.7 Bankers Trust Plaza, New York—a fully sprinklered building that, at time of completion (1974), met all requirements of New York life-safety systems *(Courtesy: Bankers Trust; Photo by Victor B. Greene)*

capita density per square foot of land. With each new building being developed, buildings such as the Empire State Building become passé and others take over the title of "Tallest Building," but only for a short period of time as a new one rises elsewhere.

With these giants come new engineering problems. In the area of plumbing and fire protection, two of the main considerations are pressure limitations and the selection of appropriate materials. The design criteria that one would normally use for low-rise buildings therefore must be modified to accommodate the high-rise building so that workable systems within general economic constraints can be achieved.

2.10 WATER SUPPLY AND DISTRIBUTION

A tall building presents numerous problems in water distribution. The taller the building, the greater the problem—solely because of the space that must be provided for the distribution equipment. Pressure limitations on fixtures, equipment, and materials must be taken into account, and increased maintenance or operation problems can be expected.

For example, when the system pressure increases, a faucet orifice opening must be decreased to supply the same quantity of water as would be delivered with less

BHP House, a 41-story building in Melbourne, Australia, the tallest steel frame in Australia
(Courtesy: G. A. Day, Australian Institute of Steel Construction; Photo by Robert Tobin Studios)

pressure. Increased pressures, therefore, require restricted orifices, and resulting velocities produce erosion of the faucet seats, thus decreasing the life of the fixture and increasing maintenance. A side effect of this restriction is a wire drawing or vibration noise that can be transmitted through the piping to other areas of the building.

Consequently, a tall building is generally zoned so as to eliminate or at least reduce the problems due to high pressures. The zoning can be accomplished by the use of gravity tanks, pressure tanks, constant pressure pumping systems, or combinations of these methods. In many instances, the zones may be established because the fire standpipe reserve and the domestic water storage can be economically combined, and the pressure limitations at which a fire hose stream can be effectively manned establish the zone pressure which becomes the maximum pressure for the zone.

When the building is subdivided by gravity tanks, the number of required pressure regulating valves is reduced. Generally, a maximum zone pressure of 1.0×10^6 N/m² to 1.1×10^6 N/m² (150 psig to 160 psig) results in the spacing of the tanks at intervals of about 100 m to 110 m (340 ft to 370 ft) so that the first floor being served from the tank is located a sufficient distance below the tank to provide a pressure of approximately 1.4×10^5 N/m² (20 psig). The use of tanks versus booster pump systems is controversial, and the major concern must be safety of life and reliability, followed by economic considerations. The tank system is designed to hold a reserve of domestic water to carry the building demand over the average peak demand while the pumps supplying the tank are sized on supplying the average hour. The tank arrangement generally provides a stored reserve of between 1/2 hr to 1 hr of domestic water, with house pumps supplying the tanks sized to maintain this reserve rather than peak demand. In addition, tank installations, in the event of a power outage, provide a reserve of water supply.

The hot water heaters or generators are usually located to zone the building in the same manner as the cold water system, so as to provide the same static pressure on the various floors. The location of the heaters can be at the high point of the zone, but below the house tanks, or at the low point at the level of the house pumps. When the heaters are placed at the top of the zone served, they will operate against normal thermal circulation, but at lower operating pressure, which results in a reduction of the initial cost of the equipment. Where the zones are spread, the heater selection would require a higher pressure rating certification and a pressure-temperature safety relief arrangement to operate at the higher pressure.

Air binding problems can be expected to develop within the circulated hot water system. While under a higher pressure at the bottom of the zone, a large amount of air can be held in solution but, as the pressure reduces near the top of the heated zone, a considerable amount of air can be released. This air, if not allowed to escape from the system, can cause an air lock, thus stopping circulation and possibly supply to fixtures or a sputtering or spurting of water at the faucet or outlet. One method of relieving the air is to provide a spill line piped to spill over the house tank. Another method employs the use of mechanical devices (air reliefs) designed for just this purpose. Still another technique suggests the installation of the hot water header a floor below the highest fixtures and connecting the fixture supply branch on a constant rise from the header, using the fixtures to purge the air from the system.

2.11   DRAINAGE AND VENTING

Because hot water is discharged into the drainage piping, the chimney or thermal effect, due to stack height, must be considered. Proper differential pressures will avoid the loss of trap seals. As long as the differential pressures are maintained in safe or tolerable ranges, the system will function adequately. For this reason, relief vents are installed. Generally, a yoke relief vent is provided at 10-floor intervals, thereby permitting air to flow from the vent to or through the soil pipe or vice versa, maintaining an equilibrium and preventing the loss of trap seals.

The other place where reliefs are required is in stack offsets. This condition, however, is not peculiar to high-rise buildings, but is present in any system where the vertical distances between or above offsets are sufficient to permit the fluid to attain terminal velocities, creating a shooting flow at the offset and the trapping of air in this hydraulic jump area which must be relieved.

Much of this air and pneumatic balancing can be accomplished by a series of

United Engineering Center, New York *(Courtesy: United Engineering Trustees)*

planned offsets and proper pipe sizing, which permits the air to be relieved without being severely compressed in such a way as to eliminate the need for both a waste or soil attending vent. This single pipe system has been used successfully in Europe under the patented name "Sovent." However, there are other areas where single pipe systems, combination waste and vent, have been used successfully without the use of patented fittings.

The storm water system produces interesting problems in high-rise buildings. One is the effect of the flow from the high roofs on the flow from low roofs. Because there is air trapped in the horizontal offsets, which is compressed between the hydraulic jumps, a pipe from a low drain that is connected into this area tends to act as a spurting fountain, because the drain acts as a relief for the compressed air. In order to eliminate this problem, it is desirable to eliminate connections between high and low drainage zones. This is especially true if there is any obstruction in the combined line, such as a valve, trap, or offset. In many instances, the higher zone

Fig. 2.8 Coca Cola Building, Atlanta, Georgia—a building that typifies latest state of art at time of construction (1979) with regard to life-safety systems *(Courtesy: Jaros, Baum & Bolles)*

roof drains are used to drain the cooling towers or receive the discharge from the tower bleed used to maintain the proper parts per million of water treatment. When this happens, the drain should be sized to receive the higher flow demand and proper consideration must be given to the fact that the line carrying the storm water is flowing approximately one-third full of water and the remainder contains entrapped air.

2.12 MATERIALS

The drainage and vent systems are generally supported at every floor, which tends to reduce the pipe loads being transmitted to the structure at any one point. Because there are fixtures with an attending waste and vent system, the maximum pressure to which any part of the system is subjected is limited. The test pressures need only approach the joint and factory testing for the material, which is 3.5×10^5 N/m^2 (50 psi), or about seven floors of piping. The testing and expansion is usually accommodated by a combination test tee and expansion joint installed at seven-floor increments. In actual operation, the drainage and vent system would seldom be subjected to pressures in excess of one story. If there is a stoppage, the fixtures would overflow and relieve the system from excessive pressures and, usually, fixtures exist on every floor.

An expansion joint or suitable offset should be provided at the top of the leader to prevent the expansion of the piping from raising the roof drain, which would damage the waterproof integrity of the roof. The storm water system should be provided with expansion test tees similar to those provided for the drainage system; however, in the event of a stoppage at a lower floor, there could be a pressure buildup in the leader piping.

The storm water piping can experience considerable movement because it can be subjected to wide temperature changes in certain areas of the world. In the winter, melting snow at low temperatures flows into the drain and the building space, where the pipe may be 22°C (72°F) or more. Because of this temperature differential, sweating is possible. To avoid the staining of ceilings from condensation, it is well to consider insulating the horizontal offsets located above finished ceilings.

Long vertical runs of piping subject to temperature changes must have provisions to permit proper expansion without placing undue stresses on the structure and piping. Usually, the length of runs between the anchors is approximately 30 m (100 ft), which tends to limit the amount of expansion and the amount of force that must be taken by the structure. In order to force the pipe movement to the expansion joint, it is necessary to provide suitable anchors and guides. The expansion can be taken by cold spring joints, multi-elbow screw joint swings, or special joints designed just for this purpose.

The amount of expansion permitted must not change or materially affect the slope of drain lines which, in turn, would affect the carrying capacity of the pipe. This is particularly true with materials that have a great amount of expansion per meter.

By dividing the building into limited vertical zones, the static pressures are reduced, permitting the selection of lighter weight materials. However, when using pressure regulating valves, it must be remembered that a failure of the mechanical device will subject the piping beyond the regulator to the maximum static pressure or pump pressure (or both) for that branch; hence, the material should be selected for such contingencies.

Table 2.1 is a list of working pressures recommended for some copper materials; however, the joint used with the material is of equal importance and must be capable of meeting the pressure requirements of the system. When reviewing these pressures, keep in mind that they are based on ANSI Standards and, therefore, other materials used in the system should be charted in the same manner.

2.13 DRINKING WATER

The use of drinking fountains in office building occupancies has been mandated by many codes. Although the need for this type of fixture is well recognized, it is difficult to locate or provide them before a floor plan of the final occupancy is made. The final floor plan affects the type selected and also the size of individual units.

If a floor layout indicates the possible installation of drinking fountains, one above the other for a number of floors, it may be well to consider the use of a central drinking water chiller.

The use of individual electric water coolers provides the most flexibility in the floor layout; however, there are many more compressors and chillers that must be maintained. In order to reduce the number of refrigeration units, a single unit can be installed to supply three fountains, one over the other.

In some cases where the static pressures are high, the chilled water may become milky due to entrainment of air. While this phenomenon can be bothersome from an esthetic standpoint, it is not detrimental to health. If the water is allowed to stand, the milky appearance disappears. It can also be reduced or eliminated by proper adjustment of the bubbler and providing the air reliefs in a piped system.

Table 2.1 Recommended working pressures

Material (1)	Working pressure, in newtons per square meter (pounds per square inch)[a] (2)
Schedule 40 Std. Wt. Threaded Brass	2.1×10^6 (310)
Schedule 40 Std. Wt. Unthreaded Brass	3.7×10^6 (540)
Schedule 80 Extra Heavy Threaded Brass	3.0×10^6 (440)
Schedule 80 Extra Heavy Unthreaded Brass	4.8×10^6 (690)
Threadless Copper	1.9×10^6 (280)
Copper Tube Type M	1.5×10^6 (219)
Copper Tube Type L	1.8×10^6 (254)
Copper Tube Type K	2.4×10^6 (350)
50-50 Solder	2.1×10^6 (300)
95-5 Tin-Antimony	3.3×10^6 (480)
Silver Solder	2.9 to 4.2×10^6 (420 to 610)

[a]Up to 65 °C (150 °F).

2.14   CONDENSED REFERENCES/BIBLIOGRAPHY

The following is a condensed bibliography for this chapter. Not only does it include all articles referred to or cited in text, but it also contains bibliography for further reading. The full citations will be found at the end of the Volume. What is given here should be sufficient information to lead the reader to the correct article: the author, date, and title. In case of multiple authors, only the first named is listed.

ASHRAE 1972, *Handbook of Fundamentals*
ASHRAE 1973a, *Standards for Natural and Mechanical Ventilation*
ASHRAE 1973b, *Experience and Applications on Smoke and Fire Control*
ASHRAE 1973c, *Systems Handbook*
ASHRAE 1974a, *Handbook and Product Directory, 1974 Applications*

ASHRAE 1974b, *Thermal Environmental Conditions for Human Occupancy*
ASHRAE 1975a, *Handbook and Product Directory, 1975 Equipment*
ASHRAE 1975b, *Transactions*
ASHRAE 1975c, *Energy Conservation in New Building Design*
ASHRAE 1976, *Handbook and Product Directory, 1976, Systems*

Au 1973, *Building Services and Systems in Hong Kong*
Banham 1974, *Engineering Services in Tall Buildings*
Baum 1971, *Service Systems in Tall Buildings*
Baum 1973a, *Building Services in Tall Buildings*
Baum 1973b, *Mutual Influences Between Building Concept and Mechanical Systems*

Baum 1973c, *Theme Report*
Baum 1971, *Service Systems*
Benazzi 1974, *Water Supply and Drainage Systems for Sears Tower*
Crabtree 1975, *Plumbing and Drainage in Tall Buildings*
Daryanari 1972, *Heating, Ventilating and Air Conditioning*

Daryanani 1973, *Heating, Ventilating and Air Conditioning*
Forwood 1974, *Development of a Data Handling Facility for a Computer Model of the Thermal*
GSA 1971, *Public Buildings Service International Conference on Fire Safety*
Ho 1974, *Hydraulic Services in a High Rise Building*
Hutcheon 1968, *Smoke Problems in High-Rise Buildings*

Inouye 1964, *Planning of Building Sevice Systems for High Rise Buildings*
Inouye 1971, *System Design of the Building Service Systems for High Rise Building*
Inouye 1974, *HVAC and Plumbing System of Japanese High Rise Buildings*
Jaros, Baum, and Bolles (staff) 1978, *The Perfect Office Building*
Jerus 1972a, *Fire Safety in Tall Buildings*

Jerus 1972b, *Plumbing*
Jerus 1973, *Plumbing and Fire Protection*
Krishnamurthy 1973, *Electrical and Mechanical Services in Tall Buildings*
Kshirsagar 1973, *Public Health Services in Tall Buildings*
Larm 1975, *A System of Computer Programs for Designing, Selecting and Analysing Air*

Lie 1975, *Control of Smoke in High-Rise Buildings*
Lloyd 1974, *Solid Waste Disposal from Tall Buildings*
Marais 1975, *Air-Conditioning in High-Rise Buildings*
McGrath 1974, *Comfort and Conservation in Large Building Environmental Control*
McGuire 1971, *Smoke Control in High-Rise Buildings*

McGuire 1970, *Factors in Controlling Smoke in High Buildings*
Murray 1975, *A Sanitary Engineer's Viewpoint on the Design, Installation, Maintenance and*
NFPA 1969, *Standard Pipe and Hose Systems*
NFPA 1976a, *Standard for the Installation of Air Conditioning and Ventilating Systems*
NFPA 1976b, *Code for Safety to Life from Fire in Buildings and Structures*
NFPA 1978, *Standard for Installation of Standpipe and Hose Systems*

NRCC 1977, *Measures for Fire Safety in High Buildings*
Norman 1973, *Service Systems*
Orvetz 1975, *Service Systems in High and Medium-High Buildings*
Rane 1973, *Water Supply and Sanitary Services in High Rise Buildings*
Reuter 1972, *Cleaning and Waste Disposal*

Reuter 1973, *Cleaning and Waste Disposal*
Rooley 1974, *Non-Environmental Engineering Services*
Rosiak 1972, *System of Natural Ventilation in Tall Buildings*
SAA 1974a, *Rules for Automatic Fire Alarm Installations*
SAA 1974b, *Rules for the Use of Mechanical Ventilation and Air Conditioning*

Sander 1973, *A FORTRAN IV Program to Simulate Air Movement*
Sharma 1973, *Recent Development of New Plumbing Systems for High Rise Buildings*
Shaw 1973, *Air Leakage Measurements of the Exterior Walls of Tall Buildings*
Spencer 1973, *The Effect of Building Design Variations on Air Conditioning Loads*
Tamura 1969, *Computer Analysis of Smoke Movement in Tall Buildings*

Tamura 1973, *The Pressurized Building Method of Controlling Smoke in High-Rise Buildings*
Tamura 1966, *Pressure Difference for a Nine-Story Building as a Result of Chimney Effect*
Tamura 1967, *Pressure Difference for a Nine-Story Building as a Result of Chimney Effect*
Tamura 1968, *Pressure Differences Caused by Wind on Two Tall Buildings*
Thoma 1972, *Service Systems in Relation to Architecture*

Thoma 1973, *Service Systems in Relation to Architecture*
von Döbeln 1975, *Air Conditioning of Tall Buildings*
Wirthensohn 1973, *Mechanical Installations in Tall Buildings*

Tall Building
Systems and Concepts

Chapter SC-3

Electrical Systems

Prepared by Committee 2C (Electrical Systems) of the Council on Tall Buildings and Urban Habitat as part of the Monograph on the Planning and Design of Tall Buildings.

Richard T. Baum	Committee Chairman
Rudiger Thoma	Vice-Chairman
Wilbur M. Herbert	Co-Editor
Albert Cho	Co-Editor

AUTHOR ACKNOWLEDGMENT

The essential initial drafts of this chapter were the work of W. M. Herbert and A. Cho. Its starting point was the set of state-of-art reports from the 1972 International Conference, held at Lehigh University. These reports were prepared by:

R. T. Baum
P. Richardson
F. S. Rohatyn
J. Strunk.

CONTRIBUTORS

The following is a complete list of those who have submitted written material for possible use in the chapter, whether or not that material was used in the final version. The Committee Chairman and Editors were given quite complete latitude. Frequently length limitations precluded the inclusion of much valuable material. The Bibliography contains all contributions. The contributors are: R. T. Baum, A. Cho, W. M. Herbert, F. R. Khan, P. K. Kwong, J. C. Okell, J. Rankine, P. Richardson, R. A. Robinson, F. S. Rohatyn, E. Skubik, J. Strunk, R. Thoma.

COMMITTEE MEMBERS

P. A. Anderson, R. T. Baum, A. Cho, W. Correalle, S. L. Daryanani, M. N. Dastur, W. M. Herbert, E. H. Hesselbert, U. Inouye, G. R. Jerus, W. Kamler, G. C. Mathur, N. O. Milbank, G. Rahulan, F. Reuter, F. S. Rohatyn, C. E. Schaffner, J. E. Snell, G. R. Strakosch, J. Strunk, R. Thoma, R. G. Werden.

SC-3   Electrical Systems

Electrical systems, equipment, and facilities which must be provided for a tall building may vary with the type of building, but will generally include lighting, power for mechanical equipment and communication systems, fire alarm, and miscellaneous control and auxiliary systems. This chapter is intended as an aid to all electrical engineers in order to select and analyze the requirements for power, illumination, and auxiliary systems. The engineer should consult with local authorities to become familiar with the local rules and regulations to select and design a reliable, safe, and functional electrical system.

3.1 LOAD DETERMINATION

The determination of the estimated electrical load for a tall building is one of the first tasks to be performed by the design electrical engineer. In addition to the normal lighting and utility loads, this estimate should include capacity for the building's mechanical systems, vertical transportation equipment, and any special systems that are planned which require electrical energy, such as computers and their associated air conditioning systems and electric heat. The load figure should also include 20% to 30% spare capacity to satisfy the load growth that might take place during the life of the building. Tables 3.1 through 3.11 contain data most commonly used as guidelines in the United States for determining electrical loads applicable to tall buildings. As a basis for comparison, for certain of these tables data that are typical of the German Federal Republic are also shown.

3.2 AVAILABLE SERVICE VOLTAGES

After the estimated electrical load has been determined for both initial and ultimate requirements, all available service voltages offered by the electric utility supplying electricity to the building should be studied in order to determine the most appropriate selection for the proposed structure.

An important requirement for the electric service in a tall building is reliability of the supply. Since the life safety of the occupants of a tall building is intimately related to the building electrical subsystems, it is necessary for the electric service to possess the highest possible degree of continuity. A building that is served by a single service (under 600 volts) naturally has a low degree of continuity when compared to a multiservice connection such as would be obtained from a transformer spot network. Accordingly, every effort should be made to obtain multiservices from a utility company spot network.

When low voltage service (under 600 volts) alternating current is offered by the utility company, consideration should be given to the possibility of having service points at the basement level and at one or more points on an upper level. This can result in an expensive installation. However, there is less likelihood of having a total building outage that would be possible with a single service point.

When electric service voltages over 600 volts (up to 13 kV) are offered by the utility company, many options are made available for study regarding the number

Table 3.1 Minimum unit lighting load applicable to tall buildings *(NFPA, 1978)*

Type of occupancy (1)	Unit load, in watts per square meter[a]	
	USA[b] (2)	German Federal Republic[c] (3)
Auditoriums	10	6.4
Banks	50	24 to 28
Barber shops and beauty parlors	30	16 to 20
Clubs	20	12
Dwellings (other than hotels)[d]		
Garages—commercial (storage)	5	2 to 4
Hospitals	20	1.8 kW/bed (100 beds)
		1.4 kW/bed (200 beds)
		1.0 kW/bed (400 beds)
		0.88 kW/bed (600 beds)
Hotels and motels, including apartment houses without provisions for cooking by tenants[d,e]	20 to 30	12 to 16
Industrial commercial	20	16
Office	25 to 50	20 to 26
Place of worship	10	6.4
Restaurants	20	12
Schools	30	16 to 20
Stores[f]	30 to 80	16 to 32
Warehouse storage	25	

    [a]Areas are gross areas.

    [b]Derived from Table 220-2(b), U. S. National Electrical Code (1978). Conversion factor: $1 \text{ W/m}^2 = 0.1 \text{ W/ft}^2$.

    [c]A power factor of 0.8 has been assumed.

    [d]All receptacle outlets of 20-ampere or less rating in single-family and multifamily dwellings and in guest rooms of hotels and motels (except those provided specifically for small appliance use) shall be considered as outlets for general illumination, and no additional load calculations shall be required for such outlets. Check local authorities for rules and regulations for outlet requirements.

    [e]Hotel guest rooms may require 25 watts/m^2 to 30 watts/m^2 to meet some luxury hotel chain requirements.

    [f]Some retail stores require up to 80 watts/m^2 because of extensive use of incandescent lamps for show window lighting.

and locations of transformers that will deliver the utilization voltage. The cost of the electrical distribution system will bear heavily on final selection of the best arrangement; however, above-grade transformer vaults create special problems that should be recognized. Some of the problems that can result from having transformer vaults located in the upper portion of a tall building are:

1. Transformer noise or vibration transmission (or both) to adjoining occupied spaces are possible unless proper design caution is exercised.

Table 3.2 General purpose receptacle loads *(Courtesy: Skidmore, Owings & Merrill)*

Type of occupancy (1)	Unit load, in watts per square meter (per square foot)[a] (2)	
Cafeteria	2	(0.2)
Drafting rooms	7	(0.7)
Gymnasiums	1.5	(0.15
Hospitals	10	(1.0)
Machine shops	15	(1.5)
Meeting halls	2	(0.2)
Office buildings	5 to 10	(0.5 to 1.0)
Place for worship	2	(0.2)
Schools	8	(0.8)

[a]Areas are gross areas.

Table 3.3 Typical loads applicable to apartments in tall buildings *(IEEE, 1974)*

Type of load (1)	USA[a] (2)	German Federal Republic (3)	India (4)
Air-conditioner (0.4 kW per room)	0.8 to 4.6 kW	1.5 to 6 kW	
Clothes dryer	1.5 to 6.5 kW	3.2 kW	
Clothes washer	0.2 to 0.4 kW[b]	3.2 kW	
Dishwasher	1 to 2 kW	2.6 kW	
Freezer	0.3 to 0.5 kW	0.3 to 0.5 kW	
Garbage disposal	0.2 to 0.4 kW[b]		
Lighting and convenience outlets[c]	30 watts/m^2 [a]	16 watts/m^2 [d]	16 watts/m^2 [d]
Range	8 to 12 kW	5 to 9.2 kW	1 to 5 kW
Refrigerator	0.3 to 0.5 kW	0.3 to 0.5 kW	0.2 to 0.4 kW
Water heater	1.5 to 9 kW	2.to 21 kW	1.5 to 3 kW
Evaporative cooler/room heater			0.2 to 3 kW

[a]From IEEE Standard 241-1944.
[b]A conversion factor of 1 hp (electric) = 0.75 kW has been used.
[c]For general lighting load use. Add at least two 1500-watt branch circuits for appliances and special circuit for kitchen cooking if required to suit the local practice. Conversion factor: 1 W/m^2 = 0.1 W/ft^2.
[d]A power factor of 0.8 has been assumed. The actual power factor may vary.

2. It is difficult to replace a defective transformer or to install additional transformers after the building is occupied.

3. The need for ventilation air to remove the heat given off by the transformers may require louvers in the building facade, not only for any outside air used, but also for any exhaust air being spilled from the building after passing the transformer vaults. This may not be architecturally acceptable.

4. The imposition of the weight of this equipment on the upper floor of the building could mandate changes and additional costs in the structural system for the building.

When transformer vaults are located below grade, problems can still arise in securing adequate ventilation for cooling and in providing space and access for replacement or addition of transformers. Also, regardless of location, fire protection requirements may be different. (Consult with local authorities.)

Table 3.4 Total connected electrical load for air conditioning in tall buildings (IEEE, 1974)

Type of occupancy (1)	Load for conditioned area, in watts per square meter[a]	
	USA[b] (2)	German Federal Republic[c] (3)
Bank	60	24 to 32
Department store	25 to 40	26
Hotel	48	26
Office	48	18 to 32
Telephone equipment	56 to 64	24 to 32
Small store (shoe, dress, etc.)	32 to 96	12 to 48
Restaurant (not including kitchen)	64	32

[a] Areas are gross areas.
[b] From IEEE Standard 241-1974. Conversion factor: $1 \text{ W}/\text{m}^2 = 0.1 \text{ W}/\text{ft}^2$.
[c] A power factor of 0.8 has been assumed. Given figures are average figures, no standard norm in Germany.

Table 3.5 Typical loads in commercial kitchens applicable to tall buildings[a] (IEEE, 1974)

Type of facility (1)	Number served (2)	Connected load, in kilowatts (3)
Lunch counter (gas ranges, with 40 seats)		30
Cafeteria	800	150
Restaurant (gas cooking)		90
Restaurant (electric cooking)		180
Hospital (electric cooking)	1200	300
Hotel (typical)		75
Hotel (modern, gas ranges, three kitchens)		150

[a] From IEEE Standard 241-1974.

3.3 SERVICE EQUIPMENT

The main service-entrance equipment for voltages over 600 volts, generally, must be compatible with the utility company's high voltage distribution equipment; therefore, the equipment selection usually is restricted. It is essential that all main service-entrance and associated distribution equipment for these higher voltages be properly coordinated with the utility and selected to achieve the utmost in safety and reliability. Furthermore, it should permit future simplified maintenance, testing, and replacement.

When electric service is 600 volts or below or from the low voltage side of the high voltage service transformer, the low voltage service equipment should be disconnectable from the power supply, either manually or automatically, without danger to the operating personnel. Usually, high short-circuit fault currents are

Gateway Center III, Chicago, Illinois: This building uses air rights over the Chicago Union Station. Railroad facilities are on ground level and basement. Transformer vaults and switching equipment are located on mezzanine level. The railroad station's central plant provides steam for heating (Courtesy: Skidmore, Owings & Merrill; Photo by Orlando R. Cabanban)

available at these service disconnect devices. When applying automatic circuit breakers as a service disconnect device, where the available fault current is in excess of the breaker interrupting rating, current limiting fuses properly coordinated with breaker tripping characteristics should be used in combination.

Table 3.6 Lighting load feeder demand factors[a] *(NFPA, 1978)*

Type of occupancy (1)	Portion of lighting load to which demand factor applies, in watts (2)	Demand factor, as a percentage (3)
Dwellings other than hotels	first 3000 or less	100
	next 3001 to 120 000	35
	remainder over 120 000	25
Hospitals[b]	first 50 000 or less	40
	remainder over 50 000	20
Hotels[b]	first 20 000 or less	50
Apartment houses without provision for cooking by tenants	next 20 001 to 100 000	40
	remainder over 100 000	30
All others	total wattage	100

[a]Derived from Table 220-11, U. S. National Electrical Code (NFPA, 1978). Refer to local rules and regulations for other requirements.

[b]The demand factors of this Table do not apply to the computed load of feeders to areas in hospitals, hotels, and motels where the entire lighting is likely to be used at one time; as, for example, in operating rooms, ballrooms, or dining rooms.

Table 3.7 Demand factors for household electric clothes dryers applicable to apartments in tall buildings[a] *(NFPA, 1978)*

Number of dryers (1)	Demand factor, as a percentage (2)
1	100
2	100
3	100
4	100
5	80
6	70
7	65
8	60
9	55
10	50
11 to 13	45
14 to 19	40
20 to 24	35
25 to 29	32.5
30 to 34	30
35 to 39	27.5
40 and over	25

[a]Derived from Table 220-18, U. S. National Electrical Code (NFPA, 1978). Refer to local rules and regulations for other requirements.

If low voltage load-break switches are used as disconnects on electric service having a high short circuit current, these units should be equipped with current limiting fuses. When using either fused circuit breakers or fused switches as the service disconnects, all equipment must be able to withstand the let-through currents of the fuses and also have adequate interrupting and withstand rating to carry all currents on which the unit can be closed or reopened before the fuse can clear the load. These disconnect devices should be equipped with an opening mechanism that will open all phases whenever a fuse is blown to prevent single phase operation.

It is important that 3-phase, 4-wire low voltage systems be solidly grounded to establish the highest degree of safety for personnel, and also to reduce dynamic and transient overvoltages which the system will develop when experiencing an arcing ground fault. Solid grounding of normal line-to-neutral crest voltage will result in a ground fault current less than the 3-phase fault current value.

Ground faults occurring on low voltage systems of 380 volts or higher, generally,

Fawkner Centre, Melbourne, Australia *(Courtesy: Rankine & Hill Consulting Engineers; Photo by Ian McKenzie)*

are not self-extinguishing and will restrike. Therefore, ground fault protective devices should be applied to low voltage service and distribution equipment.

In order to achieve maximum reliability in a tall building, and at the same time obtain a load balance for a multiservice installation, the distribution system should be so arranged that the various mechanical and electrical system loads will be served from more than one service and feeder.

It is prudent not to place all the mechanical equipment in the building on the same service connection or feeder. For instance, when a mechanical subsystem contains several redundant pumps, they should be connected in such a way that the loss of a service or feeder will not disrupt power to the entire subsystem. The same consideration should be given to other loads, such as vertical transportation, air conditioning, refrigeration compressors, lighting, etc. Provisions should be made within distribution equipment for future devices, and space reserved for future installation of feeders that might be required for load growth. Commonly used growth factors range from 20% to 30%.

3.4 POWER DISTRIBUTION SYSTEMS

Many new buildings have power supplied at two or more locations, one beneath the sidewalk and others up in the building or perhaps on the roof. Typically, these installations could provide up to 600 kVA at 208 V or up to 15 000 kVA at 480 V at one point of service. [Ratings are often given in kVA and MVA, in which $|VA| = w \cdot$ (power factor).]

Design of distribution systems divides naturally into two parts. First it is necessary to establish the utilization voltage, number of transformers, and number of service points. It is then necessary to match utility standards with customers' building designs. The design must satisfy customer and utility requirements and also meet municipal regulations, all within a framework of economics.

Numerous types of power distribution systems are commonly used to serve the needs of tall buildings. Four sample systems are briefly described in the following paragraphs.

Table 3.8 Feeder demand factors for commercial electric cooking equipment[a,b] *(NFPA, 1978)*

Number of units of equipment (1)	Demand factors, as a percentage (2)
1	100
2	100
3	90
4	80
5	70
6 and over	65

[a]Including dishwasher booster heaters, water heaters, and other kitchen equipment applicable to restaurants in tall buildings.

[b]Derived from Table 220-20, U. S. National Electrical Code (NFPA, 1978). Refer to local rules and regulations for other possible requirements.

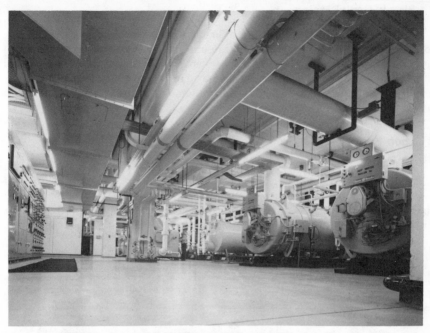

Boilers and refrigeration plant, Fawkner Centre, Melbourne, Australia *(Courtesy: Rankine & Hill Consulting Engineers; Photo by Ian McKenzie)*

Elevator equipment room, Fawkner Centre, Melbourne, Australia *(Courtesy: Rankine & Hill Consulting Engineers; Photo by Ian McKenzie)*

1 Simple-Radial System

As illustrated in Fig. 3.1, with the "Simple-Radial System" the entire building load is served from a single source. Because of the diversity among the loads, full utilization can be made of the transformer capacity allowing a minimized low-cost installation. This type of distribution is more adaptable to a building of 10 floors or less. (Note that in some countries it would be standard practice to install a load bus unit on every floor.)

2 Loop-Primary Radial System

As shown in Fig. 3.2, a primary loop is provided in this system to serve the transformers. When a transformer or primary feeder fault occurs on this type of system the main feeder breaker will open interrupting service to all loads. Through the use of the manually operated load-break switches, the faulty transformer can be disconnected from the system. The main feeder breaker can then be closed,

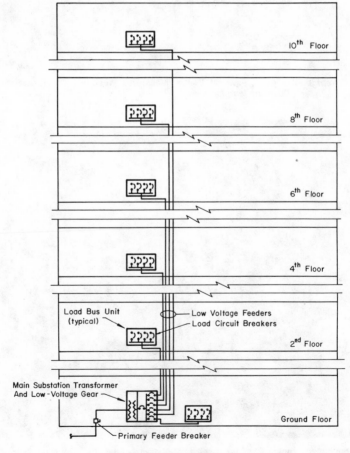

Fig. 3.1 Simple-radial system

restoring service to all other loads while repairs are made to the faulty section of the loop.

3 Primary-Selective Radial System

A primary-selective radial system (as illustrated in Fig. 3.3) uses at least two primary feeder circuits, with half of the transformers connected to each feeder. Both feeders are sized to carry the entire building load; therefore, when a fault occurs on one feeder the entire load can be transferred to the remaining feeder by means of the primary selector switches located at each transformer. When a fault occurs in one of the system transformers, the associated primary feeder breaker will open interrupting service to half of the transformers. By moving the primary selector switch at the faulted transformer to the open position and closing the primary feeder breaker, service can be restored to all loads except those served by the faulted transformer.

4 Loop-Secondary Network System

This system consists of a multiple number of transformers installed in close proximity or vertically in the structure (see Fig. 3.4). With a secondary network system, each transformer is connected to a common low voltage bus through a network protector. The advantage of this system is continuity of service. The loop-secondary network system provides the ability to install, maintain, or replace a component of the supply system without interruption of service in other parts of the network.

When a fault occurs on a primary feeder or in a transformer, the fault is isolated from the system through the automatic tripping of the primary feeder circuit breaker and associated network protectors. When the fault has been corrected, the feeder circuit breaker can be manually closed resulting in the automatic closing of the associated network protectors and restoration of service.

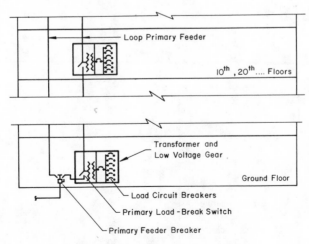

Fig. 3.2 Loop-primary radial system

Service Metering. Service metering fittings should be provided in accordance with the utility company's rules and regulations. Group mounted type metering equipment should be located in an electrical closet.

3.5 LIGHTING

It is essential in good lighting design to create a visual environment that will provide adequate visibility, desired appearance, and lighting levels to perform tasks

Table 3.9 Demand loads for household electric ranges, wall-mounted ovens, counter-mounted cooking units, and other household cooking appliances over 1-3/4 kW rating, applicable to apartments in tall buildings[a] *(NFPA, 1978)*

Number of appliances (1)	Maximum demand [b,c,d,e,f] in kilowatts (not over 12 kW rating) (2)	Demand factors, as a percentage[c]	
		Less than 3-1/2 kW rating (3)	3-1/3 kW to 8-3/4 kW rating (4)
1	8	80	80
2	11	75	65
3	14	70	55
4	17	66	50
5	20	62	45
6	21	59	43
7	22	56	40
8	23	53	36
9	24	51	35
10	25	49	34
11	26	47	32
12	27	45	32
13	28	43	32
14	29	41	32
15	30	40	32
16	31	39	28
17	32	38	28
18	33	37	28
19	34	36	28
20	35	35	28
21	36	35	26
22	37	33	26
23	38	32	26
24	39	31	26
25	40	30	26
26 to 30	15 + 1	30	24
31 to 40	for each range	30	22
41 to 50	25 + 3/4	30	20
51 to 60	for each	30	18
61 and over	range	30	16

Table 3.9 (continued)

[a]Derived from Table 220-19, U. S. National Electrical Code (NFPA, 1978). This Table, as the notes indicate, is based on USA practice. Refer to local rules and regulations for other requirements. Column (2) to be used in all cases except as otherwise permitted in Note[d] below. See Table 3.8 for commercial cooking equipment.

[b]Over 12 kW through 27 kW ranges all of same rating. For ranges, individually rated more than 12 kW but not more than 27 kW, the maximum demand in Column (2) shall be increased 5% for each additional kW of rating or major fraction thereof by which the rating of individual ranges exceeds 12 kW.

[c]Over 12 kW through 27 kW ranges of unequal ratings. For ranges individually rated more than 12 kW and of different ratings but none exceeding 27 kW, an average value of rating shall be computed by adding together the ratings of all ranges to obtain the total connected load (using 12 kW for any range rated less than 12 kW) and dividing by the total number of ranges; and then the maximum demand in Column (2) shall be increased 5% for each kW or major fraction thereof by which this average value exceeds 12 kW.

[d]Over 1-3/4 kW through 8-3/4 kW. Instead of the method provided in Column (2), it shall be permissible to add the nameplate ratings of all ranges rated more than 1-3/4 kW but not more than 8-3/4 kW, and multiply the sum by the demand factors specified in Column (3) or (4) for the given number of appliances.

[e]Branch-Circuit Load. It shall be permissible to compute the branch-circuit load for one range in accordance with this table. The branch circuit load for one wall-mounted oven or one counter-mounted cooking unit shall be the nameplate rating of the appliance. The branch-circuit load for a counter-mounted cooking unit and not more than two wall-mounted ovens, all supplied from a single branch circuit and located in the same room, shall be computed by adding the nameplate rating of the individual appliances and treating this total as equivalent to one range.

[f]This table also applies to household cooking appliances rated over 1-3/4 kW and used in instructional programs.

with minimum effort in the absence of visual discomfort. Since a tall building may consist of numerous different environments, some of which are repeated many times throughout the building, it is essential to carefully select the combination of components and systems to best satisfy the particular needs for each space. Some of the many factors affecting good lighting design are background illumination, the selection of lamps providing the desired color rendition, luminaire arrangement, fixture maintenance, floor finish, wall finish, ceiling finish, and furniture arrangements.

The illumination levels listed in Table 3.12 are recommended by the Illuminating Engineering Society for the more difficult tasks that may occur in the tall building.

Table 3.10 Lighting calculations[a] *(Courtesy: Lightolier, Inc., USA)*

Footcandles[b]	Approximate Electric Load for Various Footcandle Levels, in watts per square ft.															
	Coefficient of utilization															
	0.20	0.24	0.28	0.32	0.36	0.40	0.44	0.48	0.52	0.56	0.60	0.64	0.68	0.72	0.76	0.80
10	1.4	1.2	1.0	0.9	0.8	0.7	0.6	0.6	0.5	0.5	0.5	0.4	0.4	0.4	0.4	0.4
20	2.9	2.4	2.0	1.8	1.6	1.4	1.3	1.2	1.1	1.0	0.9	0.9	0.8	0.8	0.7	0.7
30	4.3	3.6	3.1	2.7	2.5	2.3	2.0	1.8	1.7	1.5	1.4	1.3	1.3	1.2	1.1	1.1
50	7.2	6.0	5.1	4.5	4.0	3.6	3.2	3.0	2.8	2.6	2.4	2.2	2.1	2.0	1.9	1.8
80	11.4	9.5	8.2	7.2	6.4	5.7	5.2	4.8	4.4	4.1	3.8	3.6	3.4	3.2	3.0	2.9
100	14.3	11.9	10.2	8.9	8.0	7.2	6.5	6.0	5.5	5.1	4.8	4.5	4.2	4.0	3.8	3.6

[a]This table is for use with lamps having an over-all efficiency of 50 lumens per watt (including ballast losses). Apply correction factor of Table 3.11 for specific light source. Illumination level will be increased by about 12% for airconditioned buildings in which fluorescent fixtures are used for heat extraction.

[b]Maintained (maintenance factor = 0.70); conversion factor: 1 Lux = 0.0929 footcandles = 1 lumen/ m^2.

3.6 FEEDERS

High voltage feeders should be routed vertically through a tall building in a separate fireproof shaft, preferably installed in a metal raceway and isolated from other system risers. When multiple high voltage risers are installed, the ganging of all risers at one location should be avoided, since a fire or explosion causing damage to these risers will seriously reduce the electrical capabilities of the building. Spiral wire armored high voltage cable, clamp supported at the upper end, is an excellent choice as a riser cable.

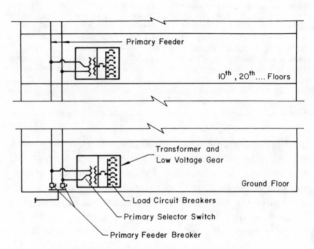

Fig. 3.3 Primary-selective radial system

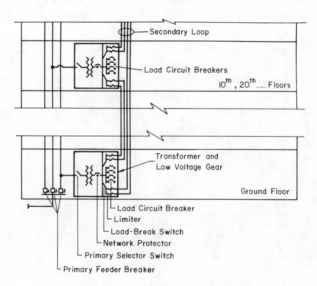

Fig. 3.4 Loop-secondary network system

There are many choices of low voltage riser feeders that might be applicable in a tall building. These include, but are not limited to, busways, cable and raceway, and interlocked armored cable in tray. The final selection from these alternatives can only be made after studying the cost, flexibility, reliability, and safety considerations that are inherent in each of the possibilities. In tall buildings, low voltage drop busways are frequently selected as the risers to supply power to individual floor lighting and apparatus loads. As busway risers usually furnish power to many floors, consideration should be given to providing dual busway risers with each busway serving one-half of each floor load, or alternatingly serving each full floor load. Either of these arrangements will minimize the chance of a blackout of a large block or space during a loss of power to one busway.

In tall buildings of approximately 40 floors or more, where the electric supply is furnished only at the bottom or top of the building, automatic voltage regulators

Australian Netherlands House, Melbourne, Australia *(Courtesy: Rankine & Hill Consulting Engineers; Photo by Ian McKenzie)*

connected ahead of the busways may be installed, to provide voltage boosting to compensate for voltage drop in busways. The cost of voltage regulators, if they are installed, should be more than offset by the cost saving resulting from the ability to install minimum size busways or riser cables. When using voltage regulators, the units may be subjected to high fault currents; therefore, this factor should also be considered.

When using voltage regulators, it is good practice to include in the design a provision to permit the installation of a temporary bypass of the regulator in the event the unit must be removed from service.

Establishing vertically alined electric closets to house the vertical low voltage risers and the floor electrical distribution apparatus is essential from the standpoint of the least possible installation cost. In addition, these closets are necessary since they create a restricted safe space for normal building maintenance and operation. Capped sleeves through floor slabs of these closets for future risers and empty wall

Table 3.11 Approximate correction factors to be applied to Table 3.10 for some typical lamps[a] (*Courtesy: Lightolier, Inc., USA*)

	Correction Factor	
Lamp type (1)	Cool white and warm white (2)	Deluxe cool white and warm white (3)
Fluorescent lamps		
40 W T12, 430 mA	0.7	1.0
8-ft slimline, 420 mA	0.7	1.0
8-ft high output, 800 mA	0.7	1.0
8-ft extra high output, 1.5 A	0.7 to 0.8	1.0
Incandescent lamps		
100 W	2.9	
150 W	2.7	
200 W	2.6	
300 W	2.5	
500 W	2.4	
750 W	2.2	
1000 W	2.1	
Mercury lamps, deluxe white		
100 W	1.4	
175 W	1.2	
250 W	1.1	
400 W	1.0	
700 W	0.9	
1000 W	0.8	
Metal Halide lamps		
400 W	0.6	
High-pressure sodium lamps		
400 W	0.5	

[a] To find the correction factor for lamps not listed here, divide 50 by the lumens per watt of the lamp (including ballast losses, where applicable). Lamp lumen data can be found in the catalogs of lamp manufacturers.

space are desirable provisions for the load growth possible in any building. *Busway risers passing through these closets must have internal firestops at the floor slab penetration. All openings through the closet floor slab must be closed to prevent spread of fire.* Closets should be constructed of at least 1-1/2-hr fire rated material or as required by the applicable local building codes. Where ventilation is required, as would be the case if a transformer is contained therein, all ventilation openings, supply and exhaust, should be protected with fire dampers consistent with the fire rating of the closet itself.

3.7 GROUNDING (EARTHING)

In a tall building of structural steel, it is common practice to use selected columns as the electrical system grounding means for transformers located in electric closets. These columns, which are located near or within the electric closets, should have their bases looped together by cable and both ends connected to the building electrical grounding point. All cable connections to these columns should be welded, not bolted.

In a tall building of reinforced concrete, the usual method employed to effectively ground transformer neutrals and other electric closet equipment is to install riser grounding conductors in a raceway from the building electrical grounding point vertically through all of the electric closets, with terminal cabinets in each closet for ground extension.

Main plant room, Australian Netherlands House, Melbourne, Australia *(Courtesy: Rankine & Hill Consulting Engineers; Photo by Ian McKenzie)*

Grounding or earthing provisions may vary from country to country. It is therefore important to refer to local rules and regulations for local requirements. For example, the practice just described is common in the United States; however, in Australia and New Zealand the preferred method for all buildings is that described above for reinforced concrete structures.

3.8 LIGHTNING PROTECTION

If a tall building constructed of structural steel is to have a lightning protection system, common practice is to use the steel columns as the down conductors for the roof ground loop and lightning arrestors. All such installations should have these columns grounded at the column base by means of a ground electrode, and have all

33 W. Monroe, Chicago, Illinois: A building management control system monitors and controls all engineering systems in this building which features three interior atriums. The standard tenant lighting provides average maintained illumination level of 55 foot-candles. An under-floor distribution system facilitates wire running for tenants' special lighting requirements. Uses primary-selective radial system *(Courtesy: Skidmore, Owings & Merrill; Photo by Hedrich-Blessing)*

electrodes interconnected by means of a buried counterpoise cable. To minimize the electrical impedance in the metallic conducting path of such grounded equipment (vertical transportation rails, plumbing risers, etc.), consideration should be given to the installation of a ground loop conductor interconnecting the down conductor columns at selected floors throughout the height of the building.

A lightning protection system applied to the roof of a reinforced concrete tall

Sears Tower, Chicago, Illinois: the tallest building in the world, the Sears Tower has over 2410 km (1500 miles) of electric wiring. Of the 102 elevator cabs, 14 are double deck elevators, each capable of lifting 4535.9 kg (10 000 lb). Uses primary-selective radial system *(Courtesy: Skidmore, Owings & Merrill; Photo by Ezra Stoller © ESTO)*

Table 3.12 Lighting illumination level[a] *(Kauffman and Christensen, 1972; DIN, 1978)*

Area	Minimum illumination on area at any time, in lux	
	USA[a]	German Federal Republic[a]
(a) Interior areas		
Art galleries		
general	320[b] ⎫	250
on paintings (supplementary illumination)	320[c] ⎬	plus special
on statuary and other displays	1080 ⎭	lights
Auditoriums		
assemblies only	160	120
exhibitions	320	250
Showrooms	1080	120
on features	5400	500
Banks		
lobby, general	540 ⎫	
lobby, writing areas	760 ⎪	
tellers' stations, posting and key punch	1600 ⎬	250
regular offices	1080 ⎭	
Courtrooms		
seating area	320 ⎫	250
court activity area	760 ⎭	
Corridors	220	60
Drafting rooms		
rough layout drafting	1600	500
detailed drafting	2200	1000
Elevators, freight and passenger	220	60
Escalators	220	60
Garages, automobile and truck		
parking garages		
entrances	540	60
traffic lanes	108	60
storage	54	120
Hotels		
bathrooms		
mirror	320[d] ⎫	120
general	108 ⎭	
bedrooms		
reading (books, magazines, newspapers)	320 ⎫	
inkwriting	320[e] ⎬	120
makeup	320[f] ⎭	
general	108	
corridors, elevators, and stairs	220	60
entrance foyer	320	250
front office	540	250
linen room		
sewing	1080	750
general	220	120
lobby		
general lighting	108	250
reading and working areas	320	250

Table 3.12 (continued)

Area	Minimum illumination on area at any time, in lux	
	USA[a]	German Federal Republic[a]
(a) Interior areas		
Libraries		
reading room		
study and notes	760 ⎫	250
ordinary reading	320 ⎬	
stacks	320	120
card files	760	120
check-in and check-our desks	760	250
Offices		
cartography, designing, detailed drafting	2200	1000
accounting, auditing, tabulating, book keeping, business machine operation, reading poor reproductions, rough layout drafting	1600	500
regular office work, reading good reproductions, reading or transcribing handwriting in hard pencil or on poor paper, active filing, index references, mail sorting	1080	500
reading or transcribing handwriting in ink or medium pencil on good quality paper, intermittent filing	760	250
reading high-contrast or well-printed material, tasks and areas not involving critical or prolonged seeing such as conferring, interviewing, inactive files, wash rooms	320	120
Place for worship		
altar	1080[h]	120
choir[g]	320[h]	120
pulpit	540[h]	120
main worship area[g]		
light and medium interior finishes	160[h]	60
for churches with special zeal	320	60
Post office		
lobby, on table	320	250
sorting, mailing, etc.	1080	250
Professional offices		
waiting room		
general	160	60
reading	320	120
examination and treatment room		
general	540	250
examining table	1080	500
dental, operatory		
general	760	250
dental chair (supplementary)	10800	4000
instrument cabinet	1600	500

Table 3.12 (continued)

Area	Minimum illumination on area at any time, in lux	
	USA[a]	German Federal Republic[a]
(a) Interior areas		
laboratory, bench	1080	500
eye, ear, nose, and throat suite		
dark room	108	30
eye examination and treatment room	540	250
eye, ear, nose, and throat room	540	250
Reception rooms	320	120
Restaurants, lunch rooms, cafeterias, dining areas		
cashier	540	250
intimate type		
light environment	108	60
subdued enviornment	32	30
for cleaning	220	120
leisure type		
light environment	320	150
subdued environment	160	60
quick service type		
bright surroundings	1080	500
normal surroundings	540	250
food displays—twice general levels, not less than	540	250
kitchens, commercial		
inspection, checking, pricing	760	500
other areas	320	250
Schools		
reading printed material	320 ⎫	
reading pencil writing	760 ⎬	250
duplicted material		
good	320	250
poor	1080	500
drafting, benchwork	1080	500
lip reading, chalkboards, sewing	1600	500
Show windows		
daytime lighting		
general	2200[i]	1000
feature	10800[i]	3000 to 4000
nighttime lighting		
main business districts, highly competitive		
general	2200[i]	1000
feature	10800	3000 to 4000
secondary business districts or small towns		
general	1080[i]	500
feature	5400	2000
open front stores (see stores, display lighting)		

Table 3.12 (continued)

	Minimum illumination on area at any time, in lux	
Area	USA[a]	German Federal Republic[a]
(a) Interior areas		
Stairways	220	60
Storage rooms or warehouse		
inactive	54	15
active		
rough bulky	108	30
medium	220	60
fine	540	120
Stores		
circulation areas	320[i]	500
merchandising areas		
service stores	1080[i] ⎫	750
self-service	2200[i] ⎭	
showcases and wall cases		
service	2200[i]	750
self-service	5400[i]	1000
feature displays		
service	5400[i]	1000
self-service	10800[i]	2000 to 3000
stockrooms	320	250
Toilets and washrooms	320	120
(b) Exterior areas		
Building exteriors and monuments		
floodlighted		
bright surroundings		
light surfaces	160	
medium light surfaces	220	
medium dark surfaces	320	
dark surfaces	540	
dark surroundings		
light surfaces	54	13 to 16 cd/m^2
medium light surfaces	108	10 to 13 cd/m^2
medium dark surfaces	160	8 to 10 cd/m^2
dark surfaces	220	6 to 8 cd/m^2
Bulletin and poster boards		
bright surroundings		
light surfaces	540	250
dark surfaces	1080	500
dark surroundings		
light surfaces	220	120
dark surfaces	540	250

building generally will require down conductors from the roof arrestors and roof ground loop to grounding electrodes connected to the counterpoise ground loop at the column footings. The reinforcing bars may be used as down conductors only if the bars are welded together and are of adequate size to achieve a low impedance path. In a reinforced concrete building it is very important to ground all metallic equipment and piping to the ground loops or down conductors in order to provide a neutralizing path to the earth.

3.9 EMERGENCY POWER

For the required movement of the occupants of a tall building (i.e., to bring elevators to floors so they may be unloaded) during the loss of normal electric power supply to the building, an emergency power system is essential. Electric power for the life-safety systems and for emergency lighting are the most important loads to be served. Emergency power sufficient to operate all of the elevators in each group on a one-at-a-time basis is desirable, especially if there are physically handicapped occupants. The connection of selected pumps to the emergency system is sometimes mandatory if the sanitary system is to be kept in working order or if

Table 3.12 (continued)

Area	Minimum illumination on area at any time, in lux	
	USA[a]	German Federal Republic[a]
(b) Exterior areas		
Loading and unloading platforms	220	60
Parking lots	10.8 to 22	10 to 15
Storage yards		
active	220	120
inactive	10.8	10

[a] Conversion factor 1 Lux = 0.0929 footcandles = 1 lm/m^2. Refer to IES Lighting Handbook (5th edition) (Kauffman and Christensen, 1972) or refer to local authorities for recommendations. Figures for the German Federal Republic are taken from DIN 5035 (DIN, 1978).

[b] Dark paintings with fine detail should have two to three times higher illumination.

[c] In some cases much more than 1080 lux is necessary.

[d] For close inspection, 540 lux.

[e] Pencil handwriting, reading of reproductions, and poor copies require 760 lux.

[f] For close inspection, 540 lux. This may be done in the bathroom, but if a dressing table is provided, local lighting should provide the level recommended.

[g] Reduced or dimmed during sermon, prelude, or meditation.

[h] Two-thirds this value if interior finshes are dark (less than 10% reflectance) to avoid high brightness ratios, such as between hymn book pages and the surroundings. Careful brightness planning is essential for good design.

[i] (1) Values are illumination on the merchandise on display or being appraised. The plane in which lighting is important may vary from horizontal to vertical. (2) Specific appraisal areas involving difficult viewing may be lighted to substantially higher levels. (3) Color rendition of fluorescent lamps is important. Incandescent and fluorescent usually are combined for best appearance of merchandise. (4) Illumination may often be made non-uniform to tie in with merchandising layout.

[j] This tabulation of information, collected by the Council, is accompanied by the warning that direct comparison between countries has been found to be difficult due to the variations in such factors as the utilization of space and the different format of recommendations.

the building has sprinkler protection. In some cases the emergency load is large due to the inclusion of such loads as computer systems and their associated air conditioning equipment, and the system requires the installation of a large generator or multiple generators. In such instances the ventilation requirement and the weight of the generator set become major factors in the selection of its location within the

John Hancock Center, Chicago, Illinois: This all electric building includes in its space heating equipment complex thirteen resistance type electric boilers. These range in size from 1600 kW to 1800 kW each for a total boiler capacity of 21 400 kW. Other space heating equipment consists of 42 electric heating coils ranging in size from 52 kW to 1300 kW, electrically heated ceiling panels, and electric heaters in window air conditioning units *(Courtesy: Skidmore, Owings & Merrill; Photo by Ezra Stoller © ESTO)*

building. Very often the ventilation air needed to satisfy cooling cannot be obtained from a below-grade area, and an above-grade source is therefore mandatory. By placing the emergency set on upper floors of a building, the weight of the set becomes a factor to be considered in the structural design. With this arrangement, consideration should be given to the use of a gas turbine generator instead of the diesel engine generator, because of the weight advantage. Another item to be taken into account for the upper story location is the fuel supply. From the fire protection standpoint, a large fuel storage tank should be buried underground; however, this means that the fuel must be pumped from a storage tank to a day tank at the generator location. Good practice would dictate that the fuel oil piping be of the pipe-within-a-pipe type construction. Dual fuel pumps would be required. They would be controlled by level devices mounted on the day tank at the generator set.

3.10 FIRE ALARM SYSTEM

A fire within a tall building must be contained within a limited space since rapid emergency evacuation of the building's occupants is very difficult because of the building's height. Therefore, the fire alarm system in the building should be capable of giving early warning to the building personnel as well as to the local fire department. (A detailed consideration of "Fire" is the subject of Chapter CL-4.) In addition, the system should include provision for transmission of voice instructions both to the occupants of the building and between the parties responsible for controlling the fire. Any fire control system in a tall building should only be detailed after reviewing all applicable codes and discussion with the local fire authorities. A typical fire alarm system in a tall building could consist of the following components:

1. A central fire control station, usually located in the ground floor lobby, which will visually display by zone any alarm condition from the alarm systems in the building. Two-way voice communication between the control station and loudspeakers on each floor, in all stairs, elevator cabs, elevator machine rooms, and mechanical equipment rooms. A recorder that will print out the type, zone, and time of alarm. Provision for either manual or automatic transmission of fire alarm signals to fire department headquarters.

2. A second panel that will visually display any alarm condition in the building can be provided in the Mechanical System Control Office.

3. Manual fire alarm stations installed on each floor at the stairs to be used for fire notification by the building occupants.

4. Smoke detectors located in the ducted return air connections to the return air shaft on each floor and in discharge of the supply fans. Requirements, for example, are given in NFPA 90A (1978). These detectors should be used to control fans to minimize the propagation of smoke through the structure.

5. Smoke detectors located in each elevator lobby over the elevator call button. These detectors, when energized, will provide a signal to the elevator controllers to automatically return the cabs to their lowest terminal floor. These are then available for use by the fire department for

dispatching fire-fighting personnel and for evacuation of the building personnel.

6. An automatic suppression system, such as sprinklers for the entire building and Halon or carbon dioxide for the special areas, such as computer centers and elevator machine rooms. Such systems should include a complete monitoring system of water flow tied into the central control station.

7. Loudspeakers located on floors throughout the entire building for issuing instruction to the building's occupants. These loudspeakers should be capable of being addressed on a floor-by-floor basis to make it possible to issue messages on a controlled basis.

8. Amplifier cabinets to contain the redundant amplifiers and alarm signal generators typically included with the system.

9. Circuitry as required to transmit the alarm signal to the loudspeakers serving the alarm floor and the floor above, and also to visually display the zone in alarm at the central fire control station and at the mechanical system control office. Alarm signals should be originated by operation of a manual fire station, smoke detector, or sprinkler system flow valve if installed.

The complete system should be tested once a month as scheduled to meet the fire marshal's requirements. The power supply for the fire alarm system should be backed up by the emergency generator. If a generator is not provided, a battery system with automatic charging features should be provided.

3.11   CENTRAL CONTROL OF MECHANICAL SYSTEMS (OPTIMIZATION)

Significant savings can be achieved in the cost of operation of the mechanical equipment used for heating, ventilating, and air conditioning in tall buildings. The savings are contingent upon the application of newly developed techniques of multiplexed data transmission of system performance in a building to a centrally located computer that is capable of analyzing the data, and either directly modifying the control of the system or advising the operator of the building of possible modifications for his action. The total system, including the local instrumentation, the data transmission link, and the computer can be called a central automated control facility. The techniques used in such an installation have been incorporated in the single word "optimization." (Mechanical systems are covered in Chapter SC-2, and operation of tall buildings is the subject of Chapter 11 of Volume PC.)

From the control aspect, the concept of optimization involves the continuous monitoring and controlling of the building. The key word is "continuous," since operating personnel in a building cannot perform the necessary operations as continuously as can a computer. The operator is time constrained to the rate at which he can sample the data necessary to perform certain operations and execute the required changes. Necessarily, he will lag behind, and the building systems will drift away from the optimal engineering path. To compensate for this lag and to eliminate possible temporary discomfort in the building, he will take short cuts and will operate the building inefficiently.

The modern computer is not time constrained and will collect the necessary data from the building, analyze it, and perform or recommend the proper changes. These changes will result in lowered operating costs without sacrifice of occupant comfort. This is the general meaning of optimization.

The savings that are projected for the computer operation of a building come from three primary areas:

1. Better utilization of energy for heating and cooling the building.

2. More efficient use of operating and maintenance personnel.

3. Improved equipment performance through proper maintenance scheduling.

A building with optimization must include the local instrumentation, the data transmission link, the central processing unit, and the computer. This system may be

A.M.P. Centre, Sydney, Australia (Courtesy: Rankine & Hill Consulting Engineers; Photo by Max Dupain)

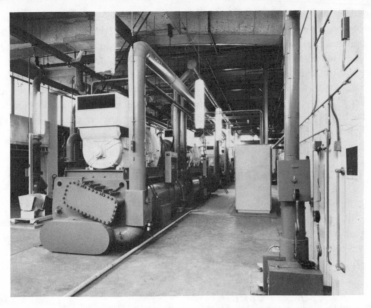

Refrigeration plant room, A.M.P. Centre, Sydney, Australia *(Courtesy: Rankine & Hill Consulting Engineers)*

Delta 2000 Computer, A.M.P. Centre, Sydney, Australia *(Courtesy: Rankine & Hill Consulting Engineers)*

extended to provide a building security system that would control entrance and egress of secured areas, as a function of time, and to advise of violations. It should be recognized that buildings with installations of this type are very rare because the technology involved is new. The development of computer software to permit the achievement of the economies possible with these systems is an ongoing effort. The availability of this software is now limited. It is hoped that the passage of time will see fuller recognition of the possibilities of these systems, and the development of more meaningful software packages that will permit greater realization of the full benefits possible than is presently the case.

3.12 CONDENSED REFERENCES/BIBLIOGRAPHY

The following is a condensed bibliography for this chapter. Not only does it include all articles referred to or cited in the text, but it also contains bibliography for further reading. The full citations will be found at the end of the Volume. What is given here should be sufficient information to lead the reader to the correct article: the author, date, and title. In case of multiple authors, only the first named is listed.

Au 1973, *Building Services and Systems in Hong Kong*
Baum 1973b, *Mutual Influences Between Building Concept and Mechanical Systems*
Baum 1973c, *Theme Report*
Beeman 1955, *Industrial Power Systems Handbook*
DIN 1978, *Artificial Lightings of Interiors Recommendations*

D'Cruz 1974, *Effect of Tall Buildings on Tele-communications Radio Link*
Dimitrios 1975, *Horizontal and Vertical Power Distribution in Large and Tall Buildings*
EEI 1978, *Glossary of Electric Utility Terms*
Felder 1973, *Electrical Installations*
Finks 1978, *Standard Handbook for Electrical Engineers*

Hye 1974, *Planning of Telecoms Services for Tall Buildings*
IEEE 1944, *Recommended Practice for Electrical Power Systems in Commercial Buildings*
IEEE 1974, *Recommended Practice for Electrical Power Systems in Commercial Buildings*
Kauffman 1972, *Lighting Handbook*
Kheong 1974, *Electricity Supply to Tall Buildings in Kuala Lumpur*

Krishnamurthy 1973, *Electrical and Mechanical Services in Tall Buildings*
McGarth 1974, *Comfort and Conservation in Large Building Environmental Control*
Muench 1975, *High Voltage Vertical Distribution System for High-Rise Residential Buildings*
Muto 1974, *The Earthquake Resistant Installing Method of Telecommunication Instruments*
NFPA 1976, *Air Conditioning and Ventilating Systems*

NFPA 1978, *U.S. National Electrical Code*
Norman 1973, *Service Systems*
Okell 1975, *Electrical Reticulation Systems in Tall Buildings*
Oravetz 1975, *Service Systems in High and Medium-High Buildings*
Richardson 1973, *Summary Report*

Rodriguez Lamus 1974, *Urban Aspect of the Construction of Tall Buildings*
Rohatyn 1973, *Automatic Voltage Drop Compensation for Tall Buildings*
Strunk 1972, *Electrical Systems*
Strunk 1973, *Electrical Systems in Tall Buildings*
Sturt 1974, *Mineral Insulated Cables*

Magazines and Standards

For additional reading and information on this subject please refer to the following magazines and standards:

Cahners Publishing Co.,
   Building Design and Construction, Cahners Publishing Co., Chicago, Ill.
Cleworth Publishing Co.,
   Electrical Consultant, Cleworth Publishing Co., Cos Cob, Conn.
FAA,
   Standards and Publications of the Federal Aviation Administration, Federal Aviation
      Administration, Washington, D.C.
IEEE,
   Standards and Publications of the Institute of Electrical and Electronic Engineers, Institute of
      Electrical and Electronic Engineers, New York, N.Y.
IES,
   Standards and Publications of the Illuminating Engineering Society, Illuminating Engineering
      Society, New York, N.Y.
McGraw-Hill Publishing Co.,
   Electrical Construction and Maintenance, McGraw-Hill Publishing Co., Inc., New York, N.Y.
NEMA,
   Standards and Publications of the National Electrical Manufacturer's Association, National
      Electrical Manufacturer's Association, New York, N.Y.
NFPA,
   Standards and Codes of the National Fire Protection Association, National Fire Protection
      Association, Boston, Mass.
ULI,
   Standards and Publications of the Underwriters Laboratories, Inc., Underwriters
      Laboratories, Inc., Northbrook, Ill.

Tall Building Systems and Concepts

Chapter SC-4

Vertical and Horizontal Transportation

Prepared by Committee 2A (Vertical and Horizontal Transportation) of the Council on Tall Buildings and Urban Habitat as part of the Monograph on the Planning and Design of Tall Buildings

Richard T. Baum   Chairman
Rudiger Thoma   Vice-Chairman
William S. Lewis   Editor

AUTHOR ACKNOWLEDGMENT

The essential first draft of this chapter is the work of W. S. Lewis. Its starting point was the collection of state-of-art reports from the 1972 International Conference, held at Lehigh University, prepared by:

> R. T. Baum
> C. L. Kort
> G. R. Strakosch.

In addition to this, other sections were based on special contributions. For the indicated sections, these individuals are:

> E. Warners, Section 2.3
> G. W. Jernstedt, Section 2.4.

CONTRIBUTORS

The following is a complete list of those who have submitted written material for possible use in the chapter, whether or not that material was used in the final version. The Committee Chairman and Editor were given quite complete latitude. Frequently length limitations precluded the inclusion of much valuable material. The Bibliography contains all contributions. The contributors are: K. Adendorff, R. Adler, R. T. Baum, J. P. Botha, G. W. Jernstedt, C. L. Kort, P. S. B. Kruger, W. S. Lewis, G. R. Strakosch, R. Thoma, E. Warners, R. G. Werden.

COMMITTEE MEMBERS

P. A. Anderson, R. T. Baum, W. Correalle, S. L. Daryanani, M. N. Dastur, B. Forwood, E. H. Hesselberg, U. Inouye, G. R. Jerus, W. Kamler, C. L. Kort, W. S. Lewis, G. C. Mathur, G. Rahulan, R. Reuter, P. Richardson, R. L. Rogers, F. S. Rohatyn, B. Rubanenko, C. E. Schaffner, J. Schroeder, J. E. Snell, G. R. Strakosch, J. Strunk, E. H. Sumka, R. Thoma, L. Tosato, E. Warners, R. G. Werden.

SC-4

Vertical and Horizontal Transportation

4.1 GENERAL OVERVIEW

The horizontal and vertical movements of people and materials have traditionally been factional disciplines which apply electromechanical assistance when time or physical demands exceed human capabilities. As the concentration of people increased in residential, commercial, institutional, and industrial environments, the value of transportation time has also markedly increased. The escalating costs of man-hours and the equipment and environments necessary to accomplish living and working tasks now require the highest level of productivity possible within each working day. The transportation time of people or materials between activity centers represents "losses" in productivity.

This chapter will consider the short-haul transportation criteria and solutions for people and materials in activity centers. The distances, therefore, will be vertically and horizontally short, compared with the horizontal long-haul between activity centers, a subject dealt with in Chapter PC-9. The relatively high cost of land in this century dictated the primary emphasis on vertical development of "environment" structures. Recent, even higher, land costs have created the need for a secondary emphasis on horizontal transportation development in the congregation of interacting vertical facilities to optimize the efficiency of these interrelated activities (Figs. 4.1 and 4.2).

Any design of an activity center demands a systems approach to the entire transportation requirement rather than the traditionally rigid and narrow product line approach. The efficient activity center must now so mesh the movement of people and materials that all the transportation subsystems must be solved simultaneously rather than separately. Today the activity center concept is exemplified by the university campus that includes a high-rise dormitory building, high-rise classroom building, high-rise administration building, high-rise student center, and perhaps even a high-rise teaching hospital. Even where land is relatively inexpensive, the high-rise campus [over 10 stories or 20 m (70 ft) above grade] is dictated by the total transit times available for the combined vertical-horizontal-vertical movement patterns.

Major airports and major commercial developments where regularized traffic patterns exist are currently the other areas of near-term planning for integrated and automated people and material movement systems. The airport of the future will borrow from the industrial sector the automated storage and retrieval concepts of warehousing to provide safe and secure baggage handling and automobile parking systems along with horizontal and vertical transportation systems. Many embryonic installations exist, and the technologies have been proven but still await economic justification for large-scale application.

The first short-haul transportation systems were for people in the vertical with technology borrowed from the long-haul railroads. Elisha Otis' "safety brake," in 1853, made the elevator as safe as the railroad car with George Westinghouse's air brake. The moving walk and the escalator soon followed for the short-haul movement of people. It has only been since the end of the first half of the 20th

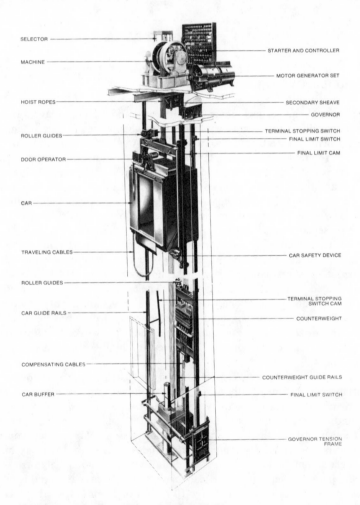

Fig. 4.1 Typical gearless traction elevator equipment *(Courtesy: Otis Elevator Company; Photo by Birlaut and Steen, Inc.)*

century that the horizontal short-haul concepts have been identified as Personal Rapid Transit (PRT), borrowing the technology of the conventional elevator and rapid transit systems (HUD, 1969; Jernstedt, 1975; Lerch, 1974).

The materials handling industry has provided the convenient further classification of these people-moving systems into categories. Short-haul, high-density moving systems must of necessity be "continuous flow" systems, while low-density moving systems are accommodated by "batch systems." The recognition of each concept, with its limitations and capital costs, is the first step in the process of selecting an appropriate solution to each facet of either a vertical, a horizontal, or a combined vertical and horizontal system. It is axiomatic in the transportation field that no single concept replaces another. It merely adds another possible solution to be tested for cost-effective feasibility. The Sherpa in the Himalayas and the mule in the Rocky Mountains have successfully defied the industrial revolution and are there still the most cost-effective material movers.

In considering the various concepts, it is desirable to discuss, separately, the use categories so as to identify the differing criteria for performance and to select the most viable solution or solutions. These are generalized into the following facilities:

1. Commercial: office, store and shops, bank, public utility.

2. Residential: apartment (rental and condominium), hotel, dormitory, hostel.

3. Industrial: warehouse, manufacture ("flatted factory"), material processing.

4. Institutional: school, hospital (health care facility), laboratory, library, museum, correctional institution, court of law, religious edifice.

Fig. 4.2 Personal rapid transit vehicle operating as a horizontal elevator between buildings
(Courtesy: Otis Elevator Company)

5. Public Assembly: theater, hall and auditorium (meeting rooms), restaurant, observation.

6. Special Purpose: transport interface (air, rail, bus, ship), garage (parking deck), mausoleum.

7. Multiple Use: megastructures that are various combinations of the above.

1 People Movers

The early vertical people movers were batch system elevators appearing about 1860. They met with gradual acceptance and became a significant factor in the development of "taller than walk-up" buildings in the 1870s and 1880s. The application of electricity to power and signal "safe" elevators led to their rapid proliferation, so that by 1900, the elevator industry had a major part in setting the stage for the increased size and height of buildings in the early years of the 20th century. Since the technology at the time was limited to single cavity (now known as single deck) elevators, the increase in passenger handling demand resulted in multiple elevator installations. These multiple batch systems grew to accommodate the continuous flow of people into and out of a building. The limitations of any reasonable number of elevators to handle large flows of people brought about the development of continuous flow moving stairways in the early 1900s. These people conveyors move large numbers of people rapidly over short vertical distances and were first known as "Escalators," an Otis trademark, and later as escalators when the trademark was lost to generic use in the English language (Strakosch, 1967).

The obvious advantages of moving stairways in department stores, office buildings, and railroad and rapid transit terminals were soon to be applied to flat escalators or moving walks. The speed of these moving stairs or walks has been limited to the ability to enter and exit safely within human limits of horizontal acceleration and deceleration. The current limitation of speed in the United States and Canada to 0.6 m/sec (120 ft per min), for safety, has obvious limitations for long horizontal distances. It has only been within the last few years that accelerating high-speed moving walks [2.5 m/sec to 5.0 m/sec (500 ft per min to 1000 ft per min)] have been studied for commercial rather than amusement applications (ANSI A17.1 Code, 1978; CSA B44 Code, 1971).

Currently (1980), feasible longer "short-haul" horizontal movement systems have had to use higher speed concepts confined to batch systems, which encapsulate or containerize the passenger. Once this "horizontal elevator" is loaded, it can be accelerated and decelerated safely. These systems have spawned a new industry called Personal Rapid Transit (PRT) to differentiate its concepts and applications from Mass Rapid Transit (MRT).

For many years the PRT concept has been used in combined vertical and horizontal applications of cable cars (Sturgeon, 1967)—more in Europe than elsewhere, apart from recreational applications. It is a mature technology that may have applications in and between some activity centers of the future. However, this concept cannot today be considered a solution for interbuilding travel in competition with the emerging PRT concepts. Since tall buildings are, and will be in the near future, ground oriented, the interbuilding transportation will be interfaced with intrabuilding transportation just below, at, or just above the pedestrian access on grade.

2 Material Movers

Material movers in activity centers have developed an industry devoted to what have become known as "Materials Handling Systems." This industry has as many concepts as there are specialized problems requiring solutions. In the last quarter of this century, the development of rapid rail, rubber, and water transport will dictate the economics of how vertical the manufacturing processes can be. When the elevator industry itself builds horizontal factories, only a few special industrial applications will use vertical materials handling systems. These will be predominantly in storage and retrieval functions for warehousing, and in retrofitting existing multistory supply systems for industrial buildings (Lewis, 1974).

Commercial and institutional buildings that were designed vertically for people purposes now demand supporting materials handling systems to reduce the time as well as the labor intensity factors. One of the basic efficiencies of the horizontal building is ease of effective supervision of employees. In vertical buildings, the employee away from his "home floor" becomes practically unsupervised and, hence, his productivity is substantially reduced. Automated and semi-automated materials handling systems have now become a major factor in maintaining a high level of productivity while reducing the over-all labor content of intrabuilding movements. As these systems become perfected and accepted in the commercial and institutional sectors, they will begin to affect the design of both transient and permanent residential buildings.

The manual freight elevator in industry has rapidly declined in importance in recent years as manual and even fork truck loading and unloading have become labor intensive. The automation of horizontal pallet and cart conveyors has only recently been extended into vertical movements with automated lifts. These lifts become slaves to "addressed" pallets or carts, which read the destinations and automatically deliver the containerized load to its destination floor. In multiple floor installations, the computer or programmable controller can select priority origins and automatically deliver the carts or pallets for maximum cost-effective throughput capacities. They have been successfully installed in both automated supply systems for the processing industries and automated storage and retrieval systems for warehousing functions.

At air terminals, these systems will combine, in the future, to automatically transport a locked motor vehicle to a secure storage "rack" and return it on demand, as well as accept baggage at the emplaning airport, store it until flight time, deliver it to the aircraft just before flight time, and reverse the procedure at the deplaning airport, with perhaps one or two aircraft or airline changes in between. Demonstration systems have already been installed, and await cost-effective justification.

At institutional buildings, the automated tote box, cart, and trash bag have joined the pneumatic message tube in moving larger discrete loads, both horizontally and vertically. As their costs reduce and their technologies increase, large-scale opportunities are waiting in commercial and residential buildings.

3 Challenge of the Future

It is generally accepted that the invention of the telephone and the elevator made possible the tall buildings of the first three-quarters of this century. The invention of the transistor, and the development of its application to logic for automation, will make obsolete previous concepts of factional design disciplines and permit the true systems approach to the design and control of interbuilding and intrabuilding movement systems for people, materials, and their environment, with a minimum of energy consumption.

Those involved with the design of people and material movers must be constantly aware of concurrent developments in the communications industry, as they change the need emphasis and time demands of all movement systems. Functional obsolescence will accelerate economic obsolescence as physical obsolescence becomes less important in the future.

4.2 PEOPLE MOVERS

People movers traditionally have been separate vertical and horizontal systems with a pedestrian interface at the modal change. Only in recent years has the concept of combination been studied, and only one installation is now under a study contract. For purposes of analysis here, the concepts will be treated separately, since the parameters of the interface have not yet been quantified as a result of human as well as mechanical experience. Until the PRT concept has been refined so that the basic suspension and propulsion systems can be standardized (as is common in both now-separate industries), there can be no specific criteria for this interface.

1 Escalators and Moving Walks

Escalators and moving walks are self-loading and self-unloading people conveyors. Currently, escalators and horizontal moving walks are limited in speed in the United States and Canada to 0.6 m/sec (120 ft per min) and 0.9 m/sec (180 ft per min), respectively, so that random passenger loading will be safe for the 805-mm (32-in.) and the 1212-mm (48-in.) widths. Recent reevaluation of escalator capacities, based on observations rather than theoretical calculations, indicate that those listed in Table 4.1 are obtainable on a daily basis, with a substantial pool of waiting passengers at the bottom for up-peak and at the top for down-peak (Strakosch, 1967; Fruin, 1970; ANSI A17.1 Code, 1978; CSA B44 Code, 1971).

Table 4.1 Escalator capacities[a]

Nominal design width, in milli-meters (inches) (1)	Rated speed, in meters per second (feet per minute) (2)	Actual capacity, number of people per hour (3)
805 (32)	0.45 (90)	2360
805 (32)	0.61 (120)	3140
1212 (48)	0.45 (90)	4720
1212 (48)	0.61 (120)	6280

[a] Moving walk capacities vary with speed, width, and angle of incline.

Present Development. Life-safety control of escalators and moving walks is long overdue. In multifloor buildings served by escalators, conveying people to a fire-involved floor is unacceptable by current life-safety concepts. The first buildings are now completed to shut down escalators remotely and safely by smoke detector or pushbutton from a fire command center. The code-required instantaneous stop will be supplemented by a controlled stop, which will decelerate the escalator at a maximum of 0.45 m/sec/sec (1.5 ft per sec per sec) and between 0.45-m (18-in.) minimum and 1.2-m (48-in.) maximum stopping distance from no-load to full-load conditions. Preliminary investigation indicates that these parameters will smoothly and safely stop an escalator under all conditions, so that passengers can return to areas of safety using the stopped escalator as a stairway. Emergency instructions are given over the public address system for correct procedures.

Future Development. Further development in North America of the escalator and the moving walk to include 0.9-m to 1.3-m (3-ft to 4-ft) flat access and egress portions after and before the comb plates may confirm the higher speeds used in the USSR with safety [1.2 m/sec (235 ft per min)]. However, the code authorities will be reluctant to change, due to successful third-party lawsuits brought against manufacturers here. Locations such as department stores, that attract people who may be unfamiliar with the dangers of soft composition soles or soft overshoes becoming wedged between the skirt and the moving step, should consider the installation of skirt switches along the entire length in excess of the codes to help prevent this common complaint (ANSI A17.1 Code, 1978; CSA B44 Code, 1971; Hiramoto and Imamaka, 1974).

Extensive development of accelerating moving walks has been underway in recent years, to provide interbuilding and long intrabuilding transport systems, but without success. While the accelerating treadway may be solved in the near future, the problem of the accelerating handrail to comply with codes will be more difficult. The intrabuilding accelerating walk with single points of access and egress will probably be the first breakthrough in this technology. The multiple access and multiple egress accelerating moving walks for interbuilding use will undoubtedly be the second phase of this concept, since the access and egress speeds will be limited to 1.0 m/sec (200 ft per min) maximum, due to human considerations.

Building Interfaces. Special consideration must be given in every escalator or moving walk installation to the access and egress area beyond the newels so that dangerous congestion in the discharge area will be avoided. The distance from the handrail at the newel to the nearest perpendicular wall or door should be not less than 3.0 m (10 ft) for ideal transfer to the floor area or to another escalator.

The number and speed of escalators in stadia or other multiple level escalator banks should be carefully designed so that congestion will not rise to a dangerous level on down-peak when an event is over. Pedestrian control under these conditions requires detailed design and operation parameters before the escalator or walk system is finally engineered.

Every escalator system with an Up and a Down unit should also include an immediately accessible stairway or elevator bank to provide alternative pedestrian circulation when an escalator is shut down to permit repairs while the building is occupied during normal working hours. In addition, many short and most elderly people object to the step-riser relationship of 400 mm (15.75 in.)—215 mm (8.5 in.) for ascending or descending fixed stairs. Most commercial buildings have found the overtime maintenance without this stairway to be extremely expensive over the life of the building (Fruin, 1970).

Except under unusual design circumstances, the standard 805-mm (32-in.) escalator should be avoided, since the width is not sufficient to permit carrying a large briefcase or traveling bag beside the pedestrian. The larger 1212-mm (48-in.) width escalator will provide this convenience, and will also permit an adult to accompany a child or elderly person standing beside them.

Standard truss designs consider only the application of lightweight exterior finish for the exposed portion. When the architectural treatment is such as to substantially increase the dead weight on the truss, the details should be specified so that the truss design can accommodate the asymmetrical loading without a detrimental truss deflection. The new modular stairway design has indicated that the drive may be sensitive to deflection.

Arrangements of escalators or moving walks are numerous, from the open single floor rise, to the multiple-parallel arrangement, to the separated criss-cross for multiple floor travel. In the selection of any arrangement, pedestrian circulation during each of the up-peak, two-way peak, and down-peak patterns, should be considered. A suitable arrangement to handle all peak conditions must be selected or congestion will occur. It is important always to consider that escalators or moving walks are people conveyors and that, once on the conveyor, there is only one exit and that is at the other end (Strakosch, 1967).

Egress qualifications of escalators vary with local codes. The accreditation of an escalator bank as a means of egress in any area of refuge is the most desirable arrangement, since the escalators may continue to evacuate the building in case of fire in another part of the building. In some cases where the elevator lobby is on the second or third level above grade and served by escalators to and from grade, it may be desirable to have one escalator available on standby power to evacuate the above-grade area quickly. The amount of energy required is small [7.2 megajoules (2kW)], particularly when down traffic regeneration is taken into consideration.

Shutting down escalators has little effect, except during the up-peak period in the morning. As seen in Fig. 4.3, only Up escalators use significant amounts of power, and then only when fully loaded. Down escalators will regenerate power to the building during the down-peak period. Over the entire day of operation, the energy consumed is small compared with other areas of potential savings.

2 Passenger and Service Elevators

Elevators with a passenger classification in the United States and Canada have two use subcategories. The passenger elevator dedicated to pedestrians is designed to maximize the passenger capacity per square meter (per square foot), and to minimize the passenger transfer time into and out of the elevator car enclosure. The service elevator is designed primarily to handle materials such as carts, stretchers, furniture, and construction repair materials, as well as passengers. It maximizes the materials handling capacity to the detriment of passenger capacity and passenger transfer time. The service elevator is hence a freight elevator with a passenger classification.

The passenger elevator is wide and shallow to provide even the rearmost passengers in a crowded elevator car with prompt access to the car and landing doors. These doors should be center opening with a 1200-mm (47-in.) clear opening to permit two passengers to enter or exit simultaneously, resulting in the minimum passenger transfer time during peak traffic periods. To complement these doors, there should be car operating panels on each side of the car.

The service elevator ideally should be narrow and deep to accommodate vehicles and materials. The doors should be two-speed, center opening to provide the maximum opening and minimum door times possible and still retain the passenger classification. For safety reasons, the passenger classification should require horizontally sliding doors, as it does in the United States and Canada. In all hospitals, in large hotels, and in large commercial buildings, this arrangement should be strictly maintained.

Commercial Office Buildings.   All large commercial office buildings with a gross area in excess of 20 000 m² (200 000 sq ft) should consider a dedicated service elevator serving dedicated service lobbies rather than the passenger lobbies. In many cases, the ideal service elevator size must be compromised by the structural framing of the passenger elevators. However, the final design should recognize the functional requirements of moving one-piece loads, such as computers or safes, both with respect to dimensions and to weight.

Selecting the office building passenger elevator system or systems starts with the evaluation of the building population when the occupancy matures over a 5-yr or 10-yr period. This will be the most significant factor in providing an acceptable waiting time for typical floor passengers. The usual method of estimating population as a function of the "elevator usable" square meters (square feet) per floor must be compared with tenant projections if they are available. In single occupancy buildings, the owner should be made aware of the impact of less than standard elevatoring on the future occupancy of the space if the design projections differ from local norms. As the population factor will vary with multiple occupancy, the

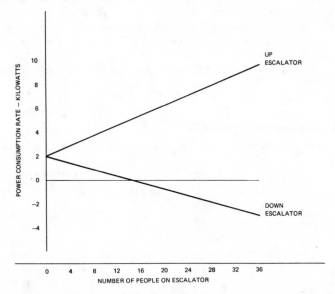

Fig. 4.3 Rate of electric power consumption and regeneration for up and down escalators under range of passenger-load conditions *(Sturgeon, 1974b)*

building occupancy on each floor should be estimated. Each floor must be assigned an "elevator net usable" area, which deletes from the gross area the following:

1. Core space for stairs, elevators, lobbies, toilets, and electrical and mechanical equipment.

2. Perimeter circulation corridor around the core.

3. Perimeter exterior space taken by convectors.

4. Interior columns.

5. Other dedicated spaces not permanently occupied.

Experience in the United States and Canada indicates that the occupancy of "elevator net usable" space will vary with use as follows:

1. Executive—14 m² to 19 m² (150 sq ft to 200 sq ft) per person.

2. Diversified—11 m² to 14 m² (120 sq ft to 150 sq ft) per person.

3. Diversified-Single Purpose—10 m² to 13 m² (110 sq ft to 140 sq ft) per person.

4. Single Purpose—9 m² to 12 m² (100 sq ft to 130 sq ft) per person.

Experience in other countries, particularly in Europe, indicates that these population factors may result in an underelevatored building if the legally permitted number of people are resident to an office floor. It is essential that local competitive and occupancy regulation factors be considered in estimating the eventual rather than initial occupancy. While the initial occupancy is important, the eventual occupancy will be one of the most important factors determining the rate of functional obsolescence.

The estimated population for each floor can then be tabulated for use in calculating the handling capacity of an elevator bank in a 5-minute period as a percentage of the total population served by each bank of elevators. A guide to estimating the variation of the average population factor as the height of the building increases is given in Table 4.2.

Since the introduction of the office skyscraper, the performance criteria used for

Table 4.2 Building population versus height

Building height, in number of floors (1)	Floors (2)	Population factor, in square meters (square feet) per person (3)
1 to 10	1 to 10	9 to 12 (100 to 130)
1 to 20	1 to 10	9 to 12 (100 to 130)
	11 to 20	9 to 13 (110 to 140)
1 to 30	1 to 10	9 to 12 (100 to 130)
	11 to 20	9 to 13 (110 to 140)
	21 to 30	11 to 16 (120 to 175)
1 to 40	1 to 10	9 to 12 (100 to 130)
	11 to 20	9 to 13 (110 to 140)
	21 to 30	11 to 14 (120 to 150)
	31 to 40	12 to 19 (130 to 200)

determining the required number of single-deck elevators have been based on the morning peak traffic requirements. Traffic studies and elevator recommendations for an office building for all types of building tenancy were usually made for the morning up-peak period, and it was then generally assumed that, if the criteria were met, the elevator system would provide good elevator service over the entire working day. New criteria have been recently formulated to identify the other critical periods.

During the 1940s and 1950s, elevator traffic counts made in office buildings with diversified tenancy frequently indicated 5-minute capacity requirements during the morning inrush which equalled about 12% of the building occupancy. However, the rapid expansion in high-rise office building construction in large urban areas during the 1970s has resulted in traffic congestion of the public transportation systems of trains, buses, highways, and streets, and pedestrian congestion on sidewalks and intersections. As a result, office buildings in these urban areas have experienced a reduction in the peak arrival rate during, but an extension of, the morning peak period. This is due to the staggering of office hours by employers, as well as to the commuters who leave home early to avoid peak vehicle congestion. A greater problem has evolved, however: the combination of heavy incoming up-peak traffic with down and interfloor traffic of persons previously arrived. As a result, the intensity of the office building morning up-peak has usually decreased, the duration of this period has lengthened, and the introduction of counterflow traffic during this up-peak has overloaded some systems designed on the basis of up-peak traffic flow only. The up-peak with 10% down traffic criterion has been introduced to check this performance when cafeteria or other traffic generators are functioning during up-peak. When work hours are staggered, the down-peak will be similarly affected.

The noontime two-way traffic demand experienced in office buildings due to interfloor traffic (movement to and from dining facilities, visitor traffic, and increased messenger and other supporting service movement) has generally increased over the years despite increased communications and improved office layout. As a result, office buildings which were originally adequately elevatored on the basis of morning peak traffic criteria alone began experiencing poor elevator service characterized by long waits at upper floors, not only during the lunch period but during the extended up-peak and down-peak periods. Tenant complaints about poor elevator service became common. The introduction of the "demand" type dispatching system in the early 1960s has improved elevator service during two-way peak traffic conditions. A great improvement in the regularity of waiting times and a substantial reduction in the number of long waits were gained by positioning rather than running the elevators in the building in anticipation of traffic.

Elevator performance criteria (office buildings). Single-deck elevator system performance is evaluated by comparing the calculated response to generally accepted standards in three separate categories. While all three should be satisfied in modern elevator systems, they are listed in order of importance. These categories for a bank of elevators are:

1. Five-minute handling capacity expressed as a percentage of total elevator bank population (this must be equal to or exceed the lobby arrival rate).

2. Average interval between cars in each elevator bank expressed in seconds (round trip time for a car divided by the number of elevators in the bank).

3. Maximum passenger Up transit time in each elevator bank, expressed in seconds.

The average interval *qualitatively* relates to the time a passenger waits at a typical landing for an elevator. It combines the speed of the elevator with the dispatching of each car to equalize the intervals between cars in all portions of the active hoistway. The average passenger waiting time at a typical floor will range from 60% to 70% of the average interval between the cars. The criteria listed in Table 4.3 relate to the quality of service in first-class office buildings.

The 5-minute handling capacity *quantitatively* relates to the handling capacity of a bank of elevators as a percentage of the building population served for morning up-peak or noon two-way peak in the heaviest respective 5-minute period (see Table 4.4).

The maximum passenger transit time *qualitatively* relates to the speed of the elevator and the probable number of stops a given size car will make. This is the one-way transit time for the last passenger during an up-peak trip to arrive at his destination, and should not exceed 150 sec for single-purpose buildings or 180 sec for diversified buildings.

Elevator performance calculations (office buildings). The calculation of single-deck elevator performance has been subject to variations due to interpretation of empirical data, manual calculations using approximations, and the use of computer simulations. The techniques of the major manufacturers have usually been safe when all the occupancy factors were known during design. The techniques of others and the results of simulations have had results ranging from good to poor.

Table 4.3 Interval criteria for passenger elevators—each bank

Building class	Interval, in seconds		
	Up-peak, with none down	Up-peak, with 10% down	Two-way peak, with 50% down
(1)	(2)	(3)	(4)
Single-purpose	20 to 25	25 to 30	30 to 40
Single-purpose diversified	23 to 28	28 to 33	33 to 43
Diversified	25 to 30	30 to 35	35 to 45

Table 4.4 Handling capacity criteria for passenger elevators—each bank

Building class	Handling capacity, as a percentage of building population served		
	Up-peak, with none down	Up-peak, with 10% down	Two-way peak, with 50% down
(1)	(2)	(3)	(4)
Diversified	11 to 12.5	11 to 12.5	10 to 12
Single-purpose diversified	12.5 to 15	12.5 to 15	12 to 15
Single-purpose	15 to 20	15 to 20	13 to 17

For the typical 10-story to 20-story building, the various techniques will all probably result in calculations that can be compared with the criteria listed in the foregoing paragraphs (Strakosch, 1967; Barney and dos Santos, 1974; Sturgeon, 1974a; Katz, 1974).

When there are more than 10 to 15 stories to be served above the main lobby, a multiple bank system should be considered in order to meet all of the criteria in all parts of the building during the calculated peak conditions. The multiple bank solution should strive for equal intervals and equal handling capacities within a ± 10% range. Since the usual office building elevator spends approximately 40% to 60% of its total round trip time stopped at a floor, these criteria cannot be met when each bank serves the same number of stops above the main landing and travels different distances in express zones.

Several arrangements should be tried to optimize the floors served with the speeds and car sizes available. This will usually result in most floors served by the low-rise bank, each higher bank serving fewer floors when the floors are of equal gross area. Before a final speed selection is made, the costs of various speeds with the final car platform size should be tested to select a speed that provides the most cost-effective performance.

The platform sizes for first-class office buildings in accordance with North American Standards should not be less than 1365 kg (3000 lb) and not more than 1800 kg (4000 lb). The preferable sizes are 1585 kg (3500 lb) and 1800 kg (4000 lb), since the elevator car enclosure is the first "room" a passenger enters in a building. If passenger transfer time is of minimum consequence, the minimum door size should be 1100 mm (42 in.). However, the optimum width for a simultaneous two-passenger transfer is 1200 mm (47 in.). This wider door will result in new platform width standards being adopted by the elevator industry in the 1135-kg, 1365-kg, and 1800-kg (2500-lb, 3000-lb, and 4000-lb) sizes. These recommended new standards with the 1200-mm (47-in.) doors are given in Table 4.5.

The speed selection for first-class office buildings in accordance with North American Standards should provide for performance to satisfy the criteria. Until recently, each elevator manufacturer recommended speeds to take advantage of machine sizes for competitive as well as for performance reasons. The evolution of

Table 4.5 Platform standards for passenger elevators

Capacity, in kilograms (pounds) (1)	Platform, in millimeters (inches) (2)	Hoistway width, in millimeters (inches) (3)
1135 (2500)	2200 × 1500 (86 × 60)	2650 (104)
1365 (3000)	2200 × 1700 (86 × 66)	2650 (104)
1585 (3500)	2200 × 1900 (86 × 74)	2650 (104)
1800 (4000)	2200 × 2100 (86 × 84)	2650 (104)
1800 (4000) alternate	2400 × 1900 (96 × 74)	2850 (114)

standard speeds has not been completed but seems to effectively reduce to those given in Table 4.6, where English or metricated English units prevail in design parameters.

The proposed standards for capacity (platform size) and speed for European Community countries are based on ratios derived from a "Renard" series of preferred numbers. The capacities are ratioed from the R5 and the R10 series. The speeds are ratioed from the R5 series. The R5 series ratio is $\sqrt[5]{10}$ or 1.5849. The R10 series ratio is $\sqrt[10]{10}$ or 1.2589. The capacities and ratios are given in Table 4.7.

Comparing the North American with the European standards, it is evident that there are fewer speeds to specify, but there is a lack of flexibility for speeds above 2.5 m/s (500 ft/min). This explains why the series is not extended beyond 2.5 m/s in the proposed ISO Standard.

When complicated circulation patterns exist or the building exceeds 20 stories, serious consideration should be given to acquiring the assistance of the traffic engineer of a major elevator manufacturer or a professional engineer in elevator consulting with experience in the type of building under consideration (Strakosch, 1967, 1972; Kort, 1972; Sturgeon, 1974a).

It is often necessary to measure the effectiveness of an installed elevator bank in responding to the day-long traffic demands. The up-peak traffic period in the morning is usually evaluated by observing the passengers handled away from and into the lobby in five-minute intervals. This performance may meet the calculation criteria, but other factors may cause complaints because of extended waiting times to respond to landing calls. The usual technique to reduce subjective complaints to objective data is to measure the day-long response of the elevator system to each up or down landing call at all the typical landings.

These results are obtained by an event recorder and either manually or computer analyzed to plot a response curve for that period of the day. Figs. 4.4, 4.5, 4.6, and 4.7 provide a guide to evaluate excellent service and a maximum limit for acceptable service. Analysis of the performance in each category will permit further study during a specific period to identify abuse by the passengers, overloading due to functions taking place in the building, or maladjustment of the elevator operating

Table 4.6 Elevator speeds for first-class office buildings

Speed, in meters per second (feet per minute) (1)	Machine type (2)	Control (3)
1.0 (200)	geared	generator field
2.0 (400)	geared	generator field
2.5 (500)	gearless	generator field
4.1 (800)	gearless	generator field
5.1 (1000)	gearless	generator field
6.1 (1200)	gearless	generator field
7.1 (1400)	gearless	generator field
8.1 (1600)	gearless	generator field
9.1 (1800)	gearless	generator field
10.2 (2000)	gearless	generator field

system which needs adjustment or reprogramming. These periods are generally identified as follows:

1. All-day average traffic, time period 1000–1800; see Fig. 4.4.

2. Balanced traffic, time period 1000–1130; see Fig. 4.5.

3. Two-way peak traffic, time period 1130–1400; see Fig. 4.6

4. Balanced traffic, time period 1400–1600; see Fig. 4.5.

5. Down-peak traffic, time period 1600–1800; see Fig. 4.7.

It should be considered when making any such analysis that special events or special periods of the week or month may not be representative. Usually, the test should be taken on a Tuesday, Wednesday, or Thursday, when the work-week is Monday through Friday, during a month when vacations are at a minimum (Jaros et al., 1978).

Double-deck elevators. The recent introduction of double-deck, local-express elevator systems as a solution to move large numbers of passengers has met with success that varies with the ability to predict the occupancy, the traffic circulation, and the mathematical probability of coincident stops. The application of double-deck, local-express elevators should be considered only when the conventional single-deck, local-express system results in elevator usable area below 65% or 70% of the gross area in the lowest typical floors. Under these circumstances, the cost of the

Table 4.7 Proposed standards for elevator capacity and speed for European Community countries

(a) Capacity (platform size)	
Capacity, in kilograms (pounds) (1)	Ratio (2)
400 (900)	—
630 (1400)	R5 × 400
800 (1800)	R10 × 630
1000 (2200)	R10 × 800
1250 (2800)	R10 × 1000
1600 (3500)	R10 × 1250
2000 (4400)	R10 × 1600
2500 (5500)	R10 × 2000
(b) Speed	
Speed, in meters per second (feet per minute) (1)	Ratio (2)
0.63 (125)	—
1.00 (200)	R5 × 0.63
1.60 (315)	R5 × 1.00
2.50 (500)	R5 × 1.60
4.00 (800)	R5 × 2.50
6.30 (1250)	R5 × 4.00
10.00 (2000)	R5 × 6.30

elevator system may be higher than its usual percentage of total building cost. However, as in the John Hancock Building in Boston and the Philip Morris Building in New York City, the concept made the project feasible on the site coverage permitted. The double-deck configuration results in a reduction of approximately 75% in the number of elevator shafts. This currently is the average reduction when comparing the same building with single-deck and double-deck systems. The concept can only be used successfully in major buildings with a number of double-deck elevators per bank, since the loss of one double-deck elevator has the same effect as simultaneously losing two single-deck elevators (Fig. 4.8) (Strakosch, 1967, 1972; Kort, 1972, 1974; Van Deusen, 1974).

The double-deck local-express elevator concept inherently has a very high

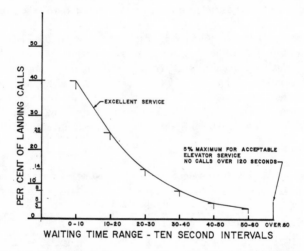

Fig. 4.4 Landing call response—all day average *(Courtesy: Westinghouse Elevator Company)*

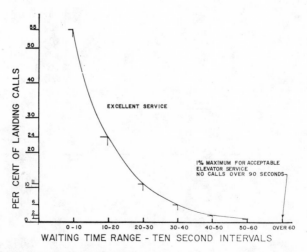

Fig. 4.5 Landing call response—balanced traffic *(Courtesy: Westinghouse Elevator Company)*

one-directional traffic handling capability for 15 to 20 local floors, as the number of probable stops per trip is reduced. Traffic studies indicate that double-deck elevator systems are capable in their special applications of carrying up to about 75% more people (rather than the theoretical 100%) during a given time period during the morning up-peak than a comparable single-deck elevator system, while reducing the hoistway space by approximately 25% (rather than the theoretical 50%). With the double-deck system, usually 20 local floors can be served, as compared to the usual 10 to 15 local floors in a single-deck system.

During two-way traffic periods, the double-deck elevator must provide service to persons traveling between odd and even floors from both the upper and lower compartments. As a result, the number of probable stops per round trip during the

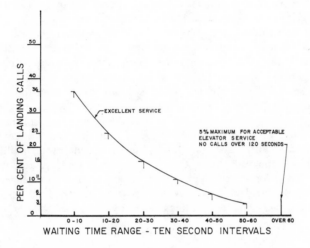

Fig. 4.6 Landing call response—two-way peak *(Courtesy: Westinghouse Elevator Company)*

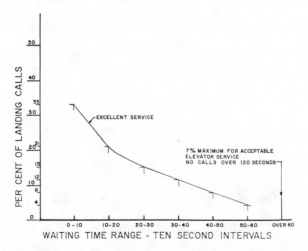

Fig. 4.7 Landing call response—down peak *(Courtesy: Westinghouse Elevator Company)*

two-way peak increases substantially over those expected during the one-directional peaks in the morning and evening. Double-deck dispatching systems minimize this effect by using the lagging car to answer landing calls, thus increasing the probability of coincident stops with the loading car. Tests have shown the average coincident stops during two-way traffic periods to be about one-third of the total stops.

The cost of a double-deck elevator, having twice the passenger capacity of a single-deck elevator and using equivalent space, is high. However, since the number of elevator shafts in the double-deck installation is 75% of those in the single-deck system it replaces, the economic evaluation of the single-deck versus the double-deck systems must compare not only the initial construction and equipment capital costs but also the rental incomes of the building. Since rental practices vary throughout the world, it is difficult to generalize as to the over-all cost effectiveness of double-deck elevators required for a particular building.

The final double-deck solution must consider whether the variations in the life-cycle occupancies of the building are similar to design criteria used to elevator the building. Double-deck installations now are operating in buildings that are considerably below their population potential. Simulation studies indicate that satisfactory service during two-way peaks will still result when the building has a mature population density. Double-deck installations, when properly applied, provide service equivalent to the conventional system they replace at improved cost-effectiveness when the total building return on investment is considered.

Sky lobby concept.   The "Sky Lobby" elevator concept, for buildings over 40 stories, utilizes high-speed shuttle cars to transport passengers express from street level to sky lobby for a local upper zone. At this point, the passengers transfer to single-deck or double-deck local elevators to arrive at their final destination. This concept creates two or more buildings vertically connected, one above the other,

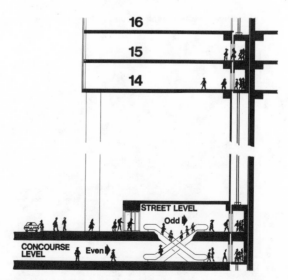

Fig. 4.8 Double-deck elevator concept showing split lobby loading at main landing *(Courtesy: Otis Elevator Company)*

each having essentially its own independent local elevator system served from the main floor by express shuttle elevators. The design criterion for the shuttle elevator system is for it to be able to handle the maximum number of people the local elevators can present within a given peak period, probably occurring during a down-peak. The World Trade Center has single-deck, double-ended 4535-kg (10 000-lb) passenger shuttles; the Sears Tower has double-deck, single-ended 2270/2270-kg (5000/5000-lb) passenger shuttles for a total capacity of 4535 kg (10 000 lb) (see Fig. 4.9).

It is essential to design any elevator system to match the anticipated maximum arrival or departure rate conditions which can be reasonably expected from the population of the building. For example, a future subway station adjacent to the building will cause more intense peak rates than a present bus station (Strakosch, 1967; Kort, 1972; Pasternak, 1974).

As the "Sky Lobby" building will be relatively large in order to justify the application, the impact from public transportation and parking facilities is significant. In order to avoid the resulting congestion, it will be necessary for tenants to stagger their working hours within the building to permit their employees to manage the down-peak congestion. The result is that the down-peak can be less than originally anticipated. Consideration of the two-way peak traffic during the day must then be emphasized to prevent improper location of eating and shopping facilities within the building complex.

When double-deck shuttle elevators are used, the location of traffic generators in the street "double lobby" and in the sky "double lobby" must be equalized for

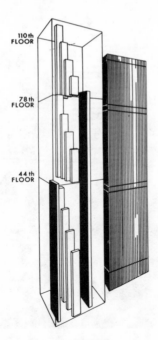

110th FLOOR

78th FLOOR

44th FLOOR

Fig. 4.9 Sky lobby concept showing express shuttle elevators to two Sky Lobbies and local elevators in three zones of World Trade Center *(Courtesy: Otis Elevator Company)*

up-peaks, two-way, and down-peaks, so as to load equally the two decks of the system. Since both levels of the street "double lobby" and the sky "double lobby" must be connected by up and down escalators, traffic that would normally use an upper street lobby to arrive at the upper sky lobby for the local elevator portion of their trip, must not be artificially attracted to the lower street lobby. The location of the coffee shop and newspaper stand in the lower lobby of the Sears Tower in Chicago results consistently in heavier loading of the lower deck during up-peak periods in the morning.

Elevator bank and lobby arrangement. The arrangement of elevators in a bank should ideally be a double-ended alcove with elevators serving the same landings facing each other. For passenger transfer time and door dwell time to be at a minimum, no more than four elevators should be in a line. When there are more than three elevators in a line or more than four elevators in a bank, two pushbutton risers should be installed where there is heavy interfloor traffic. The lobby width

The first major double-deck elevators operating as local elevators in banks, such as low-rise, high-rise, and mid-rise, are represented by the Citicorp Building, New York City *(Courtesy: Citibank)*

ideally should be from 1.75 to 2.0 times the car depth dimension to assure a large enough passenger pool in the lobby to minimize car loading time (Strakosch, 1967).

The landings served by the passenger elevators should not require travel below the main lobby. Every elevator system that is derived from relay logic gives distinctly subordinate service to landings below the main lobby. This traditional "basement service" takes an elevator out of the group system to answer "basement calls." The ideal solution is to provide local shuttle elevators to serve separately the levels below the main lobby. This solution also may prove to be the least expensive when at least two and preferably all of the main bank elevators should serve these lower floors with their deep pit requirements. The alternative solution is to have the lowest landing be the dispatching landing during the busy basement periods and shift it back to the main lobby by a time clock.

A building with anticipated total or partial single occupancy between two banks or among three banks of elevators should have transfer landings so that interfloor traffic need not travel to the main lobby to reach a destination in another bank. Dining facilities above the main floor will often demand a transfer floor if it is not low enough to be served by escalators.

The decision to serve such a major activity floor with elevators alone, or a combination of elevators and escalators, must be studied for cost effectiveness at peak traffic periods. Consideration of the handicapped will require elevators. Escalators should be added when the elevators cannot handle the anticipated peak traffic circulation.

Elevator operation. The operation of a bank of more than two elevators demands a group automatic solution. The advent of multiple zoning with both high and low call reversal during two-way traffic periods in the mid-1960s has made obsolete the coerced four or six program systems that ran elevators from top to bottom in anticipation of calls. These new "demand" systems now have reduced the "long wait" landing calls by a substantial percentage (20% to 30%) and should be standard in all new or modernized systems. The adoption of programmable controllers with minicomputers or microprocessors will provide additional flexibility in the future that will permit reprogramming of operation logic in response to changing tenant requirements. These technologies and techniques have been proven in the materials handling industry and will soon be available from all of the major manufacturers.

The location of dedicated service elevators should provide efficient access to loading docks, mail rooms, trash rooms, kitchens, storage, maintenance, and mechanical equipment rooms, as well as to the occupied floors. If a food preparation kitchen is not on the same floor as the dining facility, a dedicated food service elevator may be required to permit the service elevator or elevators to perform their basic function. The final determination of the number of service elevators in buildings larger than 47 000 m² (500 000 sq ft) gross should take into consideration a supplementary materials handling system such as a dumbwaiter, pneumatic message tubes, pneumatic trash tubes, vertical selective conveyor, automated tote box delivery system, or automated cart lift delivery system. These systems can reduce the day-long load on the service elevator system. Analysis of the work functions of the proposed occupants and their location within the building will indicate those possible intrabuilding systems that will increase the efficiency and reduce the transportation labor factor. These systems will be discussed in more detail in Section 4.3 of this chapter.

Residential Buildings.

General considerations.   The elevatoring of residential buildings has developed in two separate and distinct directions. The North American concept has been a direct derivation of the office building experience, with emphasis on retaining the dimension parameters to effect cost efficiencies to the elevator industry rather than convenience of core design. The elevator design data were the primary determinant of core design and its location. The European concept originally relegated the design of elevators to follow the residual space left over in the core, as determined by the convenience of the architect. This practice forced the elevator industry to custom build equipment for each project, resulting in inordinately higher costs. The recent high demand for residential housing and the development of European safety regulations to eliminate technical barriers between European Community countries has generated compromise standards that have permitted economies of volume, forcing architects to now consider elevator design data as a primary, rather than secondary or tertiary, determinant of core design.

It is now necessary to determine initially whether the North American standards of optimum passenger transfer efficiency at higher costs are desired, or whether the European standards of minimum costs will be the guide in core design. It has generally been accepted that, where the highest quality of efficient elevator service is required, North American standards should be followed. In geographical areas where European design influence and elevator manufacturers are present, the European standards should be considered.

North American concept.   Residential elevatoring is similar to that required for office buildings, except that the peak traffic conditions are usually two-way peaks during various periods of the day. Each building must be analyzed with respect to the location of traffic generators both inside and outside the building. The location of dining and transportation facilities must be described in detail before a traffic analysis can be generated. Rooftop dining or recreational activities that will attract traffic above the resident population must be considered when the vertical tranportation system is designed. Major recreational facilities, such as a convention ballroom, marina, or exhibit space, must be located at the main lobby level or at a level that can be served by escalators for the public and perhaps service elevators and service escalators for efficient transport of materials and service personnel. Each building with these facilities should be a "case study" by all of the design consultants involved. In 1959, The Sheraton Hotel in Philadelphia had to install two additional elevators in its second year of operation, at extensive disruption and expense, due to a communications gap at the design stage.

The basic calculation of population is again the starting point of the traffic analysis. Table 4.8 is only a guide to the ranges anticipated which should be confirmed with operating as well as design factors.

The criteria for transportation of the permanent or transient resident population are the same as the first two criteria categories of the office building (five-minute handling capacity and average interval between cars). Long passenger Up transit times are an economic necessity accepted by most residents. These criteria based on the resident population are listed in Table 4.9.

The elevator service to comply with these average criteria may exceed the level of competitive service provided in many remote locations. In the final analysis the elevator system is a major part of the capital investment, and the facility must provide an adequate return on this investment while being locally competitive with a high occupancy projection. These factors may temper the criteria to fit local conditions.

Dedicated service elevators are essential in every prestige hotel or apartment complex. The platform shape should take into consideration the cart traffic and bulk loads, not only to operate, but also initially to equip and later to refurbish the building. The location of service facilities to, from, and inside the building must be designed around the service elevator core or cores.

The increasing size of convention, resort, and guided tour hotels offers an opportunity to apply materials handling systems for baggage and room service functions. The current levels of cost and technology, however, have so far not responded to this need. It is anticipated that escalating labor costs and security considerations will justify both the development and the equipment costs in the not too distant future.

European concept. Until recently, architects determined the hoistway dimensions without consulting the elevator manufacturers, who were forced to make the

Table 4.8 Population factors for residential buildings

Building use (1)	Population factor, as number of persons per bedroom (2)
Hotel	
Prestige	1.5 to 1.7
Suburban-resort	1.5 to 1.9
Convention	1.7 to 2.0
Apartment	
In-town prestige	1.5 to 1.7
Development	1.7 to 2.0
Dormitories	1.8 to 2.0
Housing for elderly	1.2 to 1.5

Table 4.9 Interval and handling capacity criteria for elevators in residential buildings

Building use (1)	Two-way peak, with 50% up and 50% down	
	Interval between cars (each bank), in seconds (2)	Handling capacity (each bank), as a percentage of population (3)
Hotel		
Prestige without functions	40 to 50	10 to 12
Prestige with functions	40 to 50	12 to 15
Suburban-resort	40 to 60	10 to 15
Convention	35 to 45	15 to 20
Apartment		
In-town prestige	50 to 70	7 to 10
Development	60 to 90	5 to 7
Dormitories	50 to 90	12 to 18
Housing for elderly	60 to 100	5 to 7

elevator equipment fit into the available remaining space in the core. The subdivision of apartment houses and the size of staircases led to deep and narrow hoistways. The narrow width of the hoistway permitted the installation of swing landing doors in combination with collapsible gates as the only car and landing entrance protection.

About 1930, various national safety regulations were adopted to prohibit collapsible gates on automatic elevators. While retaining the narrow hoistways, which have no space for a suitable car door of any sort, the simple and cheap solution of cars without car doors and flush smooth front hoistway walls facing the car entrance was permitted with speeds up to 1.00 m/s (200 ft per min), or even higher in some countries. Surprising as it may seem, this arrangement is still permitted but will soon be prohibited.

The recent demand for dimensional standardization coincided with the important activity of drafting the "European Safety Regulations for the Construction and Installation of Electric Passenger Elevators," with the object of eliminating technical barriers to trade between the member countries of the European Community. The sifnificant decisions were that solid car doors are now required on all passenger elevators, and that the maximum car inside areas are fixed for each capacity.

The guidelines that the standardization group for elevators in apartment houses had to work to can be summarized as follows:

1. The number of size categories must be reduced to a minimum.

2. Capacities must follow the R5 and R10 (Renard) series of preferred numbers.

3. Speeds must follow the R5 series of preferred numbers.

4. Inside car platform areas must comply with the proposed European regulations.

5. Power operated car and landing doors must be provided.

6. At least one elevator must be dimensioned to accommodate an occupied wheelchair.

7. At least one elevator must be dimensioned to accommodate furniture as well as ambulance stretchers.

Local building regulations in Europe require that apartment houses having four stories or more shall be provided with an elevator. Up to six stories, these buildings usually group between two and four 4-person apartments per floor, so that a light-duty 4 to 5 passenger elevator is sufficient as the waiting time is of little importance. There has always been a wide demand in the past for this size elevator, and therefore it has been incorporated into the Standard.

Recent regulations, requiring that at least one elevator in each building should be provided dimensioned so as to carry a wheelchair, will have a significant influence in the future on the minimum size of buildings with single elevators. The recommendations for elevators in apartment houses are proposed in ISO Standard DIS 3571/1 and given in Table 4.10.

The minimum inside car depth to accommodate a wheelchair has been fixed internationally at 1.4 m (55.1 in.). For the 8-passenger elevator, this results in an internal car width of $1.66/1.4 = 1.1$ m (3.6 ft). This width also configures the

1000-kg (2200-lb) combination passenger/furniture lift, as the internal car depth of 2.1 m (6.9 ft) is obtained that will accommodate stretchers.

Hence, these three apartment house categories all have the same car width of 1.1 m (3.6 ft) and a clear entrance width of 0.8 m (2.6 ft). The hoistway width is set at 1.8 m (5.9 ft) to accommodate 0.8-m (2.6-ft) center opening car and landing doors.

Except for the small 400-kg (900-lb) passenger elevator, the result is that the cars are deeper than they are wide. The countries of continental Europe were accustomed to this configuration, as discussed previously.

The basic calculation of population is again the starting point of the traffic analysis. Table 4.11 is only a guide to the ranges anticipated, which should be confirmed with operating as well as design factors.

The criteria for transportation of the resident population are satisfied by the same first two criteria categories as those of the office building. The acceptance of long passenger up transit times is again an economic necessity, accepted by most residents. These criteria, based on the resident population, are given in Table 4.12.

The European elevator manufacturers have prepared general guidance standards in chart form to incorporate these criteria (Figs. 4.10, 4.11, 4.12). The speeds are standardized to the R5 series of preferred numbers for the various elevator capacities. The maximum speeds indicated in Table 4.13 are intended to become fixed category speeds for the speed control system employed.

Institutional Buildings.   The specialized vertical transportation solutions for many institutional buildings cannot be generalized due to the myriad of special functions served. Courthouses, libraries, laboratories, educational buildings, civic auditoriums, prisons, city halls, museums, etc., require public and private passenger elevator and specialized service elevator solutions peculiar to each specific building (Pasternak, 1974).

Hospitals.   The general and specialized hospital today requires the fine tuning

Table 4.10 Recommendations for elevators in apartment houses (European regulations)

Capacity, in kilograms (pounds) (1)	Number of passengers (2)	Maximum car floor area, in square meters (square feet) (3)
400 (900)	5	1.17 (12.6)
630 (1400)	8	1.66 (17.9)
1000 (2200)	13	2.40 (25.8)

Table 4.11 Population factors for residential buildings (Europe)

Number of rooms per apartment (1)	Population factor, as number of persons per apartment (2)
2	2.0
3	2.7
4	3.5
5	4.2

of integrated elevator and materials handling systems. The use of passenger elevators, service elevators, dumbwaiters, cart lifts, pneumatic message tubes, pneumatic trash and linen tubes, automated tote box systems, and automated cart transport systems have combined to make the modern hospital the most automated nonindustrial facility (Hesselberg, 1974).

The first step in elevatoring the new technology hospital is to separate the staff-visitor traffic from the service traffic. The circulation of staff and visitors must be considered over an entire day of operation from 0500 hours to 2300 hours. Hospital staff has statistically risen in the United States from an average of 2.0 to 3.0 employees per bed in only 20 years. Since this is only the average, each facility must be evaluated on professionally generated staff projections, especially for the specialized referral hospitals being constructed today. The staff and visitors using the various elevator banks must be apportioned and the handling requirements estimated for various peak five-minute periods. In general, 10% to 15% of the total population must be transported in this period by all the elevator systems, with traffic in both directions. The simultaneous interval criterion should be that the interval not exceed 50 sec under any of the study conditions, and ideally should be about 40 sec.

The service traffic should then be split into two categories: (1) Traffic that requires either vertical elevator or vertical cart lift transportation; or (2) traffic that can be carried by automated tote box, pneumatic message, trash, and linen tubes. The scheduled service elevator traffic must then be time-slotted to determine the critical hours of peak traffic. The number of service elevators must be designed to handle the programmed traffic with a utilization factor over an extended period of six to eight hours that does not exceed 100% when one elevator in the bank is out of service. Under such circumstances, the nonscheduled vehicle traffic will have to be transported in the appropriately sized staff-visitor bank of elevators.

Consideration should be given to handling the remaining various clean and soiled vehicle traffic by an automated cart lift system with a common design of cart base for various cart tops. The system initially should be configured to provide the vertical transportation with semiautomated inject loading at the origin floor and eject unloading at the destination floor. This system should be the basic semiautomated system for cost and performance comparison before other more sophisticated systems are studied. This level of automation reduces to the minimum the vehicles requiring a vertical transportation escort, and maximizes the productivity of service personnel since a minimum number of people leave their floor to pick up or deliver carts. If this semiautomated cart lift concept is viable against the

Table 4.12 Interval and handling capacity criteria for elevators in residential buildings (Europe)

Building use (type of apartment) (1)	Two-way peak, with 50% up and 50% down	
	Interval between cars (each bank), in seconds (2)	Handling capacity (each bank), as a percentage of population (3)
Luxury	50 to 65	7 to 8
Normal	60 to 80	7 to 8
Economy	80 to 100	7 to 8

"manual escort on service elevator" concept, other more elaborate delivery systems may be considered and tested for cost-effectiveness. This system is most effective when the vertical portion predominates over the horizontal travel portion of the total distribution distance (Fig. 4.13) (Strakosch, 1967; Hesselberg, 1974; Schachinger, 1975).

The first fully automated system for study is the cart and driverless tractor combination, which self-loads at the point of origin and self-unloads at the point of destination. This automated system can be configured so that the driverless tractor is captive to the floor and is served by the basic cart lift system, or alternatively so that it travels vertically in an automatically called and dispatched elevator and horizontally on more than one floor. This system has advantages over the basic cart lift system when there are longer horizontal runs in addition to the vertical, which would otherwise require dedicated on-floor vehicle escorts (Fig. 4.14).

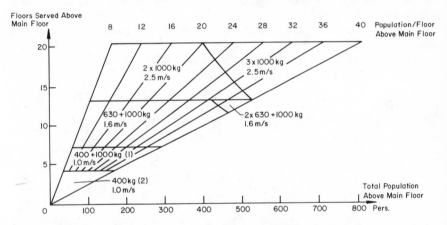

Fig. 4.10 European standard passenger elevators for apartment buildings—luxury (maximum interval 65 seconds—all local stops) *(Courtesy: Otis Elevator Company)*

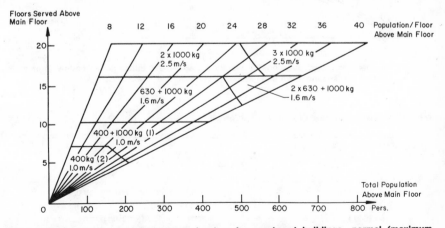

Fig. 4.11 European standard passenger elevators for apartment buildings—normal (maximum interval 80 seconds—all local stops) *(Courtesy: Otis Elevator Company)*

The second fully automated system for study, if the first alternative is viable, is the use of overhead "power and free" horizontal conveyors in conjunction with vertical lifts. These conveyors are loaded in one or more material management centers and addressed for a destination that is readable on the overhead cart carrier. The carrier with its cart can then be transported over extended horizontal distances and through one or more vertical lifts to arrive at its floor destination, where it is delivered to a "free" track to await release from the carrier and then manually pushed to the local final destination (Fig. 4.15)

Each of these automated systems should be designed and compared by those experienced in all systems, since the final system decision should be made without product line prejudice from a manufacturer of only one of these automated alternatives. Life-cycle costing with discounted cash flow methods should be used as the only valid method of making the system selection. The short payback period of the materials handling industry results in wrong decisions for the hospital industry, since it cannot shut down the materials handling system for model changes, at least during the facility's first half-life period.

The general guidelines for consideration of the selection of manual/semiautomated/automated cart systems are listed in Table 4.14.

The more popular materials handling systems are discussed in detail elsewhere.

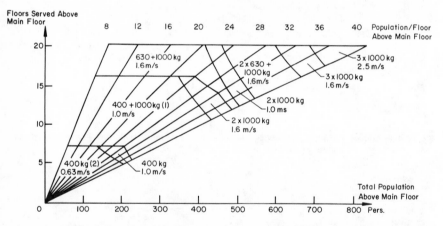

Fig. 4.12 European standard passenger elevators for apartment buildings—economy (maximum interval 100 seconds—all local stops) *(Courtesy: Otis Elevator Company)*

Table 4.13 Maximum speeds for elevators (Europe)

Speed, in meters per second (feet per minute) (1)	Speed control (2)
0.63 (125)	single speed alternating current
1.00 (200)	two-speed alternating current
1.60 (315)	generator field or alternating current—servo
2.50 (500)	generator field

The spectrum variations that current technologies and techniques provide for consideration in health care facilities are shown in Table 4.15, with general valuations for rating the efficacy of the concepts in different categories (Schachinger, 1975).

Since there are few companies that offer a systems approach, the recommendations and claims of "product line approach" companies must be viewed as subjective. The selection of a single system or a combination of systems must entail a comprehensive design selection process. The selection of a complicated system such as the overhead "power and free" conveyor may have to be proved by a computer design simulation to make sure the system configuration will stand the

Fig. 4.13 Automated inject-eject cart lift showing transfer device and typical cart *(Courtesy: American Sterilizer Company)*

Fig. 4.14 Automated driverless tractor showing cart transport by buried wire guide path *(Courtesy: American Sterilizer Company)*

anticipated traffic profiles and that all queueing will be accommodated without clogging the main delivery system.

Description of Elevator Equipment. Communication between the architectural, structural, and mechanical design disciplines with the vertical transportation

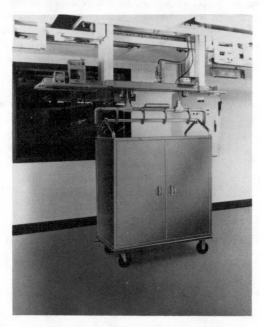

Fig. 4.15 Automated cart transport system showing cart and its transporter carried on overhead power and free conveyor *(Courtesy: American Sterilizer Company)*

Table 4.14 Hospital bulk cart system feasibility[a]

Number of beds (1)	Manual (2)	Semi-automated (3)	Automated (4)
75 to 125	A[b]	C	D
125 to 175	B	B	C
175 to 250	B	A	C
250 to 300	B	B	B
300 to 400	C	B	A
400 to 500	C	B	A
500 to 600	D	C	A
600 to 750	D	C	A
Above 750	D	C	A

[a]Predominant vertical orientation of a specific hospital may change the feasibility evaluation in this table.
[b]A = always feasible—must be considered.
  B = usually feasible—should be considered.
  C = occasionally feasible—minor consideration.
  D = rarely feasible—minor consideration.

discipline has traditionally been by word of mouth. The book published by Strakosch, formerly of Otis Elevator Company (Strakosch, 1967) has done much to bridge this communication gap. For those interested in a more detailed treatment of the basic concepts, Strakosch's book should be a continuing reference along with Annett (1960).

Modern elevator main propulsion systems fall into two categories, oil hydraulic and electric. The electric category is subdivided into geared electric traction, geared electric drum, and gearless electric traction. The various propulsion systems have responded to the need for specific solutions from architectural and structural considerations.

The first office building passenger elevators were borrowed from the freight elevator design of the winding drum elevator, with its own dedicated motor rather than the industrial jack shaft and pulley drive. By adding a car and drum counterweight, this drive could serve up to 10 or 12 stories. The possibility of limit switch failure, allowing the car or counterweights to be pulled into the overhead structure, demanded a safer design. The traction elevator solved the safety problem and the rise limitation by getting rid of the hoist ropes down the elevator shaft on the counterweight rather than trying to spool them on a mammoth drum. The bottoming of a car or its counterweight in the pit theoretically relieves the rope tension and usually destroys the traction, so that it becomes fail-safe if the propulsion unit continues to operate.

The geared machines of the drum and traction type (Fig. 4.16) uses a worm and worm gear reduction from a relatively high-speed motor. However, the car speeds are limited. The use of large slow speed, high torque traction motors from the railroad industry without intermediate gearing allowed the development of the gearless elevator, where the driving traction sheave is mounted directly on the motor armature. These gearless drives permitted higher speeds with extremely high reliability. The present speed limit in the United States is 9.1 m/sec (1800 ft per min), as demonstrated in the Sears Tower in Chicago. Japan has the world's fastest at 10.0 m/sec (2000 ft per min). The limit in Australia is 1400 ft per min.

The demand for low-cost, low-speed elevators for low-rise installations rejuvenated the early water hydraulic elevator in the form of the oil hydraulic elevator with a direct acting plunger, which required a piston equal to the length to the vertical rise. The electric motor and hydraulic pump raise the uncounterweighted elevator and gravity lowers it by controlled release of oil back to the tank. The refinement of these "oil-draulic" elevators have now replaced the market for many electric geared elevators. The current practical limitations of 0.75 m/sec (150 ft per min) in speed, and 22 m (70 ft) in rise, will undoubtedly increase to 1.0 m/sec (200 ft per min) and 30 m/sec (100 ft) of rise. Advantages of the oil hydraulic elevator are the low overhead heights in the elimination of the penthouse and the possibility, where permitted by codes, of a remote machine room. Disadvantages are the costs of drilling a precisely located plumb hole, and the larger motor required since there is no counterweight. The lack of regeneration characteristics and motor size should be carefully considered when the elevators will have intense use if electric energy and demand charges are significant compared to a geared installation in the higher speed and rise ranges (Fig. 4.17).

To compete with the advantages of the oil hydraulic, a low overhead electric elevator was configured that provides higher speeds but requires a contiguous machine room to the elevator hoistway at one of the lower levels. The location of

Table 4.15 Variations of hospital materials handling systems and relative characteristics[a]
(Courtesy: Architectural Record)

Hardware	System Characteristics					Rating			
	Horizontal speed, in feet per minute	Vertical speed, in feet per minute	Volume capacity, in cubic feet	Weight, in pounds	Mode	Management control	Asepsis control	Clean delivery	Soiled return
(1)	(2)	(3)	(4)	(5)	(6)	(7)	(8)	(9)	(10)
Carts, manually pushed	120	0	40	1000	MAN	2	2	2	2
Tote boxes, manually carried	150	0	6	35	AUTO	2	2	2	1
Freight elevators, manual	0	AR	800+	AR	MAN	2	2	2	2
Selective vertical conveyor	80+	80	3	40	MAN	3	3	3	2
Tray conveyor and lift	80	80	2	15	MAN	3	3	3	2
Tow trucks, manual	440+	AR	2000	5000	MAN	2	2	3	3
Tow trucks, driverless	440	AR	2000	5000	AUTO	3	2	3	3
Box carrier— powered, trac.	100	100	1	20	MAN	5	4	4	1
Pneumatic tube, 4 in.	2500+	2500+	0.05	2	MAN	5	4	3	0
Pneumatic tube, 6 in. spec. pur.	1200+	1200+	0.143	4	MAN	5	5	4	1
Pneumatic tube, 8 in. and larger	1200+	1200+	0.3 to 1.0	25	MAN	5	5	5	1
Pneumatic tube trash and/or linen	2000+	2000+	3.5	35	MAN	5	5	0	5
Tote box conveyor	150+	80	4	35	AUTO	4	3	3	2
Cart size dumbwaiter, manual	0	AR	28	500	MAN	2	2	2	2
Dumbwaiter, automatic, load cart	25	AR	28	500	MAN	3	3	4	4
Elevator, auto load, cart	25	AR	40	1000	MAN	3	3	4	4
Overhead monorail powered—auto.	200	100	18	220	MAN	5	4	4	4
In-floor tow conveyor, auto.	60	AR	40	1000+	MAN	4	2	3	3

the machine room in the basement requires extra hoistway space to permit the hoist ropes to reach the overhead sheaves. This machine below configuration permits either an overslung car roping arrangement with an overhead height of 5.8 m (19 ft), or an underslung car roping arrangement with an overhead height of 4.3 m (14 ft) (Fig. 4.18).

The overslung car is roped similarly (usually 1:1) to the same elevator with an overhead machine. There is usually a code requirement for an overhead floor to provide access to the governor and for lubrication of the overhead sheaves. The underslung car must be roped 2:1 with car sheaves underneath the car. The sheaves in the overhead space are placed to the sides and rear of the car to permit it to overtravel these sheaves for the lowest overhead height. The ideal basement machine configuration available from some manufacturers is the overhung machine without an outboard bearing. This permits the drive sheave to be inside the hoistway for 180° wrap of the hoist ropes on the drive sheave and for a minimum number of rope bends. The less desirable basement machine configuration is the use of a standard overhead machine in the basement with the front of the drive sheave projecting into the hoistway and a closely mounted deflector sheave to bring the ropes from the back of the drive sheave into the hoistway. This deflector is often called a "back breaker" sheave, since it bends the ropes in the opposite direction from the drive sheave and, hence, tends to shorten rope life on intensely used installations. Most basement machine installations are geared, serving up to 10 stories with only a few gearless installations at 2.5 m/sec (500 ft per min).

Previously, most speed control systems used the typical Ward-Leonard system called Generator Field Control. This system provides the smoothest acceleration to and deceleration from contract speed. It permits dynamic (regenerative) braking to stop the elevator electrically so as to use the brake only to hold the elevator at a landing. The new solid-state technology using silicon controlled rectifiers (SCR) provides equivalent performance in both the geared and gearless drives without the

Table 4.15 (continued)

Hardware	System Characteristics					Rating			
	Horizontal speed, in feet per minute	Vertical speed, in feet per minute	Volume capacity, in cubic feet	Weight, in pounds	Mode	Management control	Asepsis control	Clean delivery	Soiled return
(1)	(2)	(3)	(4)	(5)	(6)	(7)	(8)	(9)	(10)
Overhead power and free rail, auto.	40	AR	32	800	AUTO	5	5	5	5
Driverless electric car, auto.	88+	AR	34	800+	MAN	5	5	5	5

[a] All figures are representative of physical and practical limitations. AR = as required. Rating scale: 5 = excellent; 4 = good; 3 = above average; 2 = average; 1 = not practical or too limited; 0 = no present capability. Ratings are based on application, suitability, speeds, cleanliness, reliability, capacities, and management control advantages.

motor generator set. The SCR drive provides some energy savings on power absorption and increases the energy to the building on regeneration. The current design of the SCR drive, however, must be carefully applied to prevent a deleterious electrical and structure-borne noise in the building environment.

The Building Interfaces. The high-rise building of tomorrow will use every systems engineering tool to design, construct, and maintain a building with the

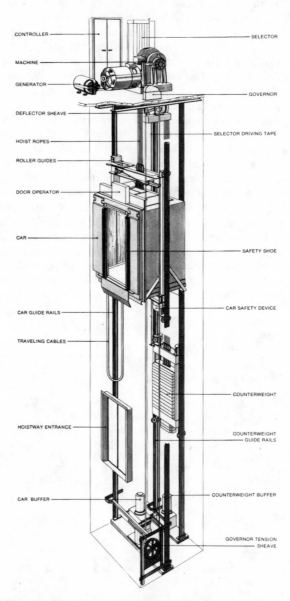

Fig. 4.16 Typical geared traction elevator equipment *(Courtesy: Otis Elevator Company)*

lowest capital and operating costs for the highest return on investment. In the past, the traditional concepts of building and vertical transportation technologies tended to be tangential in their interaction, which permitted purchasing based only on

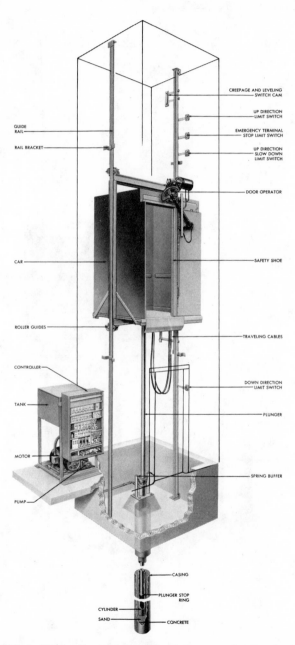

Fig. 4.17 Typical oil hydraulic elevator equipment *(Courtesy: Otis Elevator Company)*

capital costs with a bare minimum of building operation interfaces—spatial, structural, and electrical. The current level of operation sophistication in these vital building systems requires a more extensive understanding of the interfaces of these

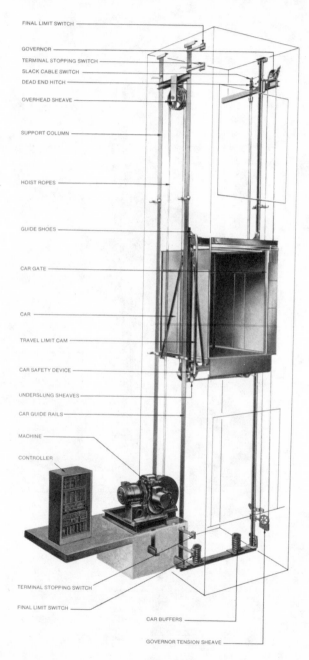

Fig. 4.18 Typical geared underslung traction elevator equipment *(Courtesy: Otis Elevator Company)*

now interacting technologies. (Chapter PC-15 deals with "Systems Methodology.") Only when the systems have been made responsive to this interaction in both the capital and operating sectors can valid cost comparisons be made.

The building-vertical transportation interfaces of the past tended to be passive. Given sufficient structural support, electrical power, and people traffic, the automatic elevator would continue to operate without regard to other conditions in the building. Today the interfaces require that the vertical transportation system react to the varied conditions occurring in the operation of a high-rise building. These conditions can be identified as belonging to two design categories: (1) Design for life safety operations in emergencies; and (2) design for special high-rise conditions. It is intended here to identify the problem areas and to indicate the direction of probable solutions. It is now of extreme importance that the various design disciplines and the elevator industry exchange freely the acquired knowledge, as private test towers can no longer thoroughly model real life high-rise conditions.

Life safety.   From now on, all elevator systems will be called upon to continue to operate safely during and after first-order emergencies. These first-order emergencies can be categorized as externally or internally generated. The external emergency conditions are total power failure or a severe climatic or earthquake disturbance; the internal are partial building power failure, fire, or mechanical equipment failure. It is suggested that an elevator system now be designed to cope with any emergency when two or three of these conditions might act simultaneously.

Standby power operation.   The elevator system must be designed for three power operational conditions under total and partial power failure to the elevator machine rooms. It is desirable in all first-class office buildings and essential in all high-rise buildings over 20 stories that a split feeder arrangement is provided, with the even numbered elevators on one feeder and odd numbered elevators on a second feeder with automatic transfer switches to standby power. In the event of a feeder failure, that portion of the building will still have elevator service during an extended restoration period.

If an odd or even feeder fails, the standby power system should feed the affected elevators with enough capacity to run them one at a time automatically to their lowest lobby floor and shut them down so as to evacuate that portion of the elevator system without normal power. When this evacuation has taken place, the elevators still on normal power operate with one or more of the affected elevators as selected manually on standby power. The elevator system must continue to operate that portion of the building or to provide partial or evacuation transportation.

When a total power failure occurs, the standby power system should automatically transfer all elevators to the standby power source and automatically, on a one-at-a-time basis, evacuate the elevator system. When this is accomplished, the system should then permit manual selection of any elevator to evacuate the building and provide transportation for emergency personnel.

This automatic switching must be coordinated between the elevator system and the electrical system to provide fail-safe interlocking at a centralized control point. All elevator car lights, ventilation fans, and communication equipment must be connected to a normal/standby power circuit so that passenger panic is prevented in temporarily stopped and occupied elevators. Emergency car lighting, with its source on the elevator car, should be provided to cover the interruption period and provide a back-up lighting system in case the standby power source fails to start or a transfer switch fails to operate.

Particular attention must be paid to providing sufficient capacity in the standby generator to evacuate the building in a reasonable length of time after the power failure. This must take into consideration any special requirements to match the evacuation capacity of shuttle elevators from a sky lobby to the total evacuation capacity of the respective local banks of elevators. This evacuation should not take longer than three hours. If an escalator is involved in the essential exit route, it should also be included on the standby power distribution bus.

When the elevator systems use silicon controlled rectifier (SCR) motor drives instead of motor generator sets, their notching effect is more pronounced on the finite bus impedance of the standby generator than on the relatively infinite bus impedance of the grid of the normal power system. Standby power loads that are sensitive to such a waveform disturbance should be put on a separate standby generator, as filtering of the notching effect may not be cost-effective (Fig. 4.19). (In Fig. 4.19, notching is indicated by vertical marks on 60-cycle sine wave.) Compare with Fig. 4.23, which shows less notching.

The service elevators that serve all local floors should have an independent feeder from the standby power distribution center direct to their machine room to provide the highest degree of reliability as the primary firemen's elevators.

Emergency firemen's service operation. Firemen's service in North America has developed into a two-phase operation that is basic to life safety and prompt service for the Fire Department regardless of the many local variations in operation details. Phase I relates to the life safety of those in the elevator system near the fire-involved floor by instantly recalling all elevators serving that floor to the lowest landing, either a ground lobby or a sky lobby. Sensor detection devices are primarily products of combustion devices (smoke detectors) located in each elevator lobby, and secondarily other smoke detectors on the floor or water flow switches in the sprinkler system on the floor. Phase II relates to the special controls that are activated by the standard firemen's key that permits Fire Department personnel to completely control the starting, running, and stopping of the elevator, as well as the opening and closing of the doors without interference from landing buttons to get to and from the fire-involved floors. Initially, it was felt that only a few elevators (three, with at least one in a separate hoistway) need be involved in Phase II, but current practice has evolved that all elevators should provide Phase I as well as Phase II operation for both above and below grade elavators (Fig. 4.20).

Earthquake operation. Soon after the Los Angeles, California, earthquakes in 1971, many regulatory authorities, manufacturers, and owners went forward to

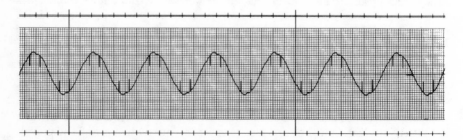

Fig. 4.19 Notching effect on elevator feeders by SCR elevator operating on standby power in major building *(Courtesy: Westinghouse Elevator Company)*

develop requirements to increase the safety of people in an elevator system during an earthquake. They sought to provide the design criteria so that at least one elevator had sufficient horizontal and vertical restraints to equal the building design; then it could be operated immediately following a disturbance of substantial proportions. These restraints must include not only the car and counterweight, but also all equipment in the pit and machine room. Whenever a high-rise building is considered, the latest deliberations of the various code and regulatory authorities should be consulted until a comprehensive advisory code has been approved for all areas of seismic activity (Sturgeon, 1967; Mitsui and Nava, 1973). (See Chapter CL-2, "Earthquake Loading and Response.")

Recently installed equipment that may eventually be adopted by regulatory authorities is shown in Figs. 4.21 and 4.22. The development of an inexpensive sliding rail clip with seismic restraint capacity is shown in Fig. 4.21. Recent codes in North America only implicitly refer to the system restraint of guide rails, whereas this potentially weak link should be explicitly required. Many elevators recently installed in earthquake zones do not have adequate rail restraints that comply with the "intent" of the local codes. The restraint of the counterweight can effectively be incorporated into new construction by installing the usual counterweight rail tie-brackets between the counterweight and the elevator car and increasing their number so that at least two brackets can restrain the counterweight at all positions in the hoistway. A recent installation is shown in Fig. 4.22.

Future life safety considerations.　The current philosophy, as a result of past experience, is that elevators must not be used to evacuate that part of a tall building above or below a fire-involved bank of elevators. Considering the current hoistway and associated building systems supporting the elevator system, this position is the only defensible one. However, as we configure taller and more multiple-use buildings, these concepts should be reevaluated with emphasis on using rather than

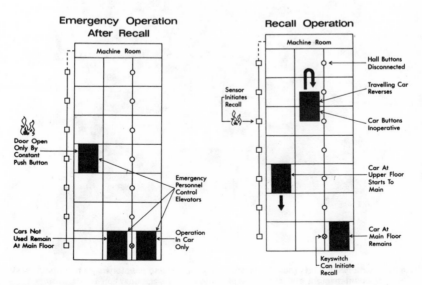

Fig. 4.20 Automatic recall and emergency fireman operation *(Courtesy: Otis Elevator Company)*

abandoning reliable evacuation equipment which also represents the psychologically instinctive human response to use the usual exit path during emergencies.

Current codes require a two-hour fire rated hoistway enclosure with one and one-half hour fire rated elevator entrances. It was 1979, however, before labeled entrances were available in the United States and Canada to be legally installed in all dry wall construction. Consideration should now be given to constructing the express portion of the hoistway as a fire bulkhead which will retain its fire integrity as a "hoistway of refuge" over a much longer period—say four hours. The stairways

Fig. 4.21 Seismic sliding rail clip using standard forged clips with shims to provide upper limit of sliding force per bracket *(Courtesy: Jaros, Baum & Bolles)*

Fig. 4.22 Counterweight tie brackets installed between car and counterweight for seismic restraint of counterweight and containment of hoist and compensation ropes *(Courtesy: Jaros, Baum & Bolles)*

could now be restricted to use by only those whose elevator service has been dedicated to the Fire Department, while all others in the building could use their normal elevator transportation to leave the building safely on an intense down-peak condition (all elevators should be arranged to handle 125% of rated capacity load as in the ANSI A17.1 Code). The location and configuration of standby power sources for each building zone might also change to increase the life safety reliability.

Sky lobbies and their dedicated shuttle elevators should be considered as extensions of the ground lobby with their own fire and power integrity, so that they will be areas of refuge for people awaiting elevator evacuation safely through a fire-involved floor in a hoistway of refuge. Pressurizing these area of refuge lobbies and hoistways of refuge could minimize possible smoke contamination due to thermal or stack effects, and is now required in some European countries.

Current design and construction technologies have substantially reduced total building weight. The over-all result of taller and more limber buildings requires more attention to phenomena that did not previously affect elevator systems adversely. Since the lower parts of a building are often occupied while the upper parts are under construction, substantial periods of transition must be tolerated with operable and reliable elevator systems. Failure to consider these factors may result in temporarily underelevatored portions of the building for a protracted period because of the construction contamination of normally clean elevators.

Wind induced building motion. While displacement amplitudes and the resulting horizontal g forces may not be greater than in previous structures, they may occur more often at lower wind velocities in currently designed structures. The anticipated dynamic response and static displacement of a building should be made a part of the contract documents; then the elevator systems can be designed so that they are not resonant with the building's oscillation. The guide rails which are erected early in construction under varying climatic conditions must be precisely alined for later satisfactory ride characteristics under building motion conditions (Mitsui and Nava, 1973).

When the building is completed and fully occupied, both linear and torsional motion may impart amplitudes to the hoist, compensation, and governor ropes, as well as the traveling control cables, which build up to self-damaging proportions. This is due to their small amount of inherent damping and to the near resonance of these rope and cable systems to the fundamental and harmonic frequencies of the building when elevators are near their terminal landings. Even though the safety of passengers may not be affected, the passenger inconvenience of removal from a stopped elevator with damaged control cables is undesirable and the noise of slapping hoist, governor, and compensation ropes hitting the car while in motion is unsettling to most passengers.

Careful layout and design should prevent the hoist and compensation ropes associated with the counterweight from hitting the car; the governor ropes from hitting the car or counterweight and from snagging on beams or brackets; and the compensating ropes from entangling the traveling cables. Vibration dampers may be needed above and rope restraint followers below the elevator and counterweight to absorb the induced rope energy and restrict rope movement.

Induced building motion on the elevator system may have the same effect as a minor seismic disturbance. The elevator system should be self-protective to the linear and torsional amplitudes that may cause damage to the hoistway equipment. In the past, a partial corrective action has been to reduce the contract speed. At this time, however, not enough is known to identify a universal cure. Each elevator system should be analyzed for performance under each condition during design and carefully observed after installation. Since modeling these conditions may not be conclusive, only research on the experience in existing buildings can point the direction of new designs to accommodate these operating conditions. These conditions are now constantly being monitored for their effect on the elevator systems at the Sears Tower and the World Trade Center. (Chapter CL-3 deals with "Wind Loading and Wind Effects.")

Building stack effect.   The stack effect in a building may seriously affect the elevator system. Even if the finished building will minimize this effect on the elevators, it may take a heavy toll in reliability during the transition construction period with sneak air circuits by preventing the power closing of landing doors. The entire shuttle elevator system to a sky lobby may shut down as a result of stack effect if lights of glass or revolving doors are lost in a gusting wind, or if mechanical equipment fails at a critical time or is not operated properly during periods of low ambient temperature.

Whenever possible, each elevator machine room should be associated with the mechanical ventilating equipment that serves its upper landings so that a sneak air circuit is not provided through the machine room. This separation precaution is also desirable between a sky lobby and local elevators that terminate in that lobby. The hoistways and machine rooms of service elevators that serve many floors or all floors should be isolated from any local or shuttle elevators.

The power door operators on each elevator should be arranged to pulse the stalled door after a certain time delay. This circuit could also be activated as a function of external air temperature or a static pressure drop across the hoistway wall. Where a stack effect may be adverse on critical elevators, the door area should be minimized, so as to reduce the horizontal force acting that increases the friction in the sill guides and door hangers that the door operator must overcome.

It is absolutely essential that the elevator system continue to operate for life safety reasons if lights of glass are lost, revolving doors collapse, or if the mechanical system has a temporary malfunction. The industry needs to relate its equipment design to pressure differentials across a door and to the area of that door. Specifications in the future should call for continued operation under specific pressure differential conditions occuring in tall buildings.

Building compression.   The compression of the building occurs primarily during construction and mechanical equipment installation, and secondarily during the loading of tenant spaces with office equipment. This has an adverse effect on the guide rail alinement, which determines to a large part the quality of the riding characteristics of a high-rise elevator. The elevator industry must develop and provide more information on the methods of bracketing, the forces to be experienced by the supporting steel, and the slide of rails during as well as after construction (Mitsui and Nava, 1973).

When sliding rail clips are free of construction debris, their interaction with the building is relatively predictable. However, significant forces may be generated during the construction phase when debris is present. Deformation of supporting steel or guide rails, or both, may be induced early during construction with current practices. Understanding the rail and beam force excursions during the construction and operation phases should be given a high priority in the next generation of elevator design. Special consideration must be given to the rigidity of perimeter supporting steel. Current assumptions are being reviewed by the code committees and may result in significant interface changes as applied to high-rise buildings. (Chapter CB-10 deals with "Creep, Shrinkage, and Temperature Effects.")

Elevator equipment induced vibration.   Structure-borne vibrations will become increasingly important as the larger elevator machines are surrounded by occupied spaces. Car and counterweight rails also transmit vibrations to the structure. All elevator machinery to be installed in these sensitive locations should be manufactured so that vibration isolation is a part of the equipment provided, or easily added in kit form (Reed, 1974).

Water damage.   An elevator system has most of its wiring and wiring devices associated with the front hoistway walls and the front of the elevator car. Ruptured pipes and fire fighting often seriously damage the elevator system unnecessarily. Typical floors that provide an island effect (raised floor slab) for the elevator hoistways and lobbies would prevent this damage at less cost than reworking the wiring and wiring devices to dripproof construction.

Machine rooms are particularly susceptible to water damage from overhead. Cutting the floor slab above a machine room should be avoided for any reason. Double and triple level machine rooms should also have the island effect to prevent water from entering from floors above.

Electrical distribution system.   The traditional motor generator set of Generator Field Control elevators has been refined to its maximum level of reliability. It has been the standard for over 75 years and will probably still have applications for the next 25 years. Today the solid state technology has already demonstrated superiority in the complex logic operation of groups of elevators with improved reliability and increased flexibility over the relay. The replacement of the motor generator sets with SCR drives has been the result of much development in both geared and gearless applications.

There is concern, however, that the application cannot yet be universally applied to every building transportation system. The motor generator set is an excellent electrical filter. The electrical feeders have always handled the starting, running, and regenerating currents unique to elevators with concern only regarding a minimum voltage drop due to regulation. The SCR, however, notches the voltage waveform to a greater or lesser extent as a function of the impedance of the source voltage. These notches can appear throughout the building during normal power operation. A typical notching effect on computer feeders with a number of elevators running during a test of a major bank building with SCR elevators is shown in Fig. 4.23.

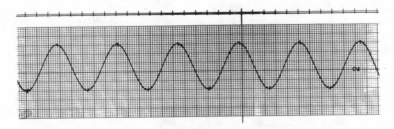

Fig. 4.23 Notching effect on computer feeder by SCR elevators operating on normal power in major building *(Courtesy: Westinghouse Elevator Company)*

During the period of this test, large main frame computers and peripherals operated a test program without failure. However, it is probable that some minicomputers and peripheral equipment could have erratic operation due to the SCR elevators without adequate filtering of their incoming line. It has been found that there are as yet no common standards for computer power supply design in the United States and probably it will take at least 5 years to field such standardized equipment. In the meantime, filters will have to be applied in the field on all equipment with a sensitivity to such disturbances, or substantial filtering equipment will have to be required on the SCR elevator drives. Experience has shown that the addition of power factor correction capacitors will substantially reduce the notching effect throughout the building.

The notching effect is much worse on standby power, since the depth of the notch is a function of the standby power source impedance. The voltage waveform in Fig. 4.19 was obtained at the same bank building with a 480-rms volt, 345-kW turbocharged diesel generator set feeding a 175-amp emergency lighting load and operating a 1585-kg (3500-lb) elevator running at 4.0 m/sec (800 ft per min) with 100% of contract load and 100% of contract speed.

The current consensus of the computer industry is that computers requiring continued operation during standby generator operation should have a dedicated generator separate from the elevator and other large inductive and cycling loads. The installation of an uninterrupted power supply (UPS) system would, of course, be the ideal but expensive solution from the computer operation standpoint.

It should be brought out that this notching also has a direct current ripple component, which tends to make the gearless machine generate magnetic noise at 120 Hz and 360 Hz without substatial filtering reactor and capacitors. Where machine rooms and secondary levels have adjacent occupied spaces, it is strongly urged that the SCR controllers, reactors, and machines be vibration isolated from the structure to prevent objectionable structure-borne sound transmission to these areas.

Energy consumption. The total energy consumed by elevators and escalators in a day is substantially less than the connected motor horsepower loads would indicate. The use of regenerative braking to decelerate an elevator and the inherent overbalance of the car when loaded in the down direction and of the counterweight with an empty car in the up direction pumps energy back into the building. Down escalators will also regenerate power when more than 15 or 16 people are on the moving portion (Sturgeon, 1974b; Cleminson and Rogers, 1974).

The elevator energy consumption of typical elevators is shown in Table 4.16 for a 10-hr day using generator field control where the motor generator is running continuously (Otis Elevator Company).

The instantaneous power for an elevator is shown for both an empty car up and down running condition to show the effects of the car-counterweight overbalance acting alone (see Figs. 4.24 and 4.25).

The instantaneous power for an escalator from no load to full load and back to no load is shown for both the up and down directions (Figs. 4.26 and 4.27).

The net energy consumed over a 10-hr period is thus entirely accounted for by the electrical and mechanical losses which show up as heat released to the elevator machine room or the hoistway.

The introduction of SCR drives will reduce energy consumption by eliminating the friction and windage losses of an idling motor generator set and its starting losses. From the preceding figures, however, it becomes apparent that the energy consumed by the vertical transportation system is a small part of the energy consumed by the total building. This tends to fall in the range of from 1.5% to 3.0% of the total building load and, hence, cannot be considered an area for energy and demand management savings. (Chapter PC-12 deals with "Energy Conservation.")

Elevator ride quality.   Recent experience with the quality of elevator ride at the Sears Tower in Chicago and the World Trade Center in New York City has demanded that there are industry acknowledged standards that are commercially acceptable. These standards must become a part of all "performance specifications" for quality equipment in first-class buildings.

The ideal times to require accelerometer tests for evaluation and specification compliance are prior to Final Acceptance, and ten to twelve months later, when the building has a mature occupancy and most of the building compression has occurred. However, the resistance by the industry to the second test conducted in the occupied building after the construction personnel has departed has forced an interim position of only one test prior to Final Acceptance. As additional experience is gained in new buildings, it is hoped that a performance specification can be generated that monitors the ride characteristics to evaluate maintenance as well as construction practice for the comfort of passengers.

The current specification that has been tentatively accepted by all major North American manufacturers in the most common speeds is quoted in the following paragraphs. It is anticipated that experience will not only modify the criteria but also extend the speed range.

Recording accelerometer tests shall be conducted prior to Final Acceptance on

Table 4.16   Energy consumption of typical elevators *(Courtsey: Otis Elevator Company)*

Type of elevator (1)	Capacity, in kilograms (pounds) (2)	Speed, in meters per second (feet per minute) (3)	Energy comsumption, in megajoules (kilowatt-hours) (4)
Geared	900 (2000)	1.0 (200)	75.6 (21)
	1135 (2500)	1.7 (350)	108.0 (30)
	1800 (4000)	1.7 (350)	133.2 (37)
Gearless	1135 (2500)	2.5 (500)	169.2 (47)
	1800 (4000)	2.5 (500)	234.0 (65)
	1580 (3500)	4.0 (800)	309.6 (86)
	1800 (4000)	5.0 (1000)	457.2 (127)
	1800 (4000)	7.0 (1400)	504.0 (140)

each elevator traveling at contract speed the full length of the hoistway between terminal landings in both the up and down directions with a maximum noneccentric load of 225 kg (500 lb). Recordings shall be taken on the platform in the plane of the car guide rails and perpendicular to the plane of the car guide rails. The accelerometer tests shall be made with the sensing unit placed in the center of the elevator car enclosure mounted directly on the top of the car platform with any carpeting removed. The accelerometer and the recording device shall be calibrated in the field prior to each test, shall provide continuous direct readings on paper tape at a speed not less than 250 mm (1 in.) per sec, and shall be sensitive to accelerations in a band width from 0.25 Hz to 2.0 Hz. One set of recordings for each elevator shall become the property of the owner as a permanent record.

The maximum horizontal acceleration permitted in each plane shall be deter-

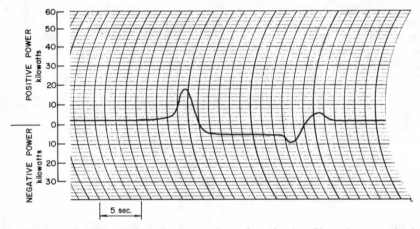

Fig. 4.24 Recording kilowatt chart of a.c. power to gearless elevator with empty car running in up direction *(Courtesy: Otis Elevator Company)*

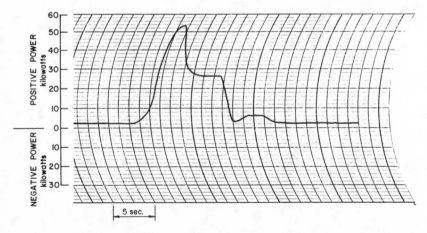

Fig. 4.25 Recording kilowatt chart of a.c. power to gearless elevator with empty car running in down direction *(Courtesy: Otis Elevator Company)*

mined from the charts in accordance with the following criteria and evaluation method. If the results exceed the maximum specified, the guide rail alinement, the guide rail joints, and the guides shall be adjusted to correct the ride characteristic in each plane separately to this maximum. The instantaneous half-amplitude acceleration recorded for a trip the full travel of the elevator in both the up and down directions shall not exceed the values shown in Table 4.17 for more than 5% of the time duration of the travel in each direction.

3 Horizontal People Movers

The horizontal elevator concept has become the goal of interbuilding transportation because of the vertical elevator's acceptance with its taken-for-granted

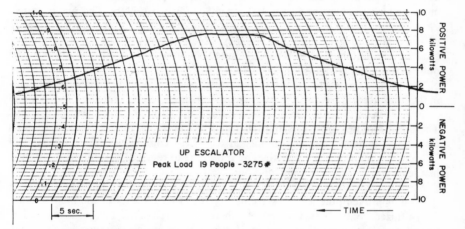

Fig. 4.26 Recording kilowatt chart of a.c. power to escalator running in up direction showing effects of progressive loading, full load, and progressive unloading operation (*Courtesy: Otis Elevator Company*)

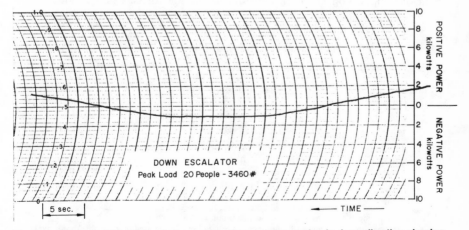

Fig. 4.27 Recording kilowatt chart of a.c. power to escalator running in down direction showing effects of progressive loading, full load, and progressive unloading operation (*Courtesy: Otis Elevator Company*)

reliability and flexibility (various HUD authors, 1969; Lerch, 1974). The Personal Rapid Transit or PRT vehicle configurations vary widely from the conventional wheel technology with rotating motor propulsion to the air or magnetic suspension technology with linear motor propulsion. However, the operation logic and human engineering interfaces developed for vertical elevators must be adopted for the successful introduction of the PRT concept. Appreciation for use of written source and photographic material is expressed from Cityscope and Mobility Company, Bolivar, Pennsylvania, U.S.A. (Jernstedt, 1975) and Otis Elevator Company, Transportation Technology Division, Denver, Colorado, U.S.A. (Figs. 4.2 and 4.28).

Urban centers have a greater capacity for serving more people and providing a broader, multifunctional range of services than is currently being practiced. The principal limitation appears to be transportation, both in quality and quantity for people and goods. Specifically, it is the quality of public and private transportation modes which inhibits the full utilization of our urban centers. The public transit systems—bus and rapid transit—do not consistently attract a large enough portion of the total trips generated, nor do they adequately participate in or precipitate growth. The automobile is severely limited by downtown traffic conditions and downtown parking capacity.

Throughout the world the urban centers represent one of the largest investments in facilities. Recent trends in most large urban centers clearly indicate a reduction in activity both in the number of functions and in the hours of utilization per day. There is a dire need for reversing this trend by improving the economic and social conditions in these vital, central city areas. These conditions can be alleviated if full-scope demand is the measurement and guide to renewed development, and not just legislation or government funding.

When measuring or projecting this demand the technology must be based on existing or proven practice. New technology must be kept out of the high-activity, daily-utilized central city because of inherent low reliability in its startup phase. New technology should be kept in demonstration locations to avoid situations demanding routinely reliable performance. New methods, however, can and must be explored. New methods imply new combinations of proven practices. Their judicious application has been the principal reason for cost improvement in our

Table 4.17 Tentative specifications for elevator acceleration

Contract speed, in meters per second (feet per minute) (1)	Half-amplitude peak acceleration, in gal (feet per second per second)[a] (2)	Adjacent peak-to-peak acceleration, in gal (feet per second per second)[b] (3)
1.5 (300)	10 (0.33)	20 (0.65)
2.0 (400)	10 (0.33)	20 (0.65)
2.5 (500)	15 (0.50)	30(1.0)
4.0 (800)	18 (0.55)	35 (1.1)
5.0 (1000)	20 (0.66)	40 (1.3)

[a]A gal is centemeter per second per second and is approximately equal to a milli-g.

[b]Adjacent peak-to-peak values of instantaneous acceleration shall be used to determine the zero reference line for the half-amplitude values.

manufacturing plants. New methods now must be the principal approach to make an urban center more cost-effective. Urban redevelopment can be considered a new method, but it also follows that only well-run projects will be successful.

Urban redevelopment alone has not caused the return of multifunction activity to the center city. What is needed now is a concept to take our urban performance up the ladder one more step. The objectives are several: (1) To improve economic conditions, by increasing private sector investment in the multifunction development; (2) to increase the capacity and quality of our downtown areas to lower the nonproductive pressures which encourage competitive and counterproductive suburban development; and (3) to create an environment that will improve social relationships.

Horizontally connected buildings.   One approach to new or renewed high-rise urban center development is the horizontally connected buildings concept. The most successful development process in downtown areas has generally been the design, construction, and use of high-rise building. However, such buildings, by and large, have stayed back of the curbside to avoid legal exposure and political entanglements. As a result, there is little joining together of downtown developments except by city streets, sidewalks, and Mass Rapid Transit (MRT). The horizontally connected buildings concept espouses a joining together of various facilities and functions according to criteria similar to those presently applied in vertically connected buildings such as the Sears Tower and the World Trade Center with their sky lobbies. These criteria include:

1. Continuously available and essentially free transportation 24 hours a day with direct access to functional space at each transportation interface.

2. Self-contained security systems, including automobile parking designed directly into the system, not across a city street or requiring ticket collection.

Fig. 4.28 Personal Rapid Transit vehicles docking at Plaza Level guideway above sidewalk serving major building *(Courtesy: Otis Elevator Company)*

3. Economic survival without direct government subsidy.

4. High degree of safety and reliability.

5. Reduction in pollution in center city.

6. Waiting time and trip length similar to the vertical elevator.

7. Passenger acceptance creating a demand.

The World Trade Center, New York City, represents the sky lobby concept using large, single-deck shuttle elevators for the first time

Mutually interdependent subsystems will now be necessary for the concept of a horizontally connected building. This concept must consist of five elements designed into one integrated unit: (1) Motor vehicle interception and parking; (2) horizontal "elevator" transportation; (3) streets and pedways; (4) developed intersection areas; and (5) business unit.

Motor Vehicle Interception and Parking. Large, freely accessible, multiple use, available parking garages (perhaps automated parking garages) at the periphery of an urban center will serve a similar function to the usual ramp parking facilities under a high-rise building. Such parking may perform its service at lower cost per parking space than in an expensive building on expensive and limited land area. Remote parking will open the capacity of the urban center for living and work functions rather than transportation functions.

Automobile parking is now recognized as being a more important common denominator to the successful plan for urban development than designers once thought. In urban centers, parking has been an auxiliary feature, never designed as a part of the total system. Now, the opportunity is available to design a parking system which provides increased capacity, greater growth potential, improved 24-hour utilization, and decreased use of center city land, with improved access and performance. When the automobile is intercepted at least 600 m to 2500 m (2000 ft to 8000 ft) away from the activity center, the capacity and usefulness of streets throughout the area can be upgraded. Also, the mass rapid transit passenger can be intercepted at the parking facilities for better access to multiple locations in the large major activity center. As a peripheral benefit this will promote increased car pooling, because a car parked in such a garage gives all occupants the same "rain or

The Sears Tower, Chicago, Illinois, represents the second sky lobby concept with double-deck elevators as shuttle elevators and single-deck local elevators, as in the World Trade Center

shine" mobility to multiple destinations on a PRT or MRT system. (Chapter PC-10 deals with "Parking.")

Horizontal "Elevator" Transportation. The modern high-rise building with its elevator system has been one of the most important elements in the high-rise growth of all cities. Providing the equivalent horizontal mobility between vertical buildings, and meeting the same functional criteria as the vertical elevator for short distances among a group of vertical buildings, can result in additional and beneficial growth through improved use of the land.

The basic criteria for vertical elevator system performance must be used for the horizontal elevator system. These criteria include: (1) Free availability 24 hours each day, with direct access to functional space preferably without contact with a city street; (2) good security resulting from functional design; and (3) quality and reliability of performance to assure continued customer demand for the service. Meeting this quality of performance can be obtained only when the customer enjoys the transportation process—witness the enthusiastic acceptance of glass-enclosed elevators, and of the new high-speed Metroliner equipment between New York and Washington, D.C. in the United States.

Streets and Pedways. In the design of the horizontal building, people must be able to flow freely. One important element of this design will be simple pedways or plazas joining the horizontal elevator with the building interior and its vertical elevators. Simultaneously, these walkways will provide a safe and uninterrupted means for people to cross streets without delaying traffic or being delayed. When the pedways are designed into the second level of a building, they will make possible the development of the new valuable second level lobby space that will be created.

Developed Intersection Areas. The most far-reaching benefit from applying the horizontally connected buildings concept will be the joining together of the buildings and functions of an activity center. This will be accomplished by creating an interface area at specific points for the intersection of the horizontal elevator and each building. The area generally will be at the elevated plaza level. It will provide direct second level access to buildings by walkways, reducing exposure to city streets. Quantitatively, only very few streets will be utilized in this joining together process, except for servicing the building. However, an area as wide as four city blocks could be readily designed into one horizontally connected center. Most urban centers could accommodate at least two such activity centers.

Summary of functions and operation of the horizontally connected center. The five separate elements of the horizontally connected center have already been demonstrated, and are in use around the world. No new technology is required, and no long development time periods are indicated to bring them together. More important, single units of a horizontally connected center can be accomplished in an incremental fashion. There should be a gradual increase in center city private investment as the process is demonstrated and as local and federal governments cooperate in providing umbrella legislation.

Under proper conditions, the first phase of a horizontally connected center in an urban environment can be designed and constructed in three to four years. It must be noted that all buildings ultimately envisioned for the plan need not be in place to complete a successful, profitable project. Subsequent developments, including private redevelopment, will come into being along the path of the horizontally connected center's corridors.

Meeting the basic and over-all planning needs of an urban center appears feasible. Most of the data and planning elements are already available. What is now required is a new interaction of responsible private developers with local and regional planning functions to demonstrate compatibility with long-range objectives and feasibility of projects. There are indications in several local governments that they will provide right-of-way and other legislation required to encourage private development. With such cooperation, these developments could be accomplished in the same time frame as, and compatibly with, the construction of a large downtown building.

One of the more advanced concepts for the horizontally connected building-vertical building interface is the Otis omnidirectional air-pad suspension, which permits docking off the main guideway. The vehicle is propelled by linear motor at a contract speed of 13 m/sec (2600 ft per min) with a contract load of 22 passengers, which is equivalent to a 1800-kg (4000-lb) passenger elevator.

An application of the horizontal elevator currently under construction by Otis-TTD employs a two-lane guideway to serve two buildings separated by about 360 m (1200 ft). Each lane is operated independently, and behaves, in effect, like separate horizontal elevator shafts. Waiting times, boarding times, and transit times are similar to those experienced in typical high-speed elevator service. One lane can be time-shared by passenger and cargo vehicles by means of lateral docking at both ends to permit one vehicle to bypass another at their respective docking or loading stations. At its destination, the cargo vehicle can be moved laterally onto a freight elevator and lowered to a cargo handling area.

4.3　MATERIAL MOVERS

1　Commercial, Residential, and Institutional Buildings

High-rise materials handling in buildings in the United States and Canada has only become important as the cost of labor has increased since 1950. Many buildings had pneumatic message tubes and tote box selective vertical conveyors to handle high-density document traffic, but the delivery of more bulky materials and the emphasis on both the vertical and the horizontal were made cost effective because of rising wages, rising fringe benefits, and the deglamorization of manual delivery labor. The typical health-care facility long declined the available benefits of office building systems, but now demands the most sophisticated equipment as health-care costs have risen rapidly. Today, the office building is using some systems that originally were health-care oriented (Schachinger, 1975; Maurer, 1974).

The early pneumatic message tube systems required a manual diverter—a person—to receive carriers and manually insert them into their destination tube. Each point of origin and dispatch was connected to "central" by two tubes. Today, these systems have computer supervision, permitting single tube stations with central loops, since the carrier can now be addressed by pushbutton through the computer, rather than on the carrier itself. The carriers have grown to accommodate the increased size of documentation, resulting in tube sizes up to 200 mm (8 in.) round and 100 mm × 300 mm (4 in. × 12 in.) rectangular for special applications.

The success of the message-tube technology has led to pneumatic trash and linen systems for interbuilding and intrabuilding systems. These systems are proving currently feasible for centralized trash handling in commercial, residential, and institutional activity centers. They can be combined gravity vertical-pneumatic horizontal when simultaneous access is required for multiple building systems.

The selective vertical conveyor with its passive tote boxes has long been a standard system for high-rise commercial and institutional buildings, with powered and gravity horizontal conveyor systems providing for both short and long travel distances from the vertical shaft. The throughput capacity of these systems, however, is rarely reached, except in industrial applications, and the operating costs are high for the horizontal portions. In recent years, the self-propelled or active tote box (Fig. 4.29) has been introduced with success when the capital costs can be justified by traffic density, flexibility, and maintenance considerations. Both these systems, however, outside the industrial sector are random delivery systems which must be supplemented with larger vehicles for scheduled bulk deliveries. Where the high throughput of the vertical selective conveyor is not needed, a self-loading inject and self-unloading eject tote box dumbwaiter should be considered as being the simplest solution when there are no horizontal runs requiring powered conveyors.

The manual cart had been the horizontal as well as the vertical transport of bulkier materials until 1952, when the inject-eject, tote box dumbwaiter concept was expanded to the inject-eject cart lift (Fig. 4.13). This concept has permitted labor savings in commercial and institutional buildings to the extent that a separate section of the ANSI Code A17.1 (Part XIV) has been written to assure safe operation by authorized personnel. These are standard systems in health-care

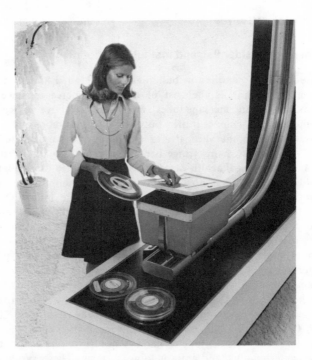

Fig. 4.29 Telelift self-propelled tote box system at typical office station *(Courtesy: Mosler Airmatic & Electronic Systems Div.)*

facilities and should now be considered in the design of office buildings, libraries, and hospitals. The cart lift has also been joined to horizontal in-floor tow line conveyors within interstitial spaces, but occupied floors should consider only a driverless tractor or overhead power and free conveyor for extended horizontal transport (Figs. 4.14 and 4.15).

The driverless tractor, which self-loads a cart at the cart lift unloading point and delivers it to a final destination, has recently become a mature product. This concept originally required horizontal travel on two floors and vertical travel by elevator. The sharing of elevators between tractors and staff was acceptable only in low-density applications. In higher-density applications, the requirement of a dedicated elevator to this traffic substantially raises the system cost (Fig. 4.14).

The driverless tractor follows a buried wire guidepath to one of many destinations, unloads a clean cart, picks up a soiled cart, and unloads it for dispatch to a return landing. It has detection devices which stop it and ring an alarm whenever it needs service, meets an obstruction, or strays off the guidepath. Success in the health-care field has generated recent interest in the on-floor delivery of mail and bulk items on large floor commercial buildings. The on-floor mail room personnel loads presorted baskets for station deliveries and dispatches the tractor at scheduled times on a loop route. The tractor stops at every station on its route, to both deliver and pick up mail. Each station operator restarts the cart by pushing the dispatch button. If the station is unattended, the tractor will stop, ring a gong, and proceed on its route after a short time delay.

The high-density transportation of carts automatically to multiple destinations has borrowed and refined the "power and free" conveyor concept from industrial materials handling. Once addressed, the cart carrier will deliver a single large or two small carts after traveling extended horizontal and vertical distances and will queue as necessary to wait out a delay. These systems involve extensive initial coordination among all the design and operating factors so that the actual will fulfill the anticipated performance. These systems can become so complex that computer simulation assistance in design to discover weaknesses should be considered as part of each manufacturer's response to a specification, since each manufacturer has built-in design parameters that may influence the selection process.

Mechanical parking systems for motor vehicles have been repeatedly demonstrated without permanent success in the United States and Canada, because of the lack of a single-source responsibility. The Pidgeon Hole, Bowser, Speed Park, and Systematic Parking attempts brought in only partial automation in the 1950s and 1960s, due to the expense of computers and due to limitations of the concepts themselves. The continuing success of these semi-automated systems in South America and Europe is attributable to the "strong box storage" feature, which protects a car from vandals and abuse. The practice in some South American countries of insuring for theft only the entire vehicle—in conjunction with initial vehicle cost—has created this market.

The first fully automated parking system, ROTOPARK, has been successfully demonstrated in Switzerland (Fig. 4.30). The lowering of a vehicle on conveyor comb fingers to a train of parking carriages for storage, and a similar return after payment, may prove to interface well with activity centers in the use of below-ground space under a high-rise building or in the use of above-ground space at airports. This concept is the only currently operating system to store and retrieve a locked vehicle with acceptance and delivery rates in excess of street capacity.

2 Industrial Buildings

The specialized and tailor-made freight elevator in the past has always been that part of the elevator industry with the least change and innovation. It has rapidly declined in the past few years, when horizontal "rubber" transportation has proliferated in the single-story manufacturing plant. The materials handling industry has reduced the direct labor content of such plants to a fraction of that in multistory plants. However, computer technology now has combined with the materials handling and elevator technologies to achieve similar results in retrofitting multistory manufacturing and warehousing facilities (Lewis, 1974).

The first such sophisticated system was completed in 1972, to handle pallets of incoming raw materials to multiple production floors and outgoing finished goods to a warehouse floor or to the shipping dock. Series of unit-powered conveyors were placed at both ends of an automatic lift on every floor. As each pallet was fork-truck loaded onto the receiving conveyor it was given a computer retained address according to its Up destination. The pallet was stepped along to its loading position in a queue until sufficient pallets were positioned for a lift load of three pallets. The computer then dispatched the lift to pick up the loads and deliver them up to the multiple destination floors. When the loads were delivered, the computer scanned the down loads available, selected those with the highest management-determined priority, picked them up, and delivered them to their destinations in order of their position on the lift. The lift was double ended at each floor with a "loading" and an "unloading" end so that the computer handled the pallet loads on the lift on a First In, First Out (FIFO) basis (Fig. 4.31).

The minicomputer and programmable controller provided a constant repro-

Fig. 4.30 ROTOPARK automated parking system under major office building *(Courtesy: ROTOPARK S.A.)*

gramming capability depending on annual manufacturing cycles and product mix. The highest degree of reliability and single-source responsibility was provided using elevator industry solid state logic and relay logic to control the lift, all the conveyor units, and the interface with the programmable controller (Fig. 4.32).

Warehouse cart lift systems have also been installed in recent years that interface with an in-floor tow line to call a lift to a waiting cart and deliver it to its addressed destination. The carts have positioned pins which determine the ultimate destination and route of the cart from the receiving dock on the multifloor tow line system. The system moves the cart both horizontally and vertically to storage positions in the warehouse or in reverse from these positions to the shipping dock.

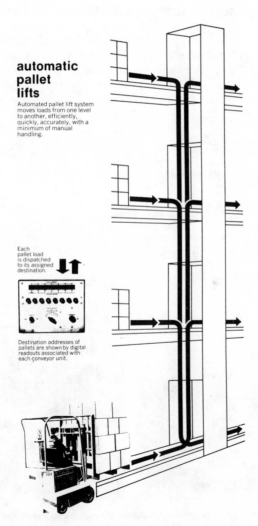

automatic pallet lifts

Automated pallet lift system moves loads from one level to another, efficiently, quickly, accurately, with a minimum of manual handling.

Each pallet load is dispatched to its assigned destination.

Destination addresses of pallets are shown by digital readouts associated with each conveyor unit.

Fig. 4.31 Automated pallet lift system *(Courtesy: Otis Elevator Company)*

4.4 CONCLUSION

The combined high-rise, residential, office, and retail structures being built today are the first step towards the integrated activity center which will combine vertical and horizontal building concepts. The next step will be the integration of light industrial or warehousing facilities to support the total complex. These activity centers will demand the simultaneous solution of all vertical-horizontal people and material movers to maximize the return on investment in structure and people. The separate and narrow "mover" disciplines of the past will have to combine to adequately support the other design disciplines to create this total environment (Jernstedt, 1975; Pasternak, 1974; Maurer, 1974; Knill, 1976).

4.5 CONDENSED REFERENCES/BIBLIOGRAPHY

The following is a condensed bibliography for this chapter. Not only does it include all articles referred to or cited in the text, but it also contains bibliography for further reading. The full citations will be found at the end of the Volume. What is given here should be sufficient information to lead the reader to the correct article: the author, date, and title. In case of multiple authors, only the first named is listed.

AIJ 1977, *Building Standard Law*
ANSI A17.1 1978, *American National Standard Safety Code for Elevators, Dumbwaiters,*
Adler 1974, *Vertical Transportation for Citicorp Center*
Anderson 1975, *Tell Me About Elevators*
Annett 1960, *Elevators*

Au 1973, *Building Services and Systems in Hong Kong*
Ayres 1973, *Criteria for Building Services and Furnishings*
BSI 1970, *Specification for Lifts, Escalators, Passenger Conveyors and Paternosters*
BSI 1972, *Electric, Hydraulic, and Handpowered Lifts*
BSI 1979, *Lifts and Service Lifts*

Fig. 4.32 Minicomputer with programmable controller operating automated pallet lift system
(Courtesy: Otis Elevator Company)

Barney 1974, *The Design, Evaluation and Control of Lift (Elevator) Systems*
Baum 1971, *Service Systems in Tall Buildings*
Baum 1973, *Service Systems in Relation to Architecture*
Benuska 1973, *Shakedown in Elevator Earthquake Safety Control*
Botha 1975, *Movement Systems for Tall Buildings*

CSA Standard B44 1971, *Safety Code for Elevators, Dumbwaiters, Escalators and Moving*
Cleminson 1974, *Elevator-Power (Energy) Consumption*
De Viaris 1973, *Passenger Elevators in High-Rise Office Buildings*
Deshpande 1973, *Lift Service in High-Rise Buildings*
Dowrick 1977, *Earthquake Resistant Design—A Manual for Engineers and Architects*

Englert 1975, *Elevator Planning in Office Buildings*
European Committee For Standardization 1977, *Safety Rules for the Construction and*
Freedom 1973, *Horizontal Transportation Systems*
Fruin 1970, *Pedestrian Planning and Design*
Gero 1970, *Interactive Lift Design-Analysis*

HUD 1969, *Tomorrow's Transportation—New Systems for the Urban Future*
Hesselberg 1974, *Major Hospital Transport*
Hiramoto 1974, *Speed Up of High-Rise Escalators*
International Organization for Standardization 1976, *Mechanical Transporting Systems for*
JIS A 4301 1970, *Size of Car and Hoistway of Elevators*

Jaros, Baum and Bolles (staff) 1978, *The Perfect Office Building*
Jernstedt 1975, *Implementing Urban Center Redevelopment by Evolution with the Horizontal*
Katz 1974, *General Design Criteria for Elevator Systems*
Knill 1976, *1976—The Real World Matches Old Predictions*
Kort 1972, *Vertical Transportation*

Kort 1973, *Vertical Transportation*
Kort 1974, *Skyscraper Transport Trends*
Lerch 1974, *Personal Rapid Transit*
Lewis 1974, *Integrated Industrial Transport*
Lewis 1976, *Oscillation of Elevator Cables*

Marmot 1972, *Towards the Development of an Empirical Model for Elevator Lobbies*
Maurer 1974, *The Transport Systems Division*
Mitsui 1973, *Analysis of Lateral Quaking of High Speed Elevators*
Norman 1973, *Service Systems*
Oravetz 1975, *Service Systems in High and Medium-High Buildings*

Pasternak 1971, *Double-Deck Elevatoring*
Pasternak 1974, *The Complex Complex-Project*
Reed 1974, *Noise: its Meaning and Measurement*
Rush 1978, *Internal Distribution Systems*
Ruzicka 1977, *Dynamics of Tuned Secondary Systems*

SAA 1975, *Rules for the Design, Installation, Testing and Operation of Lifts*
Schachinger 1975, *Evaluating Materials Handling Systems for Hospitals*
Strakosch 1967, *Vertical Transportation: Elevators and Escalators*
Strakosch 1973, *Horizontal vs. Vertical Transportation*
Sturgeon 1967, *Men and Machines Against the Mountain*

Sturgeon 1972, *Earthquakes and Elevators*
Sturgeon 1974a, *The World of Elevator Consultants*
Sturgeon 1974b, *Elevator/Escalator Energy Economy*
Swartz 1972, *Pre-engineering Elevatoring*
Tregenza 1975, *Movement of People Within Tall Buildings*

Van Deusen 1974, *Double-Deck Elevators*
Vanmarcke 1973, *Probabilistic Seismic Analysis of Equipment Within Buildings*
Veterans Administrations 1973, *Earthquake Resistant Design of Non-sturctural Elements of*
Warners 1977, *Vertical Transportation—European Concept*
Yuceoglu 1977, *Connections Between Equipment and Structure Subject to Seismic Loads*

Tall Building
Systems and Concepts

Chapter SC-5

Cladding

Prepared by Committee 12A (Cladding) of the Council on Tall Buildings and Urban Habitat as part of the Monograph on the Planning and Design of Tall Buildings.

Richard E. Lenke	Committee Chairman
Geoffrey M. J. Williams	Vice-Chairman
Howard D. Eberhart	Vice-Chairman
Anthony B. Klarich	Editor

AUTHOR ACKNOWLEDGMENT

The essential first draft of this chapter is the work of A. B. Klarich. Its starting point was the collection of state-of-art reports from the 1972 International Conference held at Lehigh University, prepared by:

O. R. Berry
E. E. Botsai
G. Essunger
S. Kajfasz
R. E. Lenke
K. Matsushita
F. Newby
S. E. Pellegrini
J. H. Polak
F. Rafeiner
P. E. Rousseau
R. L. Sharpe
Y. Uchida.

In addition to this, other sections were based on special contributions. For the individual Sections, these individuals are:

E. A. Wetherill, Section 5.10
R. L. Sharpe, Section 5.15.

CONTRIBUTORS

The following is a complete list of those who have submitted written material for possible use in the chapter, whether or not that material was used in the final version. The Committee Chairman and Editor were given quite complete latitude. Frequently length limitations precluded the inclusion of much valuable material. The Bibliography contains all contributions. The contributors are: O. R. Berry, E. E. Botsai, D. A. Button, H. D. Eberhart, G. Essunger, S. Kajfasz, A. B. Klarich, A. Kokkinaki-Daniel, R. E. Lenke, K. Matsushita, F. Newby, S. E. Pellegrini, J. H. Polak, F. Rafeiner, P. E. Rousseau, R. L. Sharpe, Y. Uchida, E. A. Wetherill, G. M. J. Williams.

COMMITTEE MEMBERS

O. R. Berry, H. D. Eberhart, G. Essunger, F. R. Estuar, I. M. Kadri, S. Kajfasz, A. B. Klarich, R. E. Lenke, K. Matsushita, F. Newby, S. E. Pellegrini, F. Penteado, P. E. Rousseau, B. Rubanenko, R. M. Schuster, R. L. Sharpe, Y. Uchida, F. Van der Woude, H. Weatherford, E. A. Wetherill, G. M. J. Williams.

SC-5   Cladding

5.1 INTRODUCTION

Close coordination has always been required between architectural and structural disciplines during the design phase of a building. As the height of buildings has increased so has the importance of this coordination.

The degree of sophistication, coordination, and integration of the architectural and structural systems has continually developed and improved in the design of structural steel or structural reinforced concrete buildings. A high degree of architectural/structural integration of building systems is accomplished with the exposed structural concrete building that embodies architectural concrete finishes. These buildings may be constructed of concrete that contains specially selected cements and aggregates to achieve a specific architectural character. Such treatment requires a high degree of coordination and understanding between the architectural and structural disciplines in order to design and construct a building that is both structurally sound and architecturally and esthetically acceptable.

The architect of today must have an intimate knowledge of the various building structural movement characteristics with respect to live loads, creep, wind loads, earthquake forces, and temperature differentials. Rigorous tolerances with respect to the movement of the structure must be designed into the various systems of architectural claddings to facilitate tall building movement so as not to break water seals and barriers, or damage architectural facings and finishes.

5.2 CLADDING MATERIALS AND SYSTEMS

With tall buildings now reaching to 100 stories or more, vast areas of exterior surfacing are created. One of the most important nonstructural or nonloadbearing architectural elements is the exterior wall, facing, or cladding system.

The separation of the structural and protective elements in a structure has concentrated attention more than ever before on the true function of the protective

191

wall, and typically the cladding is seen in terms analogous to the human skin. It is conceived as an active filter rather than a passive barrier. This cladding must be flexible as it is in constant motion.

The number of cladding or facing materials is vast, whether they are used to enclose or infill space of the structural framing elements or as facings to structural elements or nonloadbearing infill panels. Common materials used, which have developed in conjunction with tall building construction, are: steel, aluminum, bronze, stone, marble, granite, tiles ceramic and mosaic, precast concrete or other masonry materials, and glass curtain walls and cladding systems.

Each of these materials individually is of significant importance to the over-all building structure, but probably none more so than the glass curtain wall or window wall element. In this chapter we will concentrate on this element of exterior cladding, which must protect the sensitive internal environment from rapidly changing external conditions. Specifically, it must control the transfer of heat and cold, control the passage of light, and prevent the passage of moisture, dirt, vermin and, of course, people. It must also provide acoustical control and fire protection, and be capable of easy cleaning and maintenance. In addition to coping successfully with all of these tasks, the wall has to withstand enormous forces and stresses, both directly and indirectly applied, as well as absorb all movements of the building structure.

5.3 CURTAIN WALLS

Probably the single most important building innovation of the past quarter century has been the metal curtain wall. Technologically, the curtain wall makes excellent sense, and its introduction clearly underlined the developing awareness of a building structure as a highly organized assembly of prefabricated elements, contrasted with the traditional concept of building as an organized assembly of on-site trade skills.

Before the advent of the metal curtain wall, it seems that little attention had been paid to analyzing and identifying the rather complex function of an exterior building wall. Generally it was thought of as performing either one or both of two functions: (1) Providing structural support for the floors and roof if it was a bearing wall; and (2) forming a protective enclosure excluding the elements, but with openings for vision and ventilation. One of the early studies of metal curtain wall potentials pointed out the fact, now generally recognized but still sometimes overlooked, that the exterior wall of a building actually serves as a two-way filter. A properly designed curtain wall has the capability of being able to provide the degree of control desired for this filter.

In general, the metal curtain walls of today, even the simpler types, are far more sophisticated products than their early counterparts, even though many of the earliest walls are still performing admirably. Over 20 years of experience and development have eliminated the major difficulties of the pioneering designs, resulting in better products. Metal curtain wall technology has developed over the years into a proliferation of highly engineered designs.

Throughout this development, however, the basic principles of good wall design have not changed. Recognition of these principles has grown with experience and the criteria of good design are now well defined. As with any vital and developing product, the industry continues to find ways of improving performance.

The curtain wall system of cladding structures is historically associated with high-rise office buildings, and this application still remains the most dramatic expression of the concept. However, the technical sophistication and design flexibility implicit in the system have led increasingly to its use in low and medium-rise structures where its primary characteristic—lightness of weight—is not even a particularly significant design determinant.

1 Types of Curtain Walls

As a prerequisite to discussing wall types, and to facilitate communication and avoid misunderstandings, certain key terms should be defined. Three of the most commonly used terms, "curtain wall," "metal curtain wall," and "window wall," still mean different things to different people. Often they are used interchangeably with no clear distinction made between them. As their meanings are interrelated and overlapping, this will continue to be the case. For our purpose these terms are defined as follows:

1. Curtain wall: A building exterior wall, of any material, which carries no superimposed vertical loads.

2. Metal curtain wall: An exterior curtain wall that may consist entirely or principally of metal, or may be a combination of metal, glass, and other surfacing materials supported by or within a metal framework.

3. Window wall: A type of metal curtain wall installed between floors and typically composed of vertical and horizontal framing members, containing operable sash, fixed lights or opaque panels, or any combination thereof.

The five generally recognized systems or types of curtain wall are described in the following paragraphs. The classification is based upon on-site assembly. Several other classifications could be made based on structure or usage. In the former, linear bearing elements are prevalent (frame structures or joint structures), surface bearing elements (sheds or shells), or structures of mixed type. In the latter, custom-made panels, standardized panels, and factory panels are possible categories.

Stick Wall System.   In this system the wall is installed piece by piece. Usually the mullion members are installed first, followed in turn by the horizontal rail members, the panels if any, and finally the glazing or window units. However, in some designs accentuating the horizontal lines the process may be altered to install the larger horizontal member first (see Fig. 5.1).

The stick system was used extensively in the early days of curtain wall development and is still in wide use in greatly improved versions. Current designs offer considerable variation in the location of the vision panel of glass and the spandrel unit relative to the mullion and rail face. It may be virtually flush on the outside or the inside or anywhere in between the two.

The advantages of this system are its relative ease of handling and consequent low handling costs because of minimal bulk, and the fact that it offers the capability of some degree of dimensional adjustment to site conditions. It also allows for simple provision of temporary access openings in the building facade and later infill.

Among the disadvantages are the necessity of assembly on site of many components which may differ in quality from those assembled under controlled factory conditions, and the fact that preglazing is not possible.

Unit System. In this system the wall is composed of large framed units, usually a full floor height by a module width, preassembled in the factory. The units can be preglazed and spandrel panels, whether of glass or other material, can also be installed. The vertical edges of the units join to form the mullion member, and this system is generally associated with the split or the interlocking mullion. Fig. 5.2 shows a typical version.

This system offers advantages in that it can be assembled in the shop under controlled conditions where inspection is easily available, resulting in a higher class of workmanship. By this method areas of the building can be enclosed very rapidly with a minimum of site labor.

Disadvantages are that the units are more cumbersome to handle, transport, and hoist on site. Also protection during transport and prior to installation has to be more expensive. As the units are based on the interlocking mullion it can be difficult to leave openings in the facade for access purposes unless a number of units can be slid or adjusted laterally or else a special joint detail is provided at the access panel. Replacement of a damaged unit can also prove to be a problem, unless it is "built up" on site.

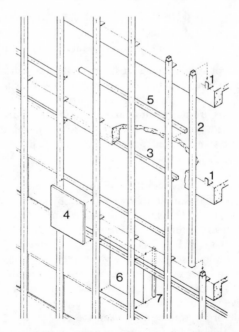

Fig. 5.1 Stick System—schematic of typical version—1: Anchors. 2: Mullion. 3: Horizontal rail (gutter section at window head). 4: Spandrel panel (may be installed from inside building). 5: Horizontal rail (window sill section). 6: Vision glass (installed from inside building). 7: Interior mullion trim. *(Courtesy: Architectural Aluminum Manufacturers Association)*

Unit and Mullion System.   This system is the combination and integration of the two previous types (Fig. 5.3). The mullion members are installed first, being either one floor height or more, and then preassembled framed units are placed between them. The framed sections may be either full floor height or divided into vision panel and spandrel unit. This system is generally adopted when the mullion is a deep member by design, or if particular attention is required to one of the advantages or disadvantages of the previous systems.

Advantages of this approach are similar to those of the Unit System, with the added facility that temporary access openings can be more readily provided. A disadvantage is that greater site labor is required, with additional jointing associated with the mullion member.

Panel System.   This system is similar in concept to the Unit System. The principal difference is that the panels need not be preassembled framed units but can be homogeneous units formed of sheet or cast metal, precast masonry, or other such materials. The jointing is reduced to an absolute minimum, with the glass vision panel inserted into the over-all panel and only the periphery jointing with adjacent panels. Fig. 5.4 shows a typical version.

The use of the panel system allows the architect to provide an over-all pattern for the facade if desired, rather than a standard grid pattern obtained by the other systems. The "molded" pattern would be custom made and consequently more expensive, but this depends on the quantity of repeat items.

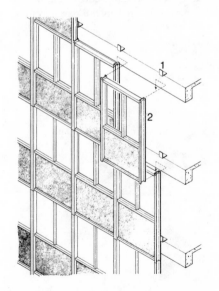

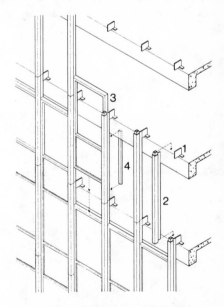

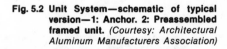

Fig. 5.2 Unit System—schematic of typical version—1: Anchor. 2: Preassembled framed unit. *(Courtesy: Architectural Aluminum Manufacturers Association)*

Fig. 5.3 Unit-and-Mullion System—schematic of typical version—1: Anchors. 2: Mullion (either one- or two-story lengths). 3: Preassembled unit lowered into place behind mullion from floor above. 4: Interior mullion trim. *(Courtesy: Architectural Aluminum Manufacturers Association)*

Advantages and disadvantages of this system are similar to those of the Unit System, but it does have the added advantage of the esthetic possibilities. The use of this system is also not limited to a metal curtain wall, although over-all weight of panels could become an important consideration.

Column and Spandrel System.   This system is the most recently developed of the five and may or may not be a true curtain wall. The column may be an applied column cover or a projecting structural column between which the windows and spandrels will extend. An example is shown in Fig. 5.5.

As the name implies, the elements of this system consist of column cover sections, or possibly a directly applied finish to the structural column, with long spandrel units spanning between the columns and infill glazing units that may be either preassemblies or separate framing members and glazing.

This system permits a wide range of esthetic expression, and unlike the others can provide a facade design that clearly expresses the structural frame of the building. The other systems all provide a superimposed grid or over-all pattern. The spandrel unit may be of a variety of materials and may incorporate other qualities, such as the necessary fire barrier required by some authorities, which cannot be incorporated in the other systems.

2   Materials and Finishes

Curtain walls of tall buildings are almost exclusively of metal construction. The one main exception is where masonry of some nature is used in the panel system.

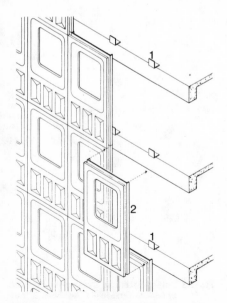
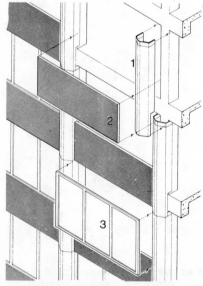

Fig. 5.4 Panel System—schematic of typical version—1: Anchor. 2: Panel. *(Courtesy: Architectural Aluminum Manufacturers Association)*

Fig. 5.5 Column Cover and Spandrel System— schematic of typical version—1: Column cover section. 2: Spandrel panel. 3: Glazing infill. *(Courtesy: Architectural Aluminum Manufacturers Association)*

Here the glazing may be glazed directly into the panel material without framing.

The metal material most commonly used is aluminum because of its lightness and wide range of possible decorative colors and finishes. Steel has also been used for curtain walls in a weathering steel form or as a core to a plastic or PVC coating that has a variety of colors incorporated. In some areas of Europe this is a reasonably economical system. Stainless steel and bronze have also been used for the facades, but generally costs associated with these materials prohibit wide usage.

It must also be mentioned here that curtain walls do exist that contain neither metalwork nor glazing. These are solid walls of natural or precast masonry utilized as a building cladding or decorative facing. Attachment to the building structure as well as jointing and weatherproofing of these walls generally follow the principles and details of metal curtain walls. Similarly, metal sandwich construction panels with or without glazing can be utilized.

Aluminum curtain walls are lightweight with consequent ease of handling. They are composed of precision-made elements that normally are shop fabricated to varying degrees of preassembly (according to type of wall selected) and to close factory tolerances. Jointing methods are predominantly mechanical, utilizing bolts and nuts of aluminum or stainless steel, self-tapping screws, rivets, and joint sealants. Where very rigid jointing is required in subassemblies, welding may be used.

Gosplan Building, Moscow, USSR *(Courtesy: B. Rubanenko)*

Spandrel panel units vary considerably in type, shape, and material. The most commonly used materials are glass or sheet metal of some nature bonded to other materials to form a laminated panel. They are pressed, stamped, or fabricated into dimensioned panels to provide facade texture and form; or they can be aluminum cast into sculptured panels. Asbestos cement sheeting with a variety of surface finishes has been used. Mosaic tiling, marble, or other natural stones are also common materials.

Aluminum curtain wall systems are extremely resistant to atmospheric corrosion —which is of vital importance due to our ever increasing and varying pollution problems—and functionally they require no protective coatings to preserve structural integrity. However, for decorative purposes or to preserve the original appearance of the metal, the aluminum is normally clear or color anodized. This assures a crisp, clean appearance over a long period of time with minimum maintenance requirements.

A variety of glass types may be used for the walls, both for the vision and spandrel panel. The glass may be clear, tinted in varying colors, reflective, laminated, heat strengthened, or fully toughened. Generally, selection of glass is for esthetic purposes and for its thermal performance and effect on internal conditions.

Finishes to the aluminum framing can be mill, etched, mechanical such as linished or polished, vitreous enamel, painted and clear, or color anodized. The most common finish of recent years is the colored hard coat anodized finish. Thickness of the coat can vary due to economic factors and degree of prestige finish required. Anodizing is an electrolytic process that changes the structure of the metal surface to impregnate the color and produce a hard surface strongly resistant to corrosion.

Temporary protective finishes are generally applied to the aluminum at time of leaving the factory to protect the surface during normal building operations and spillage of debris that may be detrimental to the surface coating. Generally these protective coatings are clear nonyellowing lacquers, wax, or petroleum jelly based liquids. Care must be exercised in not allowing these coatings to cover the metalwork that will come in contact with permanent sealants, as the adhesion properties will be seriously affected. Strippable plastic skins and protective tapes should also be avoided as they may be difficult to remove.

5.4 TESTING

Due to the custom nature of most curtain wall or cladding systems for tall buildings, it becomes necessary to verify the thermal efficiency, watertightness, and airtightness of the system as well as the structural design criteria with respect to wind load, other superimposed loads, and building movement. Therefore, extensive test procedures have been developed to verify design performance of these systems. Tests for air infiltration, water penetration, and thermal control, in addition to dynamic load performance, have become commonplace for tall building facades. Governmental research stations and building material and systems manufacturers have extensively utilized accelerated weathering tests to determine and verify the appropriateness of various materials for building construction. Figs. 5.6 and 5.7 provide some examples. [In Fig. 5.7 (partial building facade illustrating possible selection of areas to be represented in test specimen), Area A = normal choice; Area

B = better choice, but more elaborate and more expensive; Area C = most complex and expensive, but may be advisable in some cases; Area X = inadequate and unacceptable.]

Due to the tests which are available and utilized, and to extensive design development over the past quarter century, many curtain wall installers are prepared to guarantee their product and installation for periods as long as 10 years.

The need for testing depends upon the type of wall being used and the circumstances of its use. Even though a manufacturer will guarantee his wall, a custom-built wall or a previously unproven design requires thorough pretesting. The architect should be sufficiently well informed regarding the nature and value of testing to determine what procedures are appropriate.

In general, laboratory testing of metal curtain walls is aimed at evaluating performance of the wall under exposure to simulated environmental conditions before full-scale production of the wall system begins. A second advantage of such testing is that, in constructing the test specimen, or mock-up unit, an opportunity is

Fig. 5.6 Curtain wall specimen erected in chamber for conducting tests under static pressure
(Courtesy: Architectural Aluminum Manufacturers Association)

provided to evaluate the esthetics and the installation procedures. In some cases this experience in itself leads to design improvements. Although the tests provide no positive proof that the wall when installed will perform satisfactorily, they often do reveal design weaknesses, or fabrication faults, and such information in advance of general production will save many times the cost of the tests.

It must be recognized, however, that even the most extensive laboratory testing cannot predict with accuracy the performance of the wall in actual use on the building. To a large degree, actual site performance depends upon the care used in installing the wall, proper anchorage, the fit of component parts, and the effectiveness of site sealants. All of these, in turn, depend upon the alinement of the building structure, working conditions on site, and the human element of quality of workmanship and proper supervision. Proper allowance for all of these unknowns cannot be made in the tests, nor can the detrimental effects of time and aging be simulated.

The performance characteristics that are usually of greatest concern are the structural performance under wind loading and the ability of the wall to prevent water penetration. Structural failure, of course, may endanger human life, so structural adequacy is a basic essential. The occurrence of water penetration is not likely to be dangerous, but may cause discomfort and property damage.

It does not follow, however, that structural testing is more essential than testing

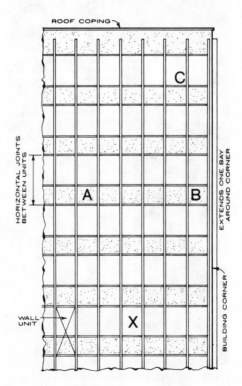

Fig. 5.7 Areas of curtain wall which can be used for test specimens are shown on an elevation of a typical curtain wall (Courtesy: Architectural Aluminum Manufacturers Association)

for water penetration. In fact, the order of importance is usually the reverse. The reason is that structural requirements are well recognized and can be calculated with reasonable accuracy. Resistance to water penetration, on the other hand, cannot be accurately calculated or predicted, but requires testing for verification.

A third common test is to determine resistance of the wall to air infiltration. This is of particular concern when the design includes operating window units. Generally leakage of air is of secondary importance, although the amount of air passing through the wall must be kept to a minimum to minimize heat loss and condensation. Contrary to some beliefs, there is no direct and constant relationship between the amount of air infiltration and the amount of water penetration occurring through a wall.

Varying degrees of importance are attached to the tests for these three characteristics, and the architect may be selective in specifying them. In addition to these, two other tests of normally minor importance are used to measure thermal transference and sound transmission.

Two methods of testing are used: dynamic and static. The dynamic method employs a wind generator, usually an aircraft motor and large propellor, to simulate wind while water is fed into the air stream and onto the wall. The wind produced also provides the test pressure. The static method utilizes an air chamber that consists of a relatively airtight assembly in the form of a large box, with the wall test specimen contained in one of the two large sides of the box. Air is then supplied into or exhausted from this assembly by means of a blower system producing a pressure differential across the specimen.

Since the inception of curtain wall testing there have been differences of opinion as to the relative merits of the two methods. Initially the dynamic test method was used, but it was soon found that the static method was capable of producing much higher and more readily measurable pressures, and often revealed leakage failures not found by dynamic tests. Consequently the static test was the one most often used. Figs. 5.8 and 5.9 are illustrative.

One of the principal advantages of the static over the dynamic method is the precision of control. The method, however, lacks the turbulence encountered in nature, which is simulated to a greater degree in the dynamic test. It has accordingly been necessary to establish the relationship between the behavior of specimens when tested both statically and dynamically. Comparative testing is continuing, but so far good correlations between static and dynamic tests have not been obtained.

Some other advantages of the suction-box method over the dynamic method are:

1. The installation and removal of specimens is more convenient.

2. Higher air pressures can be induced.

3. Operation is under cover.

4. Air infiltration, structural behavior, and water penetration can all be studied readily once a specimen has been installed.

In recent years, with the advent of pressure-equalization type wall designs, there has been considerable evidence showing that the dynamic test has important significance. Some curtain wall and window designs that have employed the pressure equalization principle to prevent leakage, and which have been tested by both methods, have been found to leak under dynamic testing. However, under static tests, run at a higher pressure, they have shown no evidence of leakage. The dynamic method more closely simulates the action of wind, producing similar gusting, buffeting, and vibrational effects, and driving the water in all directions over the surface of the test specimen. A structural test for wind loading is shown in Fig. 5.10. Unfortunately, high pressures are not generally available for the dynamic test as they are for the static method.

Further examples of infiltration, weathertightness, and structural adequacy are shown in Figs. 5.11 through 5.15.

5.5   STRUCTURAL/ARCHITECTURAL INTERACTION

Structural requirements stem principally from factors created by wind loadings. As wind pressures generally increase with height above the ground, it is common practice to specify design loads at the top of tall buildings higher than those at the lower levels. It must be remembered that negative pressures can be as critical as, and much higher than, positive pressures. In fact, this is usually the case.

Fig. 5.8 Suction-box with control panel and exhaust connection in foreground *(Courtesy: Experimental Building Station, L. M. Schneider)*

Where no primary or secondary framing is employed in the system—that is, where wall panels span from floor to floor—the cladding units must integrally accommodate the loadings. In framed systems, all cladding and glazed units must transfer their loads effectively to the primary framing. The vertical elements, or mullions, are assumed to be simply supported members.

Framing members must be designed to prevent excessive deflections or vibrations and accommodate additional superimposed loadings from maintenance and window cleaning cradles, while at the same time allowing for the structural building movement, and at all times remaining watertight. An illustrative connection is shown in Fig. 5.16.

The curtain wall, including fastenings, should be able to resist wind loads. This means that under dynamic loading, increased by coefficients, the endurance limit should stay below the accepted criteria. Deflections allowable for framing members and all components vary, but they are generally in the range of 1/240 to 1/360 of the span.

Under all conditions of loadings on the wall, both wind to its maximum gust velocity and superimposed loadings of cleaning rigs, the deflection imposed must not be permanent.

Wind loadings will vary according to the location of the building, but they are generally covered by the local regulations. Pressures due to 160 km/hr (99.4 mph) winds are very common and in some areas extend to much higher values. If a wall is required to withstand water penetration at, say, 2.6 kPa (54.3 lb/ft^2) wind pressure, then the structural requirements could easily be 1.5 or 2.0 times this figure.

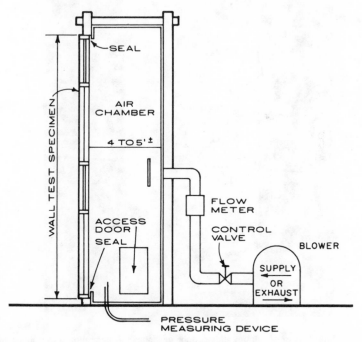

Fig. 5.9 Section through typical static pressure test assembly *(Courtesy: Architectural Aluminum Manufacturers Association)*

The attachments of a curtain wall are the connecting elements between the wall and the structural frame of the building. Since factory-fabricated curtain walls are normally produced to tight tolerances that are not normally matched by on-site tolerances of the building structure, it is necessary to erect the system using attachments that allow adjustment in three directions. The attachments usually employ slotted holes. After final alinement the attachments are welded over to assure rigidity.

The attachments should be designed so that erection is as simple and uncomplicated as possible, with the minimum number of fixing connections. The attachments have to withstand the full wind and superimposed loadings on the wall. Also they must transfer such loads to the structure, as well as withstand any earthquake forces. With the use of certain wall panels, such as precast concrete or cast metal panels, the attachments must also be able to withstand loadings due to thermal movement and deflection.

Attachments should be corrosion proof for the life of the building. Care must be taken to assure that direct contact between dissimilar metals is avoided. Steel used in the system should receive proper coatings such as hot dipped galvanizing. Condensation or weather penetration can cause ultimate failure of badly designed attachments.

Fig. 5.10 Structural test of aluminum sliding door unit showing deflection under static pressure equivalent to wind speed of 90 mph (*Courtesy: Experimental Building Station, L. M. Schneider*)

The design of attachments and curtain wall panels, irrespective of what type, should be such that the connection can be made from inside without need for external scaffolding. Hoisting of heavier panels has to be carefully planned so as not to cause damage to the panel or the attachments located on the structure.

Structural tests can be carried out on the wall by both static and dynamic methods. The static method is preferred, as greater precision is possible and approximately double the pressure can be applied, compared to the dynamic test. A uniform load is applied over the face of the specimen equal to that corresponding to a wind of velocity appropriate to the location of the building.

This structural test not only assures that the components of the metal wall meet the structural and deflection requirements of the wall design, but also tests the vision and spandrel panels and assures the structural adequacy of the glass.

The mock-up wall in the test rig is reversed and the test repeated to simulate negative or suction pressures on the wall. Gage rods are set on the mock-up wall at critical locations and deflections read electronically.

5.6 WATER LEAKAGE

The light aluminum curtain wall is in constant, if minor, movement due to structure flexing, thermal movement, and wind loads. Therefore great attention

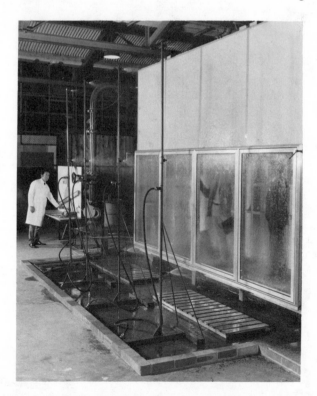

Fig 5.11 Static rain-penetration and structural test on aluminum windows in the suction box
(Courtesy: Experimental Building Station, L. M. Schneider)

must be given to joining and assembly techniques that will accommodate this movement yet avoid water and air penetration.

Driving rain is a constant hazard and failure to exclude it can be troublesome and costly. Pressures induced by the impingement of wind on the surfaces of buildings can drive water up the face of the wall quite readily; hence, both top and bottom surfaces must be sealed. The head of water that can be maintained by wind pressure increases in proportion to the square of the velocity. An average 100-km/hr (62.1-mph) wind will maintain a column of water approximately 45 mm (1.77 in.) high.

Most curtain walls leak to some degree, and it is therefore reasonable to presume that minor penetration is unimportant provided there are gutters to contain and drain the water away. The drainage of water against wind pressures can be difficult.

Curtain walls are designed generally following two principles. The first is where a full water seal is provided at the exterior face with the object of allowing no water to enter the wall. The second depends on the rain screen or pressure equalization system where the seal is provided at the inside or interior face of the wall. Under both systems all joints should be double sealed, preferably one barrier being of applied mastic and the other mechanical. Some typical details are shown in Figs. 5.17 and 5.18.

Irrespective of type, all wall systems rely heavily on efficient jointing. The joints

Fig. 5.12 Failure of window under ultimate uniform load (viewed from inside the suction box)
(Courtesy: Experimental Building Station, L. M. Schneider)

must resist water penetration, or alternatively allow penetration and subsequent escape by drainage. The joints may be of the sealed type to totally prevent water entry, or the open type designed to allow penetration. Sealed joints may employ wet or dry, or a combination of both, sealing techniques. Wet joints utilize mastics, sealants, and impregnated tapes. Dry joints utilize flexible neoprene rubber or PVC gaskets. Open joints use metal stripping or alternatively rely on joint configuration to prevent excessive weather penetration. Experience tends to show that the use of both wet and dry sealing techniques in combination offers the most effective means of achieving predictable weathertightness over long periods of time.

In designing the pressure differential system it is important that the plane of pressure differential should have as much continuity as possible. The pressure differential plane is that plane where the pressure between the interior of the building and the exterior of the building meet and change. Quite often it is a series of planes, and all too often the plane is not within the exterior skin.

The biggest cause of water penetration through the walls of a building is not the amount of rainfall but the pressure differential. Whenever possible, maintain the pressure differential plane on the interior face of the exterior walls. This keeps the internal parts of the wall as close as possible to the exterior pressure. This allows the exterior face of the wall to shed as much of the water as possible, and the external portions of the wall can freely drain to the outside instead of to the inside.

The water resistant qualities of a wall can be tested by both the dynamic and static test rigs. The static test is favored in most cases. The general criterion is that water penetration is zero under wind pressures that are called for by the regulation for the location in which the structure is to be erected.

In the static rig water is sprayed over the outer face of the specimen wall at a

Fig. 5.13 Static weathertightness test on corner window unit *(Courtesy: Experimental Building Station, L. M. Schneider)*

Fig. 5.14 Curtain wall specimen before negative pressure is applied in structural performance test *(Courtesy: Architectural Aluminum Manufacturers Association)*

Fig. 5.15 Curtain wall specimen during application of negative pressure in structural performance test—deformation of wall is shown in the reflected images *(Courtesy: Architectural Aluminum Manufacturers Association)*

controlled rate of approximately 2000 l/m²/hr (49 gals/ft²/hr), to form a curtain of water. At the same time pressure in the box is reduced so as to produce across the specimen a pressure differential that corresponds to the wind velocity prescribed for the wall. Leakage of water is observed through ports in the rear of the box. The test pressure and water are maintained for a period of 15 minutes.

5.7 AIR INFILTRATION

The infiltration of air into buildings that is induced by strong winds can prejudice comfort and impose an undue load on air conditioning and heating plants. The degree of concern about air infiltration increases where operable window units are involved.

It may be noted that curtain walls that perform well under air-infiltration tests are usually excellent in their resistance to water penetration, although the converse is not necessarily true. Air infiltration through a wall can have other associated detrimental effects on the building, such as allowing noise penetration and penetration of dust. It can also produce wind sound effects.

General criteria of allowable air infiltration through a curtain wall are not stipulated in regulations or building codes. However, the specifications for this part of the wall are chosen by the architect depending upon the class of building and the

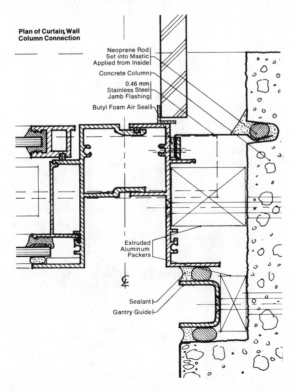

Fig. 5.16 Plan of curtain wall column connection (*Courtesy: Alcoa of Australia Limited*)

type of wall selected. The standards in some cases may be quite high, for example an allowance of 0.5 m³ (17.7 ft³) per min per meter of crack length. The allowable infiltration is generally at a wind velocity of approximately 50 km/hr to 80 km/hr (31.1 mph to 49.7 mph), which is a lot lower than the values set for structural and water penetration performances.

The test for air infiltration is always carried out by the static method, and usually in association with the structural load and water penetration tests.

In the air-infiltration test, air is exhausted from the static enclosure box to create a pressure differential between the external and internal faces of the window. The resulting air flow through the enclosure is measured with the specimen sealed and unsealed, and the difference in readings gives the air flow or leakage through the specimen.

5.8 CONDENSATION

Curtain wall systems are characterized by impervious metallic and glass surfaces, thus condensation control can become a basic design consideration. In warm or temperate climates surface condensation on windows and walls is generally of a temporary nature, but in cold climates, because of prolonged or continuous winter heating, condensation becomes a more serious problem.

Moisture, in the form of vapor, is always present in the air. It exists in warm air to

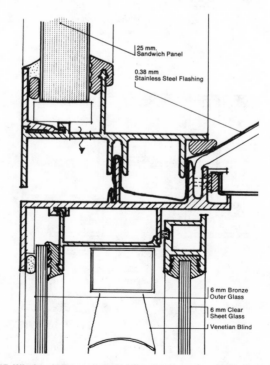

Fig. 5.17 Window head section *(Courtesy: Alcoa of Australia Limited)*

a greater degree potentially than in cold air. When water vapor cools to its dewpoint temperature, as it may do when it comes into contact with a relatively cold surface, the vapor condenses into liquid form. There can often be sufficient condensation on glass or metal panels to warrant the provision of a drain at the base of the panel.

To control condensation it is necessary to prevent the water vapor from reaching surfaces cold enough to cause condensation. This is done by the installation of an impervious vapor barrier of materials such as aluminum foil, bituminous felts or papers. These are placed in appropriate positions in the system. Condensation may also be controlled by providing ventilation behind the outer surfaces to relieve air and vapor pressure differentials, thus inhibiting vapor flow. Condensation can also be prevented by the installation of a series of materials of ascending permeability inside the panel, starting on the inner surface, in combination with insulating materials which are highly permeable and water repellent. Experience has shown that it is impracticable to construct a curtain wall system that will not permit some degree of water vapor to reach the interior face of the wall.

The problems of condensation may be reduced by the provision of insulation at the back of glass or panels in the spandrel panel areas. The vision panels may be treated by the provision of double glazed units or hermetically sealed windows. Double glazed units must be ventilated if condensation is to be avoided.

Condensation can occur inside the panel itself if it contains thermal bridges, single spots or areas with insufficient insulation. Metal screws that join different elements such as interior faces, insulators, or exterior faces in mechanically assembled panels, as well as metal panel frames and metal mullions, can act as thermal bridges. The formation of these bridges can be avoided in the case of mullions (whose larger part lies on the outside) and panels as a rule happen to be

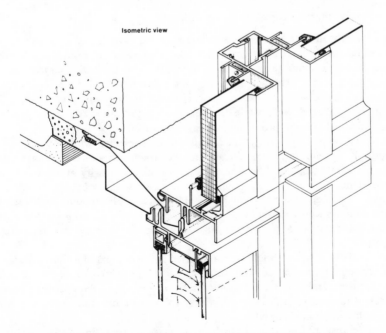

Fig. 5.18 Curtain wall details *(Courtesy: Alcoa of Australia Limited)*

thinner. In this case additional insulation should be provided on the inside part of the mullions. In panels with mechanical joints (screws that are driven into the insulating material) thermal bridges are bound to occur. The hazard of condensation can be minimized when potential thermal bridges are: (1) Uniformly distributed; (2) joined to an interior ductile surface such as tin; or (3) have a cross section that does not exceed 1/3000 of the panel surface. The temperature differential between the heated inside and the cold outside is likely to cause condensation in the interior surface of the elements.

5.9   THERMAL CHARACTERISTICS

Due to the thermal characteristics of the traditional heavy wall materials, and the thicknesses in which they are used, buildings utilizing them tend to exhibit relatively static interior thermal conditions. The curtain wall, on the other hand, utilizes thin, lightweight materials which quickly transmit thermal effects.

Thus, it is of great importance that a careful assessment of thermal control requirements of a curtain wall system be made, balancing the insulating potentialities of the system against the optimum economic degree of interior thermal control. The problem is best answered by the assessment of four factors, and the way they interrelate esthetically, functionally, and economically. The factors are:

1. The ratio of opaque to transparent areas.

2. Glazing method or type, and spandrel or wall panel design.

3. Sun control or sun shading.

4. Internal thermal control—air conditioning.

The curtain wall may be seen as a totally glass wall system, an opaque wall with minimum fenestration, or a system with a solid-to-transparent ratio lying anywhere between these extremes (Figs. 5.19, 5.20, 5.21). The thermal characteristics of buildings lying at the extremes are enormously different, and these are inevitably reflected in the economics. The most efficient is the windowless wall. The predominantly glazed wall, while best expressing the spirit of the curtain wall system, least satisfies the problems of thermal control.

The actual temperature to which a wall will be subjected when exposed to the elements will depend on its color, orientation, characteristics of the materials used, and the meteorological conditions of the locality, such as clarity of the atmosphere and prevalence or absence of cooling breezes. Lightweight curtain walls can be subjected to temperature ranges of 383 K (110 °C, 230 °F) in some locations. Not only must the wall provide thermal insulation, but also the jointing and sealants of the wall must be able to withstand the movement due to this temperature differential.

The role of the window should be reappraised in the context of efficient design for energy. Zoned lighting in deep tall buildings utilizing various degrees of integrated artificial and natural light would show significant savings in the operating costs of buildings. The positive utilization of winter solar radiation and daylight through windows should be considered.

Economic design of heating and lighting services is of paramount importance in tall buildings. The depth of plan form significantly influences the planning, structural efficiency, and performance requirements of the window. Studies of energy use in various office designs indicate that considerable savings can be achieved by careful attention to the design of artificial and natural lighting. Innovative design in artificial lighting combined with daylight can achieve savings in electrical consumption for lighting. This requires careful consideration of the size and area of fenestration and the type of glass utilized.

Problems of glare accompany the problems of thermal transmittance and radiation. The basic problems associated with large glass areas must be carefully studied and solved simultaneously.

Double glazed windows, hermetically sealed, made up of an outer pane of heat absorbing glass and an inside pane of normal clear glass, will reduce solar heat transmission by almost half as compared with clear plate glass (Fig. 5.22). In winter, when heat conservation is desirable, the same unit can provide insulation almost

Fig. 5.19 Commercial Bank of Australia Limited, Sydney, Australia, consisting of parking facilities, retail shopping arcades, main banking chamber, and 28 floors of commercial office space. The tower is triangular in plan form with the main facades strategically oriented to take maximum advantage of views available. *(Courtesy: Peddle, Thorp, & Walker Architects)*

equivalent to that of a 150-mm (5.9-in.) concrete wall. Frequently, however, the cost of such units can make them impracticable, although costs in service versus initial capital cost requires careful consideration.

Double glazed windows with an intermediate air space of approximately 60 mm (2.4 in.) to 100 mm (4 in.) have proved in many instances to be a reasonably economical installation after all factors have been considered. In many cases an integral shading device, such as venetian blinds or drapery, is incorporated.

Fig. 5.20 A.N.Z. Bank Building, Sydney, Australia *(Courtesy: Peddle, Thorp & Walker Architects; Photo by Pieter Stroethoff)*

Grey, bronze, or other colored glass can be used effectively to reduce glare. Also, solar heat transmission can be reduced by 60%. Heat absorbing glass can be economically feasible and it will reduce solar heat by approximately 50%. However, its glare reducing ability is much less than that of grey glass. This means that shading devices will frequently be necessary.

Heat reflecting glass offers advantages in the control of both heat and light transmission. Reductions of up to 75% are possible. Externally the glass presents a mirror-like appearance which may not always be esthetically acceptable or desirable. Vision from inside the building is not impaired, but from the outside, vision into the building is considerably reduced.

In the spandrel or opaque areas of the wall, thermal insulation is provided. Both sprayed-on and board type insulation is utilized for this purpose. Gypsum or fiberglass insulation is most commonly used. Plastic type insulation has been used

Fig. 5.21 Royal Exchange Building, Sydney, Australia *(Courtesy: Peddle, Thorp & Walker Architects; Photo by Diane Graham & John Garth)*

but today, despite developments by the plastics industry, the material does not meet all regulation requirements for fire safety and toxicity.

The insulation may be applied directly to the back of the curtain wall panel, by either adhesive or mechanical fixing, or it may be installed as an independent barrier. If a back-up wall is required for other purposes, such as fire rating barrier, it may incorporate the insulation barrier or have it applied to it. The back-up wall in turn can also be of assistance in the thermal control of the wall.

Tests can be carried out in the laboratory in a double chamber apparatus, which is an adaptation to the static test rig unit. The tests can determine the over-all

Fig. 5.22 Equibank Building, Pittsburgh, Pennsylvania. Double-pane reflective glass reportedly saves about 50% of the energy that would be used by comparable building with ordinary windows. *(Courtesy: PPG Industries, Inc.)*

thermal conductivity of the composite wall assembly, investigate the effect of temperature fluctuations on the exterior wall elements, measure indoor surface temperatures, and find where condensation is likely to occur. Due to the relatively high expense of this test it is not commonly used.

The advent of the energy crisis and the resulting energy conserving building codes will have a dramatic effect on the design and construction of window walls, curtain walls, and cladding systems. Generally speaking, the glass area of building exteriors in northern climates will be limited to less than 50%. Also, there will be a tendency to use more dual glazing in the glass area and to improve the insulation criteria for the opaque or cladded area.

5.10 ACOUSTICAL PERFORMANCE

The intrusion of outdoor noise into buildings is a constant problem in built-up areas, and it should be considered in both the site planning and interior planning of each building. It is often possible to locate acoustically sensitive functions so that they do not face the worst noise sources, and so may not require special wall

Hydroproject Building, Moscow, USSR *(Courtesy: B. Rubanenko)*

construction to provide the required isolation (usually termed noise reduction) from outdoor sources.

It is fairly simple to define in advance the suitability of a given wall construction for a particular noise exposure. The basic requirement for control of intruding noise is a complete enclosure of a heavy, impervious material. Openings such as operable windows or open joints clearly lessen the effectiveness of the enclosure. However, a less obvious fact is that the noise reduction capability of most office walls—even if all joints were perfectly sealed—would be governed by the window area. Unless the area of glass is very small compared to the total wall area, or unless special double glazing is used, replacement of a lightweight curtain wall panel with heavy masonry would not yield any acoustical benefit whatsoever.

As will be apparent to anyone who has flown in a jet aircraft, it is possible under certain conditions to build a lightweight wall, with windows, providing a high degree of noise isolation. Here the basic ingredients are: (1) A very stiff sandwich-panel construction consisting of sheet metal layers with sound-absorbing intermediate layers; (2) triple-glazed, very small windows; and (3) a complete absence of sound leaks.

A significant improvement in noise reduction can be achieved by changing from single to double glazing. However, ordinary heat-insulating double glazing is no better than a single layer of the same total weight in this respect. The space between glass layers should be at least 100 mm (4 in.) deep to be really effective. Unless a special laminated glass is used, the acoustical benefit to be gained by simply increasing glass thickness is in no way consistent with the increase in weight.

Any improvement in the noise isolation characteristics of a curtain wall system should be aimed at producing a balanced design. First, a gasketing system must be found to provide airtight joints, including edge gasketing for fixed and operable glazing. Next, since the area of glass normally determines the sound isolating performance of the curtain wall, double glazing with an air space of at least 100 mm (4 in.) is needed to provide a significant improvement over single glazing. Finally, reduction in glass area should be considered in conjunction with increasing the mass of the nonglazed solid wall area (Newman, 1974).

5.11 FIRE RATING

External walls by regulations are required to provide varying levels of fire resistance. They are required to be noncombustible. In tall buildings ratings for external walls can be as high as four hours.

It is frequently difficult to provide the required fire resistance level in the usual thin metal wall, especially if it is made of metal other than steel, and independent back-up walls may have to be incorporated into the structure to satisfy the ratings. These back-up walls are usually made of noncombustible or fireproof material, such as pumice stone, gypsum bars or gypsum board, cast-in-place or precast concrete, or metal panels. The curtain wall proper must not be attached to this back-up wall. Attention must also be given to the gap between the curtain wall and the back-up wall or structural floor slab, and a fire break installed to prevent the spread of fire from floor to floor.

A common regulation is that a fire rated separation 1 m high be provided between floors. This height would incorporate the structural slab thickness at the perimeter together with the height of the back-up wall. The regulations will also allow a horizontal projection beyond the facade, if it is of the same fire resistant rating, to act as the required barrier between the floors.

The attachments or fastenings of the curtain wall to the structure must also be fire protected to the same degree of fire rating as required for the wall. This protection is normally achieved by concrete encasing or by a covering of vermiculite or asbestos based fireproofing material.

Where possible radiation from an adjoining building is considered a hazard to the building, the authorities in some areas require external protection to the curtain wall or windows to counteract it. This protection is normally in the form of external fire sprinklers or fire rated windows and wired glass. The external sprinklers need to be designed so that upon operation the water will provide a complete film of water over the glass face and provide a cooling protective layer.

5.12 SHADING

The shading of glass surfaces can offer the best means of reducing the demands of internal environmental control. The economics of shading devices depend closely on good design, which must emerge from an understanding of the technical considerations involved.

Shading devices may be an integral part of the curtain wall, achieved by molded facade panels of masonry or metal, or they may be applied units. Exterior shading devices are not common, as by nature and design most curtain walls have a rather flat exterior plane. The use of applied shading devices, besides providing a benefit to the internal environment, can be a detriment to the external environment because of their effect on wind patterns and the resultant creation of turbulence.

The three basic shading systems are horizontal, vertical, and egg crate, in both fixed and adjustable configurations. Horizontal shading devices are generally horizontal overhangs, louvers in a plane at right angles to the wall, adjustable horizontal louvers, or solid or perforated strips parallel to the wall. Slanted louvers are more efficient than those set vertically.

Vertical shading devices are normally vertical fixed fins at right angles to the wall, vertical fixed fins oblique to the wall, or vertical movable fins. The fixed fins may be an expression of the columns of the building or of extended window mullions. They may also be the structural columns of the building strongly expressed on the facade with vertical strip walling between. Egg crate shading devices can consist of fixed or movable horizontal and vertical members.

An alternative to the shading devices just described is an over-all screen, fixed independently as a second wall system in front of the wall proper. A great variety of textural and sculptural effects is possible with the screen wall. This type of treatment is normally acceptable only in low or medium-rise structures.

5.13 GLASS AND GLAZING

Design criteria for glass are quite similar for both tall and low buildings, except for the more critical wind load conditions and building movement criteria in tall buildings. Interior glazing systems have been developed to solve the building problem of installing glass from the outside face of the building. This system also provides for more simple maintenance and replacement procedures. These glazing systems are composed of basically the same material as exterior glazing systems.

Single glazed units of curtain walls utilize a wide range of glass types: clear glass, heavy drawn sheet, polished plate, float, opaque, heat absorbing, heat reflecting, glare reducing, and laminated. Normal thicknesses are in the 5-mm (0.2-in.) to 8-mm (0.3-in.) range, and up to 12 mm (0.5 in.) for certain installations. Double glazed units are manufactured as required in any combination of the glass types listed.

Tinted glass has been widely used in tall buildings to reduce the heat gain through the wall. However, a substantial amount of clear glass is also used in areas where heat gain through the wall is not a critical criterion. Tempered glass and heat strengthened glass are utilized to improve the wind load characteristics of the material. Heat strengthened and laminated glasses are also used for safety factors.

The thickness of the glass is selected based on a safety factor which predicts a

Bank of Oklahoma Tower, Tulsa, Oklahoma *(Photo by A. T. Gonzales, Photography)*

certain percentage of glass failure for a given loading condition. Many manufacturers use safety factors of up to 2.5 with a predicted failure of approximately 1%.
On tall buildings the thickness of glass can vary at different levels of the building as
wind load pressures increase with the height of the building. The sizing of glass and
the depth glazed into the rebate is most important when pulsating effects are taken
into consideration in order to prevent the glass panes from being sucked out of the
wall.

Various glazing systems including both wet and dry materials and structural
neoprene gasket systems have been developed to withstand wind pressures as high
as 4903 MPa (0.711 psi, 500 kgf/m²). The wet glazing systems are more popular in
low or moderately tall buildings. Window wall systems in tall buildings which must
withstand higher wind pressures and the pumping action of the wind on the glazing
sealant require more rigid glass support, and therefore the neoprene gaskets and the
dry glazing systems involving butyl tapes have been adopted to accommodate the
more rigid wind load criteria.

Bonaventure Hotel, Los Angeles, California. Reflective glass reduces entry of the sun's light and heat for improved energy efficiency and indoor comfort. *(Courtesy: PPG Industries, Inc.)*

5.14 SEALANTS

Fabrication and erection techniques for curtain walls rely heavily on flexible compounds to assure weathersealing. The generic term for these compounds is sealant. The term mastic is by definition an oil based compound, which has only a limited use in curtain walls.

Over the past quarter century advances in the field of sealants have been extensive. Some of the initial work with caulking and sealant materials took place in the aircraft industry, and these materials were subsequently adopted by the construction industry and modified for building purposes.

It is generally conceded that the technology of sealants is the least resolved element in the curtain wall system, and in view of the wide range of properties such compounds are called upon to possess in order to fulfill their function effectively, it is not unusual that compromises must be made in their selection.

An effective sealant, to provide the necessary expansion, contraction, and movement flexibility characteristics associated with tall building design, has the

Apartment buildings in Leningrad, USSR *(Courtesy: B. Rubanenko)*

following properties:

1. Adhesion to metals, glass, and other building materials.

2. Cohesion and retention of elasticity under continuous stretching and compression.

3. Resistance to shear, both in the body of the material and at adherent surfaces.

4. Resistance to hardening, shrinkage, cracking, separation of constituents, oxidation, slumping, and polymerization.

5. Resistance to water erosion and absorption.

6. Sufficient rigidity to prevent displacement or squeezing out.

7. Resistance to ultraviolet light without hardening, cracking, or decomposition.

8. Reasonable pot life during application.

9. Optimum viscosity for application, and not excessive sensitivity to temperature.

The materials best satisfying these property requirements come from the silicone, polysulfide, polyurethane, acrylic, and butyl groups of compounds. By their nature these sealants are expensive and require careful application.

As the sealants vary in their performance regarding the various required properties, a number of different sealants may be utilized in the design of one wall. Sealant joint width, and depth and size relationships, in addition to compatibility of materials, are all very important items with respect to the proper design of an expansion or construction joint.

Resilient neoprene rubber and PVC gaskets are widely used in conjunction with or as alternatives to the expensive sealant materials discussed previously or the less effective mastic filters and tapes. The gaskets are fixed in place under pressure and rely on resilience rather than adhesion to assure weathertightness. They are most often used in metal to glass joints.

5.15 SEISMIC PERFORMANCE

Many areas of the world are subject to earthquake induced ground motions. All parts of a structure together with its contents respond nearly simultaneously when subjected to seismic ground motion. When earthquake forces must be considered, their effects on all building components, including the exterior wall enclosures, should be evaluated. In evaluating the effects it must be remembered that earthquake motions are random and occur both horizontally and vertically.

The response of a building to earthquake motion is affected by the stiffnesses and masses of the load carrying structural systems and the nonstructural exterior and interior walls, and the distribution of stiffnesses and masses of the structural and nonstructural elements. The placement and construction details of nonstructural elements can materially affect the response of the structural system during an earthquake.

The structural role which the exterior cladding is expected to perform when the building is subjected to lateral forces should be considered. The cladding may be uncoupled from the load carrying structural system by using connections which will allow the required differential movement. An alternative is to use the stiffness of the nonstructural elements to advantage. Such elements could be designed to resist building movements caused by wind and moderate earthquakes with little or no damage. The wall panels would thus resist a proportionate part of the lateral loads. This alternative may be feasible, depending on the type and geometry of the primary structural system and the magnitude of the design lateral forces. In severe earthquakes these elements would be damaged but would help the building absorb the energy from the earthquake. This approach could simplify the design of gasket sealants and panel-to-structure connections.

When deciding upon the structural participation of the exterior cladding, consideration must be given to the need for the cladding to accommodate building movement caused by wind or earthquake forces and temperature changes. Some or most of the differential movement may be taken in the wall panels (alternative noted previously) and the remainder by the connections to the structure. The differential movement resisted by the panel will tend to induce in-plane distortion, that is, change from a rectangular to a trapezoidal shape. The connections should be designed to bend or slip (if there are elongated bolt holes). Breaking of window glass due to panel distortion or failure of panel connections and subsequent falling to the ground can present a serious hazard to public safety. Thus the panels, glazing, and panel anchorage must be designed to prevent failure even when subjected to extreme earthquake motions.

Curtain walls must also be designed to provide for complete containment of the glass used in the wall. The wall panel containing the window frame must be able to deform with the building structure or have connections which permit such movement. If the panel and window deform with the structural framing systems, the glazing design must allow for differential movement between the window glass and the window frame. As noted previously, the connections of the wall panel to the building framing system must be designed to allow for differential movements caused by wind or seismic forces either by slip-type joints or ductile bending in the connection.

Factory fabrication of one-story or two-story high sections of curtain walls may be the most feasible way to assure that the glazing details required for seismic or wind forces, or both, will accommodate the specified differential movements and still remain watertight. The use of gasket seals is an effective way to permit movement without loss of watertightness. The glass should be installed so that there is sufficient space at each edge for the wall panel to deform without overstressing the glass.

Codes such as the Uniform Building Code, Los Angeles City Building Code, and San Francisco Building Code require exterior panels or cladding to be attached to the structural framing system so as to accommodate structure motions resulting from lateral forces or temperature changes. These provisions are modeled after the Recommended Lateral Force Requirements of the Structural Engineers Association of California Seismology Committee. They read as follows:

> *Exterior Elements*—Precast, nonbearing, non-shear wall panels or other elements which are attached to, or enclose the exterior, shall accommodate movements of the structures resulting from lateral forces or temperature changes. The concrete panels

or other elements shall be supported by means of cast-in-place concrete or by mechanical fasteners in accordance with the following provisions:

Connections and panel joints shall allow for a relative movement between stories of not less than two times story drift caused by wind or $(3.0/K)$* times story drift caused by the required seismic forces; or 6 mm (0.24 in.), whichever is greater.

Connections shall have sufficient ductility and rotation capacity so as to preclude fracture of the concrete or brittle failures at or near welds. Inserts in concrete shall be attached to, or hooked around reinforcing steel, or otherwise terminated so as to effectively transfer forces to the reinforcing steel.

Connections to permit movement in the plane of the panel for story drift shall be properly designed sliding connections using slotted or oversize holes or may be connections which permit movement by bending of steel.

As earthquake motions affect all elements in a building, the careful designer should provide means to adequately resist induced seismic motions in all components of the structure. Care should be exercised in planning the building to minimize, where possible, structure irregularity and nonsymmetry. A successful total design requires close coordination and cooperation among all members of the design team.

5.16 CLEANING

Most tall buildings have the vision window glass installed as a fixed unit such that exterior cleaning is required. Window washing and maintenance machines and cradles are required. These may be manually operated or fully automatic (Fig. 5.23).

The cradles which travel up and down the facade require some type of guide or attachment to hold the cradle close to the building. It is common to provide mullion guides as a part of the wall design, but guide rails may be incorporated into projecting structural columns of the building. The wall has to be designed to accommodate the additional loading of the cleaning unit, including any accompanying wind or seismic loadings.

During construction the metalwork of the wall is protected by lacquer coatings that have been applied, but the glass elements are susceptible to surface damage. Where concrete panels are used, or concrete is associated with the building structure, it should be noted that glass can be stained or etched by alkaline or fluorine materials which may be released from the concrete. Concrete frames at window heads should be designed to keep drip water away from the glass. Precast panels and other concrete wall materials should be completely cured prior to erection.

Weathering steels release oxides which, with aging, can damage the glass surface. When glass is installed adjacent to or below the masonry or steel surfaces which are exposed to the weather, the glass should be regularly examined and washed immediately if any deposits or staining are evident. Should the deposit be allowed to remain on the glass and etching occur, the only practical remedy may be glass replacement.

---

*K is a horizontal force factor varying from 0.67 for ductile space frames to 1.33 for shear wall structures.

5.17   CONDENSED REFERENCES/BIBLIOGRAPHY

The following is a condensed bibliography for this chapter. Not only does it include all articles referred to or cited in text, but it also contains bibliography for further reading. The full citations will be found at the end of the Volume. What is given here should be sufficient information to lead the reader to the correct article: the author, date, and title. In case of multiple authors, only the first named is listed.

AAMA 1970, *Aluminum Curtain Walls Publication Number 1*
AAMA 1979, *Aluminum Curtain Wall Design Guide Manual*
Aluminum Constructions 1977, *Exterior Wall Constructions, Design Principles (I)*
Aluminum Constructions 1978, *Exterior Wall Constructions, Design Principles (II)*
Aluminum Development Council of Australia undated, *Aluminum in Australia*

Berry 1973, *Architectural Seismic Detailing*
Bielek 1973, *Peripheral Walls of Tall Buildings, Their Design, Theory of Analysis*
Botsai 1973, *Designing Against Infiltration*
Building 1970, *Twin Towers Will Dominate The Sydney Skyline*
Building 1972, *External Walls: Multi-Storey: Building Construction Details*

Building Materials 1974, *Diamond Shaped Tower Dons a Special Cladding*
Building Materials 1975, *New Type Sandwich Panels Make Up a Building's Face*
Button 1975, *Considerations of Energy, Environment and Structure in Window Design*

Fig. 5.23 Exterior window washing device on high-rise building in Germany *(Courtesy: F. Rafeiner)*

CIMUR 1965, *French Light Facade Techniques: Curtain Walls And Facade Panels*
Callendar 1974, *Time-Saver Standards for Architectural Design*

Environmental Advisory Service 1976, *Energy Conservation in Commercial Buildings*
Essunger 1973, *Summary Report: Architectural—Structural Interaction*
Godfrey 1970, *Exposed Steelwork for Multi-Storey Buildings*
Ishizaki 1974, *On the Wind Resistant Design of Exterior Cladding*
Kajfasz 1973, *Interaction Approach in Poland*

Kavanagh 1974, *Architectural Structural Interaction*
Lenke 1971, *Architectural-Structural Interaction*
Lenke 1973, *Theme Report*
Lohmann 1973, *Facade Wall Design on the Tall Building*
Matsushita 1973, *High-Rise Building Construction Design in Japan and Asia*

Muszynski 1972, *A Light-Weight Curtain Wall*
Newby 1973, *Stiffness Related to Nonstructural Elements*
Newman 1974, *Acoustics*
Ortmanns 1978, *The Influence of Glass Panels on the Energy Balance of a Building*
Papadopoulos 1975, *Sun Protection in Housing—Greek Climatic Conditions*

Pellegrini 1973, *Construction in South America*
Peter 1964, *Design with Glass*
Polak 1973, *Architectural Elements in European Practice*
Rafeiner 1973, *Architectural Criteria of Tall Buildings in Germany and Europe*
Rousseau 1973, *Evolution of Conception of Curtain Walls*

SAA 1973, *Code of Practice for Installation of Glass in Buildings*
SAA 1972, *Preferred Sizes of Building Components (Metric Units)*
SEAOC 1974, *Recommended Lateral Force Requirements and Commentary*
Schall 1962, *Curtain Walls*
Schaupp 1965, *Exterior Walls, Cladding, Thermal Insulation and Humidity Protection*

Sharpe 1973, *Seismic Design of Nonstructural Elements*
Shaw 1973, *Air Leakage Measurements of the Exterior Walls of Tall Buildings*
Wojnowski 1972, *Light-Weight Metal Curtain Walls for Tall Buildings*

**Tall Building
Systems and Concepts**

Chapter SC-6

Partitions, Walls, and Ceilings

Prepared by Committee 12B (Partitions, Walls, and Ceilings) of the Council on Tall Buildings and Urban Habitat as part of the Monograph on the Planning and Design of Tall Buildings

Fritz Rafeiner   Committee Chairman
Howard D. Eberhart   Vice-Chairman
Anthony B. Klarich   Editor

AUTHOR ACKNOWLEDGMENT

Special acknowledgment is due those individuals whose contributions and papers formed the substantial first drafts of the various sections of this chapter. First are the state-of-art reporters from the 1972 International Conference whose material was published in the Lehigh Proceedings. For the indicated sections, these individuals are:

K. Matsushita, Section 6.1

J. H. Polak, Section 6.1

F. Rafeiner, Section 6.1

Y. Uchida, Section 6.1

O. R. Berry, Sections 6.1 and 6.2

R. E. Lenke, Sections 6.1 and 6.2

E. E. Botsai

S. E. Pellegrini.

CONTRIBUTORS

The following is a complete list of those who have submitted written material for possible use in the chapter, whether or not that material was used in the final version. The Committee Chairman and Editor were given quite complete latitude. Frequently length limitations precluded the inclusion of much valuable material. The Bibliography contains all contributions. The contributors are: O. R. Berry, E. E. Botsai, H. J. Cowan, H. D. Eberhart, G. Essunger, S. Kajfasz, A. B. Klarich, R. E. Lenke, K. Matsushita, W. P. Moore, Jr., F. Newby, S. E. Pellegrini, J. H. Polak, F. Rafeiner, P. E. Rousseau, R. L. Sharpe, Y. Uchida.

COMMITTEE MEMBERS

O. R. Berry, H. D. Eberhart, G. Essunger, F. R. Estuar, I. M. Kadri, S. Kajfasz, A. B. Klarich, R. E. Lenke, K. Matsushita, F. Newby, S. E. Pellegrini, F. Penteado, F. Rafeiner, P. E. Rousseau, B. Rubanenko, R. M. Schuster, R. L. Sharpe, Y. Uchida, F. Van der Woude, H. Weatherford, E. A. Wetherill.

SC-6 Partitions, Walls, and Ceilings

6.1 INTERIOR WALLS AND PARTITIONS

There are many different types of interior walls and partitions for use in high-rise buildings. They employ a wide range of materials, and they must satisfy a variety of different requirements.

High-rise building concepts cannot be based on the same criteria as those for low-rise buildings. Lateral forces, for example, must be considered. New technological concepts are required for the interior details in high-rise buildings. Safety considerations need special attention for high-rise buildings. They can draw upon the idea of safety zones, locks, and baffles, which are utilized in the construction of ships—because in high-rise building, as in ships, rescue possibilities are limited. The first task is to reduce the sources of danger resulting from the improper selection of materials.

All walls referred to in this chapter are nonloadbearing. Some are structural, assisting the main structure, but nevertheless nonloadbearing.

Walls and partitions in high-rise buildings, although built floor by floor and nonloadbearing, must withstand a completely different set of forces and satisfy different conditions from those experienced in a single-floor structure.

Careful consideration must be given at the junction of the internal wall to the structure, external walls (whether masonry or metal curtain walls), to floors, and ceilings, because of the movement associated with such buildings. This movement can be caused by a number of conditions, such as shrinkage, creep, progressive dead loading, wind load, thermal movement, and seismic forces. Such loadings can act singly, or they may be in combination. Certain of the effects can accumulate.

Dead loading of the wall or partition itself, besides being a vital factor in high-rise structural design, must also be considered since it can have a serious influence on many of the above-mentioned conditions.

Interior walls and partitions are generally classified as masonry, wood, metal, glass, plaster, drywall, or combinations thereof. The wall may be solid and fixed, or it may be classed as demountable or movable.

The qualities to be considered in the selection of a solid wall are: (1) Weight;

(2) strength; (3) fire resistance; (4) sound absorption or transmission; (5) thermal insulation; (6) ability to accept fixtures; (7) suitability for applied finishes; and (8) the labor associated with installation.

There are many types of partitions for separating different areas of the floor of a standard high-rise building, but they must all assure the utmost flexibility. The demountable or movable type wall or partition is generally selected for its modular qualities, demountability, ease of erection, stability, sound transmission, fire rating, and cost. This type of wall or partition is principally used in the fitting out of tenancies where flexibility of layout is an important requirement.

Safety of human life in the performance of building elements is of foremost importance. If other failures occur, walls can be restored to their original state by repair or replacement.

The order of priorities should therefore be:

1. Safety of human life.

2. Guarantee occupants freedom from injury.

3. Safety of property.

1   Materials and Details

Masonry or Solid Walls.   Tall buildings move due to wind loads or temperature variations. Performance criteria for interior walls and partitions must not only accommodate vertical deflection, but also accept horizontal movement and structural frame racking, without causing cracking of the wall or partition or of the architectural finishes.

Masonry and plaster walls can be designed to accommodate such building movement. This requires sophisticated details involving extensive reveals or slip joints, including metal, plastic, neoprene sealants, and other accessories, at the top and sides of the walls to isolate these elements from the building structure. Some prefabricated drywall and gypsum wall board systems have perimeter accessories; these have been developed in recent years to provide a flexible wall construction that can accommodate substantial structural movement.

Materials used for fixed or solid walls and partitions are generally clay bricks, vermiculite bricks, gypsum blocks, concrete blocks (either dense or lightweight), terra cotta tile bricks, timber stud and linings, metal stud and linings, and laminated gypsum boarding or plank systems.

The use of solid walls in high-rise buildings is generally associated with the core of the building, or the mechanical plant and machine rooms. Regulations of the various authorities having jurisdiction vary from country to country (and often also from state to state in a country). Many limit the selection of wall type and material to masonry or other high performance construction. This is especially the case in countries such as the United States and Australia, where stringent fire regulations exist. In regions where serious seismic conditions occur, most solid walls are built with stud-and-lining construction or with reinforced masonry.

In less developed or economically poorer countries, which do not have the variety or sophistication of available materials, concrete or some form of masonry or brick is most commonly used because of its local availability.

Clay bricks often undergo expansion (commonly known as "brick growth"), especially if laid into walls shortly after kiln firing while they are relatively dry. It is a distinct advantage to have the bricks stacked in the open for some time and kept damp. The more time incurred between removal of brick from kiln and its installation in a wall, the greater the reduction in the degree of movement of the completed wall. It is normally expected that one-third of the potential movement occurs within the first three months, and one-half of the movement within the first six-month period. The actual movement of expansion can continue for many years.

Concrete blocks, on the other hand, contract. Here also, the older the block, the less the potential movement. Walls constructed of concrete blocks are liable to show signs of shrinkage cracking. Block walls should be constructed in short lengths between control joints, utilizing mortars of a weaker mix than that generally used for brickwork.

Many theories exist about the type and strength of mortar that should be used with brick or block walling. Opinions vary as to whether the mortar should adhere or bond one unit to another, or whether it should separate one unit from the other.

Practical experience over many years has shown that very strong cement mortars can be more of a hazard than a benefit. If movement is to occur in a wall, the strong mortar will not prevent it, and its adherence to the masonry unit can cause spalling or fracture of that element. Experience has shown that lime cement mortar, with lime and cement in equal proportions, or with a greater proportion of lime, performs very satisfactorily.

Whether contraction or expansion occurs in a masonry wall, the "weaker" or "softer" mortar has more elasticity than a strong cement mortar, and consequently tends to minimize cracking that will occur with movement.

Demountable or Movable Partitions.   There are many proprietary modular, demountable, or movable partitions and walls. The types come under the general categories of post and infill panels of wood, metal, and glass, post and overlay panels of wood, metal, or gypsum board, postless, stud-metal or timber-and-wood or gypsum board lining, prefabricated insulated metal panels, glass in wood or metal frames, folding wood or metal doors, and wood or metal toilet partitions.

Demountable partitions utilizing the various post systems have the post extending from the floor to ceiling or structural slab. Lower height partitions are usually supported and braced by intersections of walls in the layout designs or by providing return buttresses. Long uninterrupted runs or free ends are normally minimized or eliminated because of stability problems.

Postless partitioning, whether solid timber or glass, must extend from floor to ceiling. Where lower height areas are required they cannot be provided unless adjacent panels are extended full height to provide the necessary stabilizing members.

The base or skirting section of the partitions is designed to carry service wiring for power and telecommunications. Sufficient space has to be provided to allow for the wiring to continue past supporting jacks and the skirting panel. In countries where higher voltage power is used, nominal 220 V and 440 V, the wiring space is required by the authorities to be divided by metal sheeting to separate the power, telephone, and/or intercommunications wiring.

Posts of partitions are designed to carry wiring for light switching and to contain the body of the switch box. Postless partitions must be of a type that can be internally drilled or routed to provide space for the wiring.

Some countries, principally in Europe, utilize prefabricated demountable panel systems. These systems are based on simple frame construction and infill panels of gypsum board and internal insulation material. High sound ratings may be achieved up to 45 dB, or the equivalent of a single brick masonry wall. The system is ideal for seismic areas because of movement at joints, but care has to be taken to avoid sound penetration. Neoprene fillers and caulking and sealants offer a solution.

Folding doors, vinyl fabric (or similar accordian type), or solid timber hinged panels are more frequently used in hotels, restaurants, or convention centers. This type of partition or dividing wall is used where readily movable walls are needed for frequent use, for example in adjoining conference rooms, board-dining areas, office and conversation areas. The sound rating of these panels is low unless they are specially designed and treated.

Toilet partitions are mostly constructed of prefabricated units, for example metal plastic laminate faces with core filling, or timber core, or precast terrazzo panels. The panels are ceiling suspended, floor mounted, or cantilevered from the rear wall.

One of the most commonly used types is the ceiling suspended unit, whether metal panel or plastic laminate, which leaves the floor completely unobstructed for cleaning purposes. Suspension is made at the front blade between doors, and adjustment on the suspension rods allows for alinement. Where plastic laminate is used, the internal angles are curved to provide easy cleaning.

2 Acoustics

Acoustical control is another item of great concern in tall buildings, as it is in low-rise buildings, except that in the case of tall buildings exterior acoustical control is not the major concern. Interior acoustical control through floors and walls in the building becomes a major item of concern due to the diverse occupancy in tall buildings. There are no standard sound control criteria established for these systems at the present time.

Space in a building has to be considered both as a source and a receiver of noise or sound. The need to reduce sound transference from one space to the other has to be recognized at the design stage, and the barrier or wall designed accordingly. To prevent transference at a later date is difficult and expensive.

Sound resisting requirements of a wall are dependent upon the noise level generated in one space and the acceptable level in the adjoining or receiving space. The general ambient noise level in the receiving area can affect the requirements of the wall; the lower the ambient level the greater will have to be the noise resistance qualities of the wall.

Transference of noise or sound is controlled by both sound absorption and resistance to sound transmission by a wall or partition. In broad terms, the softer and more porous the material the better its absorption performance will be, and the more dense a material the better its transmission resistance.

Masonry walls, due to their weight and density characteristics, are good for sound insulation. In most areas where masonry walls are used in high-rise buildings, such as stairwells, elevator shafts, toilets, service areas, and riser shafts, sound rating requirements are not a controlling factor in the wall design. The sound rating of a single skin brick wall is on the order of 45 dB and this satisfies most needs.

Service areas such as equipment rooms and elevator machine rooms adjacent to office space, which are enclosed by masonry walls to satisfy fire regulations, normally need some additional treatment for sound. Instead of adding additional masonry thickness or more dense wall material, it is better to treat the space that is the source, using an absorptive blanket so as to contain the noise. Thought should be given to double wall systems with sound absorbing material between them. This double skin system is most efficient in the case of nonloadbearing walls.

Noise from plant areas can be by direct transmission or by structure-borne noise. Internal acoustic treatment to the wall and ceiling surfaces in these rooms absorbs the sound so that less sound is transmitted; the noise or sound reverberation within the room is also reduced. The treatment consists of timber battening to the masonry wall surface lining, with insulating batts of rockwool or fiberglass insulation, and covering with material such as perforated metal.

Another common method, although not as effective and susceptible to damage, is

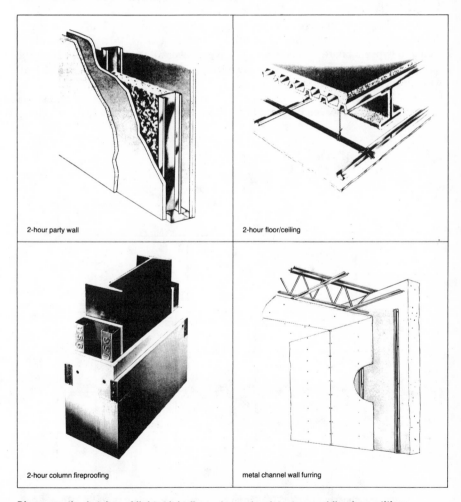

2-hour party wall

2-hour floor/ceiling

2-hour column fireproofing

metal channel wall furring

Diagrammatic sketches of lightweight fire and sound-resistant assemblies for partitions, ceilings, column fireproofing, and wall furring *(Courtesy: U.S. Gypsum Co.)*

spraying the walls with an asbestos or vermiculite plaster. In areas of constant air movement there is the likelihood of surface flaking or spalling of the fibers; a surface seal protects them, but it also reduces the absorptive qualities.

Partitions designed to allow building movement are more susceptible to noise transmission. These partition systems require a greater effort in design and detailing with regard to the amount and location of sound attenuation insulation, caulking and sealant materials, and other acoustical accessories.

The sound-rating qualities of partitions vary according to post and panel material or construction (or both), and ceiling and floor junction designs. Normal office-type partitioning has an approximate rating of 22 dB to 25 dB. Rating qualities can be raised by increasing the density of the partition by adding layers of gypsum board, and use of various dense sheet materials such as lead. In addition, the combination of dense panel material with absorptive sheeting can assist the panel sound rating. The caulking and sealing of floor, ceiling, and intersecting joints become important factors in the sound control of partitions.

It is difficult to achieve a rating greater than 35 dB to 37 dB in modular demountable partitioning without incurring exorbitant costs. Intertenancy walls of stud and gypsum board, which generally have an over-all thickness of 90 mm to 100 mm (3-1/2 in. to 4 in.), have a sound rating of approximately 27 dB to 30 dB without any special treatment.

It has been observed that noise is often transmitted from one office to another through the space between the soffit of the structural slab and the suspended ceiling,

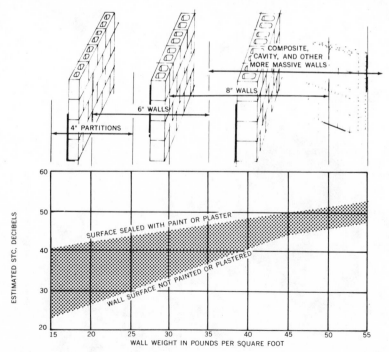

Fig. B Sound Transmission Class (STC) for concrete masonry walls (*Courtesy: National Concrete Masonry Association*)

where the partition terminates, thus creating a "sonic bridge." This occurs where the sound rating of the partition is more than twice the rating of the ceiling construction.

To solve the problem, ceiling sound baffles or a sound screen is inserted in the space above the suspended ceiling as a vertical continuation of the partition. Insertion of this sonic barrier poses, however, certain problems of construction and sound insulation at the joints with the slab, ceiling, and around air conditioning ductwork, piping, and electrical conduits.

The ceiling baffles are generally of gypsum board or sound insulation; these are dense materials which can be scribed at joints, at the junction with the ceiling structure, and at any service piping or ducting that may penetrate it. Where the space above ceilings is being used as a return air plenum, air transfer boxes, which are sound baffled, must be installed.

Sound rated walls are required in areas such as conference rooms, board rooms,

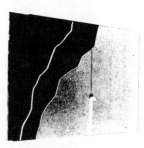

SOLID GYPSUM WALLBOARD

Gypsum wallboard face panels laminated to gypsum board core panels—nonload-bearing.

SEMI-SOLID GYPSUM WALLBOARD

Gypsum wallboard face panels laminated to narrow gypsum board ribs, single or multi-layer each side—nonload-bearing.

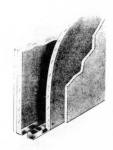

DOUBLE SOLID GYPSUM WALLBOARD

Gypsum wallboard face panels laminated to gypsum board core panels—nonload-bearing.

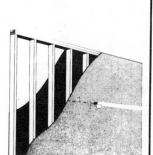

GYPSUM WALLBOARD ON WOOD STUDS

Single layer each side—load or nonload-bearing. Partitions over 8 ft. high may require fire-blocking.

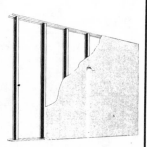

GYPSUM WALLBOARD ON METAL STUDS

Single layer attached to load or nonload-bearing metal studs.

DOUBLE LAYER GYPSUM WALLBOARD

2 ply one or both sides of wood or metal studs (metal studs shown) —load or nonload-bearing.

Typical walls and partitions: gypsum wallboard (*Courtest: Gypsum Association*)

dining areas, top executive offices, or walls surrounding noise producing spaces. Most of these rooms require containment of confidential discussions and so transmission of sound is critical. Noise producing areas may be treated by the addition of soft furnishings, carpet on the floor, or lining the walls with absorptive material like cork, felt, or acoustic tiles. Sound is thus absorbed, assisting noise control within that area, as well as reducing the degree of transmission.

3　Fire Protection and Resistance

Fire protective and fire rating requirements of high-rise buildings vary in different countries, with Australia and the United States of America possibly the most stringent. Protective devices such as sprinklers, thermal detectors, hydrants, fire telephones, pressurization systems, and evacuation systems must be incorporated into the buildings to supplement the fire resistance of the materials.

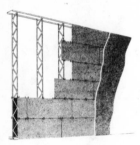

GYPSUM LATH AND PLASTER

Gypsum lath clip attached to open web steel studs—load or nonload-bearing.

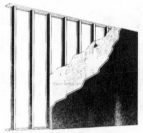

VENEER PLASTER OVER GYPSUM VENEER BASE

Single or double layer gypsum veneer base on wood or metal studs (single on metal studs shown)—load or nonload-bearing.

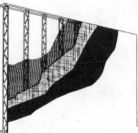

METAL LATH AND PLASTER ON WOOD OR METAL STUDS

Metal lath attached to open web steel studs shown—load or non-load-bearing.

LATH AND PLASTER ON WOOD STUDS

Gypsum plaster on metal or gypsum lath attached to wood studs —load or nonload-bearing.

SOLID GYPSUM LATH AND PLASTER WITH ½ INCH OR 1 INCH LATH

2 to 2½ inches finished thickness —nonload-bearing.

SOLID METAL LATH AND PLASTER WITH STUDS OR STUDLESS

2 to 2½ inches finished thickness —nonload-bearing.

Typical walls and partitions: lath and plaster (*Courtesy: Gypsum Association*)

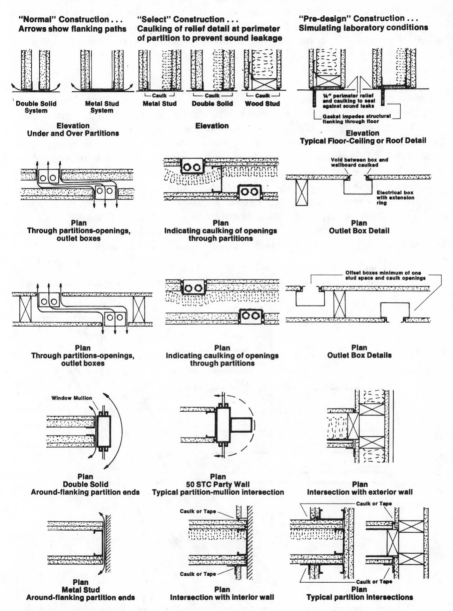

Various typical details with respect to sound insulation construction in partitions
(*Courtesy: Gypsum Association*)

Normally the structural floor construction provides the primary fire separation that is required between floors. If necessary, structural slabs can be supplemented with either spray-on fireproofing or drywall fireproofing to improve the fire rating. Masonry and gypsum board partitions normally provide the necessary fire control and protection at the shafts for stairs and air conditioning in what is commonly called the core of the building. In addition, supplementary fire protection or separation may be required by special tenant occupancy such as commercial, parking, storage, or assembly.

Regulations vary from country to country as to the actual fire ratings of walls and the manner in which shafts are treated (rated). In Australia, walls of vertical shafts in high-rise buildings, such as elevator shafts, stairwells, and service ducts must have a fire resistance of 2 hr. Walls, plant rooms or elevator machine rooms, where they are adjacent to office space, also require a 2-hr rating, whereas boiler room enclosure, and electrical transformer rooms or substations and switchrooms, are 3-hr rated. Space to be used for record storage or security rooms vary in rating requirement depending upon the client and insurance company having jurisdiction.

In the high-rise buildings of many countries any opening that connects more than two floors must be enclosed with a fire wall. Any opening connecting two floors requires protection if the total area of the interconnected space is greater than one typical floor; alternatively the space may be divided by fire rated walls.

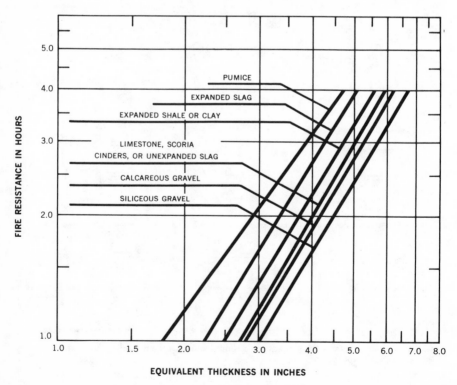

Fire resistance of concrete masonry walls as function of aggregate type and equivalent thickness of masonry (*Courtesy: National Concrete Masonry Association*)

Any doors or access openings in a fire rated wall have to be fire rated themselves to a value equivalent to that of the wall. Fire tests on doors are carried out on the assembled unit of door and frame. The actual installation in a building has to bear the manufacturer's fire test certificate on each door leaf and each frame. No modifications from the specimen tested are permitted to either the door or frame.

Only noncombustible material can be used in high-rise construction in Germany. In many other countries combustible materials are allowed, but restricted to certain areas and in limited amounts. In addition, corridor partitions have to be fire rated. Every floor and every shaft forms a separate fire zone and has to be protected. All shafts, especially stairs, have to be subdivided in sections with a maximum of four floors. In stairwells this subdivision is achieved by doors at the landings and closure of the well. This sectionalization of the shafts not only serves as fire protection, but also avoids the stack effect which disrupts the air conditioning of high-rise buildings.

Experience has shown that fire safety codes can restrict certain design selections or cause certain selections to be very expensive. For example, wood surfaces are only allowed in veneer thickness, laminated to noncombustible back-up material; and only carpets with low flame spread are allowed by high-rise building codes.

In Belgium, walls separating exits or passages from stair shafts, including the doors, require a rating of 30 minutes. Partitions separating offices, including the doors, are required to have low flame spreading surfaces.

Prefabricated products and built-in-place partitions and wall systems provide fire ratings varying from 1/2 hr to 4 hr and offer a variety of materials which include masonry, clay tile, gypsum block, drywall, and laminated gypsum plank. Prefabricated wall and partition units solve one problem which the construction industry is constantly attempting to resolve, and that is the elimination of as many "wet" trades as possible from the upper floors of tall buildings. This reduces the need to protect new construction from freezing, and it eliminates the problem of mixing wet materials on the floors.

Many paints, wall coverings, and other finishes on interior walls are manufactured from flammable and toxic materials. Recent developments in the manufacture of paints and wall coverings have resulted in materials with low flame spread and low toxic characteristics. It is most important that low flame spread/nontoxic materials be utilized for finished surfaces; the amount of flammable/toxic materials which can be installed in an area, room, or floor, should be rigidly controlled. Some building codes do not allow any flammable finish materials in public areas and restrict the use of flammable finishes to 10% of the floor area in other locations.

4 Stack Effect

Elevator shafts as well as other vertical shafts in tall buildings are susceptible to strong drafts commonly referred to as "stack action." These air currents and their associated noise—which can become quite disconcerting to the building occupants—can be controlled by minimizing the amount of air that can travel up the shafts. This can be accomplished by providing tight shaft construction, air gaskets on entrance doors, and vestibules or revolving doors in elevator lobbies.

Elevator shafts create chimney effects which disturb the heating and ventilation systems; in addition they are considered to be a fire hazard. This is the reason why the codes in Germany require the construction of elevator lobbies with vestibules which provide a smoke barrier between the shaft and the rest of the floor. The relatively low height of European tall buildings allows elevators to have a speed of not more than 3.5 m/sec to 4.5 m/sec (11.5 ft/sec to 15 ft/sec). This eliminates the need for local and shuttle elevators.

In air risers or shafts it is common to have the return air of the air-conditioning system transferred by means of a duct or shaft. With mechanical fans assisting this air flow, pressures can be exerted onto the shaft walls. These walls are usually built of masonry to comply with fire regulations.

Stairwell shafts in high-rise buildings which are required to have a fire rating and consequently are masonry enclosed, also act as air shafts. In addition to the normal stack effect created, the stair shafts are required to have mechanical air pressurization in the shaft in case of fire in the building. The purpose of the pressurization is to keep the stair shaft free of smoke. Stairs should be divided in not more than four-floor sections in order to protect against stack effect or smoke movement.

Air drafts and stack action are problems in stairwells which can be minimized by: (1) The installation of gaskets on stair doors; (2) closures to assure that doors are tightly closed; (3) vestibules to control the amount of air entering the shaft, and (4) diaphragm doors and walls at stair landings to reduce the effective height of the "stack."

5 Elevator Shafts

High-speed elevator equipment has created a new problem in shaft wall construction. In addition to fire separation, sound attenuation, and building movement, these walls must also withstand greater air pressures than are normally present in low buildings. Horizontal pressures as high as 1.2 kPa (25 psf) can be developed on the elevator shaft walls, thereby requiring masonry wall reinforcing and perimeter restraining construction to prevent damage to the shaft wall construction. Some prefabricated wall construction systems such as drywall and laminated gypsum plank construction have the capacity to span between the adjacent structural members with the additional restraint of the adjacent beams and columns, and to sustain the additional loads.

Elevator shaft enclosures are subjected to lateral pressures on the walls due to the pumping action that occurs with elevator travel. The worst condition occurs where there is a single elevator in a single shaft. In a shaft common to a number of elevators greater turbulence of air within the shaft minimizes the pressures on the walls.

As the elevator shafts themselves have to be naturally ventilated to atmosphere, strong wind drafts entering through the vent shaft can exert additional pressures on the elevator shaft. This force coupled with that of an elevator car traveling at high speeds can build up a considerable pressure. The ventilation requirement in some countries can cause problems of operation of the elevator doors in strong adverse currents in tall structures. This condition can be minimized with the use of revolving doors in vestibules in elevator lobbies.

6 Staircases

Stair construction in tall buildings is quite similar to stair construction in low buildings, except that in tall buildings there is a trend toward prefabricated stair systems such as precast concrete, metal pan, or bent plate systems. These systems have great advantages during the construction of the building with respect to both convenience and safety, by providing immediate stair construction for the building tradesmen. Stair shaft wall construction is usually masonry due to the rigorous maintenance and fire rating criteria. However, prefabricated drywall and gypsum plank systems have been developed which also satisfy these conditions.

In some countries, such as Australia, a building having fire rated enclosure walls and doors also must have fire or safety stairs. All construction within the shaft must be fireproof; a metal pan stair or bent plate stair would not be satisfactory. All finishes within the shaft have to be of a noncombustible nature, and paints must have zero flame spread rating. Buildings in the high-rise category require the stair shaft to be pressurized or ventilated to the exterior. The lower limit varies from country to country, but it is in the 50-m (165-ft) height range.

The pressure exerted upon the masonry wall by the stair pressurization, especially in very tall buildings, can be quite high. This pressure has to be withstood by the wall construction including any control joint material that has been incorporated into the stair shaft construction at the intersection of floors, columns, and beams. The pressures on the walls will vary from a maximum at the fan position location to a minimum at the furthest point from the fan. Construction of the wall must take these pressures into consideration and must be reinforced accordingly. The wall design can be adjusted according to the pressure gradients.

German fire regulations attach importance to the location of the stairway at the exterior wall because European high-rise buildings are relatively low. If the egress to a stairway is provided by an open gallery then this stairway is considered to be a "safety stairway." It is doubtful however, whether people would actually try to reach the exterior wall in case of fire. Therefore, German architects try to develop interior "safety stairways." These interior safety stairways have been pressurized or have pressurized vestibules, and the ventilation fans have been connected to emergency generators, thus avoiding smoke build-up in the stairways.

Travel distance to staircases is an important design feature in high-rise buildings, along with alternative means of escape. The distance varies from 25 m to 35 m (85 ft to 120 ft). This distance is usually increased in fully sprinklered buildings in the United States.

7   Structural/Architectural Interaction

Since all the building construction elements are designed to meet specific tasks, it is a matter of course that they should function fully to the specific imposed requirements. However, in all probability, there are qualifying conditions. For instance, there is the problem of maintaining the elastic characteristics of building elements in relation to the structural frame's displacement without lowering specified performances.

The deflection of beams or slabs—which is normally expected, and structurally acceptable—can prove troublesome to walls and partitions. (A review of the amplitude of movements actually occurring in buildings two to five years old would be of considerable value to designers.) Movement and consequent cracking may occur, especially in long continuous walls over slab and beams. Reinforcing or control jointing may be necessary in the walls and partitions. It is advantageous to allow time for satisfactory curing and settlement of the structure, and then load it by regular progressive construction of the walls, partitions, etc.

In addition to movement associated with the structure of high-rise buildings, inherent movement occurs within the masonry units themselves. The nature of the movement varies according to the type of material. The use of strong cement mortar

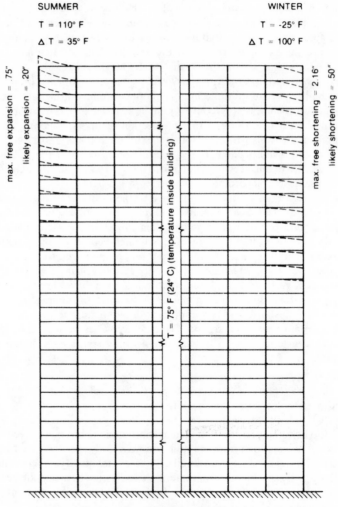

SUMMER

T = 110° F

Δ T = 35° F

WINTER

T = -25° F

Δ T = 100° F

max. free expansion = .75"

likely expansion = .20"

T = 75° F (24° C) (temperature inside building)

max. free shortening = 2.16"

likely shortening = .50"

Note: movement will be cyclic with seasons, but most severe in winter.

Section of 30-story building shows effect of differences in indoor and outdoor temperatures. Right side shows how much differential movement could be expected in top floor-slab during winter; on left, movement during summer. Numerical values assume free movement of exposed exterior column due to temperature change. Actually, free movement is restricted by bending stiffness of frame and actual movement will be considerably less (*Courtesy: Form & Function Magazine, U.S. Gypsum Co.*)

can aggravate the situation. Precautions as mentioned previously need to be taken.

The junction of partition walls with the structure or perimeter walls needs to be provided with movement or slip jointing. Plaster stop beads are installed to create a neat stop end to the plaster or any other surface finish. The beads vary in shape or form as esthetically desired.

At the junction of the head of the wall and the soffit of the slab or beam, it is advisable to provide a soft infill as a closure. The material is usually a cork or fiber board which is sealed with a sealant at the edges if exposed. Should the wall require a fire rating, the infill material must also be noncombustible, such as vermiculite or asbestos. It may or may not be topped with a sealant.

It is rare for masonry walls to stop at the underside of ceilings, as they generally extend through the ceiling to the underside of the slab above. The ceilings thus butt into the wall surface, and their treatment at this location is similar to that at any other junction of ceiling and structure.

When constructing masonry as infill units between vertical and horizontal framing it must be borne in mind that expansive movement may occur both horizontally and vertically. Full restraint of this movement must be avoided, as bowing or bulging of the wall would occur.

Should masonry infill walling be used in a reinforced concrete structure, the provision of expansion jointing is important, particularly for brick construction. Two opposing actions occur in the curing of structure and walling. Contraction and creep occur in the concrete structure, and brick growth or brick expansion in the walling.

The location of control jointing for either expansion or contraction is important. Offsets in walls can be a problem, especially if any type of restraints occur. Therefore the jointing should be located close by. Walls running continuously over slab and beam, and transverse to the beam, will need to have treatment at the beam location where no deflection occurs. At the position of large openings or dorways the wall has its weakest area. Control jointing should be located at or over the opening. This is especially true where contraction or deflection movement is to be expected in the wall.

Irrespective of the type of masonry wall, thermal variations will cause movement in the wall. In high-rise buildings which are air conditioned, interior walls are not subjected to great temperature differentials, except in special areas such as boiler room enclosures. Consequently thermal movement is generally of minor significance in interior walls.

Demountable partitioning posts and panels are usually constructed with a base jacking system between the floor runner or base channel and the underside of the panel. At the ceiling or top of the partition lateral stability is provided. This is often incorporated into the ceiling design so that physical fixing devices are not required. Provision of a groove or recess in the ceiling framing and a block or tongue in the bend of the partition is common. By expanding the jack, pressure is applied to both floor and ceiling, and the partition is stabilized.

Stability of the partition is dependent upon the design of the jacking system, the floor fixing or location, the ceiling interlocking system, and the thickness of the partition together with its associated post design. Normally it is desired to reduce the thickness of demountable partitions as much as possible, and a thickness of 35 mm to 38 mm (1-3/8 in. to 1-1/2 in.) is common.

The thinner the partition construction, the more its flexing or bowing is increased and consequently the over-all stability decreased. For the sake of stability it is advisable to provide cross walls at a maximum of 4 m (12 ft).

Modular partitioning and movable walls are ideally suited for high-rise buildings. Their dead weight is less than that of masonry, facilitating flexibility of layouts and movement of partitioning. Movement within the building structure, due to wind, thermal influences, deflection, creep and other such factors, is easily absorbed within the components of the partitioning without detrimental effect on the surface finish. However, movable partitions should be designed with a thickness of more than 80 mm (3.2 in.) if sound protection between adjacent rooms of 30 dB is required.

8 Seismic Design

Many areas of the world are subject to earthquake-induced ground motions. All parts of a structure, together with their contents, respond nearly simultaneously when subjected to seismic ground motion. When earthquake forces must be considered, their effects on all building components, including the vertical and horizontal load carrying structure, the exterior wall enclosure, interior walls and partitions, stairwells, elevator shafts, ceilings, and mechanical and electrical equipment should be evaluated. In evaluating these effects it must be remembered that earthquake motions are random and occur both horizontally and vertically. (The subject of earthquake loading and response is dealt with in Chapter CL-2.)

Seismic design codes presently apply to the main structure, and are generally based on the concept of little or no damage for minor earthquakes and to considerable damage (without collapse) for major earthquakes. Little attention, however, is paid to nonstructural items. Whether or not a building is designed to sustain minimum damage when subjected to severe earthquake motions is largely a matter of economics. This fact should be discussed with the building owner during the early planning stages so as to avoid possible serious misunderstanding should a major earthquake occur after the building is completed. In areas subject to the possibility of major earthquakes, it may not be economically feasible to design for no damage. However, damage to both structural and nonstructural elements can be minimized by careful consideration of the nature of seismic motions and the calculated displacements. It should be noted that the design of the lateral load resisting structural system may be controlled by the necessity to keep wind drift at tolerable levels.

Seismic ground motions induce building inertial forces that produce translational and torsional interstory displacements or drift. Each floor moves differentially with respect to those above and below it. Thus if damage is to be minimized, building elements that extend from floor to floor must be designed to accommodate such differential movements. The plan arrangement and the vertical distribution of lateral force resisting structural elements are important factors affecting the seismic response of a building. The response of regular symmetrical structures can be predicted with more confidence than that of irregularly-shaped buildings. Irregularities tend to increase torsional (twisting) motions, and interstory displacements will vary with horizontal location on any given floor. Such variable displacements tend to increase the likelihood of damage to nonstructural elements as well as to the structure. Such structures can be designed to minimize damage, but at greater cost than for more symmetrical buildings.

One of the basic functions of the interior, nonbearing partition is to define interior space. It is also used as an acoustical or fire barrier, or both. In addition, where the nonbearing partition extends from slab to slab, as in a core wall or a horizontal separation, it must also contend with the stress that accompanies normal building motion occasioned by thermal expansion and contraction or wind motion. Conceptually, this is normally compensated for by a resilient pad (such as vinyl or neoprene) at the base track and head channel. When a structure is located in a seismic zone, there is added the third dimension of the seismic stress, which can be vertical or horizontal or a combination of the two.

The response of a building to earthquake motion is affected by the stiffness and mass distribution of the load-carrying structure together with the stiffness and masses of the nonstructural exterior and interior walls, including stairwells and elevator shafts. Often the stiffness of nonstructural elements is not considered by the structural engineer when determining the building seismic response.

The stiffness of nonstructural elements can be used to advantage. Such elements could be designed to resist building movements caused by wind and moderate earthquake with little or no damage. (Refer to Chapters SB-5 and CB-24.) In severe earthquakes these elements would be damaged but would help the building absorb the energy from the earthquake.

When an interior partition is subjected to vertical seismic stresses and there is no provision in the partition system for vertical motion, partition failure or buckling (or both) may occur in the horizontal plane, with cracks or buckling normally parallel to the floor. This may be prevented by providing a slip joint at the head connection which will allow for about 25 mm to 35 mm (1 in. to 1-3/8 in.) vertical movement.

When the interior partition is subjected to horizontal seismic motion and there is no provision in the partition system for such horizontal motion, partition failure or buckling, or both, will normally occur in a vertical plane or on a diagonal, depending on the type of construction. This may be avoided by providing a slip joint where the partition abuts the exterior wall, at the intersection of the interior core wall, or where it joins another partition. Again, allowance for about 25 mm to 35 mm (1 in. to 1-3/8 in.) of movement is desirable.

Where ducts of any type penetrate a full-height partition, the ducts should not be tied to the partition for support. Support should be provided on either side of the partition from the building structure above. If the opening is required to be sealed because of fire resistance or acoustics, the sealant should be of a resilient noncombustible type to permit motion of the duct without affecting the partition or duct. It is important for both seismic and acoustic considerations that the duct be independently supported by hangers and horizontal restraints from the building structure.

Gypsum board apparently shows less tendency to structural damage under seismic conditions than does plaster. Apparently, this is due to the more brittle nature of plaster as opposed to the usual stress skin design of typical drywall construction.

Stairways and elevators must be designed to remain functional during and after an earthquake. Stairs and doors into stairways and elevators must be designed to permit interstory movements. If the doors will not open after an earthquake, the stairway or elevator is useless. In most buildings, because of fire exit requirements, the walls enclosing elevators and stairways are made of concrete, masonry, or other rigid materials. Such walls, unless they are designed as part of the lateral force resisting system, should not be secured to the main structure without provisions to allow building movement.

As noted previously, earthquake motions can induce inertial forces in all elements of a building, including its contents. Therefore tall bookcases, storage racks, and files should be designed and attached in a way not to collapse or topple due to seismic forces. Severe injuries have been caused by such items overturning and falling on building occupants. These items can be designed to avoid overturning by having adequate anchorage to the supporting floor or by being secured to adjacent structure. Consideration should also be given to anchoring or restraining other heavy furnishings. Heavy art objects should be restrained and should not be set on high supports where they could fall and cause injuries.

Seismic Considerations for Nonstructural Building Elements.   The design of all elements of a building, both structural and nonstructural, acted on by seismic induced forces, requires a prediction of the behavior of the total system as well as that of each element. The object of design is to prevent loss of life and to minimize damage to the structure and its contents.

Earthquake loading and the response of tall buildings are considered in Chapter CL-2. The effect on exterior cladding and criteria for its design and attachment to the primary structure are discussed in Chapter SC-5, Section 5.15.

Determination of the behavior under seismic excitation of nonstructural elements such as partitions, walls, ceilings, mechanical elements, and piping depends upon a knowledge of the magnitude of movement of the primary structure and the force resulting from acceleration. A wall or partition, for example, could be crushed by in-plane distortion of a structural frame unless provision was made for sliding connections at certain boundaries. Determination of story drift caused by wind or seismic forces is necessary to develop criteria for joint design.

Many factors are involved in predicting the seismic force to be used in the design and attachment of elements to structures. Among them are:

1. Location in an area of rated seismicity (related to earthquake risk).

2. Importance to the functioning of essential facility, such as a hospital.

3. Dynamic response of the element (related to the period of vibration).

4. Resonance between structure and site, or soil-structure interaction.

5. Weight of the element.

Based on analysis and observation of damage following earthquakes, numerical factors can be developed and assigned as an aid in determining the seismic force to be used in the design of nonstructural elements under various conditions of use and support. Such factors have been proposed, for example, by the Seismology Committee of the Structural Engineers Association of California (SEAOC,1974). They recommend that the force be computed as a combination of factors times the weight of the element, as follows:

1. A factor of 1.0 is used for an area of "high seismicity" with reduced values for areas located in zones of lower seismic risk.

2. A factor of 1.5 is recommended for facilities deemed essential to the public welfare during postearthquake operations, and a minimum of 1.0 for other elements.

3. Factors related to dynamic response depend upon the nature of support provided to the element and whether the element is connected to or part of a building. These factors vary from 1.00 for cantilever parapet walls and ornamentations or appendages, to 0.20 for walls and partitions, towers and tanks plus contents, chimneys, and equipment and machinery not considered essential, to 0.12 for units resting on the ground and for floors and roofs acting as diaphragms.

4. For soil-structure interaction the factor is estimated to be between 1.0 and 1.5 depending on the ratio of the period of vibration of the structure to the characteristic site period, the lowest value when the ratio is very low or very high, and the highest value when the ratio approaches unity.

The product of factors (1), (2), and (3) should not be less than 0.50 for equipment required to remain in place and functional in essential facilities.

Factors such as those listed are estimates based on the best available information and will change with increased knowledge and experience. It should be emphasized that better performance is not necessarily a function of higher design force. Those responsible must design, specify, and detail elements and connections that can accommodate seismic demands. Earthquake engineering requires appreciation and understanding of the uncertainties of building codes, design criteria, and materials.

6.2 CEILINGS

The function of a ceiling is to provide an esthetically pleasant finish to the underside of a structural floor. It may or may not conceal services that occur under that floor. In satisfying the esthetic requirements ceilings can perform many other functions. They can:—

1. Contribute to the reduction of sound transmission between floors.

2. Contribute to the reduction of thermal differential between floors.

3. Provide an acoustic absorption surface.

4. Provide space that may be used for transference of air.

5. Provide space to install light fixtures, ducts, piping, and other mechanical services.

6. Provide a fire protective barrier.

7. Provide a top fixing medium for partitioning.

Ceilings are of two principal types:—

1. Directly fixed ceilings. This type of ceiling is generally associated with low-cost investment buildings. It may consist of a spray finish applied directly onto the soffit of the structure and possibly over ducting or other service piping that may occur. Directly fixed ceilings can also be constructed of solid sheet or in tile form. The application would be directly onto the fixing battens or furring channels fastened to the soffit of the floor structure

above. In these cases the ceiling would have to box around any service piping or ducting distribution.

2. Suspended ceilings. This type of ceiling is by far the most common in high-rise buildings, and can be constructed in solid or tile form. The suspended ceiling conceals the underside of the floor structure and services occurring under that floor.

3. Solid ceilings are primarily used in special areas, both public and storage areas. Fire protective spaces and security rooms invariably are finished with a solid ceiling.

4. Tiled ceilings, whether modular or nonmodular, are used in office areas as the principal ceiling medium in high-rise buildings.

1 Materials and Details

Ceiling and floor finish construction in tall buildings is quite similar to that utilized in low buildings. Plaster is generally used in public areas, whereas acoustical tile ceilings are used in office areas. It is wise, however, to choose the more resilient and flexible floor and ceiling systems for tall buildings, or to isolate the more rigid floor and ceiling systems from slabs, walls, and columns to prevent damage to these elements due to building movement.

Sprayed ceilings are mainly based on gypsum, vermiculite, or similar products. The surface finish is textured and, depending upon the area occupancy, it may be required to have a surface seal to prevent displacement of fibers or particles of the spray. Sprayed finishes, by both the nature of surface finish and basic material composition, have reasonable sound absorption properties.

Solid ceilings have gypsum board or fibrous plaster as their main material in

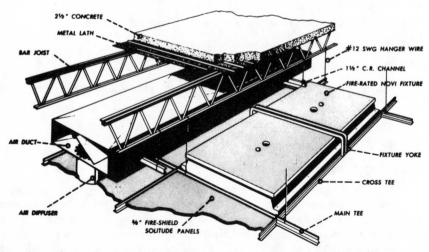

Details of typical floor with open-web joint, duct, ceiling, and fixtures (*Courtesy: Gold Bond Building Products, Division of National Gypsum Company*)

high-rise use, but timber linings or proprietary type metal ceilings are also used. This type of ceiling, used in special areas, normally has a much lower acoustic and sound absorptive quality than spray or tile ceilings.

Tiled ceilings, both modular and nonmodular, have a large and varied range of materials from which to make a choice. Those most commonly used, however, are mineral fiber, fibrous acoustic plaster, metal pan, cane fiber, or glass fiber tiles.

Modular suspended ceilings can be designed with either concealed or exposed grids, in either one or two directions. The ceilings tiles are either lay-in or infill panels, depending upon the design of the grid.

Ceiling grid material normally consists of galvanized steel, roll formed, or extruded aluminum. The exposed portions of the grid work are invariably extruded, especially for ceilings designed for infill tile panels. Finer tolerances can be achieved by the use of extrusions rather than roll-formed sections. Proprietary designed suspension systems with prepunched fixing locations and devices can maintain tight and consistent tolerances over large areas.

The module size is determined by a combination of many factors. Dimensional size of the building structure; extent of the area; proposed individual office size and variety of sizes; materials associated with the ceilings; and partitioning of floor covering can all affect the module size.

Light fittings have been an important factor in module size selection, and most high-rise buildings have a module in the range of 1230 mm to 1270 mm (4 ft 1/2 in. to 4 ft 2 in.). The standard tube size that has been available for a nominal 1220-mm (4-ft) light fitting, coupled with a requirement of recessed fittings being capable of placement end to end for more than two fittings have led to the minimum practical module dimension of 1230 mm (4 ft. 1/2 in.).

The module size has also been influenced by the partition panel unit, which is affected by elevator door dimensions and elevator car size. It is necessary for partitioning panels to be transported by the elevator to their respective floors, especially after initial completion of the building.

In many cases where the nominal 1220-mm (4-ft) module has been selected, the ceiling framing has been designed with a submodule or half-module unit, thus enabling partitioning to be located on a nominal 610-mm (2-ft) spacing. This system provides greater flexibility of office dimension in layouts together with greater ease of handling the modular units. Some limitations of layout may occur in the system at perimeter windows if they are on the base 1220-mm (4-ft) module spacing, and if partitions are required to terminate at the window mullion.

Ceilings with exposed grids, or fully concealed, may be designed to have tile panels, either lay-in or infill, which are easily removable. Ceilings with fully concealed grids are more limited in access. Access is desirable to any area of the ceiling for service work, whether maintenance or that necessitated by modification to partitioning layouts. The more flexibly a ceiling is designed, the more likely is the need for ready access to gain the full benefits.

Light fittings designed to coordinate with the ceiling tile unit are designed to alternate in any position with the tile. Sufficient length of flexible cable with plug-in type connection is allowed on each fitting so as to give the necessary range of movement. This system allows for ready removal or addition of a light fitting.

Many installations incorporate the use of light/air fittings which have air supply boots or saddles attached to the light fitting. Flexible ducting is connected to the boot. Return air to the ceiling plenum may also be gained via the light fitting. In this manner even distribution of supply and return air is achieved across open floor areas without the introduction of additional components to the ceiling system. Return air via light fittings is also a very functional design due to localized heat at the light source.

Where separate air outlet units or thermostats are utilized, connection to main duct runs is made by use of flexible ducts, allowing for ease of relocation in case of office layout alterations.

Special decorative ceilings in foyers, elevator lobbies, and other such specialized areas range extensively in material selection and type. The ceilings may be fully luminous or integrated with individual light fittings, either recessed or surface mounted, standard or special.

For fully luminous ceilings, acrylic or glass diffusers or one of the many proprietary metal crated diffusers are most commonly used. In these installations sufficient space is necessary between the light source and the ceiling space to provide a visual cut-off to the light source and to any service piping or ducting. Ideally, these should be located above the plane of the light source, so that a shadow effect will not be created.

Where acrylic is utilized, care must be taken in the framing and support design to allow sufficient room for the expansion and contraction movement of the material.

Materials used for integrated ceilings will greatly depend upon the design of the ceiling and the effect that is required by the designer. For a ceiling receiving a paint finish and in some molded form, fibrous plaster is a suitable material. It can be molded to any shape, prefabricated and flush jointed on site.

2 Acoustics

Most materials utilized in modular or tiled ceilings have some acoustical or sound absorption qualities. The materials are of perforated surface finish in some form, allowing sound penetration and absorption into the body of the tile. Materials such as plaster or metal tiles are perforated on the surface and allow sound to be absorbed into a backing batt of insulating or absorbing material. The normal suspended ceiling is installed as a unit not so much to prevent sound transmission as to provide an absorptive surface.

In open planning areas, commonly known as landscaped offices, acoustic absorption of sound is critical in order to provide the necessary privacy of conversation between working areas and individual desks. In addition to sound absorbing baffles, planting, and soft furnishings, "white" sound or background noise in the form of air noise or music can be deliberately introduced.

Solid ceilings are naturally far less absorptive than tiling, but have better sound transmission qualities. By careful design of ceilings in conjunction with remaining areas of the room, sound control can be achieved, utilizing hard reflective surfaces and soft surfaced materials for absorption. Ceilings in special areas are used as a medium to reflect or bounce sound. Solid ceilings of the correct form and angle are necessary and care must be taken to prevent reverberation within the space. Auditoriums, theaters, and lecture rooms are common areas associated with high-rise buildings where this application is utilized.

Above and below plant or machine rooms, it may be necessary to install an acoustical or sound barrier ceiling to prevent noise transmission to adjacent floors. This ceiling requires a dense or heavy ceiling material to prevent penetration of sound as well as an isolated suspension system to prevent direct transfer of sound or vibration noises. Ceiling materials using multiple layers of gypsum board with lapped joints or woodtex board (hereclith) are suitable for such installations. Should the panels be installed as lay-in panels over suspension grid work, the joints must be mastic sealed.

The ceiling grid work, concealed or exposed, is suspended from the floor above by rubber or spring mountings that are impact absorbing and nontransmitting. The junction of the ceiling barrier and either the external walls of the building or interior core walls or columns also must have an isolated joint. Foam rubber jointing strips are satisfactory for this purpose. Where the ceiling is placed below a plant room and within office space, it is ideal to have the sound ceiling above all services that occur in the ceiling space of that floor. The service piping and ducting should also be suspended on isolators or from the isolated acoustic ceiling.

3 Fire Resistance

Most of the acoustical type ceiling materials are noncombustible and have a fire rating in the order of one-half hour. When used in exposed grid installations, the ratings can be reduced to zero due to the metal exposure. Where fire rated ceilings are required, in escape corridors, fire rated security rooms, or telephone or electrical switchrooms, the rating is normally 1 hr. This requirement is satisfied by the use of gypsum board, two layers of 15-mm (5/8-in.) thickness, with lapped joints.

Structural steel frames with metal decking topped with concrete, which normally would have to be fire spray coated in order to achieve the necessary fire ratings, can have the spray eliminated if an appropriate fire rated ceiling is installed. Tiled fire rated ceilings, Fire Guard tile units and Fire Guard Grid Systems, when used in conjunction with floor systems, can receive a rating for the combination and thereby eliminate the fire spray. Where recessed light fittings occur the Fire Guard ceiling has to be carried over the fitting to fully enclose the recess. Some regulations require that the space between floor slab soffit and the suspended ceiling be compartmentized by divisional vertical baffles.

4 Structural/Architectural Interaction

Modular ceilings consisting of many small component parts not rigidly and continuously connected to each other, provide the ideal horizontal skin capable of accepting movement associated with high-rise buildings. The perimeter of the main body of the ceiling is not rigidly fixed to the exterior wall cladding. At window areas the ceiling is generally trimmed to the curtain wall or window unit by an infill member or pelmet unit which has a moving joint connection. This member caters for general building tolerances and movement which occur between the structure, the exterior wall, and the interior linings. It also acts as a medium for fixing the curtain or blind furnishings.

At the junction of ceilings and solid walls, whether exterior or interior, wall angles or shadow mold units are provided with make-up tiles or infill members. Again, the infill satisfies the variances caused by tolerances and provides space for building movements.

The ceiling grid components, which are usually clipped together regardless of whether they are the main support members or exposed or concealed secondary runners, allow for any structural movements of the building. The grid as a whole is suspended from the floor structure above, by either hanging rods or wires which are flexible and allow for movement differential between the ceiling and structure. The ceiling framing, being divorced from rigid fixing to the structure, is also used as the head stabilizing medium for movable partitioning in the building. The partitioning is also a component not rigidly fixed to the structure.

Where solid ceilings occur, over large areas or in individual rooms, plaster shop beading or shadow mold trim of some nature is provided at the perimeter. The open joint of such trim with the wall surface provides the disguise for building movement.

5 Seismic Design

Until quite recently little attention was given to the seismic design of ceilings. During two California earthquakes, Santa Rosa in 1968 and San Fernando in 1971, considerable ceiling damage occurred and injuries resulted from ceiling panels falling on people. Ceilings should be designed so that panels will not fall out in case of severe horizontal and vertical movements.

The acoustic tile ceiling normally functions in a twofold capacity. Its primary concern is to provide a light reflective surface to assist in maintaining light levels in the area defined by the ceiling. The secondary function is as an acoustical barrier to reduce sound transmission within the area.

In seismic conditions, however, the ceiling may become potentially lethal. Individual tiles or plaster may jar loose from the supports and fall. Ceiling-supported light fixtures may loosen and drop out with the possibility of serious injury or death to persons below. Therefore, alternatives to the standard ceiling construction procedures should be considered.

The horizontal components of seismic forces to which a ceiling may be subjected can be compensated for in several ways. A dimensional allowance should be made at the ceiling perimeter for this motion, so as to minimize damage to the ceiling where it abuts the walls. Additionally, the ceiling suspension system should be tied at columns and other structural elements in order to minimize ceiling motion in relation to the structural frame. By tying the ceiling system to the structure horizontally, provision is made to help prevent tiles from dropping out. There may be some slight damage to the ceiling at the walls or structural elements, but this, when compared to the over-all possibility of damage, is minimal in relation to the entire ceiling system. The vertical suspension system for the ceiling should be adequate to minimize vertical motion. In addition, any light fixtures which may be dependent upon the ceiling system for support should be securely tied to the ceiling grid members. If this is not possible, the light fixtures should be supported independently from the building structure above. Diffuser grilles, if required for the air supply system, should also be hung independently to minimize damage.

In any area where seismic conditions prevail, a lay-in T-bar system for the ceiling construction should be avoided if at all possible, as this system can permit tiles or lighting fixtures, or both, to loosen and drop out and possibly injure tenants or equipment in the structure. In both the 1964 Alaska earthquake and the 1971 Sylmar earthquake, the economical (and therefore more popular) exposed T-grid suspended ceilings suffered the greatest damage. Evidently, the differential movement between the partitions and the suspended ceilings damaged the suspension systems, and as the earthquake progressed, the ceilings started to sway and were battered against the surrounding partitions. This type of action was aggravated when the ceilings also supported lighting fixtures, and in many instances, the suspension systems were so badly damaged that the lighting fixtures fell out of the ceiling.

The need for independent support and lateral bracing of the lighting fixtures mounted in, or attached to, suspended ceilings requires further study. The City of Los Angeles has adopted an ordinance which stipulates minimum requirements for ceiling suspension systems supporting acoustical tile ceilings and lighting fixtures. It requires that ceiling suspension systems be designed to support a minimum load of 119.7 Pa (2-1/2 psf) of ceiling area, except that if the suspension system also supports lighting fixtures, this requirement is increased to 191.5 Pa (4 psf). It also stipulates that the lighting fixtures shall not exceed 50% of the ceiling area and that they be fastened to the web of the load-carrying member. It does not, however, require independent support of the lighting fixtures or any lateral bracing.

Damage to ceilings can also occur where sprinkler heads project below the ceiling tiles. One possible way to minimize this problem is to mount the heads with a swivel joint connection so the pipe may move with the ceiling.

6.3 CONDENSED REFERENCES/BIBLIOGRAPHY

The following is a condensed bibliography for this chapter. Not only does it include all articles referred to or cited in the text, but it also contains bibliography for further reading. The full citations will be found at the end of the Volume. What is given here should be sufficient information to lead the reader to the correct article: the author, date, and title. In case of multiple authors, only the first named is listed.

Ayres 1973, *Nonstructural Damage to Buildings*
Berry 1973, *Architectural Seismic Detailing*
Blume 1968, *Dynamic Characteristics of Multi-Story Buildings*
Blume 1972, *Buildings Analyzed by John A. Blume and Associates*
Botsai 1973, *Designing Against Infiltration*

Calzon 1973, *Approximate Structural Analysis of High-Rise Buildings*
Cassinello 1973, *Walls in Tall Buildings*
Devaty 1973, *Fireproof Floors with Metal Panels*
Essunger 1973, *Summary Report*
Fiorato 1970, *An Investigation of the Interaction of Reinforced Concrete Frames*

Kajfasz 1973, *Interaction Approach in Poland*
Kavanagh 1971, *Architectural Structural Interaction*
Khan 1968a, *Effects of Column Exposure in Tall Structures*
Khan 1968b, *Effect of Column Temperature, Creep, and Shrinkage*
Khan 1970, *Temperature Effects in Tall Steel Framed Buildings, Part 3*

Lenke 1971, *Architectural-Structural Interaction*
Lenke 1973, *Theme Report*
Matsushita 1973, *High-Rise Building Construction Design in Japan and Asia*
McCue 1976, *The Interaction of Building Components During Earthquakes*
McGuire 1975, *Simple Analysis of Smoke-Flow Problems in High Buildings*

Newby 1973, *Stiffness Related To Nonstructural Elements*
Opatril 1973, *Architectural Structures in Tall Buildings*
Pellegrini 1973, *Construction in South America*
Polak 1973, *Architectural Elements in European Practice*
Rafeiner 1973, *Architectural Criteria of Tall Buildings in Germany and Europe*

Rafeiner 1975, *The Development of the Structure of Tall Buildings from Single Exploitation*
Rousseau 1973, *Evolution of Conception of Curtain Walls in Relation with Flexibility*
SEAOC 1974, *Recommended Lateral Force Requirements and Commentary*
Sander 1973, *A FORTRAN IV Program to Simulate air Movement in Multi-Storey Buildings*
Sharpe 1973, *Seismic Design of Nonstructural Elements*

Sorensen 1965, *Cracking in Brick and Block Masonry*
Tamura 1969, *Computer Analysis of Smoke Movement in Tall Buildings*
Tamura 1971, *Smoke Movement in High-Rise Buildings*

Tall Building
Systems and Concepts

Chapter SC-7

Foundation Systems

Prepared by Committe 11 (Foundation Systems) of the Council on Tall Buildings and Urban Habitat as part of the Monograph on the Planning and Design of Tall Buildings

William F. Swiger   Chairman
Edward De Beer   Vice-Chairman
John T. Christian   Editor

AUTHOR ACKNOWLEDGMENT

Special acknowledgment is due those individuals whose contibutions and papers formed the substantial first drafts of the various sections of this chapter. First are the state-of-art reporters from the 1972 International Conference whose material was published in the Lehigh Proceedings. For the indicated sections, these individuals are:

> W. F. Swiger, Section 7.1
> L. Zeevaert, Section 7.3
> S. V. DeSimone, Section 7.4
> E. Horvat, Section 7.5
> C. van der Veen, Section 7.5
> G. M. Cornfield (deceased), Section 7.6
> B. H. Fellenius, Section 7.6
> J. T. Christian, Section 7.7

In addition to this, other sections were based on special contributions prepared by W. F. Swiger (Sections 7.2 and 7.8), P. F. Rocha, and W. Krol (deceased). J. A. Focht, Jr., E. De Beer, B. C. Gerwick, Jr., L. Belloni, M. B. Jamiolkowski, R. Ciesielski, and J. Kawecki prepared discussions and summaries of the state-of-the-art reports for the 1972 International Conference, and these have been incorporated throughout the chapter.

CONTRIBUTORS

The following is a complete list of those who have submitted written material for possible use in the chapter, whether or not that material was used in the final version. The Committee Chairman and Editor were given quite complete latitude. Frequently length limitations precluded the inclusion of much valuable material. The Bibliography contains all contributions. The contributors are: L. Belloni, J. T. Christian, R. Ciesielski, R. W. Cooke, G. M. Cornfield, E. De Beer, M. Delgado-Vargas, S. V. DeSimone, T. D. Dismuke, H. Y. Fang, B. H. Fellenius, J. A. Focht, Jr., B. C. Gerwick, Jr., E. Horvat, M. B. Jamiolkowski, J. Kawecki, C. F. Kee, W. Krol, S. Nikai, H. Przybyla, P. F. Rocha, W. F. Swiger, T. Tassios, C. van der Veen,L. Zeevaert.

COMMITTEE MEMBERS

Z. Bazant, L. Belloni, W. E. Blessey, J. T. Christian, R. Ciesielski, R. D. Darragh, K. R. Datye, E. De Beer, S. V. DeSimone, M. Delgado-Vargas, T. D. Dismuke, A. H. El-Ramli, S. H. K. Eusufzai, H. Y. Fang, B. H. Fellenius, J. A. Focht, Jr., B. C. Gerwick, Jr., P. M. Gery, P. Habib, E. Horvat, M. B. Jamiolkowski, R. Jelinek, K. Joustra, J. Kawecki, A. Kezd, W. Krol, A. C. Liebenberg, R. Lundgren, B. Mazurkiewicz, D. McKinley, D. Mohan, Y. Ohsaki, Y. Otsuki, H. B. Poorooshasb, H. Przybyla, D. Resendiz, P. F. Rocha, W. L. Shannon, W. F. Swiger, T. Tassios, C. van der Veen, P. C. Varghese, R. V. Whitman, T. H. Wu, L. Zeevaert.

SC-7 Foundation Systems

7.1 INTRODUCTION

Tall buildings, because of their height, stiffness, and usually urban location, encounter foundation problems requiring special consideration. Column loads tend to be very heavy. Most tall buildings have multiple, deep basements which usually are extended to the lot lines even though the superstructure may be set back. Adjoining areas are usually occupied by other structures or facilities. Streets are busy and underlain by a maze of sewers, water mains, electrical conduits, and subways. Lateral wind loads which must be delivered to the soil are large.

Where rock or strong, stable soils such as compact glacial tills are encountered at a reasonable depth, as in Chicago and New York, foundations may be carried down to these stable materials. This may be done by utilizing deep basements, caissons, or piles to carry the column loads down through poor soils to the competent materials. Such foundations provide good flexibility and freedom in architectural layout and structural systems, since large variations in column loadings and spacing can be accommodated with negligible differential settlements.

There are many cities of the world, however, where such strong, stable materials are not so readily encountered; for example, Salt Lake City, Mexico City, and Brussels. In such areas of indifferent soils, loadings of foundation elements must be limited to prevent shearing failures and excessive differential settlement. The over-all added load imposed by the structure must also be controlled to limit settlements to acceptable amounts. Usually, this is done by excavating a weight of soil equal to a significant portion of the gross weight of the structure. This is termed a compensated foundation. The allowable amount of this net added load is dependent upon the physical characteristics of the soil and its previous stress history. Where conditions are especially adverse, a weight of soil equal to the weight of the building may be excavated. In some cases, preloading may prove advantageous to reduce compensatory excavation.

The practicality and cost of compensated foundations are significantly affected by structural arrangements such as column loads and spacing and variations in structural loads over the plan area of the building. Furthermore, the soil supporting

259

these foundations will rebound during the excavation phase and then recompress under the load of the structure. Deflection or settlement at the surface of an elastic continuum is a function of the variation in moduli with depth and of the cumulative effects of all loads imposed. Settlement of a perfectly flexible uniform load placed on soil will in general be nonuniform. Further, settlements will occur as an immediate elastic response followed in most soils by time-dependent additional settlement. If the deflections (settlements) of the soil, from a given system of loads imposed upon it, are incompatible with the structural deflections used in the analysis, there will be a redistribution of stresses in the structure and, therefore, of contact pressures between soil and structure. Consequently, contact pressures at the base of foundations of relatively stiff structures such as a tall building will be nonuniform and may vary with time. These conditions must be recognized and considered in design if serious overloading of some of the columns is to be avoided.

Construction of foundations may affect adjoining structures or facilities in many ways. These effects are especially troublesome where soft, weak soils are present and occur whether the building is founded on the soil or on piles or caissons carried to competent materials. Such effects may exist only during the construction phase, such as movements from yield of sheeting or soil displacements during pile driving, or they may be of long duration, such as settlement of nearby structures from the weight of the new building.

Wind loads on tall structures both during construction and in service must ultimately be distributed to and resisted by the soils of the foundation. As structures are built higher, greater attention must be paid to the deformation which will occur under these wind loads to assure compatible performance of various elements of the structure and to limit deformation to acceptable amounts.

The intent of this chapter is to discuss, in general terms and basic approach, several foundation systems and to present recent developments and thinking to be used as a guide for those engaged in planning and design of tall buildings.

Decisions and design in these areas must be based on a sound understanding of the foundation conditions. This should include a detailed study of subsurface stratification, the pertinent physical properties of each stratum, ground-water levels in each aquifer, general site conditions, and as complete information as possible regarding structures or other facilities which might be affected by the proposed construction. These investigations should be performed by competent and experienced specialists. However, guidance regarding the general scope and objectives of such investigations can be obtained from ASCE Manual 56 (1976).

Adequate time must be allowed for these studies. They must be initiated early enough so that their findings can guide initial layouts and planning, and there must be close cooperation between foundation studies and planning and structural engineering if economy is to be achieved. This is especially necessary for soil supported structures. Soil-structure interaction can materially affect column loadings. Excessively heavy loadings, large or erratic column spacings, or variations in weight of the structure in plan may significantly increase costs where compensated foundations are planned or may even preclude using this technique. Particularly adverse foundation conditions may limit depths of excavation or dictate special procedures to minimize hazards to nearby structures. Avoiding a problem is usually cheaper than designing against it.

Thus far attention has been directed toward investigations and studies of the planning and design phase. Foundation engineering, however, encounters unique problems which are quite different from problems of other engineering disciplines involved in the design and construction of structures. Physical properties of the soil or rock, which must ultimately support the structure, cannot be specified. Rather the physical arrangement of the soils and pertinent characteristics must be determined by investigations; however, there rarely can be complete assurance that all significant geologic conditions have been considered. Furthermore, soil properties may be significantly affected by construction procedures and these effects are usually not known during design.

Investigations and studies of foundation conditions cannot terminate with completion of design drawings and specifications. Foundation studies should continue throughout the construction period to:

1. Verify that actual foundation conditions encountered are in accordance with those anticipated, or that necessary modifications are made to meet actual conditions.

2. Control construction procedures so that nearby structures are not damaged nor soil properties adversely affected.

3. Assure proper quality of workmanship and execution of the work to meet the assumptions and intent of the design.

The vagaries of deposition of soil are so unpredictable and physical properties so variable that the possibility of significant deviations from anticipated conditions should always be anticipated. The construction organization should be thoroughly advised of the anticipated conditions and design concepts so that it may readily recognize deviations. Lines of communication between field and designers should be established. Provisions should be included in specifications and contract documents to permit necessary modifications to meet actual conditions.

Construction procedures must be selected that will minimize the hazard of damaging adjoining structures or facilities. Physical conditions of such structures should be determined before starting work and means of monitoring their behavior established. Methods of excavating, dewatering, sheeting and shoring, and protection of surfaces must assure that foundation soils will not be adversely affected. For example, inadequate or improper dewatering can disturb the soils underlying a foundation so seriously as to preclude founding on such soil.

Foundations must be properly constructed at required grades, locations, and sizes of foundation. Proper materials must be used. Surfaces must be properly cleaned and prepared and foundation elements must be protected from disturbance by weather or other construction activities after their completion.

A good foundation will deliver the load of the structure to the underlying soil or rock safely and without excessive settlements. It must be constructed without adversely affecting adjoining structures or the materials upon which it is founded. Thorough foundation investigations undertaken early as well as close cooperation between foundation engineer, planner and structural engineer, and the construction organization are necessary if economical and satisfactory designs are to be developed and built.

7.2 SUBSURFACE INVESTIGATIONS

Investigations of the subsurface conditions of the site and adjoining area are necessary to: (1) Furnish data on which to evaluate suitable methods and comparative costs of foundations for the structure; (2) select the appropriate foundation; (3) furnish design parameters for the various structural elements of the foundation; (4) establish procedures for supporting walls of excavations and control ground water during and after construction; (5) determine whether there are any unusual hazards, as for example slide potential or cavernous conditions, and if so determine possible corrective measures; (6) evaluate effects of the structure on adjoining structures and facilities, both during construction and during service; and (7) if necessary, monitor behavior both during and following construction. To accomplish this, the stratification of the various soil members, and frequently rock, which underlies the site and surrounding area should be established to the degree practical. Also, pertinent physical properties should be determined for each soil type, such as shear strength, load deformation characteristics, and permeability, and ground-water levels and variation over extended periods for each aquifer (if more than one is present). Information should be collected on the locations, foundations, and physical conditions of nearby structures, roads, underground piping, transit systems, and other facilities that could be affected by the proposed construction.

The planning of such studies, direction and supervision of field work, and testing of soils or other physical tests, should be done by competent experts thoroughly trained academically and experienced in foundation investigation and design. The extent and character of such investigations will be determined by the depth and physical properties of the soils of the area, the type and possible defects such as deep weathering or solution effects in the underlying rock, topography of the site, earthquake hazards, plan and character of the proposed structure, its sensitivity to differential settlement, the loads it will impose and their distribution, and the proximity, foundations, physical condition, and performance record of nearby structures and other facilities.

Borings are the most commonly used means of determining the stratification of soils underlying a site. These may be supplemented by test pits and by on-site testing such as pile load tests or pumping tests. In making an exploratory boring, a hole is drilled and samples of soil recovered from the soil beneath the bottom of the boring as it is advanced. With careful workmanship and suitably designed thin wall samplers, samples of soil may be taken sufficiently undisturbed to permit quantitative testing of shear strength and deformation properties. Such samples may be taken in practically all fine-grained soils (clay, silts), and in sands of medium density.

Very loose sands tend to compact during sampling and test data may be nonconservative. Conversely, dense sands expand during sampling and tests performed on such samples usually show erroneously large deformations and low strengths. Undisturbed samples of gravelly soils or soils containing rock fragments such as glacial till generally cannot be taken from borings. Disturbed samples suitable for identification and classification can usually be obtained using heavy wall samplers. Approximate physical properties of soils from which undisturbed samples cannot be taken may be estimated from resistance to penetration of either static or dynamic penetrometers (Sanglerat, 1972). Among the static penetrometers the Dutch cone penetrometer and the Swedish turning penetrometer can be mentioned. The Standard Penetration Test (SPT), in which the number of blows required to drive a standard sized sampler into the undisturbed soil below the limit of drilling is recorded (ASTM D1586), is probably the most commonly used dynamic test. Also, shear moduli and compression moduli for small strains ($\pm 10^{-5}$)

can be determined by measuring transmission velocities of shear waves by using seismic survey techniques. The appropriate relations are

$$G = \frac{\rho}{g} C_s^2 \tag{7.1}$$

$$E = 2G (1 + \mu) \tag{7.2}$$

in which G = shear modulus; E = compression modulus; μ = Poisson's ratio; C_s = shear wave velocity; ρ = density; and g = acceleration due to gravity. Both shear modulus and deformation modulus decreases with increasing strain (Seed and Idriss, 1970). For the strain levels usually associated with structures, design moduli may be taken as 40% of the values obtained from Eqs. 7.1 and 7.2 for heavy structures, and 50% of these values for light structures.

Because of the cost of undisturbed sampling, it is common that most of the borings are made taking disturbed samples and undisturbed samples at only selected locations. The disturbed sample borings permit determining stratification and extrapolating tests on undisturbed samples throughout the site by using parametric relations such as penetrometer resistances or moisture content-Atterberg limit relationships. Penetrometer probes frequently are also used to supplement borings. These are especially helpful in designing pile foundations and in locating contacts between various soil layers. Vane shear tests may be used in medium to soft clay to furnish data on quick shear strengths in addition to those obtained from undisturbed samples.

It is often necessary to determine the character and condition of the rock under a site, for example if piles and caissons are to be carried to rock for support or if excavations are to be made into rock. Borings are made into the rock usually by using diamond drill bits. To assure good recovery, N size bits with double tube, nonrotating inner barrels should be used. Drillers should be instructed to work carefully to obtain maximum possible recovery. Cores should be carefully logged, care being taken to note joints, especially open joints, extent and character of weathering, pitting, vugs, or other solution effects, faults or any other discontinuities, or rock defects. Cores should be placed in proper core boxes and stored for further reference.

Rock defects which are particularly troublesome are deep weathering, solution effects, and faults or continuous joints. Because weathering develops from the joints it frequently results in blocks or slabs of hard intact rock surrounded and underlain by soft weathered material. Piles or caissons carried to such rock may not be able to penetrate the hard slabs or blocks. Thus some heavily-loaded foundation elements may be underlain by soft material, while adjoining elements are seated on hard, sound rock. This can result in damaging differential settlements. Partially weathered rock frequently is more permeable than either the intact rock or the more deeply weathered overlying material. This may cause difficult problems in ground-water control for deep excavations.

Limestone and dolomite are slightly soluble in water, especially if the water is acidic. Extensive solution may occur over geologic time, resulting in open joints or channels in the rock into which underlying soil is carried and removed by percolating ground waters. Continuing downwards motion of overlying soil or sudden collapse of soil arches over openings in the rock may result in damage to structures (Sowers, 1975). Where severe, the surface usually shows evidence of typical karst topography with many sinks and sink holes. Sometimes surface evidence is suppressed and subtle. Trying to locate cavernous rock areas by borings is usually unsatisfactory. Other means such as ground-water temperature surveys, refraction or reflection seismic surveys, resistivity tests, or acoustical holography may or may not be helpful. Usually detailed surface examination by a competent expert followed by test pits and trenches to the rock surface give the most dependable results.

Faults or continuous planar joints, especially if clay-filled, can be troublesome in excavations into rock if they dip towards the excavation. This is especially dangerous if sheeting or slurry walls are used to support soil above the top of rock and they are in turn supported by tension ties grouted into the rock. The vertical load of the sheeting or slurry walls increases the hazard of slides in the rock. Careful studies should be made of the jointing systems in the rock. Spacing and continuity of such defects must be considered in designing support systems.

Control of ground water is frequently a major problem during construction. Matters of concern are prevention of boils or loss of ground, prevention of uplift effects on the bottom of excavations, and evaluation of drawdown in surrounding areas, as it may cause settlement of buildings, streets or other facilities or expose wooden piles for deterioration. Control of ground water in such areas may be necessary to protect adjoining structures. Ground-water loadings may be very large on walls and bottom slabs of structures during their service life, especially where there are deep basements. Information to be developed during investigations on which to base structural design and systems for control of ground during construction includes:

1. Identification of potential aquifers.

2. Piezometric levels in each aquifer.

3. Yearly and long-term ranges of piezometric levels.

4. Permeability of each aquifer.

Normally, clay and clayey silt members are not of concern and attention may be directed to sands, sands and gravels, or sometimes sandy silts. Occasionally, bedrock may be permeable along joints or may have primary permeability such as occurs in course-grained sandstones.

Piezometric levels should be determined by piezometers. Usually, several should be installed in each aquifer to observe variations across the site. If more than one aquifer is present, piezometers should be installed in each and isolated from other aquifers by suitable seals. In some cases it may be necessary to measure the water pressure in layers of low permeability, for example in a varved clay. For such determinations closed piezometers should be used, in which the pressure changes can be measured with very small volume changes. Water pressure in aquifers which extend beneath excavations can cause blowup or unacceptable heave of the bottom or slides in banks unless such pressures are controlled by dewatering. Accordingly, aquifers to a depth below the bottom of excavation to about 1.5 times the depth to which excavation extends below the water table should be investigated. Borings can be converted to piezometers. If bentonite slurry has been used in drilling, extreme care will be required to remove the bentonite and destroy bentonite which has penetrated into the aquifer to assure adequate communication. Permeabilities of aquifers are best determined by pumping tests from suitable wells with drawdown curves monitored by several piezometers located at various distances from the well. Permeability may be crudely estimated by inflow tests during drilling or from grain size curves. However, such estimates may be in error by an order of magnitude or more.

Pile load tests are frequently used to verify structural capacity of piles to assure that adequate strength is available to prevent movement of the pile relative to the soil. They are described in greater detail in Section 7.6. Direct soil load tests were at one time extensively used in foundation investigations. Such tests stress only a depth of soil approximately equal to the width of the loaded test area and give no information on long-term settlements. Accordingly they provide only limited information and results are difficult to interpret. Thus they generally are rarely used.

Other on-site tests, such as refraction seismic surveys to locate bedrock, may be useful. Provision to measure heave of the bottom of excavations or lateral strains adjacent to excavations may in some cases be necessary. Information on existing nearby structures, streets, and facilities such as subways, water mains, sewers, electrical ducts, or gas pipe should be gathered. Methods of founding existing structures and their performance over the years can be of considerable assistance in deciding on methods of founding the proposed building. Decisions on how to protect such structures against disturbance during or following construction must be based on sound data. Documenting physical conditions of nearby structures may offer protection against later claims. Frequently locations of buried services such as water mains or sewers are only approximately known. They should be definitely located by test pits or trenches if clearance from construction operations is small, in order to minimize hazards of damage or disturbance.

7.3 DESIGN OF COMPENSATED FOUNDATIONS

Compensated foundations are used in deep subsoil deposits of medium to very highly compressible materials, such as lacustrine or marine sediments, in which the shear strength and, consequently, the load supporting capacity of the soil may be very low. In such deposits, it frequently is essential to limit settlement and to reduce shear stresses in the underlying soil to very small values.

1 Basic Concepts

Intuitively, one understands that if the subsurface portions of a building displaced a weight of soil and ground water equal to the total weight of the building, the structure would essentially float, proper recognition being given to coincidence between the center of buoyancy and the center of mass. Utilizing this principle, foundations of major structures may be provided for very soft soils. The principle has been known and used for many years, and many structures based on this foundation concept have been built. Such a design could be termed a "floating" foundation, but is more usually termed a compensated foundation.

In many cases, less than full flotation may be used by taking advantage of the stress-strain relations of soil. When a soil mass is loaded as by its own weight, or by an external load such as lowering of ground water, by capillary forces developed during partial desiccation, or by overlying materials, it compresses. Upon removal of the load, it will rebound to a limited extent. If the soil is then reloaded, compression will be very small until stresses equal to the previous loading are reached. This is termed the preconsolidation pressure.

Advantage can be taken of this stress-strain behavior to permit using compensation or relief of load less than the total weight of the structure, by excavating just enough material so that the final stresses induced in the soil are less than the preconsolidation values at all levels, account being taken of hydrostatic uplift. This is termed a "partially compensated" foundation. Occasionally excavation for basements will remove a weight of material including water greater than the weight of the structure. This can be termed an overcompensated foundation—for example, see Article 5 ("Case History") of this section.

Since space developed in basements necessary for compensation is usually useful, compensated foundation designs frequently are economically attractive in adverse soil conditions. However, the economics of such designs is significantly affected by the distribution of loads of the structure and the spacing of columns. Simple rectangular or similar compact geometries of uniform height and small column spacing are the cheapest. Structures of irregular shapes and loadings, as with several wings of various heights and irregular spacing of columns and wide variations in column loadings, are expensive because of the cost of, and space occupied by, necessary structural systems to distribute structural loadings to the soil.

When an excavation is made, the soil beneath the level of excavation rebounds upwards or heaves, and the sides of the excavation move inwards. Initially, these movements are elastic responses of the soil skeleton to changes in stress. They occur immediately and without change in volume. These elastic displacements are followed by time-dependent motions as water moves into the void spaces of the soil mass increasing its volume (inverse of consolidation) and, if stresses are sufficiently high, by plastic yielding. This rebound displacement is a function of the amount of load reduction (that is, the depth of excavation), the deformation moduli of the soil (both elastic and inelastic), the plan shape of excavation, and the time the excavation is open. For most cases of concern, it is maximum near the center of excavation and minimum in the corners. As load is imposed on the bottom of the excavation by the structure during its construction, these rebound displacements are quickly reduced. Thus, even when the design provides for complete compensation of load and there are no long-term settlements, significant and possibly damaging differential settlements may occur in the structural systems of a building unless heave is limited. Control of rebound or heave, during excavation and construction of the substructure, to limit possible differential settlements to tolerable amounts is therefore always a matter requiring careful investigation and design. Further, deformations carried into the plastic range can soften the structure of the clay and seriously reduce preconsolidation values. Subsequent loadings in excess of such reduced preconsolidation values may result in large settlements.

A special problem arises when dealing with sensitive soils. These are soils in which a large reduction in shear strength occurs when the soil is subjected to significant deformation. The sensitivity ratio is usually defined as the ratio of the undisturbed shear strength to shear strength after thorough remolding without loss of moisture content. Soils showing values less than four are termed low sensitivity clays. Sensitivity ratios of 20 to 50 and even more are sometimes encountered. Typical are the Leda clays of the St. Lawrence River Valley and clays in many areas of Scandinavia. Extreme care is required to avoid distortions of the soil mass which would cause significant reductions in strength; otherwise, rapid progressive failure or even flow failures may occur. Further, final loadings on the soil should not exceed more than 50% of the preconsolidation loads for sensitive clays.

When completed, the structure is supported by the sum of the hydrostatic uplift due to its submergence below ground water and the resistance of the soil skeleton to deformation. In the case of total compensation, there usually is no problem of shear failure for static loads, provided the center of loading coincides with the center of resistance. Overturning forces as from earthquake or wind loading must be considered, however, and stresses kept within safe limits. Otherwise, local failures near the edge of the structure might occur. For very tall, slender structures, the hazard of instability must be investigated (Habib, 1970).

Design of compensated foundations must be based on a thorough knowledge of stress-strain relations of each stratum of the underlying soils, both for short-term and long-term loadings, including plastic deformation characteristics. Further detailed information on ground-water regimes and realistic estimates of possible future variations are necessary. Determining this information requires a thorough and carefully executed investigational program made under constant supervision by knowledgeable experts. If there are existing structures built on the same soils using compensated foundations, a study should be made of their design and performance.

2 Effect of Construction Procedures

Compensated foundations are usually used in soft soils which deform large amounts under changes in loading. As has been previously indicated, the deformations of the soil beneath the structure during excavation and construction materially affect differential settlement of the structure in service. Soil deformations may develop from several different mechanisms. Among these are:

1. Elastic rebound from relief of stress without volume change.

2. Time-dependent inelastic movements from volume change of soil mass (inverse of consolidation).

3. Plastic deformations, especially if stresses are high.

4. Lateral movement of retaining structures for walls of excavations.

5. Seepage forces in more permeable layers.

Elastic Rebound. Elastic movements in the soil under and surrounding result in an uplift or heave of the bottom of the excavation and movements of adjoining areas toward the excavation. For most conditions where compensated foundations are considered, the upward motion of the bottom of the excavation is approximately dome-shaped as illustrated in Fig. 7.1. This may not be readily apparent since the heaved material is excavated as it moves. Reference monuments set in the soil just below the limit of excavation, however, will show such movements and permit measuring these heave motions. For further discussion of these elastic motions see Section 7.7 of this chapter.

The amount of motion is dependent upon the stress-strain relation of the various soil strata, the shape of the excavation, and its depth (that is, the amount of load removed). It should be noted that practically all soils are strain-softening; that is, their moduli of deformation decrease with increasing strain. Thus, elastic rebound motions may be modest for a small depth of excavation but be three or four times larger if the depths are doubled. The appropriate moduli may be determined from careful tests of undisturbed samples. Moduli are sensitive to sampling disturbance, and very careful workmanship should be required in taking and testing samples.

Movements Due to Volume Change.   A soil mass (including soft, normally consolidated clays) which is not reacting to recent changes in loading is in a state of stress equilibrium so that the water in the pore spaces of the soil is under hydrostatic pressure, and the soil skeleton supports the overlying weight of soil less the buoyancy from submergence of the particles. Thus, at some depth z below the surface the vertical stresses are given by:

1. Total vertical stress $= \sigma_z$, equal to total weight of soil plus water to depth z per unit of area.

2. Pore pressure of water $= u = \gamma_w d$, in which $d =$ depth of element considered below the ground-water table; and $\gamma_w =$ density of water.

3. Vertical stress in soil skeleton for element considered $= \bar{\sigma_z}$; this is termed effective stress $\bar{\sigma_z} = \sigma_z - u$.

These relations are illustrated in Fig. 7.2. For a more complete discussion, see Terzaghi and Peck (1967).

When material is excavated from above such an element, the total stress is suddenly reduced. The soil skeleton starts to rebound and to expand elastically, thus increasing in volume. This expansion can occur, however, only as water is absorbed into the soil mass to fill the voids. Otherwise, the pressure in the water is reduced or even goes negative, which places compression stresses on the soil skeleton, keeping it from expanding. This expansion is essentially the inverse of consolidation under load. It is time-dependent.

Thus, the elastic deformations of preceding paragraphs, which reflect primarily shear distortions without volume change, will be followed by further time-dependent distortions resulting from volumetric expansion of the soils, especially

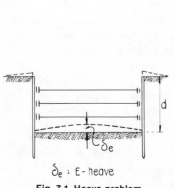

δ_e : E-heave

Fig. 7.1 Heave problem

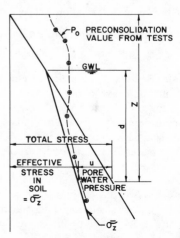

Fig. 7.2 Effective stress

beneath the excavation. The amount of such volumetric heave depends on the stress-volume relations of the soil strata affected by load reduction, the amount of load reduction, permeabilities of the several strata (especially whether any sand or coarse silt layers are present), and the time the excavation is open before significant structural weight is reimposed. Deformations are predictable based on tests of carefully taken, undisturbed samples of the soil and a thorough knowledge of stratification and ground-water conditions. Preferably, the samples should be placed in the consolidometer, loaded to slightly in excess of preconsolidation load, unloaded, and then loaded and unloaded through a second cycle. Stress-volume changes are then taken from this second load cycle.

Plastic Movements. Soft, normally consolidated clays may display time-dependent deformations which are essentially plastic in character, that is, continued yielding with no change in stress. In general, these effects are not significant for shear stresses less than about one-half or two-thirds the quick shear strength. For larger stresses, significant movements may occur.

Of particular concern are areas near the perimeter of excavations. The weight of soil adjoining the excavation plus any superimposed weight, as from an adjoining building or stockpiling of materials, induces high shearing stresses in the soil under the bottom of the excavation, as shown in Fig. 7.3. The mechanism is similar to bearing value failure of a footing [see Terzaghi and Peck (1967), p. 265 for a discussion of the analysis of this problem].

In general, if the depth of the clay below the bottom of excavation is large and does not vary significantly in shear strength—the usual conditions for compensated foundations—little is to be gained by extending the sheeting deeper. The failure plane is displaced to below the tip of the sheeting, but the factor of safety against shear failure is not increased unless the sheeting penetrates into soil having higher shear strengths.

To minimize plastic deformation, the depth of excavation should be limited to values so that shearing stresses are kept well below shear strength. These should be investigated both for near perimeter "bearing value" failure, as described, and also for general rotational slides passing below or close to the toe of the sheeting. The former usually governs.

Lateral Deformation of Retaining Structures. In most cases, support must be provided for the side walls of excavations to protect nearby structures and streets. Such retaining structures may be sheeting of wood, steel, or concrete, or slurry wall

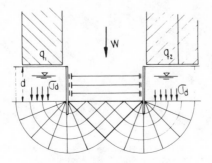

Fig. 7.3 Stability of excavation

construction. The term "sheeting" will be used to mean either.

Tiebacks to support sheeting are rarely practicable where compensated foundations are used. Rather, bracing is installed as excavation progresses. This may be installed across the excavation, bracing one wall against the other, or, if the excavation is sufficiently wide, the central portion may be excavated leaving sloping berms for stability, the central portion of the foundation mat built, and then the sheeting braced to this as the perimeter is excavated. Either method may result in significant soil deformations and lateral motions of the sheeting. Lateral deformations may develop from several different causes:

1. Elastic compression of supporting bracing.

2. Elastic and plastic deformations of berms before the bracing is installed, as shown in Fig. 7.4

3. Cumulative deflections of the sheeting as successive levels are installed.

Sheeting and bracing distort elastically as loads are imposed on them by excavations. These motions are increased if the sheeting is not properly blocked to waler systems and if bracing is not tightly wedged against the walers. Elastic distortion of support systems can be reduced to negligible amounts by preloading the bracing, for example, by jacking. Preloading of bracing systems cannot, however, reduce plastic distortions due to bottom heave and usually is not economically justified when bottom heave or distortion is apt to be significant.

Where a central excavation is used, considerable deformation of berms or slopes of the excavation may occur before the bracing is installed. These motions may be expected to be particularly large where shear stresses are high relative to shear

One Shell Plaza foundation construction, Houston, Texas: retaining structure consists of drilled-in caissons poured prior to excavation. Struts installed at two levels at 20-ft spacing
(Courtesy: Fazlur R. Khan)

strength, or if there are thin, coarse silt or sand layers present in which piezometric levels are well above the elevation of the bottom of the excavation.

Normally, bracing is installed as the excavation progresses. As the excavation progresses, the sheeting and the bracing first installed are subjected to heavier loadings. The sheeting is deflected inward, that is, toward the excavation at the next lower level of bracing. Thus, as each successive level of bracing is installed, there are successive inward deflections of the sheeting, as illustrated in Fig. 7.5. Near the bottom of the excavation, the sheeting may be deflected inwards a significant amount, especially if shear stresses are high. There are recorded cases in Mexico City of such deflection amounting to as much as 1 m.

Unless allowance is made for such deflections in layout of the sheeting, distortions from these several causes may result in serious interference with structural systems. This can result in the necessity to redesign or even refabricate structural systems which are to be below grade, with the consequences of serious delay and greatly increased costs.

In addition, such lateral deformations can seriously damage adjoining or nearby structures or streets and other facilities. There is always a hazard of rupturing underground piping. If these are carrying fluid, catastrophic failure of the walls of the excavation may occur.

Effects of Seepage Forces.   Many clays contain interbeds of coarse silt or fine sand which are several orders of magnitude more permeable than the clay. Control of seepage pressures in such strata is important during construction.

Unless seepage pressures in such permeable strata which extend under the bottom are relieved by drainage, the soil above the permeable member may be lifted and ruptured by the hydrostatic force. This, if it occurs, will disturb the soil structure. Usually there will be sand boiling from the permeable member which may so affect the foundation material as to render the site unusable.

Unrelieved pressures either under or above the bottom of excavation may result in spreading failures in soil surrounding the excavation. Deformations from such causes may extend for large distances, affecting other structures and facilities. Such coarse silts and fine sands can migrate through interlocks of steel sheeting or joints

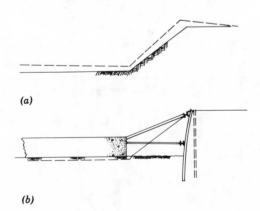

(a)

(b)

Fig. 7.4 (a) After initial excavation; (b) Completion of excavation in wood sheeting. Unless filtered drains are provided, material may be carried into the excavation, resulting in loss of ground under adjoining areas. Reductions in piezometric pressures from drainage of such permeable members may cause settlement of nearby structures and facilities. Thus, while drainage of such permeable members under and close to the excavation may be necessary, it may also be necessary to maintain piezometric levels under nearby areas by such procedures as reinjecting water by inflow wells.

3 Methods of Construction to Minimize Heave

Various methods of construction of compensated foundations, to minimize as much as possible the vertical and horizontal displacements during excavation, have been used successfully over many years in Mexico City, an area where the subsoil is of very high compressibility with expansive mechanical properties.

Excavation by Substitution.   Assume it is required to make an excavation to depth d_1, in Fig. 7.6. One finds, however, that this depth cannot be excavated fully because of bottom stability from plastic flow, and the elastic rebound would be large. Frequently, the stability conditions can be met if the excavation is performed in steps. The first step is performed to about one-half of the total depth. By doing this, the elastic heave will be reduced considerably because the subsoil material is

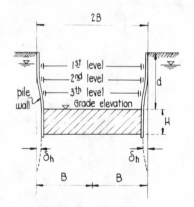

Fig. 7.5 Lateral displacement of sheet-pile wall

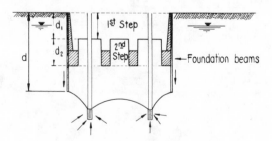

Fig. 7.6 Excavation by substitution

kept in its natural precompressed condition. The second step should be performed by substitution; for this purpose it is convenient to select a foundation structure that may be easily constructed in braced trenches. The bracing and shoring in the trenches is carefully performed, using preloading, to support horizontal earth and water pressures against the sheet piles without permitting displacements.

During the second step, the trenches are excavated step by step and the foundation structure poured into them, replacing immediately the weight of the foundation structure. This procedure is followed until the foundation structure is completed; thereafter, construction of the building is started. The foundation reaction slab is finished to grace elevation by excavating the earth panels step by step between the beams.

Pumping During Excavations.   While excavations take place, the water table is usually lowered continuously 24 hr a day, to permit construction under dry conditions. The change in effective stresses when lowering the water table should be carefully studied. Moreover, this procedure may be improved when a deep excavation is required by pumping from deep wells. The well layout may be as shown in Fig. 7.7. Pumping is performed in each one of the wells to an elevation far below the foundation grade elevation. A flow net for the wells is traced to estimate the dynamic water level that should be maintained during excavation. The lowering of the water table by the process of wells has the effect of increasing the effective weight of the soil under the foundation grade elevation and of keeping the soil in a precompressed condition, thus minimizing the elastic-heave and horizontal displacement of the sheet piles.

When sand layers are present in the subsoil, the water pumped from the wells is injected in the sand layers outside the sheet piles to preserve the effective stresses

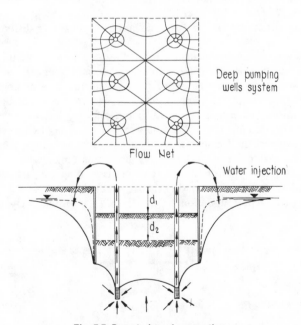

Fig. 7.7 Dewatering of excavation

and to avoid damage claims on adjacent property. The procedure just explained was introduced by Zeevaert (1949) for deep excavations in Mexico City.

Egg-Box Caissons Foundations.   In very soft soils, fully compensated (floating) foundations may be constructed by fabricating hollow raft foundations consisting of square or rectangular open bottom cells having vertical walls of a height equal to the desired depth of the foundation. This is erected on the ground surface, or in a shallow excavation, and then sunk to grade by excavating through the cells in a manner similar to that used in sinking box caissons for bridge piers (Golder, 1965). The individual cells are made sufficiently small in plan dimension to prevent plastic yielding and may be kept filled with water if necessary. When grade is reached, the soil is carefully excavated from beneath each cell and a bottom slab of concrete is installed. Considerable care must be exercised in sinking to prevent tilting. Weighting and a carefully planned sequence of excavation may be necessary.

The raft foundations may be built of normal or post-tensioned concrete. The individual cells frequently are on the order of 3 m to 4 m (10 ft to 13 ft) square. Because of this compartmentalizing, they frequently are termed "egg-box" foundations. The design provides excellent structural strength for distributing structural loads to the soil. However, the small compartments usually preclude useful occupancy.

4   Foundation Structural Design Affecting Economy

Types of Foundation Structures, Column Loads, and Spacing.   In connection with the excavation problems mentioned in the preceding articles, a choice must be made of the proper type of foundation structure compatible with the method of the excavation. Also, it is important, from the point of view of differential settlements and economy, to select the proper rigidity of the foundation structure. Three types of foundation structures may be used advantageously under different conditions (Fig. 7.8).

Fig. 7.8(a) is a foundation structure formed by structural elements in a grid. The reaction slab and the basement slab are connected monolithically to the structural elements in such a way that the entire system will provide a monolithic unit with high rigidity. The structural elements may be concrete walls or beams, or large Vierendeel trusses extending the full depth of the basement may be used (Casagrande and Fadum, 1944). The hollow spaces may be used to collect seepage water and to inspect the foundation structure. In large buildings, these spaces may be occupied or used to accommodate machinery, water tanks, sewage disposal tanks, etc. This cellular box-type foundation structure is suitable for large spans in heavy buildings and for excavations made in narrow trenches.

Fig. 7.8(b) shows a foundation of the flat-slab type that may be considered

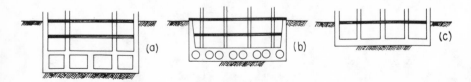

Fig. 7.8 Foundation Structures: (a) Rigid cellular-box; (b) Hollow flat-slab; (c) Flat-slab

semirigid in comparison with the cellular box-type foundation structure. Tubes are left in the concrete slab to save weight and to reduce steel in contrast to a solid flat slab construction. This foundation, however, requires that the excavation be made to full depth. Frequently, construction must be done by excavating only small portions of the area at a time to minimize distortions.

The third type of foundation structure, shown in Fig. 7.8(c), is a regular flat-slab structure, which may be considered semiflexible and which may be used for short spans in light buildings with one basement. The excavation may have to be made to full depth in areas of limited extent.

These three types of foundation structures should be analyzed for allowable total and differential settlements, for weight, and as a function of spans and depth in conjunction with the construction excavation process indicated for the specific problem in question.

Subgrade Reaction.   The contact pressures to calculate bending moments and shear forces in the foundation structure should be investigated to determine the amount of steel to be placed for reinforcement, and also to predict what can be done concerning load distribution or column distribution on the foundation to minimize bending moments.

Fig. 7.9 shows a compensated foundation under the commonly used assumptions that a unit uniform load q is imposed on the soil. From foundation engineering, however, we know that this is not the case.

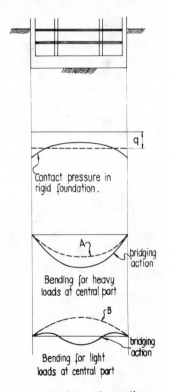

Fig. 7.9 Subgrade reaction

When the foundation is rigid by comparison with the compressibility of the soil, the contact pressures at the edges of the foundation are larger than at the center. This distribution of foundation pressure with high pressures near the edges and less in the center usually is further increased by rebound during excavation. Therefore, a bridging effect takes place in the foundation structure.

If the building loads are heavier on the central part of the foundation, the bending moments on a uniform subgrade reaction distribution will be as in the curve labeled A (Fig. 7.9). The foundation will deflect downward with tension in the lower part of the beams. Under these circumstances, the bridging effect of nonuniform reaction will increase the moment further, thus giving, in some cases, very large bending moments and shears, and possibly an unsafe design. On the other hand, if the loads at the center of the foundation are lighter, or when the structural frame spans over the foundation, then the computed bending moment in the foundation structure, assuming uniform reaction distribution, will show large tension in the upper fibers of the beams, and a large amount of steel may be indicated at these places, Curve B (Fig. 7.9). Actually, if the nonuniform distribution is properly considered, it is possible to justify substantially lower moments, and great economy may be obtained in steel reinforcement. Therefore, by determining approximately the real contact pressures on the foundation structure, one is able to obtain economy in some instances, in conjunction with a favorable distribution of the building loads, in such a way as to minimize bending moments. The column distribution, of course, will be such as to place larger loads toward the edges of the foundation. Therefore, more economy may be gained in the structural design and construction.

Where compensated foundations are used for large, heavy buildings in soft soils, the structural rigidity usually is sufficiently large, relative to load-deflection characteristics of the soil, so that structural deflections will not significantly affect contact pressures between soil and structure. For these conditions, assuming the foundation to be rigid may be used as a simplification in determining contact

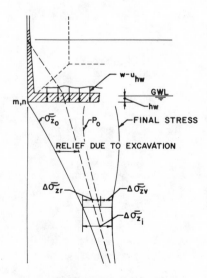

Fig. 7.10 Stresses

pressures for structural design. This condition is discussed below. If the structure is relatively flexible, which is frequently the case with partially compensated foundations, the analysis is more complex since structural deformations and soil deformations must be considered simultaneously in evaluating contact pressures for structural design. This is discussed more fully in Section 7.7 of this chapter.

The weight of the structure and the relief of load should be so designed that support, considering hydrostatic uplift and soil reaction, is coincident with the resultant of structural loads, including actual and permanent live loadings. This minimizes the hazard of tilting. The settlement as measured from the start of construction will be approximately uniform for a rigid structure. Under these conditions, the contact pressure between soil and structure must be so distributed as to cause uniform settlement at the soil surface, due to soil compression under the weight of the structure. Further, summation of contact pressures over the area of the foundation must equal the total building weight less hydrostatic uplift considering possible future variations in ground-water levels.

As shown in Fig. 7.10, the added stress $\Delta\bar\sigma_{zi}$ in element i at some depth z below point m-n is computed. The compressive deformation of the element Δ_{zi} is then computed from the stress-strain relations of the soil as determined from laboratory tests on undisturbed samples. Care must be taken to consider that the reload modulus (that is, for stresses less than the preconsolidation load value) of the soil is much higher than for stresses in excess of the preconsolidation value. The deformation at point m-n is then determined by summing

$$\Delta_{m\text{-}n} = \sum_z^0 \Delta_{zi}\,dz \qquad (7.3)$$

in which depth z is taken to an incompressible material or to a depth where added stress due to the weight of the structure is negligible. Deformation of the soil under all points of the foundation can then be determined and deformation profiles plotted. If these deviate significantly from a uniform plane, the contact pressures should be readjusted within the constraints described and the process repeated, iterating until a reasonably uniform settlement is calculated.

In practice, it is usually acceptable to use approximate deformation moduli for stresses below and above the preconsolidation load at the depth considered; thus M_{zr} = reload modulus, and M_{zv} = modulus for stresses in excess of preconsolidation load (that is, for virgin loading). Then

$$\Delta_{zi} = \frac{\Delta\bar\sigma_{zr}\,dz}{M_{zr}} + \frac{\Delta\bar\sigma_{zv}\,dz}{M_{zv}} \qquad (7.4)$$

and $\Delta\bar\sigma_{zi} = \Delta\bar\sigma_{zr} + \Delta\bar\sigma_{zv}$; $\bar\sigma_{z0} + \Delta\bar\sigma_{zr} \le p_0$; $\Delta\bar\sigma_{zv} = \bar\sigma_{z0} + \Delta\bar\sigma_{zi} - p_0$; p_0 = preconsolidation loading; and $\Delta\bar\sigma_{zv}$ = added effective stress in excess of preconsolidation values.

Depth increments are usually taken at about 3 m to 4 m (10 ft to 12 ft) and adjusted so that increment boundaries coincide with stratification and changes in physical properties, such as preconsolidation values or field moisture contents. Depth increments do not need to be of equal thickness. The number of elements to be considered in plan is dependent on the complexity of the structure. For a simple rectangular building of uniform height, a usable solution can usually be made by analyzing one quadrant, using about 16 to 20 elements in plan. Elements near the corners should be relatively small and those near the center of the structure relatively large. The contact pressures so developed may then be used by the structural engineer to analyze the structure. Stresses may be conveniently computed from the Boussinesq Solution for stress in a vertical half space. Graphs and tables for various distributed loadings are available (Poulos and Davis, 1974).

Stresses from Earthquakes and Wind. The stresses induced at the foundation grade elevation produced by horizontal forces, either by earthquakes or wind, have to be taken into consideration by the foundation engineer. It has been mentioned before that a totally compensated foundation under normal static loads has no problem of load-bearing capacity, because one is substituting or fully compensating the effective overburden stresses and water pressures with the load of the building. The resultant of the loads of the building should be coincident with the center of gravity of a rectangular loaded area to be sure that there will be no static tilting of the building. Uniform settlement, however, is only obtained for areas with two axes of symmetry. Areas of other shapes, such as triangular, trapezoidal, etc., require a variable subgrade reaction distribution to obtain uniform settlements under sustained static loading.

During earthquakes and heavy wind storms, horizontal forces occur. These forces have to be taken by subgrade reactions at the foundation elevation. The overturning moment and base shear induced by these forces push and rotate the foundation structure toward one edge. The increment of stress on the static subgrade reactions distribution because of the action of these forces may be considered to have a linear variation, as shown simplified in Fig. 7.11.

The increment of stress on the soil induced by these forces should be carefully investigated for two important reasons:

1. The increment of stress induced by these forces should be considerably less

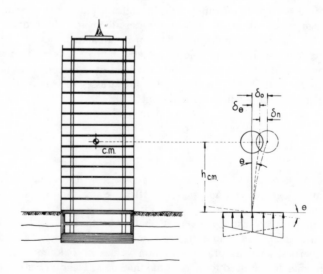

Fig. 7.11 Building subjected to earthquake

than the local shear failure pressures; otherwise, the building may tilt considerably.

2. The increment of stresses over the static subgrade reactions should be investigated to obtain elastic response of the soil during the earthquake so that the building will maintain its vertical position after the motion.

Many cases have been observed in earthquake regions in difficult subsoil conditions, like those of Mexico City, in which buildings have tilted considerably with the result that they have to be underpinned and restored to their vertical position. This is a difficult and costly process. Therefore, in these cases one has to be aware of the stresses induced in the ground by the dynamic horizontal forces on the building.

Designing against earthquake, including foundation effects, is discussed in Chapter CL-2. Design of foundations for lateral loads from wind is discussed in Section 7.4 of this chapter.

5 Case History

The results obtained for an overcompensated foundation constructed in Mexico City's highly compressible subsoil are especially interesting to illustrate the behavior of such a foundation. The foundation structure is of the rigid box type. The building has two basements and 11 stories above ground surface. The foundation grade elevation is at a depth of 10.3 m (34 ft) from the ground surface. The building average unit load is 104.9 kPa (2192 psf; 10.7 t/m²). The subsoil stratigraphy, overburden effective stresses, and hydraulic pressures are shown in Fig. 7.12. At the foundation grade elevation, the effective overburden pressure [including the weight of 39.2 kPa (820 psf; 4 t/m²) of old buildings previously occupying the site] = 115.7 kPa (2417 psf; 11.6 t/m²), and the hydraulic pressure = 85.3 kPa (1782 psf; 8.7 t/m²). Since the weight of the building is 104.9 kPa (2192 psf; 10.7 t/m²), the permanent relief of stress at the foundation grade elevation is 96.1 kPa (2007 psf; 9.8 t/m²). During demolition of the old buildings, that part of the elastic heave corresponding to 39.2 kPa (820 psf; 4 t/m²) relief took place. This effect was not measured. For heave calculations, however, it may be considered that approximately one-half of the elastic-heave due to the weight of old buildings took place. Hence, heave calculations were estimated on an average effective stress relief on the order of 76.5 kPa (1600 psf; 7.8 t/m²).

The preconsolidation values of the clay from tests, *po*, plot well above the initial effective stresses and final working stresses as shown in Fig. 7.12(b). To calculate the elastic-heave, the elastic response strain modulus of each soil stratum was determined, using the hysteresis loops from unconfined compression tests for stress relief in the range of effective stresses calculated in the soil mass from the theory of elasticity.

The excavation was performed in two stages. The first was performed to a depth of 6.0 m (19.8 ft), producing an effective stress relief of 53.9 kPa (1125 psf; 5.5 t/m²). The elastic-heave calculated for this stage of excavation was on the order of 164 mm (6.5 in.). The water table was reduced by means of 15 deep pumping wells to an average depth of 15.5 m (51 ft). The second stage of excavation was performed by substitution of weights. During this process, the soil was recompressed to approximately the initial overburden effective stresses by reducing the hydraulic pressures under the foundation grade elevation by pumping from the deep water wells. As construction proceeded and the weight of the building increased, the water table was permitted to rise until, after finishing the building, the water table was restored. The final working stress conditions in the soil mass correspond to a permanent stress relief at the foundation grade elevation of 76.5 kPa (1590 psf; 7.8 t/m²), for which the calculated elastic-heave was on the order of 261 mm (10.25 in.), Fig. 7.12(c).

From the vertical displacements observed and reported for a central point in the building, it may be noticed that slight heave of the foundation and structure

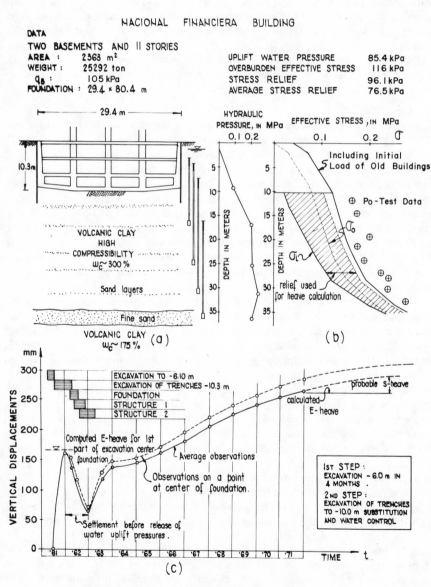

Fig. 7.12 Case history of building on over compensated foundation

continued after completing construction. The observed vertical displacement had reached the calculated elastic-heave value by 1971. The observations show that some additional vertical movement may be expected to take place in the future. This probably is due to swelling of the clay because of the permanent stress relief in the soil.

7.4   DISTRIBUTION OF WIND LOADS TO SOIL

Wind acting on tall buildings can develop large temporary loading which must be delivered ultimately to the soil. The magnitude of these wind loads and their effect and distribution within the structure will not be considered. It is assumed that the wind analysis has been completed to the point where the loads are at the foundation level. Although many elements of the structure will be defined primarily on the basis of considerations other than wind, discussions during the planning period between the structural and foundation engineers will assist in developing a design which will distribute wind to the foundations in such a manner as to allow the proper interaction between the structure and the soil without excessive deformations.

The type of foundation selected for the support of a structure is usually determined prior to wind considerations. The building will be supported either on a shallow type, such as spread footings or mats, or a deep foundation involving piles or piers. The relative merits of each type of foundation in the distribution of wind shears to the soil will not be discussed since it is assumed that the choice has been made on over-all considerations. The decision to incorporate deep basements under a building may also be made as a result of considerations other than wind loads. The absence of any deep basements will, of course, have a major effect on the method for transferring the wind shears.

Loads at the foundation level resulting from wind can be separated into vertical and lateral components and moments. The vertical component is resisted by the soil in the same manner as all other vertical structural loads and will not be discussed in this section. In general, because of the temporary nature of the wind, the allowable vertical supporting capacity of the soil is increased when considering the combined effects of structure and wind loads. The lateral component and moments resulting from wind are resisted by the following soil-structure systems: (1) Lateral soil pressure against foundation elements; (2) shear along the base of the structure; (3) lateral resistance of piles or piers; (4) batter piles; or (5) a combination of all of these.

1   Basic Considerations

Conventional Analysis.   The transmission of lateral wind loads on tall buildings to the soil has not been of particular concern to the practicing structural engineer except for the atypical structure. The conventional approach has been to determine the magnitude of the wind shears and the amount of passive resistance available from the soil surrounding the foundation. If the ratio of the available resistance and the wind load provides an adequate factor of safety, no further analysis is performed. For buildings with deep basements surrounded by soil which will not be disturbed by future construction, no valid objection to this simple approach can be made since the deformations involved in the development of the required lateral resistance are usually quite small. There are, however, special situations which require an understanding of the factors involved.

Earth Pressure Theory. Earth pressure theories on which present design practice is based were introduced in 1776 by Coulomb and 1857 by Rankine. These early theories assumed that the soil was on the verge of failure but did not recognize that substantial movements occurred in developing the shearing strength of the soil. Terzaghi (1943) demonstrated that the change in soil pressure from the original value was brought about by lateral deformations within the soil mass. The earth pressure existing in a soil deposit which has not been subjected to any lateral deformation is pressure at rest and is difficult to determine accurately since it depends on the type of soil, how it was deposited, the stress history, and other factors which cannot be easily evaluated. The change from pressure at rest to the passive state occurs when the structure moves laterally and compresses the soil until its full shearing resistance is mobilized. After this condition is reached, further deformation does not greatly affect the magnitude of the passive resistance. For analyses where only this limiting value of the soil pressure is required, without consideration of the actual deformation involved, reliable results can be obtained. Deformations can be restricted to acceptable values by the appropriate choice of a design factor of safety. However, the accurate estimation of the lateral deformation in a practical situation cannot be determined with any degree of assurance using present design methods. Pressures developed from movements less than the minimum required for full shear mobilization will be less than the passive pressure calculated.

Soil Properties. Analyses performed to determine the soil pressures and deformations must be based on knowledge of the soil properties. Engineers have generally recognized the fact that soil is not an ideal material to work with. Properties can vary materially over limited distances and simplifying assumptions necessary to allow analytical solutions often result in predicted behavior which is materially different from the actual experience of the structure. It is of great importance to define the soil properties as accurately as possible. A subsurface exploratory program involving the recovery of good quality samples of soil at various depths and locations at the site, and the testing of these samples, will provide information on the variations of soil properties throughout the site. The properties of the soil surrounding the foundation and immediately below it will control the behavior of shallow type foundations in the transfer of wind shears. For structures supported on deep foundations, the soil properties surrounding the piles or piers to some depth must also be considered. Seasonal variations of ground-water levels and the effect of this change on the soil properties must be considered.

Choice of Analytical Methods. Analytical techniques available to solve soil-structure problems all involve the substitution of a soil with ideal properties for the actual material in place. This will always limit the benefits to be derived from the use of more complicated analyses. There may be a greater advantage in using a simple procedure in which the effect of this substitution on final results can be estimated than in utilizing a more complex technique where the basic assumptions of soil properties are no more accurate but their effect cannot be evaluated. For most problems, adequate analytical results can be expected from the application of reasonable soil properties determined from soil tests and the use of analytical techniques which conform to a reasonable degree with the behavior of the soil-structure system. If the soil properties cannot be defined adequately or the soil-structure behavior is too complex to establish the validity of simplifying assumptions, tests on prototypes can be performed to develop design criteria.

Over-All Soil Deformations. In addition to knowledge of the soil properties which are directly concerned with the evaluation of resisting forces, the over-all behavior of the soil below a structure must be considered. This behavior may involve a change which is time-dependent. The most critical condition, whether it is the initial or final, must be used in the calculation of the resisting forces. For example, settlement below a pile supported structure can create a void which will eliminate the shear transfer at the base of the structure. Settlements may also develop friction at the vertical interface between soil and structure, which will have an influence on resisting pressure calculations.

Future Construction. Future construction in adjacent areas which removes soil providing lateral support to a building may create problems unless considered in the original design. This construction may include an adjacent building or an underground street structure such as a subway or sewer. An investigation should be made for shallow type foundations relying on passive pressure against the foundation walls below grade, to determine if any construction can occur below the adjacent soil in a zone defined by the ground and the rupture surface for the passive pressure. If definite information is not available on the possibility of such construction, it is prudent to assume that such construction may occur and check the lateral resistance available, disregarding whatever portion of the building foundation is above the lowest depth of adjacent excavation.

2 Passive Soil Pressure

Since most tall buildings are constructed with deep basements, the most common system for transferring wind loads to the soil involves the utilization of passive pressure against foundation elements. The principal soil properties which must be defined are the angle of internal friction, the cohesion, and the unit weight. Friction may also develop between the face of the wall and the earth mass. Calculation of passive pressure must include consideration of the ground-water level, stratification of the soil, variation of the ground surface from the horizontal, and the method of construction of the foundation. Construction procedures include consideration of whether a braced cofferdam or an open excavation will be utilized, whether backfilling will be required behind the foundation walls, the type and method of compaction of the backfill, the effect of the construction on the permanent condition of the ground water, and other factors which will influence the soil-structure interaction.

Computation of Passive Pressure. Passive pressure computations are based on the assumptions that the soil is isotropic and homogeneous and that the movement of the contact face is sufficient to change the soil from its original condition of elastic equilibrium to the state of plastic equilibrium. This last assumption may involve substantial movements which are not always experienced in practical situations. For example, tests performed on dense sand required a wall rotation of approximately 0.05 rad to develop an increase to full passive pressure. Considering a foundation wall 6.0 m (20 ft) high, this would require a movement at ground surface of 305 mm (1 ft). Obviously, a building foundation requiring development of full passive pressure for stability could not tolerate lateral movements of this magnitude. Although the importance of the relationship between the deformation and the resisting soil pressure is generally understood, and it is recognized that movements of typical structures are less than needed to develop the state of plastic equilibrium, the simplicity of the analysis makes it attractive for use by practicing engineers. The use of a high factor of safety and the development of other resisting forces on the foundation, such as friction on the base and sides to assist the resisting pressure which may be much less than the full passive pressure, allows the successful application of this method. Procedures for the calculation of passive pressures for both cohesive and cohesionless soils are available in standard soil mechanics texts. All of the variables itemized in the preceding paragraph can be incorporated into the analysis using standard procedures. For the more complex situations, the passive pressure can be determined by successive trials to determine the critical failure wedge which produces the minimum passive pressure for equilibrium.

Effect of Foundation Details. Lateral loads from wind may not be transmitted uniformly by all elements of the foundation to the soil. Most foundations for tall buildings are relatively substantial and will tend to act together as a unit. This should not be taken for granted in the analysis and a review should be made of the paths available for the wind loads to reach the soil through the foundation elements. The following examples of typical shallow foundations will illustrate this point.

A building foundation may consist of individual spread footings with a basement slab which is not adequate as a diaphragm to connect structurally all the interior footings with the exterior foundation walls. Under this condition each footing should be designed for the wind load delivered to it by its column. The lateral component will be taken by passive soil pressure against the contact face between footing and soil and the moment will result in a reduction of bearing pressure on one side and an increase on the other side of the footing.

Because of the shear load delivered to the top of the footing, an eccentric and inclined resultant loading acts on the soil. The ultimate bearing capacity of the soil is reduced by this inclined loading. Safety against shear failure under the combined loadings must be carefully investigated (Brinch-Hansen, 1961; De Beer, 1963).

If the footings are connected with a foundation slab of sufficient thickness to make the entire foundation act as a unit, the contact areas engaged in mobilizing the passive pressure are greatly increased by the area of the foundation wall in contact with the soil. The flexural rigidity of the slab will tend to distribute the effects of wind moments to a wider area, providing the slab is in contact with undisturbed soil similar to that supporting the footings and the footing to slab connections are properly designed. A structure supported on a mat will distribute wind effects in a similar manner. If the underside of the mat is a flat surface the only passive pressure mobilized will be at the foundation wall.

Elastic Design Methods. The conventional design approach discussed previously for the determination of limiting resisting pressures may not be sufficiently refined for the condition where lateral deformations must be restricted to small amounts tolerable to the building foundations. A procedure could be utilized which would involve equating a change in the horizontal pressure coefficient to the wall movement. Fig. 7.13 shows the relationship between the wall rotation and this coefficient and is based on field observations collected by Gould (1970) for predominantly granular materials. Plotted on Fig. 7.13 are the relationships as reported by Terzaghi (1936) which involve the compaction of backfill against a rigid model wall. The curves reported by Gould involve more typical field situations where the exterior foundation walls are cast against the natural soil in which the active stress state has been produced during excavation. These latter curves are based on a limited number of field observations which do not justify quantifying . this method as a design recommendation. These curves provide coefficients for a steady-state loading without regard to cyclical effects, the transient nature of the load application, or the effect of the rate of strain in the surrounding soil. The combination of these effects would probably tend to make these curves conservative for coarse grained soils. For cohesive soils, the effects would be more complicated since cyclical loading could result in strain accumulations. However, further observations are necessary to justify final design recommendations.

Assuming that it is desirable to restrict the translation at the ground surface so that the foundation wall rotation is approximately 0.002 rad, Fig. 7.13 indicates the horizontal earth pressure to be approximately 0.8 times the vertical effective earth pressure for a compact granular soil in which the active state has been produced during excavation. For most granular soils within the range of tolerable movements,

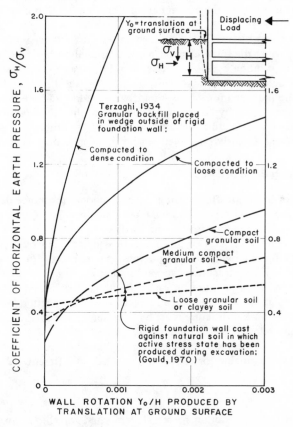

Fig. 7.13 Relationship between wall rotation and lateral earth pressure

no more than the full vertical pressure can be assumed under the same conditions.

The lateral pressure developed by a wall movement can also be approximated by considering the soil as an elastic material with a linear relation between the stress and the strain. This can be accomplished by using a horizontal modulus of subgrade reaction, as suggested by Terzaghi (1955), or by defining the soil as an elastic solid.

The coefficient of horizontal subgrade reaction k is the ratio between the pressure at a particular point on the contact surface and the lateral deformation produced by the pressure. The soil is considered to be replaced by a series of independent springs with a spring modulus equal to k. The pressure intensity at any point is therefore assumed to vary linearly with the deflection at that point and completely independent from deflections at any other point. Approximate values for different soils are suggested by Terzaghi (1955), and formulas are presented for corrections to be applied because of the size of the loaded areas. Values presented by Terzaghi were developed for resistance of wales and tie backs for bulkheads. They are conservative, that is, actual deflections usually will be less than those computed. Effects of such conservatism on stress distribution in structural systems may be nonconservative and should be investigated. Although the use of this theory may involve substantial errors as a result of the basic assumptions, these can be overcome by the judicious use of a factor of safety. Discussion of these assumptions and the errors involved in the horizontal subgrade modulus approach are presented in Article 4 of this section.

Morgenstern and Eisenstein (1970) have presented an analysis of earth pressures behind a wall using the finite element method of analysis with differing boundary conditions. The solution is based on assuming the soil as an elastic solid defined by a modulus of deformation E and Poisson's ratio μ. Results of the lateral pressure calculations are indicated for six cases under the condition where the wall is pushed into the elastic medium by an amount 0.0025 its height. Although solutions of this type are valuable in extending the understanding of the problem, it is doubtful that they will become standard design methods for practical problems in the near future.

3　Shear Along Base of Structure

Calculation of Shearing Resistance.　The frictional resistance developed along the base of a foundation depends on the type of supporting soil, the normal pressure between the soil and the foundation, and the friction angle or adhesion between the soil and the foundation. The normal pressure is determined by dividing the total dead load on a footing by the area of the footing in contact with the soil. (Note this is not applicable if the structure is supported on piles or caissons.) Wind moments causing an increase in pressure on one side of the footing with a corresponding decrease on the other side will have no effect. However, uplifting loads on footings from wind forces on the structure must be considered. The total dead load must be reduced by any buoyancy effect caused by ground water.

Friction angles (in degrees) for noncohesive soil and adhesion (in kilopascals) for cohesive soils are available for concrete supported on different soils for use in

$$F = W \tan \phi + C_a A B \qquad (7.5)$$

in which F = resisting friction force; W = normal force; ϕ = angle of internal friction; C_a = adhesion between concrete and soil; and A, B = dimensions of base.

The frictional force which is developed between the concrete base and the soil cannot be larger than the shearing resistance that can be developed within the soil mass. For cohesionless soil the shearing strength is

$$\tau = \bar{\sigma} \tan \phi \tag{7.6}$$

in which $\bar{\sigma}$ = effective normal stress, and ϕ = angle of internal friction.

For cohesive soils, the shearing strength is

$$\tau = C + \bar{\sigma} \tan \phi \tag{7.7}$$

in which C = cohesion.

Most tall buildings do not depend on the shearing resistance below the foundation as the only force resisting wind. The shear along the base is developed as part of the resisting system and must, therefore, be compatible as far as the deformation characteristics are concerned with the deformation required to develop the other forces.

For shallow foundations, such as spread footings, the inclined and eccentric resultant of the weight of the building and the force of the wind must be considered in evaluating the bearing resistance.

Pile Supported Structures. Shearing resistance along the base of pile or caisson supported structures may be completely eliminated after a period of time because of settlement of soil below the base. The effect of this settlement is shown on Fig. 7.14(a). The transfer of wind loads to the soil for pile or pier supported structures should always be accomplished by means other than the shearing resistance along the base. Fig. 7.14(b) shows one method of overcoming this problem.

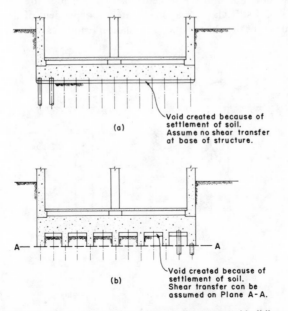

Fig. 7.14 Effects of soil settlement below pile supported buildings

4   Lateral Resistance of Piles or Piers

Piles or caissons subjected to lateral forces from wind will deflect laterally, developing pressures in the surrounding soil to resist the loads. The shape of the deflected pile will depend on the soil deformation characteristics and the length and rigidity of the pile. Fig. 7.15 shows the typical deflected shapes for both rigid and flexible members. At the present time, methods based on the concept of a coefficient of horizontal subgrade reaction are the most useful in providing a solution to the deformations and stresses in piles subjected to lateral loads. This theory assumes that the soil can be replaced by a series of independent elastic springs. The reaction in the soil f at a depth z is directly proportional to the deflection y at that point. Thus

$$f = ky \qquad (7.8)$$

in which k = spring constant or the modulus of horizontal subgrade reaction. Hetenyi (1946) derives the differential equation for the deflection curve of a beam supported by an elastic foundation as

$$EI \frac{d^4y}{dx_z^4} + ky = 0 \qquad (7.9)$$

in which EI = flexural stiffness of the pile or pier. Terzaghi (1955) has discussed the factors which affect the coefficient k and proposed reasonable values for this modulus. The errors resulting from the substitution of ideal soil properties in this analysis are considered overcome by the use of normal design safety factors, providing the coefficients selected are compatible with the deformation characteristics of the subgrade and the dimensions of the loaded area. The deformation characteristics of a stiff clay are approximately independent of depth; therefore, a uniform value for the horizontal foundation modulus can be assumed. In

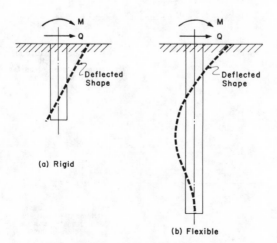

Fig. 7.15 Deflected shape of piles or piers

cohesionless soils and normally consolidated clays the pressure necessary to produce a unit displacement increases with depth and, therefore, Terzaghi (1955) recommended the use of a value for k which increased linearly with depth as

$$k = n_h z \tag{7.10}$$

in which z = distance below ground surface.

Rigidity Check.   To determine whether the pile or caisson should be considered rigid, the relative stiffness factor is determined. This value for a constant value of k is defined as

$$R = \sqrt[4]{\frac{EI}{k}} \tag{7.11}$$

For soils where k increases with depth, the relative stiffness factor is defined as

$$T = \sqrt[5]{\frac{EI}{n_h}} \tag{7.12}$$

If the embedded length of a pile or caisson L is divided by the values of R or T, the resulting dimensionless number is indicative of the rigidity of the member relative to the soil.

For values of L/R or $L/T \leqq 2$ the member acts as a rigid pole with displacements only from a rotation. For values L/R or $L/T \geqq 4$ the member is considered flexible. Piles or caissons in most practical problems will fall into the flexible category. Solutions for the deflections and moments for constant values of k and also for k increasing linearly with depth are available (Terzaghi, 1955).

Effect of Pile Head Fixity.   The effect of the amount of restraint at the top of the laterally loaded pile or caisson on the moments and deflections has also been reported. In general, the embedment of a pile or caisson is not sufficient to develop full fixity. Prakash (1962) indicates that for a free head the maximum moment occurs at a depth of $1.35T$. For a fixed head the maximum moment occurs at the top of the pile. For a fixity of approximately 50% the maximum negative and maximum positive moments are equal resulting in the most efficient use of the structural element. The soil reactions and deflections are materially reduced as the fixity of the pile at the connection to the cap is increased.

Effect of Group Action and Cyclic Loading.   The foundation modulus was found to be affected to a great degree by group action. A model study on piles embedded in sand (Prakash, 1962) reported that the effective value of k is reduced for piles with a spacing in the direction of the loading of less than 8 times the diameter of the pile. At a spacing of 3 times the diameter of the piles parallel to the loading the effective modulus is reduced to 25% of that for isolated piles. There is no effect of one pile on another in the direction perpendicular to the loading, provided this spacing is at least 2.5 times the diameter of the pile.

Cyclic loadings may also cause a large reduction in the effective foundation modulus. Mansur et al. (1964) have reported the results of tests on 2 piles subjected to 100 cycles of loading. Measured deflections of the piles at the ground surface increased up to 90% above the reading measured for the initial load. Most of this increase occurred during the first 50 cycles of loading.

Soil Modulus. The convenience of assuming either a constant value for k or one that increases linearly with depth has resulted in the use of these assumptions almost exclusively in the solution of practical problems. The fact that the soil does not behave exactly as assumed has been recognized, but because of the many factors which tend to limit the accuracy of any calculations refinements have not been thought justified.

Fig. 7.16 shows a comparison between the assumed and the actual load-deformation characteristics of typical soils. Except for very small deflections, the relationship is not linear, indicating that a variation in the foundation modulus should be considered to account for the behavior in areas where the deformation is beyond the linear portion of the curve. The transfer of wind shears to the soil through piles is controlled to a large extent by the soil near its top, which is also the region where the pile experiences its maximum deflection.

The errors resulting from the usual assumptions for the variation of foundation modulus with depth have been investigated (Davisson and Gill, 1963). They indicate that an analysis utilizing a foundation modulus constant with depth may result in an error in the values of moments and deflection of up to 100%. A comparison between the assumed constant k value with the probable variation of the modulus with depth is shown in Fig. 7.17(a) for a stiff cohesive soil. The variation near the surface is significant. The comparison for the granular soils is shown in Fig. 7.17(b) and indicates a greater compatibility between actual and assumed near the ground surface. Davisson and Gill present a nondimensional solution for the effect of a two-layered soil system on the behavior of a laterally loaded pile. The modulus of the upper layer is expressed in terms of the modulus of the lower layer, and both soft and hard upper layers are considered. Variations in thickness of the surface layer are also introduced. The results can be used to approximate the deflections and moments for soils which are layered, or to consider effects of seasonal variations in the soil properties of the soil close to the ground surface.

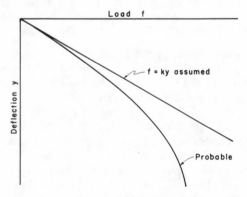

Fig. 7.16 Load deflection curve

5 Batter Piles

The use of batter piles in the foundations of tall buildings for the resistance of wind loads has been quite limited. This has probably resulted in part from economic considerations, since a large number of batter piles would be ineffective in resisting wind shears from directions near perpendicular to the plane of their inclination. To develop a system which could provide resistance from wind in all directions would require a multiple of the number of piles needed for wind in one direction. In addition, driving batter piles at a site where large numbers of vertical piles must also be installed to support vertical loads can cause many practical problems of interferences between the vertical and batter piles. Problems of the projection of pile tips beyond the limits of the property lines may also restrict the use of batter piles in this application. Batter piles should not be used where soils may settle or compress as by consolidation. In such cases, bending of the piles by the soil may rupture the piles or pull them from the pile cap.

Field tests performed to determine the relative resistance to lateral loads of various arrangements of vertical and batter piles are described by Feagin (1953). Results of these tests indicated that the least lateral resistance of all groups tested was provided by a cap with four piles battered in the direction of the load and four against the load. On two groups of vertical piles the lateral loads per pile to develop 6-mm (0.25-in.) lateral deflection were 43 kN (9.6 kips) and 52 kN (11.6 kips). The higher load occurred for the eight-pile group with four rows in the direction of the load. The equivalent configuration with all piles battered, four against and four in the direction of the load, required 140.6 kN (31.6 kips) per pile for a 6-mm (0.25-in.) deflection. If batter piles can be utilized in a foundation for a tall building, it is obvious that wind shears can be resisted with much less lateral deformation than required to develop other resisting systems.

Distribution of Loads. The distribution of lateral loads to individual piles is based on the analysis of the vertical and horizontal movement of the base and the amount of rotational movement. Such movements are a function of: (1) The physical characteristics of the piles; (2) the rigidity of the base; (3) the degree of fixity of the pile head in the base; and (4) the resistance of the soil to horizontal and vertical movements.

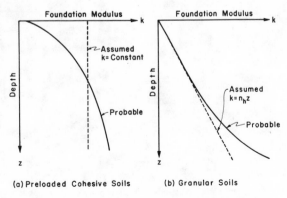

Fig. 7.17 Variation of subgrade modulus with depth

The analysis of pile groups is usually simplified by assuming that the structure is rigid and the distortions of the piles are of considerable magnitude with respect to the structure. Methods for simplified analyses are available in standard texts on foundation design. It must be recognized that these methods disregard the characteristics of the soil and piles and also the degree of fixity developed at the pile head. There are some more rational methods available for use in this analysis, including one presented by Hrennikoff (1950), which does include consideration of the factors disregarded in some of the more approximate methods. These rational methods involve time-consuming calculations and are based on assumptions of soil behavior which only approximate the actual conditions. It is, therefore, questionable to attempt to obtain loads on batter piles by the more complex methods except for the problems of substantial importance.

6 Combined Systems

Wind loads on tall buildings are generally distributed to the soil by a combination of the systems discussed previously. In order to evaluate the combined effect it is necessary to have an understanding of the deformations required to mobilize the resisting forces in each system. This understanding must be converted to a single deformation which is compatible with both systems and which is within the tolerable movement for the structure. Under this condition it is not usually possible to generate maximum resistance in more than one system. In the final analysis, resistances of the two systems acting together must provide sufficient forces to overcome the effects of the design wind loads at the acceptable limit of movement. To illustrate the procedures two examples are presented.

Vehicle Assembly Building—Florida. The Vehicle Assembly Building at Cape Kennedy, Florida is 160.4 m (526 ft) high enclosing approximately 3.5×10^6 m³ (125×10^6 ft³) of space. It is designed to resist hurricane winds of 200 km/hr (125

Launch Complex #39, Vehicle Assembly Building, Kennedy Space Center, Florida
(Courtesy: ASCE)

mph) at the 9-m (30-ft) level, and 312 km/hr (195 mph) at the roof. The maximum wind results in a total horizontal shear at the foundation level of 100 MN (22 500 kips) which is designed to be resisted by a combination of bending in the vertical piles supporting the building and passive earth pressure against the pile caps and a system of beams connecting the pile caps.

The upper 10 m (40 ft) of soil consists of loose to compact grey fine sand with moderate amounts of soft organic material in the upper 0.6 to 1.2 m (2 to 4 ft). Ground surface is at El. 0.6 m with the sands below El. -6 m (-20 ft) in a generally compact state. Ground water is at or just below the ground surface. The complete typical soil profile is shown in Fig. 7.18.

Foundation support is provided by approximately 4200 400-mm (16-in.) diam steel pipe piles with a 10-mm (3/8-in.) wall driven open ended to rock at El. -44.5 m. The soil inside the pile was not removed after driving. References used in this analysis included Design Manual No. 7 (Bureau of Yards and Docks, 1962), Reese and Matlock (1956), and Tschebotarioff and Johnson (1953). Soil properties assumed for the sand are as follows: Angle of internal friction = 33°; angle of wall friction = 0°; submerged unit weight = 960 kg/m³ (60 pcf); relative densi-ty = 50%; horizontal modulus of deformation n_h = 6.28 MN/m³ (23.2 pcf).

Further, it was recognized that settlement of the soil engaged by the beams would occur, so that an effective depth of 2.3 m (7.5 ft) was used in the calculations, although the beams were actually deeper. The following represents a summary of typical calculations.

Horizontal resistance of diaphragm walls.   Please refer to Fig. 7.19.

Movement necessary to develop full passive pressure:

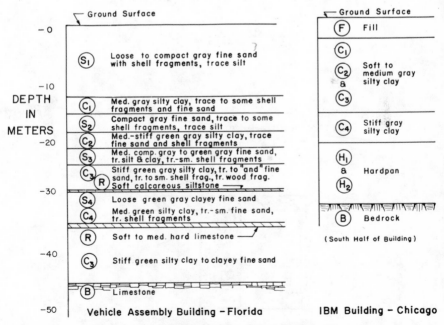

Fig. 7.18 Generalized subsurface stratification

$$0.05 \times 2.3 \text{ m} \times 10^3 = 115 \text{ mm}$$

$$(0.05 \times 7.5 \text{ ft} \times 12 = 4.5 \text{ in.})$$

If movement is restricted to 8 mm (0.3 in.) passive pressure developed is slightly more than 50% of the full passive pressure possible [see Figure 10-7 of Design Manual No. 7 (Bureau of Yards and Docks, 1962)].

Horizontal resistance of piles.

Pipe piles: 400 mm ϕ × 10 mm wall (16 in. ϕ × 0.375 in. wall).

Area of steel = 11 877 mm^2 (18.41 in.^{2}), $T = 233.96 \times 10^6$ mm^4 (562.1 in.^{4}).

Pile loading—compression: 1.1827 MN (120.6 tonnes; 226 kips).

Length = 45.7 m (150 ft), $S = 1.1513 \times 10^6$ mm^3 (70.26 in.^{3}).

Modulus of elasticity = 200×10^3 MPa (29×10^6 psi).

$n_h = 6.28$ MN/m^3 (23.2 pci).

Allowable stresses—bending = 137.9 MPa (20 000 psi).

Allowable stresses—compression = 117.2 MPa (17 000 psi). Allowable stresses may be increased by 33% ($\times$ 1.33) for combined loads of dead load + live load + wind. Bending stresses are induced only by wind loadings.

Combined stresses—bending and dead load—are

$$\frac{1.1827}{(117.2)(11.877 \times 10^{-3})} + \frac{\text{Moment}}{(1.1513 \times 10^{-3})(137.9)(1.33)} = 1$$

$$0.85 + \frac{M}{211.1 \times 10^{-3}} = 1$$

or, in kilonewtons

$$M = (0.15)(211.1) = 31.67 \text{ kNm} (23.36 \text{ kip/ft})$$

From Eq. 7.12, relative stiffness factor

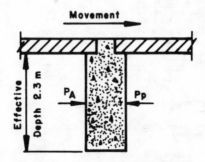

Fig. 7.19 Horizontal resistance of diaphragm walls

$$T = \sqrt[5]{\frac{EI}{n_h}} = \left[\frac{(200 \times 10^3)(234 \times 10^{-6})}{6.28}\right]^{1/5}$$

$$= \sqrt[5]{7.45} = 1.49 \text{ m } (58.8 \text{ in.})$$

$$\frac{L}{T} = \frac{45.7}{1.49} = 31\text{—flexible.}$$

Deflection = 0 at $z = 0$ [Fig. 13.4 of Design Manual 7 (1962)]

Depth for "0" deflection = $(2.4)(1.49) = 3.58$ m (11.7 ft)

From Design Manual No. 7 (Bureau of Yards and Docks, 1962)

$$F_M = \text{max moment coefficient} = 0.76$$

$$y_0 = \text{deflection coefficient at surface} = 2.3$$

$$M = F_M (P \times T)$$

in which P = horizontal force at top of pile.

$$31.67 = 0.76 (P \times 1.49)$$

$$P = 28 \text{ kN } (6.28 \text{ kips}).$$

Total pile resistance = $(28)(1652) = 46\,256$ kN (10 400 kips).

Deflection at top of pile = $y_0 = y_p(PT^3/EI)$

$$y_0 = \left\{\frac{(28 \times 10^{-3})(1.49^3)}{(200 \times 10^3)(234 \times 10^{-6})}\right\} 2.3 = 0.00455 \text{ m } (0.18 \text{ in.})$$

Height of walls = 2.3 m

$$\frac{Y}{z} = \frac{0.00455}{2.29} = 0.002$$

Passive pressure developable [see Fig. 10.7 of Design Manual No. 7 (1962)] = $1.4/3.0 = 46\%$ of maximum.

Total resistance of diaphragm walls at 4.5 mm displacement is

$$K_H = K_P - K_A$$

$$K_P = (0.46)(3.38) = 1.55$$

$$K_A = 0.3$$

$$K_H = 1.25$$

Horizontal force developed/unit length of walls

$$= \left(\frac{z^2}{2}\right)\gamma' K_H = \left(\frac{2.29^2}{2}\right)(0.96)(1.25) = 3.15 \text{ t/m} = 30.9 \text{ kN/m}$$

Total resistance:

$$\text{beams} = (30.9 \times 10^{-3})(2683) = 82.9$$

$$\text{piles} = 46.3$$

$$\text{total} = 129.2 \text{ MN.}$$

$$\text{Total wind load} = 100 \text{ MN.}$$

Therefore, satisfactory.

The analysis indicates that the structural system is adequate to develop more than the required lateral resistance using the piles and beams connecting the pile caps.

IBM Building—Chicago, Illinois. The IBM Building in Chicago, Illinois is a 52-story building on the north side of the Chicago River. The plan area of the building is approximately 82.3 m (270 ft) in the north-south and 36.6 m (120 ft) in the east-west direction. A railroad track spur crosses the site at a 45° angle from the southwest to the northeast, eliminating the basement under the south side of the building.

The absence of a basement in the southerly portion of the building required that the wind shears be transmitted to the underlying soils by bending of the caissons assisted by a system of grade beams along the column lines between caissons. The space between the grade beams was filled with a compacted granular fill. The critical wind shear in the south portion of the building has a magnitude of 9560 kN (2150 kips) with the wind in the east-west direction.

The generalized subsurface stratification is shown in Fig. 7.18. Foundations for the south portion of the building consist of 20 caissons with an average shaft diameter of 1.67 m (5 ft 6 in.). Since the caissons were widely spaced, no group action was considered.

The following assumptions and physical properties for the soil and caissons were used in the analysis.

Caissons hinged at top.

Length = 30.5 m (100 ft).

E = 20 684 MPa (3 000 000 psi).

I = 387 × 10^9 mm⁴ (93 × 10^4 in.⁴).

q_u = 47.88 kPa to 76.6 kPa (1 ksf to 1.6 ksf).

c = 24 kPa to 38 kPa (0.5 ksf to 0.8 ksf).

n_h = 3.14 MN/m³ (20 kips/ft³ = 1.16 × 10^{-2} k/in.³).

$$T = \sqrt[5]{\frac{EI}{n_h}} = \left[\frac{(20\ 684)(0.387)}{3.14}\right]^{1/5} = 4.80 \text{ m.}$$

$$\frac{L}{T} = \frac{30.5}{4.8} = 6.35 > 4, \text{ therefore flexible.}$$

$$y_0 = \frac{2.4P}{n_h^{3/5} \times (EI)^{2/5}} \qquad \text{(Broms, 1964).}$$

Now let $y_0 = 5$ mm maximum:

$$P = \frac{(5 \times 10^{-3})(1.99)(36.42)}{2.4} = 151 \text{ kN/caisson.}$$

Total lateral resistance of caissons $= (151)(20) = 3020$ kN.

Maximum moment $= (0.76)(P \times T) = (0.76)(151)(4.8) = 551$ kNm.

Grade beams must transfer remaining shear to soil with movement of 5 mm or less to be compatible with caissons.

Total length of grade beams $= 132.62$ m (435 ft).

Remaining wind shear $= 9560 - 3020 = 6540$ kN.

Required passive pressure/meter of grade beam $= \dfrac{6540}{132.62} = 49.3$ kN/m (3.35 kips/ft).

For sand fill between beams, $\gamma = 2.08$, $\phi = 32°$, $\delta = 0.5\,\phi$, $\beta = 0$.

$K_{P_{\text{ult}}} = (7.6)(0.717) = 5.5$ [see Fig. 10.3 of Design Manual No. 7 (Bureau of Yards and Docks, 1962)].

$y_0 = 5$ mm.

Calculate grade beam depth:

Try depth $z = 1.8$ m.

Rotation $\dfrac{y_0}{z} = \dfrac{5 \times 10^{-3}}{1.8} = 0.0028.$

$K_{H_{\text{mobilized}}} = 1.8$ [see Fig. 10.7 of Design Manual No. 7 (Bureau of Yards and Docks, 1962)].

$$\text{Resistance of grade beam} = \frac{1}{2} K_H Z^2 \gamma = \left(\frac{1}{2}\right)(1.8)(1.8)^2(2.08)$$
$$= 6.07 \text{ tonne /m}$$
$$= 59.5 \text{ kN/m} > 49.3 \text{ kN/m, therefore satisfactory.}$$

7 Stability Considerations

Since under the appellation "Tall Buildings" we have also included "Towers" there may be a problem of instability in some structures.

Habib (1970) has shown that for a given soil and a structure with given cross section there is a critical height which cannot be surpassed without hazard of instability.

For instance, in case of a circular tower, with a mean unit weight ρ and a radius r_o placed at the surface of a semi-infinite medium with constant modulus of elasticity

E_s, Poisson's ratio μ, and critical height h_o for the center of gravity, inducing instability is given by

$$h_c = \sqrt{\frac{2E_s r_o}{3\pi\rho(1 - \mu^2)}} \tag{7.13}$$

For instance, when E_s = 1961 MPa (2000 tonne/m², 907 ksf), μ = 0.5, ρ = 0.35 tonne/m³ (21.85 pcf), r_o = 25 m, one gets h_c = 200 m (656 ft), or H_{crit} = 400 m (1312 ft).

However, when the wind forces are also considered, the calculations show that the horizontal displacements of the top of the tower can be quite important, even for values of the height which are substantially lower than the threshold of instability. For high buildings the considerations of instability with the combination of wind forces must therefore in certain cases be considered, according to the method outlined by Habib (1970).

7.5   EFFECTS OF FOUNDATIONS ON ADJACENT STRUCTURES

Construction operations, such as excavation, dewatering, and pile driving for foundations of buildings, may cause movements of the soil adjacent. Depending on the nature of the subsoil and the distance to existing structures, such structures can be affected. The magnitude and distribution of the movements caused by the various construction operations and the allowable movements of the existing structures are important factors which must be considered in selection of the type of foundation and the method of its construction.

Although it may sometimes be economical to allow some damage to occur and to accept repair afterwards, in most cases it is best to modify the design for construction to prevent damage, or to make a provision so as to reduce or prevent movement of the structure.

Changes in stresses in the soil, after completion of the construction, may also affect nearby structures. An appreciable change in the effective soil stresses due to the foundation pressure of the new building, or a change in the pore pressure in the soil mass, can cause consolidation which results in settlements and, in most cases, differential settlements. Changes in effective stress or in pore-water pressures, even above founding level, may cause unacceptable increases in negative skin friction on piles and result in unequal settlements of adjoining structures.

Construction operations or changes in effective stress or pore pressures may cause lateral movements of nearby structures or increase lateral loads on basement walls or retaining walls.

1   Existing Structures

The first step in evaluating possible damage from construction operations for new structures is estimating allowable movements of the existing structures. The allowable settlement of a structure generally is known from available local data or by rule of thumb.

Settlement which results in a uniform tilt usually is not limited by structural considerations. Long before tilting becomes a source of possible structural damage, it will have reached the limit set by conditions of practical use or esthetic or psychological considerations.

Differential settlement between elements of the same structure is the most serious and can result in significant structural distress or damage. The maximum differential settlement between any two points in a building is not necessarily the decisive factor. The decisive factor is the angular distortion: the ratio of the differential settlement between two points to the distance between those points. Criteria suggested by Skempton and MacDonald (1956), Bjerrum (1963), D'Appolonia (1970), and Grant et al. (1974) are presented in Table 7.1.

Table 7.1 uses data obtained primarily from buildings with load bearing walls and traditional steel or reinforced concrete frame buildings with brick or block panels and partitions. It was found that no structural damage or damage to interior finish, panel walls, or partitions occurred in the 98 buildings investigated at angular distortions smaller than 1/300. In frame buildings without interior partitions or brick walls, the damage limit was about 1/150. This would imply that for a conventional structure with brick or block partitions, a differential settlement of 10 mm (0.4 in.) in any 3 m (10 ft) can be tolerated without signs of damage. The damage limit increases substantially for very slow settlement rates.

The survey just described was confined mainly to buildings with brick and block partitions; little information is available about the performance of prefabricated buildings. A prefabricated paneling structure in Rotterdam, The Netherlands, may serve as an example. For a 14-story building 70 m × 10 m (230 ft × 32 ft) with a reinforced concrete frame and prefabricated paneling, the settlements were measured for 3 yr from the beginning of construction (the construction period lasted 1 yr). The building was founded on prefabricated piles on top of a rather thin sand

Table 7.1 Damage criteria for settlement of buildings under their own weight [a]

Description of criterion[b] (1)	Angular distortion, $\dfrac{\delta}{L}$ (2)
Difficulties with machinery sensitive to settlements are of concern	1:750
Danger for frames with diagonals	1:600
Safe limit for buildings where cracking is not permissible	1:500
First cracking in panel walls is to be expected	1:300
Tilting of high, rigid buildings might become visible	1:250
Considerable cracking in panel walls and brick walls	1:100
Safe limit for flexible brick walls	1:100
Structural damage of general buildings is of concern	1:100
Severe distortion of frame	1:100

[a] From Skempton and MacDonald, 1956; Bjerrum, 1963; D'Appolonia, 1971; Grant et al., 1974.
[b] The stated limits suggest the average of a limiting range of δ/L due to the above criteria.

layer, 26 m below the surface. The live pile load was 1.11 MN (125 tons). It was necessary to calculate loadings allowing for a negative skin friction of 0.44 MN (50 tons) for the edge piles, and 0.22 MN (25 tons) for the middle piles.

The measured settlements varied between 24 mm (1 in.) and 12 mm (0.5 in.), a difference in settlements of 12 mm (0.5 in.), and the maximum angular distortion was 1/1200. All the settlements occurred in the construction period, about 1 yr; during the following 2 yr no settlements occurred. Under the given circumstances no damage at all was observed. This indicates that the angular distortion limit is more than 1/1200 for prefabricated panel construction.

The most important factors determining tolerable movements are: (1) Type of movement; (2) rate of movement; (3) magnitude, distribution, and pattern of movements; (4) age, type, and existing condition of building; (5) character and condition of the framework; and (6) character and condition of the foundation.

The following general remarks apply to these factors:

1. A horizontal movement can be more disturbing than an equal vertical movement.

2. Reversal of a movement, particularly if rapid, is more dangerous than movement in one direction.

3. Structures are usually most sensitive to rapid movement—a slow movement enables a structure to adapt itself better to the changing conditions by creep and plastic deformation.

4. Movements caused by excavation and pile driving are relatively rapid compared with settlements caused by the weight of a structure.

5. Old buildings and buildings in poor condition (that have already experienced large differential settlements) may be very sensitive to any additional movement, particularly if rapid.

6. The pattern and magnitude of the differential motions may change during pile driving and excavation along the existing building. The building may be subjected to a wave of differential settlements or lateral movements as the adjacent construction work proceeds.

7. The soil conditions also influence the behavior; under some circumstances a plastic soil may be more favorable than a stiff or brittle soil.

8. If a structure is designed as a multiple-span rigid frame, a continuous beam on many supports, or a similar rigid type of construction, the allowable differential settlements are very small (angular distortion about 1/2000), and structural rather than architectural damage tends to occur. A similar problem exists for rigid frame construction with fixed column ends at footing level.

9. Existing structures with heterogeneous foundations—that is, having: (a) Different type of foundation elements; (b) large variations in foundation pressure or pile loads; (c) significant variations in the safety coefficient —belong to the most sensitive category. This is due to the relatively high differences in the load deformation characteristics of the various (or variously loaded) foundation elements. Moreover, these structures are mostly old and varying in age.

Example. To make a small, deep excavation in the center of Rotterdam, The Netherlands, the pore pressure in the so-called first sand layer was lowered to a level of 7 m (23 ft) below normal for a period of 5 months. The subsoil consists of about 13 m (43 ft) of very soft clay and peat above the first sand layer, which is about 15 m (50 ft) thick. The pore pressure in the sand layer initially was equal to the average hydrostatic pressure caused by sea level. All structures are founded on piles that rest in the sand layer. The pore pressure in the clay and peat layers is, except for the lowest 2 m to 3 m (7 ft to 10 ft) not influenced to any great extent by the piezometric pressure in the sand layer.

The pore pressure in the sand layer had been gradually decreased by 5 m of water (49 kPa, 1024 psf, 5 t/m²). The initial lowering of the piezometric pressure was caused by pumping from a number of wells rather widely spaced. It took place gradually over a period of 10 to 15 yr. No remarkable damage to structures was observed. The drawdown line in the sand layer is very steep in the first 10 m to 15 m (30 ft to 50 ft) from the wells, and then extends gradually to about 1500 m (5000 ft) from the wells.

A second lowering of the piezometric pressure of 7 m (69 kPa, 1434 psf, 7 t/m²) was done by a number of wells located at short distances from one another, and was completed very quickly (in a few days). There was serious cracking of panel walls in a number of buildings at a distance of about 100 m (320 ft) from the wells. The buildings affected have heterogeneous foundations (wooden and concrete piles, part of the piles having a relatively low safety coefficient); they are old and of different ages.

Interestingly, other buildings closer to the wells were not damaged, even buildings 10 m (30 ft) from the well system. These buildings close to the wells have reinforced concrete frames, homogeneous pile foundations, and the safety factor for the bearing capacity of the piles (for expected loads including wind) is 2 or more.

Conclusion. The subject of allowable movements that structures can safely tolerate is complex. Much engineering judgment is needed to reach a sound conclusion in each individual case. The factors that have been mentioned should be considered when coming to a final judgment. In general, it can be stated that the movements caused by nearby construction operations which an existing structure can tolerate in most cases are less than the amount of deformation that the same structure can experience without damage during settlement due to its own weight.

2 Movements Caused by Excavation

Because of space restrictions, major foundation excavations in urban areas usually require vertical cuts with a lateral support system. The primary requirement is to prevent large movements or collapse of the side of the excavation.

Usually buildings, underground utilities, and streets are adjacent to an excavation site. Thus the design requirements are demanding, because movements must be small.

In making an excavation a mass of soil and water is removed. This produces a reduction in total stress around the sides and bottom of the cut. In many cases the ground-water level is lowered at the same time, to facilitate the construction work and to assure the vertical or horizontal (or both) stability of the excavation.

The stress changes caused by an excavation are complex. Usually soil layering is not fully determinable and soil properties may vary significantly in relatively short distances both horizontally and vertically. Thus accurate quantitative predictions of movement cannot be made on the basis of soil testing and theoretical analysis alone. Experience is essential in making predictions and to guiding judgment.

Movements which occur with excavation usually include:

1. A vertical movement in the areas adjacent to the excavation.

2. A horizontal movement toward the excavation.

3. An upward movement of the bottom of the excavation, accompanied by

4. An inward movement of the soil below the excavation level.

These movements depend on: (1) The type and character of the excavation; (2) the type of the soil; (3) factors such as the pore pressure, depth of the excavation, surcharge, and time that the excavation is left open; and (4) construction details and workmanship.

In connection with these factors, the following general remarks can be made:

1. Lateral movements above the excavation level can be controlled by the stiffness of the wall and the rigidity of the support system, or by prestressing the supports.

2. Movements occurring below excavation level are determined by the inward movements of the embedded portion of the wall and the deformation of the

Foundation excavation, AT & T corporate headquarters, New York *(Photo by Herman Bernstein Associates)*

soil below the base of the excavation. In theory, if the embedded portion of the wall extended to a great enough depth below the bottom of the excavation and were sufficiently stiff to resist any deformation due to the bending moment caused by the soil stresses acting on the outside face of the wall, then lateral movements of the soil outside the excavation would not occur, regardless of the properties of the soil. In practice, however, a wall possessing such rigidity cannot be installed prior to the general excavation. Consequently, movements depend chiefly on the properties of the soil. If the soil immediately below the base of the excavation must suffer large strains in order to develop passive resistance, or if the soil cannot develop sufficient passive resistance, the inward movement of the soil towards the excavation (and the resulting ground settlement) will be large. See also Section 7.3 of this chapter.

3. The safe depth of the excavation is a function of the shear strength of the soil below the base of the excavation. When the excavation reaches a depth where bottom stability failure (a viscoplastic flow) is approached, the movements (and subsequent settlements) increase sharply. The bottom stability can be analyzed by current methods concerning the stability of slopes and bearing capacity (Terzaghi and Peck, 1967). Bjerrum and Eide (1956) presented approximate theoretical solutions in the shape of dimensionless bearing capacity numbers, based on measurements made in Oslo.

4. The largest movements and therefore the most serious problems are encountered in excavations in soft and medium soft clay. Measurements on well designed and constructed excavations show that 60% to 80% of the total lateral wall deflection takes place below excavation level. These movements depend on the passive earth resistance to inward horizontal earth thrust that can be mobilized by the soil immediately below the base of the cut.

5. With increasing stiffness and strength of the clay, the movements caused by the excavation decrease rapidly.

6. Experiences have shown that movements associated with excavation in peat and compressible organic silt can be as large as, or even larger than, the movement caused by excavations in soft clay.

7. In the case of cohesionless sand and cohesive granular material (which have a relatively high shear strength) the movements can be expected to be small, provided there is sufficient horizontal support and seepage is properly controlled. The most important aspect of excavation in these soils is to maintain adequate control of the seepage pressure and the change in pore pressure due to ground-water flow.

8. Experiences in Rotterdam, especially in the harbor area, have shown that the occurrence of excess pore-water pressure and liquefaction (caused by surcharge along the excavation and pile driving or other types of vibration along or in the excavation) frequently result in extremely large deformations, sometimes even in failure.

9. In the case of excavations in soft soils, the initial movements will be

followed by further secondary permanent deformations as a result of creeping and horizontal consolidation below the bottom of the excavation. The magnitude of this movement, which usually is less than the initial movement, depends on the time that the excavation is left open.

10. The removal of the supports and sheeting of the excavation after construction work has been finished sometimes results in larger movements of the adjacent subsoil than the total movements during excavation and construction work. Consequently a very careful procedure of removal of the supports and the sheeting is essential. It is not unusual to leave the sheeting in the ground.

11. Sensitive clays pose especially difficult problems and advice of knowledgeable experts should be obtained if excavations are to be made in such soils.

Diaphragm Walls. Diaphragm walls, constructed by the slurry trench method, are much stiffer than sheet piles. Experience has shown that stiff walls of this type can reduce movements considerably compared to steel sheeting, especially by limiting movements below excavation level. The bending resistance of steel sheeting is not sufficient to significantly retard wall movements occurring below excavation level.

Additional technical advantages of this type of wall are that no pile driving operation during installation of the wall is needed, and that the wall will not be removed.

In France (mainly in Paris) excavations are made very close to adjacent structures, sometimes at a distance of only 0.2 m (8 in.), with a depth of excavation far below the foundation level. Due to a method of "primary wall elements" with a limited horizontal length, which are spaced at considerable distance from each other, use can be made of the favorable influence of arching during the excavation. This method is often used without any significant deformation of the adjacent subsoil or damage to the adjacent structures.

Examples. In Lyon, France, an extensive test was made in connection with the construction of future metro works. The following data and phenomena were measured: (1) The deformation of the subsoil while making a slurry trench; (2) the deformation of the subsoil, the diaphragm wall, and the horizontal support during excavation between two diaphragm walls; and (3) the stress-strain characteristics for the active, at rest, and passive earth pressure state. The test has been completed, but the interpretation of the measurements has not yet been published.

During subway construction, in Köln, Germany, part of the excavation to a depth of 18 m (60 ft) below the surface was made next to a building. The walls of the excavation were supported on four levels and the struts below the foundation level of the existing building were prestressed to assure an earth pressure at rest state below the existing foundation. There was no damage to the building.

A summary of settlements adjacent to open cuts in various soils was prepared by Peck (1969).

Conclusions. Movements in structures due to excavations are caused by inward soil movements towards the excavation above the excavation level and an upward movement at the bottom of the cut, accompanied by an inward movement of the soil below the excavation level.

The limiting depth of supported excavations is a function of the shear strength properties below the base of the cut. The occurrence of excess pore-water pressures and liquefaction can result in extremely large deformations.

The removal of the supports and sheeting of the excavation must be done very carefully.

The largest movements are to be expected in soft clay, peat, and organic silt.

Field data indicate that stiff slurry walls can reduce movements considerably as compared to steel sheeting. The rigidity of the bracing system, however, is very important.

3 Movements Caused by Dewatering

An excavation below ground-water level requires a system of dewatering which not only permits completion of the required excavation but also helps to prevent disturbance and softening of the excavation bottom.

The pore pressures in the area around the excavation are changed by the dewatering, and these changes may result in deformation of the adjacent soil because of consolidation. Uncontrolled seepage—caused by careless pumping from sumps and ditches and by leaks in retaining walls—can easily remove material and

World Trade Center, New York: view of World Trade Center bathtub area looking north (shot from 117 Liberty Street, 17th floor) *(Courtesy: Port Authority of New York and New Jersey; photo by A. Belva)*

cause subsurface erosion. Piping with heave at the bottom of the excavation is another possible cause of uncontrolled seepage.

Seepage. Damage of nearby structures from uncontrolled seepage can be caused by two different processes.

It may be due to progressive subsurface erosion (piping) that starts at springs and proceeds away from the excavation along some bedding plane. Subsidence of the adjacent ground occurs when the roof of the pipe collapses. Especially in a sandy material with clay or silt layers, which have sufficient cohesion to make a roof over the erosion area, this subsurface erosion can lead to catastrophic failures because movements usually occur rapidly and result in large differential settlements. Such subsurface erosions occur frequently in the tidal flat area formations in Holland. To avoid subsurface erosion, the ground-water flow must be under complete control and discharged through suitable collector systems provided with graded filters.

If the pore pressure below the base of the excavation (as, for example, in a thin aquifer) is greater than the weight of the overlying soil stratum, or if the hydraulic friction losses in upward percolating water in the soil near the bottom of the excavation are excessive, the bottom will be uplifted and the soil start to "boil." The erosion of soil may cause subsidence of the ground outside the excavation, or may result in a collapse of the excavation because of the loss of soil support at the base of the sheeting.

The theoretical possibility of such failure can be analyzed using a flow net analysis. However, the actual on-site flow conditions are greatly influenced by minor geological irregularities, and a high factor of safety is recommended. In the case of an artesian pressure head in a deeper lying aquifer, failure by heave can occur unexpectedly and with a high seepage gradient (due to the presence of a "weak spot" in the impervious layer).

Several measures can be taken to prevent piping by heave. Lowering the water level or pore pressure will eliminate the possibility of springs and boiling. Also the sheeting can be driven to a greater depth so that the seepage gradient is reduced.

In recent years a "clay wall" has sometimes been used instead of steel sheeting to intercept seepage. The clay wall is made by the slurry trench method and the trench is filled with a bentonite-cement mixture. It is nearly impervious and yet retains a certain amount of plasticity. These walls can be made to depths of about 30 m (100 ft). A combination of closed vertical walls with a chemically injected horizontal layer, made at a certain depth below the bottom where equilibrium exists between the hydrostatic uplift and the weight of the soil, is also being used with good results.

Decrease of Pore-Water Pressure. Pumping from pumps or wells causes a reduction in pore pressure and a corresponding increase in effective stress in the surrounding soil. Pumping from sand strata may decrease the pore pressure at large distances from an excavation (sometimes several hundred meters). The drawdown line, which defines the reduction of the pore pressure, usually is steep within the first 5 m to 25 m (15 ft to 80 ft) from the wells, followed by a nonlinear part and a much less steep linear part of the drawdown curve.

In the case of normal dewatering operations in granular soils, the increase in effective stress is too small to cause significant consolidation in all but very loose sands, especially outside the steep part of the drawdown line. However, when layers of soft clay, organic materials, or silt are present, decreasing the pore pressure may cause large settlements over a wide area.

In sand the pore pressures are quickly reduced after dewatering has started. The pore pressure in clay and organic materials, because of their low permeability, may respond very slowly; it sometimes takes years for the pore pressure in the clay to decrease noticeably. On the other hand, rather small deformations of the subsoil can cause the occurrence or increase of negative skin friction on piles.

Measures to anticipate settlements in the excavation area or around a sensitive adjacent structure are recharging by wells or the restraint of the ground-water flow by walls (clay, concrete, sheetpile, thin metal screen). Experience has shown that recharge by a relatively large number of low pressure wells (a kind of infiltration) gives less trouble than infiltration by normal high pressure wells.

4   Movements Caused by Foundation Construction

Depending on the nature of the soil being penetrated, the type and spacing of piles, and the method and sequence of pile driving, important ground movements may extend a considerable distance beyond the edge of the pile group. Pile driving near existing buildings, particularly buildings on shallow foundations, should always be viewed as a source of potential problems, regardless of the type of soil on which the foundation rests.

The most common complaints associated with pile driving involve objectionable vibrations and noise causing discomfort to people, cracking of plaster or concrete block partitions, or damage to architectural finishings. In most cases the vibrations are merely a nuisance, but hard driving at close distance can produce vibrations intense enough to cause damage. Soil vibrations are most intense in granular soils and stiff clays; within a distance of about 5 m (15 ft) from the existing structure, pile driving may give problems in these soils.

Large settlements due to pile driving in granular soil are to be expected in loose deposits of uniform fine sands and silty sands that are below ground-water level. These materials are known to be susceptible to densification and loss of strength when subjected to vibration.

Apart from reducing the level or intensity of vibration, no readily apparent means are available for reducing settlement caused by pile driving in loose sand. Low displacement piles do not appear to be particularly effective. Jetting of piles is effective in reducing vibrations, but it must be carefully controlled in order to prevent undermining of the support. It is advisable to keep to a minimum the number of piles driven close to the adjacent structure.

Pile driving in soft to medium clay causes an increase in pore pressure and heave of the ground surface during driving, and frequently lateral displacement of the soil. These displacements may affect nearby structures, or heave or displace laterally previously driven piles. Lateral pressures and displacements may damage basement walls or disturb piping (see also Section 7.6 of this chapter).

Later, the ground surface settles as the pore pressure dissipates. The end result is usually a settlement. Important movements can be expected over distances equal to the thickness of the clay being penetrated. Use of high-capacity, low-displacement piles or piles placed in precored holes is effective in reducing movements. The pile driving sequence should be controlled and proceed in a direction going away from nearby structures.

During construction of caissons or deep foundation elements other than driven piles, it is essential to maintain relatively high hydrostatic pressure in the bore hole by slurry trench, to leave the holes open as short a time as possible, and to prevent vibrations in the immediate neighborhood.

While attention has been directed in the foregoing primarily to temporary conditions during construction, permanent or long-term changes in stress, ground-water levels, or vibration may also affect nearby structures. Thus, if the weight of the new structure causes an increase in stress in soft foundations under nearby structures, distortion or damage may result. Similarly depression of the water table, as by permanent drainage systems or by wells as for air conditioning systems, may cause damaging settlement of nearby structures because of consolidation of soft soils over which they are founded or negative friction (dragdown) of the piles on which they are founded. Vibration from equipment in the new structure may also cause extensive settlement if the area is underlain by loose sands or inorganic silts.

7.6 DEEP FOUNDATIONS—PILES AND CAISSONS

Piles and caissons are structural elements, such as steel sections, pipe, concrete, or wood, which are used to transfer the load of a building from the lowest level of general excavation through soft, compressible, or unstable soils to deeper lying and usually more competent soil or to rock. Occasionally, "friction" piles are used in deep medium to soft clays which increase in strength and compressibility only slowly with depth. Friction piles may serve a useful purpose for small area, isolated loadings, such as bridge piers. For larger areas, such as most buildings, especially where minimum dimensions of the loaded area equal or exceed the length of the piles, friction piles usually do not significantly reduce settlement and may increase it because of soil disturbance. For such sites, consideration should be given to compensated foundations (Section 7.3 of this chapter).

1 Basic Concepts

The most essential difference between piles and caissons lies in the methods used to construct them. Basically, piles are emplaced by driving them from the surface, using some type of hammer. Falling weights have been used for several millennia. Alternatively, the hammer may be operated by steam, compressed air, explosion of fuel (diesel), or hydraulic pressure. Essentially, a known mass is accelerated by gravity or by gravity and pressure and strikes the top of the pile while moving at an approximately known velocity. (Vibration is used to a limited extent in several countries.)

Caissons are emplaced by excavating a hole through the unstable material and filling it, usually with concrete which may or may not be reinforced. The excavation may terminate on the bearing stratum with a base diameter equal to the caisson, or the base may be enlarged to reduce bearing pressures; or a socket may be excavated in the bearing stratum. The latter method is frequently used for very heavy loads on rock especially if the rock shows erratic or slabby weathering.

Diameters and loads imposed are secondary differences. Generally, piles are of small to modest diameters, 150 mm to 600 mm (6 in. to 24 in.), although occasionally larger diameter piles of 1.0 m to 1.2 m (3 ft to 5 ft) are driven. Loadings generally range from about 90 kN to 1800 kN (20 kips to 440 kips) or slightly higher per pile. Very high capacity piles exceeding these limits are available in some areas.

Caissons range from possibly 500 mm to several meters in diameter, and single units may be loaded to 18 MN (4400 kips) or more, depending on size and founding conditions.

2 Pile Foundations

Materials and Types. Piles are generally driven into a dense bearing stratum, such as hard clay or sand or gravel, or to end bearing on rock. They must be driven hard. This is to assure adequate penetration into the bearing stratum to enable them to carry the load by end bearing and shear along the perimeter of the portion embedded in the bearing stratum or to assure seating on or into the rock. Dynamic loads developed during driving may be several times working loads. Accordingly, the element which is driven to position must be sufficiently strong and stiff to withstand the driving stresses. Further, the piles as finally constructed must have adequate structural strength to support the working loads. If the piles are straight or nearly so, even soft soil will provide adequate lateral support so that each pile usually may be considered as a short column for strength analysis. If piles show bending, especially sharp bends, special studies and tests may be necessary to determine that the strength is adequate.

Piles may be constructed of timbers, either round or square; steel sections; pipe, either empty or filled with concrete; precast concrete, either normally reinforced or prestressed; or cast-in-place concrete. Cast-in-place concrete may be cast in a shell left permanently in place, or cast without a shell, directly against the soil, by driving a casing with a capped or plugged end, the casing being withdrawn as the concrete is placed. Shells for casting-in-place piles can be quite thin material if either an internal mandril or external casing is used for driving.

Pile Driving. Piles tend to displace a volume of soil equal to the volume of the area within their bounding perimeter times the length driven. This is true even of steel H piles, since the area between the flanges frequently becomes plugged with dense soil. Soil displacement from later piles may move earlier piles laterally or lift them from seating in the bearing stratum, which is usually termed "heave." Such movements are especially troublesome for shell-less, cast-in-place piles, since the shaft of the pile may be broken and structural failure may occur when load is placed on the pile cluster. Lateral displacements of as much as 400 mm (1.3 ft) have been observed. Lateral displacements are especially critical, since the piles may be bent, or unacceptable eccentricity of the pile group relative to the column it supports may result. Simple heave without lateral displacement may be corrected by redriving to resistance if the pile is of a type which can be redriven. Heave and displacement may be controlled by preboring for each pile. This may be done using an auger, leaving the hole filled with a clay slurry for temporary support or, exceptionally, in the dry (that is, without slurry or water). Preboring should *not* extend into the bearing stratum.

Sometimes dense strata are found above the bearing stratum which in themselves would not provide adequate support for the piles because of thickness or properties of underlying soils. Preboring or jetting with high-pressure water may be used or required to facilitate driving the piles through such strata.

Care should be taken in laying out each pile group to assure proper location. Further, each pile must be started at its proper location and held true to the desired line while being driven. This requires guides or leads for the pile and hammers which are strong and stable, and which can be made truly vertical for vertical piles and held accurately at a predetermined slope for batter piles. Piles should be checked for position after all in a group have been driven, to be sure that undesirable eccentricity between the centroid of the group and the column it supports has not occurred. If necessary, additional piles should be driven to reduce the eccentricity, or structural units installed to resist the moments developed.

Adequacy of each pile to support the load to be placed on it is usually determined by resistance to driving. Dynamic resistance to driving may be computed from formulas which equate energy expended in penetrating the soil taken as the product of the dynamic resistance times the distance driven, termed "set," by that hammer blow to the energy delivered by the hammer less energy lost in friction, ground quake, elastic and inelastic distortions, compression in the pile cap cushion, and energy reflection at interfaces. Analysis may be based on Newtonian impact, for example, Hiley Formula (Chellis, 1961), or on consideration of the longitudinal compression-rarefaction wave developed in the pile, Wave Equation (Smith, 1960; Lowery, 1969).

There may, however, be no close relation between dynamic resistance to driving and static load carrying capacity. The static load carrying capacity may be either significantly larger or smaller than the dynamic driving resistance. For example, dense sands dilate when sheared or distorted as by piling being driven into them. This dilation results in water being pulled into the zone of dilation because of the increase in volume there. If this cannot occur quickly, essentially between hammer blows, pressures in the water in the pores of the soil are temporarily reduced, increasing the effective stresses and the resistance of the soil to displacement. Under these conditions, dynamic driving resistances may be larger than static load carrying capacity. This is termed "relaxation." Usually, it is of concern only with very heavily loaded piles. Similar reduction may be observed where piles are driven to slabbily weathered rocks, such as shales or thinly bedded limestone. Later piles may break slabs of rock on which earlier piles came to rest, or irregular settlements may develop from compression of soft materials under slabs on which some piles are founded.

Conversely, loose sands become denser under vibration and displacement. This volume change can occur only as water is expelled from the zone affected. Consequently, excess pore pressures develop in such zones, and effective stresses and shearing resistance are decreased during driving. Thus, static load capacity may exceed dynamic driving resistance. Similarly, many clay soils suffer significant reduction in shear strength when disturbed or remolded at constant moisture content. Driving resistance in such clays may be significantly smaller than static load carrying capacity developed after the disturbed zone has reconsolidated.

For these reasons, depending on dynamic driving resistance can only lead to either unconservative results or to excessive costs from driving deeper than required or using lighter loadings than could be supported. Best practice, then, is to estimate required penetration into the bearing stratum from experience and from static and dynamic formulas, to drive test piles, and to verify final driving resistances by load testing selected piles.

Selection of Pile Type and Loading.   Selection of the type of piles to be driven and the loads to be imposed are developed from consideration of a number of factors. Among these are:

1. Character, density, and thickness of the bearing stratum.

2. Depth of bearing stratum below general level of excavation.

3. Ground-water levels and possible future variations.

4. Materials and types of piles economically available.

5. Sizes and types of pile driving equipment available.

6. Possible presence of deleterious or corrosive materials in soil or ground water.

7. Loads of structure and its tolerance to settlement.

8. Sensitivity of adjoining structures or the completed structure to vibration or to noise.

A relatively low strength bearing stratum, such as a clay of moderate strength or a thin bearing stratum even if of dense material, may not be able to support large individual pile loads; therefore, moderately loaded piles adapted to such conditions should be used. In general, displacement piles, such as concrete or pipe, will drive to lesser penetrations in a given soil stratum for a specified load than will low displacement piles, such as steel H sections. Constant section piles may also drive more deeply than tapered piles. The latter, however, tend to develop larger resistances in strata overlying the bearing stratum. This may be undesirable, since such resistance may be transient.

Frequently predetermining final pile lengths is not feasible. Rock surfaces may vary erratically or piles may drive to varying penetrations into the bearing stratum, depending on modest local variations in density. Erratic variations of as much as 3 m to 4 m (10 ft to 13 ft) are commonly observed. For such conditions, cast-in-place concrete piles are frequently attractive as compared with precast concrete, timber, or other materials, because of waste of the cutoff portions if piles are bought longer than the longest required, or cost and difficulty of splicing if piles are found too short.

The depth to the bearing stratum may limit types of pile which can be used on a site. Most cast-in-place concrete piles can be driven only to certain depth limits which are determined by the equipment available in the region. Timber piles may be available only to certain lengths. Precast concrete piles may be limited in length by space or handling equipment available, although it should be noted that readily spliced precast concrete piles have been developed in Sweden and are available in some other areas. These can be cast in sections of 10 m (33 ft) or other lengths and joined as the piles are driven.

Untreated wood piles in the ground totally submerged below a permanent water table are essentially permanent. Exposure above the water table will rather quickly result in deterioration of the exposed portion. Thus possible future variations in water level must be evaluated before considering untreated wood piles. Certain types of wood can be pressure-impregnated with creosote. When adequately treated with high-quality creosote, such piles may be considered permanent even above the water table.

Materials economically available for use in piles vary markedly in different areas. In some countries or regions, timber is readily available in usable lengths; in others, it is not available, or is extremely expensive. Availability and economy of steel also vary from country to country. Concrete probably is the most universally available material, either as cast-in-place or precast piles. Reinforced precast concrete piles have been extensively used in Sweden, and types developed there are becoming available in other countries (Fellenius, 1973). Extensive development of pretensioned concrete piles has been undertaken in the United States and Europe (Gerwick, 1972). Cast-in-place pilings are, in general, proprietary developments, and in many cases methods and equipment are protected by patents.

Usually it is necessary to drive piles to dynamic resistances of two to three times static load. Dynamic resistances may be calculated from Wave Equations or the Hiley Formula. Piles as driven must be able to resist such driving stresses without damage. Wood piles and, to a lesser extent, concrete piles and even pipe piles or H piles are subject to damage from driving. Limitations on driving resistance must be considered in selecting loads and pile driving equipment.

The hammer size or energy necessary to drive a pile depends on the length under the hammer, the material of the pile and its Young's modulus, the cross-sectional area, and the dynamic resistance to which the pile must be driven. Long, high capacity piles require large hammers. Such hammers are available in some regions but may not be available to a specific project. Consideration must be given to the sizes of hammers available in the area and whether pile driving rigs of adequate capacity are available. For example, very large, high capacity concrete piles might be considered well adapted to a specific project but cannot be considered if equipment able to drive them is not available.

Tests should be made routinely of soil and ground water to detect salts or other materials which would attack pile materials. Typical are sulfates, which will attack concrete. Acids may be found in industrial areas and will attack both steel and concrete. It may be noted that wood is highly resistant to either.

In general, a minimum of three piles should be used under a column, except along walls or heavy-grade beams where two piles may be usable, since the wall or grade beam will provide stability along one axis. Use of high capacity piles which cannot be fully loaded is rarely economically justifiable. Conversely, high capacity piles frequently are economical for heavy, tall buildings, especially when consideration is given to the cost of pile caps.

Occasionally, site conditions may permit either deep, high capacity piles or lower capacity piles to a higher lying bearing stratum not suitable to develop high capacity piles. Usually, then, total and differential settlements will be greater for the more lightly loaded piles on the higher stratum. This should be evaluated and the effect on the proposed structure considered in selecting the type of pile and loading.

Pile driving generates noise and vibrations which may be objectionable or even damaging to nearby structures or equipment, such as electrical relays or other delicate equipment. Vibration transmission from high frequency vibratory driving equipment is much less than from conventional equipment because of rapid attenuation of the high frequency motion, and should be considered where vibration from conventional pile hammers would be troublesome. Such equipment cannot be used with all types of piles because of difficulties in connections. Such limitations must be recognized when considering vibratory driving.

Pile Groups. Thus far, attention has been directed towards behavior of single piles. Performance of a group of piles, considering both safety against shear failure and settlement, may differ significantly from that of a single pile except where piles are driven to end bearing on rock. Unsatisfactory performance of a pile foundation may arise either: (1) From exceeding loadings which cause shear failure of the pile-soil contact or shear failure of adjoining soil permitting the pile or piles to move relative to the soil; or (2) by settlement from compression of soils underlying the group of piles or of the soil into which the piles themselves are driven.

When an areal load is placed on soil, induced stresses are highest near the center of the area and less toward the edges. As a result, a bowl-shaped settlement develops. This is pronounced in cohesive soils, but it is also observable in granular soils (Swiger, 1941). Since the pile cap is relatively rigid as compared with the deformation of the soil, the effect of such deformation is that the piles along the perimeter, and particularly corner piles, carry loads which are larger than the average, while piles near the center of the group are more lightly loaded than the average. The factor of safety against shear movement of the piles relative to the soil in which they are embedded is thus decreased for the corner piles and exterior piles of the group as compared with the factor of safety which is computed assuming all piles carry the average loading. This problem has been recognized for many years, and correction factors giving reduced loadings on pile groups to compensate for this, which are called Group Efficiency Factors, have been proposed by various investigators (Chellis, 1961, pp. 134–143). Observations strongly indicate that

One Shell Square (New Orleans, Louisiana) before placing mat on piles *(Courtesy: Fazlur R. Khan)*

deformations in granular soils usually are small enough so that consideration need be given this matter only where piles are driven into clay.

Published formulas for group efficiency probably can be used for moderate size pile groups supporting individual columns for clay soils. Group efficiency formulas, however, will lead to uneconomically low loadings where mat foundations supported on piles are considered, since the effect is significant only near the bounding perimeter of the mat. The variable contact pressures over the area of the structure can be calculated using the techniques described in Section 7.3 for Compensated Foundations to determine load concentrations along the perimeters of such mats in order that additional piles may be provided to keep average shearing stresses on piles within the acceptable limits. While group efficiency factors reduce pile loadings to minimize hazard of shear failure of individual piles, a possible nonconservatism does exist where they are used. This arises because reduced average pile loads are used in computing bending stresses in the pile caps. Actually, such a reduced average load is not achieved; the center piles are lightly loaded and exterior piles, particularly corner piles, are heavily loaded. Thus, bending stresses in the pile caps are increased to stresses even more than those which would exist if group efficiency was not considered.

As indicated, areal loads even on sand cause some bowl-shaped settlements. Consequently, there is a redistribution of loads to the piles. Such data as are available indicate that the variation in pile loading is on the order of 10%, which is within the capacity of the individual piles. Therefore, for piles driven to bearing in a medium dense to dense sand or other granular soil, consideration need not be given to group efficiency. The load capacity of n piles in a group can be assumed to be n times that of an individual pile.

An additional factor must also be considered for piles driven to clay soils. While unacceptable settlement resulting from consolidation of underlying soils may occur

Two Shell Plaza, Houston, Texas—mat foundation on clay *(Courtesy: Fazlur R. Khan)*

even at small pile loadings, true failure of piles in clay soils results almost totally from shear failure between the pile and the soil or in soil adjacent to the pile. The total load carried by the pile is proportional to the perimeter area of the pile within the bearing stratum. If piles are closely spaced, the surface area of the bounding perimeter of the pile group may be less than that of the individual piles times the number of piles. Further, disturbance by driving of a number of closely spaced piles may reduce the shearing strength of the soil. Accordingly, piles in groups driven into clay should be sufficiently widely spaced so that the bounding perimeter of the pile group is larger than the number of piles times the perimeter of each individual pile.

A somewhat similar problem can arise where piles are driven to a thin bearing stratum underlain by more compressible soils. The bearing capacity of the underlying soil should be checked to be sure a shearing capacity failure cannot occur. Bowl-shaped settlements may also develop under each pile group, due to consolidation of such underlying compressible soils, and result in excessive loading of corner and exterior piles of the group or in unacceptable settlements. Group efficiency factor should be considered wherever such conditions exist, and possible settlements due to consolidation determined.

Negative Friction.   Where piles are drawn through soils which are settling due to compression under their own weight or from some external loading, the soil tends to hang up on or to be supported by the piles, since the piles are comparatively incompressible. This is termed "negative friction." It is a complex problem which has only recently begun to be appreciated as an important problem.

For instance, both the Swedish Building Code (1967) and the National Building Code of Canada (1970) state that negative skin friction should be considered. However, it is not mentioned how the negative skin friction should be considered. Recent investigations have shown that large drag loads due to negative skin friction will develop on piles in settling soil layers (Johannessen and Bjerrum, 1965; Bjerrum et al., 1969; Bozuzuk and Labrecque, 1968; Bozuzuk, 1970, 1972). Such settlement may occur from a number of causes, including fills placed for or near the structure, or changes in ground-water level in permeable strata within or underlying the

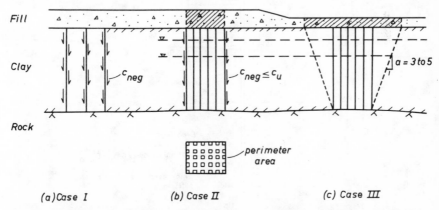

Fig. 7.20 Calculation of negative skin friction: Case I, widely spaced piles to be treated as individual piles; Case II, closely spaced piles and large surcharge on ground surface mobilizing full friction; Case III, closely spaced piles with moderate surcharge (Broms, 1971)

compressible soils. Settlements of only several millimeters are enough to cause large negative friction loadings on piles. Negative friction can be caused by the reconsolidation of clay around a driven pile because of disturbance of the soil by the piles (Fellenius and Broms, 1969). However, drag load from this last cause is normally small and usually of little concern as it is eliminated when the working load is applied on the pile (Fellenius, 1971b, 1972b).

Methods of calculating the drag load on single piles have been proposed by several authors. Zeevaert (1959) used a theoretical approach using the reduction of effective vertical pressure in the soil caused by the drag on the piles. Bjerrum et al. (1969) assumed that the negative skin friction is equal to about 0.3 times the effective vertical pressure in the soil based on full-scale investigations. Bozuzuk (1971, 1972) assumed that the negative skin friction corresponds to the horizontal effective pressure against the pile times a friction factor for the soil acting on the pile.

The uncertainty is greater when the drag load on piles in groups is estimated. Here the method of Terzaghi and Peck (1967) can be used or the approach in Fig. 7.20 after Broms (1971).

Until additional field measurements are available, a conservative method should be used to calculate the drag load. For single piles, a safe assumption is to assume that the maximum drag load is equal to the area of the pile times the shear strength of the settling soil layer as determined in a geotechnical investigation.

This drag load should in the design naturally be added to the other load on the pile. However, it must be remembered that loads from negative skin friction are different in nature from ordinary working loads. Fellenius (1971c) proposed a design method which is intended as a check that the design load arrived at by

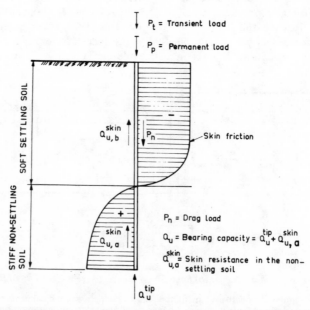

Fig. 7.21 Distribution of skin friction resistance for pile subjected to permanent and transient working loads in combination with negative skin friction

ordinary methods is not too large when negative friction is considered. The approach is that the permanent and transient working loads should be treated separately in connection with negative skin friction.

If a transient load P_t on the pile head is smaller than twice the drag load, $P_t < 2P_n$, the transient load will not be added to the load in the lower portion of the pile (Fig. 7.21). Thus, if $P_t < 2P_n$

$$P_p + P_n \leq Q_u^{\text{tip}} + Q_{u,a}^{\text{skin}} \tag{7.14}$$

in which Q_u^{tip} = ultimate capacity bearing at tip, and Q_u^{skin} = ultimate load from shear on perimeter of pile.

A design must always lie within certain margins of safety. Because of the different nature of the factors in Eq. 7.14, the method of partial factors of safety is applied. For this method, FS_p = partial factor of safety on the permanent working load P_p; FS_t = partial factor of safety on the transient working load P_t; FS_n = partial factor of safety on the drag load P_n; and FS_Q = partial factor of safety on the bearing capacity of the pile Q_u. When these partial factors of safety are applied, if $FS_t P_t < 2P_n$, Eq. 7.12 becomes

$$FS_P \leq \frac{1}{FS_Q} (Q_u^{\text{tip}} + Q_{u,a}^{\text{skin}}) - FS_n P_n \tag{7.15}$$

If the transient load is larger than twice the drag load, the bearing capacity of the pile must also be checked for the total load acting on the pile. However, positive skin friction will then develop along the entire length of the pile and the equation becomes, if $FS_t P_t > 2P_n$

$$FS_t P_t + FS_p P_p \leq \frac{1}{f_Q} Q_u \tag{7.16}$$

Especially if the transient load is cyclically applied on the pile some portion of it may reach the pile tip. Therefore it is recommended that the safety factor, FS_t in Eq. 7.15 be larger than the values normally chosen for partial factors of safety. Until further research results are available, the recommended value is 2.0. Since the drag load is normally calculated on the safe side, its partial factor of safety should be 1.00. The other partial factors of safety cannot be generally stated but must be chosen according to the requirements in each case.

When designing piles of moderate lengths the recommended approach is simple and applicable both on friction piles and end bearing piles. However, when the piles are longer, or rather when the settling layer is thicker than about 40 m (130 ft), the estimated drag load P_n can be much greater than the permanent working load P_P. In addition, the end resistance of the pile becomes more difficult to estimate. Thus, the calculated difference between the bearing capacity and the drag load may be small, of the same order as the errors that are involved in the estimations. Consequently, the design equations will not be practical. Instead, the safety factor with respect to negative skin friction can be checked by the condition that the permanent and transient loads should be smaller or equal to the bearing capacity of the full length of the pile shaft, that is

$$FS_p P_p + FS_t P_t \leq \frac{1}{FS_Q} Q_u^{skin} \qquad (7.17)$$

The safety factor FS_Q can normally be smaller than the factor FS_Q which would be applied in the previous equations.

This approach (Eq.7.17) is recommended especially for long piles driven through soft clay to end bearing on bedrock or in firm soil strata. By this approach the safety against a possible collapse of the pile is included, should the end bearing capacity of the pile be exceeded due to the effect of negative skin friction. However, large settlements will occur if the end bearing capacity is reduced. Therefore, it is important that the piles are driven to a high end bearing capacity. Consequently, much emphasis will have to be placed on the inspection of the driving. Also, it may be desirable to provide the piles with rock-shoes to assure a sound penetration into the bearing soil layers. Often a more slender pile is to be preferred to a pile of larger diameter as it is normally easier to drive a slender pile to a high end bearing capacity. The calculated maximum load in the piles under either static or dynamic stress must not exceed the strength of the pile section.

When considering negative skin friction in a design, there will be cases when the approach mentioned above indicates that the drag load is too large to be accepted or cases when only very small settlements can be accepted. Then the negative skin friction must be reduced. Field investigations have shown that this is achieved efficiently by coating the nile with a thin bitumen layer (Bjerrum et al., 1969). The bitumen can be chosen among a wide range of qualities. The important factor is to assure that the coat is intact after the installation of a coated pile. Protection against negative skin friction is therefore mainly a practical problem. It can involve large extra costs and it is recommended that protection measures should not be employed unless proven to be necessary by a detailed study.

Batter Piles.   These are piles driven at sloping orientations rather than the vertical. They are normally used to resist lateral loadings, for example a building constructed on a sloping site where lateral earth loads must be resisted because they are not balanced by earth loads on the opposite side of the building. Batter piles are not required and should not be used to resist code earthquake loadings. Code earthquake loadings are empirical factors used to provide toughness and resistance to reversals of stress in structural framing systems. "Acceleration" coefficients used in code earthquake factors may be significantly smaller than acceleration actually occurring in earthquakes. Under earthquake excitations, a building is set into vibratory motion and may be displaced relative to stable soils at depth beneath it. Thus the piles supporting it may be placed in bending. Piles used in earthquake regions should be tough and ductile. Batter piles, however, under such conditions would experience excessive heavy compression or tension loadings if designed for only code loadings, since actual lateral forces may significantly exceed code loadings. Such loadings can be approximated only from fully dynamic analyses of the structure and its foundation based on realistic earthquake spectra.

Batter piles can usually be driven to batters of 3 or 4 vertical to 1 horizontal without difficulty. Flatter slopes are possible, but special equipment may be needed and availability of such equipment should be investigated.

Maintaining the pile and hammer in proper alinement may be difficult unless proper equipment is available. Drop and single acting steam or air hammers may experience significant loss in effectiveness (energy delivered) because of friction or distortion of guides. This should be checked in evaluating dynamic driving resistance.

Batter piles should not be used through settling soils. Resistance of the piles to settlement of the surrounding soil will result in very heavy bending stresses, and either pull the pile out of the pile cap or break the pile in bending.

3 Caisson Foundations

As indicated previously, caissons for foundations consist of shafts excavated through unsatisfactory material to or into a bearing stratum and filled usually with concrete. The load is delivered to the bearing stratum either by direct bearing upon it or by end bearing combined with shear along the perimeter of the portion of the caisson penetrating the bearing stratum.

Types of Caissons. Several different procedures are used in constructing caissons. Factors which affect or guide selection of type of caisson to be used and construction method to be followed are: (1) The type and character of soil overburden; (2) ground-water control; (3) physical properties of the bearing stratum, including weathering; (4) equipment available; (5) loads to be carried; and (6) local practice and labor costs, experience, and availability.

Open caissons excavated by hand have been extensively used in the past and are being used today in many areas. They are adapted to use above the ground-water table in most soils, or below the water in stable, relatively impervious soils which will stand long enough to permit installing sheeting and bracing against the walls of the excavation for protection of workers. They may be either square or round. Sizes must be adequate for men to work in. A minimum dimension inside the walers of about 1.1 m (3.5 ft) is usually required. Maximum diameters are essentially limited only by the load to be carried. Typical construction procedures are illustrated in Fig. 7.22. Where conditions are favorable, the caisson may be enlarged at the base, termed a "belled bottom," to reduce bearing pressures on the bearing stratum yet develop economical loading stresses in the shaft. Typically, belling is used where the bearing stratum is soil such as a stiff-to-hard clay, dense glacial till, or rather soft shales.

Caissons carried to rock are usually straight sided. If the rock is irregularly or deeply weathered, is broken or slabby, or otherwise has near-surface defects, each caisson should be carried down to strong, stable material. Blasting may be necessary and can be done using drilling patterns similar to those used in rock tunnels. The final bottom should be carefully examined, and rock below the bottom should be checked for deeper lying defects by drilling before filling the caisson with concrete.

Open excavation may not be used in granular soils, such as sands or gravels carrying water, or where strata of such soils occur within generally impervious soils or underlie impervious soils. Such pervious soils must be drained as by dewatering wells before open excavation is attempted. Otherwise boiling may occur, leading to hazardous working conditions or to displacements affecting other structures or previously placed caissons.

Compressed air may be used to control ground water for caissons through pervious soils. The caisson is sealed at or below the top, and a working chamber at the bottom is provided in which air is kept at a pressure equal to the hydrostatic pressure of the ground water. Workers and materials pass through air locks. This is an extremely expensive and slow construction method and is little used today.

Some techniques have been developed for machine excavation to meet variable soil conditions and reduce labor and time. Fig. 7.23 shows a type of caisson used extensively in the United States. A heavy wall pipe with cutting edge is driven and drilled until well seated into the rock. A socket is then drilled into the rock. Drilling into rock is most commonly done using heavy percussion rock bits raised and dropped in a manner similar to that used for drilling wells in rock. Alternatively, the rock socket may be drilled using clustered percussion rock drills, Magnum Drill, or large size rotary rock bits. Any of these procedures is able to drill even hard crystalline rock such as granite. The heavy wall casing is left in place and is considered in establishing loading on the caisson. Heavy steel column sections or reinforcing cages may also be placed in the caisson for very heavy loadings or uplift. The depth of socket is computed to deliver the caisson load to the rock by shear along the perimeter. The usual design value is about 1.4 MPa (200 psi), which is conservative for most rock but should be checked by tests if sockets are to be placed in shale. This type is adapted to virtually all soil conditions; they are constructed in various diameters and carry loads of as much as 2000 tonnes per caisson, depending on diameter.

A different procedure is commonly used in Europe. A casing is driven while being excavated by a special, heavily weighted grab bucket. The grab bucket cannot excavate hard rock, but heavy percussion rock bits can be used where penetration into the rock is desired. This is illustrated in Fig. 7.24. Diameters are generally larger than for the drilled caisson described above and may be as much as 1.5 m (5 ft). The method is adapted to most soils, including soils containing boulders. Water or slurry filling may be required in pervious soils to prevent inflow of pervious soils into the

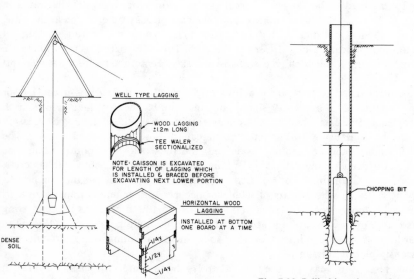

Fig. 7.22 Hand dug caissons

Fig. 7.23 Drilled in caisson *(Courtesy: Spencer, White, and Prentis)*

bottom. Usually, the casing is pulled as the concrete is placed. Shaft design is therefore based on concrete strength only.

In the mid 1930s, large-diameter earth augers were first placed in service. Development has progressed over the years. Today, equipment capable of drilling holes 2 m to 3 m (6 ft to 10 ft) in diameter and to depths of 60 m (200 ft) or more are in service. Such equipment can penetrate soft or weak rock, such as soft sandstone or shale. Further, the augers usually can be equipped with arms which fold outward to excavate an enlarged base without hand labor, as shown in Fig. 7.25.

Shafts for caissons may be drilled and cased with such large-diameter augers. Best results are obtained in stable impervious soils or above the water table. Difficulty may be experienced in excavating caissons with an auger if boulders are present in the soil. However, the large augers can accommodate larger boulders than can small augers. The augers cannot drill hard crystalline rock, but the equipment can be modified to handle large-diameter hard rock roller bits or clustered percussion bits to diameters of about 0.9 m (36 in.). For larger diameters the rock may be excavated by blasting. Casings may be left in place or removed as the concrete is placed.

Small-diameter caissons, ± 600 mm (24 in.) or larger, frequently are used for light structures. They may have belled bottoms at the bearing stratum or may be straight sided. The latter are frequently referred to as auger piles. Either auger or grab-bucket equipment may be used to excavate caisson shafts.

Bentonite slurry may be used to stabilize the walls of caisson shafts rather than using steel casings. Such procedures minimize problems of inflow from pervious strata. Inspection of the bottom of the caisson to assure that no loose soil is left or to be sure the surface on which the caisson is founded is free of defects is difficult and, at best, uncertain. Concrete is placed by tremie starting at the bottom when slurry is used, the slurry being displaced upwards by the heavier concrete.

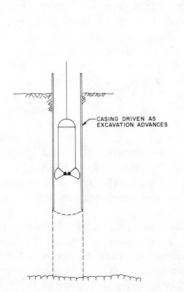

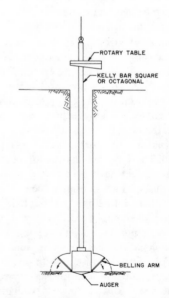

Fig. 7.24 Benoto caisson   **Fig. 7.25 Type of auger drilled caisson**

Loads on Caissons.　Loadings on caissons may be limited either by structural strength of the caisson shaft or by loadings which may be safely delivered to the bearing stratum, either in direct bearing or shear on the perimeter where the caisson penetrates the bearing stratum.

Frequently, it is possible to use a single caisson under each column. Use of multiple small caissons under a single column is feasible and is sometimes done to take advantage of equipment which is available but which is limited to certain sizes. Design of caps to accommodate multiple caissons can be difficult, and the caps expensive, because of the very large shear loadings.

Lateral loads, such as wind, may be distributed to the soil by lateral pressure against the caisson, the design considering both direct stress and bending. In general, however, the soil should not be counted on to provide sufficient lateral restraint that caissons can be assumed to be short columns regardless of length. Accordingly, stress in column action should be based on appropriate column formulas.

Construction Precautions.　In considering a caisson foundation, care must be taken to locate and determine properties of any pervious members present. If such exist, the method of construction must prevent boiling, loss of ground, or hazard to workmen. The bottoms should be checked for freedom from debris, loose soil, mud, or other objectionable materials immediately before placing concrete. Where caissons are founded on rock, the rock surface should be carefully inspected for soundness and check holes drilled, if necessary, to assure that it is not underlain by soft material, such as mud seams or weathered material. Such inspection is nearly impossible when slurry is used, and this may be a reason for not using slurry where difficulties from such causes could exist.

If there is water seepage into the caisson, the caisson should be flooded to a level where inflow from the rock or soil is stopped and the concrete then placed, using a tremie pipe extending completely to the bottom. Placing concrete with water flowing into and through it or dropping concrete through water will result in failures.

Problems with separation of the shaft of caissons have occurred in several sites where casings were removed as the concrete was placed. Such separation may result from a number of causes. Among these are squeezing and necking of the fresh concrete by plastic clays, and adherence of the concrete to the casing. Special care must be taken if casings are to be removed, and means of verifying the integrity of each caisson should be provided when casings are removed (Steinbach and Vey, 1975; Baker and Kahn, 1966).

In plastic soils, such as soft clays, plastic distortions may develop as caissons are drilled. These distortions can affect caissons already constructed. Lateral distortions of several feet have been found in some cases. Precautions should be taken to use procedures which minimize such distortions, and monitoring should be provided to detect them immediately should they start, so corrective measures may be taken before movements exceed allowable tolerances.

Since, generally, a single caisson is used under each column, any dislocation from design location can result in unacceptable eccentricities at the column-caisson junction. Care is essential to see that locations for each caisson are surveyed correctly and that location stakes are not disturbed by construction operations or plastic distortions of the soils. Caissons must be installed true to design line, which usually is vertical but sometimes may be battered.

7.7   SOIL-STRUCTURE INTERACTION

Foundation engineering is inevitably concerned with the interaction of the soil or rock and the structure. The foundation and the geologic formations supporting it are as much a part of the load-carrying system as is the superstructure of the building; this is true whether the foundation is deep or shallow. If the structure is supported by deep foundations, such as piles or caissons, the load is usually transferred to stiff formations. Thus, the deformations are small and their effects on the structure frequently may be disregarded.

However, many structures are supported by soil-bearing foundations that rest on materials which deform significantly under the weight of the structure. Also, the founding soil may deform elastically and inelastically due to reduction in stresses during excavation (heave), and then settle to or below its original position as the weight of the structure is imposed upon it. In these events, there is interaction between soil and structure affecting the deformations and stresses in both. The soil deformations modify and may control the structural deformations.

Stresses in both the structure and the soil are indeterminate. Redistribution of stresses in the structure affects the loadings delivered to the soil and, thus, the deformations of the soil, and these, in turn, further modify stress distribution in the structure.

Further complexity develops because deformations in the soil occur in two phases: (1) An immediate "elastic" response with little or no volume change; and (2) time-dependent deformations resulting from volume change of the sand and secondary distortions or creep.

Perhaps the most fundamental type of soil-structure interaction is that between the foundation engineer and the structural engineer. When each is aware that the properties of his portion of the building can affect the loads and deformations in the other, complicated problems of foundations on soft soil can be approached rationally and efficiently. Problems and distress arise when the foundation engineer simply takes his loads as given to him by the structural engineer or the structural engineer, in his analyses, assumes that all the loads and structural deformations are to be carried by an infinitely stiff material in the foundation.

Soil-structure interaction problems must consider the time-dependent nature of the phenomena. A typical situation might involve a sequence of excavation of a foundation, placement of mats and walls, backfilling, construction of the building, and occupancy and use of the building. The loads on the soil change during all these steps. Further, the response of the soils will not be instantaneous but will include time-dependent creep and consolidation effects. Therefore, detailed mathematical modeling becomes difficult, and it is essential to focus clearly on the particular problem at hand. The designer of the foundation excavation might be interested in the behavior of the bracing system and the foundation structures before the building is built. On the other hand, deformations causing cracking of plaster are those that occur after the structure is complete and involve a completely different portion of the deformation history. Different analyses would be appropriate for the different phases of soil-structure interaction.

Because the behavior can be so complex, most practical cases have involved discrete analyses of portions of the behavior, rather than comprehensive treatments of the entire problem. The development of computerized techniques, in particular the finite element method, has made it possible to consider many more aspects of the problem in one analysis. Thus, one can expect that more detailed and sophisticated treatments will be used in the future, but the engineer must resist the temptation to increase the complexity of the analysis at the expense of insight into the mechanics of the problem.

1 Static Effects

The vast majority of important problems of soil-structure interaction involves behavior under static loads. Therefore, most of the work that has been done over the years has concerned static problems. The calculation of rate of occurrence of time-dependent effects such as consolidation and creep is not very dependable. Most often, some form of the Terzaghi consolidation theory is used—for example, Terzaghi and Peck (1967)—although modifications for creep and for three-dimensional effects have been proposed. This is today (1980) a subject of theoretical and experimental investigations whose conclusions have not yet reached the point of engineering application.

Further, the rate of movement is critically dependent upon minor geologic details which affect internal drainage. Even with complete investigations, such details are usually imperfectly known. Regardless of how time-dependent effects are treated, the engineer must represent the compliance of the soil in some way. The different approaches to soil-structure interaction can be distinguished by the ways they represent the behavior of the soil and the ways they solve the resulting mathematical problem.

Analytical Methods.   One major category of methods is based on the assumption that the foundation soils can be represented adequately by a simple stress-strain law and theories derived from continuum mechanics. One of the earliest and simplest of such methods assumes the soil can be replaced by a set of discrete springs, each acting independently of the other. This is attributed to Winkler (1867). The vertical stress and the vertical motion are linearly related

$$\delta_v = \frac{\sigma_v}{k_s} \tag{7.18}$$

in which k_s = modulus of subgrade reaction. For a beam of width b transmitting a load per unit length q, the relation becomes

$$\delta_v = \frac{q}{k_s b} \tag{7.19}$$

A footing of area A carrying a load P follows

$$\delta_v = \frac{P}{k_s A} = \frac{P}{K} \tag{7.20}$$

Extensive literature has grown up around this approach, in part because it is easy to modify existing procedures for structural analysis to incorporate the Winkler springs.

Hetenyi (1946) and Allen and Severn (1960, 1961, 1963) have presented particularly useful and comprehensive results. Terzaghi (1955) describes how the values of k_s are affected by the soil properties and the geometry of the loading. He also provides empirical values for various materials and conditions. It should be noted that his values are conservative in the sense that they tend to give low values of the modulus of subgrade reaction and high values of settlement. If the problem requires computing loads that would cause prescribed settlements, his values would lead to an underestimate of the loads.

An alternative, and in many ways the preferable method, is based on the assumption that the soil is a semi-infinite, linearly elastic half-space. Using an assumed or estimated distribution of structural loads to the soil, deformations of the soil at founding level can be computed. Both "elastic" and time-dependent deformations can be considered by using appropriate moduli of deformation. From the deformations so determined and the structural stiffness, redistribution of stresses in the structure and revised load distributions to the soil can be computed. Then, further revised deformations of the soil at founding level can be determined. The iterations are repeated until there is satisfactory agreement between soil and structural deformation.

Graphs and charts of influence factors for determining added stresses in the soil mass for a wide variety of loadings have been developed by Newmark (1947) and Fadum (1948). These are available in Poulos and Davis (1974). Using these, soil stresses may be readily determined for each cycle of the iteration. The procedures are based on integration of the Boussinesq solution for stresses in a semi-infinite elastic solid.

The solution for vertical stresses is not sensitive to stratification or to lateral variations in soil properties. The procedure may be used for stratified soil by considering appropriate moduli of deformation for each stratum. Thus, for many structures the effects of soil-structure interaction on both structure and soil may be developed using simple calculations amenable to solution with hand calculators.

The approach is quite useful for manual checking of results of more sophisticated analyses. Also, in many problems, precision in computation is not warranted, as, for example, when structures are relatively flexible and stress redistribution is not sensitive to settlement; where structural stiffness, which must consider effects of walls and partitions, can only be approximated; or where soil properties are not known in detail.

The settlement of a rigid circular area loaded by a vertical force P is

$$\delta_v = \frac{P}{2aE}(1 - \mu^2) \tag{7.21}$$

in which a = radius of the circle; E = Young's modulus; and μ = Poisson's ratio. The settlement of points outside the loaded area can be described adequately by assuming P to be a concentrated load, as

$$\delta_v = \frac{P}{\pi E r}(1 - \mu^2) \tag{7.22}$$

in which r = distance from the center of the circle to the point in question.

Eqs. 7.21 and 7.22 may be used for structures founded on individual footings to estimate settlements of each footing, by calculating that due to the footing itself using Eq. 7.21; additional settlements caused by other footings may be determined from Eq. 7.22, and total settlement found by superposition. This approach is useful where the soil modulus can be approximated by a constant value. This frequently is satisfactory, especially for overconsolidated, cohesive soils.

Either the Winkler spring approach or the semi-infinite elastic half-space approach (also called the Boussinesq approach) can be used in analysis of soil-structure interaction. Both can be and have been incorporated in computer programs for structural analysis. The Winkler spring approach is easier to program because the behavior can be represented by a simple spring or elastic reaction at each nodal point of the foundation, but the Boussinesq requires coupling between the response at one point and another. On the other hand, the Boussinesq approach is clearly superior theoretically. It should be used when the foundation soils are relatively stiff, because such soils tend to behave as a semi-infinite half-space rather than as a set of independent springs. Studies by Gibson (1967) have shown that for certain nonhomogeneous distributions of modulus, the Winkler spring method may be superior to the Boussinesq method. Carrier and Christian (1973) investigated this for a range of foundation sizes, and included in their paper are charts showing when one method or the other is more realistic. For most practical cases, which involve reasonably stiff soils, the Boussinesq analysis is a closer representation of reality.

In any analysis in which the foundation soils are replaced by springs of one sort or another, there is a major difficulty in determining the properties of the soil. As mentioned previously, these properties must be selected on the basis of the particular problem to be studied. For example, if the question involves deformations during early stages of the loading, undrained material properties would be appropriate, but a study of settlements over a long term would require the use of drained properties or the use of values derived from consolidation tests. The judgment of the foundation engineer must be used in each case.

In recent years there have been several successful attempts to use foundation compliance functions to model complicated foundation behavior. In particular, Focht et al. (1971) have described the procedures used for predicting the behavior of a foundation for a high-rise building located on soft soils. They used a modified version of the Boussinesq approach, developing the "elastic" properties of the soil by means of empirical data and consolidation tests on the material. Thus, the analysis does not so much represent an elastic analysis as it does the engineer's best estimate of the moduli of deformation that are appropriate for this case. This case illustrates that the intelligent cooperation between the foundation engineer and the structural engineer can result in a substantial improvement in the design of a building. It also shows that the values of modulus that are used in such analysis need not be truly elastic properties but can be moduli of deformation.

Numerical Methods. When the properties of the soil or the geometry of the problem becomes too complicated to be handled by analytical approaches, numerical methods are necessary. The previously referenced work by Allen and Severn (1960, 1961, 1963) does use numerical methods to model the slabs themselves, and this is a common procedure for studying the stresses in slabs on elastic foundations. More recently it has been possible to represent the behavior of the soil by numerical methods, in particular the finite element method.

The finite element method, which is described in detail in some recent books, allows the engineer to divide the foundation soil into a large number of discrete elements and to describe the properties of the material in each one of those elements by different stress-strain relations. Thus, the complete, nonlinear time-dependent problem could, in theory, be analyzed. In practice, such analyses have not been carried out for several reasons. In the first place, the analyses would be extremely expensive, especially because most buildings involve a truly three-dimensional geometry which cannot be adequately represented in plane strain. In the second place, it is very difficult to determine material properties that would go into such analyses, and one doubts whether the results would be any more accurate than those that could be obtained by simpler methods. Thus, the usefulness of finite element methods is restricted to two classes of problems: (1) Those problems in which the geometry of the soil and its material properties are reasonably well known and where this geometry or the nonlinear nature of these properties is considered to have a potentially significant effect on the behavior of the structure; and (2) those problems in which a particular aspect of the foundation performance must be studied in great detail. The best examples of the latter class of problem are tied-back walls and braced excavations.

The most interesting work in application of the finite element method to problems of foundation engineering and soil-structure interaction has involved the study of tied-back walls. In particular, the work of Clough and Tsui (1974) will serve to illustrate the importance of various soil parameters on the behavior of walls. Clough has studied primarily the behavior of soft, cohesive soils, which has lent his results limited usefulness because the majority of tie-backs are installed in substantially stiffer materials. Nevertheless, his results have shown conclusively that it is difficult to obtain results by finite element methods that compare precisely with field observations and that substantially different results can be obtained by using different values of soil properties. One must conclude that the finite element method presents a powerful and useful technique for studying the behavior of foundation systems, but that it is not yet sufficiently refined to permit engineering decisions to be made solely on the basis of results from finite element analyses.

2 Dynamic Effects

The dynamic interaction of structure and soil can be initiated by a number of phenomena, including vibrations from equipment, blast loading, wind effects, and earthquakes. The earthquake effects include most of the problems associated with the other phenomena and have recently been the most extensively studied from the point of view of foundation behavior. Therefore, the discussion here will concentrate on the earthquake problem.

In Chapter CL-2 of this Monograph, there is a discussion of earthquake engineering effects on tall buildings, and it should be consulted by the reader interested in more detail. Further, this is an area of substantial ongoing research, which has the effect of making almost any article on the subject of earthquake engineering obsolescent before it is published.

Amplification Versus Interaction. Almost all earthquake engineers agree that soil conditions have a great deal to do with damage to structures during earthquakes. Comments to that effect are routine in reports of earthquakes. Most advanced countries have in their antiseismic building codes some provision for incorporating the effect of soil conditions in the design of the structure. The effect of the soil can be divided into two areas: amplification and interaction. Amplification refers to the effects of the layers of soil on the earthquake signal before it reaches the building. Amplification effects would occur regardless of whether the building were present. Interaction properly refers to the effect of the presence of the building on the motions. In other words, the building and soil together are a more complicated system than the building alone on a rigid foundation or the foundation soil alone without a structure on it. The combination of soil and structure may have a different dynamic behavior from that of the structure alone.

Engineering knowledge of both amplification and interaction is deficient in many respects. Theoretical solutions are possible for a limited number of cases, many important problems are not yet solved, field verification of theoretical and model predictions depends on the occurrence of earthquakes, and so on. Nevertheless, there have been large increases of engineering understanding, and Ohsaki (1969) and Seed (1969) have provided excellent summaries of recent advances.

The conclusion of much of this work has been that, with the exception of massive structures like nuclear power plants, the effects of soil amplification are far more important than those of interaction. In particular, analysis of the effects of the 1967 Caracas earthquake [Seed et al. (1970) and Whitman (1969a)] showed that the greatest damage occurred where the fundamental period of the structures coincided with the fundamental period of the soil beneath the building. Therefore, an early question to be asked by the designer is whether, considering both structure and soil, the structure has a vibratory frequency that corresponds to one of the characteristic frequencies of the foundation strata. Removing the structure from this condition of resonance will decrease the major effect of the foundation on the structural response.

It should be noted that calculations of amplification effects and of the corresponding resonant periods depend directly on the engineer's knowledge of the geometry of the soil and of the soil properties. Such knowledge is not easily obtained. Therefore, there is a considerable range of uncertainty in the results of amplification analyses, and the engineer is advised not to rely too confidently on the exact values of resonant period given by soil amplification analyses.

Interaction. Interaction calculations can be carried out by several techniques. The two most popular are the use of lumped springs and the finite element technique. The lumped springs technique involves replacing the soil and foundation by one or more springs, masses, and dashpots, whose properties are selected to represent the soil and the frequency range of interest. Relatively simple "equivalent springs" may be used, or complex, frequency-dependent compliance functions developed. The finite element technique involves dividing the soil into discrete elements and solving for the dynamic behavior of the resulting multiple degree-of-freedom system.

Foundation "springs" for dynamic analyses are intended to represent the behavior of the foundation as a whole and are not discrete representations of pieces of the foundation as those used in static analyses. The selection of the foundation springs requires judgment. Most selection starts from the theory of behavior of a footing dynamically excited on the surface of a half-space. Spring constants are selected from the static spring for an equivalent static condition. Richart et al. (1970) provide a summary of the spring constants, damping ratios, and equivalent soil masses for the various modes of vibration of the surface footing, and they provide solutions for most standard cases. When the foundation is not at the surface or when the soil is not very deep, these models must be modified, but the theoretical difficulties increase enormously. Another complication is introduced when the soil underlying the foundation is layered or when there is a stiff bedrock reasonably close to the foundation. Although many papers have been written on the evaluation of spring constants for these cases, finite element methods are used increasingly to evaluate the equivalent constants. Nevertheless, for a number of cases, the simplified procedures suggested by Whitman (1969b) can be used fairly rapidly without resorting to extensive computations.

The finite element method for dynamic soil-structure interaction analyses has been developed largely in conjunction with the design of nuclear power plants. It has now achieved substantial sophistication, and there are many papers describing both the details of the procedure and the numerous subtleties necessary in its use. In particular, the papers by Roesset and Kausel (1976), Kausel and Roesset (1974), Kausel et al. (1976), and Seed et al. (1975) should be consulted. As in the static case, the dynamic finite element method consists of dividing the soil into a number of discrete elements and then applying the appropriate equations of motion to each element in turn. Difficulties arise when boundaries are to be treated, and the most widely used procedures now involve boundaries at which the wave motion is allowed to pass out of the problem (Kausel and Roesset, 1975; Kausel et al., 1975; Lysmer and Wass, 1972), thus simulating an infinite layer. These are called transmitting or absorbing boundaries. Finite element programs without such boundaries are likely to trap excess energy inside the finite element mesh and should be avoided.

In general, the use of dynamic finite element methods follows lines similar to the use of static finite element methods. Because of the costs of computation, most dynamic finite element programs assume that the material is linearly elastic. Actually, moduli of soils, both granular and cohesive, are strain-dependent and soften with increasing strain, as shown by Hardin and Drnevich (1970) and Seed (1970). The effects of this nonlinear stress-strain softening are simulated by an iterative procedure in which successive solutions are obtained for different approximated values of modulus and damping, until the strains computed in the problem are compatible with the values of damping. Analyses employing such iterations can be expensive. It has been shown by Kausel et al. (1976) that iterations beyond those necessary to satisfy the strain compatibility for the amplification problem are unnecessary. Christian (1975) has given a summary of the choices that can be made in selecting a procedure for analyses of soil-structure interaction.

The general conclusion from a large number of studies is that soil-structure interaction for tall buildings is most important when the soil is soft and, in almost all cases, the effect of interaction is beneficial or unimportant. That is, it could have been ignored safely. Sarrazin (1970) summarizes the situation by stating that two or more of the following conditions must comply before interaction has a serious and harmful effect:

1. A tall building with a high aspect ratio.

2. Considerable mass in the foundation.

3. A high center of gravity in the foundation.

Nevertheless, when very strong earthquakes have to be considered for major high-rise buildings, economy and safety would both suggest that soil-structure interaction be considered in the dynamic analysis of the building. In such cases, the use of springs may well be a perfectly satisfactory way to proceed.

This is true particularly if adequately large values of damping are included to account for the radiation of energy away from the problem. In some instances, dynamic finite element procedures may be necessary for very complicated geometries.

The effect of piles on amplification and interaction has been investigated by Penzien et al. (1964) who state that the effect of the piles on horizontal swaying is negligible because the piles move with the soil. This result is generally accepted today, but the effect of soils on vertical motion or on rocking motions may be a more complicated phenomenon and has not been studied adequately.

3   Measurement of Soil Properties

A final word should be said about the methods available for determining the properties for use in soil-structure interaction analyses. For many of the older analyses, there has grown up a series of empirical methods of obtaining the appropriate parameters. Standard textbooks on foundation engineering include many of these. It should be noted that such methods as correlating the modulus of subgrade reaction with values of blow count or other tests may be adequate for many purposes. However, such a correlation should not be extended beyond the range of the data. Also, where a particular procedure has grown up for design with the assumption that a particular type of on-site or laboratory test be used to obtain the parameters, it is extremely unwise to substitute a different method of obtaining the parameters. A classic example is the use of the Terzaghi and Peck (1967) techniques for evaluating loads on braced excavations. These procedures assume that the strength of cohesive soils will be measured by unconsolidated, undrained (UU) tests. If the engineer were to substitute some other test, he would have better estimates of the shear strength of the soil, but a worse estimate of the loads on the bracing.

There are three classes of procedures for determining soil properties for soil-structure interaction analysis: (1) Empirical methods; (2) methods based on laboratory tests; and (3) methods based on on-site measurements of soil properties. The first class is described in numerous foundation manuals and texts on soil and foundation engineering. Such procedures also vary greatly from country to country because the practice of engineering and the nature of the soils are variable from place to place.

In the second procedure are included such classic methods as the use of consolidation tests or triaxial tests to determine the moduli of deformation of the soils. More recently, resonant column tests and cross-hole measurement of shear wave velocity have been developed to obtain values of the modulus of the soil at small strains. It is characteristic of most laboratory tests that even when the soil sample is supposedly undisturbed, there is sufficient disturbance of the soil structure that the values of modulus measured are substantially lower than those that will be encountered in the field. It has also been shown by Marcuson and Wahls (1971) and by Trudeau et al. (1974) that secondary compression can have a substantial influence on the measured response of the soils in the laboratory. Thus, the engineer should be skeptical of the use of laboratory results directly without reference to empirical data or personal experience in the area.

On-site tests of soil properties have been increasingly prominent in recent years. There is a great deal of promise that the development of new methods will lead to a better ability to describe the properties of the soil. Such techniques as the standard penetration test and the static cone penetrometer have been available for many years, and a large body of empirical information has been built up on these methods. In a sense, these can be considered both on-site and empirical tests. In the design of nuclear power plants, geophysical methods have also become popular. In particular, cross-hole seismic shear wave velocity measurements have proved excellent for determining the value of the shear modulus at small strain. Since this modulus can be related to other moduli, and since it dominates a great deal of the deformation behavior of the soil, this is a very important and useful measurement.

4 Conclusions

Soil-structure interaction involves both static and dynamic behavior. Static interaction effects are usually treated by simplified models of subgrade behavior, and finite element methods have become increasingly useful. However, finite element methods have been applied most often to studies of portions of the interaction problem, such as braced and tied-back excavations, rather than to the entire history of the behavior of a building and its foundation. The dynamic problem involves many complex components. It is important to distinguish between amplification effects (or coincidence of the periods of building and foundation) and interaction effects. Finite element methods, especially those with absorbing lateral boundaries, are being used to an increasing extent. The determination of appropriate soil properties continues to require great care and judgment.

7.8 SPECIAL PROBLEMS

There are some special foundation conditions that may affect planning, structural layout, or other features of tall buildings. The designer should be aware of these conditions, their significance, and possible problems which may arise in order to initiate investigations in time to incorporate necessary corrective measures early in the planning sequence. Among these conditions are subsidence, expansive soils or rocks, landslides, soils which may become unstable under certain loading conditions, and metastable soils.

Subsidence may be defined as settlement unrelated to the presence or weight of the structure. It may extend over broad areas or be sharply localized. It may occur at or extend to great depths, result from the compression of a single layer or zone, or be confined to near surface layers. Typical causes are removal of fluids, such as gas, oil, or water, or mining activities. Karst conditions, resulting from solution of limestone or other soluble rocks, pose special problems in many areas of the world (Sowers, 1975).

In a static soil-ground water system, the pressure in the water at any depth z beneath the ground-water table is equal to z times the density of water, the common hydrostatic pressure. The vertical stress in the soil, which is commonly called the effective vertical stress, is equal to the gross weight of the soil above the water table plus the weight of the soil below the water table less buoyancy. Buoyancy is equal to the volume of the soil particles times the density of water. Lowering the ground-water table, as by pumping from wells, causes an increase in stress in all soils below the original water table equal to the change in water level times the density of water. Since the soil skeleton will deform under a change in loading, compression of the soil mass will occur, resulting in subsidence of the ground surface. The rate at which this subsidence will occur is controlled, primarily, by the permeability of the various strata. Fine grained soils can drain only slowly and compression of such soils may continue over months or even many years. The total amount of subsidence is dependent on the physical properties of the various soil strata and the amount by which the water level, i.e., the stress at depth, is changed.

While reduction in water level has been used in this example, removal of oil or gas with consequent reductions in pressure will similarly result in subsidence. The eastern end of Terminal Island and some parts of adjoining Long Beach, California, have subsided approximately 9 m (30 ft) since 1942, because of oil production.

Subsidence can result in a number of undesirable effects. If soils vary markedly in compressibility within short distances, significant and possibly damaging differential settlements may occur. Such differences may result from erratic variations in types of soils; examples are lenticular deposits, or sites where streams have cut channels later filled with soils either softer or stiffer than those adjoining. Previous loading of limited areas may cause sharp variations in settlement. Thus, in Mexico City, broad areas have subsided due to pumping from wells over many years. There were many areas, however, which had been loaded by heavy Aztec temples or other structures, where the soil was less compressible than adjoining areas. Consequently, damaging differential settlements developed under some structures as a result of the difference in compressibility of adjacent foundation soils.

Piles driven through soils subject to subsidence may be seriously overloaded by the weight of soil clinging to them. Loads from this cause may be very large. Tests were conducted in Sweden on piles driven to bedrock and loaded by down drag of soft clays compressing due to small changes in ground-water level. Data for single piles showed down drag of more than 445 kN (110 kips).

Subsidence areas are usually bowl shaped. This shape results in horizontal compression of soil near the center of the bowl and tension near the edges of the bowl. Soil deformations can be serious. Thus, in the Terminal Island area horizontal compression at the center of the bowl in 1950, when subsidence was 3.3 m (11 ft), amounted to a strain of 0.001. This is sufficient to cause large lateral loads on retaining walls, basement walls, pilings, or caissons.

Many of the cities of the world are built on deltas of rivers. Commonly deltas, especially the larger ones, are characterized by large, deep seated shears caused by differential settlement due to compaction as the delta builds outward, and soft, fine grained deposits are covered by later deposits. In such areas, subsidence accompanying ground-water lowering may cause sharply differential motion across such shears. In Baton Rouge, Louisiana, 100 mm (4 in.) of differential motion occurred in 10 yr across the Scotlandville shear, causing serious damage to a school which was built across the shear. Similar problems have occurred near Houston, Texas. This possibility must be carefully investigated in areas where subsidence is a problem.

Even where structural problems as discussed previously are not of concern, subsidence may result in failures of buried piping from soil distortions. Exposure of the subsided area to flooding during heavy storms, or problems with sewers or drainage systems because of changes in gradient, may occur.

Areas underlain by mines may pose problems in serious differential settlement within short distances. In Europe, long wall mining is commonly used in coal mines. In this process, all coal is removed and the mine permitted to collapse behind the area being mined. Effects at the surface extend to a distance beyond the collapsed area equal to about half the depth of the seam below ground surface. As the mined front advances, the area subject to disturbance also advances. The advancing wave front of subsidence is especially critical and structures affected by it may be severely damaged. Structures have been constructed in the subsidence area following passage of the subsidence wave, but they may be subjected to smaller continuing settlements. Extremely sharp differential settlements may occur in the zone of disturbance. Collapse of mined areas where room and pillar techniques are used occurs quite frequently as timbering deteriorates and pillars collapse. This is a complex and difficult problem. When it is encountered, guidance of experienced experts should be retained.

Solution mining, which is commonly used for recovery of salt, potash, and sulfur, poses especially difficult problems. The shape, extent, and location of the actual area of material removal are imperfectly known. Effects may be bowl-shaped subsidence at the surface or even stoping collapse. Subsidence effects may extend for several thousands of feet beyond the area of wells, especially when the material being mined is found at depth.

Problems of several types may be encountered in karst regions. Such areas are underlain by soluble rocks, the most common being limestone with lesser regions underlain by halite, gypsum, or potash salts. Most spectacular, and damaging, is the sudden collapse of soil arches or bridges in the overburden materials above the rock resulting in formation of sinkholes. Sinkholes up to 90 m (300 ft) in diameter and many meters in depth have occurred, some under structures. Changes in ground-water level, increased seepage flow into the ground from sewers or drains, or reduction in roof thickness have precipitated such collapse. The conditions leading to sinkhole collapse, however, have developed over long periods, usually greatly outdating construction, and thus can be discovered by adequate investigation. Catastrophic failures from this cause should be avoidable.

The rate of solution of limestone is usually so slow as not to affect safety of structures. Foundations carried into sound limestone usually will be safe. Salts such as halite, gypsum, or potash are readily soluble. Localized or general subsidence may occur in areas underlain by such materials from solution caused by changes in ground-water regions, pumping, or leakage from water lines, drains, or sewers.

Extremely irregular rock surfaces may be found in these regions. Residual soils left by the solution processes may vary markedly in compressibility. Consequently, damaging settlements may develop even when sinkhole formation is not probable. If there is flow through the cavernous rock, soil may be carried downwards and then away. This can lead to long-term settlements which may be sharply differential (Sowers, 1975).

If construction is to be done in known karstic regions or areas underlain by other soluble rocks, detailed studies should be made by knowledgeable experts to determine the extent of the hazards and what precautions or corrective measures should be used.

A somewhat similar problem may be found in areas underlain by volcanic rocks. Lava tubes sometimes occur in volcanic rocks, especially the more viscous ones such as andesites. These tubes, which form when a molten interior breaks through the partially hardened shell of a flow, may be 10 m (30 ft) or more across and hundreds or more meters long. If they exist under the site of a structure, they may collapse under the added weight, or from vibrations due to construction activities or blasting.

Expansive soils and rocks are found in many areas of the world. Typical of such soils are the black cotton soils of Burma and India, the adobe soils of the southwestern United States, and gumbo soils in Texas. Expansive rocks include bentonitic shales and, to a lesser extent, shales containing pyrites which expand on exposure to the atmosphere. Such soils or rocks are susceptible to volume change with changes in moisture content or from dry to wet seasons. This may cause excessive pressures and even collapse of basement walls or disturbance of footings, and heave of grade beams or structures. Local experience is the best guide as to the possibility of encountering this hazard and of means of designing against it.

The possibility of landslides should always be carefully investigated whenever a structure is located in a hilly region or other area of significant relief. Serious damage to structures has occurred in Rio de Janeiro, San Francisco, Los Angeles, Seattle, and Hong Kong (Fang and Cheng, 1974). The advice and guidance of a competent expert knowledgeable regarding local conditions in the area of interest should always be sought.

Granular soils, especially fine sands or silty sands, subjected to cyclic shear loading as from an earthquake may show marked increases in pore-water pressure and corresponding decrease in shearing strength. In loose sands which tend to contract under shearing displacement, earthquake excitation may result in lique-fying the sands, that is, changing the sand strata to a fluid condition which persists for some period of time. Structures founded above such soils may collapse completely, as occurred in Niigata, Japan in 1964 (Seed and Idriss, 1967). Frictional support for piles driven into granular soils may be seriously reduced permitting very large settlements or footings, or structures may settle differentially. Liquefaction may also result in large landslides, as occurred in Alaska in 1964 (Seed and Wilson, 1967). If earthquake is a hazard, extensive investigation should be made on any site to determine whether liquefaction problems could occur either under the foundations or in such manner as to result in gross instabilities of the site.

Metastable soils are soils subject to spontaneous collapse. Typical are quick clays such as are found in the Laurentian Valleys of Canada or in Norway; loess which extends over large areas in the United States, China, and central Europe, especially Hungary and the Ukraine; and mud flow and alluvial fan deposits of arid and semiarid regions.

Quick clays (very sensitive clays) are subject to a large reduction in shear strength if disturbed. Reductions in shearing strengths by factors exceeding 50 have been reported. Areas underlain by such deposits are subject to flow slides with complete destruction of structures founded on the slide area or in the area covered by slide debris. Such quick clays commonly have field moisture contents approximating or exceeding the liquid limit. Comparison of moisture contents with the Atterberg limits and tests of shearing strength in the undisturbed and remolded states are useful in evaluating whether such clays are present.

Loess is a wind laid deposit of very fine sand or silt sized particles. It is widely distributed throughout the world. The most extensive deposits are believed to have developed in late Pleistocene time as fine sands and silts were eroded by wind from areas of glacial outwash before vegetation was reestablished. Deposits may vary from a few feet to hundreds of feet in thickness. In semiarid and arid regions, it typically has a very loose structure, frequently less than 1440 kg/m³ (90 pcf) gross density. Frequently, it is lightly cemented by calcite and is quite strong when dry and kept that way. Saturation may result in spontaneous collapse of the soil structure with destruction of structures founded on it. Similar very low density soils,

Landslide on residual soil, Hong Kong. Collapsing building damaged apartment building (center) *(Fang and Cheng, 1974)*

Close view of damaged building, Hong Kong landslide *(Fang and Cheng, 1974)*

subject to collapse on saturation, may be found occurring as mud flow deposits, and to a lesser extent alluvial fan deposits, in arid and semiarid regions.

On-site densities should always be investigated when sites are located in such regions. Densities less than about 1520 kg/m^3 (95 pcf) or 13.7 kN/m^3 should be investigated thoroughly against the possibility of spontaneous collapse. Because of leakage from sewers or other pipelines, effects of watering lawns or shrubbery, and discharge from systems for air conditioning or sanitary facilities, it should always be assumed such soils may become saturated during the life of the structure unless special precautions are taken and maintained.

7.9 CONDENSED REFERENCES/BIBLIOGRAPHY

The following is a condensed bibliography for this chapter. Not only does it include all articles referred to or cited in the text, but it also contains bibliography for further reading. The full citations will be found at the end of the Volume. What is given here should be sufficient information to lead the reader to the correct article: the author, date, and title. In case of multiple authors, only the first named is listed.

Alexander 1964, *Vertical Assembly Building*
Allen 1960, *The Stresses in Foundation Rafts I*
Allen 1961, *The Stresses in Foundation Rafts II*
Allen 1963, *The Stresses in Foundation Rafts III*
Andersen 1947, *Substructure Analysis and Design*
ASTM 1964, *Method of Test for Load-Settlement Relationship for Individual Piles Under Vertical*

Baker 1965, *Raft Foundations*
Baker 1966, *Caisson Construction Problems and Method of Correction*
Bazant 1973, *Foundations of Tall Buildings*
Begemann 1963, *The Use fo the Static Soil Penetrometer in Holland*
Belloni 1973, *Soil-Structure Interaction*
Bhaskaran 1974, *Effect of Pile Driving on Pile-Soil Interaction and Bearing Capacity Prediction*
Bjerrum 1956, *Stability of Strutted Excavations in Clay*
Bjerrum 1957, *Norwegian Experience With Steel Piles to Rock*
Bjerrum 1963, *Discussion, Section VI*
Bjerrum 1969, *Reduction of Negative Skin Friction on Steel Piles to Rock*
Blomdahl 1968, *Piles and Piling Methods at NYA Asfalt AB*
Bozuzuk 1968, *Downdrag Measurements on 270-Ft Composite Piles*
Bozuzuk 1970, *Field Observations of Negative Skin Friction Loads on Long Piles in Marine Clay*
Bozuzuk 1971, *Downdrag Measurements on a 160-Ft Floating Pipe Test Pile in Marine Clay*
Breth 1970, *The State of Loading of Grouted Anchors in Clay*
Brinch-Hansen 1960, *Major Problems of Soil Mechanics*
Brinch-Hansen 1961, *The Ultimate Resistance of Rigid Piles Against Transversal Forces*
Briske 1968, *Measurements on the Stresses in the Strutted Excavation During Construction of the*
Brodeur 1971, Private communication, *Information on Pile Projects*
Broms 1964a, *Lateral Resistance of Piles in Cohesive Soils*
Broms 1964b, *Lateral Resistance of Piles on Cohesionless Soils*
Broms 1965, *Design of Laterally Loaded Piles*
Broms 1966, *Methods of Calculating the Ultimate Bearing Capacity of Piles, a Summary*
Broms 1968, *End Bearing and Skin Friction Resistance of Piles*
Broms 1970, *Methods Used in Sweden to Evaluate the Bearing Capacity of End-Bearing Precast*
Broms 1971, *Design of Pile Groups With Respect to Negative Skin Friction*
Budzianowski 1965, *Bending of Low Buildings on the Mining Basin Slope*
Budzianowski 1972, *Design of Tall Buildings in Mining Subsidence Areas*
Bureau of Yards and Docks 1962, *Soil Mechanics, Foundations and Earth Structures*

Capatu 1975, *The Direct Foundation of a Tall Building on Weak Soils with Partial*
Carrier 1973, *Rigid Circular Plate Resting on a Non-Homogeneous Elastic Half Space*
Casagrande 1944, *Application of Soil Mechanics in Designing Building Foundations*

Cederwall 1962, *Six Factors That Make Piling High Quality Work*
Chamecki 1956, *Structural Rigidity in Calculating Settlements*
Chamecki 1957, discussion on *Foundation of Structures*
Chamecki 1969, *Calculation of Progressive Settlements of Foundations*
Chellis 1961, *Pile Foundations*
Christian 1973, *Soil-Structure Interaction for Tall Buildings*
Christian 1975, *Choices Among Procedures for Dynamic Finite Element Analysis*
Ciesilski 1973, *Dynamic Influences on Foundation Calculations for Tower Shaped Structures*
Ciongradi 1975, *Soil-Foundation-Structure Interaction at Reinforced Concrete Tall Buildings*
Clark 1966, *Evaluation of Pile Capacity and the Effect of Negative Friction*
Clough 1974, *Performance of Tied-Back Walls in Clay*
Cooke 1974, *The Settlement of Friction Pile Foundations*
Cornfield 1973, *Deep Foundations—Piles and Caissons*
Correa 1969, *A Telescopic Type of Pile for Subsidence Conditions*
Cosovliu 1975, *Interaction Problems at Tall Buildings Constructed on Moisture-sensitive Soils*
Cuevas 1936, *The Floating Foundation of the New Building of the National Lottery of Mexico*
Cunningham 1974, *Rock Caissons for the Northern Building in Chicago's Loop*

D'Appolonia 1971, *Effects of Foundation Construction on Nearby Structures*
Davisson 1963, *Laterally Loaded Piles in a Layered Soil System*
Davisson 1969, *Energy Measurements for a Diesel Hammer*
Davisson 1970, *Static Measurements of Pile Behaviour*
De Beer 1948, *Calculation of Beams Resting on the Soil, the Coefficient of Stiffness K of the Soil*
De Beer 1957, *The Influence of the Width of a Foundation Raft on the Longitudinal Distribution*
De Beer 1963, *Bearing Capacity Calculation for Shallow Foundation with Inclined and Eccentric*
De Beer 1970a, *Soil Mechanics*
De Beer 1970b, *Experimental Determination of the Shape Factors and Bearing Capacity Factors*
De Beer 1971, *Problems Presented by the Construction of the Tunnel under the Scheldt at Antwerp*
De Beer 1972, *Methods of Determining the Bearing Capacity of a Tile on the Basis of the Results*
De Beer 1973, *Summary Report: Foundation Design*
Delgado-Vargas 1975, *Large Diameter Foundation Piers in Colombia*
DeMello 1969, *Foundations of Buildings in Clay*
DeSimone 1973, *Distribution of Wind Loads to Soil*
Dismuke 1973, *Excavations and Deep Foundations*
Duncan 1971, *Finite Element Analyses of Port Allen Lock*

Engineers Handbook 1975, *Subsidence*

Fadum 1948, *Influence Values for Estimating Stresses in Elastic Foundations*
Fang 1973, *Landslides and Foundation Design*
Fang 1974, *Landslide and Tall Building Foundation Design*
Fang 1975, *Basic Consideration of Design, Construction and Maintenance of Tall Buildings*
Fang 1975, *Tall Building Foundation Problems in Limestone Regions*
Feagin 1953, *Lateral Load Tests on Groups of Battered and Vertical Piles*
Fellenius 1963, *Driving Tests With Rock-Shoes Equipped with Rock Tips*
Fellenius 1969, *Negative Skin Friction for Long Piles Driven in Clay*
Fellenius 1969, *A New Pile Force Gauge for Accurate Measurement of Pile Behaviour*
Fellenius 1969a, *Negative Skin Friction on Piles in Clay, a Literature Review*
Fellenius 1969a, *Modulus of Elasticity for Precast Piles*
Fellenius 1971a, *Bending of Piles Determined by Inclinometer Measurements*
Fellenius 1971b, *Negative Skin Friction on Long Piles Driven in Clay*
Fellenius 1971c, *Influence of Pile Driving on Soil Compaction, Soil Movement and Bearing*
Fellenius 1973, *Precast Concrete Piles*
Fenoux 1971, *Excavations in Congested Urban Areas*
Focht 1964, *Observed Heave of Three Excavations in Houston, Texas*
Focht 1971, *Performance of Deep Mat Foundation of 52-Story One Shell Plaza Building*
Focht 1973, *Soil-Structure Interaction for Tall Buildings*
Focht 1974, *Performance of Deep Mat Foundation for the 52-Story One Shell*
Frohlich 1953, *On the Settling of Buildings Combined with Deviation From Their Originally*
Fuller 1970, *Methods and Equipment for the Installation of Piles in Foreign Countries*

Gerwick 1972, *Prestressed Concrete Piles*
Gerwick 1973, *High Capacity Prestressed Concrete Piling*
Gibson 1967, *Some Results Concerning Displacements and Stresses in a Non-Homogeneous*
Glick 1936, *Foundations of the New Telephone Building at Albany*
Girault 1964, *A New Type of Pile Foundations*
Goble 1970, *Prediction of Pile Behaviour From Dynamic Measurements*

Goble 1971, *A New Testing Procedure for Axial Pile Strength*
Golder 1963, *Floating Foundations for a Factory Building*
Golder 1965, *State of the Art of Floating Foundations*
Golder 1971, *The Allowable Settlement of Structures*
Gould 1970, *Lateral Pressures on Rigid Permanent Structures*
Grabowski 1972, *Interaction of Subsoil and Structure of Tall Buildings*
Grabowski 1973, *The Influence of Varying of Subsoil Deformability Moduli for Estimating*
Granholm 1967, *The Bearing Capacity of Reinforced Concrete Piles Driven to Bed Rock*
Grant 1974, *Differential Settlement of Buildings*
Grasshof 1957, *Influence of Flexural Rigidity of Superstructure on the Distribution of Contact*

Habib 1970, *Stability of Foundations of Structures of Great Height*
Hanna 1968, *The Bending of Long H-Section Piles*
Hanna 1971, *The Distribution of Load in Long Piles*
Hardin 1970, *Shear Modulus and Damping in Soils*
Hellers 1971, *Stresses, Cracks and Material Fatigue When Driving Reinforced Model Concrete*
Hellman 1967, *On Driving End Bearing Piles to Refusal*
Hellman 1971, *Investigation of Piles for Norrkoping Kraftvarmeverk*
Helmfrid 1971, *Automatic Pile Driving, Testing of Equipment and a Comparison of Automatic*
Hetenyi 1946, *Beams on Elastic Foundation*
Horvat 1972, *Foundation Design*
Horvat 1973, *Effects of Foundations on Adjacent Structures*
Hrennikoff 1950, *Analysis of Pile Foundations With Batter Piles*
Hui 1974, *Foundation of a 17-Story Building on a Pinnacled Limestone Formation in Kuala Lumpur*
Huntington 1957, *Earth Pressures and Retaining Walls*

Ionescu 1975, *Considerations of the Analysis of Silos and Tower Construction on Raft Foundation*

Johannessen 1965, *Measurement of the Compression of a Steel Pile to Rock Due to Settlement*
Johnson 1971, *A Technique for the Settlement and Stress Analysis of Mat Foundations*
Joustra 1971, *Precast Piles in Holland*

Kanjanavanit 1974, *Investigation of the Settlement of Kian Gwan Building and the Underpinning*
Kang 1959, *Analysis of Shallow Foundations*
Kausel 1974, *Soil-Structure Interaction Problems for Nuclear Containment Structures*
Kausel 1975, *Dynamic Stiffness of Circular Foundations*
Kausel 1975, *Dynamic Analysis of Footings on Layered Media*
Kausel 1976, *Nonlinear Behavior in Soil-Structure Interaction*
Kee 1974, *The Behavior of Raft Foundations in Lateritic Soils*
Krol 1964, *Statics of Reinforced Concrete Foundations with Consideration of the Rigidity of the*
Krol 1966, *On Piling in Mining Subsidence Areas*
Krol 1970, *Protection of Buildings Against Destruction Due to Mining*
Krol 1975, *On the Prefabricated Basements of Buildings in Mining Subsidence Areas*
Krol 1974, *Design of Tall Buildings in Mining Subsidence Areas in Poland*
Krsmanovic 1965, *Foundation Beams Resting on Homogeneous and Isotropic Soil*
Kubo 1974, *A Tall Building on Deep and Inclined Bearing Stratum*

Lo 1975, *Subsurface Investigation—Honolulu Municipal Building*
Lousberg 1957, *Calculation of the Distribution of Soil Reactions Underneath Eccentrically Loaded*
Lowery 1969, *Pile Driving Analysis—State-of-the-Art*
Lysmer 1972, *Shear Waves in Plane Infinite Structures*

Mansur 1964, *Pile Driving and Loading Tests at Lock and Dam No. 4*
Marcuson 1972, *Time Effects on Dynamic Shear Modulus of Clays*
Marwah 1973, *Construction Problems of Foundations of Tall Buildings*
Masopust 1973, *Problems of the Calculation of Footing Slabs on a Deformable Soil Foundation*
Matallana 1973, *Foundation Within the Urban Perimeter*
Meyerhof 1947, *The Settlement Analysis of Building Frames*
Meyerhof 1951, *The Ultimate Bearing Capacity of Foundations*
Meyerhof 1960, *The Design of Franki Piles With Special References to Groups in Sand*
Moller 1968, *Piling and Pile Design*
Moretto 1971, *Deep Foundations—Selected Synthesis of the Present State of Knowledge About*
Morgenstern 1970, *Methods of Estimating Lateral Loads and Deformations*

National Building Code of Canada 1970, *National Building Code of Canada, Section 4.2.5*
Newmark 1947, *Influence Charts for Computation of Vertical Displacements in Elastic*
Norwegian Geotechnical Institute 1962-1966, *Measurements of a Strutted Excavation*

Ohsaki 1969, *Effect of Local Soil Conditions Upon Earthquake Damage*
Ouyang 1973, *Structural and Foundation Design in Hong Kong*

Paez 1973, *Foundations*
Peck 1953, *Foundation Engineering*
Peck 1969, *Deep Excavation and Tunneling in Soft Ground*
Penzien 1964, *Seismic Analysis of Bridges on Long Piles*
Plantema 1967, *Influence of Pile Driving on the Cone Resistance in a Deep Sand Layer*
Popov 1950, *Successive Approximations for Beams on an Elastic Foundation*
Poulos 1974, *Elastic Solutions for Soil and Rock Mechanics*
Prakash 1962, *Behavior of Pile Groups Subject to Lateral Load*
Przybyla 1973, *Static Calculations of Buildings Subjected to Undermining Influences*
Przybyla 1973, *Passanger Lifts in Middle-Height Houses in Mining Subsidence Areas*
Przybyla 1974a *Characteristic of Technical Conditions Concerning Planning and Design of*
Przybyla 1974b, *Safety Evaluation of Structure of a Building Subjected to Mining Influences*

Rao 1974, *Stability of Foundations of Tall Structures under Earthquakes—A Case Study*
Reese 1956, *Non-Dimensional Solutions and Laterally Loaded Piles With Soil Modulus Assumed*
Rehnman 1968, *The Bearing Capacity of Sloping Rock Surface Loaded Statically by a Rock Tip*
Rehnman 1970, *The Strength of Rock Tips, Results from Statical Load Tests*
Rehnman 1971, *Bearing Capacity of Piles Driven into Rock*
Rocha 1970, *Geotechnical Aspects of the Project of Section 3 of the Metro of Saõ Paulo*
Rocha 1974, *Settlement of High Rise Buildings Due to the Construction of a Subway*
Richart 1970, *Vibrations of Soils and Foundations*
Roesset 1976, *Dynamic Soil Structure Interaction*
Romana 1973, *A Semicompensated Foundation for the New Social Security Hospital in Barcelona*
Romanoff 1962, *Corrosion of Steel Piling in Soil*

Sanglerat 1972, *The Penetrometer and Soil Exploration*
Sarrazin 1970, *Soil-Structure Interaction in Earthquake Resistant Design*
Schmidbauer 1970, *Drying of Deep Excavations Beneath the Groundwater Level by Temporary*
Scott 1970, *Soil Mechanics and Engineering*
Seed 1967, *Analysis of Soil Liquefaction: Niigata Earthquake*
Seed 1967, *The Turnagain Heights Landslide, Anchorage, Alaska*
Seed 1969, *Influence of Local Soil Conditions on Earthquake Damage*
Seed 1970, *Soil Moduli and Damping Factors for Dynamic Response Analyses*
Seed 1970, *Relationships Between Soil Conditions and Building Damage in the Caracas*
Seed 1975, *Soil-Structure Interaction Analyses for Seismic Response*
Severinsson 1965, *Practical Experience from Driving High Quality Precast Concrete End-Bearing*
Skempton 1956, *The Allowable Settlements of Buildings*
Smith 1960, *Pile Driving Analysis by the Wave Equation*
Souto Silveira 1969, *Written Contribution to the VII International Conference on Soil Mechanics*
Sowers 1975, *Failures in Limestones of Humid Subtropics*
Steinbach 1975, *Caisson Evaluation by Stress Wave Propagation Method*
Stermac 1968, *Unusual Movements of Abutments Supported on End-Bearing Piles*
Sundberg 1968, *Round Pretensional Piles*
Swedish Pile Commission 1964, *Driving and Test Loadings of Long Concrete Piles, Tests at*
Swedish Building Code 1967, *Pile Foundations. Requirements, Advice and Recommendations*
Swedish Pile Commission 1970, *Recommendation for Pile Driving Test and Routine Load Testing*
Swedish Pile Commission 1971, *Statistics of Piles Driven in Sweden 1962, 1966, 1968 and 1970*
Swiger 1941, *Foundation Tests for Los Angeles Steam Plant*
Swiger 1971, *Foundations*
Swiger 1971, *Foundations of Tall Buildings*
Swiger 1973, *Theme Report: Foundation Design*

Tassios 1974, *Investigations of Difficult Soils in Seismic Regions*
Teng 1962, *Foundation Design*
Terzaghi 1934, *Large Retaining Wall Tests*
Terzaghi 1936a, *A Fundamental Fallacy in Earth Pressure Computations*
Terzaghi 1936b, *Settlement of Structures*
Terzaghi 1943, *Theoretical Soil Mechanics*
Terzaghi 1944, *Discussions of Application of Soil Mechanics in Designing Building Foundations*
Terzaghi 1955, *Evaluation of Coefficients of Subgrade Reaction*
Terzaghi 1967, *Soil Mechanics in Engineering Practice*
Tettinek 1953, *A Contribution to Calculating Inclination of Eccentrically Loaded Foundations*
Timoshenko 1951, *Theory of Elasticity*
Trow 1967, *Analysis of Pile Load Test Results*

Trudeau 1974, *Shear Wave Velocity and Modulus of a Marine Clay*
Tschebotarioff 1970, *Bridge Abutments on Pile Driven Through Plastic Clay*
Tschebotarioff 1953, *The Effects of Restraining Boundaries on the Possible Resistance of Sand*
Tsytovich 1961, *Foundation of Structures*

Van der Veen 1968, *Soil Mechanics*
Van Weele 1957, *A Method of Separating the Bearing Capacity of a Test Pile into Skin Friction and*
Varga 1973, *Foundations for Tower-Shaped Structures*
Vargas 1973, *Foundation Problems of Tall Buildings*
Vesic 1961a, *Beams on Elastic Subgrade and the Winkler's Hypothesis*
Vesic 1961b, *Bending of Beams Resting in an Eleastic-Isotropic Solid*
Vesic 1965, *An Experimental Study of Dynamic Bearing Capacity of Footings on Sand*
Vesic 1967, *A Study of Bearing Capacity of Deep Foundation*
Vesic 1970, *Tests on Instrumented Piles, Ogeechee River Site*
Vetter 1939, *Design of Pile Foundations*

Wasilkowski 1951-1955, *The Full Protection of Buildings Agianst Destruction Due to Mining*
Wasilkowski 1966, *The Influence of Ground Creeping on Buildings Foundations in Mining*
Whitman 1969a, *Effect of Soil Conditions Upon Damage to Structures, Caracas Earthquake of 29*
Whitman 1969b, *Equivalent Lumped System for Structure Founded Upon Stratum of Soil*
Winkler 1867, *The Laws of Elasticity and Strength*
Wong 1974, *Evaluation of Settlement under Earthquake Loading Conditions of Buildings Founded*
Wynne-Edwards 1968, *Cracks in Reinforced Concrete Piles*

Zeevaert 1944, Discussion of *Application of Soil Mechanics in Designing Building Foundations*
Zeevaert 1945a, *Elastic-Plastic Equilibrium in the Surface of Contact of Rigid Plate and a Clay*
Zeevaert 1945b, *Fundamental Theories and Experiments That Apply to the Design of Foundations*
Zeevaert 1947, *The Outline of a Mat Foundation Design on Mexico City Clay*
Zeevaert 1949, *Present Building Foundation Problems in Mexico City*
Zeevaert 1950, Discussion of *Effects of Driving Piles into Soft Clay*
Zeevaert 1952, *Stratigraphy and Engineering Problems of the Deposits of Lacustrine Clay of the*
Zeevaert 1953a, *Outline of the Stratigraphical and Mechanical Characteristics of the*
Zeevaert 1953b, *Pore Pressure Measurements to Invistigate the Main Source of Surface*
Zeevaert 1956, *Heavy and Tall Building Problems in Mexico City*
Zeevaert 1957a, *Compensated Friction-Pile Foundation to Reduce the Settlement of Buildings*
Zeevaert 1957b, *Foundation Design and Behavior of Tower Latino Americana in Mexico City*
Zeevaert 1957, *Consolidation of Mexico City Volcanic Clay*
Zeevaert 1959a, *Compensated Foundations*
Zeevaert 1959b, *Reduction of Point-Bearing Capacity of Piles Because of Negative Friction*
Zeevaert 1960, *Base Shear in Tall Buildings During Earthquake of July 28, 1957, in Mexico City*
Zeevaert 1961, *Large Compensated Foundations on Volcanic Clay With High Compressibility*
Zeevaert 1962, *Foundation Problems Related to Ground Surface Subsidence in Mexico City*
Zeevaert 1963, *The Effect of Earthquakes in Soft Subsoil Conditions*
Zeevaert 1964a, *Strong Ground Motions Recorded During Earthquakes of May 11 and 19, 1962, in*
Zeevaert 1964b, *Structural Steel Building Frames in Earthquake Engineering*
Zeevaert 1964c, *The Engineering of Large Structures*
Zeevaert 1967a, *Consolidation Theory for Materials Showing Intergranular Viscosity*
Zeevaert 1967b, *Free Vibration Torsion Tests to Determine the Shear Modulus of Elasticity of Soils*
Zeevaert 1973, *Design of Compensated Foundations*

Tall Building Systems and Concepts

Chapter SC-8

Construction Systems

Prepared by Committee 4 (Construction Systems) of the Council on Tall Buildings and Urban Habitat as part of the Monograph on the Planning and Design of Tall Buildings.

Sherwin P. Asrow   Committee Chairman
W. H. Arch   Vice-Chairman
L. Richard Shaffer   Editor

AUTHOR ACKNOWLEDGMENT

Special acknowledgement is due those individuals whose contributions and papers formed the substantial first drafts of the various sections of this chapter. First are the state-of-art reporters from the 1972 International Conference whose material was published in the Lehigh Proceedings. These individuals are:

S. P. Asrow, Section 8.1
F. M. Bowen, Section 8.2
R. C. Halpern, Section 8.2
T. N. Subba Rao, Section 8.2
P. F. Moon, Section 8.3
R. K. Rainer, Section 8.3
E. E. White, Section 8.4

W. H. Arch, Section 8.5
K. D. Cunningham, Section 8.5
S. Nikai, Section 8.5
E. E. F. Taylor, Section 8.5
W. S. Bellows, Jr., Section 8.6
J. F. Camellerie, Section 8.7
J. A. Roret, Section 8.7

In addition to this, other sections were based on special contributions prepared by:

G. McCollam, Section 8.6   W. Beard, Section 8.8

CONTRIBUTORS

The following is a complete list of those who have submitted written material for possible use in the chapter, whether or not that material was used in the final version. The Committee Chairman and Editor were given quite complete latitude. Frequently length limitations precluded the inclusion of much valuable material. The Bibliography contains all contributions. The contributors are: W. H. Arch, S. P. Asrow, W. Beard, W. S. Bellows, Jr., F. M. Bowen, J. F. Camellerie, K. D. Cunningham, W. E. Fisher, R. C. Halpern, J. Healy, G. McCollam, P. F. Moon, S. Nikai, R. K. Rainer, J. A. Roret, L. Sadoff, L. R. Shaffer, L. U. Simon, G. G. K. Smith, W. K. Stockdale, T. N. Subba Rao, E. E. F. Taylor, A. Tedesko, E. E. White, G. Williamson, Sr.

COMMITTEE MEMBERS

W. H. Arch, S. P. Asrow, W. Beard, W. S. Bellows, Jr., F. M. Bowen, F. Brunner, J. F. Camellerie, W. F. Conlin, Jr., M. Crane, R. W. Crenshaw, K. D. Cunningham, C. A. DeBenedittis, S. V. DeSimone, R. C. Halpern, R. Krapfenbauer, G. Lacombe, J. Loizeaux, A. F. Margarido, G. McCollam, J. F. Murphy, S. Nikai, H. Paschen, T. Perzynski, B. M. Radcliffe, R. Rainer, J. A. Roret, L. R. Shaffer, L. U. Simon, G. G. K. Smith, T. N. Subba Rao, E. E. F. Taylor, E. E. White.

SC-8   Construction Systems

8.1   INTRODUCTION

The construction of tall buildings has developed out of the need for space in crowded urban areas. Accordingly, constructing a tall building has evolved into a complex function. Interaction is required among the public, government officials, contractor, owner, architect, planner, and engineer in order to make tall buildings economically feasible and functionally acceptable as well as to introduce innovative contracting and construction practices into tall building construction. This chapter presents the essential elements in tall building construction to be utilized as the basis for interaction by the public, government officials, and the others.

The construction of tall buildings is presented in terms of the following seven systems: (1) Control of the construction process; (2) safety; (3) foundations; (4) steel construction (see Fig. 8.1); (5) concrete construction (see Fig. 8.2); (6) mixed construction (see Fig. 8.3); and (7) demolition. The information presented in each section represents worldwide construction practices, although the greatest emphasis is given to practice in the United States. Construction management—a vital emerging mechanism in the system for construction of tall buildings in many countries—is not reported here, but rather as a separate subject of Chapter PC-14. Each system is subdivided into the major subelements that must be considered in any detailed examination of the system. These subelements are too numerous to list here but are identified in each presentation.

8.2   CONTROL OF THE CONSTRUCTION PROCESS

System selection and integration is the critical element to the economic success of the high-rise building. The construction manager, relying on his experience and on critical study, advises the architect and the owner on the most economic integrated set of building elements, such as foundation items, exterior walls, interior walls, floor systems, ceiling systems, electrical systems, and mechanical systems, based primarily on their constructability, that is, construction control process. The factors considered in choosing and scheduling systems and in the high-rise building are presented in terms of the three major stages in the process wherein control on such selection is centered: (1) Control during the design phase; (2) control of the subcontractors; and (3) control at site. The construction control theme is played and replayed at each stage in every successful project.

1 Control During Design Phase

Selection of Foundation System. During the design phase involving the foundation system, the construction manager strives for less expensive and faster ways to complete the foundation. Preliminary foundation plans may indicate a double gridwork of beams tying together a system of pile or caisson caps, but it may be less expensive and faster to substitute a thick mat area even though the quantity of concrete and reinforcing will probably increase. These added material costs must be carefully reviewed against possible savings in excavation time, or simpler bracing support systems. In this example the construction manager substitutes one strategy for another. On the other hand he might suggest a construction change wherein the temporary support system would be incorporated into the design of the foundation

Fig. 8.1 Typical steel frame building: I.B.M. Building, Chicago, Illinois *(Courtesy: American Bridge Division)*

wall itself. Examples of this approach occur in the use of a slurry wall to supplant the normal foundation wall plus sheeting, or use of permanent building framing instead of temporary walers and bracing. The working level for the project is of prime importance. It may pay, for example, to drive a longer pile and cut it off or drill caissons through an overburden, if these actions will keep the working level in the dry and preclude extensive dewatering.

In setting the basic design parameters one of the most common questions asked by the construction manager is, "How many basements?" The construction manager provides a quick, preliminary estimate of various schemes of basements from both construction cost and time bases. The owner can then weigh these cost and time requirements against income, cost of building additional stories, and cost of money over an extended construction period. In a recent project involving such an analysis, the owner was given the option of schemes from three to five

Fig. 8.2 Water Tower Place, Chicago, Illinois (John Hancock Center to left). Associated Architects-Engineers; Loebl, Schlossman, Dart and Hockl; C. F. Murphy Associates (*Photo by Shimer, Hedrich-Blessing*)

basements. The engineer forwarded suggested foundation sketches covering the various depths. Against these sketches various temporary sheeting and bracing designs were applied. These studies led to the report in Table 8.1.

Table 8.1 Report on basement schemes

(a) Description

Three-basement scheme (1)	Four-basement scheme (2)	Five-basement scheme (3)
Interlocking steel sheet pile, walers, and diagonal bracing into the lot. Finished basement foundation wall poured reinforced concrete.	Reinforced concrete slurry trench wall 1 m (3 ft) thick to hardpan with waler and diagonal bracing into the lot. Finished basement walls utilize slurry wall with patching.	Reinforced concrete slurry trench wall 1 m (3 ft) thick with diagonal drilled tie-back system to rock. Finished basement walls utilize the slurry wall with patching.

(b) Cost comparisons, calculated in United States dollars

Cost item (1)	Three-basement scheme (2)	Four-basement scheme (3)	Five-basement scheme (4)
Sheeting	360 000		
Diagonal bracing	280 000	550 000	
Slurry wall		810 000	1 470 000
Tie backs			750 000
Foundation wall	210 000		
Ramps, pumping	150 000	240 000	325 000
Excavation	350 000	700 000	850 000
Miscellaneous		35 000	45 000
Subtotal	1 350 000	2 345 000	3 440 000
Foundation timing	7.5 months	8.75 months	11 months
Escalation at 7% of total project cost beyond 7.25 months	0	750 000[a]	1 875 000[a]
Subtotal	1 350 000	3 095 000	5 315 000
Omit "standard" foundation	1 350 000	1 350 000	1 350 000
Premium add for deeper basement	0	1 745 000	3 965 000

[a]Escalation figures are based solely on construction costs and do not reflect carrying charges, land taxes, etc.

The study for cost comparisons in Table 8.1 includes only those phases normal to the foundation wall or sheeting system or both, bracing, excavation, dewatering, and ramping. Building items such as structure, interior work, caissons, elevators, grade beams, pits, sumps, and building services, common to all schemes, are not included. Based on the data shown in Table 8.1, the owner chose the three-basement scheme.

Structural System Selection.   Over 20% of total project dollars is spent on structure. The structure is usually of structural steel or concrete. In structural steel, the construction manager strives for the system that results in least cost per ton erected. One of the most misleading guidelines utilized by high-rise designers today is the weight per square foot of structural steel; a design is thought to be economically sound if the weight per square foot is low. The most important

Fig. 8.3 Building using mixed construction: Gateway 3, Chicago, Illinois *(Courtesy: Sherwin P. Asrow)*

guideline, however, is the cost per ton, erected. The amount of shop fabrication required and the ease of erection are two prime considerations in the cost of steel; raw steel itself is less than 40% of the cost. Another factor would be the use of field welding in geographic areas where certified welders are not available. Where metal deck is utilized, requirements for shoring should be reviewed at great length, eliminating their use if at all possible by the addition of filler beams or heavier gaged deck. Deck systems can be designed so that there is no requirement for wood forming on a floor, either at shafts, stairs, or perimeter conditions. If deck is bought with integral metal stops and detailed properly, carpenter labor on a typical floor can be held to protection work only during the basic structural frame erection.

In a concrete structure the construction manager also strives for the system that is most economical. In concrete his most important guideline is cost per yard, in place. However, in concrete he must be alert to detailed specifications that will overprice an apparent minimum cost concrete structure. For example, specifications commonly call for expensive sealers on all surfaces. This is not required on many buildings, such as office buildings which later receive composition flooring. In addition, when concrete is a fill, and not acting in composite design with the deck, the need for a full mesh needs careful evaluation, because cracking over girders and beams is common with mesh or without it.

Selection of Mechanical Systems.   The location of the mechanical rooms can be another control area to be reviewed by the construction manager. If the major equipment room is located at roof level, the construction period will be extended beyond that required if the basic equipment, such as boilers and chillers, were located in a lower level of the building with only the cooling and related equipment towers on the roof; however, a basement machine room may require a deeper excavation, a flue for the full height of the building, or an extensive system of air intakes and exhausts. The construction input must be weighed against the mechanical design considerations as well as the owner's operating and F.A.R. (floor area ratio) restrictions. In certain areas a rooftop mechanical room does not count in the F.A.R. computation. Where the building is the maximum building area possible on a given plot, this may be an overriding consideration. Another advantage to a lower mechanical room is the possible use of permanent systems for temporary construction heating.

A further concern for the construction manager with regard to mechanical systems often comes from vendor engineering. With today's technology and increasing complexity of various building systems, the architect and engineer must utilize technical data and design furnished by equipment suppliers and manufacturers. To keep a competitive atmosphere the construction manager must ferret out any "one of a kind" specification. The "or equal" phrase works only when more than one exists.

Conclusion.   These are only samples of the kind of questions which the construction manager must have addressed during the design phase. Other questions may arise on cost differentials between structural steel and concrete frames, and between heat by light electrical system versus other energy systems (gas, fuel oil). Questions on core design, such as backing up of plumbing fixtures, location of electrical closets, shaft locations, ease of duct distribution, and vendor engineering are other examples. The construction manager must apply himself to the review of the reasonable spectrum of alternatives to maintain an economic and time control of the project in this first phase.

2 Control of Subcontractors

The construction manager's task in this stage is the selection and interfacing of independent corporations (subcontractors), all experts in their particular field of endeavor. The ability of these subcontractors, and the manner in which they are coordinated or managed, play a key role in the success or failure of the project.

Basis for Selection.   Obviously, the size, experience, and economic strength of each potential subcontractor must be investigated, together with his current workload and the type of work in which he is experienced. Government projects require a different procurement and management policy from private construction; thus it is not uncommon for subcontractors to specialize in either government or private work, and negotiated subcontracts, those based on preliminary drawing, will require a "meeting of the minds" between the construction manager and the subcontractor. The price is obviously an important basis for selection. The construction manager, however, should not take prices until he has predetermined his value of the work. This should be done by him on an in-house basis predicated on his own current and past experience. The best situation involves a subcontractor anxious to do the job and submitting a price that requires the attention of his top management and an efficient operation to realize a fair profit. When a construction manager buys too cheaply, he will have problems maintaining quality, manning the job, and negotiating changes.

The subcontractor is the efficiency and monetary master of his particular trade. The pricing phase is an excellent opportunity for the construction manager to look for those last-minute changes which can reduce cost or speed production, or both. The construction manager should extract as much of this information as possible, discarding any suggestions that would tend to downgrade quality, and reviewing the others with the building team for possible incorporation into the project documents.

Subcontractor Obligations.   The special conditions for the project which must be known when prices are taken include the following:

1. Schedule requirements.

2. Deliveries (how made, how stored, how hoisted).

3. Shop drawings (when are they to be submitted?).

4. Special temporary equipment (predetermine location).

5. Temporary facilities (electric power, heat, water).

6. Protection (who provides).

7. Escalation (until when, formula thereafter).

These conditions identify the subcontractor obligations to the project that are of particular import to the construction manager.

An example of these conditions in a structural steel subcontract would be a determination of steel derrick location; in the spray-on fireproofing subcontract, a decision as to who provides the enclosures for heat and excess material. Other typical questions are, "What is each subcontractor's obligation regarding cleaning, both of their work, and of what is adjacent to it?" "Is there a rubbish chute, or is their waste material to be put into containers?" "How is the hoist controlled; is it on a reserved time and charge basis?" "Will the subcontractor provide power to a welding machine?" "Does the subcontractor remove utility lines to bring cranes into the site?" "Is the subcontractor doing the concrete testing?"

This list is very long. The construction manager should keep a current checklist of special condition items for each trade as a checkoff before awarding the project. After a project is completed, any extra orders issued during the project should be reviewed, and if they were written due to an omission of a special condition item, then the checklist should be supplemented and updated. The proper and complete use of special conditions in a subcontract is the most effective and easiest way to exercise project control.

Monitoring Subcontractor Performance.   When the subcontractors have been selected the monitoring process begins. The first step in monitoring is to assure that scheduled dates are met. If the construction manager calls for shop drawings on the day they are due, chances are they'll be late. The call should be made well enough in advance so that if they have not been started, the promised date can still be met. The same condition holds true in expediting shop drawings through the architect's and engineer's office within a required time span. There is no trick to this. What it requires is accurate and monitored charting, follow-up, and "follow-through." When the shop drawings are approved and returned, the manager must make periodic visits to the site of any fabrication or manufacture, to check off-site fabrication progress against the project schedule. This is the only way to avoid unpleasant surprises. During these visits specific delivery scheduling can be established.

Approximate manpower requirements should have been established during the pricing process. Normally, the construction manager is responsible, not for the number of workmen a subcontractor utilizes, but only for the work they turn out. However, since the two are closely linked, the monitoring of project manpower is imperative to project the subcontractor's progress accurately.

Another aspect of monitoring is coordination among the trades. A prime example is in the mechanical trades. Who goes where, in what shaft, can be a vexing and sometimes expensive problem. The construction manager must arrange for mechanical subcontractors to meet periodically. However, he should strive to have them solve their own problems, among themselves, rather than under his control. If he devises the solution to the problem, there is a tendency for a subcontractor to request additional payment for items that are obviously field conditions.

Quality Control.   The prime guideline here for the construction manager is that a job not done properly, within acceptable tolerances, should be corrected immediately. A high-rise building builds upon itself, hides mistakes, makes delayed corrections difficult, or impossible, and if delayed too long endangers the total schedule. It is at the early stages, when a subcontractor is first on the job, that the standards must be set for the quality of work that the project demands.

Quality control in many countries is invariably strict, and periodic tests are carried out on concrete and steel to assure they are of satisfactory quality. In some countries specialists for quality control are employed, such as a welding engineer or concrete engineer. These specialists must be known to the construction manager.

3 Control at Site

The plans are drawn, the subcontracts awarded, and work is ready to begin. Management of the site, monitoring of material, hoist provisions, and level of safety provided are all responsibilities of the construction manager. Well planned and executed general conditions allow the construction manager to control manpower and material in an expeditious fashion, permitting the work to proceed on the most efficient and economic schedule possible.

Access to Site and Foundation Staging. In establishing points of project access, entrance and exit ramps should favor the excavation operation since it involves the greatest traffic, but consideration must be given to all types of trucking and equipment entering the project, such as the less-maneuverable concrete, formwork, and rebar trucks. Site entrances should be kept to a minimum if at all possible. The ideal is one gate which would facilitate control over all material deliveries. The construction manager must try to select a site entrance on the least congested space, thereby causing minimum traffic and pedestrian disruption. A flagman is essential on a large city project. He helps control the pedestrian traffic, controls the deliveries entering the project site, moves trucks out of the site into city traffic, and keeps records of trucks leaving and entering. This information enables the construction manager to estimate earth and rock yardage removed on any given day. Only those materials to be used within a specific work week along with continually used items should be allowed on the site. This keeps the site open for additional areas to be started, and gives the project an appearance of planned productive progress.

After foundation and excavation are complete, the type of access must permit deliveries of structural steel and equipment to erect the structure up to derrick starting level. Consideration should be given to a temporary structural ramp if such a ramp will allow the completion of the foundation and still give access to lower levels of the project. The final excavation and concrete work can then be completed allowing access for the erection equipment deliveries of structural steel and derricks. The ramp should be situated so that as excavation equipment backs out of the hole the ramp is removed and the structure completed in the ramp area.

A high-rise building will have at least two derricks and possibly three, depending on the area and coverage required. The derricks will probably be the creeper stiffleg type mounted on jumping towers. The placement of these derricks will require two sides of the building for taking steel, with an in and out driveway at each location, and a storage space in the receiving area. Because the structural steel contract is awarded early in the project, this planning and layout must be a first step in job phasing on site.

Curtain-wall hoisting and material tower layout must be carefully coordinated with steel derrick and delivery areas. In addition, derrick engine locations should be considered with an eye toward completion of the lower areas of the building. The lobby is usually one of the most difficult spaces to complete. The construction manager may find that steel is still being erected on upper floors, and lobby work cannot proceed due to the derrick engine location.

Proper Hoisting of Material and Manpower. The main cranes and man and material hoists are generally provided by the main contractor, although in Great Britain there are numerous plant hire contractors who provide such equipment if the general contractor requires an addition to his fleet. In India and other countries where manpower is readily available at reasonable costs and plant is expensive, buildings up to 30 m (100 ft) high are constructed using labor for the lifting operations, but increasing use is being made of mechanical lifting equipment. Supplies are also limited by a shortage of foreign exchange to import them.

Material hoisting.   Hoisting operations should be placed on an elevation away from steel derricks to avoid hoisting steel over the material towers. Recommended number of material towers for a high-rise project could be three, with one pouring concrete, one normal three-wheelbarrow size hoist with a 4-m (13 ft) high cage, and the third a platform large enough to handle full sheets of gypsum board. The concrete equipment would be removed after concrete operations are complete and a typical hoist cage installed. Each tower has its own engines, with one possibly having a double drum operating a tower boom. The placement of the material towers and engine locations is important, because they must have complete access and free movement to and from a staging area. Also, the towers and areas around them will be the last spaces to be completed, which means this area should be selected with full knowledge that the hoist areas will be unfinished until first occupancy.

Cranes are commonly used in pairs or are self-elevating to facilitate their upward movement as the building progresses. Tower cranes are increasingly used in Europe, but much use is also made of Scotch or stiffleg derricks working on climbing gabberts or tower frames. Guy derricks are often used, but have the disadvantage of having to clear the guys when the jib is being slewed. Mobile cranes, either track or rubber-tire mounted, are commonly used for ground handling, but are only of value for the actual erection at the lowest levels.

In areas where shift work is economical, stocking materials on a second shift should be encouraged. Items such as drywall, masonry, and mass pipe to a mechanical floor are all prime candidates.

Manpower hoisting.   Manpower hoisting is a completely different problem. Facilities are provided to move the men at peak hours. Elevator subcontractors are now providing jumping elevators which are fast becoming the most efficient way to move manpower. Care must be exercised to keep the total weight of the jumping equipment within the capacity of the steel derricks. This enables the elevator to be raised to its new location in one clean move and returned to operation in a matter of hours. The speed of the jumping equipment is also important. Elevator codes for temporary elevators are now being changed, and speeds of 150 m (500 ft) per min are common. The selection of the elevators and use of shafts must be planned in advance so that the temporary elevators interface with the turnover of final elevators. Some other considerations when planning manpower hoisting are:

1. Owner's requirement for first occupancy.

2. Selection of shafts which will allow cars in the same bank to be completed for final use.

3. Scheduling the return of temporary elevator for completion with the completion of other permanent cars to replace the temporary manpower hoisting.

4. Temporary elevators arranged in permanent shafts so they will not interfere with completion of the core.

5. Elevators should be run express at peak hours, morning, noon, and night.

Material Handling Within Project. Equipment for handling material within the project, such as front-end loaders, could be effectively utilized if pallets are required on all types of material. Material can then be placed in a staging area from the trucks, and placed on hoist with forklifts. This cuts down not only on truck unloading time, but also improves the loading and unloading efficiency of material hoists.

The entire building will be brought to the site by truck, so the jobsite must be prepared to receive, unload, and return empty trucks without clogging street traffic and the small project staging area. This is where other decisions regarding general conditions yield their benefits. Night hoisting, concrete batch plants instead of ready-mix (with night bulk sand and gravel delivery), and material handling at the loading areas, all help to unload trucks and keep access clear.

There is general provision of an office—in France a "Bureau de Trafic"—to coordinate and plan the supplies of material on the site and the off-loading of road vehicles with the requirements of materials. Cranes and hoists are often invoiced to the subcontractors making use of them on either an hourly or a per capita basis, depending on the type of plant.

Jobsite Communications. In a high-rise project, communications will affect its progress, and preplanning will be extremely important. Telephone systems can be used effectively with a phone on each floor (together with a separate paging device), one in each subcontractor's office, and one in the construction manager's office. This system would permit complete floor-by-floor and shanty-by-shanty communication, which is essential to a controlled operation.

In other cases communications are provided by telephone from fixed points. Orders are transmitted to mobile teams by loudhailer, and to the drivers of cranes from those mobile teams by radio. There are difficulties in the use of radio in some countries caused by a shortage of frequencies, or by a shortage of the necessary equipment on the market.

Day-to-day communication between contractors and their subcontractors is maintained by regular meetings attended as required by the client's agents or outside public utility representatives.

Temporary Heat and Power. In all climatic zones where a cold winter construction period exists, the project planning must include temporary heating. On the other hand temporary power is required on all locations, and is normally provided by the main contractor who must lease with the executing authority to assure that the necessary supplies are available. Where they are not, temporary generators are provided.

Each subcontractor is nominally responsible for his own men and normally pays the costs of installation and consumption in proportion to his requirements. This arrangement is dependent on the terms of his contract.

A system to enclose the building should be engineered both to contain the fireproofing operation and to enclose for winter heating. A system of light framework with plastic inserts mounted in tracks and hoisted as floors are completed has proved more effective than tarpaulin. Temporary electric entry and power requirements must also be preplanned, and included as part of the contract documents.

8.3 SAFETY

Safety is one of the most important planning items a project can have. Preplanning safety into the project is a critical requirement and is a joint effort between the construction manager and the subcontractors. Each subcontractor can contribute to protection as his work progresses. The structural steel erector can furnish and install perimeter cable at each floor, the deck erector can furnish a large perimeter angle to act as a toe board, the concrete installer can protect shaft openings, and so on. The control of safety can be achieved with early planning.

Safety in the construction of tall buildings involves two major categories: (1) Protection of men in the work areas; and (2) protection of public at the work site.

In France the methods used to assure safety are laid down by government edict of January, 1965. In Great Britain, similarly, there are statutory instruments which lay down safety rules. The application of the rules is assured in both cases by regular visits of inspectors who carry out inspections of working sites. Contractors normally employ a full-time safety officer who is helped by private safety organizations, such as the Royal Society for the Prevention of Accidents in Britain and OPBTP in France, in the interpretation of the law. In Japan, in addition to employing a safety officer, companies hold regular meetings with their subcontractors with all the work crews attending in order to discuss safety.

At this time (1980) each location has national, state, and local codes and laws. Attempts are being made by such bodies as the American National Standards Institute Committees in writing codes covering many phases of construction operations and equipment. Other countries also have safety codes applicable to construction. An international organization of standards (ISO) is active in formulating standards.

1   Protection of Workers in Work Areas

Certain safety practices are minimal and these must be shared by the general contractor and the subcontractors: working platforms, safety nets, safety belts, helmets, and other protective equipment. Each subcontractor must contribute to the safety of his work as it progresses. The structural steel erector can institute the following safety practices:

1. Provide a floor area for the erectors on the top floor erected, known as the derrick floor, and an additional floor two floors below. This flooring may be temporary or permanent floor deck material. All flooring is attached for wind conditions. All the openings are either fenced off or covered with wire mesh.

2. Each floor that is decked should have a wire cable railing stretched around the perimeter.

3. Plan operations to eliminate working over the top of other workmen; otherwise, special overhead protection should be provided.

4. Protect the public by barricades and overhead protection.

5. Personal protection involves equipment such as belts for tying-off, hard hats,

and glasses for specific hazards. Safety training is an important phase of personal protection.

6. Place protective fencing around areas where contact with running cables is likely.

Safety nets and belts are provided and are used as conditions dictate. In Great Britain it is mandatory to provide belts, but their use is a matter for the individual workman. Increasing emphasis is being placed on the use of safety nets.

The stability of a framework while it is partly erected should be considered at the design stage. In Great Britain the provision of temporary bracing and other supports is nominally the responsibility of the contractor erecting the frame. The contractor is also responsible for ascertaining the stresses that are being induced in the frame by the particular erection method he is using. There are regulations governing such things as access gangways, scaffolds, and the provision of toe boards and guard rails.

Horns advising of back-up motions of trucks, forklifts, and other mobile equipment should be installed and utilized to warn workers of unexpected motions.

2   Protection of Public at Work Site

The protection of the public begins with the erection of fences or barriers around the excavation to preclude spectators from toppling into the hole. When the structure is above ground, safety practice must include covered walkways or streets for the public to pass adjacent to the site without fear of injury from falling materials or tools from the construction. In addition, fog horns in staccato bleeps should be installed on vehicles entering streets in city sites and flagmen should control traffic. Finally, signs displaying both dangers and precautions must be prominently displayed for the public to be protected while adjacent to the site.

3   Inspection Practices

The regulations in Great Britain and other countries lay down regular inspection routines for lifting equipment, and tests include overload tests to assure the safety of anchorages as well as the structure of the lifting appliance. Inspections and tests are required at regular intervals, in addition to others each time the appliance is re-erected. In France the crane driver is subjected to stringent medical and physiological tests to assure his suitability for employment in a position of great responsibility.

8.4   FOUNDATIONS

Tall buildings present many foundation construction problems because of their heavy column loads and deep basements. These loads have been increasing in magnitude as architects use wider spacing of exterior and interior columns to provide uninterrupted floor space in modern high office buildings. It is not unusual to have column loads of 27 000 kN (6 000 kips) to 36 000 kN (8 000 kips) for a tall building. Since tall structures are built in many cities along rivers, lakes or harbors, foundation conditions are usually not ideal. It is often necessary to carry these heavy loads through deep poor layers of ground to reach a proper bearing stratum.

The heavy loads of these structures where poorer ground is present have made spread footings or mat foundations impossible; and the use of conventional piling, with moderate loads of 534 kN (120 kips) or 890 kN (200 kips) per pile, requires so many piles under a column that there is often not enough room to install the required number of piles.

Even if enough piles can be placed under a column, the use of so many piles causes disturbance to the surrounding areas. If they are displacement piles, the heave caused by the installation can be very destructive. Even low-displacement piles in large quantities can cause consolidation of material. This occurred in the lower Manhattan area of New York City during the installation of piles for a tall building founded on a substratum of loosely consolidated sand. The sand was compacted during the driving of over a thousand piles, causing settlement of adjacent structures. It was necessary to stop work, condemn these structures, and demolish them to continue with the project.

As a result of this need for heavy load-bearing elements various machines and techniques have been developed in different areas of the world, and each has its application and, unfortunately, its limitations. There is no universal unit, and the experienced foundation practitioner has to be able to realize the proper application of these techniques and equipment. The design aspects of foundations are covered in Chapter SC-7.

1 Caissons

One of the primary means of providing good foundations for heavy loads, where the construction site is overlain with deep layers of poor soil, is the use of caissons to bedrock, hardpan or similar material. Originally the word "caisson" referred to the hollow shaft or box that supported the soil laterally while the hole was being dug, and that then became the outer part of the finished pier. It was also used to describe the method of installation of these piers. Now, however, the word is more often used to describe the structural element (the pier) that carries the load from the building to the supporting soil layer. This article describes the current state of the art in the use and installation of caissons.

Hand-dug Caissons.   Hand-dug caissons are utilized for deep foundations where access to site or obstructions preclude the use of machines. The Chicago Well Method of constructing a hand-dug caisson requires the installation of wood lagging and steel rings as the hand excavation takes place. A round hole is dug approximately the required diameter of the caisson plus the lagging thicknesses. Normally, lagging 1.3 m (5 ft) long is used. The tongue and groove lagging is placed vertically tight to the earth. The curved two-piece steel rings are wedged apart at the joints to press against the lagging. Generally, these are steel channels bent about the weak axis so that radius to the back of the channel which presses against the lagging is that of the caisson. Two rings are used per set of lagging. Successively the hole is dug and lagged to the bearing strata or top of a bell, using a bucket and motor-driven winch supported by a tripod, for access to the bottom of the hole and removal of the soil. When belling is required, the bells are hand excavated and the soil must be suitable for belling. Special procedures are used when water, water-bearing runny silts, or sand are encountered.

The bottom of the hole is cleaned and the bearing capacity verified. The caisson is completed by placing the reinforcing steel and concrete. A short tremie is used to prevent segregation of the concrete. Continuous operations for both excavation and concrete placement are essential to a safe and successful installation.

Similar hand-dug caisson construction methods are being used in Hong Kong, India, and other parts of the world.

Auger Caisson Machines. One of the most important developments in large-diameter caissons has been the truck and crane mounted bucket or auger equipment which in the last fifteen years has been used in clay areas of the United States in the vicinity of the Great Lakes. This equipment has made great inroads into the use of conventional piling in that part of the country. In recent years the foundations for large buildings in Chicago, Cleveland, and Detroit as well as other areas in the United States, such as Texas and California, have been constructed using augers. This equipment is also widely used in London clay, which has proved to be very suitable for it. The caisson method works best in cohesive ground that will stand open until a protective casing can be installed or until concrete is poured into the drilled excavation to form a concrete shaft to good bearing material. The auger machines are not suitable in glaciated areas where there is wet, running granular material with silt and boulders, such as the northeastern part of the United States. Therefore the installation of caissons with auger equipment is limited.

The equipment to install these caissons is based on oil-well drilling techniques using a square section steel column called a Kelley bar which is rotated by a turntable. To the bottom of the Kelley bar are fastened various types of tools, such as a bottom dump bucket to pick up the spoil, an auger which is turned into the ground, belling buckets, core barrels, and many other types of ingenious devices (see Fig. 8.4). The equipment to dig these holes is either truck or crane mounted. The crane-mounted equipment is used for deeper and heavier work or in excavations where it is difficult to move truck-mounted equipment. With the large crane-mounted caisson it is possible to dig holes 3 m (10 ft) in diameter to a depth of over 45 m (150 ft) using telescoping Kelley shafts. The weight of the heavy Kelley bar plus a downward force, or crowd, helps the digging tools penetrate hard strata and improves their speed in digging (see Fig. 8.5).

The cranes to install large caissons must have a capacity of 91 000 kg (100 tons) to handle the turntable, Kelley bar, and auger, which weigh about 36 000 kg (40 tons). The torque of the turntable is as much as 490 000 N.m (360 000 lbf-ft). The equipment is very heavy and expensive, costing up to $200 000 (US) for a crane and drill unit to install large-diameter caissons. It is possible, however, to install a larger number of smaller units of less capacity to take advantage of less expensive equipment. The turntable units can be mounted on standard cranes, which is a great advantage as the cranes can also be used for other types of work.

The caissons are belled by special tools to increase the bearing area on the hardpan for larger capacity caissons. The limit by machine for a bell is about 9 m (30 ft) in diameter. Hand digging is necessary for larger bells, and to clean up the machine bells for proper bearing of the concrete on either rock or hardpan. The concrete is usually 35 000 kPa (5 000 psi) with 25% f'_c allowed. Reinforcing of the shafts is usually eliminated except for top cages, as it is more economical to have concrete carry the loads rather than steel.

Method of Construction of Caisson. The basis of operation of caisson auger machines is to take advantage of the ability of the ground to stay open for a short duration until a steel casing can be dropped into place. The augers or buckets will dig an oversize hole to rock. This hole is larger in diameter than the steel casing, which is usually 13 mm (1/2 in.) to 25 mm (1 in.) thick, depending on the type of ground, hole diameter, and depth of the caisson. The annular ring between the steel casing and the clay is a source of difficulty as the clay gradually squeezes against the steel and causes loss of ground and subsidence of adjacent areas or streets. Attempts to correct by grouting or by installing sand fill have not been very successful. In Chicago there is an additional problem caused by a 3-m (10-ft) layer of wet sand above the impervious clay. By using an auger and bentonite, however, it is not difficult to churn up the sand layer so that a steel casing can be forced into the clay, sealing off this wet layer. This casing has to be larger in diameter than the bottom casings so that the lower ones can be installed within the top casing.

If there is a problem with water at the top of the rock surface, belling on the rock is difficult and large straight-sided caissons are used. The steel casing is equipped with tungsten carbide teeth making an excellent core barrel, which can be rotated into the rock to effect a seal so that men can work in the bottom of the caisson to excavate poor rock and clean off the rock for proper bearing of the concrete shaft. It is possible to cut as much as 3 m (10 ft) into the rock to attempt to seal off water or material inflows. However, they cannot always be sealed off, and a certain percentage of caissons may be troublesome. For example, on one tall building in Chicago about 10% of the caissons were difficult to seal against water and material inflows. Several large-diameter 3-m (10-ft) caissons took several months to complete and blew several times before completion. The loss of ground resulting from this blowing is translated into settlement of streets and adjacent structures, which may move as much as 150 mm (6 in.) to 300 mm (12 in.) laterally and twice as much vertically.

It is not unusual during the installation of caissons to have the loss of ground affect adjacent structures. A very heavy old building in Chicago had to be underpinned due to the loss of ground caused by the installation of deep caissons

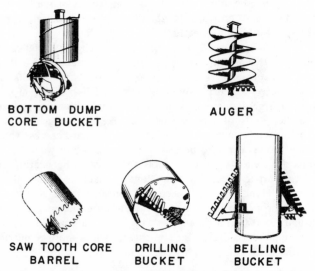

BOTTOM DUMP   AUGER
CORE BUCKET

SAW TOOTH CORE   DRILLING   BELLING
BARREL   BUCKET   BUCKET

Fig. 8.4 Machine-drilled caisson tools

across a narrow street (see Fig. 8.6).

The core barrels will seal off into soft or medium rocks, but will have difficulty in hard rocks, boulders, steep sloping rock, decomposed rock, fractured rock, or rock that has water in its seams. Even a small quantity of water will cause difficulty in the installation of a caisson.

Concreting of Caissons. Concreting of caissons is extremely important. In the past some improper techniques have been used that have caused many failures and a great deal of expense and delay on some major structures founded on caissons.

Great care must be taken in the installation of each caisson as there is usually only one high-strength concrete unit under each column. If one caisson is defective great difficulty occurs, as was discovered in 1961 where settlement was discovered in the vicinity of one column while a building in Chicago was being erected. Probings disclosed that caisson concrete just under the column was missing, only clay being present. It was necessary to institute emergency measures immediately to shore the column and install permanent underpinning to provide adequate support for the building.

Other difficulties have arisen while concreting wet caissons where the bottom concrete was segregated into its component parts of cement, sand, and gravel. If there is a flow of water into the caissons exceeding a 6-mm (1/4-in.) rise per minute in the caisson, it is advisable to flood the caisson and concrete the caisson subaqueously with a 200-mm to 250-mm (8-in. to 10-in.) tremie pipe using concrete with a 180-mm to 200-mm (7-in. to 8-in.) slump. A bottom dump bucket should not

Fig. 8.5 Crane-mounted auger machine *(Courtesy: Calweld, Inc.)*

be used for tremie concrete as it can accidentally open prior to reaching bottom, ruining the concrete. Even if the water flow can be handled with a pump, the process of simultaneously pouring concrete and pumping water is dangerous.

A great source of trouble is the pulling of the caisson shell during concreting of the caisson as an economy measure to save the expensive casing for use on other caissons. This is a difficult process and has caused voids in the concrete when the concrete arched against the sides of the casing and the concrete shaft was pulled apart when the steel casing was extracted (see Fig. 8.7). The void is filled in with soft clay when the casing is fully extracted. This is not an unusual situation, and a void of as much as 4.25 m (9 ft) was detected in a caisson of a major tall building. This is most likely to occur on a hot day when there is a delay in concreting and initial set of the concrete has taken place. Old concrete clinging to the side of the casing increases the friction and contributes to the problem. As a result of these failures, it is advisable to leave the steel casing in place for rock caissons.

Since caissons bearing on hardpan in Chicago are usually dry and deep, they do not have serious problems, and it is usually proper to pull the casing. Even so, a careful check of the actual quantity of concrete in each caisson poured against the theoretical quantity should be made to see if clay seams are possibly present in the concrete. Careful inspection is vital, and in addition a core boring in the concrete should be made in a few random caissons and all suspect caissons to determine

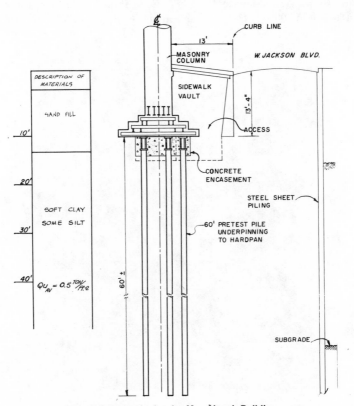

Fig. 8.6 Underpinning for Monadnock Building

whether the concrete is defective or there is proper contact of the concrete and the rock.

Benoto Machines.   Another caisson machine is the Benoto machine (see Fig. 8.8), which is excellent in penetrating granular materials such as silt, wet sand, and gravel that present difficulties to the auger rigs described previously. The Benoto machine works on the principle of continuously rotating the special shell or casing to reduce the side friction of the casing against the ground. This is done by a pair of jacks which rotate the casing in a back and forth circular motion. The shells are forced into the ground with vertical jacks and the earth within the shell is excavated by ingenious single line grab buckets and chopping tools.

The concreting of a Benoto caisson is greatly facilitated by the rotation and jacking of the caisson and the special bolted reusable casings. These casings are 6 m (20 ft) in length. Care must be taken, however, to keep from pulling the concrete shaft apart when the casing is extracted.

The Benoto machine is relatively expensive, has high maintenance costs and is limited in diameter, making it unsuitable for heavy loads. Its use has been greatly diminished by the development of the auger rigs.

Drilled-In-Caissons.   An excellent high-capacity system for carrying heavy loads is the drilled-in-caisson, which has been used for many heavy buildings in the United States since the early 1950s and has a remarkable record of successful applications. This type of caisson is used where depth of caisson or difficult ground conditions are encountered, such as wet granular material, boulders, obstructions, or sloping hard rock which cannot be coped with by auger techniques.

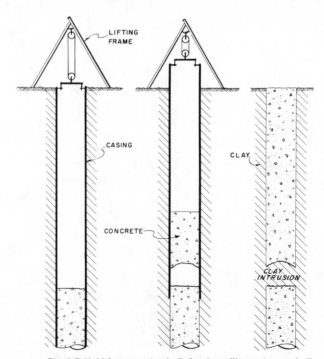

Fig. 8.7 Void in concrete shaft due to pulling caisson shell

Drilled-in-caissons are installed by driving a steel cylindrical pipe to rock using a pile hammer. The pipe, which is 610 mm to 1100 mm (24 in. to 42 in.) in diameter and 13 mm (1/2 in.) thick, has a 30-mm (1-1/4-in.) steel shoe welded at the bottom to reinforce its tip. The cylinder is excavated by blowing with compressed air, augered out with a standard caisson rig, or evacuated by a cable drill rig with suction buckets.

If there are obstructions in the overburden it is possible to break them up with the chopping tools of a cable drill rig. Very large obstructions can be penetrated in this manner. These heavy cable tools will also penetrate hardpan over the rock. When bedrock is reached, a socket is churn drilled into the rock slightly smaller in diameter than the cylindrical pipe. A heavy steel H-beam core or equivalent area in reinforcing rods is installed to extend from the top of the cylinder to the bottom of the rock socket. The entire assembly is concreted in place, producing a fixed-end caisson locked into the rock (see Fig. 8.9). Techniques for concreting under water have been developed, making it unnecessary to dewater the caisson if there is leakage of water into the caisson—one of the great advantages of this method.

The drilled-in-caisson can also be socketed into sharply sloping rock by placing granite blocks into the pipe after it has been excavated to rock permitting the drilling of a socket. This gives a solid area for the heavy drill bits to chop into the solid rock.

Drilled-in-caissons have been used to great depths, having been installed over 61 m (200 ft) long in Boston and Cleveland for tall buildings where other methods would have had great difficulty in reaching a sound bearing on rock. However, the

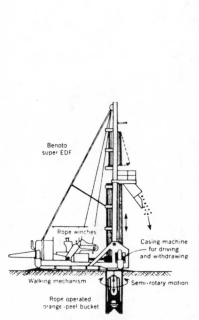

Fig. 8.8 Benoto caisson machine

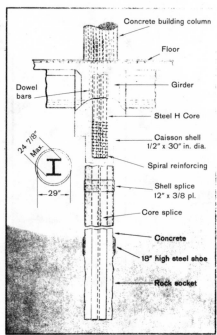

Fig. 8.9 Detail of drilled-in-caisson

drilled-in-caisson has the disadvantage that expensive steel carries its loads. For that reason it is expensive in areas of the world where steel is scarce.

The basic principle of using bond and bearing for caissons has many applications and does not have to be confined to rock alone. In California it has been applied to caissons in hard granular materials and dense clays with values assigned for bond of 480 kPa (70 psi). There has been experimental work on this type of installation in varying materials, including London clays. The carrying of load by bond or friction used in the drilled-in-caisson design will certainly be increasingly used in the future.

Slurry Caissons. An interesting new foundation element is the application of the slurry wall technique, which is described in more detail later. In this case a rectangular trench is dug to rock using bentonite slurry to keep the earth sides of the trench from collapsing. The area required for load bearing is obtained by widening or lengthening the trench. In the construction of the Maine-Montparnasse building in Paris, slurry caissons were used for this tall structure. The caissons ranged from 1.2 m to 1.5 m (4 ft to 5 ft) wide and 2.1 m to 4.9 m (7 ft to 16 ft) long. The unit load carried was approximately 5.7 kPa (60 tons/ft²). Only the top of the slurry foundation was reinforced. Two small pipes were installed in the unit to within a short distance from the bottom of the concrete in order to core the lower concrete and its contact with the chalk-bearing stratum. This makes an excellent test of the concrete poured by tremie methods into the slurry.

The slurry caisson method does not rely on suitable cohesive soil as required by the auger technique, it eliminates dewatering, and uses less complicated equipment. It is, however, a method that must be carefully installed to obtain good concrete properly seated on its bearing stratum. The slurry caissons can be of various shapes, such as crosses or tees to provide horizontal stability.

2   Other Foundations

If soil conditions at the building site are favorable, piles or a mat foundation might be more economical than caissons for a tall building.

Piles. There are so many types of piles that space does not permit adequate coverage of this important field. In recent years the carrying capacity of piles has been greatly increased, particularly of the end-bearing piles. For example, the allowable stress for H beams has increased from 62 MPa (9 000 psi) to 86.8 MPa (12 600 psi), and in two instances (based on tests) increased to 152 MPa (22 000 psi). The use of heavier hammers with a more rapid stroke, a better understanding of soils, and better application of test procedures have contributed to this increase in capacity. There also has been an important development in precast concrete piles. The use of piles for large structures, however, has been supplanted in many cases by use of the large-capacity units described previously.

Mat Foundations. Concrete mats for tall buildings can be used where there is a good bearing stratum, such as dense sand or hardpan. The mat foundation, instead of caissons or piles, should be investigated for suitability, and if it is suitable, for economy.

Mat foundations, depending on soil properties and column spacing and loading, can vary greatly in thickness. Thicknesses of 1.8 m (6 ft) for a mat foundation are not uncommon. Reinforcing steel is heavy because unequal loading is generally the case. Careful consideration must be given to locations of construction joints and to the effect of temperature.

3 Deep Excavations

While deep building foundation excavations are not limited to tall buildings, a study of tall buildings makes it quite clear that they usually have deep and large foundations. Most are large structures constructed in deep excavations, the area of which is larger than the building itself. An example is the new Sears Tower in Chicago, Illinois which is a 70-m (225-ft) square tower in an excavation area 100 m wide × 120 m long × 15 m deep (324 ft × 398 ft × 50 ft). These deep and large foundations present new and difficult problems and have been responsible for the development of new techniques to solve them.

Many foundations of large structures are located in difficult ground and have to be carefully designed and constructed. It is one of the great risks in the project. An error in foundation construction methods or design can add many months to the time of construction. Such delays, because of the large amount of money, invested without profit, can have serious financial consequences to the owners. Experience has shown that when something goes wrong, it is usually in the foundation.

Since large buildings are usually constructed in congested cities, it is necessary to use braced sheeted systems to protect the streets, buildings, utilities, and sewers. Underpinning is often necessary to support adjacent subways or buildings. There is usually not enough room to slope the earth naturally and eliminate sheeting.

There is a great variety of sheeting and support systems that may be used for these excavations, depending on type of ground encountered, availability of materials, and the structure to be constructed. The basic systems are interlocking steel piling, steel soldier beams with horizontal sheeting, and concrete slurry walls. Each method has its application and limitation. No description of vertical wood sheeting is given here as this type of sheeting is used for shallow excavation.

Interlocking Steel Sheet Piling. Interlocking steel sheet piling, or steel sheeting as it is called in the United States, is probably the most basic type of sheeting for deep cuts and is usually the first type of sheeting to be considered by engineers, although it is expensive and has its limitations. Steel sheet piling can penetrate to reasonable distances and is able to resist bending stresses, particularly the deep web types of Z sheeting. It is generally watertight when driven and sealed in an impervious layer (see Fig. 8.10).

Sheeting will not hold back water, however, when driven in a thick layer of pervious sand extending below the sheeting. An example is a building in New York constructed in a deep stratum of permeable sand. When the interior of the excavation was pumped out, piezometers outside and inside the sheeting showed only a foot or two difference in levels. The pumping had reduced the water level only a little from the level outside the sheeting because of the water flowing under the sheeting.

Steel sheeting, in spite of its great acceptance, has a number of disadvantages. It is difficult to install in dense material and more expensive than horizontal wood sheeting and soldier beams unless it can be removed after use. This is often not possible because the construction of the building interferes with this operation. The pulling of the sheeting also causes a disturbance of the ground, and it is difficult to pull if the driving was hard.

Steel sheeting, because of its ability to hold back water when sealed properly, causes water pressure to build up against the sheeting. In this case a larger and more expensive bracing system is required to hold back both water and earth pressure than if the sheeting is against drained ground.

Sheeting has to be carefully installed as ripped sheets or jumped interlocks will affect the watertightness of the system. Sheets should be driven with a minimum of 1.5 m (5 ft) or less between tips of adjacent pieces to prevent the jumping of interlocks. The resistance of the interlocks makes it much more difficult to drive steel sheeting than soldier beams which are free to move and accommodate themselves to obstructions in the ground. Obstructions in the ground can easily damage sheeting by ripping the sheets or causing jumping of the interlocks.

Steel Soldier Beams and Horizontal Timber Sheeting. Soldier beams and horizontal timber sheeting make a flexible and economic method adaptable for many situations. This technique is called the Berlin Method in Europe since it was used there first. It consists of driving vertical steel beams on centers varying from 2 m to 3 m (6 ft to 10 ft) apart, depending on ground conditions, and then installing untreated wooden sheeting placed in the flange of the beam to support the ground (see Fig. 8.11). The planks, spaced 50 mm (2 in.) apart, eliminate water pressure. The drainage also reduces the earth pressure by increasing the shearing resistance of the ground. The soldier beams can penetrate denser material than steel sheeting and can be extended if the beams hang up or are damaged on boulders or obstructions. This is done by underpinning and welding a section to the bottom of the beam.

In recent years, with the development of augers, it has become possible to install the soldier beams in auger holes and backfill the hole with lean concrete of 1 bag weighing 94 lb (43 kg) per 1 cu yd (0.76 m^3) of concrete. The auger can penetrate in hard ground. It also has the advantage of eliminating noise in construction, a new and important consideration as more and more restrictions to driving seem likely in the future, such as exist in London at the present time. The soldier piles can be more accurately installed by augering than with driving. It is also possible to install in the auger holes special steel sections that cannot be easily driven, such as split channels, and these can be used to install ground anchors or deep beam sections with a high section modulus.

In sand the steel beams are installed a distance of 2 m (7 ft) to 3 m (10 ft) apart depending on the ground. In soft clays the spacing is usually 1.5 m to 2 m (5 ft to 7 ft) apart. The horizontal wood sheeting is 75 mm (3 in.) thick, although in soft clays 100 mm (4 in.) is used. Wood sheeting of this thickness has been used successfully for years. While it does not appear to be thick enough based on accepted theories of earth pressures, it does work as the ground arches from soldier beam to soldier beam. It is also possible to use 50-mm (2-in.) sheeting for spans ranging up to 1.5 m (5 ft) in width. The sheeting thickness used does not have to be increased with depth of excavation even up to 15 m (50 ft).

The 50-mm (2-in.) louvers or spaces between the boards provide drainage and prevent building of hydrostatic pressure from either ground water or leading sewers and water mains. The latter two are a common source of water in city work. The louver is wide enough to pack sand behind the boards to have tight contact between the ground and the timbers, or to install hay if necessary to prevent soil from running out between the planks. If wood is difficult or expensive to obtain, as it is in many parts of the world, concrete planks can be used instead. Concrete planks are

Fig. 8.10 Interlocking steel sheet piling and bracing *(Courtesy: E. E. White)*

Fig. 8.11 Steel soldier beams and horizontal timber sheeting *(Courtesy: E. E. White)*

heavier to handle and hard to cut but can be a suitable substitute. If the ground will stand unsupported for 1 m (3 ft) or over it is possible to fasten a mesh to the soldier beams and use gunite to support the wall. This is a common technique in California.

Bentonite Slurry Walls. In recent years the use of bentonite slurry walls has developed to the point where they have been used for many important structures, including the World Trade Center in New York. It was the method used in that project for 976 m (3 200 lin ft) of a 21.4-m (70-ft) deep, 1-m (3-ft) thick perimeter wall of the huge excavation of this structure. The process was developed in Europe and consists of the construction below grade of a cast-in-place reinforced concrete wall up to 1.2 m (4 ft) in thickness and over 30 m (100 ft) deep. It can serve a dual function of supporting the earth in a manner similar to steel or wood sheeting and acting as the permanent foundation wall of the building.

Specially designed clamshells or reverse circulation excavating equipment dig a slot in the ground normally 0.75 m to 1 m (2-1/2 ft to 3 ft) wide. These rigs are able to dig through difficult ground containing obstructions, boulders, and hardpan, and can, with special drilling tools, penetrate into bedrock. The trench is supported by being filled with a slurry mixture of bentonite and water. This slurry is carefully mixed and controlled as to specific gravity, viscosity, sand content, and chemical contamination which occurs during concreting. The slurry level is kept above the ground-water level. Maintaining this level with a slurry with a specific gravity of approximately 1.05 to 1.10 maintains the walls of the trench. The slurry walls are dug in short panels about 6 m (20 ft) in length in alternate or consecutive sections, using concrete guide walls at the top of the trench or ground level to guide the buckets and prevent the top earth from collapsing or unraveling.

When the trench has been dug to subgrade, reinforcing steel is prefabricated into rigid cages and positioned in the trench prior to concreting. The concrete is tremied through steel pipes into the trench to create a reinforced concrete wall. The bentonite is displaced by the concrete and pumped into tanks for reuse. It is possible to have excellent concrete in the walls. The fact that the reinforcing is installed in slurry does not affect its performance and reasonable bond stresses can be obtained.

Special treatment is provided for the panel joints using a variety of methods, such as steel pipes which are withdrawn prior to the setting up of the tremie concrete, steel beams to form the ends of the panels, or other techniques. These joints are very important to maintain the integrity of the concrete wall at the wall connections. It is difficult, however, to have completely watertight joints, and some leakage can be expected.

Slurry walls are not economically competitive with steel sheeting or soldier beams with horizontal wood sheeting in firm ground or ground that is easily dewatered and excavated. Slurry walls are excellent, however, in certain installations such as the World Trade Center site, where walls had to be installed in a waterfront area which had been filled with riprap, old timber cribs, and other obstructions overlying a soft Hudson River silt, with open water channels directly connected to the Hudson River. The reinforced slurry wall was installed through this difficult ground and was seated about 1 m (3 ft) to 3 m (10 ft) deep into the mica schist bedrock. It would have been impossible to drive soldier beams or steel sheeting in this area due to the obstructions. The slurry wall was an excellent solution (see Figs. 8.12 and 8.13).

Slurry walls have also been used with great success for deep cuts in soft Chicago clay. Here the slurry wall is economical to install, using clamshell buckets to excavate the soft clay. The completed wall is heavily reinforced, very rigid, and will not move nearly as much as flexible steel sheeting when the cut is excavated, although some movement will occur in the unloading of the clay, or if ground is lost in caisson installation.

The slurry walls are excellent in areas of the world where steel sheeting or soldier beams are expensive or unavailable. The basic materials used are concrete and steel reinforcing, and for that reason slurry walls are more widely used in Europe than in the United States.

Simple machines consisting of a small tripod and winch to operate the cable buckets do the digging. This type of equipment has performed excellent work, including the digging of the World Trade Center slurry wall, although the present trend is to use large cranes with leads to lift the Kelley bars fastened to the clamshell bucket. The Kelley bar guides the bucket better than free-hanging cables and gives a downward force to facilitate digging. The clamshell buckets are specifically designed to work in the bentonite slurry using either hydraulic or cable operation. The buckets have special teeth for various types of ground, are as wide as the width of the trench to be dug, and may vary from 2 m to 4.6 m (7 ft to 15 ft) in length.

If hardpan, dense ground, boulders or rock must be penetrated, special rigs must be used. One is a reverse circulation drilling rig with a chopping bit to break up the obstructions. There are ports in the bit through which slurry and rock cuttings are sucked up by pumps from the trench, facilitating the drilling. These cuttings are screened out at ground level and the slurry is returned to the trench. It is possible to use standard churn drills to break up hard material and remove the cuttings with clamshell buckets.

A new technique has recently been developed in France using precast special

Fig. 8.12 World Trade Center—general view of foundation (Courtesy: World Trade Center)

reinforced concrete walls which are installed in the slurry trench. A mixture of bentonite, cement, and additives is used in the slurry trench. This mixture is fluid during the excavation and placing period but sets up later to a hard medium holding the precast panels in place. The panels have a special tongue and groove joint to make a continuous wall. Anchors can be placed in the precast wall similar to those used in standard slurry walls.

The slurry wall can be braced or tied back similarly to other methods, and special inserts can be installed in the wall to attach permanent steel to the concrete. These inserts are fastened to the reinforcing rods. Tolerances have to be large as it is difficult to set the cages accurately, and the inserts must be well fastened to prevent movement.

Special Methods of Sheeting. In addition to the methods described previously there are other techniques of sheeting an excavation, including tangent auger caissons. In this process auger caissons are installed tangent to each other to form a wall. The process will work in stiff clay or dry cohesive ground. It is not watertight as a small deviation from the vertical of adjacent caissons will open gaps in the wall. In stiff clay these gaps are easily plugged and no damage will be done, but in wet granular ground this type of construction can have serious consequences and should be avoided. It is interesting to note that the tangent auger caisson method preceded

Fig. 8.13 World Trade Center—slurry wall with rock tie-backs (Courtesy: E. E. White)

the slurry wall, which was developed due to the difficulties in wet granular ground. The tangent auger caisson can be reinforced and form an excellent structural wall. It has been used in hard clay with success.

A specialized auger caisson wall has been used in Houston, Texas. An auger hole was dug in the ground. It was enlarged with a specialized broaching tool to form an extension to the auger hole which then held the permanent wall to the concreted auger hole. This method is applicable in firm, cohesive material.

Bracing of Walls.   Bracing is basically the same problem, with steel sheeted walls, soldier beams and horizontal wood sheeting, slurry walls, and other types of walls, and it is crucial to the success of the work. In most cases when trouble arises it is due to inadequacies in the bracing of the walls and in the sequence of construction.

The horizontal pressure diagram which is the basis for the design of the bracing system is very important. It is usual now to use trapezoidal or rectangular pressure distribution rather than triangular pressure in well drained ground. This distribution has been substantiated many times by field measurements and is considered the best practice in soil mechanics.

The trapezoidal or rectangular pressure diagram gives a different distribution with more load at the top of the cut than the triangular diagram, although the total load does not differ greatly. It makes the top brace the most critical. The top brace is the longest, is subject to damage from excavation operations, and the method of installation causes it to take heavy loads. For example, in a typical cut the top brace must support virtually two-thirds of the excavation height until the bottom brace is installed. This includes a distance of several feet below the lower waler for working room to install the brace. It is good practice to design for this interim construction step as it may cause a greater loading condition in the bracing system than the final excavation pressures.

A comparison is given in Fig. 8.14 of the earth pressures obtained in predominantly granular material in Washington, D.C., and that in soft clay with an unconfined compression stress of 38 kN/m² (800 psf) to 67 kN/m² (1 400 psf) in Chicago, Illinois. In the clay a three-tier system is required against a two-tier system in the sand, since the load in the clay soil is over 40% greater than that in sand.

The bracing members are the most critical and have to resist the earth pressures without any benefit from arching. It is necessary with rolled steel braces to use cross lacing, intermediate pin piles, and ties to reduce the length factor of the braces and prevent a buckling failure in compression. These secondary members must be installed in the proper sequence. For example, pin piles must be driven in a clay cut to reduce the unsupported length of the top brace when it is first installed, rather than waiting until the lower brace is placed to connect secondary members from the first to second brace. This is necessary because the load may cripple the top brace before the secondary members can be installed.

As deep cuts develop heavy loads, details must be carefully considered structurally and from a soil mechanics viewpoint. Proper stiffeners and connections are essential. The bottom reaction of the braces has to be against an adequate foundation, either against the permanent concrete slab of the building or against a temporary concrete pad in the ground. It is best not to brace to clay or poor material as settlement will occur, damaging the system. Walers are designed on the basis of uniform distribution of earth pressure using a steel stress of 170 MN/m² (25 000 psi), and designing for simple spans even though the walers are continuous.

Continuity is important as a safety measure in case of damage to the bracing system caused by equipment digging around the braces, blasting, and other factors. It is also possible to have greater loads than computed because of leaking water mains and sewers, unfortunately a common condition in urban areas.

When inclined braces react against the walers, bracket connections have to be properly designed to prevent the waler from rolling over or overturning and causing a failure of the system.

In recent years steel pipe bracing has been used in place of rolled steel beams to cut down on the expense of installing lacing and intermediate piles which also interfere with the excavating operation (see Fig. 8.15). The pipe bracing has the steel distributed most efficiently for column action and huge unsupported spans can be obtained. For example, a 450-mm (18-in.) diam 9.5-mm (0.375-in.) wall pipe with 15-m (50-ft) unsupported span can carry a load of 1360 kN (305 kips), and a 600-mm (24-in.) diam 9.5-mm (0.3L75-in.) wall pipe 25 m (80 ft) long can support a load of 1491 kN (335 kips). The connections for pipes with large diameters are expensive but have been worked out successfully.

When diagonals are used for bracing in the corners of an excavation it is important to design for the large axial loads that the diagonals transmit to the walers, increasing the size of the walers needed for safe design. Diagonals should not be used for corners that are over a 90° angle as there is likely to be an inward movement of the entire corner. It is difficult to analyze and design for these axial loads. In the Sears Building in Chicago the axial load was transmitted into heavy plates which were installed in the slurry wall. Where the diagonals framed into a temporary wall of soldier beams and horizontal lagging, the load was not expected to be dissipated because the soft clay would not be able to resist the huge forces involved. In a good granular material the steel sheeting or soldier beams will be able to absorb part of the axial load by friction against the ground, and it is not necessary to carry the axial load from one side to the other.

The excavation technique in deep excavations—particularly in soft clay—is of

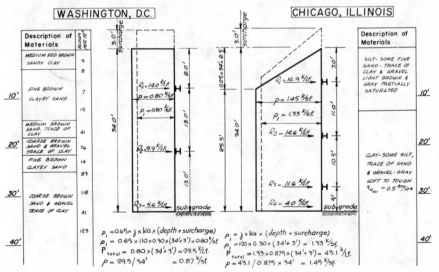

Fig. 8.14 Comparison of sand and clay earth pressures

vital importance, and the best designed system can be destroyed by improper procedure. The design of the berms and sequence of excavation must be carefully planned and supervised; as excavators are notorious in their desire to take out material and ignore plans. Modern machines work so fast that they can be destructive to the over-all excavation plan if the operators are not supervised well.

In sand it is usual to provide a level area of 1 m (3 ft) to 1.5 m (5 ft) against the sheeting and a slope of 1 vertical to 1-1/2 horizontal. The waler is located 2 m (7 ft) to 2.7 m (9 ft) below the street level. This cantilever must not be too large or settlement will occur at the very start of the work: a lateral movement of 25 mm (1 in.) will result in a 50-mm (2-in.) settlement of the surface outside the sheeting. To check on the behavior of the sheeting and bracing, it is important to have careful periodic surveys of the area to determine movements horizontally or vertically in the sheeting, streets, and adjacent utilities and buildings. Inclinometers are excellent to determine deep-seated movements behind the sheeting, particularly when excavating in soft clay. This survey has to be made on a daily basis sometimes, and is the best way to determine the performance of the system. A strain gage survey of bracing is advisable to determine the stresses in the bracing. This also gives excellent information on member stresses in extreme changes in temperature.

In soft clay as found in Chicago or Boston, deep excavations are very difficult and should only be undertaken by experienced engineers and contractors who have had previous experience in this type of work and are ready to work quickly and carefully. While it is not possible to eliminate all movements in this type of ground, good practice will keep movements to a minimum.

Sloped berms in soft clay are a source of difficulty as the clay does not have the stability to stand on even moderate slopes of 2-1/2 to 1. In the interval before the top braces can be installed the berms will slowly creep into the cut. For example, at

Fig. 8.15 Steel pipe bracing of slurry walls for deep excavation in clay *(Courtesy: E. E. White)*

the Civic Center Building in Chicago it took about 20 to 25 days to excavate the earth and install the bottom slab and the top inclined braces (see Fig. 8.16). In this interval the berms moved into the cut 50 mm (2 in.) to 75 mm (3 in.), causing the sheeting to move in and the streets to settle. It was anticipated that there would be movements of this type and the soldier beam system was given a tolerance of 100 mm (4 in.) to 130 mm (5 in.) behind the building line to accommodate this movement. The actual movement used up this tolerance in certain areas.

Time is of the essence when working in soft clay and the operation should be planned to keep the foundation construction time to a minimum. The caissons should be installed from the upper levels to reduce the working time in the bottom of the cut. Driven piles should be avoided, as they must be driven from the top of the excavation and the final excavation among the piles is expensive and slow due to the many piles protruding into the slab. It is difficult to work mechanical excavating equipment around the protruding piles. The piles present a special problem in this case because the length of pile above subgrade will be greater than normal due to the difficulty in estimating the necessary pile length prior to driving.

Movement in soft clay will occur with all types of sheeting, including slurry walls. The critical period is the installation of the first inclined brace. This can be eliminated to some degree by using horizontal diagonal pipe braces at the corners. Cross lot bracing is an excellent method of eliminating movement as the sloped berms are eliminated, but this system makes the excavation and concrete work expensive and slow. Unless the excavated area is small, it is not usually feasible.

4 Tie-Backs or Ground Anchors

Since the mid-1960s an important development in the construction of large, deep foundations has been the tie-back or ground-anchor system. This eliminates the use

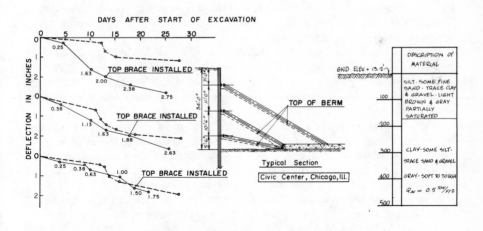

Fig. 8.16 Movement of sheeting during excavation and installation of concrete mat

of braces which have in the past interfered with excavation, concrete, and other operations of foundation construction. It is no wonder that these systems which provide unobstructed excavation areas have become so important.

Due to the complexity of earth and rock, tie-back systems are hard to standardize. There is a great variety of methods adaptable to the special ground conditions where they are used, and a system excellent in one area will not be practical in another. There is a demand from builders for tie-backs, and it requires an excellent technical organization to realize the limitations of the tie-backs and not use them improperly. A large failure of a tie-back system in a city with crowded streets, adjacent buildings, and utility lines can be a disaster.

Tie-backs have been used successfully in firm ground, hardpan, glacial till, and rock. They should not be used in soft clay or unconsolidated granular material, or low values should be assigned to anchors in material of this type, making the system uneconomic. One problem with tie-backs is that they extend beyond property lines, making it necessary to obtain authority for the encroachment. In deep cuts facing narrow streets it is often necessary to install the ties under private property on the other side of the street. Difficulty in obtaining the necessary permission often prevents the use of this method.

Rock Tie-Backs. Rock tie-backs were the first ties to be developed. They are used in excavation where there is a mixed face of earth overlying rock, or where rock is at or near subgrade. Rock is an excellent medium to anchor into and even poor shales give good values to tie-back anchors, where a working load of 890 kN (200 kips) is easily obtained. In this process a 100-mm (4-in.) to 150-mm (6-in.) pipe is advanced through the earth overburden on a 45° angle until rock is reached, using the conventional rock drilling crawler percussion equipment. A 90-mm (3-1/2-in.) hole is drilled into the rock about 4.6 m (15 ft) in length, and either high-strength bars of 999 MPa (145 000 psi) ultimate strength or, for greater design loads, a number of seven-wire strands 13 mm (1/2 in.) in diam of 1790 MPa (260 000 psi) ultimate strength are used. The ties are grouted into the rock and each is tested to a stress 25% higher than the working stress of the wire, which is usually about 60% of ultimate strength. The test is an excellent way to assure that proper workmanship has been performed in the tie installation.

Very heavy loads can be used for these rock ties. At the World Trade Center rock ties with a working load of 3115 kN (700 kips) were used. They were installed in a 150-mm (6-in.) pipe through overburden with a 140-mm (5-1/2-in.) hole, 10.7 m (35 ft) long into rock. These ties held back a 21-m (70-ft) deep slurry wall in a very large excavation (see Fig. 8.17).

When excavation in the rock is below the bottom of the sheeting system it is important that the rock face be carefully maintained to prevent a failure of the rock. The downward force of the 45° ties is considerable, being equivalent to the horizontal earth pressure of the overburden. This great force can shear off the rock face, causing failure of the sheeting system. Ties can be installed to hold back the rock, or inclined braces can be used to take the vertical force of the soldier beams when the rock excavating depth from subgrade to the bottom of the sheeting is not very great. Another method was used in Pittsburgh because the shale rock would not support the tie-back downward force. There it was necessary to underpin the steel sheeting system with 1-m × 1.2-m (3-ft × 4-ft) concrete piers excavated in rock to the subgrade of the excavation.

If soldier beams can be drilled below subgrade in soft shale rocks, it is well worth the expense to do this to eliminate the difficulty caused by maintaining rock faces. Rock is an unreliable material and a cleavage plane or fault in the wrong place can cause a sudden failure of the system.

Earth Ties. An interesting development has been the earth tie-back, which is far more difficult to anchor than rock. The anchorage loads are lower, but it is not possible at the present time to anchor economically into soft clay, fill, or unconsolidated sands. Special situations such as boulders in the ground and water problems can also make the installation of earth ties very difficult. There are now a great many different earth anchorages which have important applications for tying back sheeting systems. They are based on different types of equipment adapted or developed for these tie-backs. Earth tie-backs have the advantage that flatter angles can be used, thus reducing the downward forces of the system. It is usual to use 30° from the horizontal, and at times a tie angle as low as 15° from the horizontal is used.

Large-Diameter Tie-Backs. Large-diameter tie-backs have been used success-fully on many large installations in Los Angeles and San Francisco because of the favorable ground conditions there. An example is the Atlantic Richfield Building in Los Angeles where the foundation was 184 m wide × 102 m long with a maximum depth of 26 m (600 ft × 335 ft × 84 ft). The soldier beams to support the cut were installed in augered holes. Concrete was installed in the bottom of the hole to take the downward thrust and lean concrete was placed in the balance of the auger hole. The tie holes were 300-mm (12-in.) diam auger holes up to 20 m (65 ft) deep at an angle of 30° to the horizontal with a 910-mm (36-in.) bell at the bottom of the anchor. The equipment to install these anchors was caterpillar-mounted augers similar to standard drilling machines using continuous flight augers, and belling buckets to form the enlarged bell at the bottom of the anchor (see Fig. 8.18).

In caving formations, continuous hollow-stem augers are excellent to excavate the hole and support it simultaneously. When the required depth is reached the tendons

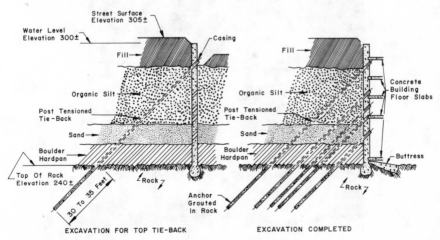

Fig. 8.17 Rock ties (World Trade Center): diagram of construction sequence for perimeter wall tie-backs

or rods can be inserted into the hollow stem and the system grouted in place while the auger is withdrawn without rotation.

It is usual for these installations to use one Stress Steel or McAlloy rod per tie. The maximum length of the ties is 20.4 m (67 ft) with a diameter up to 35 mm (1-3/8 in.) and a working capacity of 420 kN (94 kips). All the ties are tested to an overload of 50% and certain ties are tested to 100% overload.

The ties are designed to resist trapezoidal or rectangular lateral earth pressures. They are anchored back to beyond a 35° slip plane from vertical, starting at or below subgrade. Anchors must be at least 11 m (35 ft) beyond this slip plane. No concrete should extend above this line, to assure that the reaction is below the slip plane (see Fig. 8.19).

In recent work there has been a trend to eliminate the tie-back bells, which are difficult to form or maintain until the tendon is concreted in place. To take the place of the bell, longer ties are installed, or the concrete is placed under pressure and depends on the friction of the concrete and ground. On a garage extension to the Atlantic Richfield Building cables were used for higher loads. The ties were used for a working load of 556 kN (125 kips) using a bond of 3.3 kPa (70 psf). The ties extended 15 m (50 ft) behind the slip plane.

Small-Diameter Tie-Backs. For small-diameter tie-backs in caving ground, percussion air tracks (as for rock drilling) or soil exploration rotary drills are used to

Fig. 8.18 Earth tie-backs—90 ft deep cut (Atlantic Richfield Building, Los Angeles, California) *(Courtesy: E. E. White)*

install 100-mm (4-in.) diam casing. Stress Steel rods or three or four 13-mm (1/2-in.) seven-wire strands are placed and grouted into the casing. The casing is extracted during the grouting operation. The grout is carried to the slip plane and the tie is tested to 25% above its working load. The working load is 270 kN (60 kips) to 450 kN (100 kips) depending on the ground conditions. In the United States, as a result of high labor costs and low material costs, the casing is usually left in the ground. In the Bauer or lost point method, developed in Germany, a percussion drill hammers a 75-mm (3-in.) OD casing into the ground. At the end of the casing is a loose fitting cast steel point designed to have threaded into it a high-tensile steel Stress Steel or McAlloy rod. After the system is grouted through the steel rod, hydraulic jacks remove the steel casing. The rods are tested to a 25% overload and working loads of 180 kN (40 kips) to 360 kN (80 kips) are used, depending on the ground conditions.

In Sweden a system has been developed where a percussion crawler rig drives a special hollow bit drill rod and couplings to the required depth. The system is grouted in place through the drill rod and bit to form an anchorage at the tip. This is an easy method to install but the light loads used, 220 kN (50 kips) to 270 kN (60 kips) and the high cost of the steel left in place makes the system expensive even in a high labor cost area such as the United States.

Another type of tie-back has been developed in France using the tube-à-Manchette principle to grout at high pressure. It has been found that the carrying capacity of the tie can be increased in soil by high grouting pressures. If the tie does

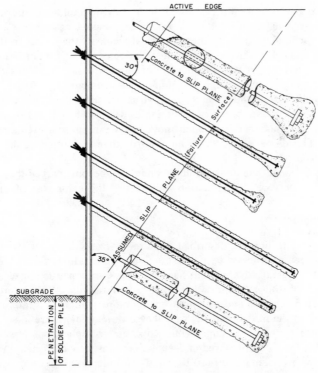

Fig. 8.19 Belled and straight shaft earth tie-backs

not test properly the system can be regrouted until the proper capacity is obtained. This system, however, is more elaborate and sophisticated than the systems described above and it is questionable whether it will be in general use in the United States with its high labor and craft organization of work.

Space will not permit the discussion of other successful earth tie-back systems. As earth tie-backs are in an empirical stage and in their infancy, there will be new developments to improve their reliability and capacity. More experimental work will be necessary to arrive at proper standards for this type of work.

5   Mined Excavation

Mined excavation refers to the use of permanent floors of a structure to brace the sheeting or support system of the excavation sides. These floors of concrete are poured in the ground and excavation is made under them, hence the term "mined excavation." The floors are supported on piles or permanent columns during the work. This system has applications in soft clay areas such as Chicago where cross-lot bracing is desirable. It has the disadvantage that the excavation must be done under the floors and in a difficult manner, making it more expensive. An economic study must be made to determine how extra cost of excavation and other expenses compare with the cost of the steel bracing.

6   Underpinning

Large excavations often are adjacent to and below buildings, subways, or other structures. Systems of sheeting, bank protection, bracing, or tie-backs are usually no substitute for underpinning in these cases. Movements that occur in the deflection of sheeting and soldier beams prior to installation of the first set of braces will cause damage to adjacent structures if they are not underpinned. It is difficult to install a bracing system that will completely eliminate movement.

Slurry walls will provide a more rigid structure than sheeting, or soldier beams and horizontal bracing, but even this method will also be subject to movements in soft clay or granular material. Such movements can cause great damage to other buildings. This damage may be far more costly than underpinning the buildings by conventional means.

In many instances the underpinning system can become part of the over-all bank protection to serve a dual function and reduce the extra cost of underpinning.

7   Conclusion

Many of the techniques described, such as tie-backs, auger caissons, and slurry walls have been in general use in construction of foundations within the last decade and reflect the great advance that has been made in construction technique.

The field of soil mechanics has also grown rapidly. With improvements in construction machinery and techniques many more changes and improvements can be expected in the next decade as well. These developments are likely to be in the use of bentonite slurry for subaqueous work, better applications of soil mechanics theory to the forces encountered in deep excavations, new construction machines to perform the work more efficiently, and the increased development of earth tie-backs.

8.5 STEEL CONSTRUCTION

There has been intense development associated with the construction of multistory buildings. From a construction time point of view, which is decisive for the choice of the load-carrying system of a building, the steel frame is preferred for multistory buildings. Examples of all-steel structures are the Maison de la Radio, Paris (Figs. 8.20 and 8.21), the Esso Standard France Building, Paris (Fig. 8.22), and the "Steel Builders" Building, Paris (Fig. 8.23).

The design of the structural steelwork for tall buildings is carried out by consulting engineers appointed by the client, or alternatively by the steelwork fabricator's design office staff. (See Volume SB.)

The construction contract documents will state the date for work to start on site and the date for completion. In order to meet these dates it is essential for all parties concerned to plan the program for ordering, detailing, fabrication, and erection of the steelwork. Constant liaison is required between the fabrication shop and the erection site to assure a smooth flow of steelwork, in the correct sequence, from shops to site.

Before commencing any tall building project the steelwork contractor considers the Specifications Conditions of Contract. A detailed examination of these documents will be carried out to assure that he fully understands and can comply with the various clauses.

Paramount to the successful completion of the steelwork erection of tall buildings is the planning that takes place shortly after the contractor receives a contract for the structure. This planning includes scheduling all activities, the preliminary erection scheme, and planning for fabrication. This section will follow the sequence of construction for tall buildings from the initial planning through fabrication and erection.

1 Planning

In the early stages of preparing the fabrication drawings, close coordination is required between the drawing office and the architect to assure that all architectural features are accommodated. The various floor plans are prepared and the main material is listed and ordered from the mills. Occasionally economically designed sections may be infrequently rolled, and in order to meet the building program it is necessary to substitute alternative sections. After fabrication drawings are prepared for each item of steelwork and are submitted to the architect or consulting engineer for approval the fabrication drawings are sent to the steel fabrication shops.

To retrogress, the preparation of the estimated costs for tall buildings, in general, follows the same path of preparation as postcontractual planning and operations of the contractors. Therefore, a complete set of architectural design drawings is important at the time of bidding. These eliminate guesswork as to the structural features of the building and thereby provide the basis for more realistic costs and time scheduling of fabrication and construction.

Upon receiving a contract, the contractor must schedule his operations to maintain an even flow of material orders, drawings, delivery of material for fabrication, fabrication, shipment, and erection. The structure is divided into sections called "shipping divisions," which are representative of the erection sequence to be followed.

The erector plans his erection scheme based on height and area of building, size and weight of shipping pieces, and the configuration of the structure. At this time, structural details will be investigated for possible combinations of pieces—reducing the total pieces to be erected, duplication of fabrication, and feasibility of erection entry. The erector and fabricator must decide which parts of the connection will be shop fabricated, including, when permitted by the owner's representative, a preferred type of connection. Erection procedures affecting the structural stability must be investigated. The addition of temporary members is costly and time consuming. The erector's final plans are dependent in various degrees on the

Fig. 8.20   Maison de la Radio, Paris, France—all steel structure. Architect: H. Bernard *(Courtesy: Compagnie Française d'Entreprises Métalliques; Photo by Mazo)*

Fig. 8.21 Maison de la Radio, Paris, France—finished building *(Courtesy: Compagnie Française d'Entreprises Métalliques; Photo by G. M. Lavalette)*

activities of others. Provision must be made for access to the site.

Prior consideration of access for men and material by the owner's representative can expedite the work and save duplicating costs to the owner created when each contractor must provide his own facility. Sufficient access areas must be available for all contractors who will work simultaneously.

Access to the upper stories of the structure must be made available as the steelwork progresses. Here again, the owner or general contractor should make provision for sufficient elevator service for all.

Provision for accessible areas within the structure should be made for the contractors' equipment. Specifically, hoists should remain at one level for from 1 to 50 floors, including the wire rope leads passing through the floors from hoist to derrick.

The scheduled activities of other contractors may dictate scheduled erection rates and utilization of more or less equipment. When design criteria and working conditions are restrictive relating to individual contractors' activities, the owner's representative should emphasize these restrictions in the bidding documents and be prepared to assist the contractors jointly in scheduling and planning their activities.

Closely related to the erection planning and scheduling are the scheduling and planning of fabrication. Division by division, the steel orders must be prepared and the shipment of the structural steel planned for delivery to the fabricator. Sufficient lead time must be available from start of work to start of erection so that once erection has commenced, a continual flow of fabricated steel will arrive to support a planned erection schedule.

In planning, the fabricator must determine the work load of various plant facilities and direct the material and fabrication to those facilities which can meet the schedule and, at the same time, accurately and economically produce the results. In planning for fabrication, as in erection, the details of the structure must be reviewed. Duplication and simplification of details are considered. The owners or their representatives should be receptive to the contractors' requests for alternate designs of members and details when the characteristics or strength of the structure are not affected.

Thus far, advance planning has been presented relating to fabrication and construction. Each of these will be dealt with independently hereafter, except it should be understood that a close planning and coordinating relationship should exist between fabricator and erector throughout the project.

2 Fabrication

Bills of Material. Advance bills of material using the design drawings are prepared. These advance bills are translated into computer readout. This information is then sent to a central mill ordering office where similar orders are received from various sources. The computerized data then summarize total quantities of different items and a mill rolling quantity is available, including dates of delivery necessary. These orders include multiple lengths and widths where possible. Each piece of mill rolling ordered is given an item number at this time. This item number is also used on the detail drawing bill of material. In addition to item numbers being placed on the steel, each piece shipped from the mill is color coded for identifying the steel specification and stenciled with the mill heat number. Generally, material

Fig. 8.22 Esso Standard France, Paris la Defense—all steel structure. Architect: P. Greber *(Courtesy: Compagnie Française d'Entreprises Métalliques)*

Fig. 8.23 CTICM, Paris la Defense—all steel structure with columns outside the curtain wall. Architect: Binoux and Folliasson *(Courtesy: Compagnie Française d'Entreprises Métalliques; Photo by G. M. Lavalette)*

obtained from fabrication plant stocks is kept to a minimum; therefore, the receiving yard in the fabricating plant contains only materials labeled for a specific assembly in the completed structure.

Cambering of beams where required can be carried out during erection, but it is common practice to order beams already cambered, as this is a service provided by the mills.

Various types of steel have specific advantages, such as the corrosion resistance of ASTM A588. Similarly, various types of steels require specific fabrication processes. For example, ASTM A36 and some grades of ASTM A572 normally do not require preheating prior to flame-cutting, whereas other types require preheating. A shearing machine that shears plates 25 mm (1 in.) thick of ASTM A36 material, will only shear 14.3-mm (9/16-in.) thick ASTM A514 material. Punching machines that normally punch 22.2-mm (7/8-in.) thick ASTM A36 material, will only punch 9.5-mm (3/8-in.) thick A514. Various grades of steel are used where economies can be effected.

Material Handling.   Each fabricating shop has its own characteristics for handling materials. The size of fabricated assemblies is limited in the shop by weight, length, height, and shipping clearances. Fabricated assemblies are transferred through the shop by single or dual overhead cranes. The maximum length of these pieces is limited by column spacing within the shop and sometimes the stiffness of the member. A rule of thumb is that the member is sufficiently stiff to lift when the length divided by the flange width is less than 80. The weight of the piece is limited by single or multiple crane capacity. Plant planning must include lifting hitches for oddly shaped sections where normal slings will not properly support the member. Special hitches are welded or bolted. In addition to overhead cranes, rubber-tired and rail-mounted vehicles are used.

The flow of material from the stockyard is generally through the material preparation bay to the material assembly bay and then to the painting and dispatch bay. The main object of this procedure is to minimize the movement of material from one operation to another.

Rolled steel has allowable geometric tolerances. Provisions in detailing and fabricating the steel make it possible to erect and aline the structure within erection tolerances. These provisions include: (1) For columns, truss members, and bracing, the center line of the member is the straight line connecting the working points at the center of either end of the member; and (2) for beams, the center line is the straight line connecting the points established by the intersection of the center line of web and flange at each end. When the rolling tolerances exceed those required for fabrication, corrections or compensations are made in the shop.

Shearing and Cutting.   The preliminary work of fabricating consists of shearing or flame-cutting individual pieces from multiple length material. Connection and detail material is punched or drilled. Welded construction may require edge preparation, depending on the type of welds. Blast-cleaning and a wash coat primer to protect the steel from rust and provide the proper surface for welding may be required. Material may require bending or curving. Cardboard, wood, or metal templates are laid out and used for drilling. Metal templates are used when frequent duplication is needed.

The first operation in the material preparation bay is to cut to exact length the main material. For beams and columns this is done by cold sawing, but angles are often cropped in shearing machines.

Floor beams are passed through an automatic sawing and drilling production line in which several holes are drilled in the web or flanges in one operation. Holes in angles are often punched on an automatic cropping and punching machine.

Floor girders and columns outside the normal range of rolled universal beams and columns are fabricated by welding three plates together, two flange plates and a web plate. This can be carried out manually or in a special plant where the components are automatically assembled and welded.

Castellated beams are fabricated by cutting through the web of the beam with a profile burning machine to a predetermined profile. When the two halves of the beam are separated they are adjusted by moving one half along until the "teeth" of the castellations coincide and the two halves are tack welded together. Deep penetration welding is used on the top side of the web first, and then the beam is reversed for welding the second run along the other side of the web.

Shop equipment includes saws which are generally employed to cut all rolled shapes, such as beams, channels, and angles. Cold saws utilize a blade traveling at a slow rate that actually cuts away the material. A friction saw is a high-speed saw in which the teeth actually melt away the material. Shears cut the material and are limited to use on plates and angles.

When plates are ordered in multiple widths, the cutting of the narrower widths is done by flame-cutting with a plate stripper. A traveling gantry carries several gas-cutting torches set at desired widths. The plates may be cut to a required camber with this equipment. Shape cutters also make use of multiple cutting torches and cut circles or other shapes as directed by a template or numerical controls. Portable machines, which consist of a motor-driven carriage mounted on a small track, can be placed wherever necessary to cut a straight line. The torch can be tilted to provide a beveled edge. Manual gas-cutting is done for miscellaneous trimming and cutting beam copes.

The beam-to-column connections play an important part in the over-all stability of any steel frame. They should be simple and have as much work as possible performed in the shops with minimum work on site. These connections are generally made with bolts for economic reasons. On rigid frames the beam-to-column connections are made using high-strength friction grip bolts, or alternatively are welded.

Punching and Drilling.   Punching is usually the quickest means of making holes. Multiple controlled punching is provided for plates, beams, and large angles. Connection angles are punched on single hole punches.

Drilling is achieved by manually operated or automatic numerically controlled single or multiple drills. Manually operated drills usually are set up with a 75-mm (3-in.) spacing. Numerically controlled drilling employs the use of a perforated tape to direct the drill head, working on its own traverse horizontally and vertically. Also the tape directs the piece being drilled to move a specific amount forward when the drill head has horizontally traversed its limit of travel. This operation is automatically repeated until the total length of the piece being drilled is finished. Multiple drills opposing each other or one-sided can be directed to drill individually or collectively on the numerically controlled drill.

Circular or rectangular holes can be flame cut in the webs of beams to facilitate services, pipes, and ducting. Where holes are cut into webs of members in high-yield steel it is necessary to grind off about 3.2 mm (1/8 in.) of material from the flame-cut edge.

Welding. Many varieties of welding processes are available, as well as many means of motion control. Stationary automatic welding machines utilizing single or multiple welding heads are positioned over the piece to be welded, which is moved past the welding position. Preheat torches can also be easily adapted to this method. The submerged arc process is used in this instance. Fillet welds as large as 13 mm (1/2 in.) are deposited in one pass. Welding head manipulators of various types are rail-mounted on column and boom supports. The welding head can be manipulated to provide flat or horizontal welds. The motion is controlled by the movement of the column and boom past the work, which is stationary in this case. The submerged arc, gas-shielded, or self-shielded welding process is adaptable to this method. The electroslag welding process is used for full penetration welds. This process involves positioning the joint to be welded in a vertical position and placing weld metal between the two surfaces to be welded. Removable copper shoes are placed as dams across the open sides of the space to be welded. Welding is started at the bottom of the joint and moves vertically to the top as the weld metal is deposited. On large welds, the copper shoes may be made to move vertically as the welding proceeds. Semiautomatic hand welding is done on detail material where automatic welding is limited. The submerged arc, gas-shielded, or self-shielded processes are adaptable to semiautomatic welding. Manual welding is used for tacking, repairing welds, and other miscellaneous welds.

Bending. Methods of bending shapes and plates are press bending, press braking, rolling, and heat curving. Press bending, consisting of press and die, is used for curving rolled shapes and limited-width heavy plates. Brake bending, consisting of press and die, produces a bend of small radius such as is found in detail connection material; also, wider plates are handled in brake bending. The plate is moved over the die, receiving numerous strokes of the press until the desired shape is obtained. Bending by rolling is primarily done on plates. Bending by rolling can be performed on plates up to 150 mm (6 in.) thick.

The type and thickness of the steel dictate the amount of bending and degree of heating that may be done when bending plates and shapes. Heat curving or cambering is a process used for providing large radii in beams and also camber. Heat is applied to that side or edge of the steel which is to be shortened. Generally, the material is heated to approximately 893 K (1 150°F). As the steel is heated, it expands, creating compression which effects an upsetting of the metal in the heated zone. When cool, the expanded metal contracts but the final length of the heated side is shorter than it was originally.

In recent years, steel girders have been curved using heat. Heat curving provides camber or curvature, whereas otherwise the material would have to be cut in a curved pattern. The latter method creates considerable scrap and complicates fitting and welding operations.

Machining. It is considered best practice to machine the ends of columns to obtain smooth square ends so that close contact between upper and lower lengths can be achieved. Finishing of bearing surfaces is accomplished on various types of equipment such as planers, lathes, boring mills, and milling machines. The type of equipment utilized is generally dependent upon degree of finish, type of surface, size and weight of member to be finished, and availability of equipment on the fabrication line.

The foregoing includes only a limited variety of the fabricating shop equipment but deserves some comment as to usage. Other fabricating equipment includes annealing and heating furnaces, blast cleaning, boring machines, forging equipment, a variety of machine shop equipment, reaming, riveting, bolting, and stud welding equipment.

Assembly.   The assembly work of fabrication includes collecting all the steel with preliminary fabrication completed and connecting it together in an assembly piece. At this time, connection material is attached, splice material is placed, and holes are drilled or reamed full size. Connections for beams to columns are a significant factor in the total cost of a structure. Apart from mentioning current shop fabrication of connections, welded or bolted, there will be no special discussion in detail of the practice other than some economic consideration. Connections should provide the strength requirements for soundness of the structure, provide a ready connection for the erector, allow for adjustment, and be as simple as possible to fabricate and erect. Preferably, the shop should provide the major work at a splice. Field assembly should be relatively simple.

To require reamed assembled joints is costly. Shop floor space is limited and a material flow rate must be maintained. When reamed assemblies are required, the steelwork is moved to an assembly area. This is an extra move for two or more pieces which probably were initially fabricated in two unrelated shops and now have to be specially handled to bring them together. Before requiring the use of reamed assembled joints, consideration should be given to the use of holes reamed to a metal template. Bolted connections should have all the same diameter bolts, not only for a specific joint, but for the complete structure. Only when a sufficient quantity of smaller bolts appreciably affecting the cost are usable should they be considered, and then never in material having larger bolts, because then there would be holes of several different sizes in one detail. Design of welding should consider positioning for welding. Preferably, down-head welding should be done. Avoid welding requiring several positions of the steel. Bolted connections may include ordinary bolts and high-strength bolts. Worth mentioning is the use of pinned connections.

When there is sufficient duplication of large assemblies, jigs are used. These jigs may be stationary or rotatable. Where access is necessary to both sides of an assembly for bolting or welding, the jig may be mechanically revolved. The use of jigs further assures accuracy.

Inspection.   Inspection within the fabricating plant is conducted through a medium known as quality control, whereby the plant inspection personnel, independent of production personnel, inspects the work regulating accuracy based on the contract specifications. In building work, the common standard code is that of the American Institute of Steel Construction (1971a). Various methods of inspection are applied to welds. The first consideration is the critical nature of the joint and the severity of inspection necessary. Equipment is available in the fabrication shops for carrying out various inspections, such as ultrasonic testing of plates and welds, radiographic weld tests, and magnetic crack detection tests. Adequate inspection of a weld may sometimes be made by magnetic particle, dye penetrant, or visual inspection. Prior to inspecting welds, criteria should be agreed upon relating to acceptable standards. Otherwise, results may be misinterpreted causing unnecessary delay.

Painting. Cleaning and painting prior to shipment are generally done in a separate building. The methods of cleaning are by blast, flame, power tool, hand tool, and solvent. Normally, cleaning is done to remove loose mill scale, dirt, grease, and other foreign material from the steel prior to painting. Blast cleaning may be manually or automatically applied using shot or grit. Certain automatic facilities can blast clean and apply a rust inhibitor. Painting methods are by brush, spray, or roller. Painting is done in conformance with the recommendations of the Steel Structures Painting Council (1954, 1964).

Shipping. Before completing fabrication and painting, advance clearance must be arranged with the shippers and cars ordered to meet the schedule. All material must be secured for shipment and inspected for tie-down and clearance dimensions.

Shipping bills are made up in advance. These bills list the shipping pieces to be loaded on the same car. Following shipment, a shipping statement is mailed to the erector notifying him of the carrier, car number, shipping pieces in the car, and the weight of each. Miscellaneous material, such as bolts not fabricated by the steel fabricator and supplied by another vendor, is shipped direct to the erector by the vendor.

Exterior Facades. Fabrication of exterior structural facades differs to some extent from normal fabrication. Mill orders should specify that the material is for architectural use, thereby giving the mill an opportunity to furnish satisfactory surface quality. The tolerances for camber and sweep are about one-half those of normal tolerances. Handling operations must be kept to a minimum and the exterior architectural surface protected from abrasions. Stud bolting is frequently used for connecting. The diameter of the studs should not be more than 1.6 mm (1/16 in.) greater than the thickness of the plate they are attached to, in order to avoid weld distortion on the architectural face. Exterior butt welds are often left recessed. The recess is then filled with plastic steel. After painting, this process leaves an unnoticeable joint.

3 Erection

Erection Techniques. It is essential that close liaison is maintained between the fabricating shop and the erection personnel to assure that steelwork is delivered to the site in the correct sequence in accordance with the erection program. Storage of steelwork on site can pose problems, and where the storage area is limited it is necessary to deliver only those sections of steelwork required for the work in hand.

Steelwork can be erected relatively quickly, and for over-all economy it is necessary for other contractors to be able to follow up with their work of fixing floors and walls as soon as the steelwork has been plumbed and levelled. This requires close cooperation between the main contractor and all other parties concerned.

The erector plans his method of construction depending upon the characteristics of the tall buildings. The most common method is tier by tier. Each tier represents a column height of usually two or three building floors. Another method used may be erecting the structure in vertical segments. This method is used on buildings which can be reached from the ground to the roof by ground-based lifting equipment. Frequently, a combination of the tier by tier and vertical segment methods is employed. This applies when the tower tiers are erected by ground-based mobile equipment within the structure to about street level, followed by derricks supported on the steel erecting tier by tier. Structures consisting of a core erected prior to the surrounding steelwork sometimes have the surrounding steelwork erected from the top down. In this case, the peripheral floor areas are generally suspended from structural cantilever members over the top of the core. Erecting rigs atop the cantilever hoist the suspended steelwork for attachment to the cantilever members.

Push-up construction has been used on tall buildings of lesser height. This method involves erecting the top floor first at about ground level. Jacks push the completed structural frame upward and additional steel is placed underneath and attached to that previously jacked. Other materials are added into the structure at several locations above the ground; however, relatively close to the ground. In this manner, no material is hoisted more than several stories and, with proper scheduling and expediting completion of various crafts' work, a floor is essentially complete after it is about six or eight stories from the ground. Considerable erection equipment, including temporary horizontal stabilizers, is required for this type of construction.

Hoisting Equipment—Selection Criteria. Numerous types of hoisting equipment are utilized in the erection of tall steel buildings. Before describing them, it is worth mentioning the operational considerations to be made before choosing a specific type of equipment for a structure. The hoisting equipment must be able to pick the maximum fabricated assembly piece and also a reasonable truckload of steel from the delivery point at ground level. Where pieces of extraordinarily heavy weight (few in number) are involved, usually at very low levels in the structure, additional or special splices may be introduced to limit their weight. However, the prime erecting rig must be able to hoist the equivalent weight of a truckload of steel throughout the height of the building as it proceeds upward. Once the steel is hoisted to floor level, the erecting rig must reach out a reasonable radial distance and erect individual pieces. The rated capacity based on the reach necessary for "steel loads" and reach capacity for erecting individual pieces will determine the size and number of erecting rigs necessary on a given structure. Structural offsets in the building plan will also affect the number of rigs.

The method of erection is mainly governed by the size of the site, the height of the building, the weight of pieces, and number of crane lifts. These factors dictate the type of crane to be used.

Mobile Crane. Mobile cranes are often used for erecting the heavy steel members at the lowest level of the building. Guy derricks are sometimes used as they have the advantage of the mast and jib being so arranged that one can be used to lift the other as the work proceeds. Tower cranes are most commonly used for erection of tall buildings in the United Kingdom. Their main advantage is that they can operate above the top level of the structure and are able to cover a complete circle. The tower crane is equipped with a telescoping cage at the top to facilitate erecting further sections of mast itself.

Special attachments are applied to mobile cranes that increase the height to which loads may be picked or increase load capacities, or both. Tower attachments up to and over 61 m (200 ft) with a luffing boom are especially fitted for use on structures within their scope of reach and capacity. Other attachments may increase normal boom length with added load capacity, such as special masts with portable counterweights, or special boom supports placing the boom further from the crane, thus providing greater counterweight.

Derricks. The guy derrick, probably the most common type of erecting rig now utilized, consists of a vertical mast which rotates, a luffing boom, wire rope guys stabilizing the mast, and load falls. The power is supplied by a base-mounted hoisting engine. For building work, this type of derrick has capacities ranging from approximately 15 000 kg (16 tons) to 82 000 kg (90 tons) with boom lengths from 18 m to 38 m (60 ft to 125 ft). Guy derricks provide a relatively easy adaptability to building structures, are quickly erected and dismantled, and easily "jumped" vertically—tier by tier, as the building is erected. The structural members in the floor of the building must be investigated to provide support for the dead load, live load, and hoist leads of the derrick. The structure must be analyzed for the vertical and horizontal components of guy stresses. Caution must be observed in analyzing composite beams regarding the horizontal distribution of guy stresses.

Stiffleg derricks consist of a mast and luffing boom which rotate approximately 290°, two diagonal stifflegs capable of resisting tension and compression which act as guys, and stiff horizontal sills connecting the lower end of the stiffleg to the mast base. A base-mounted hoisting engine supplies the power. The stiffleg derrick departs all its dead weight and live-load weight, except wind, vertically to the building structure.

Advantages of the stiffleg derrick not inherent in the guy derrick are: (1) An unrestricted swing within the 290°, whereas the guy derrick has to clear the guys with the boom end; (2) by mounting it on a tower, the derrick operates above the steelwork at all times; and (3) the derrick may be located anywhere within the structure or mounted on the side of the structure and operate as a "creeper."

Disadvantages of the stiffleg derrick are: (1) The limited swing of 290°; (2) additional fabrication of a base mounting for the derrick to adapt it to the building; (3) erection and removal time; and (4) the use of special handling rigging to fill in the building structure under the derrick which the derrick cannot reach. The stiffleg derrick mounting platform is supported either on the building beams near the columns or pinned to special plates welded to the columns. Uplift as well as gravity loads must be provided for. These derricks may either carry the hoisting engine on the frame as it moves vertically up the building or leave the hoist at a lower floor area.

Tower derricks consist of a vertical tower mounted within the structure or adjacent to the structure, and a horizontal swinging boom with load-carrying trolley and counterweight jib usually supporting the hoisting mechanism. Another type of tower derrick may consist of a similar tower supporting a luffing boom which swings, a self-adjusting counterweight, and hoist support. Tower cranes vary widely in capacity and may be adapted to almost any structure. The tower is supported by the building structure for gravity and uplift loads. Lateral supports within the height of the tower may or may not be required for capacity loads and wind loads. The tower may be telescoped or "jumped" as the structure rises. Tower cranes provide full swing and operate above the erected structure.

Jacks. Jacks utilized for push-up construction are of high capacity, mechanically operating, and synchronized. When planning the use of jacks, the floor space available is important because of the size of the jacks, special support material required, material handling equipment used, and room needed for erecting additional column lengths. Column splices must be located for access and length increments. Critical path scheduling must be accurately planned because each craft is dependent upon others finishing their work within time limits, thus avoiding layoffs of various operations.

Special Erection Aids.   Successful steel erection is dependent on detail planning and execution of the plans. Special erection aids are important features of these plans. Hitches for attachment of the hoisting equipment should be added to heavy sections, such as columns, and large sections that are not readily adaptable to the use of slings. The design of hitches should include the complete handling operation, such as tipping-up a piece as well as hoisting and landing it. Wherever possible, a mechanical release of the hoist load and hitch should be used. An example of such a release is the lanyard method of pulling the column hitch pin loose, thereby eliminating the necessity of a man climbing the column. The analysis of hitches, particularly welded hitches, should consider eventual side loading. Inspection of hitch welds is important.

Erection aids include such devices as special plate or angle clips, and are added in the fabricating shop to the top and bottom of welded columns. These column aids are connected when the column is erected and provide stability for the column until floor framing is added. They should be clear of future welding operations at the column splice. Erection aids may be left in place when they are in areas where they do not interfere with welding, fireproofing, and other operations.

Site Delivery.   Tall buildings are generally located in city areas where little space is available for storage of steel at the site. Ideal steel delivery is direct shipment by carrier to the site. Direct delivery from the fabricating plant requires constant scheduling and communication. Since there is no area for ground storage available or within the reach of the derricks, the steel is hoisted from the carrier on delivery and placed on the top floor. Delivery of maximum weight loads permissible on streets and within derrick capacity save hoisting time and costs. These shipping loads consist of column and beam shipments in prearranged numbered segmental areas of the building. The load of steel is hoisted to the building floor and landed for future sorting and erecting in the area where it belongs. The building floor steel must be investigated to be certain the loads landed for storage will not overstress the members. Frequently, particularly in composite design, special shores or additional supports must be added to the structure to carry the weight of the steel loads.

Generally, fabricated steel for a building is shipped to a yard area several miles from the building. At this yard, the steel for derrick loads may be sorted. Either trucks or straddle carriers may transport the steel from the yard to the building site. Sorted steel for shipment to the site by straddle carrier should be stored on bolsters. The straddle carrier can then pick up a load without outside aid. The importance of efficient and correct yarding and shipping of steel to the site should not be underestimated.

Field Connections.   Field connections are primarily of two general types, fastener and welded. The predominant fastener is the high-strength bolt. These bolts are delivered to the site direct from the manufacturer in containers marked with number of bolts, diameter, length, and floor designation. As the steel is erected, the "connector" will generally aline the holes using the pointed end of his wrench and then place a minimum quantity of bolts to safely connect the member. In the event that difficulty is encountered alining the holes, drift pins will be used. Later, the bolting gang will complete the connection. At this time, the plumbing gang will have placed plumbing guys and adjusted the tier for plumbness. Bolting is done according to the specifications for structural joints using ASTM A325 or A490 high-strength bolts as approved by the Research Council on Riveted and Bolted Structural Joints (AISC, 1971b). The turn-of-the-nut method is widely preferred. Air-driven impact wrenches are used to tighten the bolts. Various wrenches are available depending on the torque required for the type and diameter of bolt. Advance planning is necessary to assure that wrench clearance is available at all joints. Hand wrench tightening of bolts is inefficient and costly.

Field connections may be accomplished in a way similar to fabrication shop practices. Positioning of members is not possible; however, advance planning can in some instances eliminate overhead welds or other conditions by revising designs and details. The installation of equipment is a major feature in efficient field welding operations. Where public power is available, a main switch rack with circuit breakers and distribution terminals must be installed. Distribution circuits clear of other operations must be properly installed to portable switch racks which, in turn, distribute the power to the individual welding machines. In the event no public power is available, the power can be generated at the site.

Erection Planning and Equipment. Advance planning must determine the number of welding machines necessary to maintain the schedule of the erecting derricks. Total power must be calculated. Usually, 440-V service is used. Local codes must be reviewed regarding the type of electrical service installation. Certain steels require preheating for welding. This may be accomplished using gas heating, which requires a gas source and distribution, or electrical heating. Protection from wind exposure is required for field welding. Gas metal arc welding using core gas requires a gas distribution system for the CO_2 shielding.

Welding creates shrinkage at each joint. When the structure is plumbed, an allowance for this shrinkage must be made. Generally, the structure is plumbed starting at the center bay and working outward. Derrick locations must be considered first because these areas must be welded before the derricks can be "jumped" and operated. As welding commences on a structure, the amount of shrinkage should be observed. Field weld inspection methods are similar to shop inspection. Stud welding is used in the field for placing shear connectors and floor decking.

The geometric and framing characteristics of a building significantly affect the erection. Derricks generally operate in a circular pattern over a radius determined by the derrick capacity. A structure of a square or rectangular plan that can be covered by one or more derricks is ideal. Additional building "ells" may require an additional derrick which may only actively erect 30% of the circular pattern it covers. Uniform column spacing throughout the height of a building, with header beams framing to the column flanges and webs, is ideal. When header beams frame parallel to the column web or support other header beams, the erection sequence is limited or temporary material must be added to facilitate erection. Continuity throughout the building is ideal. When beam or column spacings change, the erection scheme and derrick locations may have to be modified.

As previously mentioned, composite design presents problems in placing the steel loads temporarily on the floor. The lack of lateral stiffness of beams may require temporary cross-bridging until the floor decking is placed. Consideration should be given to preassembling sections of floor with the decking attached.

Erection engineering must include investigation of the entire structure under erection conditions, which include the superimposed loads of derricks. Limitations may exist regulating the rate of erection with respect to concreting floors. Special bracing may have to be installed and removed. On occasion, it has been necessary to leave plumbing guys in place to provide stability. Field control to maintain vertical and horizontal tolerances of steel buildings is very important.

4 Construction Management

The general management of a tall building must be vested in one person. Contributing to this manager must be people knowledgeable in the various phases of operations and planning. This level of management is the responsibility of the owner or his architect or engineer. More specific to this section on construction of the structural steel is the management of the contractors' operations for the fabrication and erection of the structural steel.

Where one contractor is responsible for the fabrication and erection of the structural steel, a Project Manager is assigned to manage the contract. It then becomes his responsibility to plan the erecting procedure, review the designs and make recommendations to the owner's representative, schedule the fabrication and erection, and procure the equipment necessary. This work is done in cooperation with the fabricating plant management, District Construction Manager, Contracting Manager, and Engineering Department. The schedule and operations must be compatible with the plans of the owner's management.

The field erection forces report directly to the Project Manager through a General Superintendent and Project Engineer. As required, Assistant Superintendent and Field Engineers are assigned.

8.6 CONCRETE CONSTRUCTION

The development of high-strength concrete and reinforcing steel led to the concept of high-rise concrete structures. For widespread utilization of these materials, changes in construction methods and equipment were required. (See Volume CB of this Monograph for structural design aspects.) The construction industry met the challenge. Improvements in method and development of the logistics for moving materials rapidly and economically to great heights have occurred primarily since World War II. The introduction of flat-plate construction has greatly enhanced the economies of concrete construction, allowing that system to become competitive with structural steel in multistory buildings. New equipment has been conceived, produced, and developed to take advantage of the new expertise of the building designer. These advances in methods and finished products could not have been achieved without the invaluable technical assistance of equipment manufacturers and the cooperation of progressive labor unions.

1 Development of High-Rise Concrete Construction

To appreciate new developments, an understanding is important of the nature of construction practices that prevailed before 1946. Buildings above 20 stories in height were, almost without exception, steel structures. The Empire State Building at 381 m (1 250 ft) was the tallest of the giant buildings. Since approximately 1950, and particularly during the past 20 years, concrete buildings have begun to rival the height of many steel buildings. Water Tower Place, in Chicago, at 76 stories is about two-thirds the height of the tallest steel buildings.

Prior to World War II, the movement of materials was accomplished by means of wood frame hoisting towers; gasoline hoist motors were the source of power. Concrete was mixed on the jobsite, usually in 3/4-yd^3 mixes, with all the ingredients hand charged. Placing of concrete usually required push buggies, ramps, and much hand labor.

The early 1950s saw the advent of steel hoisting towers containing sophisticated electrical hoists. These towers could transport concrete and other materials from the ground to a 150-m (500-ft) level at a rate of 120 m (400 ft) per min. Next came the introduction of the Chicago Boom to lift pipe, reinforcing steel, and other similar materials to the appropriate floors. The present approach to construction of tall concrete buildings utilizes large, fast climbing cranes of the Australian type, with steel towers and electric hoists as auxiliary equipment.

The production of ready-mixed concrete at highly mechanized central plants, and efficient transportation to the jobsite, made available a virtually unlimited supply of concrete which could be placed at a rapid rate. It became possible to complete placements of 230 m^3 (300 yd^3) at locations high above ground level in less than 6 hr. Hand mixing of concrete and crude hoisting systems quickly became obsolete. The capability of placing concrete for an entire floor within a single day was a significant breakthrough.

Today, reliable, 62 MPa (9 000 psi) high-strength concrete is available. These high-strength concretes, coupled with modern construction methods, have so reduced structural costs and increased usable floor space that they no longer impose severe limitations on the height of concrete frame structures.

Plant and Equipment for Tall Concrete Buildings.   The proper selection of construction equipment for tall buildings is vitally important. Once it is set in place 30 m (100 ft) or more above the ground, a change presents enormous difficulties. The primary equipment must accommodate various types of loads. If the equipment is purchased, rather than rented, consideration should be given to its future usefulness. Equipment that is on an evolutionary dead end should be acquired strictly on a rental basis whenever possible. One example of a poor purchase would be a rail-mounted tower crane for a medium-height, long building.

Example Selection of Plant and Equipment.   The climbing crane is becoming the primary tool used by the majority of contractors for high-rise buildings. This is evident in any panoramic view of the skyline of a large city experiencing a building boom. The climbing crane is a versatile piece of equipment, which will handle every type of load. The only limitation on its effective working height is the length of cable the drums will spool.

The crane should be at least large enough to handle a 1.5-m^3 (2-yd^3) concrete bucket with a double part line at the building extremities. The contractor should realize, however, that a crane having a 53 300-N (12 000-1bf) pound, or 2.3-m^3 (3-yd^3) capacity, may be a bargain, because although its rental cost is \$1 200 to \$1 500 (US) more per month, it has approximately the same operational cost as the smaller crane, and it can be used to hoist heavier mechanical and elevator equipment directly into the penthouse. Whatever the size of the crane, it is well to remember that it still has only one hook, and hook time is critical in meeting two-day to four-day floor schedules. On a three-day sequence, each crane will handle between 930 m² (10 000 ft²) and 1 400 m² (15 000 ft²) of deck: 930 m² (10 000 ft²) of deck if the structure is complicated by exterior exposed columns, wall spandrels, and interior shear walls; and 1 400 m² (15 000 ft²) if the structure is very simple with masonry or curtain-wall facades.

The crane mast should be located at a midband in an open part of the deck, so that the jumping crews will have ample working space. With careful planning it can usually be situated so that it will top out on a long, flat part of the roof where it may be jacked down to the roof and readily dismantled and lifted to the ground with a stiffleg derrick. The crane openings should be located in closets or storage rooms when possible. The joints that remain after the openings are poured continue to open and close as the building moves under the action of wind forces. This movement will cause unsightly cracks that will be a nuisance in occupied areas.

Although the concrete frame itself can be erected with the climbing crane alone, there are compelling reasons why a steel hoisting tower should also be utilized. Hoisting of materials and equipment for the finish trades cannot be accomplished efficiently with the climbing crane for the following reasons: (1) Crane availability is minimal until the concrete work has been completed; and (2) a load attached to an extended crane cable is difficult to handle effectively—the problem becomes particularly acute when the object being lifted must be placed into a small opening in the building facade. Although the steel hoisting tower is not as necessary for the concrete work as for the operations of the finish trades, it can be a singularly useful tool for the concrete contractor as well, provided it is installed at an early stage of construction.

A personnel elevator installed in a steel tower or within a permanent elevator shaft should be erected to minimize stair climbing. Economic considerations aside, trade unions may require a man hoist after about eight floors. The elevator should have a landing platform every fifth floor to reduce stopping time; the operation must provide express service to the top at critical times. The top of the hoisting tower should be kept beneath the boom of the climbing crane.

A combination elevator and material cage will service an 18 600 m² (200 000 ft²) building. A single material tower having two platforms and a single personnel elevator will service about 46 000 m² (500 000 ft²). For areas between 46 000 m² (500 000 ft²) and 74 000 m² (800 000 ft²), two large combined man and material cages will be the most efficient installation. Both cages can transport peak loads of personnel in the morning and at noon, and then can revert to material handling. On still larger buildings, it is best to separate the personnel and material cages, with both towers being provided for each 37 000 m² (400 000 ft²) of building.

The hoisting towers should be located so as to minimize interference with the entrance and loading deck facilities of the building; the owner may want occupancy before the towers can be removed. Braces and ties to the structure should be planned to facilitate the erection of the finish facade behind the tower without interference from these braces. It is disconcerting to see portions of buildings left incomplete on every floor because of the interference of hoisting towers. On one well-planned Chicago office building with a glass and marble facade, a material hoist was kept in operation to facilitate tenant work for more than a year after contract completion. This was accomplished without interference with the building operation; nor did it interfere with substantial completion of the facade.

Compressed air required for form cleaning prior to concrete placement and for other purposes can be supplied by a portable compressor lifted to the working area by the climbing cranes. Having the capability of placing the compressor anywhere it is needed, the contractor need not install a stationary compressor and a standpipe on every floor. Thus it is possible to eliminate the inefficiency and high cost of a stationary compressor that must be operated continuously.

An electrical panel can be attached to the interior of the crane tower to provide electrical service for concrete operations. The crane requires 440-V service; therefore, with a step-down transformer, convenience outlets for 110 V, 220 V, and 440 V can be provided on a power panel. Extension cords no longer than the length of the crane boom will reach anywhere on the deck. Floodlights should be attached to the tower. Once installed on the mast, the power panel and the floodlights are automatically jumped with the crane and are always available at the concreting level. It is customary to trail a loose cable of approximately 60 m (200 ft). Provisions must be made for plugging in the cable at various locations within each 60 m (200 ft) of building height.

2 Concrete Placement

As a rule, the designer of tall structures will prescribe many concrete mixes in order to achieve economy of design. Standard weight concrete will vary from 62 MPa (9 000 psi) columns to 14 MPa (2 000 psi) mud slabs, while lightweight slabs and fills will vary from 41 MPa (6 000 psi) to 20 MPa (3 000 psi).

Water Tower Place in Chicago has eleven mixes; concrete hoisting is handled by six cranes. The ready-mix plant which supplies the job serves the entire central city. It has over 700 mixes on file, and uses 60 to 70 of these every day. To guard against pouring errors, the concrete contractor has an engineer whose full-time responsibility is to schedule and receive the concrete; the structural engineer checks all ordering and placing; a full-time representative from the testing lab checks truck tickets and makes job tests and samples. These cooperative efforts have succeeded in preventing any mixing or placing errors.

The usual rate of concrete pouring varies between 30 m³ and 45 m³ (40 yd³ and 60 yd³) per hr on most high-rise buildings. The maximum pour size should be restricted to 260 m³ (350 yd³). Contractors in countries that do not have a concrete ready-mix industry can achieve placements of this size through careful planning of the mixing equipment setup and materials handling system. Columns and walls in buildings with short story heights are poured one hour ahead of the slab; tall story heights are poured a day in advance. Pouring columns with the slab eliminates setup and cleanup cost, and also tends to prevent shrinkage cracks in the slabs by reducing the restraint factor.

High-strength concrete will allow upturned beams poured monolithically with the floor slabs to be installed to a height of 1.2 m (4 ft) by ordinary production methods. With special pouring techniques, a 1.8-m (6-ft) spandrel or beam height is possible. Lower-strength mixes and standard production methods will produce upturned beam heights to 1 m (3 ft). The placement sequence in the construction of high-rise reinforced concrete structures may soon no longer be a decision of the contractor, but will be determined in conjunction with the design engineer. Recent analyses have shown that final stresses in members are influenced by the concrete placement sequence. The deviation of the final stress from the calculated stress is significant enough to warrant consideration.

Using hoisting towers with ground and deck hoppers in combination with conveyors can increase the rate (and size) of pours. This procedure has the following disadvantages:

1. Spraying the surrounding area (cars, both moving and stationary, are a common target) with little droplets of cement, borne by the inevitable high winds prevailing at higher elevations.

2. Higher rigging costs for both the climbing crane and the hoisting tower because of interference between the climbing crane boom and the hoisting tower. [The hoisting tower must rise 11 m (35 ft) above the deck, and the crane boom has a maximum distance, depending upon size, above its last support. This incompatibility necessitates jumping both pieces of equipment every three floors.]

3. Higher setup and cleanup costs. Concrete pumping techniques have been developed that permit pumping to heights in excess of 150 m (500 ft).

3 Forming Techniques

The most significant advances in forming techniques have been flying forms for decks and gang-hinged forms of steel for facades and walls. Slip forms, which were originally developed for tower type construction, have found application in concrete building construction, and are widely used. Improved adaptations of "stick framing" are still being used. Steel scaffold supports are replacing individual shores, and adjustable steel joists have claimed a percentage of the deck framing market. These advances in forming techniques require careful preplanning of form removal or reshoring (or both) consistent with the construction progress. The faster the vertical rate of construction, the greater the number of floors that must be left shored below.

Flat Slab Forming. Steel scaffold frames 1.5 m (5 ft) wide set 3 m (10 ft) on center each way with 200-mm (8-in.) steel girts, flat 50-mm × 100-mm (2-in. × 4-in.) boards on 200-mm (8-in.) centers and 6-mm (1/4-in.) finn form make an excellent framing system. The scaffold frames are equipped with an adjustable head staff with a channel head to receive the 200-mm (8-in.) steel girts. The 50-mm × 100-mm (2-in. × 4-in.) joists which are 4.9 m (16 ft) long are laid flat and the ends run wild over the 200-mm (8-in.) steel supports. The 50-mm × 100-mm (2-in. × 4-in.) joists, although weakened structurally when laid flat, never tip and the ends rest alongside each other without requiring cutting. The 6-mm (1/4-in.) plywood is light, easy to cut, and it is not a calamity when the mechanical trades cut it up to make room for pipe stacks. About 5% of the plywood sheets are replaced on each floor. For a three-day pouring cycle, three or four sets of forms are needed.

Flying forms are prefabricated deck forms comprising sheeting, joists, and usually, scaffold supports which remain intact after each use. They are obtainable in either half-bay or full-bay sizes. The name "flying forms" is derived from the dramatic view the public sees when a large section of a prefabricated deck form is being propelled through the air by a climbing crane. A climbing crane is a prerequisite to the use of flying forms.

In determining whether a flying form system is feasible, the following considerations are pertinent: (1) Make-up cost dictates that there should be at least ten uses, for example, a 30-story building on a three-day schedule, or a 20-story building on a five-day schedule; (2) the interior and exterior columns of the building must be in line; (3) the building must have an open facade through which to pass the forms; and (4) prefabricated components which will impede moving of the forms, such as plumbing stacks, cannot be used.

Equipment manufacturers have devised ways of collapsing the flying forms to enable them to pass through restricted openings in the facade. However, these methods add to the cost of the system and make its use questionable. If obstructions cause the amount of fill-in between the flying forms to exceed 20% of the total area formed, the cost of the piecemeal operation will negate the labor savings otherwise realized from use of the flying forms.

Structural slab systems more complex than the flat plate can be handled expeditiously with flying forms. Two-way slabs with deepened column bands, custom dome slabs, custom joist slabs, and even free shaped slab soffits are economical if the higher make-up cost is amortized over many reuses. Fiberglass reinforced plastics have proved cost effective for these types of form construction. The moving cost of the flying forms remains the same as that of a flat plate. The designer should take precautions to allow for at least a 1 in 3 draft of vertical surfaces to accommodate easy stripping. The use of precast elements considerably reduces formwork requirements.

Steel Gang-hinged Forms.   Column, spandrel, or wall forms constructed so that all of the sides fold back for easy stripping, moving, and erection are called "hinged" forms. Usually, the forms for all the vertical surfaces of each bay are moved in one piece. Because there are few loose parts and a large area of formwork is moved at one time, there can be a substantial saving in labor.

These forms cost between $10 and $15 per 1 ft^2 (0.09 m^2) of contact area. Therefore, if the purchase of forms for one complete floor is being considered, an economic advantage will be seen only if the building contains approximately 30 typical floors.

4   Quality Control of Concrete

The problems associated with the removal of unsatisfactory concrete in high-rise construction are enormous and costly. Accelerated (heat) curing methods for test specimens assist in determining form stripping schedules, but are of no help in preventing the placement of unspecified concrete. Chemical and neutron activation systems have been developed in several countries that will determine the water and cement content of fresh concrete before it is placed. The results can then be used to predict the 28-day strength with acceptable accuracy. These systems can be particularly helpful on projects that employ numerous design mixes. Cumulative sum (CUSUM) control charts are used in the United Kingdom to provide a continuous evaluation of concrete strengths, and for early detection of changes in concrete quality.

5   Conclusion

Before the tallest existing concrete building has had time to enter the record book, even before it receives its last pour, the equipment manufacturers are marketing climbing cranes more than twice as large as their predecessors. Field concrete of 69

MPa (10 000 psi) can now be produced, and laboratory samples of 207 MPa (30 000 psi) have been made. With more finely ground cement, a better understanding of cement chemistry, and the development of more effective additives, 83 MPa (12 000 psi) concrete will be a reality in the near future. These advances, coupled with reinforced concrete designs that emulate the tall steel building designs by making the structural concept the central design theme, will allow concrete to become the most desirable and economical material for the tallest buildings. The concrete industry is ready and waiting for the corporate giant to plan its temple of the future, the high-rise building.

8.7　MIXED CONSTRUCTION (STEEL AND CONCRETE)

Mixed construction of tall buildings (sometimes referred to as "hybrid" and in which the structure is partly concrete and partly structural steel) can provide savings in both cost and time in addition to other benefits which cannot be realized using either all steel or all concrete structural systems. Such systems, properly designed, may yield one or more of the following advantages in the construction process:

1. Compact simplified foundation configurations resulting in savings in foundation cost, construction time, and quantities of sheeting and bracing materials.

2. Reduced danger to surrounding buildings, more room and better access for handling and storage of construction equipment and materials.

3. Less interference with existing buildings, railroads, highways or communication lines which must be maintained in operation.

4. Rapid construction to satisfy requirements for early occupancy or scheduling to avoid adverse weather conditions.

5. Early development of temporary and permanent vertical transport facilities.

6. Optimum balance between cast-in-place and prefabricated construction.

7. Performing a significantly greater amount of construction work at ground level.

There is an almost unlimited number of combinations of concrete and steel construction used in this system, to say nothing of combinations of other construction materials, such as nonferrous metals, plastics, and glass products. This section will be limited to a consideration of steel and concrete frames which have been successfully used in building construction. Structural design aspects for "Mixed Construction" are covered in Chapter SB-9.

1　Major Structural Systems

Those structural systems in common use include the following:

1. Structural systems that utilize a central concrete core or shear wall combined with steel framing. Steel framing systems may be constructed either simultaneously with or after construction of the core.

2. Multiple concrete cores or shear walls, or both, constructed with steel girders or beams spanning between the cores.

3. Steel frames suspended on a central concrete core in a configuration resembling a tree.

4. Individually cantilevered floors or a cantilevered transfer girder or truss at the first typical floor with column construction above.

5. Industrialized construction of buildings using concrete or structural steel frames with box modules of precast concrete, steel, or other material, which contribute to the stability of the building.

6. Concrete or steel cores with steel or concrete floors constructed at grade or intermediate floors and raised into position.

7. Structural steel frames with concrete encasement.

8. Tube-in-tube construction using the exterior of the building as a structural element to reduce the overturning moment requirements of the inner core tube.

2   Erection Sequence

Tall Buildings Having Concrete Cores or Shear Walls, or Both, and Steel Framing. This type of construction is probably the most prevalent hybrid construction in the western hemisphere, Europe, and Africa. The cores (and sometimes shear walls) are constructed using either gang forming or slip forms, the latter being the more common for the tallest buildings. Cores may be constructed at the rate of one floor per two to four days using gang forms, and one to two floors per day using slip forming. Such cores speed up erection of the steel by reducing the weight of steel to be handled and the number of bolts and rivets or length of welds required, and sometimes eliminate the necessity to jump derricks.

Cores Constructed Ahead of Steel Erection. The cores may be built completely to the top before starting steel erection or they may be built simultaneously in echelon with the steel erection, one or the other lagging by a few floors. Completing the core before starting the steel has the advantage that one crew does not have to work below the other. Another advantage is the reduced interference between the concrete and steel subcontractors. It must be kept in mind, however, that unless the core is constructed rapidly using slip forms on a 24-hr five day per week basis, the delay in starting steel erection may well be excessive. Furthermore, in some areas where two or three shifts of men are not available, or where premium pay for overtime is unusually high, the cost of such rapid construction may not be balanced by the saving in the cost of steel erection. Lastly, the cost and time advantage of starting elevator and mechanical work shortly after completion of the core must be given proper consideration.

Cores Constructed Simultaneously with Steel Erection. Conducting the placement of concrete for the core and steel erection simultaneously will reduce or eliminate premium pay and will allow the choice between slip forms and gang forms. This must be weighed against complications arising from a two-level, two-subcontractor operation and dual logistical systems for feeding materials into both operations simultaneously. Whether the core precedes the steel or lags behind is a matter of study for each particular construction, as there are advantages and problems in either sequence. That solution must be utilized which results in the best economy and minimum danger to personnel for that particular structure in that particular locality at that particular time. Fig. 8.24 shows the 170-m (556-ft) high core for the United States Fidelity and Guaranty Company building at Baltimore, Maryland. This core was slip-formed the full height with a tower crane suspended from the slip form. Fig. 8.25 shows the second phase of the work, the erection of the structural steel. Concrete columns are being cast in each corner of the building using gang forms. The column construction is an example of simultaneous construction with the concrete lagging behind the steel erection. Note also the erection derricks at the top of the core.

Multiple Concrete Cores or Shear Walls with Steel Girders or Beams Spanning Spaces Between.   This type of structure has the same basic characteristics as single-core construction and may be sequenced in the same manner, except that the cores must always precede the steel. The logistics of supplying materials at several high locations not yet connected by the floor system must be given careful study. Means for distribution of material and emergency mutual logistical support between cores must be devised. This applies also to personnel; a system of bridges is often provided to allow efficient movement of the various trades from core to core, without requiring a complete crew comprising all trades for each core.

Concrete Cores and Suspended Steel Frame Structures.   This system is similar to those already described, but has the potential of producing a building with minimum area at the base, that is to say with a configuration resembling a tree. Such construction has been suggested for urban renewal projects where a minimum dislocation of existing facilities is desired. It allows the structural steel members to be raised vertically into position working from the top down and using hoisting equipment mounted on the cantilevered girder system. In very tall buildings it is possible to have cantilevered girders or trusses at several levels and to erect the steel simultaneously from all of these levels if desired.

The major difficulty with this type of framing is the problem of raising the heavy cantilever girders or trusses into position for suspending the steel framing. These beams or trusses may be structural steel, cast-in-place concrete, or precast concrete. The weight involved in raising precast girders is such as to make this type of girder impracticable unless each girder is cast and raised in sections and erected in place using sophisticated connections or post-tensioning, or both. The same technique may be used for steel trusses or girders with greater facility as they are lighter in weight and can be welded together. Cast-in-place girders require forms to be constructed in place under difficult conditions; the support of the cantilevered section is an especially difficult feat. If sliding forms are used, there is the possibility of raising the girders as part of the slip form working deck, utilizing the same hydraulic system. Fig. 8.26 shows the 76-m (250-ft) high West Coast Transmission Tower in Vancouver, B. C., Canada. This frame hangs all floors directly from the top of a central core without trusses.

Fig. 8.24 Concrete core for United States Fidelity and Guaranty Co. Building, Baltimore, Maryland
(Courtesy: Huber, Hunt & Nichols; Photo by Tadder)

Fig. 8.25 Steel erection for United States Fidelity and Guaranty Co. Building, Baltimore, Maryland
(Courtesy: Huber, Hunt & Nichols; Photo by Tadder)

Concrete or Steel Cores and Cantilevered Floors of Other Structural Material. This type of structure includes: (1) Individually cantilevered floors; (2) one cantilevered transfer girder (or truss) at the first typical floor with column construction above; (3) cantilevered girders (or trusses) at intermediate levels with vertical column construction of several floors supported on each; and (4) alternate cantilever floors paired as trusses. These structural frames do not have the problems nor the advantages of suspended floors. The main advantage in construction is in eliminating or reducing the difficult task of raising the heavy girders and trusses to the top of the core. The main disadvantage is the need for somewhat heavier floor members and more complex floor to core connection.

Industrialized Construction of Buildings. Such buildings have concrete or structural steel frames with box modules of precast concrete, steel or other material contributing to the structural stability of the building. This is one of the latest developments in mixed construction. Buildings are being constructed where modules are piled on each other like children's building blocks. In other instances, cores and frames have been devised on which or to which the box modules have been attached. Neither of these is a hybrid structural system. The systems referred to here are systems in which the box modules actually contribute to the structural frame. Such systems are the next generation to the stacked module system.

Special equipment must be developed for handling the box modules horizontally from the factories or from the site fabrication areas to the points of pickup for erection. This equipment must have built-in jacking equipment for picking up and

Fig. 8.26 West Coast Transmission Tower, Vancouver, B.C., Canada (*Courtesy: Vancouver Sun photo*)

depositing the modules without use of cranes. Cradles must also be designed for lifting and controlling the ascent of the modules into position. Jacking equipment must also be integrated into the cradles to allow fine vertical and lateral movements of the module for final attachment to the core and to each other. Fig. 8.27 shows a model of the NAVA-QUIN System to be used for construction of housing units at Rio Piedras, Puerto Rico. On the right, the two structural cores and the central utility core are being slip formed. In the foreground is the precasting operation for box construction and the storage area. Erection of the boxes is proceeding from the top down on the left side of the photograph. This is not a suspension system, as each box is structurally attached to the core at each level for support, and to each other to form continuous diaphragms. These boxes are precast concrete; in other areas of the world steel can be just as easily used and may have some weight and connection advantages.

Concrete or Steel Cores with Steel or Concrete Floors Constructed at Grade or Intermediate Floors and Raised into Position. The advantages of building at grade are obvious and highly desirable as long as the cost of raising the completed floors and connecting them to the columns, cores, and shear walls does not become excessive. The methods, problems, and advantages of core construction, as well as connection considerations, have been adequately covered. The comments in these paragraphs will therefore be confined to the construction aspects of the floor

Fig. 8.27 Model of NAVA-QUIN System for construction of housing units at Rio Piedras, Puerto Rico *(Courtesy: J. F. Camellerie)*

fabrication and erection. There are basically two types of floors to be considered, steel and concrete, but fiberglass reinforced plastic members are not to be forgotten as they are an imminent possibility.

Concrete floors may be cast on a flat floor at or near grade or even at some intermediate level. These floors must be of a "flat slab" type without beams, girders, or drop panels. Each floor is cast on the one before, using an effective bond breaker to prevent bonding to each other. The only formwork required is the marginal formwork, which is minimal. These slabs may be up to 20 m × 60 m (60 ft × 150 ft) in area, or larger, and in stacks of as much as 20 slabs, possibly more. If beneficial or required, post-tensioning can be economically applied while the slabs are still in the stacked position. The slabs are then hydraulically lifted as a stack to slightly above the floor to be placed, climbing on the steel columns. The lowest slab is then separated from the stack, lowered into its final position, and connected to the column. Because of heavy shear concentration at the columns (without help from drop panels) the reinforcing requirements become oppressive or impossible; structural shear distribution frames must therefore be cast into the slabs at column connections. Fig. 8.28 shows such construction in progress. Steel floors of the beam and girder type may be erected on the ground in proper plan location one above the other. A corrugated metal deck form with concrete placed at grade (or at final elevation) or a steel tubular deck completes the assembly of each floor. These floors may then be raised vertically upward and attached to the suspension system or core, depending on structural frame design. As an alternate, sections of steel floor may be prefabricated anywhere on or off jobsite, transported horizontally and vertically into place, and then attached to core, columns, and to each other. The cores furnish an excellent space platform for hoisting facilities at the top. Fig. 8.29 shows such construction at Berkeley, California utilizing a concrete core with structural steel floors.

Tube-in-Tube Construction Using Exterior of Building as Structural Element. A recent innovative solution to the design of tower structures is a symmetrical three-dimensional interaction tube structure. It is composed of two basic elements: an outer tube and an inner braced core. Typically, large perimeter columns are spaced around the perimeter to support the weight of the outer zone of floors. Internal floor loading is supported at the core. The facade of the building acts as a vertical tube of high stiffness. The two elements, the braced core and the facade tube, are rigidly connected by floor diaphragms and act as an integral unit to resist wind deformation.

An interesting example of this type of construction is the Collins Place project, Melbourne, Australia. The office towers incorporate the dual economies of reinforced concrete vertical systems and steel beams in horizontal systems.

Two towers 183 m (600 ft) high, 47 and 49 stories above ground, contain 1020 m² and 1700 m² (11 000 ft² and 18 000 ft²) of rentable space, respectively. The center core is a reinforced concrete wall system with clear span floors using steel beams (with sprayed fireproofing) and cast-in-place slabs of 130-mm (5-in.) lightweight concrete composite with the beams.

The precast structural facade has T-shaped architecturally finished units 4.3 m × 3.7 m (14 ft × 12 ft) with a hollow column and solid spandrel. The columns incorporate a very light steel U.C. section for erection of floor systems four floors ahead of the facade. Hollow columns act as forms for reinforced concrete.

Fig. 8.28 Lift slab construction (East Chicago, Indiana) *(Courtesy and photo: Orlando R. Cabanban)*

Fig. 8.29 Concrete core and steel floor framing, building under construction at Berkeley, California *(Courtesy: J. F. Camellerie)*

The sway system for the towers is that of a "tube in tube," wherein the central core and facade act together to reduce the overturning movement on the core to a value approximately 50% of that which would have been had it been acting by itself.

The construction sequence for these towers involved slip forming the core, keeping several floors above the floor slab levels. Steel beams and light columns were erected to a maximum of four levels above the concrete column. Table forms, the full dimension of the slab bay, are supported at the bottom flange of the steel beams. The table forms have rollers which move on the bottom flange of the steel beam.

Structural Steel Frames with Structural Concrete Encasement (Composite Construction).   This type of construction has long been in use in the construction industry throughout the world. Concrete filled pipe columns; concrete columns with structural steel cores; piles and drilled-in-caissons of both types, are common hybrid components. Composite floors utilizing concrete slabs with shear connected steel beams, as well as leave-in-place steel forms structurally designed to act compositely with the concrete, are also in general use. The most general and varied use of composite frame construction is to be found in Japan and is covered in Chapters SC-1 and SB-9.

Encasement of parts or all of a structural steel frame with concrete allows the use of lighter steel frames, simpler connections, and reduction in bracing, thereby speeding and reducing the cost of steel erection. The height to which the steel framing may precede the concrete work will depend on design and lateral loading conditions, but a range of 6 to 12 stories may be expected. As concrete or another material is needed for architectural, enclosure, and fireproofing reasons, the encasement economically performs several functions at once. Early encasement of the steel also results in earlier occupancy of the building.

The problems associated with this type of construction include the use of two types of subcontractors working one above the other, and a proneness to cracking due to initial shrinkage of concrete and continuing deflection of the steel frame due to increased loading.

The forming for the encasing concrete is much more difficult to design, install, and remove than that for normal concrete forming. "Wrecking Strips" or section of forms which cannot be removed without destroying them must be built in so as to make as much formwork as possible removable for reuse. Gang forming and form handling generally are also complicated.

Construction of Tall "Hybrid" Buildings from the Top Down.   Since one of the major costs in the construction of tall buildings is that of raising and lowering equipment, men, and materials to the great heights involved, and a degree of inefficiency results from labor working at these heights, construction of an entire building at ground level is greatly to be desired. This would require building the structure from the top down and raising the building as construction proceeds. Such a construction was in fact effected at Barras Heath in Coventry, England using a method of construction known as the "Jackblock" method. This method was used to construct a 17-story apartment building, 55 m (180 ft) high, with a composite structural framing integrating cast-in-place concrete with precast blocks. The structural system was a central core with cantilevered prestressed floors.

The foundation was first constructed together with the ground floor and a system of hydraulic jacks in the basement level. The ground floor slab acted as the casting bed for the floors and roof; the core walls were erected in the basement on the hydraulic jack system and raised as construction progressed. The roof was cast on the ground floor slab with the penthouse structures built on the roof slab and the top floor walls built in the basement. The core was raised, roof and all, to the top floor and the top floor slab was cast. This process was repeated to the top, in effect extruding the building upward.

Once the cycle was in operation, all trades were operating simultaneously without interfering with one another, and substantially at ground level. The core walls were constructed in the basement level, floors were formed at ground level, partitions, mechanical and electrical work, outside skin and finishing were completed on the second and third floors. The whole area up to and including the third floor was completely enclosed to allow all trades to work in the dry.

3   Connections and Tolerances

Steel to Concrete Connection.   Special attention must be given to the connections between the structural steel and the concrete. Proper allowance must be made for construction tolerances allowed in both steel and concrete when designing these connections, and the adjustability must be carefully worked out to prevent field problems and yet not make connections excessively expensive. The use of weld plates cast in the concrete with field welded connection angles has proved most advantageous in many instances. Pockets are often used when stresses are almost purely vertical, but these tend to disrupt wall reinforcement and usually require filling with concrete. In connecting steel to concrete, the use of header beams running parallel and close to the wall is often desirable to reduce the number of concrete to steel connections. Moment connections and connections not absolutely required are to be avoided. For lighter reactions, stair carriages, elevator spacer beams, and other such steel to concrete connections, drilled-in inserts are highly recommended.

Steel Girders Spanning Between Multiple Cores.   The connections or bearings, or both, for the steel members on the concrete cores must be designed to compensate for the tolerances allowed, and to allow the members to be easily swung into position and then quickly released from the crane to allow the crane to prepare for placing the next member. For this purpose, pockets or at least seat angles are highly desirable. When anchor bolts are used, slotted or oversized holes must be used to assure quick safe seating despite variations in the beam length and misplacements of the anchor bolts. Temporary bolted connections are sometimes used for erection, with a follow-up crew making the permanent connection by welding. In designing the forms and logistics systems, an eye must be kept to the method for economically and safely returning this equipment to earth when it is no longer required. Fig. 8.30 shows the four corner columns 8.5 m (28 ft) in diameter, and the 9.1-m (30-ft) square central core slipformed to the full 102-m (335-ft) height for the Knights of Columbus Headquarters in New Haven, Connecticut. Runways connected all towers. Crane and hoist were integral with the slip-form system and automatically rose with the construction. Fig. 8.31 shows the architecturally exposed girders spanning tower to tower a distance of 24.3 m (80 ft) erected after the concrete was finished, using hoisting equipment mounted at the top of the cores.

The geometry of the structure must be carefully maintained, especially as to the clear dimensions that must be spanned by the structural steel members. Dependable positive measures for physically tying the core forming systems together, or a system of forms possessing adequate adjustability to hold tolerance, are an absolute necessity. With slip-form operations the bridges between cores may be designed as horizontal trusses and spacers to hold dimension and angle between cores, in addition to affording foot bridges and runways for material distribution at work level.

Steel Frames Suspended on Concrete Cores. When erecting frames suspended from a central core, particular attention must be given to compression and creep in the concrete core and elongation of the steel suspensors. This action tends to be minimal when erection starts, but accelerates to significant proportions at the lower levels when both stresses and lengths involved are at a maximum. As the steel stresses allowed are higher than the compressive stresses normally used, enclosure, partitioning, and mechanical work may have to be delayed until satisfactory vertical dimensional stability is achieved.

Industrialized Buildings Having Frames Supporting Box Modules. These systems will of course have the advantage of using factory methods on site or at a

Fig. 8.30 Corner and center concrete cores, Knights of Columbus Headquarters Building, New Haven, Connecticut *(Courtesy: J. F. Camellerie)*

more or less distant factory. Since they are structurally integrated, the jointry problems become much more difficult than those associated with nonstructural modules. The most serious construction problem lies in the connection problems that arise in tying the modules to each other as well as to the core.

These boxes may be suspended from the top of the core or attached directly to the core at each floor level. When the modules are attached at each level, the cantilever beams required at the top (if any are required at all) will be much shorter in length and lighter in weight, as only one module need be supported at any time. The box modules themselves are capable of acting as beams between cores, cantilevers from cores, or diaphragms produced by joining the box modules together using the cores as columns.

8.8 DEMOLITION

Consideration must be given to cleaning the site selected for the erection of a high-rise building. Since most high-rise construction is of necessity in existing urban areas, and on prime property that is occupied by an existing high-rise structure that must be removed, the cost and time required for this operation must be analyzed.

Fig. 8.31 Completed structure showing steel girders, Knights of Columbus Headquarters Building, New Haven, Connecticut *(Courtesy: J. F. Camellerie)*

The leases involved with the tenants in the existing building and their relocation are important to the time schedule and the costs of the project, and require the assistance of specialized real estate personnel.

Due to the costs of taxes and the maintenance of the building, the demolition of the existing building may take place well in advance of the new construction.

Depending upon the time element, the contract for the demolition work may be directly with the owner or the architect, or as a subcontract to the general contractor for the entire project.

1 Estimating

The cost for demolition is determined by unit costs acquired in prior operations applied to the "in place" quantities of the structure, similar to the costs involved in new construction. Information comes either from plans obtained from the previous owner or from plans on file at municipal departments. In the event that no plans are available, a field inspection of the structure is required to obtain the information desired.

A major item in the cost is for the protection of pedestrians and adjacent structures during the demolition operation.

The type of construction of the building determines the method to be used in the demolition operation. For an analysis of the costs in the New York City area (circa 1975) for demolition based on the cubic content, see the following:

1. Brick walls with bearing wood joists—$2.47/m^3 to $4.24/m^3 ($0.07/ft^3 to $0.12/ft^3).

2. Steel frame with concrete floor arches—$5.30/m^3 to $8.83/m^3 ($0.15/ft^3 to $0.25/ft^3).

3. Reinforced concrete—$7.07/m^3 to $10.60/m^3 ($0.20/ft^3 to $0.30/ft^3).

An analysis based on the cubic content can vary according to the floor heights; therefore, a quantity take-off is required.

Salvageable items, such as wood beams, brick, and steel that are recovered during the demolition operation are credited to the cost of the work. The market for these items fluctuates and will affect the costs accordingly. It follows that in a reinforced concrete structure there is very little salvage and this will cause the costs to be higher.

2 Safety

Building demolition is one of the most dangerous phases of construction. Safety cannot be neglected.

The type of protection in general use in the demolition of high-rise buildings is a steel sidewalk shed that supports a tubular steel scaffolding on the exterior of the building. Steel scaffolding supported on the roof of adjacent lower structures, or on outriggers, serves as protection in the removal of the exterior walls. The scaffolding is topped with three levels of wood plank and wire mesh screening, enabling it to be used as a work platform as well as for safety.

On taller buildings, the steel scaffold may be started on the upper floors, using either setbacks or outriggers. Together with the sidewalk shed, the demolition work can proceed at an earlier time.

The glass windows are removed and the openings are boarded up to control the debris. Floor openings are covered with timber for additional control. Since buildings to be demolished are usually old, the construction materials are often dried out and highly combustible. Therefore, the existing standpipes are maintained to assure fire protection in the building.

During demolition, continuing inspections are made as the work progresses to detect hazards resulting from weakened or deteriorated floors or walls, or loosened material. No worker is permitted to work where such hazards exist until they are corrected by shoring, bracing, or other effective means.

3 Method

Prior to starting demolition operations, an engineering survey of the structure is made by a properly qualified person to determine the type and condition of the framing, floors, and walls, to prevent collapse of the structure. When indicated as advisable, any adjacent structures are also similarly checked. Next, existing utility services such as gas, electricity, and water are cut off. However, water and electricity may be retained on a limited basis to serve the needs of the demolition operation for lighting areas, wetting down debris to eliminate flying dust, and to provide water for fire protection. The building is serviced by an exterminator to prevent the spread of rodents and vermin to adjacent buildings.

A chute is then constructed to convey the debris generated from the upper floors to the ground, or to a truck-size hopper located on a lower floor. An existing masonry shaft, such as a stairwell, may be used for this purpose, or else it may be constructed. Materials should not be thrown out of windows and left to fall free.

After all the protection timber is in place, a stripping operation of all tenant construction (hung ceilings, partitions, and furnishings) is normally begun, starting at the top floor of the building. This operation proceeds and leaves behind only the basic structure.

The roof slab is removed by pneumatic tools and falls to the floor immediately below. It is then removed by means of payloaders to the chutes. However, prior to initiating this type of demolition practice each floor must be thoroughly inspected by a qualified inspector in order to determine that it can support the impact load of the dropped slab, as well as the weight of men, equipment, and material resting on that floor. The walls are removed next, but only to windowsill height to allow a backstop for the removal of the debris.

The steel frame that is left exposed is next to be removed. The steel is cut with acetylene torches. By precutting the beams and columns prior to dismantling, an appreciable time saving can be realized. The steel is then removed by crane or derrick, depending on site conditions. Upon completion of the steel removal, the next floor slab is removed and the progression is the same for the remainder of the building.

The major quantity of debris generated is removed from the site, and the dumping areas are usually landfills in swamps. The basement of the building may be backfilled with masonry debris to serve as a retainer for the foundation walls until such time as the foundation contractor for the new building starts his work. In the interim the site can be used as a parking lot for other construction workers. As the demolition work proceeds, all party walls with adjacent buildings are pinned to the frame of the remaining building.

The method set forth is for a steel frame and concrete arch building. This method is a basis for all types of buildings.

A ball swung by means of a crane is used extensively in areas where pedestrian traffic and adjacent structures are not a factor in the demolition operation. The recent use of explosives for this purpose would apply only in the same areas.

4 Conclusion

In the future, because of the height and type of construction, the demolition of buildings should require that more information be made available to the contractor. In the case of prestressed members and cantilevered sections, the method of demolition would be safer if the original design information were a matter of record.

8.9 CONDENSED REFERENCES/BIBLIOGRAPHY

The following is a condensed bibliography for this chapter. Not only does it include all articles referred to or cited in the text, but it also contains bibliography for further reading. The full citations will be found at the end of the Volume. What is given here should be sufficient information to lead the reader to the correct article: the author, date, and title. In case of multiple authors, only the first named is listed.

Control of the Construction Process

Bonny 1973, *Handbook of Construction Management and Organizations*
Clough 1972, *Construction Project Management*
Clough 1975, *Construction Contracting*
Foxall 1971, *Professional Construction Management and Project Administration*
Kittides 1974, *Construction Management: State of the Art in 1974*
O'Brien 1971. *Contractors Management Handbook*
Reiner 1972, *Handbook of Construction Management*
Wass 1972, *Construction Management and Contracting*

Safety

Associated General Contractors 1971, *Manual of Accident Prevention in Construction*
Construction Methods & Equipment 1975, *Construction Safety Handbook*
deStivolinski 1969a, *Occupational Health in the Construction Industry*
deStivolinski 1969b, *A Survey of the Safety Environment of the Construction Industry*
Institution of Civil Engineers 1969, *Safety on Construction Sites*
Levitt 1969, *Effect of Top Management on Safety Construction*

Foundations

Baker 1971, *Caisson Construction Problems and Correction*
Chellis 1961, *Pile Foundations*
ENR 1961, *Tiebacks—Remove Clutter in Excavation*
Gerwick 1967, *Slurry-Trench Techniques for Diaphragm Walls in Deep Foundation Construction*
Institution of Civil Engineers 1966, *Large Bored Piles*
Peck 1943, *Earth Pressures Measurements in Deeper Cuts*
Peck 1969, *Deep Excavations and Tunneling in Soft Ground*
Prentis 1950, *Underpinning*
The Consulting Engineer 1970, *Ground Anchors*
Weinhold 1970, *Machine-bored Caissons for Earth Retaining Systems in Europe*

White 1958, *Deep Foundations in Soft Chicago Clay*
White 1962, *Underpinning*
White 1962, *Cofferdams*
White 1964, *Design and Construction of Braced Cuts*

Concrete Construction

ACI 1971, *Building Code, Requirements for Reinforced Concrete*
ACI 1974a, *Manual of Standard Practice for Detailing Reinforced Concrete Structures*
ACI 1974b, *Placing Concrete by Pumping Methods*
Fintel 1974, *Handbook of Concrete Engineering*
Hurd 1973, *Formwork for Concrete*
Komendant 1972, *Contemporary Concrete Structures*
Waddell 1974, *Concrete Construction Handbook*

Mixed Construction

ASCE 1974, *Composite Steel-Concrete Construction*
Knowles 1973, *Composite Steel and Concrete Construction*

Demolition

Akam 1972, *Demolition: Erecting a Framework—Results of a BRS Survey*
Consulting Engineer 1975, *Brute Force Without Ignorance*
Higgins 1973, *Demolition: Newest Dimension of Modern Blasting*
Irwin 1974, *Planned Obsolescence and Demolition of Tall Buildings*
Price 1972, *Demolition: the Art of Science*

Additional References

AISC 1971a, *Quality Criteria and Inspection Standards*
AISC 1971b, *Specification for: Structural Joints Using ASTM A325 or A490 Bolts*
ANSI, *Various Standards Applicable to Construction Safety*
ASTM 1971, *1971 Annual Book of Standards*
Abdallah 1974, *The Progressive Strength Method*
Anastasescu 1975, *Slip Form Constructed Lightweight Expanded Clay Concrete Tall Buildings*
Arch 1973, *Summary Report: Construction Systems*
Aristy 1973, *Prefabricated Housing*
Asrow 1973, *Theme Report: Construction Systems*

Balaguru 1974, *Project Planning and Control for Tall Buildings*
Bellows 1973, *Concrete Frame Construction*
Bruna 1973, *Structures of Tall Buildings Using Precast Concrete Skeleton*

Camellerie 1973, *Hybrid Frame Construction (Steel and Concrete)*
Chow 1974, *Pour-in-Place Prestressed Concrete Construction for High Rise Buildings*
Chye 1974, *The Constructional Aspects of a Tall Building*
Cole 1975, *A Review of Research into Learning Curves and Their Application*
Constructional Review 1974a, *MLC Project, Sydney*
Constructional Review 1974b, *390 St. Kilda Road, Melbourne*
Cunningham 1974, *Rock Caissons for the Northern Building in Chicago's Loop*
Cunningham 1973, *Steel Construction*

Da Costa 1973, *Calculation of High Buildings for Loads During Construction*
Despeyroux 1975, *Construction of Prefabricated Panels in Tall Buildings*
Diaz-Caneja 1973, *The Preflex System in the Structures of High Buildings*
Drakatos 1975, *The Influence of Mechanical Vibrations on the Construction of Tall Buildings*
Duncan 1970, *Rebuilding of the Stock Exchange: 1st Phase*

Fang 1975, *Basic Consideration of Design, Construction and Maintenance of Tall Building*

Feld 1974, *Building Failures: Floor Support Shoring in Multi-Storey Construction*
Finzi 1973, *The Structural Design of Tall Steel Buildings*

Garnett 1973, *The AMP Center, Sydney*
Giangreco 1973, *General Report on Italian Contribution to Tall Buildings*

Halpern 1973, *Control of the Construction Process*
Hunt 1970, *Skyscraper Frame Welded by a Semi-Automatic Process*

Ikeda 1974, *Construction Methods for High-Rise Buildings*

Jackson 1974, *Concrete Quality Control*
Jackson 1974, *Foundation, Construction and Performance for a 34-Storey Building*
Jain 1973, *Effect of Construction Stages on the Stresses in Multi-Storied Frames*
Jendele 1971, *High Buildings with a Concrete Bearing System in Czechoslovakia*
Jorg 1975, *The West German State of Art of Tall Buildings, Questions Concerning*

Kawasaki 1974, *Construction of the D.B.S. Building, Singapore*
Kebo 1973, *Some Experience Acquired by Assembly of Steel Structures of Multi-Storey Buildings*

Libbey 1975, *Design and Construction of the Pacific Trade Center Building*

McMillan 1975, *Optimum Design of High-Rise Buildings—A Multi-Disciplinary Engineering*
Mikos 1972, *Structural, Physical and Technological Unity of Erection of Monolithic*
Miller 1973, *Qantas Center, Sydney, Design and Construction Planning*

Nakamura 1974, *Present Problems over HPC Method*
Navodariu 1975, *The Actual Stage and New Tendency in the Construction of Flatstall Buildings*
Nisbet 1973, *Whickham Tower Block: The Design and Construction of a 30-Storey Block of Flats*

Ohta 1974, *Research and Development of HPC Tall Building System*
Orczykowski 1972, *The Problems of Tall Concrete Buildings Realization*
Osborne 1975, *Precast Panels for Centre Rising Sixty Levels*

Pancewicz 1972, *Steel Pin-Jointed Structures with Hexagonal Column Arrangement*
Penn 1974, *Vertical Movement of Materials in Highrise Buildings*
Peyton 1974, *Collins-Wales Project—A 500 Ft. Tower in Simple Hybrid Construction*
Pozzi 1975, *Planning of Structures and its Relationship with Construction Methods*

Rainer 1973, *Safety Practices*
Ranada 1975, *Design and Construction of the Honolulu Municipal Building*
Robertson 1973, *Design Opportunities in Construction Safety*
Roret 1973, *High Rise Construction in France*

SSPC 1954, *Steel Structures Painting Manual*
SSPC 1964, *Steel Structures Painting Manual*
Selvaraj 1974, *Influence of Construction Sequence on the Stresses in Tall Building Frames*
Simon 1973, *Tall Buildings in Australia—Construction Trends*
Skinner 1971, *50 Storey Office Tower in Hong Kong*
Smith 1973, *Construction Practices in the United Kingdom*
Smith 1973, *The Bank of New Zealand, Concept and Design*

Takenami 1974, *Hotel New Otani Tower Project*
Tank 1973, *Steel-Reinforced Concrete Structure—Prefabricated (HPC)*
Taylor 1973, *Steel Construction*
Taylor 1974, *Joints in Multi-Story Steel Framed Buildings*
Tedesko 1973, *Unusual Solutions*

Wargon 1973, *Centerpoint Project, Sydney*
Wheen 1973, *Positive Control of Construction Floor Loads in Multistorey Concrete Buildings*
Wheen 1974, *Practical Aspects of the Control of Construction Floor Loads in Tall Buildings*
White 1973, *Foundations*

Appendix

High-Rise Building
Data Base

1 INTRODUCTION

Since the inception of the Council, various surveys have been made concerning the location, number of stories, height, material, and the use of tall buildings around the world. The first report on these surveys was published in the Council's Proceedings of the First International Conference (Joint Committee, 1973b). The present document brings the information as up to date as possible.

The purpose of the collection of the data is as follows:

1. For a variety of reasons, one simply needs to know what tall buildings exist, where they are located, their principal characteristics, and the functions they serve. The data base serves as a form of "census" of tall buildings.

2. They are an indicator of the state of economic development and industrialization of a city or country.

3. The information forms a statistical base from which trends can be drawn about material of construction, the use to which tall buildings are put, and where they are built. In addition, it provides a chronological and historical record of tall building construction.

4. It provides a frame of reference for consideration of the impact of natural hazards such as earthquake, flood, and severe wind.

5. Eventually it may form a basis for correlation with other aspects of urban development.

The information is presented, then, for the potential use of: (1) Engineers, architects, and planners; (2) investors, owners, and managers; (3) officials of public and private organizations; and (4) product and material producers and suppliers.

2 SOURCES OF DATA

The survey is based mainly on information collected from individuals in the major cities of the world. The criterion for the selection of a city is generally its population, and at the same time the availability of a Council member or other contact who

415

might provide the needed information. In addition to information collected by questionnaires, data were also obtained from a few selected references (Condit, 1969; Delury, 1980; William Clowes & Sons, Ltd., 1972).

In certain instances the data are incomplete. This is due to the fact that information came from a number of sources. Also, some of the sources reported only the height or number of stories. The remainder of the information had to be obtained separately. Because the data came from so many sources, complete accuracy cannot be guaranteed. Buildings change names from time to time, and this information is sometimes slow in reaching the Council headquarters. In this sense the survey keeps its nature as a "living document."

Additions and corrections to the information presented herein are welcomed, and should be brought to the attention of headquarters staff at Lehigh University.

3 FUTURE WORK

The data base contains a total of 3206 buildings in 405 cities and 62 countries. As contacts are made in more and more cities and countries, the data base becomes more complete. It is anticipated that at an appropriate time an updated report will be made available.

A beginning has been made in collecting information on megastructures (multiuse buildings) and multibuilding developments (such as the Ikebukuru Business Center in Tokyo). Future reports will identify these. A list of "decentralized concentrations" and "new towns" would also be useful.

A longer-term objective is to expand the scope of the surveys and to collect more complete information for each building. The work would be done under the guidance of the Council's Standing Committee 14, "Surveys." As has been described in FitzSimons (1973), there are three major categories of characteristics that are of possible interest. They are as follows:

1. Physical Characteristics: Site (location, size, shape, and geological profile); size (over-all dimensions); shape and disposition; systems (structural, mechanical, and electrical).

2. Economic Characteristics: Land costs; construction costs; operating costs; revenue.

3. Performance Characteristics: Tenant satisfaction; management satisfaction; adequacy of service systems; public acceptability (esthetics, safety).

4 TABULATED DATA

The high-rise building data base is presented in the form of four tables as follows:

Table 1: World's Tallest Buildings. This is a listing of the world's 100 tallest buildings. In common with the other similar tables in this appendix, the information presented includes the country and city in which located, year of completion, number of stories, height (in meters and feet), material, and use of each building. Even where some data are missing, the building is listed if the height, at least, is available.

Table 2: Historical Developments. This table is a chronological listing of the tallest buildings in various categories at the time of their construction. (The characteristic for which the building is the tallest at the time of construction is identified by an asterisk in the table.) Thus, for example, in 1904 the Times Square Building was the tallest building in the world. Also identified in this table are the tallest buildings on each continent.

Table 3: Tallest Building in Each Country. This is a listing of the tallest building in each country, the countries being alphabetically arranged. The city in which the building is located is also identified. A total of 63 countries is represented in the tabulation.

Table 4: Tallest Buildings in Major Cities. This is a listing of the tallest buildings for which data are available in cities around the world. It is the complete information available to the Council. Buildings shorter than nine stories are excluded.

Some additional notes are appropriate with regard to the scope and coverage of the material presented in the tables.

Country. The objective was to include data from every country in the world. Data are reported for 62 countries out of the total of 165 in the world.

City. The cities included in the tabulation for each country (where data are available) are at least the capital and the largest city. (In "city-states," of course, there will be but one listing.) Generally a city is not listed if the population is less than 10,000, even though the definition of "urban area" is customarily as low as 5,000 individuals (Delury, 1980).

Buildings. A "building" is considered to be a structure that is designed for residential, business, or manufacturing purposes (Joint Committee, 1973a). An essential characteristic of a building is that it has floors. A list of the types of tall buildings and their functions is given in Mongraph Chapter PC-1 (Council on Tall Buildings, Committee 28, 1978). The survey does not include structures such as TV towers, even though there may be floors in them.

As noted elsewhere, a "tall building" is not strictly defined by the number of stories or its height. The important criterion is whether or not the design, use, or operation of the building is influenced by some aspect of "tallness." In some design approaches a building is tall if it has three or more stories. In the case of elevators it is tall if it is five stories or more in height. In the various surveys, data were requested on buildings nine or more stories in height. (The reason for this limit is that, in many cities, this is the height at which fire-fighting equipment at street level becomes ineffective.)

5 TRENDS

Table 1 shows that out of the world's 100 tallest buildings, only four are over 100 stories, one in Chicago and three in New York. Eight of the buildings are over 300 m (~1000 ft), three in Chicago, four in New York, and one in Houston, all in the USA. The 300-m mark was passed in 1930 by the Chrysler Building, followed by the Empire State Building in 1931. However, it was not until 1968 that another building over 300 m was completed. All 100 buildings listed are over 190 m in height and have at least 40 stories. The oldest building in this group is the Woolworth Building (22nd tallest) completed in 1913. This means that all 100 were built within the last 70 years. Most of them are framed in steel. Likewise, with few exceptions they are all office buildings. The oldest skyscraper on record was built less than 100 years ago (Home Insurance Building, 1885).

Table 2 shows that all buildings that have held the record for height at the time of construction are framed in steel, except the Monadnock Building, in which load-bearing masonry walls were used (the interior was a braced iron frame). Two of the buildings that hold the record for height in their category are found outside the United States. These are the tallest lightweight concrete and prefabricated concrete buildings, both in Australia.

Although steel is the predominant material used in the world's tallest buildings, an examination of Table 3 shows that concrete is the predominant material for the tall buildings outside the USA. Office buildings are still the tallest in most countries, but there is also a significant number of hotels and apartments in this group.

6 ACKNOWLEDGMENT

The survey itself and this particular update of the report have been prepared by members of the headquarters staff at Lehigh University, working under the leadership of Lynn S. Beedle and George C. Driscoll. Staff members have included the following:

>   Research Assistants: Narciso L. Abaya, Tom Brinker, Perry Green, Reinhard Gsellmeier, Ashok M. Gunda, J. Patrick McHugh.

>   Research Associates: M. Nuray Aydinoglu, Ryszard M. Kowalczyk, Erkan Ozer, Umur Yuceoglu.

>   Undergraduate Students: Barry Anderson, Mark Follet, Randy Haist, Craig Menzemer, Curt Timmerman.

>   Staff: Barbara R. Bryan, Elaine T. Moore, Jamie I. Moyer, Joanne Smyth, Mary E. Snyder.

Special acknowledgment is extended to those who have contributed material and who have responded to the survey. The information is difficult to obtain—as those who have participated in the survey can appreciate. Thus, special thanks are due them. Some were members of the Council. Some were building commissioners. Some were professionals not otherwise connected with the Council. To all we are most grateful.

In the following, the name of each person who participated is listed according to the the country. Unfortunately, during the early days of the survey, complete records were not maintained. As a result, there may be some omissions for which apology is made, and the request that such individuals make their names known to us, in order that suitable acknowledgment may be made at a future time.

Contributors

Argentina *Buenos Aires:* Carlos P. A. Cortes, H. B. Yentel.

Australia *Adelaide:* Ken Dunstan, Public Buildings Department, G. Sved;
          Brisbane: Chief Building Surveyor, Ken Dunstan, Sydney City;

Canberra: K. J. Curtis; *Melbourne:* Chief Building Surveyor, Ken Dunstan, Sydney City; *Sydney:* Chief Building Surveyor, Ken Dunstan, Sydney City, George A. Day.

Austria *Linz:* Theodore Müller.

Bangladesh *Chittagong:* J. R. Choudhury; *Dacca:* J. R. Choudhury.

Barbados *Bridgetown:* Chief Technical Director.

Belgium *Antwerp:* P. Borchgraeve; *Brussels:* P. Borchgraeve.

Brazil *Campinas:* Nilo Amaral; *Caxilas Do Sul:* Hugo Theodorico Grazziotin; *Porto Alegre:* Raul Rego Faillace; *Rio De Janeiro:* Sergio Marques De Souza; *Salvador:* Nilo Amaral; *Santos:* Nilo Amaral, Sergio Marques De Souza; *São Paulo:* Nilo Amaral.

Bulgaria Milcho Brainov.

Canada Michael Gilmor; *Calgary:* Dennis Willson, Norman Massé; *Edmonton:* Norman Massé, S. C. Rodgers; *Hamilton:* Norman Massé; *Montréal:* Paul Drolet, Léopold Laurin, Norman Massé; *Ottawa:* R. F. Buckingham, Corp. City of Ottawa; *Québec:* M. Giroux, Norman Massé; *Toronto:* D. J. MacMaillan, Norman Massé, H. F. Microys, R. Milne, J. Springfield; *Vancouver:* Norman Massé; *Winnipeg:* M. Dmytriw.

Chile *Santiago:* E. Calcagni, R. Saragoni.

Colombia *Medellín:* Jaime Muñoz Duque.

Czechoslovakia *Bratislava:* František Faltus, Svetozár Lichardus; *Brno:* František Faltus; *Bystrica:* František Faltus; *Gottwaldov:* František Faltus; *Kosice:* Svetozár Lichardus; *Liberec:* František Faltus; *Most:* Svetozár Lichardus; *Ostrava:* František Faltus; *Povázská:* František Faltus; *Praha:* František Faltus, Svetozár Lichardus.

Denmark *Copenhagen:* Kampmann, Kierulff & Saxild A/S.

Germany *Berlin:* Karl Kordina; *Braunschweig:* Karl Kordina, Konrad Weiss, Stadtbaurat; *Düsseldorf:* Karl Kordina; *Frankfurt:* Karl Kordina; *Hannover:* Karl Kordina; *Köln:* Karl Kordina, Stahlbau Lavis Offenbach; *München:* D. Jungwirth, Karl Kordina, Lokalbaukommission Munich.

Ghana *Accra:* A. Babah-Alargi.

Greece *Athens:* Demetre N. Coroneos, John Vassiliou; *Halandri* (suburb of Athens): John Vassiliou; *Island:* John Vassiliou; *Rhodes:* John Vassiliou.

Hong Kong *Hong Kong:* Ouyang & Associates, H. K. Cheng, J. J. Robson, E. E. F. Taylor.

Hungary *Budapest:* Iran Erényi.

India *Bangalore:* J. K. Sridhar Rao; *Bombay:* Charles M. Correa, J. K. Sridhar Rao; *Calcutta:* J. K. Sridhar Rao; *Hyderabad:* J. K. Sridhar Rao; *New Delhi:* J. K. Sridhar Rao.

Indonesia *Jakarta:* Poerwo Soeparman.

Iran *Tehran:* Hassan Barmak.

Israel J. Gluck.

Italy Leo Finzi.

Japan *Ashiya:* Masami Sakai; *Fukuoka:* Masami Sakai; *Hiroshima:* M. Wakabayashi; *Kita-Kyushu:* Masami Sakai; *Kobe:* Seigoro Seyama, M. Wakabayashi; *Nagoya:* Masami Saki, Seigoro Seyama, M. Wakabayashi; *Naha:* M. Wakabayashi; *Ohgaki:* Masami Sakai; *Osaka:* Seigoro Seyama, M. Wakabayashi; *Sapporo:* Masami Sakai, M. Wakabayashi; *Sendai:* M. Wakabayashi; *Shizuoka:* Masami Sakai; *Tokyo:* U. Inouye, Kiyoshi Muto, Masami Sakai, Seigoro Seyama, Medori Ueda, M. Wakabayashi; *Yokohama:* Naokazu Koiwai, Masami Sakai, M. Wakabayashi.

Kenya *Mombasa:* Ministry of Works; *Nairobi:* Ministry of Works, J. C. Braithwaite, A. A. Ngotho.

Korea *Seoul:* Won Kim.

Luxembourg Bob Frommes.

Malaysia *Kuala Lumpur:* G. Rahulan.

Mali *Bamako:* Abdoulaye Deyoko.

Mexico *Acapulco:* J. Alvarez Ordoñez; *Mexico City:* J. Alvarez Ordoñez; *Monterrey:* Federico Villarreal, Graciano A. Dieck.

Netherlands *Amsterdam:* J. Strating; *Delft:* H. van Koten; *Eindhoven:* H. van Koten; *The Hague:* H. van Koten; *Rotterdam:* H. van Koten, J. Strating; *Ryswyk:* H. van Koten; *Zandvoort:* H. van Koten.

Norway *Bergen:* Inge Lyse; *Oslo:* Finn Fluge, Inge Lyse; *Trondheim:* Inge Lyse.

Pakistan *Karachi:* Zafar & Associates, Fazluddin Syed.

Papua New Guinea *Lae:* D. S. Mansell; *Port Moresby:* D. S. Mansell.

Peru *Lima:* Carlos Casabonne, Héctor Gallegos, Raúl Rios.

Philippines *Makati:* G. P. Formoso & Assoc., Angel E. Nakpil, Nakpil & Nakpil, Jose M. Zaragoza & Assoc.; *Manila:* G. P. Formoso, Angel E. Nakpil, Nakpil & Nakpil, Jose M. Zaragoza; *Pasay:* Angel E. Nakpil, Nakpil & Nakpil; *Pasig:* G. P. Formoso, Jose M. Zaragoza; *Queyon City:* Angel E. Nakpil.

Poland R. Kowalczyk; *Gdansk:* Z. Pawlowski; *Katowice:* Z. Pawlowski; *Kraków:* Janusz Murzewski; *Lódź:* Z. Pawlowski; *Warsaw:* Z. Pawlowski; *Wroclaw:* Z. Pawlowski.

Romania *Bucarest:* D. Anastasescu; *Timisoara:* D. Anastasescu.

Singapore *Singapore:* G. Rahulan.

South Africa *Cape Town:* A. C. Liebenberg; *Johannesburg:* A. C. Leibenberg; *Pretoria:* A. C. Liebenberg.

Spain Juan Batanero García Geraldo.

Sri Lanka *Colombo:* P. C. Varghese.

Switzerland Gertsch Alain; Karl Keller.

United Arab Emirates *Dubai:* Robert W. Turner.

United Kingdom—England *Liverpool:* City Building Surveyor, J. B. Bennett; *London:* Greater London Council, Scott Wilson Kirkpatrick & Partners, R. J. W. Milne, G. M. J. Williams; *Manchester:* City Architect, Greater London Council.

United Kingdom—Scotland *Glasgow:* A. Coull.

U.S.A. *Akron:* D. H. Sall; *Albany:* Milton Musicus; *Atlanta:* L. Z. Emkin; *Baltimore:* A. K. Bhandari, R. C. Embry, Jr.; *Baton Rouge:* Robert C. Groht; *Bethlehem:* David Fenstermacker, James Halkins, E. K. Muhlhausen, Robert Spillman, C. Zumas; *Birmingham:* Robert J. Schaffhausen; *Boston:* Lee Lim; *Boulder:* Kurt H. Gerstle; *Chicago:* Sherwin Asrow, F. R. Khan, D. Stanton Korista; *Columbia (MO):* James W. Baldwin, Jr.; *Dallas:* Tony Eiler, J. Tom Jones, John L. Tanner III; *Dayton:* James A. Danda; *Detroit:* Lin Y. Huang, Creighton C. Lederer; *El Paso:* Dept. of Public Inspection; *Honolulu:* Howard M. Shima, Ernest T. Yuasa; *Houston:* Walter J. Moore, Jr., Velesa Sullivan; *Huntington:* J. F. Camellerie; *Indianapolis:* Joseph W. Honan; *Jersey City:* Anthony A. Varsalone; *Kansas City (MO):* C. Dale Albert; *Las Vegas:* Clay Hymer; *Los Angeles:* Robert Ayers, Walter A. Brugger, R. L. Hohman; *Milwaukee:* James F. Brengosz, Constantine Diplaris, Alex P. Legrand; *Manchester:* James A. Moynihan; *New York City:* Robert F. R. Ballard, Vincent R. Bray, Raymond C. Heun, Roderick K. Johnson, Emanuel Pisetzner, Leslie E. Robertson, Bob Young; *Oklahoma City:* C. Michael Pugh; *Omaha:* Robert Ramsey; *Philadelphia:* Dominic Sabatini, Al Strobl; *Phoenix:* Ross Hildebrandt, M. J. Sienerth; *Pittsburgh:* J. A. Gilligan; *Portsmouth (VA):* William Froehlich; *Providence:* Vincent Dimase; *Richmond:* F. Ayers Williamson; *Rochester:* Edward J. Ribson; *Rockville:* Kurt Haldane; *St. Louis:* T. V. Galambos; *San Diego:* R. L. Christopherson; *San Francisco:* Henry J. Degenkolb, Charles deMaria, Nancy Garvin; *Seattle:* Alfred Petty; *Toledo:* John Marlais; *Tuscon:* James R. Singleton; *Tulsa:* Betty R. Overton.

U.S.S.R. B. Rubanenko.

Venezuela *Caracas:* Mario Paparoni.

Yugoslavia *Ljubljana* Milos Marincek, Andrj Pogacnik; *Zagreb:* D. Anicic.

7 REFERENCES

Condit, C. W., 1969
  AMERICAN BUILDING, The University of Chicago Press, Chicago, Illinois.
Council on Tall Buildings, Committee 28, 1978
  PHILOSOPHY OF TALL BUILDINGS, Chapter PC-1, Vol. PC of Monograph on Planning and Design of Tall Buildings, ASCE, New York.
Delury, G. E., Ed., 1980
  THE 1980 WORLD ALMANAC, BOOK OF FACTS, Newspaper Enterprise Association, Inc., New York.

Engineering News-Record, 1972
  BUILDING AND HOUSING TRENDS, Engineering News-Record, Vol. 188, No. 3, January, pp. 57–60.
Field Enterprises Education Corporation, 1976
  WORLD BOOK ENCYCLOPEDIA, Field Enterprises Education Corporation, Edition No. 14, p. 411.
FitzSimons, N., 1973
  COMMITTEE ON THE SURVEY OF TALL BUILDINGS, Theme Report, Planning and Design of Tall Buildings, Proceedings of Conference held at Lehigh University, August 1972, Vol. C, ASCE, New York, pp. 87–91.
Joint Committee, 1973a
  COMMITTEE STRUCTURE, PROCEDURE, AND ROSTERS, Fritz Laboratory Report 369.7, Lehigh University, Bethlehem, Pa.
Joint Committee, 1973b,
  PLANNING AND DESIGN OF TALL BUILDINGS, Proceedings of ASCE-IABSE International Conference held at Lehigh University, August 1972, ASCE, New York (5 volumes).
Kidder, F. E., 1911
  ARCHITECTS' AND BUILDERS' POCKET BOOK, John Wiley & Sons, New York.
Ozer, E., Abaya, N., and Driscoll, G., 1973
  TALL BUILDINGS: MAJOR CHARACTERISTICS, Planning and Design of Tall Buildings, Proceedings of Conference held at Lehigh University, August 1972, Vol. C, ASCE, New York, pp. 93–112.
Preece, W. E., Ed., 1968
  ENCYCLOPEDIA BRITANNICA, Encyclopedia Britannica, Inc., 14th Edition, Vol. 20, pp. 620–621.
William Clowes & Sons, Ltd., 1972
  WHITAKER'S ALMANAC 1972, 104th Edition, William Clowes & Sons, Ltd., London, England.

Table 1 The one-hundred tallest buildings in the world

Building	City	Year completed	Number of stories	Height meters	feet	Material	Use
Sears Tower	Chicago	1974	110	443	1454	steel	office
World Trade Center South	New York	1973	110	412	1350	steel	office
World Trade Center North	New York	1972	110	412	1350	steel	office
Empire State	New York	1931	102	381	1250	steel	office
Standard Oil (Indiana)	Chicago	1973	80	346	1136	steel	office
John Hancock	Chicago	1968	100	344	1127	steel	multiple
Texas Commerce Plaza	Houston	1981	75	318	1049	mixed	office
Chrysler	New York	1930	77	319	1046	steel	office
American International	New York	1931	66	290	950	steel	office
First Bank Tower	Toronto	1975	72	285	935	steel	office
Citicorp Center	New York	1977	59	278	914	steel	multiple
Water Tower Place	Chicago	1976	74	262	859	concrete	multiple
United California Bank	Los Angeles	1974	62	260	858	steel	office
40 Wall Tower	New York	1966	66	259	851	steel	office
RCA Rockefeller Center	New York	1933	70	259	850	steel	office
First National Bank	Chicago	1968	60	257	844	steel	office
Transamerica	San Francisco	1972	48	257	843	steel	office
U.S. Steel	Pittsburgh	1970	64	256	841	steel	office
One Chase Manhattan Plaza	New York	1960	60	248	813	steel	office
Pan American	New York	1963	59	246	808	steel	office
Woolworth	New York	1913	57	242	792	steel	office
1 Palac Kultury i Nauki	Warsaw	1955	42	241	790	steel/concrete	office
John Hancock Tower	Boston	1973	60	241	790	steel	offiḟe
M.L.C. Centre	Sydney	1976	70	240	786	concrete	office
Commerce Court West	Toronto	1974	57	239	784	steel	office
Bank of America	San Francisco	1969	52	237	778	steel	office
3 First National Plaza	Chicago	1980	58	236	775	mixed	office
IDS Center	Minneapolis	1972	57	235	772	mixed	office
One Penn Plaza	New York	1972	57	234	766	steel	office
Maine Montparnasse	Paris	1973	64	229	751	mixed	office
Prudential Center	Boston	1964	52	229	750	steel	office
Federal Reserve	Boston	1975	32	228	750	steel	office
Exxon	New York	1971	54	229	750	steel	office

Table 1 The one-hundred tallest buildings in the world (continued)

Building	City	Year completed	Number of stories	Height meters	feet	Material	Use
First International Plaza	Houston	1980	55	228	748	mixed	office
1 Liberty Plaza (U.S. Steel)	New York	1972	54	227	743	steel	office
Ikebukuro Office Tower	Tokyo	1978	60	226	742	steel	office
20 Exchange Place (Citibank)	New York	1931	55	226	741	steel	office
Renaissance 1	Detroit	1977	73	225	739	concrete	hotel
Security Pacific National Bank	Los Angeles	1974	57	225	738	steel	office
Toronto Dominion Bank Tower	Toronto	1967	56	224	736	steel	office
Shinjuku Center	Tokyo	1979	54	223	733	concrete/steel	office
One Astor Plaza	New York	1972	54	222	730	mixed	office
9 West 57th Street	New York	1972	50	221	725	steel	office
Peachtree Center Plaza	Atlanta	1975	71	220	723	concrete	hotel
Carlton Centre	Johannesburg	1973	50	220	722	concrete	office
One Shell Plaza	Houston	1971	52	218	714	concrete	office
First International	Dallas	1973	56	216	710	steel	office
Terminal Tower	Cleveland	1930	52	216	708	steel	office
Union Carbide	New York	1960	52	215	707	steel	office
General Motors	New York	1968	50	214	705	steel	office
Metropolitan Life	New York	1909	50	213	700	steel	office
Atlantic Richfield Plaza A	Los Angeles	1972	52	213	699	steel	office
Atlantic Richfield Plaza B	Los Angeles	1972	52	213	699	steel	office
One Shell Square	New Orleans	1972	51	212	697	steel	office
500 Fifth Avenue	New York	1931	58	212	697	steel	office
Shinjuku Mitsui	Tokyo	1974	55	212	696	steel	office
IBM	Chicago	1973	52	212	695	steel	office
Shinjuku Nomura	Tokyo	1978	53	210	690	steel	office
Neiman-Marcus	Chicago	1981	65	210	690	concrete	multiple
55 Water Street	New York	1972	53	209	687	steel	office
Chemical Bank Trust	New York	1964	50	209	687	steel	office
Three Allen Center	Houston	1980	50	209	685	steel	office
One Houston Center	Houston	1978	46	208	681	mixed	office
Chanin	New York	1929	55	207	680	steel	office
Gulf+Western	New York	1970	44	207	679	steel	office
Southern Bell	Atlanta	1981	46	206	677	concrete	office
Marine Midland Bank	New York	1966	52	206	677	steel	office
Metropolitan Tower	New York	1909	50	206	675	steel	office

Table 1   The one-hundred tallest buildings in the world (continued)

Building	City	Year completed	Number of stories	Height meters	feet	Material	Use
Lincoln Bldg	New York	1930	55	205	673	steel	office
McGraw-Hill	New York	1972	51	204	670	steel	office
1633 Broadway	New York	1972	48	204	670	steel	office
Bank of Oklahoma Tower	Tulsa	1976	50	203	667	steel/concrete	office
Civic Center	Chicago	1965	38	202	662	steel	office
Overseas-Chinese Banking Corp.	Singapore	1976	52	201	660	concrete	office
First City Tower	Houston	1981	49	200	660	mixed	office
Shinjuku Sumitomo	Tokyo	1974	52	200	656	steel	office
Parque Central Torre Oficinas	Caracas	1979	56	200	656	concrete	office
1100 Milam	Houston	1974	47	198	651	steel	office
Michigan + Oak	Chicago	1981	60	198	650	concrete	multiple
Ukraine Hotel	Moscow	1961		198	650	steel/concrete	hotel
American Brands	New York	1967	47	198	648	steel	office
Lake Point Towers	Chicago	1968	70	196	645	concrete	apartment
A.T. & T.	New York	1982	37	197	645	steel	office
1000 Lakeshore Plaza	Chicago	1964	60	195	640	concrete	apartment
Irving Trust	New York	1930	53	195	640	steel	office
345 Park Avenue	New York	1968	44	193	634	steel	office
Yasuda Kasai	Tokyo	1976	43	193	633	steel	office
Belmont Centre	Kuala Lumpur	U.C.	50	193	632	concrete	multiple
Place Ville Marie	Montréal	1962	47	192	630	steel	office
One New York Plaza	New York	1968	50	192	630	steel	office
Grace Plaza	New York	1972	50	192	630	steel	office
Home Insurance Company	New York	1966	45	192	630		office
N.Y. Telephone	New York	1975	40	192	630	steel	office
One Dag Hammar-skjold Plaza	New York	1972	49	191	628		
888 7th Avenue	New York		42	191	628		
First National Bank	Dallas	1964	52	191	625	steel	office
First Wisconsin Center	Milwaukee	1973	42	190	625	steel	office
Burlington House	New York	1969	50	191	625	steel	office
Waldorf Astoria Hotel	New York	1931	47	191	625		hotel
Place Victoria	Montréal	1964	47	190	624	concrete	office

U.C. = Under construction in 1980.

Table 2 Historical developments

Building	City	Year completed	Number of stories	Height meters	feet
Home Insurance	Chicago	1885	10*	55	180
Rand McNally	Chicago	1889	9	37	121
Monadnock	Chicago	1889	17	66	216
Tacoma	Chicago	1889	13*		
American Surety	New York	1895	20*	92*	303
St. Paul	New York	1896	26*	95*	313
Park Row	New York	1898	30*	118*	386
Ingalls	Cincinnati	1903	16	64	210
Times Square	New York	1904		114*	375
Singer	New York	1907	47*	187*	612
Metropolitan Tower	New York	1909	50*	206*	675
Woolworth	New York	1913	60*	242*	792
Chrysler	New York	1929	77*	319*	1046
Empire State	New York	1931	102*	381*	1250
1 Palac Kultury i Nauki	Warsaw	1955	42	241	790
Ilikaii	Honolulu	1963	27	79	260
Australia Square	Sydney	1968	51	183	600
Lake Point Towers	Chicago	1968	70	196	645
John Hancock	Chicago	1968	99	344	1127
One Shell Plaza	Houston	1970	52	218	714
Park Towers	Melbourne	1970	31	90	296
World Trade Center (two buildings)	New York	1972 and 1973	110*	412*	1350
Carlton Centre	Johannesburg	1973	50	220	722
Sears Tower	Chicago	1974	110*	442*	1450
M.L.C.	Sydney	1976	70	240	786

Table 2 Historical developments (continued)

Material	Use	Notes
cast iron, wrought iron, Bessemer steel	office	first iron- and steel-framed curtain-walled skyscraper
steel*	office	first tall building with all-steel frame
masonry *, iron	office	first masonry-iron skyscraper
steel*	office	first use of riveting in a major building
steel*	office	first complete steel skyscraper
steel*	office	
steel*	office	tallest building of the 19th century
concrete*	office	first reinforced concrete skyscraper
steel	office	tallest building ever to have been demolished
steel	office	first building taller than pyramid of Giza (147 m)
steel	office	
steel	office	
steel*	office*	
steel*	office*	the world's tallest for 40 years
mixed*	office	tallest building in Europe
prestressed concrete*	hotel	
lightweight concrete*	multiple	
concrete*	apartment*	tallest apartment building
steel	multiple*	
lightweight concrete*	office	
prefabricated concrete*	apartment	
steel*	office*	
concrete	office	tallest building in Africa
steel*	office*	the world's tallest building
concrete	office	tallest building in Australia

Table 2 Historical developments (continued)

Building	City	Year completed	Number of stories	Height meters	feet
Water Tower Place	Chicago	1976	76	262	859
Renaissance 1	Detroit	1977	73	225	739
Ikebukuro Office Tower	Tokyo	1978	60	226	742
Parque Central Torre Oficinas	Caracas	1979	56	200	656
Texas Commerce Center	Houston	1981	75	318	1049

*The characteristic for which the building is the tallest at the time of construction.

Table 2 Historical developments (continued)

Material	Use	Notes
concrete*	multiple	tallest reinforced concrete building
concrete	hotel*	tallest hotel
steel	office	tallest building in Asia
concrete	office	tallest building in South America
mixed*	office	tallest mixed construction buidling

Table 3 Tallest buildings in each country

Name of country, city, and building	Year completed	Number of stories	Height meters	feet	Material	Use
Argentina						
Buenos Aires						
Atlas	1950	42	141	462	concrete	apartment
Australia						
Sydney						
M.L.C. Centre	1976	70	240	786	concrete	office
Austria						
Vienna						
IAKW	1974	21	118	387	concrete	office
Bangladesh						
Dacca						
BADC	1973	11	40	133	concrete	office
Barbados						
Bridgetown						
National Insurance	1973	6	33	100	concrete	office
Belgium						
Brussels						
Tour Cité Administrative	1970	36	150	492	concrete	office
Brazil						
São Paulo						
Palacio Zarzur Kogan	1960	50	170	557	concrete	office
Bulgaria						
Sofia						
TV Tower	1959	17	105	345	steel/concrete	office
Canada						
Toronto						
Bank of Montréal	1976	72	290	952	steel	office/retail
Chile						
Santiago						
Santiago Central Building B		24	81	268	concrete	office
China						
Shanghai						
International Hotel	1930	24				hotel
Colombia						
Medellín						
Coltejer	1972	37	175	574	concrete	office
Czechoslovakia						
Bratislava						
Shopping Centre		30	113	371	steel/concrete	office
Denmark						
Copenhagen						
K.A.S. Herlev	1973	30	116	380	concrete	hospital
Ecuador						
Quito						
Benalcazar	1973	22	66	216	concrete	office
Egypt						
Cairo						
Belmont	1954	32	102	334	concrete	multiple

Table 3 Tallest buildings in each country (continued)

Name of country, city, and building	Year completed	Number of stories	Height meters	feet	Material	Use
France						
Paris						
Maine Montparnasse	1973	64	229	751	mixed	office
German Democratic Republic						
Leipzig						
Karl Marx Universität	1971	36	153	502	concrete	office
Germany, Federal Republic of						
Frankfurt						
Hochhaus Platz der Republik	1973		143	469	concrete	office
Ghana						
Accra						
Kwame Nkrumah Conf. Centre	1965	12	40	132	concrete	office
Greece						
Athens						
Athens Tower	1972	27	87	285	concrete	office
Hong Kong						
Hong Kong						
Sun Hung Kai Centre	1980	50	183	600	concrete	multiple
Hungary						
Budapest						
Semmelweiss Medical University	1976	26	88	288	concrete	university
India						
Bombay						
Hotel Oberoi Sheraton	1973	35	116	383	concrete	hotel
Indonesia						
Jakarta						
Wisma Nusantara	1972	25			steel/concrete	office
Iran						
Teheran						
Saiman	1973	24	70	230	prefab	apartment
Israel						
Tel-Aviv						
IBM	1978	27	112	363	concrete	office
Italy						
Milan						
Centro Pirelli	1958	35	128	420	concrete	office
Japan						
Tokyo						
Ikebukuro Office Tower	1978	60	226	742	steel	office
Kenya						
Nairobi						
Kenyatta Conference Centre	1974	33	105	345	concrete	office
Korea						
Seoul						
Lotte Hotel	1978	37	138	453	steel/concrete	hotel

Table 3 Tallest buildings in each country (continued)

Name of country, city, and building	Year completed	Number of stories	Height meters	feet	Material	Use
Lebanon						
Beirut						
Shell	1962	20	70	233	concrete	multiple
Luxembourg						
Luxembourg						
Centre Européen	1966	23	71	233	concrete	office
Malaysia						
Kuala Lumpur						
Belmont Centre	U.C.[a]	50	193	632	concrete	multiple
Mali						
Bamako						
Hotel de l'Amitié	1967	17				hotel
Mexico						
Mexico City						
Hotel de Mexico	1972	48	175	573	concrete	hotel
Netherlands						
Rotterdam						
Erasmus University	1969	27	112	367	concrete	office/laboratory
Norway						
Oslo						
Post Office	1975	22	83	272	concrete	office
Pakistan						
Karachi						
Habib Bank Plaza	1971	23	100	328	concrete	office
Papua New Guinea						
Port Moresby						
Ang House	1967	11	45	147	concrete	multiple
Peru						
Lima						
Centro Civico	1976	34	102	335	concrete	office
Philippines						
Makati						
FNCB	U.C.[a]	20	79	259	concrete	office
Poland						
Warsaw						
1 Palac Kultury i Nauki	1955	42	241	790	steel/concrete	office
Portugal						
Lisbon						
Sheraton Hotel	1972	27	85	278	concrete	hotel
Romania						
Bucharest						
Continental Hotel		24	88	289		hotel
Saudi Arabia						
Jeddah						
National Commercial Bank	1981	27	122	400	steel	office
Singapore						
Singapore						
Overseas-Chinese Banking Corp.	1976	52	201	660	concrete	office

Table 3 Tallest buildings in each country (continued)

Name of country, city, and building	Year completed	Number of stories	Height meters	feet	Material	Use
South Africa						
Johannesburg						
Carlton Centre	1973	50	220	722	concrete	office
South Vietnam						
Saigon						
National Library	1970	13	50	163	concrete	office
Spain						
Madrid						
Building of Offices	U.C.[a]	50	175	574	steel	office
Sri Lanka						
Colombo						
Central Wholesale Establishment	1978	14	59	195	concrete	office
Sweden						
Malmö						
K.V. Kronprinsen	1964	29	83	272		multiple
Switzerland						
Bern						
Laboratory-Forschung/ Versuchsa	1965	21	93	305	steel/concrete	laboratory/ office
Taiwan						
Taipei						
Hilton		22			concrete	hotel
Thailand						
Bangkok						
Bangkok Bank	U.C.[a]	35	134	439	concrete	office
Turkey						
Istanbul						
Sheraton Hotel	1973	25	87	285	concrete	hotel
UK						
London						
National Westminster Bank	1980	52	182	600	concrete	office
USA						
Chicago						
Sears Tower	1974	110	443	1454	steel	office
USSR						
Moscow						
Ukraine Hotel	1961		198	650	steel/concrete	hotel
United Arab Emirates						
Dubai						
Dubai International Trade Centre	1978	38	150	500	concrete	multiple
Venezuela						
Caracas						
Parque Central Torre Oficinas	1979	56	200	656	concrete	office
Yugoslavia						
Zagreb						
Vranica	1975	25	85	278	concrete	office

[a]U.C. = Building under construction in 1980.

Table 4 Tallest buildings in major cities

Building	Year Completed	Number of stories	Height meters	feet	Material	Use

Argentina
Buenos Aires

Building	Year Completed	Number of stories	Height meters	feet	Material	Use
Atlas	1950	42	141	462	concrete	apartment
Viamonte No. 147/153	1949	38	125	410	concrete	apartment
U.I.A.	1974	32	116	384	concrete	office
Catalinas Norte	1976	30	115	376	concrete	office
Torre Dorrego	1970	34	111	363	concrete	apartment
Kavanagh	1935	32	105	346	concrete	apartment
Pirelli	1974	26	104	340	concrete	office
Florida 1035/95	1936	32	101	330	concrete	apartment
Brunetta	1962	32	101	330	concrete	office
Dorrego 2699	1967	32	99	325	concrete	apartment
Conurban	1974	27	92	303	concrete	office
Sheraton Hotel	1973	23	91	297	concrete	hotel
Av. Alem, S. Martin y Madero	1969	25	89	292	concrete	hotel
Las Heras 1738/50	1969	30	87	287	concrete	apartment
Posadas 1258/62	1969	28	83	272	concrete	apartment
M.O.P.	1936	23			concrete	office

Australia
Adelaide

Building	Year Completed	Number of stories	Height meters	feet	Material	Use
Grenfell Centre	1975	26	104	340	concrete	office
Ansett Centre	1976	21	75	246	concrete	office
Government Office	1980	19	73	240	concrete/steel	office
A.M.P.	1966	16	73	240	steel/concrete	office
Adelaide House	1970	19	71	232	concrete	office
Education Building	1976	17	67	220	concrete	office
Reserve Bank	1966	17	67	220	concrete	office
State Administration Centre	1966	16	67	220	steel/concrete	office
Communications Centre	1970		67	220	concrete	telephone exchange
King William Tower	1975	19	65	212	concrete	office
Sun Alliance House	1975	19	64	210	concrete	office
I.M.F.C.	1971	19	19	210	concrete	office

Brisbane

Building	Year Completed	Number of stories	Height meters	feet	Material	Use
State Govt. Ins. office	1970	30			steel	office
160 Ann Street	1974	21			concrete	office

Canberra

Building	Year Completed	Number of stories	Height meters	feet	Material	Use
M. L. C. Tower			82	270		
Lakeside Hotel			56	183		hotel
Juliana House			50	163		
Darwin 3			48	158		
AMP Building			48	157		
Russell: Bldg. 14			45	146		

Hobart

Building	Year Completed	Number of stories	Height meters	feet	Material	Use
Wrest Point Casino	1973	21	70	230	concrete	hotel
Commonwealth Centre	1974	18	61	200	concrete	office
A.M.P.	1970	17	61	200	concrete	office
S.B.T.	1975	14	59	196	concrete	office
Public Buildings	1969	17	58	190	concrete	office
Reserve Bank	1977	12	54	177	concrete	office/bank
Hydro Electric Commission	1972	13	49	160	mixed	office
Lands Building	1976	14	47	153	concrete	office
Marine Board	1972	10	46	151	concrete	office
T.G.I.O.	1976	11	37	135	concrete	office
M.L.C.	1962	11	32	107	concrete	office

Melbourne

Building	Year Completed	Number of stories	Height meters	feet	Material	Use
Collins Place—AMP Tower	U.C.	51	183	602		office/hotel
Collins Place—ANZ Tower	1978	47	183	602		office
Nauru House	U.C.	47	137	550	concrete	office
State Bank	U.C.	45	167	548		office
B.H.P. House	1972	41	153	504	steel	office
Commonwealth Bank	1974	35	152	500	steel	office
Collins Wales	1978	36	150	492		office
City Mutual	1973	35	124	406	concrete	office
M.L.C.	1973	35	121	397	concrete	office
Marland House	1972	33	118	390	concrete	office
M.M.B.W.H.O.	1972	24	113	372	mixed	office
A.M.P. St. James	1970		113	372	concrete	office
500 Collins Street	1972	27	105	345	concrete	office
C.R.A.	1962	23	98	324	mixed	office
Park Towers	1970	31	90	296	concrete	apartment
444 St. Kilda Road	1974	13	45	148	concrete	office
T and G Building	1974	19			concrete	office

Sydney

Building	Year Completed	Number of stories	Height meters	feet	Material	Use
M.L.C. Centre	1976	70	240	786	concrete	office
A.M.P. Centre	1973	44	187	614	concrete	office

Table 4 Tallest buildings in major cities (continued)

Building	Year Completed	Number of stories	Height meters	feet	Material	Use
Sydney, Australia (continued)						
Australia Square	1968	51	183	600	concrete	multiple
Hyde Park Square	1976	48	180	588		office
Nauru House	1973	47	168	550	concrete	office
Park Regis	1969	45	140	458	concrete	multiple
City Mutual	1972	35	124	406	concrete	office
National Mutual	1978	38	122	400		office
N.S.W. Bank	1971	32	119	390	steel	office
Royal Exchange Assurance	1967	29	100	329	steel	office
State Govt. McKell Building	1979	27	100	328		office
Goldfields House	1966	29	98	321	steel	office
Central Square	1972	29	92	300	concrete	multiple
CBA Centre	1979	38	14	48		office
Sydney Office Tower	1975	32			concrete	office
State Office Block	1967	30			concrete	office
Norwich Union Insurance	1970	29			steel	office
Exchange Centre	1973	29			concrete	office
Austria						
Linz						
Lentia 2000, A-Block	1976	21	80	262	concrete	multiple
Apartment Houses at Hart	1975	20	67	220	steel/concrete	apartment
Lenauerstrasse	1958	21	64	210	concrete	apartment
Harter Plateau	1973	20	61	200	concrete	apartment
Vierthalerstrasse	1959	18	56	184	concrete	apartment
Niedernhart	1968	17	56	184	concrete	apartment
Vienna						
IAKW	1974	21	118	387	concrete	office
A. K. Bettentrakt	1978	19	116	380	mixed	hospital
Ringturm	1955	20	70	230	concrete	office
A. K. Personalwohnhaus	1967	18	63	207	concrete	apartment
Philipshaus	1964	14	63	207	concrete	office
A. K. Schwestrenschule	1967	18	61	200	concrete	apartment
Chemiehochhaus	1964	11	51	167	mixed	office
United Nations Complex	1978					
Wels						
Maria-Theresiastrasse	1964	27	82	267	concrete	apartment
Zeltweg						
Hochhaus D. OAMG	1960	12	40	131	mixed	office
Bangladesh						
Chittagong						
Sadharan Bima	1969	9	29	94	concrete	office
Dacca						
BADC	1973	11	40	133	concrete	office
WAPDA	1963	11	40	130	concrete	office
Hotel Intercontinental	1965	11	34	112	concrete	multiple
Sadharan Bima	1971	10	34	112	concrete	office
EIC House	1974	11	33	108	concrete	office
Modern Mansion	1970	10	32	106	concrete	office
HBFC	1974	10	31	102	concrete	office
Islam Chamber	1974	10	31	102	concrete	office
Janata Bank	1969	9	31	102	concrete	office
Samabaya Sadan	1964	9	30	100	concrete	office
Hotel Purbani	1965	10	30	98	concrete	multiple
Ispahani	1964	9	30	97	concrete	office
Barbados						
Bridgetown						
National Insurance	1973	6	33	100	concrete	office
Treasury	1966	6	27	92	concrete	government
Cable and Wireless	1972	8	27	92	concrete	office
Holiday Inn	1967	8	27	90	concrete	hotel
Belgium						
Antwerp						
Boerentoren	1930	26	87	285	mixed	motel
B.P.	1963	12	57	187		office
Brussels						
Tour Cité Administrative	1970	36	150	492	concrete	office
Tour du Midi	1967	38	145	476	steel	office
Madou	1965	33	112	367	mixed	office
Manhattan	1972	29	102	335	mixed	hotel/office
World Trade Center Tour No 1	1972	28	102	335	mixed	office
World Trade Center Tour No 2	1973	28	102	335	steel/concrete	office
Brusilia		36	100	328	concrete	apartment

Table 4 Tallest buildings in major cities (continued)

Building	Year Completed	Number of stories	Height meters	feet	Material	Use
Brussels, Belgium (continued)						
International Rogier Center	1960	30	100	328	mixed	office
Tour IBM	1978	23	97	318	steel/concrete	office
Hilton	1967	30	94	308	concrete	hotel
Westbury Hotel	1962	23	80	265	steel/concrete	hotel
I.T.T.	1973	25	80	262		office
Tour Trieste-Louise	1966	23	68	224	mixed	office
Philips	1969	18	68	223	steel	office
Centre Monnaie	1971	15	63	207	concrete	office
Berlaimont		12	55	180		office
Complexe Machtens	1967	18	53	174	steel	apartment
Le Prévoyance Sociale	1957	17	52	171	steel	office
La Royale Belge	1971	10	51	167	steel	office
Galilee	1971	14	50	164	mixed	office
Institut Sociologie ULB	1968	13	49	161	mixed	office
Assurances Générales	1961	12	45	148	steel	multiple
Caisse Patronale	1971	12	40	131	steel	office
Banque Lambert	1965	9	35	115	concrete	office
Crédit Communal	1970	14			mixed	office
Charleroi						
Centre Albert	1966	25	82	269	mixed	office
Ghent						
Zonneweelde	1966	21	70	230	concrete	apartment
Liège						
Résidence Simenon	1963	25	73	239	concrete	apartment
Cité Administrative	1968	18	67	220	steel	office
Mons						
Nurse Training Center	1969	18	64	210	mixed	apartment
Ostend						
Europacentrum	1969	35	100	328	concrete	apartment
Brazil						
Belo Horizonte						
Ed. Acaiaca	1940	30	120	394	concrete	office
Othon Palace Hotel	1978	32	110	330	concrete	hotel
Ed. Banco Real	1965	25	80	264	concrete	office
Banco Com. Indust. Minas Gerai	1955	15	75	246	concrete	office
Ed. Vicente de Araujo	1970	20	70	231	concrete	office
Hotel del Rey	1962	18	62	203	concrete	hotel
Ed. Boa Esperanca	1960	15	55	180	concrete	multiple
Ed. Niemeyer	1958	13	45	148	concrete	apartment
Campinas						
Ed. José Guernelli	1956	24	60	197	concrete	apartment
Ed. Cev Azvl	1972	23	57	187	concrete	apartment
Caxias do Sul						
Parque do Sol	1975	36	117	384	concrete	apartment
Galeria JC	1974	29	95	312	concrete	apartment
Guadalupe	1974	29	93	305	concrete	apartment
Estrela	1973	22	71	233	concrete	office
Marina	1974	20	62	203	concrete	apartment
Da Ercilia	1965	18	59	194	concrete	apartment
Muratory	1969	16	54	177	concrete	apartment
Aplub	1972	16	54	177	concrete	apartment
Alfred Palace	1977	15	54	177	concrete	hotel
Banco do Brasil	1976	15	54	177	concrete	office
São José	1976	15	54	177	concrete	office
Porto Alegre						
Centro Adminis. do Estado	U.C.	33	119	390	concrete	office
Santa Cruz	1960	32	115	377	steel	multiple
Coliseu	1972	28	90	295	concrete	office
Banco do Estado do RGS	1966	23	85	279	concrete	office
Galeria do Rosario	1970	27	84	276	concrete	multiple
Cacique	1960	25	84	276	concrete	multiple
Formac	1962	26	81	266	concrete	office
Jaguaribe	1959	25	77	253	concrete	apartment
Mal. Trpompovski	1959	23	77	253	concrete	apartment
Vila Rica	1968	21	70	230	concrete	apartment
Galeria di Primio Beck	1965	20	65	213	concrete	office
Rio de Janeiro						
Rio Sul Center	1980	50	163	538	concrete	office
Ed. Lineu de Paula Machado	1980	34	138	453	concrete	office
Ed. Banerj	1965	34	136	446	concrete	office
Ed. Arenida Centra	1958	34	136	446	steel	office
Ed. São Sebastiao	1980	45	148	438	concrete	office

Table 4 Tallest buildings in major cities (continued)

Building	Year Completed	Number of stories	Height meters	feet	Material	Use
Rio de Janeiro, Brazil (continued)						
Ed. Frederico Bokel	1970	33	120	394	concrete	office
Ed. Christian Barnard	1972	33	120	394	concrete	office
Hotel Nacional	1972	36	113	373	concrete	hotel
Hotel Meridien	1976	40	110	363	concrete	office
Ed. de Paoli	1957	30	110	361	concrete	office
A Noite	1928	22	77	253	concrete	office
Salvador						
Apolo XXVIII	1973	32	90	295	concrete	apartment
Marte	1973	24	70	230	concrete	apartment
Quinta da Graça	1972	23	70	230	concrete	apartment
Florentino	1972	22	65	213	concrete	apartment
Parque Julio Cesar	1972	22	65	213	concrete	apartment
Solar 2 de Julho	1970	21	63	206	concrete	apartment
Valerio Carvalho	1970	19	55	180	concrete	apartment
Pedro Ribeiro	1972	18	55	180	concrete	apartment
Fund. Politecnica	1968	17	50	164	concrete	office
Braulio Xavier	1964	16	48	157	concrete	office
Santos						
Edif. Excelsior	1970	19	62	204	concrete	office/apartment
Edif. Kennedy	1971	19	58	192	concrete	office
Edif. Holiday	1965	19	58	190	concrete	apartment
Ed. Pombeva	1955	18	57	188	concrete	apartment
Ed. Crumau	1955	18	57	188	concrete	apartment
Ed. Universo Palace	1972	22	57	187	concrete	apartment
Tertulta	1970	18	55	180	concrete	apartment
Edif. Igarata	1969	19	53	175	concrete	apartment
Edif. Pedro 2	1970	15	53	175	concrete	office/apartment
Edif. Romoel	1973	18	52	171	concrete	apartment
Edif. Preludio	1967	16	53	164	concrete	apartment
São Paulo						
Palacio Zarzur Kogan	1960	50	170	557	concrete	office
Banco do Estado	1947	35	150	492	concrete	office
Bank of Brazil	1955	24	134	440	concrete	office
Italia	1970	45	120	394	concrete	office
Copan	1959	37	115	376	concrete	office
Conde de Prates	1955	33	112	366	concrete	office
Moreira Salles	1959	32	100	328	concrete	office
Secretaria da Fazenda	1950	23	100	328	concrete	office
San Siro	1968	36	91	298	concrete	parking
Grande São Paulo	1971	25	85	279	concrete	office
Edificio Andraus		30				office/shops
Bulgaria						
Blagoevgrad						
Apartment houses (2)	1976	12	39	128	concrete	apartment
Administration Building	1972	11	38	125	concrete	office
Apartment house	1970	10	33	108	concrete	apartment
Hotel	1972	10	33	108	concrete	hotel
Administration Building	1970	9	30	98	concrete	office
Apartment houses (6)	1977	9	30	98	concrete	apartment
Commercial/Service Building	1970	9	26	85	concrete	office/shops
Botevgrad						
Hotel	U.C.	14	42	138	concrete	hotel
Clock Tower			33	108	stone/brick	monument
Bourgas						
Hotel Bulgaria	1977	20	65	213	steel/concrete	hotel
Apartment houses	1972	18	60	197	concrete	apartment
Apartment houses	1965	14	47	154	concrete	apartment
Apartment houses	1977	15	43	141	brick	apartment
Administration Building	1973	13	41	135	concrete	office
Administration Building	1960	12	38	125	concrete	office
Railway Station Tower	1906	8	36	118	stone	clock tower
Hospital	1967	11	35	115	concrete	hospital
Hotel	1960	9	30	98	steel/brick	hotel
Clock Tower	1700	5	20	66	stone	clock tower
Gabrovo						
Hostel	1971	20	60	197	concrete	hostel
Hotel	1973	15	45	148	concrete	hotel
House of Technics	1976	13	45	148	concrete	office
Hotel	1973	13	42	138	concrete	hotel
Hospital	1968	12	40	131	concrete	hospital
Administration Building	1973	10	30	98	concrete	office
Jambol						
Church Tower-Sveti Georgi	1890		75	246	stone/brick	church
Apartment house	1977	15	45	148	concrete	apartment
Hostel	1976	14	44	144	concrete	hostel
Apartment house	1971	14	42	138	concrete	apartment
Hotel	1969	13	42	138	concrete	hotel/rest.

Table 4 Tallest buildings in major cities (continued)

Building	Year Completed	Number of stories	Height meters	feet	Material	Use
Jambol, Bulgaria (continued)						
Apartment house	1975	13	40	131	concrete	apartment
Apartment houses (5)	1971	11	37	121	concrete	apt./shops
Administration Building	1972	10	29	95	concrete	office
Kardjali						
Hotel Arpezos	1978	16	47	154	concrete	hotel
Apartment house	1964	11	36	118	concrete	apartment
Apartment houses (2)	1978	11	36	118	concrete	apartment
Apartment houses/shops (4)	1977	12	35	115	concrete	apt./shops
Hospital	1977	10	30	98	concrete	hospital
Apartment house	1964	9	30	98	masonry	apartment
Kjustendil						
Apartment houses (7)	1977	15	45	148	concrete	apartment
Administration Building	1974	12	38	125	concrete	office
Lovech						
Apartment house	1977	14	43	141	concrete	apartment
Apartment houses (3)	1977	11	37	121	concrete	apartment
Hospital	1975	10	36	118	concrete	hospital
Apartment houses (8)	1969	10	34	112	concrete	apartment
Apartment houses (4)	1977	9	29	95	concrete	apartment
Mihajlovgrad						
Administration Building (2)	1970	10	40	131	conc./brick	office
Apartment houses (2)	1976	10	34	112	conc./brick	apt./rest.
Apartment houses (2)	1976	9	30	98	conc./brick	apt./rest.
Pazardjik						
Apartment houses (2)	1971	12	40	131	concrete/brick	apt./rest.
Clock Tower	U.C.		36	118	stone/brick	clock
Pernik						
Apartment houses (3)	U.C.	18	48	157	concrete	apartment
Adimistration Building	1975	15	40	131	concrete	office
Apartment houses (2)	1970	12	34	112	concrete	apartment
Administration Building	1973	11	39	98	concrete	office
Apartment houses (9)	1974	9	26	85	concrete	apartment
Pleven						
Apartment house	1970	17	56	184	concrete	apartment
Administration Building	1978	19	54	177	concrete	off./labs
Apartment houses (6)	1972	16	50	164	concrete	apartment
Apartment houses (4)	1976	14	45	148	concrete	apartment
Hotel	1966	14	40	131	concrete	hotel
View Pleven Epopee	1977		40	131	concrete	museum
Apartment house	1974	11	33	108	concrete	apartment
Administration Building	1962	10	32	105	concrete	office
Apartment houses (3)	1978	10	30	98	concrete	apartment
Hotel	1978	10	30	98	concrete	hotel
Plovdiv						
Apartment houses	1975	17	50	164	concrete	apartment
Apartment house	1978	15	48	157	concrete	apartment
Hotel Maritsa	1966	13	47	154	concrete	hotel
Administration Building	1968	12	40	131	concrete	office
Administration Building	1968	12	40	131	conc./alum.	office
Apartment house	1963	11	33	108	concrete	apartment
Razgrad						
Apartment houses (4)	1975	16	48	157	concrete	apartment
Apartment house	1974	13	39	128	concrete	apartment
Rousse						
Hotel Riga	1974	22	71	233	concrete	hotel
Administration Building	1977	17	61	200	concrete	office
Apartment houses (4)	1973	15	50	164	concrete	apartments
Manufacturing	1971	14	48	157	steel	workshops
Apartment houses (2)	1969	12	42	138	concrete	apartment
Administration Building	1973	10	28	92	concrete	office
Samokov						
Apartment houses	1977	9	27	88	steel/brick	apt./shops
Sliven						
Hotel Sliven	1973	16	60	197	steel/concrete	hotel
Apartment houses (3)	1977	13	43	141	concrete	apartment
Apartment houses (4)	1977	12	40	131	concrete	apartment
Apartment house	1976	11	37	121	concrete	apartment
Sofia						
TV Tower	1959	17	105	345	steel/concrete	office
Hotel Moskva	1976	23	78	256	concrete	hotel

Table 4 Tallest buildings in major cities (continued)

Building	Year Completed	Number of stories	Height meters	feet	Material	Use
Sofia, Bulgaria (continued)						
Administration Building	1969	20	70	230	concrete	office
Trade Unions/Administration	1978	21	68	223	concrete	office
Vitosha	1978	21	68	223	concrete	hotel
Administration Building	1968	17	56	184	concrete	office
Gynaecological Institute	1976	14	53	174	concrete	hospital
Apartment houses (3)	1971	16	50	164	concrete	apartment
Hotel Pliska	1966	15	48	157	concrete	hotel
Apartment houses (3)	1978	14	42	138	concrete	apartment
Stara Zagora						
Hospital	1978	18	58	190	concrete	hospital
House of the Builders	U.C.	15	50	164	concrete	office
House of Trade Unions	1978	15	45	148	concrete	office
Apartment house	1975	15	45	148	concrete	apartment
Apartment houses (4)	1973	14	42	138	concrete	apartment
Svishtovy						
Hospital	1977	11	42	138	brick	hospital
Apartment houses (3)	1978	11	38	125	concrete	apartment
Administration Building		10	38	125	concrete	office
Apartment house	1978	9	33	108	concrete	apartment
Varna						
Hotel Cherno More	1978	22	74	243	conc./alum.	hotel/rest.
Hotel International	1968	18	60	197	conc./alum.	hotel/rest.
Apartment houses (2)	1974	17	52	171	concrete	apartment
Apartment houses (4)	1976	16	48	157	concrete	apartment
Apartment houses (4)	1972	15	46	151	concrete	apartment
Apartment houses (8)	1978	14	45	148	concrete	apartment
House of Scientists	1961	14	45	148	concrete	hotel
Apartment houses (3)	1972	13	40	131	concrete	apartment
Internat. House of Journ.	1964	10	40	131	concrete	hotel
Palace of Sport	1968		21	69	conc./alum.	sport/fest.
Veliko Tirnovo						
Hotel Etar	U.C.	15	46	151	concrete	hotel
Apartment house	1978	14	41	135	concrete	apartment
Administration Building	1969	11	40	131	concrete	office
Apartment houses (3)	1978	10	32	105	concrete	apartment
Vidin						
Apartment houses (2)	1973	18	60	197	concrete	apartment
Administration Building	1970	17	55	180	concrete	office
Hotel	1975	15	55	180	concrete	hotel
Apartment houses (3)	1969	13	36	118	concrete	apartment
Apartment houses (2)	1973	9	30	98	concrete	apartment
Vratsa						
Apartment houses (3)	1978	18	60	197	concrete	apartment
Hostel	1966	13	52	171	concrete	hostel
Apartment house	1970	9	32	105	concrete	apt./rest.
Hotel	1974	9	28	92	conc./alum.	hotel
Tower	17 C	3	14	46	stone/wood	monument
Tower	17 C	3	11	36	stone/wood	monument
Canada						
Calgary						
Norcen Tower	1976	33	155	508	steel/concrete	office
Scotia Tower	1975	38	154	504	steel/concrete	office
Toronto Dominion Square- North	1976	34	141	463	steel/concrete	office
Shell Tower	1977	34	140	460	steel/concrete	office
Toronto Dominion Square- South	1976	33	137	449	steel/concrete	office
Three Bow Valley Square	1979	35	132	432	steel/concrete	office
Sun Oil	1975	34	121	397		office
Western Centre	1971	40	117	385		apartment
Two Bow Valley Square	1975	39	115	378	steel/concrete	office
Mobil Tower		29	113	369		
One Palliser Square		28	107	350		
Mount Royal House		34	101	330		
Standard Life		25	100	327		
Place Concorde (Twin Towers)		36	98	321		
Penthouse Towers		34	95	312		
International Hotel		34	92	301		
Two Calgary Place		24	91	300		
Edmonton						
AGT Tower	1971	34	134	441	concrete	office
Toronto Dominion Bank Tower	1976	30	122	400	steel/concrete	office

Table 4 Tallest buildings in major cities (continued)

Building	Year Completed	Number of stories	Height meters	feet	Material	Use
Edmonton, Canada (continued)						
CN Towers	1966	26	111	365	concrete	apartment
Royal Trust Tower		25	99	325	steel/concrete	office
Edmonton House	1971	34	96	315	concrete	apartment
Century Place	1974	22	81	267	steel/concrete	office
Canada Towers	1978	45			concrete	
Avord Arms	1966	27			concrete	apartment
Chateau Lacombe	1968	26			concrete	hotel
Macdonald Place		26			concrete	apartment
Imperial Oil	1970	24			concrete	multiple
Centennial	1967	22			concrete	office
Garneau Towers	1965	20			concrete	apartment
Cambridge	1969	18			concrete	office
Viking Arms Apartments		15			concrete	apartment
Guelph						
Student housing	1969	12			masonry	dormitory
Halifax						
Fenwick Towers		31	91	300		
Barrington Street Project		15			concrete	apartment
Hamilton						
Stelco Tower	1973	26	107	350	steel/concrete	office
London						
Senior Citizens Apartments	1969	9	25	81	masonry	apartment
Montréal						
Place Ville Marie	1962	47	192	630	steel	office
Place Victoria	1964	47	190	624	concrete	office
Royal Bank	1962	45	187	612	steel	office
Canadian Imp. Bank of Commerce	1962	43	184	604	steel	office
Pl. Desjardins la Tour du Sud	1976	40	152	498	concrete	multiple
Chateau Champlain Hotel	1966	37	143	470	steel/concrete	hotel
Holiday Inn Hotel	1977	38	137	450	concrete	hotel
C.I.L. House	1962	32	131	430	steel	office
Pl. Desjardins la Tour du l'Est	1976	32	130	428	concrete	multiple
Le Port Royal	1964	33	130	425	concrete	apartment
Le Cartier Apartments	1964	32	130	425	concrete	apartment
Tour Terminal	1966	30	122	400	steel	office
Royal Bank		22	121	397		
Banque Canadienne National		32	119	390		
Sun Life		26	119	390		
Place Internatl de l'Aviation	1975	28	116	380	concrete	office
Place du Canada		33	113	372		
Pl. Desjardins la Tour du Nord	1976	27	108	355	concrete	multiple
Le Chatel	1967	30	107	350	concrete	apartment
Alexis Nihom Plaza		33	101	331		
Bell Telephone		22	99	324		
Le Cartier	1965	31	132	315	steel	office
Résidence Mont Carmel	1978	16	52	170	concrete	apartment
La Tourelle	1979	14	49	161	concrete	office
Tour Crown Trust	1978	15	47	153	concrete	office
La Villa du Pont	1978	13	37	120	concrete	apartment
Habitations Jarry	1979	10	30	100	concrete	apartment
Habitations Terrassee Ontario A	1978	11	29	97	concrete	apartment
Habitations Montmorency	1978	9	29	94	steel	apartment
Complex Olympic	1976				concrete	stadium
Ottawa						
Tower C-Place de Ville	1971	29	112	368	steel	hotel
Place Bell Canada	1972	26	97	318	steel	office
Holiday Inn	1972	28	94	308	concrete	hotel
DBS Tower	1973	26	94	308	concrete	office
Skyline Hotel	1967	25	87	286	concrete	hotel
L'Esplanade Laurier (2 towers)		22	87	285		
DND Headquarters	1972	22	84	275	concrete	office
Arts Tower-Carleton Univ.	1971	23	77	253	concrete	school
Bromley Square	1972	26	70	231	concrete	apartment
Riverside Terrace	1971	26	70	231	concrete	apartment
Island Park Towers	1968	24	68	222	concrete	apartment
Twin Towers-The Highlands		24	67	219	concrete	apartment
Park West	1971	23	64	210	concrete	apartment
Québec						
Complexe G	1972	33	126	415	concrete	office
Place Haute Ville	1975	32	107	350	concrete	office

Table 4 Tallest buildings in major cities (continued)

Building	Year Completed	Number of stories	Height meters	feet	Material	Use
Québec, Canada (continued)						
Le Concorde	1974	29	91	300	concrete	hotel
Place Québec	1974	23	85	280	concrete	hotel
Place Montcalm	1975	26	82	270	concrete	hotel
Québec Hilton	1974	26	81	265	concrete	hotel
Place de la Capitale	1974	21	80	263	concrete	office
Edifice Price	1930	18	77	254	steel	hotel
Price Building	1930	18	77	254	steel	office
Immeubles St-Cyrille	1974	18	76	248	concrete	office
Banque de Montréal	1971	21	73	240	concrete	office
Chateau Frontenac	1921	21	73	240	steel	hotel
Edifice Montcalm	1970	21	73	240	concrete	office
Le Méridien	1975	22	65	213	concrete	hotel
La Laurentienne	1963	14	56	185	steel	office
Le Louisbourg	1975	21	55	180	concrete	apartment
Samuel Holland	1971	18	52	170	concrete	apartment
Regina						
Roberts Plaza Apartments		20			concrete	apartment
Richmond						
Park Tower Apartments		17			concrete	apartment
Toronto						
First Bank Tower	1975	72	285	935	steel	office
Commerce Court West	1974	57	239	784	steel	office
Toronto Dominion Bank Tower	1967	56	224	736	steel	office
Toronto Dominion	1969	46	185	609	steel	office
Royal Trust Tower	1969	46	183	600	steel	office
Royal Bank Plaza	1976	41	173	567	concrete	office
Manufacturers Life Centre	1971	51	166	545	concrete	apartment
Manulife Centre	1973	55	160	525	concrete	off./retail
Simpson Tower	1968	33	148	486	concrete	apartment
Two Blook Street West	1974	34	146	480	concrete	off./retail
Old Bank of Commerce	1930	34	145	477	steel	office
Two Blook Street East		35	135	442		
Harbour Castle Hotel		38	134	438		
Four Seasons Sheraton Hotel	1972	45	130	428	concrete	hotel
Commercial Union Tower	1974	32	128	419	steel/concrete	office
Leaside Towers	1970	43	125	410	concrete	apartment
Royal York Hotel		28	124	407		
Harbour Square Apartments		34	123	403		
Eaton Centre	1976	31	122	400	steel/concrete	office
390 Bay Street	1972	33	120	394	steel	office
100 Bloor Street West		29	113	370		
Hyatt Regency Hotel		31	111	365		
Royal Bank Plaza	1976	26	111	365	concrete	office
Carlton Court		29	108	355		
Summerhill Square Apartments		37	108	354		
Hotel Toronto		32	107	350		
Macdonald Block		24	106	349		
York Centre	1971	27	105	343	steel	office
Richmond Adelaide Centre	1966	25	102	333	concrete	office
Toronto Star	1970	25	102	333	concrete	office
Sutton Place	1967	33	100	328	mixed	hotel
City Hall	1965	27	99	326	concrete	government
Commonwealth Towers	1967	32	85	280	concrete	apartment
Mounted Police Headquarters		12			concrete	headquarters
Vancouver						
Harbour Centre	1976	28	146	479	concrete	office
Royal Bank Tower		37	143	468		
Scotiabank Tower		36	138	451		
200 Granville Square		30	123	403		
Toronto Dominion Bank Tower	1970	32	122	400	steel	off./retail
Sheraton Landmark Hotel		41	120	394		
First Bank Tower		30	118	386		
Hyatt Regency Hotel		36	109	357		
Hotel Vancouver		22	108	352		
Oceanic Plaza		26	104	342		
Board of Trade Tower		26	104	342		
Macmillan Bloedel		28	104	340		
Guinness Tower		23	100	328		
Marine Building		21	98	321		
Four Seasons Hotel		30	95	311		
Martello Tower		31	91	300		
West Coast Transmission	1969	12	82	270	steel/concrete	office

Table 4 Tallest buildings in major cities (continued)

Building	Year Completed	Number of stories	Height meters	feet	Material	Use
Canada (continued)						
Winnipeg						
Trizec	1980	32	148	494	concrete	office
Richardson		34	134	439	concrete	office
55 Nassau Street		39	108	354	concrete	apartment
York Estates	1979	24	96	319	concrete	apartment
North Star Inn		36	91	300	concrete	hotel
1 Evergreen Place		32	90	294	concrete	apartment
Legislative Building	1920		76	253		office
Holiday Tower-North	1971	27	75	250	concrete	apartment
Holiday Tower-South	1973	27	75	250	concrete	apartment
Chateau 100	1970	22	75	250		apartment
Terra Heights Apartments	1972	14	45	146	concrete	apartment
Mercantile Bank	1974	10	44	144	concrete	bank
Chile						
Osorno						
Kauak		20	58	191	concrete	multiple
Rancagua						
General Freire		20	57	188	concrete	apartment
Santiago						
Santiago Central Bldg. B		24	81	268	concrete	office
Tajamar-Tower A	1967	29	74	245	concrete	apartment
Endesa	1968	21	71	234	concrete	office
Unidad Vecinal Providencia	1968	24	70	230	concrete	apartment
San Luis-Towers C1 and C2		25	68	224	concrete	apartment
San Borja-Tower 22	1972	25	68	223	concrete	office
San Borja-Towers 1 to 3	1971	21	63	206	concrete	apartment
Los Trabajadores	1970	15	58	192	concrete	office
Serrano		18	58	189	concrete	office
San Borja-Tower 12	1971		58	189	concrete	apartment
Ines de Suarez	1972	20	57	188	concrete	apartment
San Borja-Towers 4 to 8	1971	22	57	186	concrete	apartment
San Borja-Tower 11	1971	21	56	184	concrete	apartment
Baquedano	1970	21	54	178	concrete	apartment
Tajamar-Tower C	1967	20	54	177	concrete	apartment
Seminario	1968	19	52	171	concrete	apartment
Rotonda Vitacura	1971	16	45	146	concrete	apartment
Viña del Mar, Chile						
Hexagonal Tower		23	61	199	concrete	apartment
China						
Beijing						
Beijing Hotel	1974	17				hotel
Shanghai						
International Hotel	1930	24				hotel
Colombia						
Bogotá						
Las Americas	1974	47	174	571	concrete	office
La Nacional		47	171	561	concrete	office
Avianca	1969	41	161	528	concrete	office
Colseguros	1974	36	140	459	concrete	office
Bogotá Hilton	1970	38	123	403	concrete	office
Seguros Tequendama	1970	38	122	400	concrete	office
Edif. el Parque	1972	38	117	384	concrete	apartment
Seguros Fenix		36	115	377	concrete	office
Seguros Colombia	1974		106	348	concrete	office
Torres de Fenicia	1970	31	100	328	concrete	apartment
Bavaria	1966	29	89	292	concrete	office
San Martin	1972	33	88	289	concrete	office
Panorama	1972	29	77	253	concrete	apartment
Edif. Edisa	U.C.	26	72	236	concrete	apartment
Edif. Forfa	U.C.	24	72	236	concrete	apartment
Office Building	1975	22	58	190	mixed	office
Medellin						
Coltejer	1972	37	175	574	concrete	office
Cafeterels Band	1975	36	130	426	concrete	office
Camara de Comercio	1974	32	102	335	concrete	office
Nacional		25	80	262	concrete	office
Coltabaco	1968	23	74	243	concrete	office
London Bank	1972	22	70	230	concrete	office
EDA Building	1970	20	64	210	concrete	office
Fenalco	1971	20	64	210	concrete	office
Casablanca	1968	20	58	190	concrete	apartment
Villanueva	1973	20	58	190	concrete	apartment
Czechoslovakia						
Bratislava						
Shopping Centre		30	113	371	steel/concrete	office
Czech Television Building		27	108	354	mixed	office

Table 4 Tallest buildings in major cities (continued)

Building	Year Completed	Number of stories	Height meters	feet	Material	Use
Bratislava, Czechoslovakia (continued)						
Press Centre	1977	27	104	341	steel/concrete	office
Highrise TV Centre	1975	29	103	338	steel/concrete	office
TV	1974	29	103	337	steel/concrete	TV/office
Military Hostel		25	82	269	steel/concrete	hotel
University in Bratislava		24	78	256	concrete	school
Faculty of Civil Engineering		22	72	236	concrete	school
Slovak Technical University	1970	22	72	236	concrete	school
Broadcast-Radio	1978	17	56	185	steel/concrete	office
Brno						
Administrative Building	1969	19	53	174		
Gottwaldov						
Office Building	1937	16	72	236	concrete	office
Kosice						
Hospital Monoblock		19	83	272	steel	hospital
Liberec						
SVUT		18	78	256	steel/concrete	office
Research Institute	1965	18	54	177	steel/concrete	res. inst.
Martin						
Matice Slovenska	1965	14	42	138	concrete	office
Most						
Technical Services SHD		23	86	282	steel/concrete	office
Ostrava						
Apartment House	1969	22	60	197		
Povazska Bystrica						
Office Building		13	56	185	steel/concrete	office
Prague						
Motokov	1977	27	105	346	steel/concrete	office
Telecommunication Building		18	80	262	steel/concrete	office
Residential Building	1973	23	65	213	concrete	apartment
Hotel Olympic	1974	21	63	207	concrete	hotel
Computer Research Inst.	1965	17	51	167	concrete	research
Faculty of Civil Engineering	1972	15	50	164	concrete	school
Mathematical & Physical Faculty	1975	13	43	141	steel/concrete	school
Apartment House		21			concrete	apartment
Denmark						
Aalborg						
Vanforehojhuset	1964	18	50	164	concrete	apartment
Arhus						
Langenaeshus		14	42	138	concrete	apartment
Marselisvaenget	1969	14	42	138	concrete	apartment
Copenhagen						
K.A.S. Herlev	1973	30	116	380	concrete	hospital
Domus Vista	1969	30	90	295	concrete	apartment
Hotel Scandinavia	1973	27	84	276	concrete	hotel
Royal Hotel	1970	22	70	230	concrete	hotel
Rigshospitalet	1970	17	70	230	mixed	hospital
Falkonercentret	1958	17	60	197	concrete	hotel
Lyngby Storcenter	1973	14	48	157	concrete	mutliple
Hoje Gladsaxe	1966	16	45	148	prefab	apartment
Vanforehjemmet	1960	14	40	131	concrete	apartment
Milestedet	1956				concrete	apartment
Esbjerg						
Ungdomsbo	1975	14	42	138	concrete	apartment
Vestbo	1967	10	29	95	concrete	apartment
Haderslev						
Varbergparken	1973	11	33	108	concrete	apartment
Sitkeborg						
Silkeborghus		14	42	138	concrete	apartment
Ecuador						
Guayaquil						
Banco del Pichincha	1973	18	54	177	concrete	office
Gran Passaje	1969	16	48	157	concrete	multiple
Calero	1950	14	42	138	concrete	multiple
Noboa	1972	14	42	138	steel	office
Caja del Seguro	1969	12	36	118	concrete	office
Reed y Reed	1964	12	36	118	concrete	multiple
Quito						
Benalcazar	1973	22	66	216	concrete	office

Table 4 Tallest buildings in major cities (continued)

Building	Year Completed	Number of stories	Height meters	feet	Material	Use
		Quito, Ecuador (continued)				
Granda Centeno	1973	20	60	197	concrete	multiple
Caja del Seguro	1961	14	50	164	concrete	office
Torres de la Colon	1972	16	48	157	concrete	multiple
Hospital Militar	1973	14	42	138	concrete	hospital
Salazar Gomez	1972	14	42	138	concrete	multiple
Filantropica	1973	12	36	118	concrete	office
Jaramillo Arteaga	1972	12	36	118	concrete	office
Previsora Norte	1967	12	36	118	concrete	office
Hotel Colon	1971	10	30	98	concrete	hotel
Hotel Quito	1961	10	30	98	concrete	hotel
Palacio Legislativo	1960	10	30	98	concrete	office
		Salinas				
Tiburon	1972	16	48	157	concrete	apartment
Torre Blanca						
		Egypt				
		Aswan				
New Cataract Hotel	1962				concrete	hotel
		Cairo				
Belmont	1954	32	102	334	concrete	multiple
TV Tower	1957	30	100	328	concrete	
Sheraton		26	100	328	concrete	hotel
El Nasr Tower	1974	25	84	280	concrete	
Meridian	1974		72	238	concrete	hotel
Maaroof	1974	18	64	210	concrete	office
Nile Hilton	1958		60	196	concrete	hotel
MISR Apartments	1956	18	58	190	concrete	apartment
Wahba	1954	18	58	190	concrete	apartment
Ministry of Agriculture	1956	17	58	190	concrete	office
Cleopatra	1960	15	55	180	concrete	multiple
Immobilia	1936	15	55	180	concrete	apartment
Office Building	1972	14	55	180	concrete	office
Al Ahram	1968	14	50	164	concrete	
Office Building	1970	13	45	148	concrete	office
El Nile Hotel	1965	12	45	148	concrete	hotel
Ministry of Labour	1972	12	45	148	concrete	office
Mobil Oil	1957	11	45	148	concrete	office
Shawarbi Block	1925				concrete	apartment
		Giza				
El Galaa	1974	22	72	238	concrete	
Apartment Building	1973	17	65	213	concrete	
		Heliopolis				
Merryland Block A	1967	22	72	238	concrete	
Roxy Tower	1967	17	57	188	concrete	
Roxy Building	1966	13	41	136	concrete	
Merryland Block B	1968	11	35	106	concrete	
		Nasr City				
Office Building	1969	13	45	148	concrete	office
		France				
		Bordeaux				
City Administration	1967	27	90	295	mixed	office
		Marseille				
Le Grand Pavois	U.C.	30	100	328	concrete	apartment
		Nantes				
Bretagne	1974	32	105	344	concrete	office
		Paris				
Maine Montparnasse	1973	64	229	751	mixed	office
La Tour Fiat	1974	45	180	590	concrete	office
CB 21	1973	42	165	541	mixed	office
UAP (CB 312)	1973	41	150	492	concrete	office
Tour Blanche	1973	42	139	456	concrete	apartment
Les Poissons	1970	42	129	423	mixed	multiple
PB 2	U.C.	33	111	364	concrete	office
PB 34	U.C.	32	111	364	concrete	office
Nobel (PB 11)	1966	32	106	348	mixed	office
Euope (CB 14)	1969	27	90	295	concrete	office
Faculty of Sciences	1970	27	90	295	mixed	school
Tour Apogée		60			steel	office
Palais des Congrès Hotel		33				hotel
Lafayette Hotel					concrete	hotel
		Rennes				
Les Horizons	1970	30	96	315	concrete	multiple

Table 4 Tallest buildings in major cities (continued)

Building	Year Completed	Number of stories	Height meters	feet	Material	Use
		German Democratic Republic				
		Berlin				
Stadt Berlin	1970	41	132	433	concrete	hotel
Wohnhochhaus Leipziger Str.		27	78	256	concrete	multiple
Wohnhochhaus Liebknecht Str.	1968	26	77	254	concrete	apartment
Wohnhochhaus Leninplatz	1969	27	77	251	concrete	apartment
Haus des Reisens	1971	19	76	249	concrete	office
Wohnhochhaus Fischerkietz	1969	24	72	235	concrete	apartment
Wohnhaus Spandauer Str.	1970	20	62	203	concrete	multiple
		Halle				
Wohnhochhaus Thalmann-platz	1970	23	68	222	steel	apartment
		Jena				
Forschungshochhaus	1972	30	133	435	concrete	office
		Karl Marx Stadt				
Interhotel	1970	29	97	317	concrete	hotel
		Leipzig				
Karl Marx Universität	1971	36	153	502	concrete	office
Wohnhochhaus Winter-garten Str.	1972	31	100	328	concrete	apartment
		Magdeburg				
Wohnhochhaus Jacob Str.	U.C.	22	70	230	concrete	apartment
		Rostock				
Wohnhochhaus Lutten Klein		27	77	252	concrete	apartment
		Germany, Federal Republic of				
		Berlin				
Steglitzer Kreisel	1977	30	126	413	mixed	office
Bundesversicherungsanstalt	1977	24	97	313	mixed	office
Wohnhochhaus Ideal	1969	31	91	293	concrete	apartment
Kurfurstendamm Karree	1974	21	90	290	mixed	office
Postscheckamt Berlin	1971	23	89	287	concrete	office
Europa Center	1965	21	86	277	mixed	office
Wohnhochhaus Waldsas-senerstr.	1971	28	85	274	concrete	apartment
Wohnhochhaus Zwickauer Damm	1969	28	85	274	concrete	apartment
Wohnhochhaus Wutzki Allee	1968	27	80	258	concrete	apartment
Telefunken Haus	1960	22	80	258	concrete	university
		Bonn				
Parliament Office	1968	31	109	357	mixed	office
		Braunschweig				
Landesbank	1973	17	73	238	concrete	office
Schwarzer Berg	1969	24	70	230	prefab	apartment
Techn. University	1956	19	62	203	concrete	office
Atrium 3	1971	22	62	202	prefab	apartment
I Punkt	1971	19	56	182	concrete	apartment
T. U. Elektrotechnik	1973	17	55	180	concrete	office
Atrium 1 and 2	1971	17	48	157	concrete	apartment
Studenten Wohnhaus	1967	10	27	89	concrete	apartment
		Düsseldorf				
Thyssen Adm. Building	1956	30	106	348	steel	office
Phonix Rheinrohr		25	98	321	steel	office
Mannesmann Adm. Building	1958	26	89	292	mixed	office
		Essen				
Rheinstahl Adm. Building	1960	25	80	263	mixed	office
		Frankfurt				
Hochhaus Platz der Republik	1973		143	469	concrete	office
AFE		33	116	381		
Commerzbank		31	103	338		
Unterliederbach Cheruskerweg	1974	8	22	73	concrete	apartment
		Hamburg				
Unilever Adm. Building	1963	26	103	338	mixed	office
Polizeiprosidium	1960	15	80	262	concrete	office
Jduna	1967	23	75	246	concrete	office
Breite Str.	1972	24	70	230	concrete	apartment
Nobistor	1972	19	57	187	prefab	multiple
		Hannover				
Continental	1953	18	66	216	mixed	office

Table 4 Tallest buildings in major cities (continued)

Building	Year Completed	Number of stories	Height meters	feet	Material	Use
Karlsruhe, Germany, Federal Republic of (continued)						
Badenwerk	1965	22	72	236	steel	office
Köln						
Concordia	1972	49	137	450	concrete	apartment
Buroturm	1976	34	120	394	concrete	office
Herkules Apartment House	1972	35	95	313	concrete	apartment
Klinikum	1971	23	89	292	concrete	hospital
Studioturm	1976	24	86	282	steel	TV/radio
Rundfunkanstalten Dtsch. Welle						
Leverkusen						
Bayer Adm. Building	1962	37	122	400	steel	office
Ludwigshafen						
BASF Adm. Building	1961	27	110	360	concrete	office
Munich						
BMW	1972	22	100	328	concrete	office
Arabella	1971	24	68	223	concrete	apartment
Sheraton	1971	23	68	223	concrete	hotel
Siemens	1964	21	62	204	concrete	office
Deba Hotel Solln	1970	19	56	184	concrete	hotel
Deutscher Kaiser	1960	17	51	167	concrete	hotel
Deba Westendstr.	1973	17	49	161	concrete	multiple
Schwabylon	1973	15	44	144	concrete	multiple
Theresienhohe	1973	15	44	144	concrete	multiple
Klanzestrasse	1973	13	41	135	concrete	apartment
Siemens Sternharser	1960	13	41	135	concrete	apartment
Ghana						
Accra						
Kwame Nkrumah Conf. Centre	1965	12	40	132	concrete	office
Greece						
Athens						
Athens Tower	1972	27	87	285	concrete	office
Apollo Tower	1973	24	80	263	concrete	apartment
Hilton	1967	15	65	213	concrete	hotel
OTE Telecom Center	1966	14	56	188	concrete	office
EDOK-ETER	1978	13			concrete	office
Rhodes Island						
Mediterranean	1972	19	65	213	concrete	hotel
Hong Kong						
Hong Kong						
Sun Hung Kai Centre	1980	50	183	600	concrete	multiple
Connaught Centre	1974	50	183	599	concrete	office
New Alexandria House	1978		124	408	concrete	multiple
Furama	1977	33	109	359	concrete	hotel
Pearl City Mansion	1971	34	109	356	concrete	multiple
Century Towers	1971	31	109	356	concrete	apartment
Murray	1970	25	92	303	concrete	office
International Building	1967	31	92	302	steel	multiple
Realty Building	1967	31	91	300	steel	multiple
Wu Sang House	1966	28	86	283	concrete	multiple
Sun Hing	1966	27	86	283	concrete	multiple
Ping Shek Housing	1970	28	83	271	concrete	apartment
Container-Handling Warehouse	1976	16	80	264		warehouse
Causeway Centre		43				comm/apt.
Mei Foo Apartments (100)	1976	20			brick	apartment
Hungary						
Budapest						
Semmelweiss Medical University	1976	26	88	288	concrete	university
Tall Dwellinghouse w/ reservoir	1975	19	68	222	concrete	apartment
B 42	1974	18	64	210	concrete	apartment
Trade Union	1973	22	72	236	mixed	office
India						
Bangalore						
Municipal Corporation		24	106	348		multiple
Highpoint	1978	12	41	134	concrete	apartment
Bangalore Municipal Corp.		15			concrete	multiple

Table 4 Tallest buildings in major cities (continued)

Building	Year Completed	Number of stories	Height meters	feet	Material	Use
		India (continued)				
		Bombay				
Hotel Oberoi Sheraton	1973	35	116	383	concrete	hotel
Air India		24	105	345	mixed	office
Jupiter	1974	31	91	300	concrete	apartment
Venus	1974	31	91	300	concrete	apartment
Grand Paradi No. 1		28	91	297	concrete	apartment
Grand Paradi No. 2		28	91	297	concrete	apartment
Grand Paradi No. 3		28	91	297	concrete	apartment
Lands End (1)	1968	29	88	290	concrete	apartment
State Bank of India		22	88	289	concrete	office
Kanchanganga		28	85	280	concrete	apartment
Urvashi No. 1	1973	27	82	270	precast	apartment
Urvashi No. 2	1973	27	82	270	precast	apartment
Kanchanjunga Apartments	1976	27	82	269	concrete	apartment
Woodlands	1970	26	79	260	concrete	apartment
Taj Intercontinental	1972	23	76	250	concrete	hotel
Akash Ganga	1969	24	73	240	concrete	apartment
Administrative Office Building	1974	22	71	234	concrete	office
Skyscraper No. 1	1970	23	70	230	concrete	apartment
Waibhav	1973	23	70	230	concrete	apartment
Dalamal Park	1972	22	67	220	concrete	apartment
Neelambar	1973	22	67	220	concrete	apartment
Hotel President	1973	20	67	220	concrete	hotel
Sterling	1971	21	66	215	concrete	apartment
Darya Mahal No. 1	1971	21	64	210	concrete	apartment
Darya Mahal No. 2	1971	21	64	210	concrete	apartment
Jaslok	1973	21	64	210	concrete	hospital
Manek	1970	21	64	210	concrete	apartment
Persepolis	1974	21	64	210	concrete	apartment
Skyscraper No. 2	1971	21	64	210	concrete	apartment
Venus Apartment No. 1	1971	21	64	210	concrete	apartment
Palm Spring	1970	21	61	200	concrete	apartment
Cuffe Castle	1971	20	61	200	concrete	apartment
Mehr-Dad	1971	20	61	200	concrete	apartment
Shanti Nagar	1974	20	61	200	concrete	apartment
Venus Apartment No. 2	1971	20	61	200	concrete	apartment
Venus Apartment No. 3	1971	20	61	200	concrete	apartment
Lands End (2)	1968	19	58	190	concrete	apartment
Mehr Naz	1972	19	58	190	concrete	apartment
Shanaz	1967	19	58	190	concrete	apartment
Basant	1974	18	55	180	concrete	apartment
Iris	1971	17	52	170	concrete	apartment
Officers' Quarters	1973	17	51	168	concrete	apartment
Usha Kiran		26				apartment
Indian Express		24				office
Meenakshi Chambers		22				office
Shipping Corporation of India		18			concrete	office
Videsh Sanchar Bhavan		16			concrete	office
		Calcutta				
The Tata Centre		18	79	260	concrete	office
Birla Brothers		15	60	200	concrete	office
Industry House		24			concrete	office
Calcutta 16	1956	18			concrete	apartment
Shipping Corporation of India	1972	13				
Calcutta 1	1966	12			concrete	office
Basant Investment Corp.		11			concrete	office
Corp. Housing Society Ltd.		11			concrete	apartment
Flats		11			concrete	apartment
CPWD		10			concrete	office
Lake Corp. Housing Society	1971	10			concrete	apartment
Staff Qrs. Singhee Park		10			concrete	apartment
		Hyderabad				
Hindustan Ideal Insurance Ltd.	1971	12	44	144	concrete	office
Gagan Vihar		14			concrete	multiple
HMT Ltd.		13			steel	office
Deepak Estate		11			concrete	multiple
		Madras				
LIC Building	1958	14	47	154	concrete	office
Housing Board	1974	10	37	120	concrete	office
Nandanam Tower Block	1966	11	35	115	concrete	apartment
Turnbulls Tower Block	1966	12	35	114	concrete	apartment

Table 4 Tallest buildings in major cities (continued)

Building	Year Completed	Number of stories	Height meters	feet	Material	Use
Madras, India (continued)						
Queens Court	1973	10	35	114	concrete	apartment
Cambrae East	1975	10	35	114	concrete	apartment
Chesney Nilgiri	1975	10	35	114	concrete	apartment
Khaleel Shirazi Estate	1976	10	35	114	concrete	office
Hotel Kanchi	1978	10	35	114	concrete	hotel
Hotel Taj Coromandel	1975	10	35	114	concrete	hotel
Hotel Chola	1975	10	35	114	concrete	hotel
Kannammai Buildings	1975	10	35	114	concrete	hotel
Ram Apartments	1975	10	35	114	concrete	apartment
Life Insurance Corp.	1957	13				office
Madras 18	1966	11			concrete	apartment
New Delhi						
Hansalya	1971	21	89	290	concrete	office
Delhi Development Authority	U.C.	23	82	269	concrete	office
Hindustan Times House	1973	18	81	264	concrete	office
Bank of Baroda	1971	15	64	210	concrete	office
Vandan	1972	14	55	180	concrete	office
State Bank of India	1970	14	53	175	concrete	office
Kailash Apartments	U.C.	12	53	173	concrete	office
Himalaya House	1970	14	52	170	concrete	multiple
Jeevan Prakash	1973	11	51	168	concrete	office
Food Corporation of India	U.C.	13	50	164	concrete	office
Suryakiran	1972	13	46	150	concrete	office
Akash Deep	1969	12	43	140	concrete	office
Ansal Bhawan	1973	12	43	140	concrete	office
Asha Deep	1970	11	40	130	concrete	apartment
Indonesia						
Jakarta						
Wisma Nusantara	1972	25			steel/concrete	office
Town Hall of Jakarta		24			concrete	office
Iran						
Teheran						
Saiman	1973	24	70	230	prefab	apartment
ASP	U.C.	23	68	223	prefab	apartment
Doma	U.C.	22	64	210	mixed	apartment
Hilton Hotel	1971	20	62	203	concrete	hotel
Iranian Bank	1973	20	62	203	concrete	office
Bank Car	1962	19	59	194	mixed	office
SAAI	1973	14	42	138	concrete	apartment
Asia Insurance Co.	1974	12	35	115	prefab	office
Chamber of Commerce	1972	12	35	115	steel	office
Swissair	1972	12	35	115	mixed	office
Chamber of Commerce	1972	9	24	79	mixed	office
Israel						
Haifa						
Eshkol Tower	1976	31	86	279	concrete	office
Sihchun Dvdim	1978	22	62	201	concrete	apartment
Izraelia	1977	18	52	170	steel/concrete	apartment
Jerusalem						
Hilton Hotel	1975	26	95	308	concrete	hotel
Town Tower	1978	24	83	269	concrete	office
Office Building	1978	18	79	256	concrete	office
Ramat-Gan						
Diamond Boursa 2	1978	32	100	323	concrete	office
Diamond Boursa 1	1966	25	78	254	concrete	office
Tel-Aviv						
IBM	1978	27	112	363	concrete	office
Shalom Tower	1962	24	68	220	concrete	office
Italy						
Brescia						
Complesso Via S. Giovanni Bosco	1979	13	40	131	mixed	office
Genoa						
SIP Teti	1967	23	105	343	mixed	office
La Platea	1959	18	65	214	mixed	apartment
INA	1960	14	47	155	mixed	apartment
Lecco						
La Moderna	1957	14	48	158	mixed	apartment
Milan						
Centro Pirelli	1958	35	128	420	concrete	office
Piazza Repubblica	1957	30	117	385	concrete	multiple

Table 4 Tallest buildings in major cities (continued)

Building	Year Completed	Number of stories	Height meters	feet	Material	Use
Milan, Italy (continued)						
Galfa	1958	33	109	356	concrete	office
Torre Velasca	1958	28	106	348	concrete	multiple
Torre Romana	1965	27	94	308	concrete	apartment
Servizi Tecnici Comunali	1963	25	90	295	concrete	office
Torre Monforte	1962	24	82	269	concrete	apartment
Centro Svizzero	1950	23	78	256	concrete	office
Torre Turati	1967	22	74	244	steel	office
Torre Porta Volta	1969	19	64	210	concrete	office
Sede INPS	1965	20	60	197	steel	office
Torri Gratosoglio	1970	19	60	197	concrete	apartment
Centro ENI	1957	16	55	180	steel	office
Torri Ca Granda	1976	17	51	168	concrete	apartment
Torri Gallaratese	1969	15	46	151	concrete	apartment
Naples						
Soc. Cattolica di Assicurazion	1958	30	105	344	concrete	multiple
Direzione Ff. Ss.	1965	18	88	269	concrete	office
Torre Nuovo Policlinico	1964	21	74	243	mixed	office
Torre del Politecnico	1964	12	55	180	concrete	university
ENEL—SME	1953	15	50	164	concrete	office
Alfa Romeo-Alfasud	1974	10	48	157	mixed	office
Palermo						
Complesso Florida	1980	15	49	161	mixed	apartment
Rome						
ENI	1962	23	80	263	steel	office
Financial Ministry	1961	21	70	230	mixed	office
Alitalia	1966	20	67	220	mixed	office
Torre Grassetto	1962	17	57	188	concrete	
Turin						
RAI—TV	1963	19	72	237	steel	office
Japan						
Ashiya						
Ashiyahama High-Rise	1977	29	84	276	steel	apartment
Fukuoka						
Tenjin Center	1976	18	65	213	steel	office
Fukuoka DNT	1976	18	65	213	mixed	multiple
Nishi Nihon Shinbun	1975	17	65	213	steel	office
Nishinippon Watanabe	1975	17	65	213	steel	multiple
Chiyoda Life Ins.	1978	15	55	180	steel	office
Fukuoka Asahi	1970	14	51	167	mixed	office
Nishitetsu Grand Hotel	1974	14	51	167	mixed	hotel
Fukuoka Bank	1975	11	45	148	mixed	office
Asahi Life Insurance	1975	12	44	144	mixed	office
Tenjin	1960	11	42	138	mixed	office
Hiroshima						
Motomachi Apartment House	1975	20	63	207	steel	apartment
Hiroshima Meiji Life Ins.	1972	15	61	200	mixed	office
Holiday Inn Hiroshima		18	59	194	mixed	hotel
Hiroshima Mitsui		16	58	190	steel/concrete	office
Chugoku Nippon T + T Public Corp.	1974	14	55	180	mixed	office
Kita-Kyushu						
Kita-Kyushu Municipal Building	1972	15	58	190	steel	office
Kobe						
Kobe Trade Center	1969	26	107	351	mixed	office
Shinnagataeki Apartment House	1976	25	82	269	mixed	multiple
Sannomiya West	1975	19	75	246	mixed	multiple
Nagoya						
Nagoya Sumitomo	1974	26	106	348	steel	office
Takihyo Marunouchi	1973	25	87	286	steel	office
Hirokoji Denden Toghin	1976	18	80	263	steel	office
Nagoya Terminal Hotel	1974	20	79	260	steel	hotel
Nihon Life Ins. Co. Sasajima	1974	19	79	260	steel	office
Nagoya Kanko Hotel	1973	19	70	230	mixed	hotel
Meiji Life Insurance	1973	16	60	197	steel	office
Nishiki-Sako	1977	14	47	154	steel	office
Naha						
Ryukai		20	70	230	mixed	hotel/off.

Table 4 Tallest buildings in major cities (continued)

Building	Year Completed	Number of stories	Height meters	feet	Material	Use
Japan (continued)						
Ohgaki						
Ohgaki Kyoritsu Bank	1972	18	71	233	mixed	office
Osaka						
Hankai Nanbaeki Hotel	1978	38	134	440	steel	multiple
Nankai Namba Station Hotel	1978	38	134	439	steel	hotel
Osakaekimae Shigaichibaizo		34	132	433	steel	office
No. 3 (in front Osaka Station)	U.C.	34	132	433		office
Nakanoshima Center	1975	30	122	400	steel	office
Osaka Kokusai	1973	32	121	397	steel	office
Vmeda Hankyu	1976	32	121	397	steel	office
Osaka Ohbayashi	1973	32	120	394	steel	office
Osaka Data Communication	1974	24	120	394	steel	office
Dojima Den-Den	1974	24	120	394	steel	office
Yoshimoto	1976	30	114	374	steel	hotel
Osaka Royal Hotel	1973	32	108	355	steel	hotel
Fujitakanko Hotel Taikoen		27	90	295	steel	hotel
Nissho-Iwai	1975	21	88	289	steel	office
Morinomiya Apartment Houses	1977	25	77	253	mixed	apartment
Asahi Hoso		22	77	253	mixed	hotel
Sony Tower	1976	18	72	236	steel	office
Osaka Merchandise Mart	1969	20	71	233	mixed	multiple
Sapporo						
Zen-Nikku Hotel	1974	25	96	315	steel	hotel
Shinkyosai	1974	25	88	289	mixed	hotel
Sumitomo Life Ins. Sapporo	1972	23	80	263	steel	office
Sapporo City Administration	1970	18	78	256	steel	office
Dai-Ich Life Insurance	1973	18	64	210	mixed	hotel
Tokyo Hotel	1974	15	57	187	mixed	hotel
Hokkaido Pref.	1967	12	54	177	mixed	office
Sanko	1973	10	54	177	mixed	shopping
Meiji Life Insurance	1972	13	52	171	mixed	office
Mitsui	1967	11	52	171	mixed	office
Sapporo Telephone	1971	10	52	171	mixed	office
Sapporo Grand Hotel	1975	17			steel	hotel
Sendai						
Sendai Kowa		17	68	223	steel	office
Sumitomo Life Ins. Co. Sendai	1974	13	66	216	mixed	office
Nanajunana Bank	1973	14	57	187	steel	bank
Harihisa			54	177	mixed	apt./office
Sendai Sakuragaoka Apt. House	1973	17	51	167	mixed	apt./office
Shizuoka						
Shizuoka Broadcasting	1970	18	66	217	steel	office
Shizuoka Pref.	1970	17	60	197	mixed	office
Tokyo						
Ikebukuro Office Tower	1978	60	226	742	steel	office
Shinjuku Center	1979	54	223	733	concrete/steel	office
Shinjuku Mitsui	1974	55	212	696	steel	office
Shinjuku Nomura	1978	53	210	690	steel	office
Shinjuku Sumitomo	1974	52	200	656	steel	office
Yasuda Kasai	1976	43	193	633	steel	office
Keio Plaza Hotel	1971	47	170	557	steel	hotel
Internatl Telecommunication	1974	32	165	541	steel	telecom.
KDD	1974	34	162	530	steel	office
Tokyo World Trade Center	1970	40	152	499	steel	office
Kasumigaseki	1968	36	147	482	steel	office
Dai-Ichi Kangyo Bank	U.C.	32	132	433		office
Ikebukuro Hotel	1978	36	130	427	steel	hotel
Hotel New Otani Tower	1974	39	127	417	steel	hotel
Toho Life Insurance	1975	31	122	400	steel	office
Hotel Pacific Tokyo	1971	30	113	371	steel	hotel
Asahi Tokai	1971	29	113	371	steel	office
Mita	1975	26	106	348	steel	office
Tokyo Miyako Hotel	U.C.	32	104	341	steel	hotel
G-Building	1976	21	102	335	steel	office
Imperial Hotel	1970	26	101	331	mixed	hotel
Sanwa Bank Tokyo	1973	25	100	328	steel	office
Tokyo Kaijo	1974	25	100	328	steel	office
Mitsui Bussan	1976	24	100	328	steel	office
Mitsubishi Bank Head Office	1973	24	100	328	steel	office
Taiyo Gyogyo		24	100	328	steel	office
Takehira Office of T + T Corp.	1970	21	96	315	steel	office

Table 4 Tallest buildings in major cities (continued)

Building	Year Completed	Number of stories	Height meters	Height feet	Material	Use
Tokyo, Japan (continued)						
Morinaga	1974	24	89	292	steel	office
Nakano Wireless Telegraphy	1976	18	71	233		office
Tokyo Fire Station Head Office	1976	15	62	203	mixed	office
Kajima Const. Co. Shinmachi Apt.	1973	20	54	177	concrete	apartment
Yokohama						
Yokohama Tenri Kyokan	1972	27	102	334	steel	office
Sumitomo Denki (Totsuka)	1972		82	268	steel	manufacturing
Dai-Ich Life Insurance	1967	18	80	261	mixed	office
Empire Hotel	1965	21	78	255	steel	hotel
Tokai Fudohsan	U.C.	22	75	246	steel	multiple
Kanagawa Pref. Sohgo Center	1972	15	56	184	steel	office
Sangyo Rodo Center	1972	15	55	180	steel	
Yokohama Kyoiku	1973	13	52	172	mixed	office
Kyoiku	1973	13	52	172	mixed	office
Sangyo Boeki Center	1975	12	52	172	mixed	office
Nihon Jutaku Kodan (Isogo)	1971	16	45	148	mixed	apartment
Jutaku Kodan (15060)	1971	16	45	148	mixed	apartment
Yokohama Nikko Hotel	U.C.	13	45	148	mixed	hotel
Yokohama Civic University	1969	12	45	148	mixed	hospital
Iwasaki Gakuen	1973	12	45	148	mixed	multiple
Iwasaki Gakuen (Mitsukoshi)	1973	12	45	147	mixed	multiple
Nihon Jutaku Kodan (Kosugaya)	1972	15	43	141	mixed	apartment
Isogo Apartment House	U.C.	14	41	134	mixed	apartment
Nihon Jutaku Kodan	1975	14	40	131	mixed	apartment
Marutan	U.C.	11	40	131	mixed	multiple
Nippon Kokan (Kishiya)	1970	14	39	128	steel	apartment
Tokai Bussan	U.C.	9	36	118	mixed	multiple
Isogo Apartment House	U.C.	11	31	102	mixed	apartment
Nihon Jutaku Kodan	U.C.	11	31	102	mixed	apartment
Nara Fudosan	U.C.	9	31	102	concrete	multiple
Ginyo Shoji	1973	9	31	102	mixed	office
Isogo Apartment House	U.C.	10	29	95	mixed	apartment
Prefectural Housing Supply Co.	1975	14	20	66	mixed	apartment
Nihon Jutaku Kodan	1975	14	20	66	mixed	apartment
Kenya						
Mombasa						
Ambalal House	1976	9	35	115	concrete	office
New Coast Provincial Hqs.	1975	9	31	100	concrete	office
Nairobi						
Kenyatta Conference Centre	1974	33	105	345	concrete	office
Govt. Office Conference Hall	1972	32	97	320	concrete	multiple
National Bank of Kenya Hqs.	1976	21	82	268	concrete	office
Uchumi House	1972	21	71	232	concrete	office
International House	1971	17	66	215	concrete	office
Hilton House	1969	20	61	200	concrete	hotel
Bruce House	1971	17	55	179	concrete	office
Union Tower	1977	14	48	156	concrete	office
Hotel 680	1972	14	47	153	concrete	hotel
Office of the President	1967	14	43	140	concrete	office
Ministry of Works Hqs.	1968	14	43	140	concrete	office
Bima House	1975	13	41	136	concrete	office
Harambee House	1962	12	40	130	concrete	office
Development House	1972	12	39	128	concrete	office
Kenya Charity Sweepstake	1975	13	38	126	concrete	office
Kencom House	1977	10	38	126	concrete	office
Extelcoms House	1973	10	34	110	concrete	office
IPS	1971	10	33	108	concrete	office
Electricity House	1974	9	31	102	concrete	office
Korea						
Seoul						
Lotte Hotel	1978	37	138	453	steel/concrete	hotel
Sam-Il	1971	31	110	361	steel/concrete	office
Lotte Dept. Store	1978	25	106	346	steel/concrete	commercial
Dong-Bank Life Insurance	1976	26	102	337	steel/concrete	office
President Hotel	1974	27	98	332	steel/concrete	hotel
Korea Exchange Bank	1978	24	98	320	steel/concrete	bank
Dae-Kyo	1979	25	97	319	steel/concrete	office
Kuk-Dong	1978	22	96	316	steel/concrete	office
Tokyu Hotel	1971	25	95	312	steel/concrete	hotel
KAL	1969	23	95	312	steel/concrete	office
Plaza Hotel	1978	21	87	284	steel/concrete	hotel
Silla Hotel	1978	22	85	280	steel/concrete	hotel
Koreana Hotel	1971	24	84	276	steel/concrete	hotel

Table 4 Tallest buildings in major cities (continued)

Building	Year Completed	Number of stories	Height meters	feet	Material	Use
Seoul, Korea (continued)						
Nam-Gang	1973	20	83	272	steel/concrete	office
Koreana Dept. Store	1977	22	77	253	steel/concrete	commercial
Bank of Seoul & Trust Co.	1975	18	75	247	steel/concrete	office
Youth Hostel	1978	20	73	241	steel/concrete	hotel
Royal Hotel	1970	21	72	236	steel/concrete	hotel
Capitol	1970	22	72	235	steel/concrete	office
Mirama Hotel	1978	18	71	234	steel/concrete	hotel
Trade Association	1973	22	70	230	steel/concrete	office
Luckry	1973	20	70	230	steel/concrete	office
Korea Automobile Insurance	1973	19	69	226	steel/concrete	office
Dong-Hwa	1971	19	68	224	steel/concrete	office
Dae-Woo	1977	23	68	223	steel/concrete	office
Victoria Hotel	1974	20	68	223	steel/concrete	hotel
Ambassador Hotel	1974	18	68	222	steel/concrete	hotel
Korea Stock Exchange	1978	15	67	220	steel/concrete	office
National Library	1973	18	67	219	steel/concrete	library
Ssang-Yong	1969	19	65	213	steel/concrete	office
New Seoul	1971	18	65	213	steel/concrete	office
Hanyang University Hospital	1972	18	63	207	steel/concrete	hospital
Kyong-Gi	1969	18	63	207	steel/concrete	office
Kyong-Hee University Hospital	1971	17	63	207	steel/concrete	hospital
M.B.C. TV.	1971	16	63	207	steel/concrete	office
Seoulin Hotel	1973	18	62	203	steel/concrete	hotel
Jinyang Arcade	1970	17	61	199	steel/concrete	arcade
KAL New Building	1976	17	61	199	steel/concrete	office
Grand Palace Hotel	1978	15	60	198	steel/concrete	hotel
Walker Hill	1979	15	60	198	steel/concrete	hotel
Min-Kyong-Eok	1975	17	60	197	steel/concrete	office
Seong-Bo	1969	17	60	195	steel/concrete	office
New Seoul Hotel	1971	17	60	195	steel/concrete	hotel
Jumbo Mansion	1974	19	59	194	steel/concrete	apartment
Chosun Hotel	1974	18	59	194	steel/concrete	hotel
Lex Mansion	1974	18	59	194	steel/concrete	apartment
Sejong Hotel	1970	16	59	194	steel/concrete	hotel
Hyundai Construction Co.	1976	16	58	192	steel/concrete	office
Taihan Electric Wire	1978	15	58	191	steel/concrete	office
Dongwa	1969	16	58	190	steel/concrete	office
Dae-Il	1970	16	58	190	steel/concrete	office
Myong-Ji University	1972	15	57	187	steel/concrete	school
Villa Mansion	1974	17	57	185	steel/concrete	apartment
Woo-Seong Apartment	1971	16	56	185	steel/concrete	apartment
Tae-Heung	1969	16	56	184	steel/concrete	office
Tae-Yang	1969	15	56	183	steel/concrete	office
Cho-Chun	1969	15	56	183	steel/concrete	office
The Cho-Heung Bank	1966	15	57	182	steel/concrete	office
Naeway Business Journal	1959	15	56	182	steel/concrete	office
Han-Il	1970	15	55	181	steel/concrete	office
Sam-Won	1969	15	55	180	steel/concrete	office
Sam-Koo	1971	15	55	180	steel/concrete	office
Heung-Hwa	1969	15	55	180	steel/concrete	office
Sam-Yun Parking	1971	15	55	180	steel/concrete	parking
Jeil Life insurance	1976	15	55	180	steel/concrete	office
Hwa-Bo	1977	15	55	180	steel/concrete	office
Jeil	1976	15	54	177	steel/concrete	office
Seo-Heung	1968	15	54	177	steel/concrete	office
Sam-Jeong	1971	17	54	176	steel/concrete	office
Public Procuration Office	1974	15	53	174	steel/concrete	office
Se-Dae	1965	15	53	174	steel/concrete	office
Namsan Mansion	1974	15	53	174	steel/concrete	office
Namsan Foreigners Apartment	1972	16	52	172	steel/concrete	apartment
Bolim	1969	15	53	172	steel/concrete	office
Kookmin University	1974	15	53	172	steel/concrete	office
Center Building	1971	18	52	171	steel/concrete	office
Kwang-Hak	1970	15	52	171	steel/concrete	office
Soo Woon	1970	15	52	171	steel/concrete	office
Sam-Boo Apartment (4 dong)	1975	15	52	171	steel/concrete	apartment
Sam-Boo Apartment(2 dong)	1976	15	52	171	steel/concrete	apartment
Sam Young	1967	15	52	171	steel/concrete	office
Sam-Boo Apartment		15	52	171	steel/concrete	apartment
Arirang Hotel		15	52	170	steel/concrete	hotel
Lee-Jonk-Rok Apts. (11 dong)	1974	15	52	169	steel/concrete	apartment
Ankook	1969	15	52	169	steel/concrete	office
Namsan Foreigners Apartment	1972	15	50	163	steel/concrete	apartment
Tower Hotel	1967	18	49	161	steel/concrete	hotel
Nak-Won Arcade	1972	15	49	161	steel/concrete	apartment
Joo-Gong Apartment (10 dong)	1978	15	49	161	steel/concrete	apartment
Citizens National Bank	1969	16	48	157	steel/concrete	office

Table 4 Tallest buildings in major cities (continued)

Building	Year Completed	Number of stories	Height meters	feet	Material	Use
\multicolumn{7}{c}{**Seoul, Korea (continued)**}
Hongik University	1973	16	48	157	steel/concrete	school
Hyundai Mansion (3 dong)	1975	15	46	152	steel/concrete	apartment
Hyundai Mansion (6 dong)	1976	15	46	152	steel/concrete	apartment
Asia Hotel	1973	16	46	151	steel/concrete	hotel
Kwang-Il	1972	15	46	150	steel/concrete	office
Tower Mansion	1974	15	42	138	steel/concrete	apartment

Lebanon
Beirut

Building	Year Completed	Number of stories	Height meters	feet	Material	Use
Shell	1962	20	70	233	concrete	multiple

Luxembourg
Luxembourg

Building	Year Completed	Number of stories	Height meters	feet	Material	Use
Centre Européen	1966	23	71	233	concrete	office
Kredietbank	1977	13	49	160	concrete	multiple
Forum Royal	1977	14	44	144	concrete	multiple
Rubis Kirchberg	1976	13	44	144	concrete	apartment
Le Carrefour	U.C.	12	39	128	concrete	multiple

Malaysia
Kuala Lumpur

Building	Year Completed	Number of stories	Height meters	feet	Material	Use
Belmont Centre	U.C.	50	193	632	concrete	multiple
City Hall	U.C.	31	133	435	concrete	office
Hotel Hilton	1973	36	123	402	concrete	hotel
Wisman Stephens	U.C.	29	106	348	concrete	multiple
UMBC	1973	26	103	337	concrete	off./shops
Hotel Hilton Extension	U.C.	27	99	324	concrete	hotel
Angkasa Raya	U.C.	24	99	324	concrete	off./shops
Flats in Jalan Batai	U.C.	28	96	314	concrete	apartment
Wisma MPI	U.C.	22	96	314	concrete	off./shops
Wisma Lee Rubber	U.C.	29	95	310	concrete	office
Hotel Regent	1973	25	93	305	concrete	hotel
Oriental Plaza	1974	22	78	256	concrete	office
Equatorial	1973	17	67	221	concrete	hotel
Campbell Complex	1975	20	64	210	concrete	office
Fitzpatrick S.	1974	18	64	210	concrete	office
Merlin (new block)	1973	20	63	206	concrete	hotel
Wisma Damansara	1971	16	58	183	concrete	office
Holiday Inn	1973	13	53	174	concrete	hotel
3 blocks of flats	1975	17	46	150	concrete	apartment
Ming	1974	19			concrete	office

Mali
Bamako

Building	Year Completed	Number of stories	Height meters	feet	Material	Use
Hotel de L'Amitié	1967	17				hotel

Mexico
Acapulco

Building	Year Completed	Number of stories	Height meters	feet	Material	Use
Paraiso Marriott		21	96	314	concrete	hotel
Plaza International		25	92	303	concrete	hotel
Estrella del Mar	1972	26	87	285	concrete	apartment

Mexico City

Building	Year Completed	Number of stories	Height meters	feet	Material	Use
Hotel de Mexico	1972	48	175	573	concrete	hotel
Latin American Tower	1955	45	139	456	steel	office
Nonoalco Tlatelolco Tower	1962	25	127	417	concrete	office
National Lottery	1972	30	102	334	steel	office
Hotel Fiesta Palace	1970	31	96	314	concrete	hotel
Miguel e Abed	1952	29	94	308	steel	office
Communications Tower	1968	19	87	286	concrete	
Foreign Affairs Ministry	1964	24	86	283	steel	office
Anabnac	1960	24	86	282	steel	office

Monterrey

Building	Year Completed	Number of stories	Height meters	feet	Material	Use
Condominio del Norte	1964	30	100	328	concrete	office
Condominio Acero Monterrey	1959	20	87	285	steel	office
Edificio de las Instituciones	1977	15	58	190	concrete	office
Hotel Rio	1970	16	55	180	concrete	hotel
Condominio Confia	1973	14	53	174	concrete	office
Hotel Ambasador	1974	13	50	164	concrete	hotel
Financiera del Norte	1958	11	44	144	concrete	office
Hospital de Gineco-Obstet- ricia	1972	11	39	128	concrete	hospital
Centro Medico San José	1973	9	37	121	concrete	office
Hotel Monterrey	1976	9	32	105	concrete	hotel
C.F.E. Div. del Golfo	1971	8	28	92	concrete	office
Condominio Monterrey		17			concrete	office
Edificio Monterrey		15			concrete	office
Edificio Chapa	1949	12			steel	office

Table 4 Tallest buildings in major cities (continued)

Building	Year Completed	Number of stories	Height meters	feet	Material	Use
Monterrey, Mexico (continued)						
Hotel Yamallel		11			concrete	hotel
Hos de Zona del Seguro Social	1957	10			concrete	hospital
Netherlands						
Amstelveen						
Zonnehuis	U.C.	12	38	125	concrete	hospital
Amsterdam						
Stationspostgebouw	1968	11	49	161	concrete	office
Arnhem						
Research-Laboratorium A.K.U.	1971	16	71	233	prefab	office
Postcheque-en Girodienst	1970	14	70	230	concrete	office
Delft						
Electro Techniek	1969	23	90	295	mixed	school
Eindhoven						
Philips	1965	15	66	216	mixed	office
Hoofdgebouw Tech. Hoge-school	1963	13	62	193	concrete	office
Gebouw Electro Tech. Hoge-school	1963	14	59	184	concrete	school
Gebouw Scheikunde Tech.	1965	10	59	184	concrete	school
Technische Dienst	1973	11	48	156	concrete	office
Winkelcentrum Vaartbroek	1967	10	33	108	concrete	apartment
Enschede						
Gebouw Werktuigbouw Tech.	1968	11	53	174	mixed	multiple
Rotterdam						
Erasmus University	1969	27	112	367	concrete	off./laboratory
Medical Faculty	1970	26	104	341	concrete	hospital
Shell	1977	27	95	312	concrete	office
Europoint II	1977	22	95	312	concrete	office
Europoint I	1974	22	95	312	concrete	office
Europoint III	1977	22	95	312	concrete	office
Erasmus Univ-Economics Dept.	1969	20	75	246	concrete	office
Nederland Economic Hoge-school	1974	18	74	243	concrete	office
Bouw Center	1971	16	63	207	concrete	multiple
Adriaan Volkerhuis	1974	17	62	203	concrete	office
Phs. van Ommeren	1963	16	60	187	concrete	office
Stationspostgebouw	1959	14	60	187	concrete	office
Overbeekhuis	1965	14	53	174	mixed	office
Witte Huis	1897	13	45	148	steel	office
St. Franciscus Gasthuis	1977	13	44	144	concrete	hospital
Ryswyk						
Octrooi Raad	1972	24	83	272	concrete	office
CRM	1966	18	65	213	jack block	office
Schiedam						
Stadhuis	U.C.	17	55	180	concrete	office
The Hague						
Schedeldoekshaven	1979	20	76	249	mixed	office
Nationale Nederlanden	1967	19	74	243	mixed	office
Transitorium	1969	21	73	240	mixed	office
Paleis van Justitie	1975	16	64	210	concrete	office
Westeinde Zickenhuis	1979	17	58	190	concrete	hospital
Babylon	1978	14	52	171	concrete	mulitple
Ministerie van Buitenlandse Zaken	U.C.	13	47	154	concrete	office
Grand Hotel	1977	11	44	144	concrete	apartment
Werkgeversverbond	1967	14	40	131	concrete	office
Arendsdorp	1970	9	28	92	concrete	apartment
Utrecht						
Hoofdkantoor Amev	U.C.	10	45	148	concrete	office
Voorburg						
Centraal Bur. v.d. Statistiek	1973	17	70	230	concrete	office
Zandvoort						
Bouwes	1965	19	61	200	concrete	office

Table 4 Tallest buildings in major cities (continued)

Building	Year Completed	Number of stories	Height meters	feet	Material	Use
Norway						
Bergen						
NKP Office	1972	14	45	148	concrete	office
City Hall	1974	13	43	141	concrete	office
Vest-Bo	1975	13	38	125	concrete	apartment
Oslo						
Post Office	1975	22	83	272	concrete	office
SAS Royal Hotel	1975	25	67	221	concrete	hotel
Okern Center	1969	20	65	213	steel/concrete	office
Trondheim						
Hospital	1974	15	53	174	concrete	hospital
City Administration	1970	14	52	171	concrete	office
Pakistan						
Karachi						
Habib Bank Plaza	1971	23	100	328	concrete	office
National Shipping Corp.	1971	17	69	227	concrete	office
National Bank	1965	14	61	200	concrete	office
KMC Super Market	1976	10	41	135	concrete	off./shops
Twin Stars (Rimpa Apartments)	1975	12	39	127	concrete	apartment
Papua New Guinea						
Lae						
Boug Copper Mine	1972	5	36	119	steel	industrial
Port Moresby						
Ang House	1967	11	45	147	concrete	multiple
PNG Cen. Govt. Offices	1974	7	28	91	concrete	office
Peru						
Lima						
Centro Civico	1976	34	102	335	concrete	office
Petro Peru	1971	23	71	233	concrete	office
Ministerio de Industria + Turism	1971	21	69	226	concrete	office
Torre del Olivar	1975	24	66	217	concrete	apartment
Esq. La Colmena y Wilson	1958	23	63	207	concrete	off./apt.
Hotel Sheraton	1974	21	63	207	concrete	hotel
Ministerio de Educacion	1956	21	63	207	steel	office
Hotel Crillon	1964	20	60	197	concrete	hotel
Oropes	1970	20	55	180	concrete	office
Lafayette	1972	20	53	174	concrete	apartment
Philippines						
Makati						
FNCB	U.C.	20	79	259	concrete	office
PAL		14	63	207	concrete	office
Soriano/SMB		11	58	189	concrete	office
Tuason	1965	13	55	182	concrete	office
AIU	1965	13	54	179	concrete	office
Sikatuna	1965	13	54	179	concrete	office
Phil. Bank of Commerce	1970	15	52	171	concrete	office
Bank of P.I.		10	50	164	concrete	office
The Chartered Bank	1972	11	49	161	concrete	office
Tele. Co. Makati	1968	10	45	147	concrete	office
Hotel Inter-Con	1968	14	44	146	concrete	hotel
Dona Narcisa	1967	11	44	144	concrete	office
Rufino Office Building	1962	10	44	143	concrete	office
Ayala Building 2	1960	11	43	141	concrete	office
Commercial Bank and Trust Co.		9	37	122	concrete	office
Makati Stock Exchange	1972	10	35	114	concrete	office
Manila						
Central Bank Multi-Storey		17	73	240	mixed	office
Philbanking Corp.		11	46	151	concrete	office
Philippine Savings Bank	1960	12	41	134	concrete	office
Avenue Theatre and Office	1936	10	38	124	concrete	office
Cultural Center of the Phil.	1969		35	116	mixed	theater
Manila Royal Hotel	1972	24			concrete	hotel
Manila Hilton	1966	22			concrete	hotel
Pasay City						
Asian Development Bank	1972	14	44	145	concrete	office
Hyatt Regency	1967	12	42	138	concrete	hotel
Philippine Village Hotel	1974	9	34	111	concrete	hotel
Lopez Museum	1959	8	30	98	concrete	museum

Table 4 Tallest buildings in major cities (continued)

Building	Year Completed	Number of stories	Height meters	feet	Material	Use
		Philippines (continued)				
		Pasig				
Meralco Adm. Building		13	76	249	concrete	office
Manila Chronicle	1970	7	29	95	concrete	office
		Quezon City				
S.S.S. Office Building	1965	12	55	182	mixed	office
		Poland				
		Bydgoszcz				
Administration Building	1969	14	47	154	prefab	office
		Gdansk				
1 Rajska Street	1976	19	75	246	concrete	office
1 Waly Piastowskie Street	1972	21	70	230	concrete	apartment
1 Centr. Osr. Przem. Okret.	1967	20	70	230	concrete	office
1 Rajska Street	1976	17	66	216	concrete	apartment
		Katowice				
2 Rozdzienski Housing Estate	1975	25	74	243	concrete	apartment
1 Rozdzienski Housing Estate	1974	24	70	230	concrete	apartment
1 Zawadzki Street	1970	24	70	230	steel	apartment
1 Armii Czerwonej Square	1968	17	57	187	concrete	apartment
		Krakow				
NOT Building	1978	24	91	300	steel	office
Book and Press Building	1977	18	65	213	mixed	office
Biprostal	1963	15	59	194	concrete	office
Olimp	1969	16	48	156	steel	stud. hall
Bablyon	1971	16	48	156	steel	stud. hall
		Lodz				
1 SDM	1976	24	78	256	concrete	apartment
		Warsaw				
1 Palac Kultury i Nauki	1955	42	241	790	steel/concrete	office
Bank and Foreign Trade Bldg.	1978	46	146	479	concrete	office
1 Intraco Stawki 3 Street	1975	38	138	453	concrete	office
1 Forum	1974	31	95	312	concrete	hotel
3 Sciana Wschodnia	1964	24	75	246	steel	apartment
Marszalkowska Street Apt.	1967	25	74	243	steel	apartment
1 Riviera Polna 4 Street	1963	22	69	226	steel/concrete	dormitory
Student Hostel	1962	21	69	226	mixed	multiple
1 Osiedle Wolska Poludniqua	1974	18	65	213	concrete	apartment
Skocznia 7 Street	1974	18	65	213	concrete	apartment
1 Tamka Street	1967	22	64	210	concrete	apartment
1 Smolna Street	1973	20	60	197	concrete	apartment
3 Kepa Potocka	1965	19	55	180	concrete	apartment
1 Dworkowa Street	1972	19	55	180	concrete	apartment
1 Hotel Warszawa Powstancow	1951	17	51	167	steel	hotel
2 Zelazna Brama	1971	17	51	167	concrete	apartment
3 Torwar C	1971	17	51	167	concrete	apartment
Osiedle Batorego	1973	17	51	167	concrete	apartment
1 Torarowa Street	1973	17	51	167	concrete	apartment
1 Targowa 49 Street	1971	16	48	157	concrete	apartment
1 Czerniakowska Street	1974	16	48	157	concrete	apartment
1 Komarowa Street	1974	16	48	157	concrete	apartment
Staroscinska Street	1974	16	48	157	concrete	apartment
		Wroclaw				
1 Grunwaldzki 5 Squaere	1972	16	48	157	concrete	apartment
Grabiszczynska 9 Street	1973	16	48	157	concrete	apartment
1 Grunwaldzki Squaere	1974	16	48	157	concrete	apartment
1 Grabiszczynska	1973	16	48	157	concrete	apartment
1 Grunwaldzki Square	1975	16	48	157	concrete	apartment
		Portugal				
		Lisbon				
Sheraton Hotel	1972	27	85	278	concrete	hotel
		Lourenço Marques				
Montepio de Moçambique	1974	35			concrete	multiple
		Luanda				
Banco Comercial de Angola	1967	21			concrete	office
		Portimao				
Tarik	1973	21	70	230	concrete	hotel

Table 4 Tallest buildings in major cities (continued)

Building	Year Completed	Number of stories	Height meters	feet	Material	Use
		Portugal (continued)				
		Porto				
W. Graham	1974	23			concrete	apartment

Romania
Bucharest

Building	Year Completed	Number of stories	Height meters	feet	Material	Use
Continental Hotel		24	88	289		hotel
Casa Scinteii	1953	17	78	255	mixed	office

Timisoara

Building	Year Completed	Number of stories	Height meters	feet	Material	Use
Continental Hotel	1971	15	50	164	concrete	hotel
Isim Building	1975	11	43	141	concrete	office/lab.
The County Hospital	1974	10	40	131	concrete	hospital
Marasti Square	1973	11	38	125	concrete	shops/apt.
47 Circumvalatiunii Zone	1974	11	37	121	concrete	shops/apt.
A2, A3, G. Lazar Street	1973	11	35	115	concrete	shops/apt.
5, 1 December Street	1975	11	35	115	concrete	shops/apt.
C5 Giroc Way	1976	11	35	115	concrete	shops/apt.
Electromotor	1975	9	35	115	concrete	shops/apt.

Saudi Arabia
Jedda

Building	Year Completed	Number of stories	Height meters	feet	Material	Use
National Commercial Bank	1981	27	122	400	steel	office

Singapore
Singapore

Building	Year Completed	Number of stories	Height meters	feet	Material	Use
Overseas-Chinese Banking Corp.	1976	52	201	660	concrete	office
International Plaza	1976	50	190	624	concrete	shops/off.
Development Bank of Singapore	1975	50	187	612	concrete	office
CPF	1976	45	171	560	concrete	office
Hong Leong	1976	45	159	520	concrete	multiple
UIC	1974	40	152	500	concrete	office
Mandarin Hotel	1973	40	152	500	concrete	hotel
Communication Centre	U.C.	32	140	460	concrete	office
Admore Park	U.C.	36	137	450	concrete	apartment
Shaw Tower	1974	34	134	440	concrete	multiple
Ocean Building	1974	29	119	390	concrete	office
High Street Centre	1974	31	116	380	concrete	multiple
Pearl Bank Apartments	1976	38	113	372	concrete	apartment
Peace Centre	1974	35	110	363	concrete	multiple
Shenton House	1974	24	108	355	concrete	multiple
Peoples Park Complex	1973	31	99	326	concrete	multiple
Robina House	1973	23	97	318	steel	multiple
Tunas	1973	29	97	317	concrete	office
OUB	1974	30	91	300	concrete	multiple
Golden Mile Tower	1974	24	90	295	concrete	multiple
Shing Kwan House	1973	22	86	283	concrete	multiple
Peoples Park Centre	1974	28	86	282	mixed	multiple
Textile Centre	1974	24	86	282	concrete	multiple
Hotel Summit	1971	28	85	280	concrete	multiple
Shangri-La Hotel	1972	24	85	280	concrete	hotel
Shenton Plaza	1974	21	85	278	concrete	multiple
Goldhill Plaza	1973	26	76	250	concrete	office
Apollo Hotel	1972	19	76	249	concrete	multiple
Specialists Centre	1973	25	75	245	concret	office
Crawford Tower	1974	21	74	245	concrete	multiple
Hilton Hotel	1969	24	73	240	concrete	multiple
Selegie Complex	1972	18	64	210	concrete	multiple
Hyatt Hotel	1971	20	61	200	concrete	multiple
Manhatten House	1974	15	59	193	concrete	multiple
Golden Mile Shopping Centre	1972	16	57	188	concrete	multiple
Hotel Miramar	1970	16	57	188	concrete	multiple
Kings Hotel	1970	12	52	170	concrete	multiple
Anson Centre	1971	14	49	163	concrete	multiple
Maxwell House	1971	13	49	162	concrete	multiple
Supreme House	1971	13	44	146	concrete	multiple
Regal House	1973	12	40	133	concrete	multiple
Og Building	1972	10	35	110	concrete	multiple
United Overseas Bank	U.C.	30			concrete	office
Futura		25			concrete	apartment
Straits Trade	1974	22			concrete	office
Yen San	1973	20			concrete	office
Asian Development Bank	1974	13			concrete	office

Table 4 Tallest buildings in major cities (continued)

Building	Year Completed	Number of stories	Height meters	feet	Material	Use
South Africa						
Cape Town						
B. P. Centre	1972	31	125	409	concrete	office
Shell House	1976	29	119	390	concrete	office
Trust Bank	1970	33	107	350	mixed	office
Provincial Administration	1976	26	101	330	concrete	office
Civic Centre	1978	26	98	320	concrete	office
Mobil House	1970	24	93	306	concrete	office
Sanlam	1962	22	93	306	concrete	office
Mobil House	1969	22	93	305	concrete	office
Cartwrights Corner House	1969	24	92	303	concrete	office
Cape Town Centre	1976	23	88	289	concrete	office
S.A. Reserve Bank	1975	23	87	284	concrete	office
H.F. Verwoerd	1969	20	85	280	concrete	office
Gardens Centre	1973	22	81	265	concrete	residential
Durban						
Nedbank Centre	1974	21	94	310	concrete	office
Johannesburg						
Carlton Centre	1973	50	220	722	concrete	office
Standard Bank Centre	1970	31	160	525	concrete	office
Trust Bank Centre	1970		150	459	concrete	office
African Eagle Life Centre	1976	30	138	453	concrete	office
Ponte Investments Apartment			125	410		apartment
Schlesinger	1965	21	110	360	concrete	office
Pretoria						
Volkskas Bank Centre	U.C.		175	574		office
Volkskas Bank Building	1978	38	132	432	concrete	office
Agricultural Union Centre	1968		110	360		office
Poytons Centre	1968		110	360		
Hallmark			70	230		
South Vietnam						
Saigon						
National Library	1970	13	50	163	concrete	office
Ind. Commercial Bank	1973	12	46	150	concrete	office
Spain						
Alicante						
Comp. Vistahermosa	1966	16	51	167	concrete	apartment
Andorra						
Chimenea Conica de Andorra	1978		105	343		industrial
Badajoz						
6 Torres Sta. Marina	1972	12	40	131	concrete	apartment
Sta. Marina Housing	1977	11	35	115	concrete	apartment
Badalona						
INP in Badalona	1978	15	55	180	concrete	hospital
Barcelona						
Residencia Principes de España	1972	21	65	213	concrete	hospital
Viviendas para Policia Armada	1971	19	60	197	concrete	apartment
Benidorm						
Edif. Solana	1975	15	48	157	concrete	apartment
Bilbao						
Bank of Vizcaya	1968	21	106	348	steel	office
Viviendas Renfe	1971	15	57	187	concrete	apartment
Caceres						
Viviendas Covisemca No 4	1979	12	40	131	concrete	apartment
Jerez						
Jerez Housing	1977	16	55	180	concrete	apt./off.
Ceret Housing	1976	12	40	131	concrete	apartment
San Benito Housing	1972	11	35	115	concrete	apartment
La Coruna						
Torre Galicia	1972	21	57	187	steel	apartment
Las Palmas						
Hotel Don Juan	1971	24	84	276		hotel
Hotel Cristina	1970		52	171		hotel
Red Crown Apartments	1972	15	50	164	concrete	apartment
Sical	1967		45	148		office
Logroño						
Torre de Logroño	1973	18	48	157	steel	apartment

Table 4 Tallest buildings in major cities (continued)

Building	Year Completed	Number of stories	Height meters	feet	Material	Use
Spain (continued)						
Madrid						
Building of Offices	U.C.	50	175	574	steel	office
Bank of Bilbao	1979	31	107	351	steel/concrete	bank
Reyzaca	1977	29	105	343		office
Ministry of Trade	1979	25	100	328	concrete	office
Entrerrios Apartments	1973	25	100	328	concrete	apartment
Banco de Santander	1977	20	70	230		bank
Housing in Madrid	1976	18	65	213	concrete	apartment
Cristaleria	1977	18	64	210		office
Hotel Princesa Plaza	1976	14	55	180		hotel
Ministry of Industry	1979	14	55	180	concrete	office
Viviendas Alberto Alcocer	1967	17	50	164	concrete	apartment
Residencia Sur	1973	16	50	164	steel	hospital
Centro Ramon y Cajal.	1977	15	48	157	steel	hospital
Torre de Madrid	1950	35				multiple
Tower of Madrid	1960	32				multiple
Edificio España	1952	25				multiple
Ciudad de los Periodistas	1972	18				apartment
La Union y el Fenix	1967	18				
Banco Español de Credito	1970	11				bank
Galerias Preciados	1960	10				office
Malaga						
Playamar Apartments	1971	16	45	148	concrete	apartment
San Enrique Hotel	1971	11	35	115	concrete	hotel
Don Pablo Hotel	1975	11	30	98	concrete	hotel
Orense						
Orense Tower	1969	20	65	213	steel/concrete	apartment
Sevilla						
Bloques Coveca	1972	15	45	148	concrete	apartment
Tenerife						
Rascacielos Tenerife	1963	25	75	246	concrete	apartment
Apart. Melo	1974	17	50	164	concrete	apartment
Torremolinos						
Los Manantiales	1972	20	63	207	concrete	apartment
Tres Torres los Manantiales	1973	18	54	177	concrete	hotel
Valencia						
Viv. Fuente San Luis	1977	15	48	157	steel	apartment
Vivis. Blasco Ibanez	1978	15	47	154	concrete	apartment
Valladolid						
Hotel Duque de Lerma	1973	24	70	230	steel	hotel
Zaragoza						
Templo del Pilar Dos Torres	1950		95	285		library
Sri Lanka						
Colombo						
Central Wholesale Establishment	1978	14	59	195	concrete	office
Sweden						
Gothenburg						
Frolumdatore	1967	18	57	188		multiple
Sahlgrenska	1961	17	56	182		hospital
Stora Badhusgat	1946	16	53	173		office
Axel Dahlstroms Torg	1955	16	49	162		apartment
SKF	1967	14	46	149		office
Dragspelsgat	1961	14	42	136		apartment
Park Aveny	1949	12	41	133		hotel
KV Tonfisken	1972	13	40	130		apartment
Kviberg	1958	13	38	125		apartment
Mandolingatan	1960	13	37	122		apartment
Malmö						
K.V. Kronprinsen	1964	29	83	272		multiple
Stockholm						
Dagms Nyhelm	1963	26	82	269		office
Skalhmesel	1960	26	80	263		office
Folksam	1959	24	74	243		office

Table 4 Tallest buildings in major cities (continued)

Building	Year Completed	Number of stories	Height meters	feet	Material	Use
		Switzerland				
		Basel				
Bank-Intern. Zahlungsausg-leich	1977	20	70	230	steel/concrete	office
		Bern				
Laboratory-Forschung/Ver-suchsa	1965	21	93	305	steel/concrete	lab/off.
		Geneva				
Lignon	1965	31	91	298	steel/concrete	apartment
Bâtiment/Tour SSR	1970	19	60	197	steel/concrete	office
		Lausanne				
Valemont	1962	17	54	178	concrete	apartment
Rouveraie	1973	15	44	144	concrete	apartment
Valentin 34	1976	14	44	144	concrete	apartment
		Montruex				
Tour d'Ivoire	1962	25	79	259	concrete	off./apt.
Eurotel	1966	17	54	177	steel/concrete	hotel
		Morges				
Tour Résidence	1969	18	55	180	concrete	off./apt.
		Prilly				
Clair-Logis	1969	17	49	161	concrete	apartment
		Regensdorf				
Zentrum Regensdorf B1	1973	19	55	180	concrete	apartment
		Renens				
Longemalle 20	1969	16	44	144	concrete	apartment
		Winterthur				
Sulzer Hochhaus	1965	25	92	302	conc./alum.	office
Stadtkirche Turme	1959	11	64	210	stone/wood	church tower
Winterthur Unfall Turm	1930	8	35	115	brick/conc.	office
Wohnhochhaus Mattenbach	1960	13	34	112	brick/conc.	apartment
Ueberbauung Gruzefeld	1967	11	32	105	concrete	apartment
		Zürich				
Hardau	1975	33	93	303	concrete	apartment
Hotel International	1972	28	85	279	concrete	hotel
Hotel Zürich	1972	21	70	230	concrete	hotel
Triemli	1970	21	70	230	concrete	hospital
Lochergut	1966	23	62	203	concrete	apartment
Frohes Wohnung	1976	18	55	180	concrete	apartment
Heumatt	1973	18	53	174	concrete	apartment
SIA	1970	13	47	154	concrete	office
Murg	1972	13	40	131	masonry	apartment
Spreiteubach						
		Taiwan				
		Taipei				
Hilton		22			concrete	hotel
		Thailand				
		Bangkok				
Bangkok Bank, Ltd.	U.C.	35	134	439	concrete	office
Chokechai International		24	100	328	concrete	office
Dusit Thanee Hotel and Office		23	82	269	concrete	multiple
Hau Chiew Hospital	U.C.	22	82	269	concrete	hospital
Indra Regent Hotel		17	70	230	concrete	multiple
U.N. Office (ECAFE)	U.C.	15	62	203	concrete	office
Kiannguan		16	60	197	concrete	office
South East Insurance		13	59	194	concrete	office
Rama-Hilton Hotel		16	56	184	concrete	hotel
Cathay-Trust (Esso)		14	50	164	concrete	office
Bangkok Boonmit	U.C.	13	50	164	concrete	office
Jetro		15	46	151	concrete	multiple
Chulalongkorn's Student Dorm.	U.C.	14	43	141	concrete	dormitory
Jilom Building and Service		11	40	131	concrete	office
Thaniya		11	40	131	concrete	office
A.I.A. Bangkok		10	40	131	concrete	office
Thani Danu Bank		10	39	128	concrete	office

Table 4 Tallest buildings in major cities (continued)

Building	Year Completed	Number of stories	Height meters	feet	Material	Use
Turkey						
Ankara						
Kizilay Is Hani	1962	26	72	236	concrete	office
Istanbul						
Sheraton Hotel	1973	25	87	285	concrete	hotel
UK—England						
Beaconsfield						
Army School of Education	1967	16			mixed	school
Birmingham						
ATV Offices	1972	27	82	270	concrete	office
Sentinel Tower	1971	32	79	260	concrete	apartment
Kennedy Tower		21	70	228	concrete	office
Aston Student Hall	1971	21	57	187	concrete	
Swan Office Center		11			concrete	office
Cambridge						
Univ. Library Tower	1935	15	49	160	masonry	
Addenbrooks Hospital Tower	1968		37	120	concrete	
Peterhouse Dormitory	1967	9	27	90	masonry	dormitory
Essex						
Essex University Towers	1965	15			mixed	school
Hatfield						
Goldings House	1968	15			masonry	apartment
French Horn Lane	1967	15			brick	apartment
Liverpool						
St. Johns Beacon	1965		135	442	concrete	restaurant
Liverpool Cathedral			106	347	sandstone	cathedral
Royal Liver	1909	13	94	308	steel/concrete	office
Whiteacre House	1974	20	78	257	steel/concrete	office
Royal Insurance Company	1976	18	77	251	steel/concrete	office
Post and Echo	1973	18	73	240	concrete	office
Old Hall Street Development	1974	18	70	230	mixed	office
Metropolitan Cathedral	1967		66	216	concrete	cathedral
J.M. Centre	1962	17	64	210	steel/concrete	office
St. Georges Hill	1964	22	63	206	concrete	apartment
Silkhouse Court	1970	15	58	190	concrete	office
Rice Lane/Zante Street	1968	16	47	154	concrete	apartment
London						
National Westminster Bank	1980	52	182	600	concrete	office
Post Office Tower	1965		177	580	concrete	office
Guys Hospital	1971	35	143	468	concrete	hospital
Barbican	1970	40	126	412	concrete	apartment
Euston Centre	1970	34	124	407	concrete	office
Britannic House (B.P. House)	1970	35	121	395	concrete	office
Commercial Union	1968	28	118	387	mixed	office
Vickers Tower Block			117	385		
Millbank Tower	1961	34	117	382	concrete	office
Centre Point	1964	36	116	380	concrete	office
Kings Reach Development	1972		111	365	steel	office
Shell	1961	26	107	351	steel	office
Berkeley Hambro Bishops-gate Tr	1975	29	104	341	mixed	office
Southwark Towers	1976	25	100	327	concrete	office
Angel Court	1977	24	93	306	concrete	office
Kleinwort Benson			87	286		
Manchester						
CIS	1965	30	126	425	mixed	office
Co-op Insurance	1970		122	400	steel	office
Piccadilly Plaza		32	118	390	concrete	office
Albert Bridge Hosue		18	60	200	concrete	office
UK—Scotland						
Glasgow						
Gallowgate Flats	1968	31	87	285	concrete	housing
Red Road Flats	1969	32	85	280	steel	housing
Balornock	1969	31	85	280	steel	apartment
Springburn Flats	1967	24	67	220	concrete	housing
Anniesland Cross	1971	20	67	220	concrete	housing
Garscadden Flats	1970	22	63	205	concrete	housing
Laurieston	1972	24	62	202	concrete	apartment
Gorbals Flats	1972	24	62	202	concrete	housing
Townhead Flats	1969	24	61	200	concrete	housing

Table 4 Tallest buildings in major cities (continued)

Building	Year Completed	Number of stories	Height meters	feet	Material	Use
Glasgow, UK—Scotland (continued)						
Cowcaddens Flats	1972	24	61	200	concrete	housing
Hutcheson Flats	1972	22	61	200	concrete	housing
Dumbreck Flats	1970	22	59	195	concrete	housing
Cleeves Road		13			brick	apartment
Lanarkshire						
Hamilton Training College	1966	16			mixed	school
USA						
Akron, Ohio						
First National Tower		28	101	330		office
Cascade		24	96	316		office
Edison Tower		19	85	280		office
Albany, New York						
Office Tower, South Mall	1973	44	180	589		
State Office Building	1930	34	118	388		
Agency Bldgs. 1, 3, 4	1973	23	95	310	mixed	office
Agency Bldg. 2	1974	22	87	286	mixed	
Univ. Towers Dutch I	1965	22	87	286	concrete	dormitory
Univ. Towers Indian II	1971	22	87	286	concrete	dormitory
Univ. Towers Colonial III	1966	22	87	286	concrete	dormitory
Univ. Towers State IV	1968	22	87	286	concrete	dormitory
Allentown, Pennsylvania						
Pennsylvania Power & Light	1929	23	96	315	steel	office
Episcopal House	1965	19	62	202	steel	apartment
Atlanta, Georgia						
Peachtree Center Plaza	1975	71	220	723	concrete	hotel
Southern Bell	1981	46	206	677	concrete	office
First National Bank	1967	44	171	562	steel	office
Equitable	1969	34	138	453	steel	office
101 Marietta Tower	1975	36	136	446	steel	office
National Bank of Georgia	1961	32	134	439	concrete	office
Peachtree Summit No. 1	1976	31	124	406	concrete	office
Coca-Cola Headquarters	1979	28	123	403	concrete	office
Tower Place	1975	29	122	401	steel	office
Atlanta Hilton Hotel	1976	32	117	383	concrete	hotel
Richard R. Russell Fed. Bldg	1979	26	117	383	steel	office
Peachtree Center Harris Bldg	1976	31	116	382	steel	office
Trust Company Bank	1968	28	115	377	steel	office
Coastal States Insurance		27	115	377		
Peachtree Center Cain Bldg		30	115	376		
Peachtree Center Building		31	114	374		
Life of Georgia Tower	1968	29	113	371	steel	office
Georgia Power Tower	U.C.	24	106	349		
Peachtree Center South		27	101	332		
Gas Light Tower		27	101	331		
Hyatt Regency Hotel	1966	22	101	330	concrete	hotel
100 Colony Square		25	100	328		
Georgia Power		22	97	318		
Colony Square Hotel		28	95	310		
400 Colony Square		23	94	308		
Atlanta Center		23	92	301		
Coca-Cola Headquarters	1979	28	93	300	steel	office
Merchandise Mart		22	91	300	concrete	mart
Fulton National Bank	1954	22	90	295	steel	office
Grady Hospital	1959	22	84	277	steel	hospital
Peachtree Towers	1962	24	82	270	concrete	apartment
C and S Bank	1970	20	81	266	steel	office
Southern Bell Telephone	1930	14	78	257	steel	equipment
State Capitol	1889	4	77	252	steel	government
Rhodes/Haverty	1929	22	76	250	steel	office
City Hall	1930	15	67	219	steel	government
Candler	1906	17	64	210	steel	office
Hurt	1913	17	64	210	steel	office
Martin Luther King Tower	1971	12	30	100	masonry	apartment
Colony Square Hotel	1978	25				
Twin State Office Towers	1980	22			steel	office
Omni International Hotel	1977	14			steel	hotel
Austin, Texas						
Austin National Bank		26	100	328		
American Bank		21	95	313		
State Capitol			94	309		
Univ. of Texas Admin.		29	94	307		
J. Frank Dobie Univ. Center		29	91	299		
Westgate		24	80	261		
Holiday Inn	1966	13	38	122	masonry	hotel

Table 4 Tallest buildings in major cities (continued)

Building	Year Completed	Number of stories	Height meters	feet	Material	Use
USA (continued)						
Baileys Crossroads, Virginia						
Skyline Plaza						apartment
Baltimore, Maryland						
U.S. Fidelity and Guaranty Co.	1973	40	161	529	steel	office
Maryland National Bank	1929	34	155	509	steel	office
World Trade Center	1977	28	123	405	concrete	office
Blaustein	1962	30	110	360	steel	office
Arlington Fed. Savings and Loan	1967	28	106	350	steel	office
Federal Building	1967	28	103	338	concrete	office
St. Paul Apartment	1966	37	100	330	steel	apartment
Charles Center South	1977	26	101	330	steel	office
Tower Building	1912	16	101	330	steel	office
Baltimore Arts Tower	1911	15	97	319		office
Lord Baltimore Hotel	1928	22	96	315	steel	hotel
Mercantile Safe Deposit + Trust	1968	21	96	315	concrete	office
Chesapeake and Potomac Tele. Co.	1977	16	91	300	steel	office
No. 1 Charles Center	1962	22	90	294	steel	office
Baltimore Gas and Electric	1916	21	88	287	steel	office
Hilton Hotel	1967	24	86	281	concrete	hotel
Charles Plaza Apts. South	1967	31	85	280	concrete	apartment
Hilton Hotel (Addn)	1974	28	85	280	concrete	hotel
Mercy Hospital	1961	21	85	280	steel	hospital
First Natl Bank of Maryland	1972	22	81	265	concrete	office
Equitable Bank Centre	1979	17	79	260	steel	off./retail
Charles Plaza Apts. North	1967	28	78	255	concrete	apartment
First National Bank	1923	20	77	254	steel	office
Fidelity	1912	16	70	220	steel	office
Munsey	1912	20	65	215	steel	office
Social Security Administration	1979	14	62	208	steel	office
Stanblat	1921	16	62	205	steel	office
Commercial Credit	1956	20	61	200	steel	office
Court Square	1927	19	61	200	steel	office
Maryland National Bank	1968	17	61	200	steel	office
Baton Rouge, Louisiana						
State Capitol		34	140	460		office
American Bank	1974	25	95	310		off./bank
Hilton Hotel	1976	28	88	290		hotel
Louisiana National Bank	1968	21	84	277		off./bank
Bethlehem, Pennsylvania						
Martin Tower	1969	21	101	330	steel	office
Bethlehem Steel 3rd St.	1905	13	60	197	steel	office
First Valley Bank	1974	11	49	162	steel	office
Moravian I	1973	14	45	146	steel	apartment
Rooney	1978	14	42	138	steel	apartment
Monocacy Tower	1973	11	39	127	steel	apartment
Lutheran Manor	1978	11	38	126	steel	residence
Union Bank	1967	10	35	114	steel	off./bank
Hotel Bethlehem	1921	9	34	112	steel	hotel
Moravian II	1979	9	30	98	steel	apartment
Birmingham, Alabama						
First Natl Southern Natural		30	119	390	steel	off./bank
South Central Bell Hqs.		30	119	390	steel	office
City Federal Building		27	99	325	steel	office
Cabana Motel		21	88	287	steel	apartment
Daniel		20	86	283	concrete	office
First Alabama Bank		17	65	212	steel	bank/off.
Hyatt House		15	55	180		hotel
Central Bank		14	52	170	concrete	bank/off.
Beacon Towers		11	34	111	concrete	
Boston, Massachusetts						
John Hancock Tower	1973	60	241	790	steel	office
Prudential Center	1964	52	229	750	steel	office
Federal Reserve	1976	32	228	750	steel	office
Boston Company	1970	41	183	601	mixed	office
First National Bank of Boston	1970	37	180	591	steel	office
One Post Office Square	1981	40	161	525	steel	office
Shawmut Bank	1975	38	158	525	steel	office
Sixty State	1978	38	155	509	steel	office
Employers Commercial Union Co.	1977	40	155	507	steel	office
N.E. Merchant Bank	1968	40	152	500	steel	office
U.S. Custom House		32	151	496		

Table 4 Tallest buildings in major cities (continued)

Building	Year Completed	Number of stories	Height meters	feet	Material	Use
Boston, Massachusetts, USA (continued)						
John Hancock Building	1973	26	151	495	steel	office
State Street Bank	1966	34	145	477	steel	office
100 Summer Street	1975	33	137	450	steel	office
McCormack		22	122	401		
Keystone Custodian Funds	1971	32	122	400	mixed	office
Harbor Towers (2 buildings)		40	121	396	concrete	residential
Saltonstall Office Building		22	121	396		
John F. Kennedy Building	1964	24	118	387	steel	office
State Office Buidign		22	107	350		office
Federal Building + Post Office		22	105	345		
Suffolk County Courthouse		19	101	330		
Sheraton Boston Hotel		29	95	310		
State Service Center		23	91	300		
Bozeman, Montana						
Married Student Housing	1969	9	23	76	masonry	apartment
Buffalo, New York						
Marine Midland		40	161	529		
City Hall		32	115	378		
Rand		29	107	351		
Erie County Savings Bank		26	107	350		
Manufacturers + Trades Trust Co.		21	97	317		
Liberty Bank		23	93	305		
Electric Tower		18	90	294		
Churchil Academic Tower	1972	11			steel	office
Cambridge, Massachusetts						
MIT Center for Earth Sciences	1964	21	90	295	concrete	research
Camden, New Jersey						
Westfield Towers	1969	10	26	86	masonry	apartment
Charlotte, North Carolina						
NCNB Plaza		40	153	503		
Jefferson First Union Tower		32	132	433		
Wachovia Center		32	128	420		
Southern National Center		22	91	300		
NCNB Building		18	91	299		
Bank of North Carolina		20	85	280		
Chicago, Illinois						
Sears Tower	1974	110	443	1454	steel	office
Standard Oil (Indiana)	1973	80	346	1136	steel	office
John Hancock	1968	100	344	1127	steel	multiple
Water Tower Place	1976	74	262	859	concrete	multiple
First National Bank	1969	60	257	844	steel	office
3 First National Plaza	1980	58	236	775	mixed	office
IBM	1973	52	212	695	steel	office
Newman-Marcus	1981	65	210	690	concrete	multiple
Civic Center	1965	38	202	662	steel	office
Michigan & Oak	1981	60	198	650	concrete	multiple
Lake Point Towers	1968	70	196	645	concrete	apartment
1000 Lakeshore Plaza	1964	60	195	640	concrete	apartment
Prudential	1953	42	183	601	steel	office
Marina City	1962	60	179	588	concrete	multiple
Mid-Continental Plaza	1972	50	175	582	concrete	office
Newberry House	1972	58	171	560	concrete	apartment
CNA Towers	1972	40	171	560	steel	office
Harbor Point	1975	54	170	558	concrete	apartment
Pittsfield Building	1927	38	170	557	steel	multiple
Kemper Building (Opera House)	1929	45	169	555	steel	office
30 North La Salle	1975	43	169	553	steel	office
Xerox	1979	45	168	550	concrete	office
2 First National Bank	1972	40	168	550	steel	office
La Salle National Bank	1934	44	163	535	steel	office
Frontier Towers	1973	55	163	533	concrete	apartment
One La Salle Street	1930	49	162	530	steel	office
River Plaza	1978	56	160	524	concrete	apartment
Board of Trade Building	1930	44	160	524	steel	office
Pure Oil Building	1926	40	159	523	steel	office
United Insurance Company	1962	41	159	522	steel	office
111 East Chestnut	1973	57	156	520	concrete	apartment
Lincoln Tower		42	158	519		
Carbide and Carbon		37	153	503		office
Marriot Hotel	1978	45	152	500	concrete	hotel
Walton Colonnade		44	152	500	concrete	apartment

Table 4 Tallest buildings in major cities (continued)

Building	Year Completed	Number of stories	Height meters	feet	Material	Use
Chicago, Illinois, USA (continued)						
Edgewater Beach Apartments		39	152	499		apartment
La Salle Wacker		41	150	491		
American National Bank		40	146	479		
Brunswick Building	1964	38	146	478	concrete	office
Park Tower	1974	54	145	476	concrete	apartment
Bankers Building		41	145	476		
Continental Companies		45	145	475		
American Furniture Mart		24	145	474		
Sheraton Hotel		42	144	471		
Harris Bank II	1976	35	143	470	steel	office
Playboy		37	143	468		
188 Randolph Tower		45	142	465		
Tribune Tower		36	141	462		
Equitable Life	1964	35	139	457	steel	office
Roanoke		37	138	452		
Gateway III	1972	35	137	450	mixed	office
168 N. LaSalle	1975	35	133	435	concrete	office
150 S. Wacker	1970	35	131	430	concrete	office
1100 S. Michigan	1970	35	122	400	concrete	apartment
Continental Plaza Hotel	1974	27	122	400	concrete	hotel
Outer Drive East Apts.	1969	40	122	400	masonry	apartment
Dewitt-Chestnut Apts.	1965	43	120	395	concrete	apartment
St. Clair Building	1979	30	114	375	concrete	office
33 W. Monroe	1980	29	114	375	steel	office
Montgomery Ward	1972	27	114	375	concrete	office
Connecticut Mutual	1966	25	104	340	steel	office
500 N. Michigan	1970	25	99	325	concrete	office
U. of Illinois Administration	1964	25	99	325	concrete	university
Harris Bank I	1961	25	99	325	steel	office
200 West Monroe	1973	23	85	280	concrete	office
120 S. Riverside	1968	20	84	275	steel	office
100 S. Riverside	1964	20	84	275	steel	office
Inland Steel	1959	20	82	270	steel	office
100 S. Wacker	1962	20	72	235	concrete	office
Illinois Center	1975	54			concrete	apartment
Monadnock Building	1889	16	66	216	masonry	office
Restaurant House		14				restaurant
Home Insurance	1885	10			iron	office
Cincinnati, Ohio						
Carew Tower	1932	49	175	574	steel	multiple
Central Trust Tower	1913	34	151	495		office
Dubois Tower		32	129	423	steel	office
Central Trust Center		27	111	364		
Kroger	1959	25	105	345	concrete	office
Stouffer's Cincinnati Tower		33	98	324		
Federated Building		21	93	305		
U. of Cinn. Sander Hall	1971	27	91	297	steel	dormitory
CG and E	1929	20	85	280	steel	office
Terrace Hilton Hotel		19	83	273		
Provident Tower	1968	19	82	268	steel	office
American Building	1928	18	78	255	concrete	office
Celestial Apts.	1967	24	76	250	steel	multiple
Tri-State	1903	15	76	250	steel	office
Crosley Tower A-2	1968	16	74	244	concrete	laboratory
Post Times	1931	16	70	231	concrete	multiple
Stouffers Inn	1969	21	70	230	steel	hotel
First National Tower	1903	19	70	228	steel	office
Edgecliff Apts	1969	16	69	225	concrete	apartment
Transit	1903	16	64	210	concrete	office
Ingalls	1903	16	64	210	concrete	office
Telephone Company	1975	12	62	204	concrete	office
Enquirer	1926	14	58	189	concrete	office
Mabley and Carew	1923	16	56	184	concrete	retail
Madison House	1957	19	56	183	steel	apartment
Formica	1970	13	55	180	steel	office
Procter and Gamble	1955	11	55	180	steel	office
Telephone Company	1914	11	54	176	steel	office
Quality Motor Inn	1973	18	53	173	concrete	motel
Race Street Tower	1972	14	51	168	concrete	office
Central Trust No. 11	1970	12	50	165	concrete	office
Fifth/Third Bank	1969	17	50	164	steel	office
Dixie Terminal	1923	11	50	163	concrete	office
Queen Towers	1965	15	49	160	steel	apartment
Insight Tower	1927	12	49	160	steel	office
Calhoun Hall	1968	16	48	157	concrete	dormitory
Mercantile Library		13	48	156		office
Morgen Hall	1966	13	47	154	concrete	dormitory
Sawyer Hall	1966	13	47	154	concrete	dormitory

Table 4 Tallest buildings in major cities (continued)

Building	Year Completed	Number of stories	Height meters	feet	Material	Use
Cincinnati, Ohio, USA (continued)						
Scioto Hall	1966	13	47	154	concrete	dormitory
Queengate Highrise	1975	17	46	152	concrete	apartment
Queengate No. 2	1975	17	46	152	concrete	apartment
Stanley Rowe Apts		14	46	150		
Gwynne	1914	13	46	150	steel	office
Fourth National Bank	1905	12	44	143	steel	multiple
Pan Am East		15	43	140	concrete	
Pan Am West	1972	15	43	140	concrete	
Siddall Hall	1965	14	43	140	concrete	dormitory
Board of Education	1921	12	43	140		office
Procter and Gamble	1915	10	42	138	steel	office
Daniels Hall	1968	14	41	135	concrete	dormitory
Page Towers	1973	14	41	134	steel	apartment
Wiggins	1905	10	41	134	steel	office
River Terrace	1964	12	40	130	steel	apartment
Power		10	40	130		multiple
Provident Bank	1906	11	37	121	steel	office
Alms Apts	1962	11	37	120	steel	apartment
Stanley Rowe Apts	1964	13	35	116	concrete	apartment
City-County	1970	9	35	114	concrete	office
Marquette Manor	1967	15	34	111	concrete	apartment
Holiday Park	1971	12	34	110	concrete	office
Riverview House	1935	10	31	103	concrete	apartment
Park Eden	1973	10	27	90	concrete	apartment
Netherland Hilton		29				
Terrace Hilton		20				
Hammond North Apts		18				
580 Building		17			steel	office
Golden Towers	1972	15			concrete	
Belvedere Apts		12				
Garfield Towers		12				
Lytle Tower		12				
Mid-Towne Apts		12				
Phelps Apts	1926	12				apartment
Second National Bank		12				
Textile		12				
Merchants		11				
Schott Hall		11				
Sheraton Gibson		11				
Atlas Bank		10				
Schmidt		10				
Temple Bar		10				
Clarksburg, West Virginia						
Elderly Housing Complex 27-1	1967	11	32	108	masonry	apartment
Cleveland, Ohio						
Terminal Tower	1930	52	216	708	steel	office
Erieview Plaza Tower		40	161	529		
Justice Center		26	128	420		
Federal Building		32	128	419		office
Cleveland Trust Tower 1		29	117	383		
Ohio Bell Telephone Co.		22	111	365		
Cleveland State Univ. Towers		10	107	352		
Park Centre		26	98	320		
Central Natl Bank		23	93	305		
Diamond Shamrock		23	91	300		
CEI		22	91	300		
Union Commerce		21	88	289		
Standard		21	86	282		
East Ohio		21	84	275		
Bond Court		20	82	270		
Case W. Reserve U. Mens Dorm.	1969	12	40	130	masonry	dormitory
Parmatown	1972	10	27	90	masonry	apartment
Columbia, Missouri						
Paquin Tower	1973	15	43	142	concrete	apartment
Tiger Hotel	1929	10			concrete	hotel
Oak Tower	1967	9			concrete	apartment
Bingham Group (2 towers)	1964	9			concrete	dormitory
Blair (2 towers)	1962	9			concrete	dormitory
Dobbs Group (3 towers)	1959	9			concrete	dormitory
Lewis Hall	1964	9			concrete	office
Clark Hall	1964	9			concrete	office
Columbus, Ohio						
State Office Tower	1973	41	190	624		
State Office Building	1973	42	180	592	steel	office
Leveque Lincoln	1930	47	170	555	steel	office
Nationwide Plaza		40	148	485		

Table 4 Tallest buildings in major cities (continued)

Building	Year Completed	Number of stories	Height meters	feet	Material	Use
Columbus, Ohio, USA (continued)						
Bordens	1974	34	134	438	steel	office
Columbus Center	1964	26	109	357		office
Franklin County Mun. Courts		19	108	357		
Ohio Bell Telephone	1973	26	107	350	steel	office
88 East Broad Street	1963	20	99	324	concrete	office
Bancohio Plaza		25	97	317		
Motorists Mutual	1973	21	87	286	steel	office
Midland Mutual	1970	21	85	280	concrete	office
Lincoln	1965	24	79	260	concrete	dormitory
Morrill	1965	24	79	260	concrete	dormitory
Sheraton	1961	22	76	250	concrete	hotel
IBM	1973	17	67	220	steel	office
St. Anthony	1970	17	58	190	concrete	hospital
Summit Chase	1962	20	55	180	concrete	apartment
8 E. Broad	1914	16	55	180	steel	office
Buckeye	1927	15	52	170		office
House of Studies	1970	18	51	165	concrete	apartment
Christopher Inn	1963	16	46	150	concrete	hotel
Canterbury	1968	15	46	150	concrete	apartment
Huntington, West	1965	10	46	150	mixed	office
Riverside	1966	10	46	150	concrete	hospital
Grant Nursing	1969	16	43	140	concrete	dormitory
Atlas	1906	12	43	140	mixed	office
Huntington Bank	1901	12	43	140		office
University	1950	10	43	140	concrete	hospital
Brunson	1904	12	40	130	steel	office
High Long	1926	12	40	130	steel	office
Grant Hosptial	1959	10	40	130	concrete	hospital
16 E. Broad St.	1914	12	38	125	steel	office
Neil House	1925	11	38	125	concrete	hotel
Taylor	1961	13	36	120	concrete	dormitory
Beggs	1928	12	37	120	steel	office
Center for Tomorrow	1970	10	36	120	concrete	hotel
Ohio Depts. Building	1928	10	37	120		office
Seneca Towers	1920	10	36	120	concrete	apartment
Hall of Justice	1972	9	37	120	steel	multiple
Drackett	1958	12	33	110	concrete	dormitory
Harrison	1960	12	33	110	concrete	dormitory
Jones	1962	12	33	110	concrete	dormitory
Morrison	1958	12	33	110	concrete	dormitory
Thurber Tower	1962	12	33	110	concrete	apartment
145 N. High St.	1915	11	33	110		office
Cols. Metro. Hsg.	1972	10	33	110	concrete	apartment
Fort Hayes	1920	10	33	110		hotel
Hartman	1912	10	33	110	steel	office
Nationwide	1949	10	33	110	mixed	office
Southern	1910	10	33	110		hotel
Park Tower	1958	10	30	100	concrete	apartment
33 N. High St.	1908	9	30	100		office
Jay-Cee Arms	1972	11	28	95	masonry	apartment
Connellsville, Pennsylvania						
Elderly Hous. Complex (Pa 25-3)	1967	11	33	110	masonry	apartment
Cumberland, Maryland						
Elderly Housing Project 16 1	1967	9	28	93	masonry	apartment
Dallas, Texas						
First International	1975	56	216	710	steel	office
First National Bank	1964	52	191	625	steel	office
Republic Bank Tower	1964	50	182	598	steel	office
Southland Life Tower	1958	42	168	550	steel	office
Harwood Tower		14	167	550		office
2001 Bryan Street	1972	40	156	512	steel	office
Republic Bank Building	1954	36	138	452	steel	office
One Main Place	1968	34	136	445	steel	office
Ling Tempco Vought Tower	1964	31	132	434	steel	office
Mercantile National Bank	1937	31	131	430	steel	office
Mobil	1921	31	131	430	steel	office
Fidelity Union Tower	1959	33	122	400	steel/concrete	office
One Dallas Centre	1979	30	113	372	concrete	office
S. W. Bell Telephone	1927	22	113	372	concrete	office/exch.
Courthouse and Fed. Office	1970	16	110	362	stl./masonry	office
Mercantile Dallas	1958	22	110	360	masonry	office
Sheraton Hotel	1958	29	107	350	masonry	hotel
Reunion Hyatt Hotel	1977	30	105	343	steel	hotel

Table 4 Tallest buildings in major cities (continued)

Building	Year Completed	Number of stories	Height meters	feet	Material	Use
Dallas, Texas, USA (continued)						
Elm Place		22	104	341		
Main Tower	1973	26	102	336	masonry	office
Adolphus Tower	1912	27	100	327	masonry	hotel
Park Central No. 3	1975	20	100	327	steel	office
Bell Telephone	1964	23	99	326	stl./masonry	office
Davis Building	1925	21	98	323	masonry/conc.	office
Manor House, Bank of S.&T.	1966	26	97	319	masonry	multiple
Preston Tower	1966	29	96	316	stl./brick	apartment
Adolphus Hotel	1912	25	95	312	concrete	hotel
Penney Regnl Credit Bldg	1975	23	95	310	steel	office
Fairmont Hotel	1968	24	94	308	steel	hotel
Tower Petroleum Building	1930	23	93	305	concrete	office
Baptist Annuity Center		17	92	303		
Life Building	1951	22	92	302	stl./brick	office/rtl
Santa Fe Building	1946	20	91	300	masonry	office
Two Turtle Creek Village	1972	18	91	300	steel	office
Holiday Inn	1969	22	82	268	stl/brick	hotel
Fidelity Union Life	1953	20	82	268	concrete	office
Campbell Center	1971	20	79	258	steel	office
Baker Hotel	1925	19	75	247	masonry	hotel
Statler Hilton Hotel	1956	18	71	234	concrete	hotel
Reunion Center	1978	30	66	217	mixed	multiple
Zales	1969	17	63	205	concrete	office
Registry Hotel	1974	14	51	168	masonry	hotel
Cliff Towers	1927	13	46	150	masonry	multiple
Stemmons Tower	1964	12	46	150	masonry	office
Mockingbird Towers (2)	1974	12	45	148	steel	office
Le Baron	1973	13	42	138	masonry	hotel
Sheraton Hotel	1970	10	39	128	steel	hotel
Campbell Center II	1977	10	37	122	steel	office
Reunion Center	1978					
Dayton, Ohio						
Winters Bank	1970	30	123	404	steel	ofc./store
Mead Tower	1975	28	111	365	mixed	office
Centre City Office Building	1927	21	91	297	concrete	ofc./store
Hulman	1931	23	90	295	concrete	office
Miami Valley Tower	1969	22	88	290	mixed	office
First National Bank		21	81	265	mixed	office
Biltmore Tower	1928	19	55	180	concrete	apt/office
Talbott Tower	1958	16	55	180	mixed	ofc./store
American Building	1932	15	52	170	stl/masonry	ofc./store
Third National	1924	15	52	170	mixed	office
Good Samaritan Hospital	1975	16	49	162	steel	hospital
Stouffer's Dayton Plaza	1976	14	46	150	concrete	hotel
YMCA	1929	15	43	140	conc./masonry	multiple
Dearborn, Michigan						
Regency-Hyatt	1975	13	40	130	steel	hotel
Parklane Towers	1972	15			steel	office
Denver, Colorado						
Columbia Plaza	U.C.	50	183	600		
Anaconda		40	176	580		
Brooks Tower	1965	42	154	504	concrete	apartment
Amoco		36	137	450		
First of Denver	U.C.	32	132	431	steel	office
Energy Center 1		29	123	405		
Colorado National Bank		26	119	389	concrete	office
First National Bank		28	117	385		
Security Life	1967	32	117	384		office
Energy Plaza		28	112	370		
Lincoln Center		30	112	367		
Brooks Executive Tower	U.C.	30	110	360	concrete	multiple
Western Federal Savings		27	108	354		
Colorado State Bank	1971	27	107	350	mixed	office
410 Building		24	102	335		
Mountain Bell		21	101	330		
D and F Tower		20	101	330		
Prudential Plaza	1972	25	96	312	concrete	office
Mountain States Telephone	U.C.	24	96	312	steel	office
Denver Club		23	84	277		
Park Central	1973	16	71	230	steel	office
Park Lane No. 1	1970	20	62	206	masonry	apartment
Park Lane No. 2 and No. 3	1972	20	62	206	masonry	apartment
Park Lane No. 4	1973	20	62	206	masonry	apartment
Park May Fair East	1967	17	50	165	masonry	apartment
Des Moines, Iowa						
Ruan Center		36	139	457		
Financial Center		25	105	345		
Equitable Building		19	97	318		
3000 Grand Apts.	1971	10	29	96	masonry	apartment

Table 4 Tallest buildings in major cities (continued)

Building	Year Completed	Number of stories	Height meters	Height feet	Material	Use
USA (continued)						
Detroit, Michigan						
Renaissance 1	1977	73	225	739	concrete	hotel
City Natl Bank (Penobscot)	1928	47	171	562	steel	office
Renaissance 2	1976	40	163	534	steel	office
Renaissance 3	1976	40	163	534	steel	office
Renaissance 4	1976	40	163	534	steel	office
Renaissance 5	1976	40	163	534	steel	office
Guardian	1928	40	148	485	steel	office
Book Tower	1925	35	144	472	steel	office
Cadillac Tower	1928	40	133	437	steel	office
David Stott	1930	38	133	436	steel	office
Consolidated Gas Co.	1963	32	131	430	steel	office
Fisher	1928	28	128	420	steel	office
Town Center	1975	32	123	405	steel	office
J. L. Hudson		28	121	397		store
McNamara Fed. Office Building	1974	27	120	393	concrete	office
Detroit Bank and Trust Co.	1963	28	113	370	steel	office
Edison Plaza		25	111	365		
David Broderick	1927	34	109	358	steel	office
Buhl	1925	26	107	350	steel	office
Big Beaver Office	1975	25	106	346	steel	office
Michigan Bell Telephone	1920	19	104	340	steel	office
First Fed. Savings and Loan	1965	23	103	338	steel	office
Pontchartrain Hotel	1965	23	102	336	concrete	hotel
Blue Cross/Blue Shield	1970	23	101	332	steel	office
Michigan Bell Telephone	1973	17	100	327	steel	office
1300 Lafayette East	1960	30	99	325	concrete	apartment
Commonwealth		25	99	325		
Walker Cisler	1973	24	99	325	steel	office
First National Building	1922	25	97	319	steel	office
City County Building	1953	20	97	317	steel	ofc/courts
American Motors	1975	26	95	312	steel	office
Sheraton Cadillac Hotel	1924	28	94	310	steel	hotel
The Jeffersonian	1965	29	93	305	concrete	apartment
Executive Plaza	1971	21	85	280	steel	office
Travelers Tower	1971	18	78	256	steel	office
Manufacturers Bank	1970	14	66	217	steel	office
North Park Plaza	1973	17	62	203	steel	office
333 Fort Street	1970	14	56	184	steel	office
El Paso, Texas						
State National Bank of El Paso	1971	22	90	296	steel	multiple
El Paso Natural Gas	1954	18	72	235	steel	office
El Paso National Bank	1961	19			steel	multiple
El Paso Natural Gas	U.C.	18			mixed	office
Plaza Hotel	1930	18			conc./brick	hotel
First National	1920	15				office
Bassett Tower		15			conc./brick	office
Mills	1909	12				office
Fairbanks, Alaska						
Alaska Building	1976	5	14	46	wood	apartment
Fairfax County						
Woodlake Towers No. 1	1970	9	27	91	masonry	apartment
Woodlake Towers No. 2	1973	9	27	91	masonry	apartment
Fort Wayne, Indiana						
Fort Wayne National Bank		26	103	339		
Lincoln National Bank		23	95	312		
Fort Worth, Texas						
Fort Worth National Bank		37	138	454		
Continental National Bank		30	116	380		
First National Bank		21	91	300		
Continental Life Insurance		23	86	282		
Electric Service		20	84	275		
W. T. Waggoner		22	82	270		
Service Life Center		19	82	270		
Tandy Plaza						office
Greensboro, North Carolina						
Jefferson Building	1923	18	75	245	mixed	office
Wachovia Building	1967	15	71	233	mixed	office
Southeastern	1919	9	61	199	stl/masonry	office
Southern Life Insurance	1980	10	45	146	mixed	office
Towers Apartment	1964	14	43	141	concrete	apartment
Gateway Plaza	1975	14	41	135	concrete	apartment
Howard Johnson Motel	1975	14	41	135	concrete	hotel
Guilford	1929	12	41	134	mixed	office

Table 4 Tallest buildings in major cities (continued)

Building	Year Completed	Number of stories	Height meters	feet	Material	Use
Greensboro, North Carolina, USA (continued)						
First Union Bank	1971	11	41	134	mixed	office
Housing for the Elderly	1969	9	23	77	masonry	apartment
Guttenburg, Iowa						
Galaxy Complex (3 bldgs)	1976	44			steel	multiple
Harrisburg, Pennsylvania						
State Office Tower No. 2		21	101	334		office
City Towers		25	88	291		
State Capitol		6	83	272		
Presbyterian Apartments		23	79	260		
Hartford, Connecticut						
Travelers Insurance Co.		34	161	527		
Hartford Plaza		22	128	420		
Hartford Natl. Bank and Trust		26	110	360		
One Financial Plaza		26	102	335		
Honolulu, Hawaii						
Ala Moana Hotel	1970	38	119	390	concrete	hotel
Pacific Beach Hotel	1979	45	107	350	concrete	hotel
Ala Wai Sunset	1979	44	107	350	concrete	hotel
Waikiki Lodge II	1979	43	107	350	concrete	hotel
Waikiki Ala Wai Waterfront	1979	43	107	350	concrete	hotel
Regency Tower II	1979	43	107	350	concrete	apartment
Mehelani Waikiki Lodge	1978	43	107	350	concrete	hotel
Discovery Bay	1976	42	107	350	concrete	apartment
Regency Tower	1974	42	107	350	concrete	apartment
Century Center	1978	41	107	350	concrete	apt/office
Yacht Harbor Towers	1972	40	107	350	concrete	apartment
Cantorbury Place		40	106	350		
Hyatt Regency Waikiki	1976	39	107	350	concrete	hotel
Hemmeter Center		39	107	350		
Royal Iolani	1978	38	107	350	concrete	apartment
Iolani Towers		38	106	350		
Diamond Head Tower		38	106	350		
Pacific Trade Center	1972	30	107	350	concrete	office
Chateau Waikiki	1975	39	106	349	concrete	apartment
Rainbow Plaza		37	106	348		
Contessa	1971	37	106	348	concrete	apartment
2121 Ala Wai Boulevard	1977	41	106	347	concrete	apartment
Waikiki Beach Tower		39	105	347		
Royal Kuhio	1973	39	105	346	concrete	apartment
Waipuna	1970	38	105	343	concrete	apartment
Iolani Court Plaza	1979	40	104	341	concrete	apartment
Waikiki Sunset Makai	1979	37	104	341	concrete	apartment
Waikiki Banyan	1979	36	104	341	concrete	apartment
The Villa on Eaton Square	1974	37	102	335	concrete	multiple
The Skyrise	1972	38	102	333	concrete	apartment
Kukui Plaza	1976	33	102	333	concrete	apartment
Ke Aloha at Waikiki	1978	35	101	330	concrete	apartment
Grosvenor Center	1979	30	101	330	concrete	office
Marco Polo	1971	36	100	328	concrete	apartment
Diamond Head Vista	1975	35	98	322	concrete	apartment
Reed and Martin Apartment	1971	36	98	321	concrete	apartment
Waikiki Islander Inn	1979	34	98	321	concrete	hotel
Sheraton Waikiki	1971	29	96	315	concrete	hotel
Prince Kuhio Towers	1979	36	95	311	concrete	apartment
1350 Ala Moana	1968	32	94	308	concrete	apartment
Mott Smith Laniloa	1976	34	92	303	concrete	apartment
Ala Moana Building	1960	23	91	300	concrete	office
Harbor Square	1971	26	84	275	concrete	multiple
Ilikaii Apartments	1963	27	79	260	concrete	apartment
Amfac Tower	1970	20	78	256	concrete	office
Financial Plaza	1969	27	78	255	concrete	multiple
Houston, Texas						
Texas Commerce Plaza	1981	75	318	1049	mixed	office
First International Plaza	1980	55	228	748	mixed	office
One Shell Plaza	1971	52	218	714	concrete	office
Three Allen Center	1980	50	208	685	steel	office
One Houston Center	1978	46	208	681	mixed	office
First City Tower	1981	49	200	660	mixed	office
1100 Milam	1974	47	198	651	steel	office
Exxon	1964	44	185	606	steel	office
Two Houston Center	1974	40	177	579	steel	office
Dresser Tower	1974	40	168	550	steel	office
Pennzoil Place	1976	38	159	523	steel	office
Two Allen Center		36	158	521		
Entex		35	158	518		
United Gas	1972	35	157	516	steel	office

Table 4 Tallest buildings in major cities (continued)

Building	Year Completed	Number of stories	Height meters	feet	Material	Use
Houston, Texas, USA (continued)						
Tenneco	1963	32	153	500	steel	office
Conoco		32	142	465		
One Allen Center	1973	34	138	452	steel	office
Summit Tower West		32	134	441		
Summit Tower East		32	134	441		
Gulf Building	1929	37	130	428	steel	office
First City National Bank	1961	32	125	410	steel	office
Houston Light and Power	1967	27	125	410	steel	office
Neils Esperson		31	125	409		
Hyatt Regency Houston		34	122	401		
Houston Natural Gas	1967	28	118	386	steel	office
Hyatt House	1973	29	113	370	concrete	hotel
Bank of the Southwest	1956	24	113	369	steel	office
Sheraton Lincoln Hotel		28	107	352		
Two Shell Plaza	1971	26	104	341	concrete	office
American General	1965	25	103	337	steel	office
Transco		25	102	333		
Allied Chemical		25	100	328		
Holiday Inn	1971	30	99	325	concrete	hotel
609 Fannin		22	99	325		
Post Oak Central 2		24	97	321		
Capital National Bank		21	98	320		
Post Oak Central		25	97	318		
St. Lukes Hospital		26	96	316		
500 Jefferson		21	96	316		
Marathon Manufacturing Co.		21	95	313		
Sterling		22	95	312		
Belrose		21	94	308		
Chamber of Commerce		22	93	306		
Control Data Center		22	92	303		
First National Life		22	92	302		
Kellogg		22	91	300		
Prudential		21	91	300		
Huntington, West Virginia						
Holiday Inn	1973	13			mixed	hotel
Indianapolis, Indiana						
American Square	U.C.	37	163	533		office
Indiana National Bank Tower	1971	37	154	504		office
City County Building	1962	26	115	377		office
Indiana Bell Telephone	1932	20	98	320		office
Blue Cross/Blue Shield	1970	18	92	302		office
Riley Towers (2)	1962	30	90	294		apartment
Indiana Bell 220 Building	1974	20	87	284		office
Monument Circle	1902		87	284		museum
Market Square Office Building	1975	20	86	283		
Merchants Plaza/Regency Hyatt	1977	17	83	271		hotel/off
Jacksonville, Florida						
Independent Life & Accident Ins.	1974	37	163	535	steel	office
Gulf Life Tower	1967	27	132	433	concrete	office
Prudential Ins. Co. of America	1954	22	90	295	steel	office
Blue Cross/Blue Shield	1974	20	88	287	steel	office
Atlantic National Bank	1974	19	85	278	steel	office
Universal Marion	1963	20	82	268	steel	office
Seaboard Coastline	1958	15	74	242	steel	office
Independent Life	1953	16	69	227	steel	office
City Hall	1959	15	64	210	steel	office
Cathedral Townhouse	1970	18	56	185	concrete	apartment
Riverside Presbyterian	1973	18	56	185	concrete	apartment
Federal Offices	1967	11	55	181	steel	office
Florida National Bank	1960	11	55	181	steel	office
Cathedral Tower	1966	17	54	177	concrete	apartment
Barnett Bank	1961	12	51	166	steel	office
Mount Carmel	1972	17	45	147	concrete	apartment
Hilton Hotel	1968	10	43	140	concrete	hotel
Presbyterian Tower	1972	13	42	137	steel	office
Baptist Towers	1972	12	39	127	concrete	apartment
Twin Towers (two bldgs)	1970	11	37	120	masonry	apartment
Robert Meyer	1957	21	33	107	concrete	hotel
Broadview Terrace	1961	15	29	95	concrete	apartment
Jersey City, New Jersey						
JCMC Medical Bldg	1940	23	91	300	mixed	hospital
JCMC Surgical Bldg	1936	22	87	286	mixed	hospital
Murdock Hall	1944	21	83	273	mixed	hospital

Table 4 Tallest buildings in major cities (continued)

Building	Year Completed	Number of stories	Height meters	Height feet	Material	Use
Jersey City, New Jersey, USA (continued)						
JCMC East Hall	1936	21	83	273	mixed	hospital
JCMC Clinical Bldg	1940	20	79	260	mixed	hospital
Pollack Hospital	1942	18	71	234	mixed	hospital
JCMC Clinical Bldg	1940	18	71	234	mixed	hospital
JCMC Staff	1936	16	63	208	mixed	hospital
JCMC Dental Bldg	1942	10	40	130	mixed	hospital
M. Hague Maternity	1933	10	40	130	mixed	hospital
Johnston, South Carolina						
Low Rent Housing for Elderly	1971	15	44	147	masonry	apartment
Kansas City, Kansas						
Federal Office Building	1964	18	90	296	steel	office
Ten Main Center	1968	20	84	275	concrete	office
Kansas City, Missouri						
Kansas City Power and Light	1931	33	145	476	steel	office
City Hall	1936	29	135	443	steel	office
Fidelity Bank and Trust	1931	35	130	426	steel	office
Hyatt Regency Hotel	1980	42	126	413	concrete	hotel
Commerce Towers	1963	31	124	407	steel	office
Southwestern Bell	1913	28	116	379	steel	office
Mutual Benefit Life	1977	28	107	352		office
Bryant Building	1931	26	101	331	steel	office
A.T. and T. Long Line		20	101	331		
City Center Square	1977	30	92	302	concrete	office
Holiday Inn	1968	28	91	300	concrete	hotel
Federal Reserve	1921	21	87	287	steel	office
Continental Hotel	1915	24	87	284	steel	hotel
Federal Office Bldg	1968	19	85	280	steel	office
Traders National Bank	1963	21	85	278	steel	office
Jackson County Court House	1933	15	83	272	steel	multiple
Ten Main Center	1966	21	83	271	concrete	office
Mercantile Bank Tower	1975	21	80	263	steel	office
Kansas City Bank Tower		21				office
Las Vegas, Nevada						
Las Vegas Hilton		30	114	375		hotel
MGM Grand Hotel		26	110	362		hotel
Landmark Hotel		27	94	308		
Sahara Hotel		27	90	308		
Dunes Hotel		24	84	277		
Mint Hotel		26	84	275		
Union Plaza Hotel		22	83	272		
Highlands Univ. Hi Rise Dorm.	1969	9	24	80	masonry	dormitory
Lawrence, Kansas						
McCollum Hall (K.U. Dorm.)	1967	10	32	105	concrete	dormitory
Lexington, Kentucky						
Crestline Apartments	1973	21			steel	apartment
Lincoln, Nebraska						
National Bank of Commerce	1976	11			concrete	office
Little Rock, Arkansas						
First National Bank		33	138	454		
Worthen Bank and Trust	1969	28	114	375	concrete	office
Union National Bank		24	101	331		
Tower Building	1960	18	91	300	steel	office
Union Bank	1969	21	85	279	steel	office
Donaghey Building	1930	14	73	240	concrete	office
Grady Manning	1929	14	61	200	concrete	hotel
Lakewood House	1965	16	48	156	concrete	apartment
SW Bell Office	1972	10	47	154	steel	office
SW Bell Toll	1967	8	44	143	steel	
Summit House	1963	14	41	136	concrete	apartment
Fred Parris Tower	1972	14			concrete	apartment
Holiday Inn	1972	12			concrete	hotel
Boyle Building	1915	11			steel	office
Heritage House	1968	11			concrete	apartment
Lafayette Hotel	1927	11			concrete	hotel
Union Life	1925	11			steel	office
Arkansas Highway Office	1966	10			steel	office
Pyramid Building	1927	10			concrete	office
Lockport, Illinois						
Elderly Housing	1967	11	33	110	masonry	apartment

Table 4 Tallest buildings in major cities (continued)

Building	Year Completed	Number of stories	Height meters	Height feet	Material	Use
USA (continued)						
Los Angeles, California						
United California Bank	1974	62	260	858	steel	office
Security Pacific National Bank	1974	57	224	738	steel	office
Atlantic Richfield Plaza A	1972	52	212	699	steel	office
Atlantic Richfield Plaza B	1972	52	212	699	steel	office
Crocker Citizens Plaza	1969	42	188	620	steel	office
Theme Towers (2)	1974	44	175	575	steel	office
Union Bank Plaza	1966	41	156	512	steel	office
Equitable Life	1969	34	138	454	steel	office
City Hall	1923	28	138	454	steel	office
Occidental Life	1965	32	138	452	steel	office
Mutual Benefit Life	1970	31	133	435	steel	office
Broadway Plaza	1973	33	126	414	steel	office
1900 Avenue of Stars	1970	27	121	398	steel	office
One Wilshire	1968	28	120	395	steel	office
California Federal Savings	1962	28	111	363	steel	office
Century City Office Bldg	1970	24	111	363	steel	office
Bunker Hill Towers	1969	32	106	349	steel	apartment
City National Bank	1968	24	106	348	steel	office
International Industries Plaza	1970	24	106	347	steel	office
L.A. Bonaventure Hotel	1977	34	100	327	steel	hotel
Wilshire West Plaza	1969	24	100	327	steel	office
Century Park Plaza	1973	23	93	304	steel	office
Century Plaza Hotel	1966	20	58	190	steel	hotel
Western International Hotel	1977	35			steel	hotel
Barrington Plaza		25			steel	apartment
Federal Office Building	1969	17				office
Signal Oil and Gas Company	1959	16				office
9200 Sunset Tower	1972	13			steel	office
Louisville, Kentucky						
First National Bank		40	156	512		
Citizens Plaza Bank	1972	30	128	420	concrete	office
Galt House		25	99	325		
Louisville Trust		24	95	312		
800 Apartments		29	88	290		
Macon, Georgia						
St. Pauls Apartments	1971	15	46	152	masonry	apartment
Low Rent Hi Rise for Elderly	1972	11	37	123	masonry	apartment
Manchester, New Hampshire						
Hampshire Plaza	1972	20	79	259		office
New Hampshire Insurance	1971	14	53	173		office
Amoskeag Bank	1979	10	44	144		office
Carpenter Center	1919	12	38	126		apartment
Burns Apartments	U.C.	13	36	119		apartment
Pariseau Apartments	1974	11	33	109		apartment
O'Malley Apartments	1970	9	26	85		apartment
Kalivas Apartments	1973	9	33	81		apartment
Memphis, Tennessee						
100 N Main		37	131	430		
Commerce Square		31	121	396		
Clark 5100 Poplar		32	111	365		
Sterick Building		31	111	365		
First National Bank		25	101	332		
Hyatt Regency Hotel		28	100	329		
Lowensteins Towers		25	90	296		
Lincoln American Life Tower		22	88	290		
White Station Tower		24	85	280		
Miami, Florida						
One Biscayne Corporation		40	139	456		
First Federal Savings and Loan		32	114	375		
Dade County Courthouse		28	108	357		
Ferre Building		30	104	340		
Plaza Venetia		33	101	332		
Flagler Center		25	97	318		
Omni Intl Hotel		29	90	296		hotel
Brickell Bay Club		29	87	286		
Palm Bay Club		24	85	279		
Retirement Center		9	23	77	masonry	apartment
Milwaukee, Wisconsin						
First Wisconsin Center	1973	42	190	625	steel	office
City Hall	1895	9	107	350	steel	office
Wis. Telephone Co.	1930	19	95	313	steel	office

Table 4 Tallest buildings in major cities (continued)

Building	Year Completed	Number of stories	Height meters	feet	Material	Use
Milwaukee, Wisconsin, USA (continued)						
Carl Sandburg Dorm (U. of Wis.)	1973	26	94	310	concrete	dormitory
Marine Plaza	1962	22	88	288	steel	office
Allen Bradley Company		19	85	283		
Marshall and Ilsley Bank	1969	21	83	277	concrete	office
Bayview Terrace		25	84	275		
Regency House	1969	27	75	272	concrete	apartment
Prospect Tower Apartments		23	81	268		
Juneau Village Bldg. B	1968	28	81	265	concrete	apartment
Marc Plaza Hotel	1927	24	81	265	steel	hotel
Carl Sandburg Dorm (U. of Wis.)	1973	20	79	259	concrete	dormitory
Locust Court Apartments		24	76	250		apartment
Arlington Court Apartments		24	76	250		apartment
Wis. Tower	1930	21	76	250	steel	office
Wis. Gas Co.	1930	20	76	250	steel	office
Northwestern Mutual Life		16	76	248		office
Clark Bldg.	1966	20	73	239	concrete	office
Pfister Hotel & Tower		21	72	235		hotel
Cudahy Tower Apartments		14	70	231		apartment
1st Wisconsin National Bank		16	70	230		office
Carl Sandburg Dorm (U. of Wis.)	1973	16	68	224	concrete	dormitory
1st Federal Plaza		19	68	222		office
Hyatt Regency Hotel		17	67	221		hotel
YMCA		18	64	209		recreation
Catholic Knights Tower		18	63	207		
Minneapolis, Minnesota						
IDS Center	1972	57	235	772	mixed	office
Pillsbury		40	161	529		
Foshay Tower		32	136	447		
Hennepin County Gov. Center		24	123	403		
First National Bank		28	112	366		office
Municipal Building		14	108	355		
Northwestern Bell Telephone		26	107	350		
Cedar Riverside		39	103	337		
Dain Tower		26	95	311		
Northwest Financial Center		24	91	300		
Midwest Federal Savings & Loan		20	84	276		
Federal Reserve Bank						bank
Sheland Tower					concrete	
Muskegon, Michigan						
Muskegon Retirement Apts	1969	11	29	96	masonry	apartment
Nashville, Tennessee						
National Life & Accident Ins. Co.		31	138	452		
Nashville Life & Casualty Tower		30	125	409		
First American National Bank		28	108	354		
Hyatt Regency		28	91	300		
Third National Bank		20	89	292		
Andrew Jackson St. Office Bldg		17	87	286		
"Death Hilton"	1973	20				mausoleum
New Haven, Connecticut						
Knights of Columbus Hqs.		23	97	319		
New Orleans, Louisiana						
One Shell Square	1972	51	212	697	steel	office
Plaza Tower	1970	45	162	531	steel	office
Marriott Hotel	1974	42	137	450	concrete	hotel
Canal Place One		32	134	439		
Bank of New Orleans	1970	31	134	438	concrete	office
International Trade Mart	1967	33	124	407	steel	office
225 Baronne Street		28	110	362		
Hyatt Regency Hotel	1975	25	109	360		hotel
Hibernia Bank	1921	23	108	355	steel	office
1250 Poydras Plaza		24	104	341		
Hilton Hotel, Intl River Cent.	1977	29	103	340	steel	hotel
American Bank	1929	23	101	330	steel	office
Pan American Life		27	98	323		
Canal La Salle	1972	24	88	288	steel	office
Charity Hospital of Louisiana	1939	19	85	279	steel	hospital

Table 4 Tallest buildings in major cities (continued)

Building	Year Completed	Number of stories	Height meters	Height feet	Material	Use
			**New Orleans, Louisiana, USA (continued)**			
Lykes Center	1973	22	84	276	steel	office
Masonic Temple	1930	18	69	228	steel	
Texaco	1953	17	64	210	steel	office
Rault Center	1967	16	64	210	concrete	hotel
Pere Marquette	1925	18	62	202	steel	office
Fairmont Hotel Annex	1924	15	58	190	steel	hotel
Monteleone Hotel	1908	16	57	188	steel	hotel
Howard Johnson	1968	18	54	178	steel	hotel
Saratoga Building	1957	14	48	156	concrete	office
Monteleone Annex II	1958	15	46	150	steel	hotel
Hawthorn Tower	1928	16	41	135	concrete	dormitory
Monteleone Annex	1928	14	41	135	steel	hotel
Fisher Apartments	1966	13	41	135	concrete	apartment
Barnett Furniture	1927	9	41	134	concrete	store
Warwick Hotel	1951	12	40	130	concrete	hotel
234 Loyola	1905	10	38	125	mixed	office
234 Loyola Building Addition	1961	10	38	125	steel	office
Security Homestead	1971	10	38	125	concrete	office
Gust Homes	1963	12	37	120	concrete	apartment
Baronne Building	1915	10	34	113	concrete	office
The Wohl	1951	13	34	110	concrete	hotel
Hilton Hotel	1978	30			steel	hotel
International River Center	1977	30			steel	multiple
Louisiana Southern Life	1960	28			steel	office
Hyatt-Regency	1975	21			concrete	hotel
Braniff Place Annex	1952	18			brick	hotel
Commerce Building	1958	18			steel	office
Delta Towers	1953	18			brick	hotel
Delta Towers (2nd building)	1956	18				hotel
Holiday Inn	1969	18			brick	hotel
Natl Bank of Commerce	1927	18			steel	office
International American	1974	17			concrete	hotel
Elk Place Medical Tower	1975	16			steel	office
International Hotel	1974	16			concrete	hotel
Charity School of Nursing	1939	15			brick	dormitory
Executive Towers	1973	14			steel	office
Exxon	1954	14			concrete	office
Federal Building	1959	14			mixed	office
Odeco	1968	14			concrete	office
Oil and Gas	1960	14			steel	office
Orleanian Hotel	1950	14			mixed	apartment
Richards	1925	14			steel	office
Sheraton Inn	1973	14			steel	hotel
Travel Center	1973	14			concrete	office
Whitney Building	1910	14			steel	office
Carol Apartments	1965	13			concrete	apartment
Carondelet	1916	13			steel	office
Hale Boggs Federal Building	U.C.	13			steel	office
Maison Blanche	1908	13			steel	store
Fairmont Hotel	1907	12			concrete	hotel
First National Life	1961	12			steel	office
Medallion Tower	1920	12			concrete	office
Pontchartrain Hotel	1926	12			concrete	hotel
ICB	1920	11			steel	office
LSU School of Med. Resid. Hall	1962	11			concrete	apartment
Maritime Building	1895	11			steel	office
3421 Causeway	1975	10			steel	office
AAA	1971	10			steel	office
Braniff Place	1925	10			mixed	hotel
Causeway Plaza	1972	10			concrete	office
F. Edward Hebert Federal Bldg.	1939	10			steel	office
Heal Garage	1975	10			concrete	parking
International Building	1931	10			steel	office
Jefferson Bank	1969	10			steel	office
Lapavillon Hotel	1906	10			concrete	hotel
LSU Medical Center	1933	10			concrete	hospital
Napoleon Fin. and Med. Center	1975	10			concrete	office
Ramada Inn	1972	10			steel	hotel
Southern Savings	1975	10			concrete	office
State Welfare	1972	10			steel	office
Touro Infirmary	1972	10			mixed	hospital
Touro Infirmary Addition	U.C.	10			steel	hospital
Veterans Admin. Hospital	1949	10			concrete	hospital
YMCA	1931	10			steel	
210 O'Keefe	1956	9			aluminum	office

Table 4 Tallest buildings in major cities (continued)

Building	Year Completed	Number of stories	Height meters	feet	Material	Use
New Orleans, Louisiana, USA (continued)						
Baptist Hospital	1925	9			concrete	hospital
City Hall	1955	9			steel	office
LSU Med. Cent. Dentistry Schl.	1971	9			concrete	school
Regency Hotel		9			mixed	hotel
Selma Gumble		9			concrete	dormitory
Tulane School of Medicine		9			brick	school
New York, New York						
World Trade Center South	1973	110	412	1350	steel	office
World Trade Center North	1972	110	412	1350	steel	office
Empire State	1931	102	381	1250	steel	office
Chrysler	1930	77	319	1046	steel	office
American Intl	1931	66	290	950	steel	office
Citicorp Center	1977	59	278	914	steel	multiple
40 Wall Tower	1966	71	259	851	steel	office
RCA Rockefeller Center	1933	70	259	850	steel	office
One Chase Manhattan Plaza	1960	60	248	813	steel	office
Pan American	1963	59	246	808	steel	office
Woolworth	1913	57	242	792	steel	office
One Penn Plaza	1972	57	234	766	steel	office
Exxon	1971	54	229	750	steel	office
1 Liberty Plaza (U.S. Steel)	1972	54	227	743	steel	office
20 Exchange Place (Citibank)	1931	55	226	741	steel	office
One Astor Plaza	1972	54	222	730	mixed	office
9 West 57th St.	1972	50	221	725	steel	office
Union Carbide	1960	52	215	707	steel	office
General Motors	1968	50	214	705	steel	office
Metropolitan Life	1909	50	213	700	steel	office
500 Fifth Avenue	1931	58	213	697	steel	office
55 Water Steet	1972	53	209	687	steel	office
Chemical Bank Trust	1964	50	209	687	steel	office
Chanin	1929	55	207	680	steel	office
Gulf-Western	1970	44	207	679	steel	office
Marine Midland Bank	1966	52	206	677	steel	office
Metropolitan Tower	1909	50	206	675	steel	office
Lincoln Bldg	1930	55	205	673	steel	office
McGraw-Hill	1972	51	204	670	steel	office
1633 Broadway	1972	48	204	670	steel	office
American Brands	1967	47	198	648	steel	office
A.T. & T.	1982	37	197	645	steel	office
Irving Trust	1930	53	195	640	steel	office
345 Park Avenue	1968	44	193	634	steel	office
One New York Plaza	1968	50	192	630	steel	office
Grace Plaza	1972	50	192	630	steel	office
Home Insurance Company	1966	45	192	630		office
N.Y. Telephone	1975	40	192	630	steel	office
One Dag Hammarskjold Plaza	1972	49	191	628		
888 7th Avenue		42	191	628		
Burlington House	1969	50	191	625	steel	office
Waldorf Astoria Hotel	1931	47	191	625		hotel
Olympic Tower	1975	51	189	620	mixed	multiple
10 East 40th Street	1929	48	189	620		office
101 Park Avenue	U.C.	46	188	618	concrete	office
General Electric	1930	50	188	616		office
New York Life	1928	33	188	615		office
Penney Bldg	1964	46	186	609		office
560 Lexington Avenue		46	183	600		
Celanese	1973	45	180	592		office
United States Courthouse	1933	37	180	590		office
Time and Life	1959	47	179	587	mixed	office
Federal Bldg	1966	41	179	587		office
1185 Avenue of the Americas	1971	42	177	580		office
Cooper Bregstein	1969	38	177	580		office
Municipal Building	1913	34	177	580		office
One Madison Square Plaza	1973	42	176	576		office
Westvaco	1967	42	175	574		office
Socony Mobil	1956	42	174	572	steel	office
Sperry Rand	1963	43	174	570		office
600 Third Avenue	1971	42	174	570		office
One Bankers Trust Plaza	1974	40	172	565		office
New York General	1928	35	172	565		office
30 Broad Street	1932	48	171	562		office
Sherry Netherland	1927	40	171	560		office
Continental Can Co.	1962	41	170	557		office
No. 3 Park Avenue	1975	42	169	556	concrete	multiple
Sperry and Hutchinson	1964	41	169	555		office
Galleria	1976	57	168	552	concrete	multiple

Table 4 Tallest buildings in major cities (continued)

Building	Year Completed	Number of stories	Height meters	feet	Material	Use
New York, New York, USA (continued)						
Interchem		45	168	552		office
919 Third Avenue	1970	47	168	550		office
N.Y. Telephone		45	168	550		
Burroughs	1963	44	168	550		office
Bankers Trust	1912	37	167	547		office
Transportation Bldg	1928	44	166	546		office
1166 Avenue of the Americas	1974	44	165	540	steel	office
Equitable Life	1959	42	165	540		office
Ritz Tower	1926	41	165	540		hotel
Bankers Trust	1912	37	165	540		office
Equitable	1915	42	164	538		office
1700 Broadway	1969	42	163	533		office
Downtown Athletic Club	1930	45	162	530		
Nelson Towers	1931	46	160	525		office
Hotel Pierre	1931	44	160	525		hotel
Seagram	1959	38	160	525		office
Random House	1969	42	159	522		office
Du Mont		42	159	520		
North American Plywood		41	158	520		
26 Broadway		31	159	520		office
Newsweek	1931	42	158	518		office
964 Third Street	1969	39	155	518	concrete	office
Sterling Drug	1964	41	157	515		office
First National City Bank	1959	41	157	515	mixed	office
Navarre	1930	44	156	513		office
Bank of New York	1927	31	156	513		office
Williamsburg Savings Bank	1929	42	156	512		office
1407 Broadway Realty Corp.	1950	41	156	512		office
International Bldg	1935	41	156	512		office
ITT American	1967	40	156	512		office
Park Vendome Tower		48	154	505		
United Nations	1952	39	154	505	steel	multiple
2 New York Plaza	1970	40	154	504		office
22 East 40th Street	1931	43	153	503		office
60 Broad Street	1962	39	153	503		office
Sheraton Centre		51	153	501		
World Apparel Center		42	153	501		
Americana Hotel	1962	50	150	500	concrete	hotel
CBS	1964	38	148	491	concrete	office
Excelsior House	1964	47	145	483	concrete	apartment
Broadway & 64th St.	1969	42	141	471	concrete	apartment
Park Row Building	1898	30	119	390	mixed	
Allied Chemical Bldg (Times Sq)	1904		114	375		office
Manhattan Life Insurance	1925	16	107	350		office
Continental Corporation	U.C.	38	95	313	mixed	office
Flatiron Bldg	1902	20	87	286	steel	office
New Astor Hotel	1977	54				hotel
Olympic Tower	1975	51			mixed	multiple
Palace Hotel	1980	51				hotel
Tracey Towers		42			concrete	apartment
Linden Plaza Apartments	1970	40				apartment
Finland House		38				office
Waterside Towers	1974	37				apartment
Bristol	1974	32				apartment
Roosevelt Hospital	1973	30			steel	hospital
Seven Pines	1974	27			mixed	apartment
St. Paul Building	1896	25				
Newark, New Jersey						
National Newark and Essex Bank		36	142	465		
Raymond Commerce		36	137	448		
Prudential Corporate Building		27	113	369		
Western Electric		31	109	359		
Gateway I Tower		30	108	355		
Prudential Insurance Company		21	108	353		
American Insurance Company		21	99	326		
Raymond Plaza West		26	94	310		
Prudential Insurance		15	91	300		office
N.J. Bell Telephone Company		21	84	275		
Gateway 2 Tower		20	83	272		
Mutual Benefit Life Ins. Co.		18	83	271		
Oakland, California						
Ordway		28	123	404		
Kaiser	1960	28	119	390	steel	multiple
Clorox		24	101	330		
City Hall		15	97	319		

Table 4 Tallest buildings in major cities (continued)

Building	Year Completed	Number of stories	Height meters	feet	Material	Use
Oakland, California, USA (continued)						
Tribune Tower		21	93	305		
United California Bank		18	91	297		
Blue Cross		21	90	296		
Telephone Building		15	88	289		
565 Bellevue Apartments		25	82	270		
Oklahoma City, Oklahoma						
Liberty Tower		36	152	500		
First National Bank		33	150	493		
City National Bank Tower		32	134	440		
Kerr McGee Center		30	120	393		
Fidelity Plaza		15	95	310		
Southwestern Bell Telephone Co.		15	92	303		
Hotel Oklahoma		24	91	298		
The Regency Tower		25	88	288		
United Founders Tower		20	83	275		
Citizens Tower		20	76	250		
One Galleria Plaza	U.C.	19	75	247		
Mid America Plaza	U.C.	12	56	184		
Oil Center		12	48	160		
Omaha, Nebraska						
Woodmen Tower	1970	30	134	440	steel	office
Northwestern Bell Admin.	1980	17	76	250	steel	office
Hilton HOtel	1972	19	61	200	concrete	hotel
Mutual of Omaha	1970	13	59	194	steel	office
Omaha-Douglas Civic Center	1975	12	54	175	steel	office
Union Pacific RR	1970	12	52	170	steel	office
Clarkson Hospital	1968	9	42	138	concrete	hospital
Orlando, Florida						
Travel Lodge	1972	18	60	196	concrete	hotel
CNA Regional Office Building		19			mixed	office
Pasadena, California						
Pacific Telephone	U.C.	20			mixed	office
Pasadena Hilton	1970	13			mixed	hotel
Union Bank	1971	12			concrete	office
Philadelphia, Pennsylvania						
City Hall	1901	7	167	548	masonry	office
1818 Market Street	1974	40	152	500	concrete	office
Phila. Savings Fund Society	1932	39	150	492	steel	multiple
Fidelity Mutual Life	1972	38	150	492	steel	office
Centre Square (2 towers)	1973	38	149	490	concrete	multiple
No. 5 Penncenter	1970	36	149	488	concrete	office
Industrial Valley Bank	1969	32	147	482	concrete	multiple
Franklin Plaza	1980	30			steel	multiple
Philadelphia National Bank	1931	25	145	475	steel	office
Two Girard Plaza	1930	30	137	450	steel	office
2000 Market Street	1973	29	133	435	steel	office
Fidelity Bank	1927	30	123	405	steel	office
Lewis Tower	1929	33	122	400	steel	multiple
Academy House	1976	41	119	390	concrete	multiple
1500 Locust Street	1973	44	119	390	concrete	multiple
Philadelphia Electric Company	1970	27	117	384	steel	office
The Drake	1928	33	114	375	concrete	apartment
Penn Mutual Life	1975	20	114	375	concrete	office
Medical Tower	1931	33	111	364	steel	multiple
State Building	1957	18	107	351	steel	office
United Engineers	1975	20	105	344	steel	office
Packard Building	1924	25	104	340	steel	office
Inquirer Building	1947	18	104	340	concrete	office
Dorchester	1962	32	103	339	concrete	apartment
Transportation Center	1957	18	102	336	concrete	office
Land Title Building	1897	22	102	334	steel	office
Suburban Station Building	1929	21	101	330	steel	office
IBM	1964	16	82	270	mixed	office
Municipal Service Building	1965	18	81	264	concrete	office
Stock Exchange	1966	14			concrete	office
Phoenix, Arizona						
Valley Center	1972	40	148	483	steel	office
Arizona Bank Downtown	1976	31	124	407	steel	bank
First National Bank	1971	27	113	372	stel	bank
Phoenix Center	1979	28	110	361	concrete	off./bank
United Bank Plaza		27	108	356		
First Federal Savings	1964	25	101	330	steel	svgs. & loan
Regency Apartmentsf	1963	24	95	312	concrete	apartment
Hyatt Regency Hotel	1976	26	89	293	steel	hotel

Table 4 Tallest buildings in major cities (continued)

Building	Year Completed	Number of stories	Height meters	feet	Material	Use
Phoenix, Arizona, USA (continued)						
Great Western Plaza	1980	17	89	293	steel	off./bank
Rosenzweig Center	1963	22	86	281	concrete	office
Del Webb Towne House		23	85	280		
United Bank Square		20	83	272		
Townhouse Hotel	1964	20	83	271	concrete	htl./office
Del Webb Building		17	83	271		
Executive Towers		22	81	265	concrete	apartment
Arizona Title		20	73	240	steel	office
Guarantee Bank	1959	18	71	234	concrete	office
County Bldg Addition	1978	13	71	234	steel	office
Security	1927	17	64	209	steel	office
Pittsburgh, Pennsylvania						
U.S. Steel	1970	64	256	841	steel	office
Gulf	1931	44	177	582	steel	office
University of Pittsburgh	1936	42	163	535	steel	school
Mellon Bank	1951	41	159	520	steel	office
One Oliver Plaza	1968	40	156	511	steel	office
Grant	1928	40	148	485	steel	office
Koppers	1929	34	145	475	steel	office
Equibank Bldg	1975	34	135	442	steel	office
Pittsburgh National Building	1972	30	130	428	steel	office
Alcoa	1953	30	125	410	steel	office
Westinghouse	1969	23	108	355	steel	office
Oliver	1910	25	106	347	steel	office
Gateway Bldg No. 3	1952	24	105	344	steel	office
Center City Tower (Smithfield Plaza)	1971	26	104	341	steel	office
Federal Bldg	1964	23	104	340	steel	office
Bell Telephone	1923	20	103	339	steel	equipment
Hilton Hotel	1959	22	102	333	steel	hotel
Frick	1902	20	101	330	steel	office
301 Fifth Avenue	1903	24	98	322	steel	office
Washington Plaza Apartments	1964	23	91	300	concrete	apartment
Commonwealth Bldg	1906	21	91	300	steel	office
635 Grant St. Telephone	1969	16	85	280	steel	equipment
Lawrence Hall	1927	21	67	220	steel	adm./dorm.
Liberty Park Tower	1973	23	64	210	masonry	apartment
East Liberty		20	52	173	masonry	apartment
IBM	1963	13	52	170	steel	office
Chateaugay	1970	12	30	100	masonry	apartment
Penn Plaza	1967	9	23	78	masonry	apartment
Portland, Oregon						
First National Bank of Oregon	1972	40	163	536	steel	multiple
Georgia Pacific		27	112	367		
Portsmouth, Virginia						
U.S. Naval Hospital		16				
No. 1 Crawford Parkway	1965	18	55	179	concrete	apartment
Providence, Rhode Island						
Industrial Trust	1927	26	130	428	steel	office
R.I. Hospital Trust Company	1973	28	120	394	steel	office
40 Westminster		24	92	301		
First Hartford Realty	1969	23	84	275	concrete	office
Turks Head	1913	16	64	208	steel	office
Biltmore Hotel	1921	18	61	200	steel	hotel
R.I. Hospital Ambulatory Center	1974	12	52	170	concrete	hospital
Brown Univ. Science Library	1969	16	48	157	concrete	library
Union Trust	1900	12	48	157	steel	office
Smith Elderly Housing	1973	16	46	150	concrete	apartment
Tobey Street Elderly Housing	1973	16	46	150	concrete	apartment
Reading, Pennsylvania						
Episcopal House	1972	15	46	152	masonry	apartment
Richmond, Virginia						
Federal Reserve Bank		26	120	393		
Medical Coll Virginia-Univ Hos.	U.C.	12	115	376	steel	hospital
First Merchant National Bank		26	95	313	steel	office
City Hall		18	95	310		
One James River Plaza		21	92	302		
Central National Bank		24	86	282		
First National Bank		19	80	262		
Fidelity Bankers Life		23	80	261		
14th Street Tower	U.C.	26			steel	office
Vepco Hqtrs	1978	22			concrete	office
McGuire VA Hospital	U.C.	14			concrete	hospital

Table 4 Tallest buildings in major cities (continued)

Building	Year Completed	Number of stories	Height meters	feet	Material	Use
USA (continued)						
Rochester, New York						
Xerox Tower	1967	30	135	443	concrete	office
Lincoln First Tower	1972	26	119	390	mixed	office
Eastman Kodak Office Bldg	1912	19	110	360	mixed	office
First Federal Plaza	1976	22	93	305	mixed	office
Marine Midland Bank Plaza	1969	22	85	280	concrete	office
Alliance	1926	15	80	261	mixed	office
Times Square	1930	10	78	256	steel	office
Midtown Tower	1962	18	77	251	steel	multiple
New York Medical-Surgical	1958	19	67	221	concrete	hospital
Genesee Crossroads Office	1969	16	66	215	steel	office
Seneca Tower	1968	22	65	212	concrete	apartment
Rock Island, Illinois						
Housing for the Elderly	1967	11	28	92	masonry	apartment
Rockville, Maryland						
Town Center Office Bldg		23	73	238	steel	office
Salt Lake City, Utah						
L.D.S. Church Office Building		30	128	420		
Beneficial Life Tower		27	107	351		
City and County			88	290		
State Capitol			87	285		
University Club		24	84	277		
Kennecott		18	81	267		
San Antonio, Texas						
Tower of the Americas			190	622		
Tower Life		30	123	404		
Nix Professional Building		23	114	375		
National Bank of Commerce		24	95	310		office
First National Bank Tower		20	92	302		
Frost Bank Tower		21	91	300		
Alamo National		23	88	288		
Milam		20	85	280		
San Diego, California						
So. Cal. First Natl Bank	1967	24	118	446	steel	office
Financial Square	1974	24	103	339	steel	office
Union Bank	1968	22	98	320	mixed	office
Central Federal	1977	22	98	320	steel	office
Crocker Bank	1962	25	93	306	steel	bank
San Diego Federal	1974	24	93	306	steel	office
Charter Oil	1963	23	86	281	concrete	office
Home Tower	1962	18	85	278	steel	office
Security Pacific Plaza	1973	18	85	278	steel	office
San Diego Gas and Electric	1966	21	84	276	steel	office
Bank of California	1971	18	81	265	steel	office
Little America Westgate Hotel	1970	19	92	245	steel	hotel
Chamber Bldg	1963	23	73	240	concrete	office
Del Prado	1973	17	46	150	concrete	apartment
Century Plaza Towers	1973	18	42	139	concrete	apartment
Catamaran Apartments	1968	13	37	122	masonry	apartment
Westgate Executive House	1968	9	33	108	steel	hotel
San Francisco, California						
Transamerica	1972	48	257	843	steel	office
Bank of America	1969	52	237	778	steel	office
Embarcadero Center		51	181	595	steel	office
Security Pacific Bank	1973	45	173	569		office
One Market Plaza	1975	43	172	565		
Wells Fargo	1966	43	171	561	steel	office
Standard Oil	1975	41	168	551	steel	office
Crocker Plaza	1978	38	162	553	steel	office
First and Market Building	U.C.	38	161	529	steel	office
Metropolitan Life	1974	38	160	524	steel	office
Hilton Hotel	1971	46	150	493	steel	hotel
Pacific Gas and Electric	1970	34	150	492	steel	office
Union Bank	1972	37	149	490	steel	office
Pacific Insurance Co.	1972	34	145	476	steel	office
Bechtel Building Annex	1978	33	145	475	steel	office
Hartford Insurance	1964	33	142	465	steel	office
Mutual Benefit Life	1969	32	134	438	steel	office
Telephone Building		26	133	435	steel	office
Embarcadero Center No. 3	1976	31	126	412	steel	office
Levi Strauss	1975	31	126	412	steel	office
Russ Building	1928	31	124	409	steel	office
California State Auto. Assn.	1974	29	122	400	steel	office

Table 4 Tallest buildings in major cities (continued)

Building	Year Completed	Number of stories	Height meters	feet	Material	Use
San Francisco, California, USA (continued)						
Alcoa	1967	27	121	398	steel	office
Shell	1930	29	118	386	steel	office
St. Francis Hotel (Addition)	1972	32	115	378	steel	hotel
Del Monte	1975	28	115	378	steel	office
Mills Tower	1930	22	114	376		
Great Western Savings	1968	26	109	359	steel	office
Union Square Hyatt House Hotel	1971	35	108	355	steel	hotel
Grosvenor Plaza		29	108	354		
450 Sutter Street		26	105	343	steel	office
Cathedral Apartments		21	104	340	concrete	apartment
Fairmont Hotel Tower	1961	29	101	330	steel	hotel
Royal Towers	1961	24	101	330	steel	apartment
Bechtel Building	1968	23	100	327	steel	office
Standard Oil International Building	1964	22	99	325	steel	office
California First	1974	23	99	324		
Equitable Life	1955	25	98	320	steel	office
450 Sutter Street	1929	26	96	315		
Bank of California	1967	21	96	314		
California Commercial Union	1921		94	309		
111 Sutter Street	1926	24	94	308		
Tishman Cahill	1974	38			steel	office
Fox Plaza	1966	29			steel	multiple
Lombard and Chestnut Apts		25			steel	apartment
Pacific Telephone	1967	16	88	288	steel	office
St. Francis Hotel	1901	13	57	186	steel	hotel
San Jose, California						
1625 Alameda		13			concrete	
Seattle, Washington						
Seattle First National Bank	1969	50	186	609	steel	office
Rainer Tower	1976	42	174	570	steel/concrete	office
Bank of California	1974	43	166	543	steel	office
L.C. Smith Tower	1925	42	159	520	steel	office
Federal Office Building	1973	38	152	499	steel	office
1600 Bell Plaza	1976	33	146	480	concrete	office
One Union Square	U.C.	38	139	456	steel/concrete	office
1111 Third Avenue	1980	35	138	454	steel	office
Washington Plaza Hotel	1969	40	116	380	steel	hotel
Financial Center	1972	33	113	372	concrete	office
Fourth and Blanchard	1980	24	110	360	steel	office
Park Hilton Hotel	1980	33	107	352	concrete	hotel
Pacific N.W. Bell Telephone	1976	33	107	350	steel	office
Seattle Tower/Northern Life Tower	1929	28	107	350	steel	office
Grandview Condominium	1979	27	99	325	concrete	condominium
Safeco Tower	1972	26	98	320	concrete	office
Norton Building	1959	21	95	310	steel	office
Pacific Building	1969	22	91	298	steel	office
Washington Building	1960	21	88	289	steel	office
Exchange Building	1929	23	84	275	concrete	office
Park Place	1971	21	82	270	concrete	office
Plaza 600	1969	20	82	270	steel	office
Peoples Bank	1973	20	81	266	steel	office
Hilton Inn/Garage	1971	25	79	260	concrete	hotel/parking
King County Stadium	1973	25	76	250	concrete	athletics
IBM Seattle	1964	20	76	250	mixed	office
Washington Park Tower	1969	24	73	240	concrete	apartment
Tower 801	1970	24	72	237	concrete	apartment
Washington Athletic Club	1972	23	71	232	steel	club
Royal Crest	1973	26	70	230	concrete	apartment
Royal Manor	1970	21	55	181	concrete	apartment
Pacific Northwest Bell	1969	11	50	164	steel	office
Springfield, Massachusetts						
Valley Bank Tower		29	113	370		
Chestnut Towers		34	88	290		
St. Louis, Missouri						
Mercantile Trust	1975	35	148	485	steel	office
Laclede Gas	1969	34	122	400	concrete	office
Bell Telephone	1926	33	121	398	steel	office
SW Bell Telephone		31	121	398		office
Civil Courts	1929	13	118	387	steel	government
Queeny Towers		19	98	321	steel	hospital
Council House Plaza		27	98	320		hotel

Table 4 Tallest buildings in major cities (continued)

Building	Year Completed	Number of stories	Height meters	feet	Material	Use
St. Louis, Missouri, USA (continued)						
Chase-Park Plaza	1930	30	95	310	steel	hotel
Pierre Laclede Center	1965	17	93	309	steel	office
Stouffers	1968	30	92	301	steel	hotel
Pet Inc.		22	91	300	concrete	office
River Front Holiday Inn	1968	28	88	290	steel	hotel
500 Broadway	1971	22	86	282	steel	office
Clayton Inn Center	1969	24	85	280	concrete	hotel
Breckenridge Inn	1976	23	85	280	concrete	hotel
Continental	1930	23	84	277	steel	office
Railway Exchange	1912	21	84	277	steel	multiple
Pierre Laclede Center	1969	25	84	276	steel	office
University Club Tower	1974	23	84	276	steel	office
Equitable	1973	21	84	276	steel	office
77 Bonhomme		25	84	275		office
Lennox Hotel		25	84	275		hotel
Boatmans Bank Tower	1976	22	84	275	steel	office
Park Tower Apartments		24	82	270		apartment
Missouri-Pacific	1927	23	81	265	steel	office
Gateway Towers	1967	20	80	261		apartment
Executive Office	1963	20	76	250	concrete	office
Mart	1931	20	72	235	concrete	office
Pet Milk	1969	15	67	225	concrete	office
Ralston-Purina	1969	15	64	210	concrete	office
Helio Colony Hotel		17			steel	hotel
Chromalloy	1973	17			steel	office
Clayton Club		13			steel	office
Westport Building	1976	12			steel	office
Wainwright	1892	10			steel	office
St. Paul, Minnesota						
First National Bank		32	127	417		
Osborn		20	112	368		
Kellogg Square Apartments		32	112	366		
Northwestern Bell Telephone		15	104	340		
American National Bank		25	102	335		
St. Paul Cathedral			94	307		
U.S. Post Office		12	84	274		
St. Paul Hilton Hotel		24	83	273		
City Hall and Courthouse		18	80	261		
Housing for the Elderly	1971	14	44	145	masonry	apartment
Stamford, Connecticut						
Landmark Towers		21				
Syracuse, New York						
State Tower		22	96	315		
MONY Office Building		19	82	268		
Carrier Tower		19	82	268		
Lincoln National Bank	1972	18			steel	office
Tampa, Florida						
First Financial Tower		36	140	458		
Exchange National		22	85	280		
Toledo, Ohio						
Owens Illinois Headquarters	1982	30	123	404	steel	office
Owens Corning Fiberglass Tower	1970	30	122	400	steel	office
Owens Illinois Bldg	1932	27	112	368	steel	office
Toledo Trust	1915	21	79	258	steel	off./bank
Toledo Edison Plaza	1972	17	68	223	mixed	office
National Bank	1921	17	64	210	steel	off./bank
Libbey-Owens-Ford	1960	15	64	209	steel	office
Commodore Perry	1925	17	57	187	steel	hotel
Holiday Inn	1970	19	55	180	concrete	hotel
Ohio Bldg	1930	13	48	158	steel	office
Ramada Inn	1970	9	32	108	steel	hotel
Alpha Towers	1976	9	27	90	concrete	apartment
Topeka, Kansas						
Merchants National Bank	1969	16			steel	office
Tucson, Arizona						
Arizona Bank Plaza	1977	16	80	262	concrete	office
Tucson Federal Savings	1967	20	74	242	steel	office
Great Western Bank	1977	16	59	193	concrete	office
Federal Bldg	1974	8	58	190		office
Pima County Administration	1970	11	49	162	concrete	office
City Hall Tower	1967	10	43	142	steel	office
Clinical Sciences and Teaching	1971	9	43	142	concrete	multiple
Tucson House	1964	16	43	141	concrete	apartment
Valley National Bank	1929	10	40	132	steel	office

Table 4 Tallest buildings in major cities (continued)

Building	Year Completed	Number of stories	Height meters	feet	Material	Use
Tucson, Arizona, USA (continued)						
University of Arizona Adm.	1967	7	37	122	steel	office
Marriot Hotel	1974	11	37	121	mixed	hotel
Redondo Towers	1961	9	37	121	concrete	apartment
First Natl Bank	1972	8	33	109	concrete	office
Tucson Electric	1968	6	33	107	mixed	office
Arizona Hall	1964	11	30	99	concrete	dormitory
Sonora Hall	1963	11	30	99	concrete	dormitory
Coronado Hall	1965	11	30	97	concrete	dormitory
College of Education	1968	9	28	91	steel	school
University Hospital	1971	10	27	89		hospital
Pioneer International Hotel	1930	11			concrete	hotel
Transamerica	1962	11			steel	office
Lawyers Title	1958	9				office
Almeda Plaza	1961					office
Tulsa, Oklahoma						
Bank of Oklahoma Tower	1976	50	203	667	steel/concrete	office
First National Tower		41	157	516		
Fourth National Bank of Tulsa		21	126	412		
National Bank of Tulsa		24	122	400		
Cities Service		28	118	388		
University Club Tower		32	115	377		
Philtower		23	105	343		
Helmerich, Payne, Bland Dev. Co.	1979	16	48	159	masonry	condos
Service Corp of Tulsa	1979	10	43	140	concrete	office
Williams Plaza Hotel	1978	12	40	130	mixed	hotel
R.J. LaFortune Tower	1975	11	32	104		apartment
Washington, D.C.						
Lafayette Centre		8				off./retail
Weirton, West Virginia						
Low-Rent Housing Proj.16-1	1966	9	27	89	masonry	apartment
White Plains, New York						
Westchester County Courthouse	1973	20	79	260	concrete	office
Wilmington, Delaware						
Hercules Tower		23	88	287		
American Life Ins. Co.		21	86	282		
Dupont Brandywine Building	1972	18			mixed	office
Winston-Salem, North Carolina						
Wachovia		30	125	410		
Reynolds		21	96	315		
USSR						
Arkhangelsk						
Construction & Design Building	1977	23	82	269	concrete	office
Baku						
Azerbajdzhan	1970	17	50	167	mixed	hotel
Housing		16	48	157	concrete	apartment
Erevan						
Anee	1975	15	47	156	mixed	hotel
Gorky						
Housing (E-277)		16	48	157	concrete	apartment
Jalta						
Jalta	1977	17	50	167	mixed	hotel
Kemerovo						
Housing (1-464)	1970	12	36	118	concrete	apartment
Housing (EHI-3)	1970	12	36	118	concrete	apartment
Khabarovsk						
Orgtechstroy	1972	14	53	173	concrete	office
Kiev						
Ministry of Light Industries	1976	22	78	256	concrete	office
Lebed	1971	19	60	200	mixed	hotel
Slavoutich	1972	18	57	190	mixed	hotel
Kiev	1975	19	55	154	mixed	hotel
Kishenev						
Intourist	1977	17	50	152	mixed	hotel

Table 4 Tallest buildings in major cities (continued)

Building	Year Completed	Number of stories	Height meters	feet	Material	Use
USSR (continued)						
Leningrad						
Sovetskaya	1967	19	55	183	mixed	hotel
Institute Lengyprogor	1969	14	51	167	concrete	design org.
Retchnaya	1975	17	48	160	mixed	hotel
Housing (1-LG-602)		16	48	157	concrete	apartment
Housing (Series 137)		16	48	157	concrete	apartment
Housing (Series 141)		16	48	157	concrete	apartment
Housing (Series 122)		16	48	157	concrete	apartment
Leningrad	1970	15	44	146	mixed	hotel
Pribaltiskaya Hotel	1978	13			concrete	hotel
Minsk						
Housing	1977	20	59	194	concrete	apartment
Housing (M-111-90)		16	48	157	concrete	apartment
Housing		16	48	157	concrete	apartment
Moscow						
Ukraine Hotel	1961		198	650	steel/concrete	hotel
Moscow State University		37	170	559		school
Ministry of Foreign Affairs	1952	26	170	558	concrete	office
Ministry of Transport	1953	20	134	440	concrete	office
Ukraina	1957	30	128	426	mixed	hotel
CMEA	1967	30	103	337	concrete	office
Hydroproject Building	1968	25	97	319	concrete	design org.
Kotelnicheskaya Nab.	1950	24	90	295	brick/lime	apartment
Ministry Transport Development	1974	24	88	287	concrete	design org.
Vernadsky Prospect Bldg	1972	22	85	280	concrete	design org.
Structural Design-Izmailovo	1977	23	79	259	concrete	design org.
Vosstania Square	1950	21	75	246	brick/lime	apartment
Setunsky Proezd	1970	25	73	240	concrete	apartment
Prospect Mira	1970	25	73	240	concrete	apartment
Izmailovo	1977	25	73	240	concrete	apartment
Semenovskaya Square	1977	25	73	240	concrete	apartment
Kalinin Prospect	1970	23	67	220	concrete	apartment
National	1969	23	65	216	mixed	hotel
Vodocanalproyect	1975	18	65	213	concrete	design org.
State Committee of Standards	1970	16	65	212	concrete	office
Troparevo	1972	22	64	210	concrete	apartment
Belgrad	1972	21	60	200	mixed	hotel
Gosplan	1967	16	61	198	concrete	office
Ministries in Kalinin Prospect	1967	25	58	190	concrete	office
Lenin Prospect		19	56	184	concrete	apartment
Red Gate		16	56	184	brick/lime	apartment
Housing (E-264)		17	50	164	concrete	apartment
Housing (II-3/16)		16	48	157	concrete	apartment
Housing (II-42)		16	48	157	concrete	apartment
Housing (II-43)		16	48	157	concrete	apartment
Housing (II-44)		16	48	157	concrete	apartment
Housing (II-22)		16	48	157	concrete	apartment
Housing (II-3)		16	48	157	concrete	apartment
Housing (II-23)		16	48	157	concrete	apartment
Butirskaya Square (K-446)	1977	16	48	157	concrete	apartment
Housing ((11-68)		16	48	157	concrete	apartment
Chertanovo		16	48	157	concrete	apartment
Housing		16	48	157	concrete	apartment
Housing (Series 16)		16	48	157	concrete	apartment
Akademicheskaya	1974	16	47	156	mixed	hotel
Orleonok	1977	16	46	153	mixed	hotel
Housing (U-209A)		14	42	138	concrete	apartment
Housing		14	42	138	brick/concrete	apartment
Drouzba	1969	14	40	133	mixed	hotel
Housing (Series 1605)	1970	12	36	118	concrete	apartment
Housing (II-28)	1970	12	36	118	concrete	apartment
Housing (II-29)	1970	12	36	118	concrete	apartment
Housing (II-30)	1970	12	36	118	concrete	apartment
Housing (II-31)	1970	12	36	118	concrete	apartment
Housing (II-32)	1970	12	36	118	concrete	apartment
Housing (II-35)	1970	12	36	118	concrete	apartment
Housing (II-46)	1970	12	36	118	concrete	apartment
Housing (II-47)	1970	12	36	118	concrete	apartment
Housing (II-50)	1970	12	36	118	concrete	apartment
Housing (II-53)	1970	12	36	118	concrete	apartment
Housing (11-68)	1968	12	36	118	concrete	apartment
Housing (E-433)	1965	12	36	118	concrete	apartment
Hotel Intourist	1973	21			steel	hotel
Soviet Trade Center	1978	20			steel	multiple

Table 4 Tallest buildings in major cities (continued)

Building	Year Completed	Number of stories	Height meters	feet	Material	Use
USSR (continued)						
Naberezhnie						
Housing	1977	25	73	240	concrete	apartment
Housing (E-298)		12	36	118	concrete	apartment
Ordjonikidze						
Housing (111-92-C/1-OP)	1977	12	36	118	concrete	apartment
Orsk						
Housing (E-377)		16	48	157	concrete	apartment
Housing (E-376)		12	36	118	concrete	apartment
Riga						
Latvia	1976	26	75	250	mixed	hotel
Rostov-Don						
Intourist	1973	17	48	160	mixed	hotel
Sochi						
Zhemchouzhina	1970	19	60	200	mixed	hotel
Kamelia	1971	12	35	116	mixed	hotel
Moscwa	1975	12	35	116	mixed	hotel
Tallin						
Viru	1971	23	100	333	mixed	hotel
Tashkent						
Ministry Building in Lenin Sq.	1974	19	70	229	concrete	office
Publishing House	1975	15	63	206	concrete	office
Togliatti						
Housing (11-60)		16	48	157	concrete	apartment
Housing (E-241)		12	36	118	concrete	apartment
Tula						
Housing		16	48	157	concrete	apartment
Uljanovsk						
Venets	1970	23	64	214	mixed	hotel
Volgograd						
Housing (E-268)		16	48	157	concrete	apartment
Zelenograd						
Housing	1977	22	64	210	concrete	apartment
Zhukovsky						
Housing (1-464A)	1971	12	36	118	concrete	apartment
Housing (E-54)	1971	12	36	118	concrete	apartment
Zvezdni						
Housing (E-54)		16	48	157	brick	apartment
United Arab Emirates						
Dubai						
Dubai Intnl Trade Centre	1978	38	150	500	concrete	multiple
Venezuela						
Caracas						
Parque Central Torre Oficinas	1979	56	200	656	concrete	office
Parque Central Edif. Viviendas	1972	42	120	394	concrete	multiple
La Previsora	1972	32	117	385	concrete	office
Centro Res Sonia	1967	26	74	243		
Don Manuel	1968	24	65	214		
Los Ortega	1961	22	60	197		
Catleya	1968	20	60	197		
Petunia	1967	21	41	133		
Normandie	1972	30			concrete	multiple
Centro Empresarial Edif. B.O.	1969	26				
CANTV	1972	25				
Banco Caracas	1966	24				
Patricia	1967	23				
El Conde	1970	21				
Yugoslavia						
Belgrade						
Bldg of Public Organisation	1974	29	100	215	concrete	multiple

Table 4 Tallest buildings in major cities (continued)

Building	Year Completed	Number of stories	Height meters	feet	Material	Use
		Yugoslavia (continued)				
		Ljubljana				
Bavarski Dvor	1976	17	64	210	steel/concrete	office
Ruski Car (housing highrise)	1970	13	61	199	concrete	housing
Neboticnik (skyscraper)	1932	12	57	187	concrete	off./apt.
Bank of Ljubljana	1971	12	55	182	concrete	office
Iskra	1971	12	55	182	concrete	office
Metalka	1967	14	44	144	concrete	office
Avtotehna	1970	14	44	144	concrete	office
BS 6 Housing Highrise in Siska	1969	15	39	127	concrete	housing
		Zagreb				
Vranica	1975	25	85	278	concrete	office
Udarnik Srednjaci	1974	22	67	220	concrete	apartment
Industrogradnja Utrine	1972	18	53	174	concrete	apartment
Tempo Utrine	1976	18	53	174	concrete	apartment
Vjesnik	1965	17	53	174	concrete	office

Summary Statistics

Number of Countries: 62
Number of Cities: 405
Number of Buildings: 3206

Current Questions, Problems and Research Needs

This appendix identifies problem areas for further study and research. It constitutes an update of Council Report No. 5, first issued in 1972, as part of its mission to identify such problems for interested investigators and organizations. The sequence of headings is the same as that used in this Volume. Numbers in parentheses refer to the Committee responsible for the topic. Additional suggestions of study areas should be forwarded to Council Headquarters for transmission to the appropriate Committee for possible inclusion in the next revision of the Council's report on the subject.

STRUCTURAL SYSTEMS (3)

1. The impact of industrialization and mass production of structural systems on the planning and design of tall buildings.
2. The effect of nonstructural partitions on damping and stiffening characteristics of the building.
3. Performance of various structural systems with respect to expansion, contraction, deflection, wind sway, vertical movement, and differential settlement.
4. When is it feasible to use "mixed" structural beams and columns (reinforced concrete with steel core)?
5. What improved structural schemes can enhance economical construction of tall buildings?
6. How is design modified by virtue of multiple use? (Garages on first floor, combined residence and business use with attendant delivery problems.)
7. Evaluation of the structural systems used in the existing tall building structures, and delineation of the range of story heights for which different forms of construction are most suitable.
8. Use of box girders for wide-span floors as airducts.
9. Generally, designing of structures and detailing of ducts and cables are done independently of each other and are not properly integrated.
10. What is the actual and required ductile behavior of structural system (including shear walls and braced frames) when subjected to seismic events?
11. What is the actual and required strength and stiffness of floor diaphragms for high-rise buildings?

12. Work on techniques to evaluate vibration characteristics of floor systems. (Research work to date has been limited to steel floors).
13. The effect of composite action between steel beams and concrete slab on plastic hinge formation and ductility under seismic loading.

MECHANICAL AND SERVICE SYSTEMS (2B)

1. How does one optimize the mechanical-electrical system with respect to structural design?
2. In what ways can pollution be decreased? (Centralized HVAC, power, and trash disposal systems.)
3. How can the environmental problems created by unusual mechanical systems be solved? Architectural solution?
4. As a means of conserving power requirements, what are the criteria for needed illumination levels and air-circulation characteristics?
5. How can energy consumption in a tall building be minimized?
6. Effect of omission of dampers on smoke distribution throughout an air-conditioned building.
7. How can solar water heaters be utilized in tall buildings?
8. What savings can be made on mechanical-electrical systems if the building is fully protected by an automatic sprinkler system?

ELECTRICAL SYSTEMS (2C)

1. Since "electrical" is not necessarily a part of Heat, Ventilating, and Air Conditioning, how can the electrical system be made more effective?
2. Automation and life safety systems. This includes the future improvements in automatic warning systems and communications in case of emergency such as fire, etc.
3. Automatic communications of security violations. This would require a new approach to using communication techniques within the buildings to signal warning of any violations of present security levels.
4. Automation in light-meter-controlled shading, heating, and cooling systems. Light-meter-activated control systems need to be developed for efficient use of energy in the building. Such control systems could also maintain predetermined lighting levels throughout the building, thereby utilizing natural light when available.
5. For large tall buildings, electrical generation for the entire building may totally support the requirements or support peak requirements. A method needs to be developed to analyze the extent and efficiency of standby electric generating systems.

VERTICAL AND HORIZONTAL TRANSPORTATION (2A)

1. How can one overcome the trend that "the height of the building fits the elevator"?
2. What is an effective scheme for total evacuation in an emergency?
3. How can traffic within a building be moved more rapidly, especially at rush hours?
4. Optimum methods of handling parking in multiple levels.
5. Secondary transportation systems integrated into building design (such as "people-mover" system), using air cushion linear induction motors and interconnected to vertical transportation in the buildings.
6. Criteria for determining "waiting time" for elevators.
7. What is essential for emergency services in elevators—e.g., battery operated lights and fans as well as emergency generator for all buildings?

CLADDING (12A)

1. What can be done about the ice-sheets that form on the sides of tall buildings (with exposed steel) that then fall to the street as the building warms up?
2. How can one better integrate the cladding into the structure? (Experience broken stone and broken windows after a relatively short life.)
3. Review various aluminum, steel, masonry, and glass, curtain wall and perimeter cladding systems, including fire resistance, insulation, vapor barrier, and heating criteria.
4. In the case of prestressed concrete cladding, determine whether or not galvanized reinforcement is needed to prevent spalling of concrete in the early life of a building.

PARTITIONS, WALLS, AND CEILINGS (12B)

1. What are acceptable vibration limits of partitions?
2. Generate a list of recommendations for architectural materials, systems, and details with regard to earthquake design, flammability, and toxicity.
3. How are the air drafts and/or stack action in elevator shafts, mechanical shafts, and stairwells controlled?
4. How can methods of construction be improved to avoid the damage of nonstructural elements due to wind load, earthquake, vibration, temperature variation, or construction?
5. The stiffening effect of internal partitions and curtain walls, particularly where openings or other irregularities are present. Examine (a) Unit purpose made to provide structural action; and (b) conventional nonstructural units.
6. Connections with nonstructural elements.
7. Further work is necessary to permit the stiffness and damping of nonstructural elements to be included in the calculation of structure response for serviceability checks.
8. Mechanism of load transfer between deep shear walls and floor slabs.
9. Joint between lintel beams and deep shear walls.

FOUNDATION DESIGN (11)

1. How does the interaction of the building with its foundation influence its design, especially under lateral loads?
2. What is consistent foundation safety as compared with the superstructure safety: (a) from standpoint of deformation; and (b) from standpoint of rupture?
3. Lateral load criteria on earth retaining structures.
4. Pressure distribution at the base of tall building foundation.
5. Soil-structure interaction under static and dynamic forces.
6. Mechanism of interaction of piles with soil.
7. How does the nonuniform settlement of foundation influence the superstructure?
8. Concrete plates on soft soil for bearing of heavy load.
9. Differential settlement (or lack of it) when low-rise buildings adjoin high-rise buildings.

CONSTRUCTION (4)

1. How to best move construction workers and equipment within a tall building during the construction process.
2. Difference in construction techniques depending on story height. (Can this be catalogued for various ranges of story heights? Note influence of industrialization.)
3. Effect of past failures on improved construction techniques.

4. Support of adjacent work during installation of large foundations.
5. Protection of the public at work site.
6. How to incorporate prefabricated systems into tall building construction.
7. Is there a way to design for demolition?
8. Methods to eliminate annoying floor vibrations. Devices or techniques are needed which can be used at the time of construction or after the structure is occupied.
9. How to speed up construction time. In the field of reinforced concrete one floor per week seems about "standard" for industrialized countries, but for many others—and even some fairly advanced countries—it can take up to three weeks per floor.
10. Evaluation of workmanship in the field.
11. During mixing, what technique is available to determine how strong concrete will be after it is in place?
12. Compile information concerning actual straightness of columns after erection.
13. How do the results of fire affect mechanical properties of reinforced concrete and prestressed concrete?
14. More information and research are needed on the fire rating of bare steel members as part of a structural system.
15. Comparison of cost and time expenditures between lift-slab construction and conventional reinforced concrete construction.

Nomenclature

GLOSSARY

Accelerating moving walk. A horizontal or inclined moving walk which at points of access accelerates to, and at points of egress decelerates from, the constant speed portion running at a speed faster than 1.2 m/sec (235 ft per min).

Acrylic. A group of thermoplastic resins formed by polymerizing the esters of acrylic acid.

Activator. A material which, when added to the base compound or the curing agent, as in the case of a two-part system, will speed up or initiate the curing mechanism.

Activity center. A group of structures and the interacting support systems that provide multiple services in a dedicated environment.

Adhesion. The ability of a coating or sealant to stick or bond to the surface to which it is applied.

Adhesion failure. Failure of a compound by pulling away from the surface with which it is in contact.

Adhesion peel-back test. The separation of a bond, whereby the material is pulled away from the mating surface at a 90° angle or a 180° angle to the plane to which it is adhered. Values are generally expressed in pounds per inch width and as to whether failure was adhesive or cohesive.

Air, return or exhaust. Air returned or exhausted from each or any space in the system.

Air, supply. The quantity of air delivered to each or any space in the system, or the total delivered to all spaces in the system.

American Institute of Steel Construction. A U.S. organization founded in 1921 for the purpose of technical specifications and trade organization for the fabricated structural steel industry in the United States.

Amortization. A method of liquidating a debt by making annual payments to a sinking fund, in a given time with the accumulated interest, which becomes equal to debt.

Anchor bolt. A bolt used to secure frameworks, stanchion bases, etc., to piers or foundations, and having a 90° bend hook or a washer at the embedded end for anchorage.

Apparent power. Apparent power is proportional to the mathematical product of the volts and amperes of a circuit. This product generally is divided by 1 000 and designated in kilovoltamperes (kVA). It is comprised of both real and reactive power.

Appliance. An appliance is utilization equipment. It is generally other than industrial; normally built in standardized sizes and types; installed or connected to perform one or more functions, such as clothes washing, air-conditioning, food fixing, and cooking.

Application life. The period of time during which a sealant, after being mixed with a catalyst or exposed to the atmosphere, remains suitable for application. Also referred to as work life.

Aquifer. A layer of soil or rock that conducts ground water.

Area-of-refuge. An internal area in a building, safe from fire and smoke contamination, that may include avenues of egress.

Arrival rate. The rate of arrival of the transient and permanent population, including visitors to service personnel, at the building for use of vertical transportation system.

Asphalt base. Descriptive of a compound whose liquid content is composed of Asphaltic materials resulting from distillation of petroleum.

Atterberg limits. The water content of a cohesive soil at two critical points: the Plastic Limit, which is the driest state at which the soil acts as a plastic mass, and the Liquid Limit, which is the wettest state at which the soil has significant shear strength.

Auger caisson. A large-diameter caisson drilled by a technique derived from oil drilling.

Auger machine. A powered, screw type rotating drill used to transport loose material, usually earth, away from the cutting face.

Automated cart transport system. A cart-sized automated supply system.

Automated storage and retrieval system. A "hands-off" electromechanical materials handling system to temporarily warehouse containerized or palletized raw or finished goods for subsequent retrieval and use.

Automated parking system. A "hands-off" electromechanical system to park, store, and unpark motor vehicles, including the automated ticket dispensing and ticket payment subsystems.

Automated supply system. A "hands-off" electromechanical materials handling system to deliver containerized or palletized raw or finished goods from a point of origin to a point of destination without warehousing.

Automated tote box system. A tote-box-sized automated supply system.

Back-up material. A compressible material placed in a joint before applying a sealant, to limit the depth of the sealant and assist in providing the proper sealant configuration. This material may also act as a bond breaker.

Base track. The bottom section of a nonbearing wall or partition which can accommodate some movement without damage to the wall or partition.

Batch flow. The reduction of people or material flow to manageable and transportable sizes in the origin-to-destination flow of traffic.

Batter piles. Piles driven at an angle from vertical to provide lateral support to a structure.

Bauer or lost point method. A drilled-in earth tie-back using a grouted tip.

Bead. A sealant or compound after application in a joint irrespective of the method of application, such as caulking bead, glazing bead, etc. Also a molding or stop used to hold glass or panels in position.

Bearing capacity. The load that a foundation member (such as a footing or pile) can carry without rupture of the ground. Usually expressed as force per unit area.

Bearing value. The allowable load per unit area on a foundation member.

Bed or bedding. The bead of compound applied between sight bar glass or panel and the stationary stop or sight bar of the sash or frames, and usually the first bead of compound to be applied when setting glass or panels.

Bedding of stop. The application of compound at base of channel, just before the stop is placed in position, or buttered on inside face of stop.

Benoto machine. A caisson machine that works on the principle of continuously rotating the special shell to reduce the side friction of the casing against the ground, while excavating within the shell with grab buckets.

Bentonite. A very plastic clay composed largely of the mineral montmorillonite which adsorbs water and swells. Bentonite has a very low permeability and is, therefore, used to restrict the flow of water.

Berm. A portion of an embankment placed against a wall or other embankment to improve stability.

Bevel of compound bead. Bead of compound applied so as to have a slanted top surface so that water will drain away from the glass or panel.

Bite. Amount of overlap between the top of the stop and the outer edge of panel or light.

Bitumen. A mixture of hydrocarbons occurring both in native state and as a residue of petroleum distillation. Used in coatings, adhesives, paints, sealants and roofing.

Bleeding. A liquid coating or drops of a liquid component that migrate to the surface of a sealant.

Block. A small piece of wood, lead, Neoprene or other suitable material used to position the panel in the frame.

Bond breaker. A release type of material (such as polyethylene film sheet with adhesive on one side) used to prevent adhesion of the sealant to the back-up material or back of the joint.

Boring. A hole drilled in the ground from which samples are taken to determine the nature of the soil or rock.

Braced frames. Usually refers to frames which derive their stability primarily from truss action. Most elements have pinned ends and do not develop bending resistance. (These frames usually develop minor bending forces.)

Bracing. Structural members provided to support sheeting or slurry walls against lateral earth pressures.

Branch circuit. That portion of a wiring system extended beyond the final over-current device protecting the circuit.

Bubbling. Open or closed protuberances in a sealant caused by the release, production or expansion of gases.

Building operator. Owner, Manager, Agent, or Trustee responsible for the operation and maintenance of the building.

Bulk compound. Sealants in containers or cartridges capable of being extruded in place.

Bunching. The propensity of elevator cars to operate close together under heavy traffic conditions through lack of sophisticated logic controls.

Busway. A ventilated or nonventilated housing which encases insulated copper or aluminum conductors of bar, rod or tube construction.

Buttering. Application of compound or sealant to the flat surface of a member before placing it into position.

Butyl. Synthetic rubber formed by the co-polymerization of isobutylene with isoprene.

Caisson. A reinforced concrete pier usually excavated by auger which may have a shell to laterally support the soil. (a) A deep foundation member used to deliver structural loads to the founding material, installed by excavating. [Note: In the United Kingdom the caisson can refer to the temporary structure which may or may not form part of the temporary structure which in a temporary state is used to support excavation. Excavation within the caisson can either take place with free air or compressed air conditions.] (b) A large box used to advance an excavation while men work in it.

Caisson, belled. A caisson [definition (a)] with the diameter of the lower portion increased.

Caisson, casing supported. A caisson [definition (a)] which is kept open during emplacement by a steel casing.

Caisson, drilled-in. A caisson [definition (a)] whose lower end is in a hole drilled into the supporting rock.

Caisson, open. A caisson [definition (a)] that is excavated without support or has support installed as work progresses, usually excavated by hand.

Caisson, slurry supported. A caisson [definition (a)] which is kept open during placement by the presence of a bentonite slurry in the hole.

Camber. Upward convex curvature of slabs and beams to counteract service load deflections.

Capacity. The specified and design capacity in kilograms (pounds) of an elevator or lift that legally constitutes the normal full passenger load.

Car call. A call register in an elevator car operating panel to indicate that the elevator should stop at that landing.

Car platform. The horizontal structural base of an elevator car that supports the car enclosure, doors, and door operator, and provides a surface for the passenger flooring.

Cart lift. A classification of lift that is restricted to the substantially vertical transport of carts with automated transfer device to load and unload the lift.

Cast-in-place. A term applied to concrete elements where the element is cast in the exact location where it will be used (sometimes called cast-in-situ).

Castellated beams. Beams fabricated by cutting through the web of the beam with a profile burning machine, separating the two halves, moving one half along the other until the "teeth" of the castellations coincide and tack welding the two halves together. Deep penetration welding is then used to weld both sides of the web.

Castor-Severs test. Performed with a Castor-Severs rheometer and measures the rate of flow of a compound under controlled conditions of temperature, pressure, and orifice size. Of value in work for the measurement of the internal cohesive force of pumpable sealers.

Catalyst. A material which markedly speeds up the cure or reaction of another substance when added in minor quantities.

Caulking. The process of making a joint watertight. The term originally implied stopping up joints with oakum (loose fiber got by picking old rope) and melted pitch. It is now also applied to stopping joints with lead, mastics, rubber, and other flexible materials.

Central automated control facility. A computerized central system which monitors, analyzes, and automatically and/or indirectly controls the operation of building facilities.

Ceiling. The divider between the ductwork and the structural system of the floor above and the usable interior space below.

Ceiling grid. The structural system from which the panels of the ceiling are hung.

Chain stopper. A material which, when added during the polymerization process, will stop the molecules from continued growth to still longer lengths.

Channel. A three-sided, U-shaped opening in sash or frame to receive light or panel, with or without removable stop or stops. Contrasted to a rabbet, which is a two-sided, L-shaped section, as with face glazed window sash.

Channel depth. The measurement from the bottom of the channel to the top of the stop, or measurement from sight-line to base of channel.

Channel glazing. The sealing of the joints around lights or panels set in a U-shaped channel employing removable stops.

Channel width. The measurement between stationary stops (or stationary stop and removable stop) in a U-shaped channel.

Chemical cure. A change in the properties of a material due to polymerization or vulcanization, which may be effected by heat, catalysts, exposure to the atmosphere, or combinations of these.

Chlorinated rubber. A synthetic resin produced by the chlorination of natural rubber or of a synthetic rubber, such as polyisoprene.

Cladding. The opaque areas of an exterior window wall or curtain wall; i.e., the column cladding or spandrel cladding of a building exterior.

Clamshell grab. A grab shaped like a clamshell, used for excavation.

Cleavage plane. Any joint, crack, or change of quality of formation along which rock will break easily when dug or blasted.

Cohesion. The component of strength of soil that is independent of normal stress.

Cohesive failure. Splitting and opening of a compound resulting from over-extension of the compound.

Coincident stops. The stop of a double-deck elevator to simultaneously answer car and landing calls on two contiguous floors.

Cold sawing. Sawing a piece of metal with a blade traveling at a slow rate with the teeth tearing the metal.

Comb plate. The stationary toothed edge of the top and bottom plates of an escalator that engages the ribbed tread of the steps so as to prevent footwear from wedging between the landing plate and the moving steps.

Compartmentation. Dividing a building into compartments to limit the size of fires.

Compatibility. The ability of two or more materials to exist in close and permanent association for an indefinite period with no adverse effect of one on the other.

Compensated foundation. A foundation constructed by excavating material equal or nearly equal in weight to the finished structure, often called a "floating foundation." If the weight of excavated material is less than that of the finished structure, the foundation is "undercompensated." If it is more, the foundation is "overcompensated."

Composite beam. A beam which acts with a floor slab as though they were one single unit. Usually a positive method of horizontal shear force transfer is required at the interface.

Compression, secondary. That portion of the decrease in volume of a soil under load that is time-dependent but independent of hydraulic lag in the pore water pressure.

Compression, virgin. Compression under stresses larger than those previously carried by the soil.

Concrete slurry walls. Reinforced concrete wall, created by displacing the lighter slurry fluid by placement of denser concrete mix through a tremie at bottom of trench excavation.

Consolidation. Time-dependent change in volume of a soil as the result of applied load. Volume change can occur only as fluid, usually water, is forced from the voids of the soil. Thus, the time rate is dependent on soil permeability and location of drainage paths.

Consolidation coefficient. The coefficient (in units of length/time squared), describing the rate at which consolidation occurs.

Consolidation, normal. Consolidation (complete dissipation of excess pore pressure) under current effective stresses that have never been exceeded in the past.

Consolidation, over. Previous consolidated under effective stresses larger than those which now exist in the soil mass.

Constrado. The British organization for research and development pertaining to structural steelwork in the United Kingdom.

Contact pressure. The pressure exerted by the soil on a foundation member.

Continuous flow. The accommodation of passenger or material flow at the natural or normal rate of arrival or departure.

Continuous hollow stem augers. A boring tool with a hollow shank connected to the bit.

Contract load. The specified and design capacity in kilograms (pounds) of an elevator or lift that legally constitutes the normal full passenger load.

Contract speed. The specified and design speed in meters per second (feet per minute) of an elevator or lift that legally constitutes the normal full speed under contract load conditions.

Control. The speed control system of an elevator which provides the acceleration, contract speed, deceleration, and leveling functions.

Control jointing. Small separations in walls or partitions which allow movement without damage to either the wall or partition. The most common cause of movement results from temperature change.

Core. The portion of a building floor reserved for elevators, fire stairs, toilet rooms, mechanical rooms, etc. This area is usually, but not always, in the middle of a building.

Cost-effective. The value judgment of operating and capital expenditures for, versus the benefits derived from, a proposed new method of operation.

Cripple. A part of a frame which is cut less than full size.

Cross-braced panel. A panel fitted with crossed diagonals to resist the shear, as distinct from a shear wall.

Cross-bridging. Bridging consisting of transverse rows of small diagonal braces or struts set in pairs, and crossing each other between the members.

Crosshole test. A test in which shear waves are propagated horizontally between borings to measure the stiffness of soil on rock.

Curing agent. Generally a part of a two-part system which when added to the base material cures by a chemical reaction.

Curtain wall. A building exterior wall, of any material, which carries no super-imposed vertical loads.

Custom-designed. Individually designed (like a suit made to measure) as opposed to a pre-engineered (or mass-produced) system.

Cyclic loading. Loading in which the forces or stresses are applied repeatedly.

Damping. The dissipation of energy for dynamic loading.

Damping, hysteretic. Damping that is independent of the frequency of dynamic loading but related to displacement.

Damping, viscous. Damping that is dependent on the velocity and, hence on the frequency of dynamic loading.

Dead load. The actual weight of the structural elements. (This is a gravity load.)

Deformation modulus. A modulus, relating axial stress to axial strain, that is similar to Young's modulus but does not imply reversibility of behavior.

Demand factor. The ratio of the maximum demand of a system, or part of a system, to the total connected load of a system or the part of the system under consideration.

Demand system. A group automatic operation system that programs the position and direction of cars to prevent bunching and to promptly respond to car and landing calls.

Derrick. Any hoisting device used for lifting or moving heavy weights.

Dewatering. Removal of ground water from an excavation.

Diaphragm wall. A concrete wall designed to retain soil and water from an excavation.

Differential settlements. Settlements of a building that have different magnitudes at different locations.

Discounted cash flow (DCF). The discounting of future income or savings for financial evaluation of proposed expenditures and savings as a function of a fixed interest rate.

Dispatching landing. The landing at which the dispatching system holds the elevator cars, usually the main lobby of a building.

Dispatching system. A time interval release of cars from the main lobby to prevent more than one partially loaded car from leaving before the expiration of the interval.

Disturbed sample. A sample of soil taken from a boring in a manner such that, while all materials are present, the properties of soil are severely altered by remolding during sampling.

Diversified occupancy. The classification of office building occupancy that contains multiple tenants, without interacting pedestrian or material traffic, with varied starting and finishing times for their work functions, and without internal dining facilities.

Door close time. The time necessary to close an opened set of car and landing doors within the legal code requirements of kinetic energy and stall force.

Door open time. The time necessary to open a closed set of car and landing doors.

Double-deck elevator. A double cavity passenger or freight elevator serving equally spaced landings so that both cavities can be simultaneously loaded or unloaded, that is installed within a single car frame and provided with a single driving machine.

Down conductor. A conductor used to connect the lighting air terminals and roof mounted loop conductor to the provided electrodes at the column and/or building base.

Down-peak. The traffic pattern caused by passenger traffic predominantly in the down direction.

Drilled-in caisson. Caisson installed by driving a steel tube with a pile hammer.

Ductility. The ability of structural elements or frames to absorb energy through deformation without failure.

Dumbwaiter. The materials handling classification of vertical transportation limited by code to platform not greater than 0.84 m² (9 sq ft) and to a door height of 1.2 m (4 ft). Personnel are not permitted to ride on dumbwaiter.

Durometer. A device used to measure hardness. Also a word used to describe hardness of a material.

Dwell time. The variable time a set of car and landing doors are in the fully open position in response to car or landing calls.

Earth pressure, active. The minimum pressure exerted by the earth against a wall.

Earth pressure, at rest. The pressure exerted by the earth against a wall when no lateral movement of the wall has occurred.

Earth pressure, lateral. The pressure exerted by the earth against a wall.

Earth pressure, passive. The maximum pressure exerted by the earth against a wall. This develops when the wall moves against the soil, for example, when supporting a bracing element.

Elastomer. An elastic rubber-like substance.

Electrical load. Any electrically connected material, device or system that uses electrical energy.

Elevator. A passenger or freight classification of vertical transportation for the movement of passengers or freight with an operator between floors.

Elevator recall. The automatic smoke detector, including water flow alarm or the manual key switch recall of all elevators in a bank to the landing closest to the street.

Elevator net usable area. That area on the floor of an office building that is occupied by people requiring vertical transportation to and from the street level by elevator.

Emergency power. That power which is available within ten (10) seconds of a normal power failure to operate emergency, or portions of the normal, lighting in a building (see "standby power").

Emulsion. Suspension of microscopic particles in water, as contrasted to chemical solutions.

End-bearing pile. A pile carried on a load-bearing layer, such as rock, as opposed to a friction pile.

Epoxy. A thermoplastic resin formed by combining epichlorohydrin and biphenols. Requires a curing agent for room temperature or elevated temperature hardening.

Erection. The assemblage of structural elements into an integrated structural system.

Escalator—moving stairs. A people conveyor accomplishing vertical transportation by discrete moving steps along an incline approximately 30°. The steps gradually form at the point of embarkation and disappear at the point of debarkation.

Express zone. That portion of an elevator hoistway landing doors in which the elevator bypasses floors served by another elevator.

Extender. A relatively inexpensive material, added to a compound for the purpose of reducing the cost and/or improving certain desirable characteristics.

Fabrication shop. Workshop for the preparation of structural steel components from mill shapes and plates by detailed operations such as drilling, bending, cutting, and assembling.

Facade. The principal face of a building.

Facade grid. A grid of closely placed columns and girders on the facade of a building, which forms a compromise between a shear wall and a frame.

Fault. A discontinuity in geologic material along which relative motion has occurred parallel to the plane of the fault.

Fault current. Current occurring because of a fault to ground or short circuit in an electrical system.

Feeders. All circuit conductors between the service equipment, or the generator, switchboard of an isolated plant, and the final branch circuit overcurrent device.

Fill. Rock or soil dumped to bring a site to the required level.

Finite element method. A numerical method of solving problems in mechanics in which the continua are divided into discrete elements.

Fire command center. A centralized street level indicator and control station to operate emergency and security building systems during a fire alarm condition. This normally includes the elevator and escalator status, control, and communication functions.

Fire control station. A central communication point for monitoring emergency conditions, two-way communications between floors and critical areas, and fire department alarm.

Fire rating. External walls by regulations are required to provide varying levels of fire resistance. They are required to be noncombustible. In tall buildings ratings for external walls can be as high as four (4) hours.

Firemen service. The mode of operation that provides dedicated transportation to Fire Department personnel under their complete control from within each car, individually.

Fire resistance rating. The time in minutes or hours that materials or assemblies have withstood a fire exposure as established in accordance with approved test procedures.

Fire stopping. The application of material barriers in construction to limit the spread of fire.

Flame-cutting. Cutting of ferrous metals by torch or gas flame.

Flame spread rating. The flame spread rating of materials is determined by the Method of Test of Surface Burning Characteristics of Building Materials (NFPA 255-1972, ASTM E84, 1970). Such materials are listed in the Underwriters' Laboratories, Inc., Building Materials List under the heading "Hazard Classification (Fire)." The propagation of flame over surface.

Flow net. A graphical solution for flow through porous media consisting of lines of equal head and of continuous flow.

Foot jack. An adjustable device in the posts or mullions between individual pieces or panels of a wall system which can be used to stabilize interior wall systems. The adjusting device or "jack" is located at the bottom of the post.

Formwork. A temporary structure or mold for the support of wet concrete while it is setting.

Foundation. Structural elements located beneath the lowest habitable space used to deliver the load of structure to the foundation material.

Foundation material. The soil or rock on which the foundation is supported.

Friction angle. The angle whose tangent relates shear strength to normal stress on the plane of the shear.

Friction pile. A pile supported by friction between the surface of the pile and the surrounding soil, as opposed to an end-bearing pile.

Ganged hinged forms. Prefabricated panels joined to make a much larger unit with hinges for a convenience in erecting and stripping.

Gasket. Preformed shapes, such as strips, grommets, etc., of rubber and rubber-like composition, used to fill and seal a joint or opening either alone or in conjunction with a supplemental application of a sealant.

Grade beam. A beam, used for a part of a foundation, resting directly on the soil. Usually extends between footings or pile caps.

Gravity loads. The loads which act in a vertical plane and are associated with the weight of the building. (This includes both dead and live loads.)

Grounded (earthings). Connected to earth or to some conducting body that serves in place of the earth.

Grounding conductor. A conductor intentionally grounded (earthed) in any manner.

Ground-water level. The level at which the top of the ground water is found in the ground.

Grout. A cement mortar with sand or small aggregate.

Group. The behavior of groups of piles acting as a unit.

Group automatic operation. The response of a bank of two or more elevators to respond to car and landing calls in such a manner that only one car will answer an up or down landing call without long wait landing call at the top or bottom hoistway.

Gun consistency. Compound formulated to a degree of viscosity suitable for application through the nozzle of a caulking gun.

Gunite. A material composed of cement and sand which is mixed together with water in a nozzle of a pressure gun.

Guy derricks. An erecting rig consisting of a vertical mast which rotates, a luffing boom, wire rope guys stabilizing the mast, and load falls.

Hall (landing) calls. A call registered at a landing to indicate the direction of desired travel so that the next available elevator will stop.

Handling capacity. The capacity of a bank of elevators in people in a five-minute period, and compared to the total population served by the bank requiring vertical transportation which must accommodate the arrival rate or departure rate of pedestrian traffic.

Hanger. A slender, linear, vertical member suspended from the main structure to carry the floor loads.

Hardpan. An extremely dense hard layer of soil, boulder clay or gravel, difficult to excavate.

Head channel. The top section of a nonbearing wall or partition which can accommodate some movement without damage to the wall or partition.

Header beam. A beam used to support free ends of beams and to transfer their loads.

Heave. Vertical, upward motion of soil due to reduced load during excavation, influx of water, or both.

Heel bead. Sealant applied at the base of channel, after setting light or panel and before the removable stop is installed.

High-rise building. A building that has occupied floors above the normal operation of an aerial ladder fire truck. This is usually all buildings with the top floor higher than 20 m (70 ft) above the adjacent street level permitting truck access.

Hoistway. The substantially vertical space in a building through which an elevator travels, that usually is surrounded by a fire-rated wall enclosure with fire-rated hoistway landing doors. (See "Shaftway".)

Hoistway-of-refuge. An internal elevator hoistway in a building, safe from fire and smoke contamination, as a means of transporting people through fire involved doors.

Horizontal connected building concept. A group of multifunction buildings, generally arranged in a corridor of an urban area joined together with intercept parking and integral, continuously available, above grade, horizontal transportation and walkways for direct access to buildings reducing pedestrian traffic at street level.

Horizontal elevator. An automatic vehicle mechanically locked on a horizontal guideway system connecting buildings and activity centers in a corridor providing performance and operation by the public, generally similar to conventional vertical elevator systems.

Horizontal lagging. Timbers placed between vertical steel soldier beams for support of soil excavations.

Hybrid frame construction. The frame construction composed of different structural building materials, such as concrete and steel.

Hypalon. Trade mark for chlorosulfonated polyethylene—a synthetic rubber.

Inclinometers. An instrument for indicating the inclination from the horizontal or vertical plane.

Infiltration. Air flowing inward as through walls or cracks.

In-situ. In place, characterizes operations done on the construction site, as opposed to fabrication shops.

Institution of Civil Engineers. A British organization founded in 1818 for general advancement of mechanical science, and more particularly for promoting the acquisition of that species of knowledge which constitutes the profession of a Civil Engineer.

Interface. The compatibly designed connection between two different modes of transportation or between two different building components, such as electrical or structural interfaces.

Interval. The calculated as well as the observed average time, in seconds, between the arrival or the departure of random elevators at a typical floor in a bank during peak traffic periods. The calculated average interval equals the calculated average round trip time divided by the number of elevators in the bank.

ISO. International Organization for Standardization that provides standards among the European Community Countries.

Joint. A discontinuity or crack in a geologic material along which relative motion has not occurred.

Jump derricks. A derrick which can be moved upwards on tiers of steel for high-rise work.

Karst. A terrain underlain by limestone with caverns into which overlying material may fall to create cavities at the surface.

Knife consistency. Compound formulated in a degree of firmness suitable for application with a glazing knife such as is used for face glazing and other sealant applications.

Landing call. See Hall (landing) calls.

Lanyard. A short piece of rope used for fastening various objects.

Lateral loads. The loads which act in a horizontal plane. (These loads normally are associated with either wind or earthquake.)

Latex. A collodial dispersion of a rubber resin (synthetic or natural) in water, which coagulates on exposure to air.

Level luffing boom. The boom on a crane with an automatic device which causes the load to move horizontally with any alteration of the operating radius.

Life safety. The emerging discipline dedicated to providing the maximum safety of persons during fire, smoke or earthquake activity in a high-rise building among all design disciplines and building systems.

Lift. The materials handling classification of vertical transportation for the dedicated movement of containerized or palletized freight, with a platform and landing door larger than the dumbwaiter classification.

Lighting outlet. An outlet intended for the direct connection of a lamp holder, a lighting fixture (fitting), or a pendant cord terminating in a lamp holder.

Liquefaction. The conversion of soil from a solid to a liquid state.

Live load. The vertical loads which represent the weight of objects that the structural elements will support. (This is a gravity load.)

Load, estimated design. In a heating or cooling system, the sum of the useful heat transferred, plus heat transfer from or to the connected pipe, plus heat transfer occurring in any auxiliary apparatus connected to the system.

Load growth. Incremental increase of electrical load over a designated period of time.

Load indicating bolt. A bolt whose head is fitted with four pads which are compressed when the bolt is tightened. The required tension is achieved when a feeler gage indicates that the gap below the bolt head has been reduced to a specified dimension.

Load indicating washer. A washer with protrusions on one side which are compressed when the bolt is tightened. The required tension is achieved when a feeler gage indicates that the gap below the washer has been reduced to a specified dimension.

Main entrance service equipment. Power equipment such as circuit breakers, switches, fuses and their accessories for controlling electric service at the utility entrance point.

Make-up. Quantity of supply air required to balance the amount of exhaust air removed from a designated space.

Mastic. Descriptive of heavy-consistency compounds that may remain adhesive and pliable with age.

Mat foundation. A foundation consisting of a slab or continuous mat as opposed to individual pile caps or footings.

Mechanical systems. Those systems required for introducing, circulating, or removing liquids, solids, and air.

Metal curtain wall. An exterior wall which may consist entirely or principally of metal, or may be a combination of metal, glass and other surfacing materials supported by or within a metal framework.

Mica-schist. Mica mixed with quartz. A dry mineral of a specified screen grading.

Migration. Spreading or creeping of a constituent of a compound onto adjacent surfaces.

Mined excavation. The use of permanent floors of a structure to brace the sheeting or support system of the excavation sides. The floors of concrete are poured on the ground; excavation is made under the floors.

Modulus of elasticity. The ratio of the direct stress of a linearly elastic material to its strain, also called Young's modulus.

Module. A planning dimension which allows flexible layout of space with the exterior wall system and interior partitions.

Moisture content. The ratio between the weight of water in a soil and the weight of soil solids.

Moment connection. A rigid connection capable of transmitting the bending moment imposed on it.

Moment resistant frames. An integrated system of structural elements possessing continuity and hence capable of resisting bending forces. (These frames usually develop minor axial forces.)

Moving walk. A horizontal or limited incline (12°) smooth belt or flat step (pallet) people conveyor with design similar to an escalator.

Mullion. The horizontal or vertical member of a window wall or curtain wall system that is normally attached to the floor slab or beams, and supports the glass and/or elements of a window wall.

Muntin. In sash having horizontal and vertical bars that divide the window into smaller lights of glass, the bars are termed muntin bars.

Needle glazing. Application of a small bead of compound at the sight-line by means of a gun nozzle about 1/4 in. $\times$ 1/8 in. in opening size.

Negative skin friction. Friction exerted downward on a pile by the surrounding soil, resulting usually from settlement of the soil.

Neoprene. A synthetic rubber having physical properties closely resembling those of natural rubber but not requiring sulfur for vulcanization. It is made by polymerizing chloroprenes, and the latter is produced from acetylene and hydrogen chloride.

Nitrile rubber. A class of rubber-like copolymers of acrylonitrile with butadiene. There are many types. A few of the trade names are: Buna N, Butaprene and Chemigum. It has high resistance to solvents and oils, greases, heat, and abrasion.

Non-sag (sealant). A sealant formulation having a consistency that will permit application in vertical joints without appreciable sagging or slumping.

Non-skinning. Descriptive of a product that does not form a surface skin.

Non-staining. Characteristic of a compound which will not stain a surface.

Notching. The short voltage transient reduction of alternating current line voltage below normal caused by the firing of a silicon controlled rectifier.

Oleoresinous. A mixture of natural or synthetic resins mixed with drying oils.

Operation. The logic system governing the sequence in which landing calls and car calls are answered by a single elevator or group of elevators.

Optimization. The function of an automated central control facility to effect the best operating condition in accordance with preset requirements.

Organic. Compounds which consist of carbon and generally hydrogen, with a restricted number of other elements, such as oxygen, nitrogen, sulfur, phosphorous, chlorine, etc.

Organisol. Essentially a plastisol which contains solvent that must be evaporated prior to exposing the material to the elevated temperature necessary for fusion or curing.

Outlet. A point on the wiring system at which current is taken to supply utilization equipment.

Overhung machine. A geared or gearless elevator or lift driving machine that has a driving sheave outboard of the machine bearings.

Overslung car. An elevator or lift car frame that is supported from a rope system attached to the top member (crosshead) by a dead-end hitch for 1:1 roping or by a sheave for 2:1 roping.

Pallet lift. A class of lift dedicated to the substantially vertical movement of loaded or empty pallets in a materials handling system, with an automated transfer conveyor to load and unload the lift.

Partition. A divider of space within the interior of a building. It can be bearing or nonbearing and it can extend from floor to floor or from floor to ceiling.

Pedway. A dedicated horizontal path for pedestrian circulation between activity center nodes.

Permeability. The relation between the velocity of flow of ground water and the gradient of the head.

Penetrometer. A device pushed into the ground to measure its resistance to penetration.

Personal rapid transit (PRT). The discrete medium size pedestrian or material vehicle that travels substantially horizontally at intermediate speeds among stops in an activity center.

Phenolic. Term refers to synthetic resins formed by the condensation of phenol and formaldehyde.

Pier. A solid support for a building structure.

Piers. Large caissons used to support massive structures.

Piezometer. An instrument for measuring pressure head, usually consisting of a small pipe tapped into the side of a conduit and flush with the inside, connected with a pressure gage, mercury, water column or other device for indicating pressure head.

Piezometer level. The level to which water rises in a standpipe.

Piezometer pressure. The pressure in the pore water.

Piggy-back system. A system of progressively pumping liquids up the height of a building in steps.

Pile. A long, heavy post of timber, concrete or steel, driven into or cast in the ground to compact the soil, shut out water, support a vertical load or withstand a horizontal force.

Pile, end bearing. A pile which derives substantially all load-carrying capacity by direct bearing on a resistant stratum such as a rock.

Pile, friction. A pile which derives a substantial portion of its load-carrying capacity through friction or shear with the soil in which it is embedded.

Pile cap. A structural member used to deliver load of the structure to two or more piles acting together.

Pile hammer. A mechanical device for driving piles by impact of repeated blows or by vibration.

Pile head. The top end of a pile.

Pile tip. The bottom end of a pile.

Piping. Displacement or moving of soil particles by seepage flow tending to open channels or voids in the mass. Loss of soil may be to an open face, or fine particles may be washed into voids of coarser soils. The latter is termed internal piping.

Plastisol. A physical mixture of resin (usually vinyl) compatible plasticizers, stabilizers, and pigments. Mixture requires fusion at elevated temperatures in order to convert the plastisol to a homogeneous plastic material.

Poisson's ratio. The ratio of lateral strain to longitudinal strain when a material is subjected to a uniform and uniaxial stress.

Polybutene. Straight chain aliphatic hydrocarbon polymer. Non-drying and widely used as a major component in sealing and caulking compounds. Being essentially nonreactive and inert under certain conditions it will migrate.

Polyester resin. Any of a group of thermosetting synthetic resins which are polycondensation products of dicarboxylic acid and dihydroxy alcohol.

Polyethylene. A straight chain plastic polymer of ethylene.

Polyisobutylene. See Polybutene. Frequently associated as having higher molecular weight.

Polymer. An organic product of polymerization composed of an indefinite number of monomers.

Polysulfide. Polysulfide liquid polymers (Thiokol) are mercaptan terminated, long chain aliphatic polymers containing disulfide linkages. They can be converted to rubbers at room temperature without shrinkage upon addition of a curing agent.

Population. The population in a building that requires vertical transportation.

Population factor. The population factor is the number of square meters (square feet) per person, as the result of the resident population on a floor to be elevatored divided into the elevator net usable area of that floor.

Pore pressure, pore water pressure. Pressure in the fluid, usually water, contained in the void of the soil, at a given point in the mass, expressed in terms of force per unit area. It acts equally in all directions.

Post-tension. A term applied to prestressed elements when the reinforcement is stressed after the concrete is cast and has reached specified strength.

Pot life. The time interval following the addition of an accelerator before a chemically curing material will become too viscous to apply satisfactorily. Synonymous with work life.

Power (electric). The time rate of generating, transferring, or using electric energy, usually expressed in kilowatts.

Power factor. The ratio of real power (kW) to apparent power (kVA) for any given load and time. Generally, it is expressed as a percentage ratio.

Precast. A term applied to concrete elements where the element is cast at a remote location and then transported to the site and lifted into place (in tilt-up construction the element is cast at the site and later is lifted into place).

Pre-engineered. Mass-produced, as opposed to a custom-designed system.

Prefabricate. A term applied to structural elements or components which are built at a remote location, usually a factory, and then transported to the site and erected.

Prestress. A method whereby the reinforcing steel is stressed prior to the application of any external loads.

Pre-tension. A term applied to prestressed elements when the reinforcement is stressed prior to casting the concrete.

Primer. A special coating designed to enhance the adhesion of sealant systems to certain surfaces.

Protective coating. A film to protect the surface from destructive agents or environments (abrasion, chemical action, solvents, corrosion and weathering). Such coatings may be either temporary or permanent. Temporary protective coatings include methacrylate lacquers.

P-Δ effect. Secondary moments produced by horizontal deflection and vertical loads.

Queue. The waiting line or pool of pedestrians or the materials handling containers at an interface between the horizontal and the vertical portions of a movement pattern.

Quick shear test. A test to determine apparent shear strength of cohesive soil. The test may be made by direct shear or axial compression. It is run quickly to prevent changes in the moisture content.

Raceway. Channel for routing electrical cables, bus bars, and wires.

Racking. Movement and distortion of sash or frames because of lack of rigidity.

Radiographic weld test. A nondestructive method for the internal examination of a metallic body exposed to a beam of x-ray or gamma radiation in which the registration of images is made on a radiogram.

Raft foundation. See Mat foundation.

Reaction. A mutual action of chemical agents upon each other resulting in a chemical change.

Reactive power. The portion of "Apparent Power" that does no work. It is commercially measured in kilovars. Reactive power must be supplied to most types of magnetic equipment, such as motors. It is supplied by generators or by electrostatic equipment, such as capacitors.

Real power. This is the energy or work-producing part of "Apparent Power." It is the rate of supply of energy, measured commercially in kilowatts. The product of real power and length of time is energy, measured by watthour meters and expressed in kilowatthours.

Receptacle. A contact device installed at the outlet for the connection of a single attachment plug.

Refraction seismic survey. Use of refraction of compression-rarefraction waves in soil or rock estimate stratification. Denser, stronger materials exhibit higher wave velocities, which can be correlated with stratification as determined from boring.

Regeneration. The transfer of mechanical kinetic energy from an escalator or elevator system back to the electrical supply system.

Reglect. Any slot cut into masonry or formed into poured concrete or precast stone. May also be an open mortar joint left between two courses of bricks or stones, or a slot cut or cast into other types of building materials.

Relative density. A means of comparing qualitatively the density in situ of a noncohesive soil with the loosest and most dense states it can assume. Expressed in relative terms, such as "very loose" or "medium dense."

Resilient tape. A preshaped, rubbery sealing material furnished in varying thicknesses and widths, in roll form. May be plain or reinforced with scrim, twine, rubber or other materials.

Resonant column test. A means of measuring shear modulus of a soil by measuring torsional response of a cylinder of the soil to dynamic loads.

Retrofit. The modernization of an existing facility with current technologies or techniques for improved performance.

Riprap. Small pieces of rock used for making a revetment.

Riser. Vertical pipes or ducts.

Riser feeder. Conductor from the service equipment running to the panel boards or branch circuits on the upper floors.

Rock. A natural aggregate of minerals connected by strong and permanent bonds.

Rolling tolerances. The amount of variation in the finished product of the rolled structural shape to the published profiles of the member's cross section.

Round trip time. The calculated as well as the observed average time in seconds between the departure of an elevator from the main dispatching lobby and its return to that lobby.

Safe area. An interior or exterior space that serves as a means of entry to or egress from an assembly space, and which also provides a transitional area.

Sag and flow test. Involves vertical applications of compounds to specified surfaces or shapes under predetermined conditions of temperature and time intervals. Tendency to run or sag is observed and is reported as none, very slight, slight, etc. or may be reported as a lineal movement.

Sagging. Caused by a compound not capable of supporting its own weight in a joint, or by application in joints larger than the compound is designed for, or by improper application.

Sash. The frame including rabbets and muntin bars if used, to receive lights of glass whether with or without removable stops, and designed either for face glazing or channel glazing.

Sealant. Material used to exclude water and solid foreign matter from joints.

Self-leveling (sealant). A sealant formulation having a consistency that will permit it to achieve a smooth level surface when applied in a horizontal joint.

Service systems. Those systems required for providing sanitation, power, lights, heat, cooling, ventilation, air conditioning, refuse disposal, fire-fighting, transportation or similar facility for a building.

Setting block. Small blocks of composition, lead, Neoprene, etc. placed under bottom edge of light or panel to prevent its settling down onto bottom rabbet or channel after setting, thus distorting the sealant.

Settlement. Displacement downward of a structure, surface or reference plane, usually as a result of compression or shear distortion of underlying materials.

Shaftway. A number of contiguous elevator hoistways without separating walls. A maximum of four are permitted by Code.

Shear connector. A stud or similar protrusion from a steel girder, usually attached by welding, used to resist the horizontal shear in composite steel-concrete construction.

Shear modulus. Measure of resistance of a body to shear distortion.

Shear strength. The limiting (failure) resistance of soil to shear.

Shear wall. A concrete or masonry wall (with or without window openings) resisting the shear, as distinct from a panel with crossed diagonals.

Shear wave velocity. The velocity of transmission of seismic shear waves through soil or rock.

Sheet piling. Closely spaced piles of timber, reinforced concrete, prestressed concrete or steel driven vertically into the ground to support earth pressure, to keep water out of an excavation and often to form an integral part of a permanent structure.

Sheeting. Members, usually of steel, wood, or concrete, used to support the walls of an excavation. Commonly used for temporary support.

Shim. Small blocks of composition, Neoprene, etc. placed on each face of lights or panels to center them in the channel and maintain uniform width of sealant.

Shore "A" Hardness. Measure of firmness of a compound by means of a Durometer Hardness Gage. (Range of 20–25 is about the firmness of an art gum eraser. Range of 90 is about the firmness of a rubber heel.)

Shoring. Props or post of material in compression used for the temporary support of excavations, formwork, or unsafe structures.

Shuttle elevator. An express elevator between two or among three landings to transport pedestrian traffic from the street lobby to a sky lobby above, where a transfer is made to a bank or banks of local elevators.

Siamese connection. A fitting connected to a fire extinguishing system and installed on the outside of a building with two hose inlets for use of the fire department, to furnish or supplement the water supply to the system.

Sight line. Imaginary line along perimeter of lights or panels corresponding to the top edge of stationary and removable stops, and the line to which sealants contacting the light or panels are sometimes finished off.

Silicone sealant. A sealant having as its chemical composition a backbone consisting of alternating silicon-oxygen atoms.

Silt. A granular material which is finer than sand, yet coarser than clay, ranging from 0.002 mm to 0.060 mm.

Single deck. A single cavity passenger of freight elevator serving landings above the street.

Single occupancy. The classification of office building occupancy that contains interacting pedestrian or materials traffic in a building with common management and integrated work functions with substantially simultaneous starting and finishing times; may include internal dining facilities.

Size of bead. Normally refers to the width of the bead, but there are many situations in which both the width and the depth should be taken into account in design, specification, and application.

Sky lobby. A major lobby above the street to permit transfer from a bank of express shuttle elevators to a bank or banks of local elevators.

Slewing. The rotation of a crane jib so that the load moves through the arc of a circle on a horizontal line.

Sloped berm. An artificial ridge of earth. The space between the toe of a slope and an excavation.

Slurry. A fluid mix of bentonite and water to support the walls of an excavation trench.

Slurry caisson. A caisson whose walls consist of bentonite slurry which is later replaced by concrete using a tremie.

Slurry trench. A trench in which the walls are supported by the outward pressure of a slurry, usually of bentonitic material. May be used to cut off seepage, or concrete may be placed by displacing the slurry to provide structural walls.

Soffits. The underside of any subordinate member of a building, such as the under surface of an arch, cornice or stairway.

Soil amplification. Vibratory motion transmitted through rock may be increased by resonant response to certain frequencies as it propagates through the overlying soil, thus subjecting structures founded in the soil to larger motion than if they had been founded on rock.

Soil-structure interaction—dynamic. Effect on dynamic response of a structure from its support on an elastic or quasielastic medium.

Soil-structure interaction—static. Redistribution of stresses and deformations of a structure, contact press at the soil-structure interface, and deformation of the soil resulting from relative stiffness of soil and structure.

Soils. Defined by grain size:

1. Gravel. Cohesionless aggregate of particles of more or less unaltered minor rocks grading in size from 3 mm (1/8 in.) to about 150 mm (6 in.) in size.
2. Sand. Cohesionless aggregate particles of more or less unaltered minerals or rock grading in size from 0.06 mm to 3 mm in size.
3. Silt. (Inorganic) aggregate of particles, usually unaltered, grading in size from 0.06 mm to 0.002 mm in size. Coarse grained silt is nonplastic. Fine grade silt, containing significant flaky particles, may exhibit some or moderate plasticity.
4. Clay. Very fine grained soil, generally containing a substantial content of particles finer than 2 and which is plastic to highly plastic. Plasticity, the capacity to deform at constant stress, results in large measure from adsorbed water bound to the surface of the very fine grains by molecular forces.

Soils. Defined by mode of deposition:

1. Residual. Derived in situ by mechanical or chemical weathering (or both) of rock.
2. Transported. Material eroded from its original position and redeposited by some agent, such as flowing water.
3. Loess. A wind-deposited soil of silt-sized particles. As deposited, the soil may be of very low density, and collapse of the soil structure may occur on wetting.
4. Alluvial. Deposited by water.
5. Colluvial. Soil developed on slopes and moved from position by gravity.
6. Till. An unsorted mass of soil ranging in grain size from clay size to large boulders deposited under ice, especially of the Glacial Period.
7. Lacustrine. Deposited by sedimentation in a lake.
8. Varved Clay. A soil showing alternating thin, parallel layers of finer-grained and coarser-grained materials, e.g., clay and silt layers. Commonly, the layering is annual, and deposition derives from glacial outwash. The coarser-grained layers then result from warm summer conditions and the clay layers quiescent, winter conditions.
9. Organic. Soils containing substantial quantities of finely divided organic materials, typically soils found in estuarine deposits and mud flats.
10. Peat. Fibrous organic material mixed with more or less fine-grained soil.
11. Fill. Deposited by man.

Soils. Defined by structure:

1. Sensitive. (Quick Clays). Clay soils which exhibit marked loss of strength when disturbed. The ratio of strength undisturbed to strength when throughly remolded at constant moisture ranges from 4 to more than 50.
2. Metastable. Soils which show collapse of soil structure, resulting in sudden

reduction in volume and frequently in strength when saturated. Typical are loess deposits, some playa, alluvial fan deposits, and slide deposits.

3. Expansive. Soils containing certain clay minerals, especially montmorillonite and halloysite, which expand markedly on wetting and shrink on drying.

Soldier beam. A beam used to carry the force from a horizontal sheeted earth bank.

Solids content. A determination of the nonvolatile matter of a compound at a specified temperature and time interval. Usually expressed in percentage by weight and the difference between this figure and 100% represents the volatile matter or loss by evaporation.

Spacers. Small blocks of composition, Neoprene, etc. placed on each face of lights or panels to center them in the channel and maintain uniform width of sealant.

Spandrel. In skeleton frame buildings, the panel of wall between adjacent structural columns and between the windowsill and the window head next below it.

Spot network. An electrical network system with two or more transformers arranged so that failure of any one transformer or incoming line does not interrupt power to the load.

Spread footing. Structural member used to deliver column or wall load to soil.

Sprinkler system. A system of piping and sprinkler heads connected to one or more sources of water supply.

Stack effect. The flow of air at room temperature and density to the outside air at low temperatures and high density traveling predominantly through the vertical shafts of the building.

Staining (associated with sealing). A change in color or appearance of masonry adjacent to sealant.

Standard penetration test (SPT). A dynamic penetration test in which the number of blows required to drive a sampler 600 mm long and 50 mm OD the final 300 mm of a total penetration of 450 mm into undisturbed soil at the bottom of a boring is recorded. The sampler is driven by a ram weighing 63.4 kg and falling 760 mm.

Standby power. That power which is available within 60 seconds on normal power failure to operate major building systems for life safety or continuously operating functions.

Standpipe system. The system of piping for fire-fighting purposes, consisting of connections to one or more sources of water supply and serving one or more hose outlets.

Steel soldier beam. A rolled steel section driven into the ground to carry the force of a horizontal sheeting earth bank.

Stick wall system. In this system the wall is installed piece by piece. Usually the mullion members are installed first, followed in turn by glazing or window units. However, in some designs accentuating the horizontal lines the process may be altered to install the larger horizontal member first.

Stiffleg derrick. A type of erection rig consisting of a mast and luffing boom which can rotate approximately 290°, two diagonal stifflegs which act as guys, and stiff horizontal sills connecting the lower end of the stiffleg to the mast base.

Straddle pole. A sloping scaffold pole laid along a roof line in a straddle scaffold from an upright to meet another straddle pole at the ridge of the roof.

Straight chain polymer. A polymer containing groups of molecules attached to each other in a straight line.

Stratum. A layer of soil of similar character, physical properties, and origin extending over a significant area.

Stress. Force per unit area. A tensor quantity which may be resolved for a plane of any orientation into a component normal to the plane and two mutually orthogonal shear components parallel to the plane. For any solid, three mutually orthogonal planes may be determined on which there are no shear stresses. These are termed planes of principal stress.

Stress, total. Stress at a point resulting from combining body stresses, pore water pressures, and external loads.

Stress effective. Stress at a point acting through soil skeleton and thus capable of causing intergranular frictional resistance and resistance to compressional deformation; that is

$$\bar{\sigma} = \sigma - u$$

in which $\bar{\sigma}$ = effective stress; σ = total stress; and u = pore water pressure.

Structural rubber gaskets. A synthetic rubber section designed to engage the edge of glass or other sheet material in a surrounding frame by forcing an interlocking filler strip into a grooved recess in the face of the gasket.

Subgrade reaction, coefficient, or modulus. A theoretical ratio between the applied vertical stress on the surface of a foundation material and its displacement.

Subgrade reaction, coefficient, or modulus of horizontal. The coefficient of subgrade reaction for horizontal loading.

Subsidence. Settlement of an area, usually due to removal of solids or fluids, e.g., subsidence caused by mining.

Superstructure. The portion of the structural framing system which is above the ground.

Synthesis. Creation of a substance which may either duplicate a natural material or be a unique material not found in nature.

Systems approach. A concept of design that takes into consideration the effect of all the environmental and human factors and phenomena that affect the operation of that piece of equipment or that system.

Terminal (landing). Strictly, the highest and lowest landing of an elevator, but often referring to the top and main lobby landings.

Test pit. An excavation made for the purpose of exploring near-surface soil properties; undisturbed samples of soil may be taken during excavation.

Thixotropy. The ability of a compound to maintain a jelly-like form when at rest and flow freely when force is applied.

Throughput. The qualification of pedestrian or materials traffic capacity of a handling system.

Tie backs. Mechanical devices for supporting sheeting, consisting of post-tensioned rods extending to anchor points in the soil surrounding the excavation or to rock.

Tower derricks. A type of erection jig consisting of a vertical tower mounted within the structure or to adjacent structures, and a horizontal swing boom with load-carrying trolley and counterweight jib.

Transfer girder. A horizontal framing member which transfers vertical loads, for example, at one of the lower floors where some of the columns need to be eliminated to create larger open spaces.

Transfer time. The passenger transfer time at an elevator landing when the elevator is at rest with the doors open.

Trap seal. A liquid seal to prevent flow of objectionable odors or gases.

Traveling gantry. A movable gantry built on wheels for traveling on rails and supporting a grab.

Tremie. A large funnel made of sheet steel by means of which concrete can be placed in fluids of lighter density.

Triaxial test. A system of interrelated tests to determine shearing resistance by compression of cylindrical samples. Intermediate and minor principal stresses are maintained equal by fluid pressure on an external, impervious membrane.

Truss. The fabricated structural member that supports and contains the escalator or moving walk equipment.

Two-part compound. A product comprised of a base and the curing agent or accelerator. The two components are uniformly mixed just prior to its use since, when mixed, it cures and its useful life is quite limited from the standpoint of application characteristics.

Two-way peak. The traffic pattern caused by passenger traffic in both up and down directions simultaneously.

Ultrasonic testing. Technique using crystal which can be made to vibrate at frequencies ranging from 1/2 MHz to 10 MHz. When the crystals are held against a piece of steel the vibrations travel through the steel and are reflected back from the opposite side or from intervening defects. The echoes are made visible on a cathode-ray tube.

Ultraviolet. The invisible rays of the spectrum which are outside of the visible spectrum at its violet end. Sometimes called Actinic Rays.

Underslung car. An elevator or lift car frame that is supported from a rope system passing under the car sheaves, with the dead-end hitch as the top of the hoistway for 2:1 roping.

Undisturbed sample. A sample taken from a boring in such a manner that it is changed as little as possible.

Underpinning. The operation of supporting a structure while deepening a foundation without disturbing or damaging the structure.

Unit. Term normally used to refer to one single light of insulating glass.

United inches. The sum of the dimensions of one length and one width of a light of glass.

Up-peak. The traffic pattern caused by passenger traffic predominantly in the up direction.

Up transit time (trap time). The calculated as well as observed average time, in seconds, that the last passenger to leave an up traveling elevator spends in the car.

Vane shear test. A test of shear strength in which an X-shaped rake is rotated in the sample around a vertical axis; used to determine quick-shear strength.

Vendor. A person or organization who furnishes materials or equipment not fabricated to a special design.

Venting. Providing circulation of air or ventilation between two walls or partitions. Venting accomplished by the use of tubes, breather vents or openings left in wall.

Vinyl. Derived from ethylene (hydrocarbon gas) the compounds of which are polymerized to form high molecular weight plastics and resins such as vinyl acetate, vinyl chloride, styrene, etc. It is a base material for plastisols and organisols.

Vinyl glazing. Holding glass in place with extruded vinyl channels or roll-in type.

Viscosity. The internal resistance to flow exhibited by a fluid.

Volatile. The property of liquids to change into a gas and pass away by evaporation, under normal atmospheric conditions.

Voltage regulation. The reduction of voltage at a point of use compared to the voltage at the source point.

Waiting time. The time a passenger waits for elevator service at a typical floor after a call is registered until an elevator answers that call.

Wall. An encloser of space. It can serve as a partition but can also serve as the divider between the exterior and the interior of a building.

Weathering. The change of properties and constituents of a rock and soil by the effects of heat, water, chemicals, freezing, and other similar factors.

Whaler (alternative spelling—waling). A horizontal bracing member used in form construction and open excavation.

Window wall. A type of metal curtain wall installed between floors and typically composed of vertical and horizontal framing members, containing operable sash, fixed lights or opaque panels, or any combination thereof.

Work life. The time interval following the addition of an accelerator before a chemically curing material will become too viscous to apply satisfactorily. Synonymous with pot life.

Young's modulus. The modulus of direct elasticity.

SYMBOLS

The numerals in parentheses refer to the chapters in Volume SC in which the given symbol is used.

A, B, b	= horizontal dimensions	(7)
C.M.	= center of mass	(7)
C_u	= shear strength	(7)
c	= cohesion	(7)
c_{neg}	= negative skin friction or cohesion on pile	(7)
c_v	= shear wave velocity	(7)
d, h, z	= vertical dimensions	(7)
d_1, d_2	= incremental depths of excavation	(7)
E	= modulus of elasticity (Young's modulus)	(7)
e	= void ratio of soil	(7)
e_0	= initial void ratio	(7)
e_0'	= void ratio after excavation (apparent)	(7)
e_{0z}	= initial void ratio at depth Z	(7)
F	= total force	(7)
FS	= factor of safety	(7)
f	= unit force	(7)
G	= shear modulus	(7)
g	= acceleration due to gravity	(7)
H	= depth of wall	(7)
H	= thickness of foundation mat	(7)
$h_{C.M.}$	= height of center of mass	(7)
hw	= height of ground water table above elevation of foundation	(7)
I	= moment of inertia	(7)
K	= a horizontal force factor varying from 0.67 for ductile space frames to 1.33 or shear wall structures	(5)
K_A	= coefficient of lateral earth pressure—active	(7)
Ka	= active-earth pressure coefficient	(8)
K_0	= coefficient of lateral earth pressure at rest	(7)
K_P	= coefficient of lateral earth pressure—passive	(7)
k	= modulus of subgrade reaction	(7)
L, l	= length	(7)
M	= modulus of deformation, may be inelastic	(7)
m, n	= geometric coordinates or dimensions	(7)
n_h	= rate of increase of the coefficient of horizontal subgrade reaction with depth	(7)
P	= load per unit pile or caisson	(7)
P_A	= forces due to active earth pressure	(7)
P_d	= total uplift pressure	(7)
P_m	= drop load	(7)
P_P	= forces due to passive earth pressure	(7)
P_p	= permanent load	(7)
P_t	= transient load	(7)
P_{total}	= total earth pressure	(8)
p_0	= preconsolidation stress, i.e., stress to which soil element has been previously subjected	(7)

p, p_1	= earth pressure	(8)
Q_u	= bearing capacity $Q_u^{tip} + Q_{ue}^{skin}$	(7)
Q_u	= ulimate or failure load	(7)
$Q_{u,a}^{skin}$	= load carried by skin friction on section a	(7)
$Q_{u,b}^{skin}$	= load carried by skin friction on section b	(7)
q, w	= unit loading	(7)
q_u	= compressive strength from unconfined compression test; q_u = $2c$, in which c = undrained shear strength	(7)
$q_{u_{av}}$	= average bearing capacity	(8)
q_1, q_2	= surchanges outside excavation	(7)
R	= relative stiffness factor, constant modulus	(7)
$R_{1,2,3,4}$	= resultant force on strut	(8)
T	= relative stiffness factor, modulus increasing with depth	(7)
U_D	= uplift fluid pressure	(7)
u	= pressure in water contained in pore spaces of soil	(7)
u_{hw}	= pressure due to ground water on bottom of foundation	(7)
W	= total weight	(7)
w_c	= water content of soil expressed as fraction or percentage of dry weight	(7)
Y_o	= horizontal translation of top of wall	(7)
y	= deflection	(7)
Z	= depth	(7)
γ	= unit weight or density	(7, 8)
Δ, δ	= deflection or deformation; subscript e or E indicates "elastic" response; subscript s indicates long-term inelastic response from volume change	(7)
$\Delta\bar{\sigma}_{exc}$	= change in vertical effective stress due to excavation	(7)
$\Delta\bar{\sigma}_{-i}$	= increment of vertical effective stress from initial to final case	(7)
$\Delta\bar{\sigma}_{zr}$	= increment of vertical effective stress from initial to preconsolidation	(7)
$\Delta\bar{\sigma}_{zv}$	= increment of vertical effective stress from preconsolidation to final	(7)
δ_h	= horizontal movement	(7)
δ_n	= horizontal displacement of center of mass due to distortion of building	(7)
δ_o	= horizontal displacement of center of mass	(7)
δ_θ	= horizontal displacement of center of mass due to rotation of foundation	(7)
θ	= angle of rotation of foundation	(7)
μ	= Poisson's ratio	(7)
ρ	= unit weight or density	(7)
σ	= total stress; orientation may be shown by subscript, as z or v for vertical and h for horizontal	(7)
σ_d	= vertical stress outside excavation at level of bottom of excavation	(7)
σ_H	= horizontal stress	(7)
σ_l	= vertical stress when excavation is open	(7)
σ_0	= initial vertical stress without old buildings	(7)
$\bar{\sigma}$	= effective stress (Terzaghi and Peck, 1967, p. 58); stress in soil skeleton	(7)

$\bar{\sigma}_{bz}$	= critical overburden effective stress	(7)
$(\bar{\sigma}_{bz})_p$	= critical overburden effective stress—preconsolidated	(7)
$\bar{\sigma}_{od}$	= original vertical uplift effective stress	(7)
$\bar{\sigma}_{oz}$	= overburden effective stress	(7)
$\bar{\sigma}_z$	= vertical effective stress	(7)
$\bar{\sigma}_{zo}$	= initial vertical effective stress	(7)
τ	= shear stress	(7)

ABBREVIATIONS

AIA	American Institute of Architects
AIJ	Architectural Institute of Japan
AIP	American Institute of Planners
ANSI	American National Standards Institute
ASCE	American Society of Civil Engineers
ASHRAE	American Society of Heating, Refrigerating and Air Conditioning Engineers
ASME	American Society of Mechanical Engineers
BSI	British Standards Institute
CB	Volume CB of Monograph, Concrete Buildings
CL	Volume CL of Monograph, Criteria and Loading
CSA	Canadian Standards Association
DIN	Deutsche Industrie Normen, German Industrial Standards
EEI	Edison Electric Institute, USA
FAR	Floor Area Ratio
FIFO	First In, First Out system
HUD	U.S. Department of Housing and Urban Development
HVAC	Heating, Ventilating and Air Conditioning
IABSE	International Association for Bridge and Structural Engineering
IEEE	Institute of Electrical and Electronic Engineers, USA
IFHP	International Federation for Housing and Planning
JIS	Japanese Industrial Standard
K/LF	Kips/linear ft
K/SF	Kips/ft^2
MRT	Mass Rapid Transit
NFPA	National Fire Protection Association, USA
NRCC	National Research Council of Canada
NSF	National Science Foundation, USA
PC	Volume PC of Monograph, Planning and Environmental Criteria
PRT	Personal Rapid Transit
PVC	Polyvinyl chloride
SAA	Standards Association of Australia
SB	Volume SB of Monograph, Steel Buildings
SC	Volume SC of Monograph, Systems and Concepts
SCR	Silicon-controlled rectifiers
UIA	International Union of Architects

UNITS

In the table below are given conversion factors for commonly used units. The numerical values have been rounded off to the values shown. The British (Imperial) System of units is the same as the American System except where noted. Le Système International d'Unités (abbreviated "SI") is the name formally given in 1960 to the system of units partly derived from, and replacing, the old metric system.

SI	American	Old Metric
Length		
1 mm	0.03937 in.	1 mm
1 m	3.28083 ft	1 m
	1.093613 yd	
1 km	0.62137 mile	1 km
Area		
1 mm^2	0.00155 in.^{2}	1 mm^2
1 m^2	10.76392 ft^2	1 m^2
	1.19599 yd^2	
1 km^2	247.1043 acres	1 km^2
1 hectare	2.471 acres[1]	1 hectare
Volume		
1 cm^3	0.061023 in.^{3}	1 cc
		1 ml
1 m^3	35.3147 ft^3	1 m^3
	1.30795 yd^3	
	264.172 gal[2] liquid	
Velocity		
1 m/sec	3.28084 ft/sec	1 m/sec
1 km/hr	0.62137 miles/hr	1 km/hr
Acceleration		
1 m/sec^2	3.28084 ft/sec^2	1 m/sec^2
Mass		
1 g	0.035274 oz	1 g
1 kg	2.2046216 lb[3]	1 kg
Density		
1 kg/m^3	0.062428 lb/ft^3	1 kg/m^3
Force, Weight		
1 N	0.224809 lbf	0.101972 kgf
1 kN	0.1124045 tons[4]	
1 MN	224.809 kips	
1 kN/m	0.06853 kips/ft	
1 kN/m^2	20.9 lbf/ft^2	
Torque, Bending Moment		
1 N-m	0.73756 lbf-ft	0.101972 kgf-m
1 kN-m	0.73756 kip-ft	101.972 kgf-m

SI	American	Old Metric
Pressure, Stress		
1 N/m^2 = 1 Pa	0.000145038 psi	0.101972 kgf/m^2
1 kN/m^2 = 1 kPa	20.8855 psf	
1 MN/m^2 = 1 MPa	0.145038 ksi	
Viscosity (Dynamic)		
1 N-sec/m^2	0.0208854 lbf-sec/ft^2	0.101972 kgf-sec/m^2
Viscosity (Kinematic)		
1 m^2/sec	10.7639 ft^2/sec	1 m^2/sec
Energy, Work		
1 J = 1 N-m	0.737562 lbf-ft	0.00027778 w-hr
1 MJ	0.37251 hp-hr	0.27778 kw-hr
Power		
1 W = 1 J/sec	0.737562 lbf ft/sec	1 w
1 kW	1.34102 hp	1 kw
Temperature		
K = 273.15 + °C	°F = (°C × 1.8) + 32	°C = (°F − 32)/1.8
K = 273.15 + 5/9(°F − 32)		
K = 273.15 + 5/9(°R − 491.69)		

(1) Hectare as an alternative for km^2 is restricted to land and water areas.
(2) 1 m^3 = 219.9693 Imperial gallons.
(3) 1 kg = 0.068522 slugs.
(4) 1 American ton = 2000 lb.   1 kN = 0.1003612 Imperial ton.   1 Imperial ton = 2240 lb.

Abbreviations for Units

°C	degree Celsius (centigrade)	kW	kilowatt
cc	cubic centimeters	lb	pound
cm	centimeter	lbf	pound force
°F	degree Fahrenheit	MJ	megajoule
ft	foot	MPa	megapascal
g	gram	m	meter
gal	gallon	ml	milliliter
hp	horsepower	mm	millimeter
hr	hour	MN	meganewton
Imp	British Imperial	N	newton
in.	inch	oz	ounce
J	joule	Pa	pascal
K	kelvin	psf	pounds per square foot
kg	kilogram	psi	pounds per square inch
kgf	kilogram-force	°R	degree Rankine
kip	1000 pound force	sec	second
km	kilometer	slug	14.594 kg
kN	kilonewton	W	watt
kPa	kilopascal	yd	yard
ksi	kips per square inch		

CONVERSION TABLE FOR COMMITTEES AND CHAPTERS

The Council maintains an ongoing bibliography organized according to subject areas that are identified by the committee number. For this reason (and also because future editions of the Monograph may have different chapter numbers) the *committee* designations have been retained in the parenthetical information at the end of each bibliographic citation. The following conversion table is supplied for reference as is needed.

Committee	Chapter Number	Chapter Title
2A	SC-4	Vertical and Horizontal Transportation
2B	SC-2	Mechanical and Service Systems
2C	SC-3	Electrical Systems
3	SC-1	Structural Systems
4	SC-8	Construction Systems
11	SC-7	Foundation Systems
12A	SC-5	Cladding
12B	SC-6	Partitions, Walls, and Ceilings

References/Bibliography

The citations that follow include both references and bibliography. The list includes all articles referred to or cited in the test and it also includes bibliography for further reading. The material is arranged alphabetically by author, followed by the year of publication. Since the citation in text is to author and year, there will be instances in which reference is made to two different articles published in the same year by the same authors. In those instances it has been necessary to affix letters to the year to provide proper identification.

Where articles are published in a language other than English, the translation of the title is given first, followed by the title in the original language.

The numbers in parentheses designate the committee for which the citation is appropriate. (See facing page for committee/chapter conversion table.)

Additional bibliographies are available through the Council.

AAMA, 1970
    ALUMINUM CURTAIN WALLS PUBLICATION NUMBER 1, Architectural Aluminum Manfacturers Association, Chicago, Ill. (12A)
AAMA, 1979
    ALUMINUM CURTAIN WALL DESIGN GUIDE MANUAL, Architectural Aluminum Manufacturers Association, Chicago, Ill. (12A)
ACI, 1971
    BUILDING CODE REQUIREMENTS FOR REINFORCED CONCRETE (ACI 318-71 AND 1975 SUPPLEMENT), American Concrete Institute, Detroit, Mich. (4)
ACI, 1974a
    MANUAL OF STANDARD PRACTICE FOR DETAILING REINFORCED CONCRETE STRUCTURES (ACI 315-74), American Concrete Institute, Detroit, Mich. (4)
ACI, 1974b
    PLACING CONCRETE BY PUMPING METHODS Manual of Concrete Practice, Part 1, American Concrete Institute, Detroit, Mich., pp. 304–55—304–73. (4)
ACI Committee 442, 1971
    RESPONSE OF BUILDINGS TO LATERAL FORCES, ACI Committee 442, M. Fintel, Chmn., Title No. 68-11, ACI Journal, Vol. 68, No. 2, pp. 81–106. (3)
AIA, 1970
    BUILDING SYSTEMS—WHY CONCRETE? Architect/Researcher's Conference, American Institute of Architects, November. (3)

AIJ, 1977
BUILDING STANDARD LAW, Architectural Institute of Japan, Maruzen Co. Ltd., Tokyo, Japan. (2A)
AISC, 1971a
QUALITY CRITERIA AND INSPECTION STANDARDS, American Institute of Steel Construction, New York. (4)
AISC, 1971b
SPECIFICATION FOR: STRUCTURAL JOINTS USING ASTM A325 OR A490 BOLTS, American Institute of Steel Construction, New York. (4)
ANSI A17.1, 1975
AMERICAN NATIONAL STANDARD SAFETY CODE FOR ELEVATORS, DUMB-WAITERS, ESCALATORS AND MOVING WALKS, American Society of Mechanical Engineers, New York. (2A)
ANSI, undated
VARIOUS STANDARDS APPLICABLE TO CONSTRUCTION SAFETY, American National Standards Institute, New York. (4)
ASHRAE, 1972
HANDBOOK OF FUNDAMENTALS, American Society for Heating, Refrigerating, and Air Conditioning Engineers, New York. (2B)
ASHRAE, 1973a
STANDARDS FOR NATURAL AND MECHANICAL VENTILATION, Standard 62-73, American Society for Heating, Refrigerating, and Air Conditioning Engineers, New York. (2B)
ASHRAE, 1973b
EXPERIENCE AND APPLICATIONS ON SMOKE AND FIRE CONTROL, Symposium LO-73-2, American Society for Heating, Refrigerating, and Air Conditioning Engineers, New York. (2B)
ASHRAE, 1973c
SYSTEMS HANDBOOK, American Society for Heating, Refrigerating, and Air Conditioning Engineers, New York. (2B)
ASHRAE, 1974a
HANDBOOK AND PRODUCT DIRECTORY, 1974 APPLICATIONS, American Society for Heating, Refrigerating, and Air Conditioning Engineers, New York. (2B)
ASHRAE, 1974b
THERMAL ENVIRONMENTAL CONDITIONS FOR HUMAN OCCUPANCY, Standard 55-74, American Society for Heating, Refrigerating, and Air Conditioning Engineers, New York. (2B)
ASHRAE, 1975a
HANDBOOK AND PRODUCT DIRECTORY, 1975 EQUIPMENT, American Society for Heating, Refrigerating, and Air Conditioning Engineers, New York. (2B)
ASHRAE, 1975b
TRANSACTIONS, Vol. 81, Part 2, American Society for Heating, Refrigerating, and Air Conditioning Engineers, New York. (2B)
ASHRAE, 1975c
ENERGY CONSERVATION IN NEW BUILDING DESIGN, Standard 90-75, American Society for Heating, Refrigerating, and Air Conditioning Engineers, New York. (2B)
ASHRAE, 1976
HANDBOOK AND PRODUCT DIRECTORY, 1976, SYSTEMS, American Society for Heating, Refrigerating, and Air Conditioning Engineers, New York. (2B)
ASTM, 1964
METHOD OF TEST FOR LOAD-SETTLEMENT RELATIONSHIP FOR INDIVIDUAL PILES UNDER VERTICAL AXIAL LOADS, Book of American Society of Testing and Materials (ASTM) Standards, Part II, Designation 1143-61T, pp. 377–380. (11)
ASTM, 1971
1971 ANNUAL BOOK OF STANDARDS, American Society for Testing and Materials, Philadelphia, Pa. (4)
Abdallah, N., 1973
THE MLC CENTRE, SYDNEY, Proceedings of the National Conference on Tall Buildings (Sydney, Australia), Lehigh University, Bethlehem, Pa. (3)

Abdallah, N., 1974
THE PROGRESSIVE STRENGTH METHOD, Proceedings of the National Conference on Tall Buildings (Kuala Lumpur, Malaysia, December), Institution of Engineers, Kuala Lumpur, Malaysia. (4)

Acier-Stahl-Steel, 1971
NEW HOTELS IN AMSTERDAM, *Acier-Stahl-Steel*, Brussels, Belgium, May. (3)

Acier-Stahl-Steel, 1972
RADISON HOTEL SOUTH, MINNEAPOLIS, MINNESOTA, *Acier-Stahl-Steel*, Brussels, Belgium, February. (3)

Adler, R., 1974
VERTICAL TRANSPORTATION FOR CITICORP CENTER, unpublished communication to the Joint Committee. (2A)

Akam, A., 1972
DEMOLITION: ERECTING A FRAMEWORK—RESULTS OF A BRS SURVEY, *Civil Engineering and Public Works Review*, Vol. 67, No. 789, pp. 377–381. (4)

Alexander, W. D., Tedesko, A. and Rutledge, P. C., 1964
VERTICAL ASSEMBLY BUILDING—PROJECT DESCRIPTION, ORGANIZATION AND PROCEDURES, *Civil Engineering*, ASCE, Vol. 35, No. 1, pp. 42–45. (11)

Allen, D. N. deG., 1963
THE STRESSES IN FOUNDATION RAFTS III, *Proceedings*, Institution of Civil Engineers, London, England. (11)

Allen, D. N. deG. and Severn, R. T., 1960
THE STRESSES IN FOUNDATION RAFTS I, *Proceedings*, Institution of Civil Engineers, London, England, Vol. 15, pp. 35–48; and discussion, Vol. 17, pp. 339–350. (11)

Allen, D. N. deG. and Severn, R. T., 1961
THE STRESSES IN FOUNDATION RAFTS II, *Proceedings*, Institution of Civil Engineers, London, England, Vol. 20, pp. 293–304. (11)

Aluminum Constructions, 1977
EXTERIOR WALL CONSTRUCTIONS, DESIGN PRINCIPLES (Leichte Aussenwand Konstruktionen, Grundlagen für Planung und Ausführung), Part I, Aluminum Verlag GmbH, January, pp. 9–31. (12A)

Aluminum Constructions, 1978
EXTERIOR WALL CONSTRUCTIONS, DESIGN PRINCIPLES (Leichte Aussenwand Konstruktionen, Grundlagen für Planung und Ausführung), Part II, Aluminum Verlag GmbH, January, pp. 16–41. (12A)

Aluminum Development Council of Australia, undated
ALUMINUM IN AUSTRALIA, State of Art, Series A, No. 7, Aluminum Development Council of Australia. (12A)

Anastasescu, A., Ionescu, I. and Koreck, I., 1975
SLIP FORM CONSTRUCTED LIGHTWEIGHT EXPANDED CLAY CONCRETE TALL BUILDINGS IN TIMISOARA (Structuri Multietajate din Beton Usor de Granulit Realizate Prin Glisare in Orasul Timisoara)(Iasi, Romania, October), Consiliul National al Inginerilor si Tehnicienilor, Iasi, Romania, Vol. 2. (4)

Andersen, P., 1947
SUBSTRUCTURE ANALYSIS AND DESIGN, The Roland Press Co., New York. (11)

Anderson, P., Ed., 1975
TELL ME ABOUT ELEVATORS, Otis Elevator Co., Philadelphia, Pa. (2A)

Annett, F. A., 1960
ELEVATORS, 3rd ed., McGraw-Hill Book Co., Inc., New York. (2A)

Arch, W. H., Nikai, S., Subba Rao, T. N., Roret, J. A., Taylor, E. E. F. and Bowen, F., 1973
SUMMARY REPORT: CONSTRUCTION SYSTEMS, Planning and Design of Tall Buildings, Proceedings of the 1972 ASCE-IABSE International Conference, ASCE, New York, Vol. 1a, No. TC-4. (4)

Aristy, E. M. R., 1973
PREFABRICATED HOUSING (Sistema Constructivo de Estructuras Prefabricadas Sacmo), Proceedings of the National Conference on Tall Buildings (Madrid, Spain, September), Typografia Artistica, Alameda, Madrid, Spain. (4)

Asrow, S., 1973
THEME REPORT: CONSTRUCTION SYSTEMS, Planning and Design of Tall Buildings, Proceedings of the 1972 ASCE-IABSE International Conference, ASCE, New York, Vol. 1a, No. TC-4. (4)

Associated General Contractors, 1971
MANUAL OF ACCIDENT PREVENTION IN CONSTRUCTION, 6th revised ed., Associated General Contractors. (4)

Au, F., 1973
BUILDING SERVICES AND SYSTEMS IN HONG KONG, Proceedings of the Regional Conference on Tall Buildings (Hong Kong, August), Lehigh University, Bethlehem, Pa., pp. 146–155. (2A, 2B, 2C)

Ayers, J. M. and Sun, T. Y., 1973
CRITERIA FOR BUILDING SERVICES AND FURNISHINGS, National Bureau of Standards, Building Science Series No. 46, *Building Practices for Disaster Mitigation*, February, pp. 253–285. (2A)

Ayers, J. M., Sun, T. Y. and Brown, F. R., 1973
NONSTRUCTURAL DAMAGE TO BUILDINGS, *The Great Alaska Earthquake of 1964: Engineering*, National Academy of Sciences, Washington, D.C., pp. 346–456. (12B)

BSI, 1970
SPECIFICATION FOR LIFTS, ESCALATORS, PASSENGER CONVEYORS AND PATERNOSTERS, British Standard 2655, British Standards Institution, London, England. (2A)

BSI, 1972
ELECTRIC, HYDRAULIC, AND HANDPOWERED LIFTS, British Standard Code of Practice CP 407, British Standards Institution, London, England. (2A)

BSI, 1979
LIFTS AND SERVICE LIFTS, British Standard 5655, British Standards Institution, London, England. (2A)

Baker, A. L. L., 1965
RAFT FOUNDATIONS, 3rd edition, Section XXVIII, pp. 141. (11)

Baker, C. N. and Khan, F., 1966
CAISSON CONSTRUCTION PROBLEMS AND METHOD OF CORRECTION, presented at ASCE Annual Meeting (Chicago, Ill., October). (11)

Baker, C. N. and Khan, F., 1971
CAISSON CONSTRUCTION PROBLEMS AND CORRECTION IN CHICAGO, *Journal of the Soil Mechanics and Foundations Division*, ASCE, Vol. 97, No. SM2, Proc. Paper 7934, pp. 417–440. (4, 11)

Balaguru, P. and Sathyamoorthy, K., 1974
PROJECT PLANNING AND CONTROL FOR TALL BUILDINGS, Proceedings of the National Conference on Tall Buildings (Bangkok, Thailand, January), Asian Institute of Technology, Bangkok, Thailand. (4)

Bandel, H., 1973a
STRUCTURAL SYSTEMS FOR VERY TALL BUILDINGS, Planning and Design of Tall Buildings, Proceedings of the 1972 ASCE-IABSE International Conference, ASCE, New York, Vol. 1a, No. 3-D3. (3)

Bandel, H., 1973b
COMPOSITE CORE AND COLUMNS, Planning and Design of Tall Buildings, Proceedings of the 1972 ASCE-IABSE International Conference, ASCE, New York, Vol. 1a, No. 3-D4. (3)

Banham, R., 1974
ENGINEERING SERVICES IN TALL BUILDINGS, Proceedings of the Regional Conference on Tall Buildings (Bangkok, Thailand, January), Asian Institute of Technology, Bangkok, Thailand, pp. 83–95. (2B)

Barney, G. C. and dos Santos, S. M., 1974
THE DESIGN, EVALUATION AND CONTROL OF LIFT (ELEVATOR) SYSTEMS, Lift Design Partnership, Bolton, England. (2A)

Baum, R. T., 1971
SERVICE SYSTEMS IN TALL BUILDINGS, 5th Regional Conference Proceedings (Chicago, Ill., November/December), Lehigh University, Bethlehem, Pa., pp. 27–29. (2A, 2B)

Baum, R. T., 1973a
BUILDING SERVICES IN TALL BUILDINGS, Proceedings of the Regional Conference on Tall Buildings, (Hong Kong, August), Lehigh University, Bethlehem, Pa., pp. 156–161. (2B)

Baum, R. T., 1973b
MUTUAL INFLUENCES BETWEEN BUILDING CONCEPT AND MECHANICAL SYSTEMS IN TALL BUILDINGS, Planning and Design of Tall Buildings, Proceedings of Conference (Sydney, Australia, August), Lehigh University, Bethlehem, Pa., pp. 483–498. (2B, 2C)

Baum, R. T., 1973c
THEME REPORT, SERVICE SYSTEMS IN RELATION TO ARCHITECTURE, Planning and Design of Tall Buildings, Proceedings of the 1972 ASCE-IABSE International Conference, Vol. 1a, ASCE, New York, pp. 305. (2A, 2B, 2C)

Baum, R. and Thoma, R., 1971
SERVICE SYSTEMS, 2nd Regional Conference Proceedings, (Bled, Yugoslavia, May), Lehigh University, Bethlehem, Pa., pp. 23. (2B)

Bazant, Z., 1973
FOUNDATIONS OF TALL BUILDINGS, 10th Regional Conference Proceedings (Bratislava, Czechoslovakia, April), CSVTA-Czechoslovak Scientific and Technical Association, Bratislava, Czechoslovakia. (11)

Beeman, D., ed., 1955
INDUSTRIAL POWER SYSTEMS HANDBOOK, McGraw-Hill Book Co., Inc., New York. (2C)

Begemann, 1963
THE USE OF THE STATIC SOIL PENETROMETER IN HOLLAND, *New Zealand Engineering*, February. (11)

Bellows, W. R., Jr., 1973
CONCRETE FRAME CONSTRUCTION, Planning and Design of Tall Buildings, Proceedings of the 1972 ASCE-IABSE International Conference, ASCE, New York, Vol. 1a, No. 4–6. (4)

Belloni, L. and Jamiolkowski, M. B., 1973
SOIL-STRUCTURE INTERACTION, Planning and Design of Tall Buildings, Proceedings of the 1972 ASCE-IABSE International Conference, Vol. 1a, ASCE, New York. (11)

Benazzi, R. Z. and Reilly, R. J., 1974
WATER SUPPLY AND DRAINAGE SYSTEMS FOR SEARS TOWER, presented at ASCE National Meeting on Water Resources Engineering, Los Angeles, Ca., January 21–25. (2B)

Benuska, L., Solberg, M. and Schroll, W., 1973
SHAKEDOWN IN ELEVATOR EARTHQUAKE SAFETY CONTROL, *Buildings: The Construction & Building Management Journal*, Stamats Publishing Co., Cedar Rapids, Iowa, March. (2A)

Berry, O. R., 1973
ARCHITECTURAL SEISMIC DETAILING, Planning and Design of Tall Buildings, Proceedings of the 1972 ASCE-IABSE International Conference, Vol. 1a, ASCE, New York, pp. 1115–1131. (12A, 12B)

Bhaskaran, R., 1974
EFFECT OF PILE DRIVING ON PILE-SOIL INTERACTION AND BEARING CAPACITY PREDICTION, Proceedings, Conference on Tall Buildings (Kuala Lumpur, Malaysia, December), Institution of Engineers, Kuala Lumpur, Malaysia. (11)

Bielek, M., 1973
PERIPHERAL WALLS OF TALL BUILDINGS, THEIR DESIGN, THEORY OF ANALYSIS OF THEIR PERFORMANCE FROM THE POINT OF VIEW OF THEIR PHYSICAL PROPERTIES, 10th Regional Conference Proceedings (Bratislava, Czechoslovakia, April), Vols. I & II, CSVTA-Czechoslovak Scientific and Technical Association, Bratislava, Czechoslovakia (two editions: English and Czech), pp. 215–239. (12A)

Bjerrum, L., 1957
NORWEGIAN EXPERIENCE WITH STEEL PILES TO ROCK, *Geotechnique*, London, England, Vol. 7, pp. 73–100. (11)

Bjerrum, L., 1963
DISCUSSION TO SECTION VI, Proceedings of the European Conference on Soil Mechanics and Foundation Engineering (Wiesbaden, West Germany), Vol. II. (11)

Bjerrum, L. and Eide, O., 1956
STABILITY OF STRUTTED EXCAVATIONS IN CLAY, *Geotechnique*, London, England, Vol. 6, No. 1. (11)

Bjerrum, L., Johannessen, I. J. and Eide, O., 1969
REDUCTION OF NEGATIVE SKIN FRICTION ON STEEL PILES TO ROCK, Proceedings, 7th International Conference on Soil Mechanics and Foundation Engineering (Mexico City, Mexico), Vol. 2, pp. 27–34. (11)

Blomdahl, T., 1968
PILES AND PILING METHODS AT NYA ASFALT AB (in Swedish), *Cement och Betong*, Malmö, Sweden, pp. 84–105. (11)

Blume, J. A., 1968
DYNAMIC CHARACTERISTICS OF MULTI-STORY BUILDINGS, Report No. NVO-99-30, John A. Blume and Associates, Research Division, San Francisco, Calif. (12B)

Blume, J. A. and Associates, 1972
BUILDINGS ANALYZED BY JOHN A. BLUME AND ASSOCIATES, Report for EERI/NDA San Fernando Earthquake Investigation Committee of the EERI, San Francisco, Calif. (12B)

Bonny, J. B., 1973
HANDBOOK OF CONSTRUCTION MANAGEMENT AND ORGANIZATIONS, Van Nostrand Reinhold, Inc., New York. (4)

Botha, J. P., Adendorff, K. and Kruger, P. S., 1975
MOVEMENT SYSTEMS FOR TALL BUILDINGS, Proceedings of the South African Conference on Tall Buildings (Johannesburg, South Africa, November), Hortors Printers, Johannesburg, South Africa. (2A)

Botsai, E. E., 1973
DESIGNING AGAINST INFILTRATION, Planning and Design of Tall Buildings, Proceedings of the 1972 ASCE-IABSE International Conference, Vol. 1a, ASCE, New York, pp. 1131–1135. (12A, 12B)

Bozuzuk, M., 1970
FIELD OBSERVATIONS OF NEGATIVE SKIN FRICTION LOADS ON LONG PILES IN MARINE CLAY, Proceedings of the Conference on Design and Installation of Pile Foundation and Cellular Structures, H. Y. Fang, ed., Envo Publication Co., pp. 273–280. (11)

Bozuzuk, M., 1971
DOWNDRAG MEASUREMENTS ON A 160-FT FLOATING PIPE TEST IN MARINE CLAY, presented at the 24th Annual Geotechnical Conference, held at Halifax, England. (11)

Bozuzuk, M. and Labrecque, A., 1968
DOWNDRAG MEASUREMENTS ON 270-FT COMPOSITE PILES, Special Technical Publication No. 444, ASTM, Philadelphis, Pa., pp. 15–40. (11)

Brainov, M., 1975
THE PROBLEM TALL BUILDINGS—ARCHITECTURE, STRUCTURES, INDUSTRIALIZATION—A UNIFIED OPENED UNIVERSAL BUILDING—STRUCTURAL SYSTEM, Darzhavno Izdatelstvo Technika, Sofia, Bulgaria. (3)

Breth, H., 1970
THE STATE OF LOADING OF GROUTED ANCHORS IN CLAY (Das Tragverhalten von Injektionsankern in Ton), Vorträge der Baugrundtagung 1970 in Düsseldorf, Deutsche Gesellschaft für Erd und Grundbau, Essen, Germany. (11)

Brinch-Hansen, J., 1961
THE ULTIMATE RESISTANCE OF RIGID PILES AGAINST TRANSVERSAL FORCES, Bulletin No. 12, Danish Geotechnical Institute. (11)

Brinch-Hansen, J. and Lundgren, J., 1960
MAJOR PROBLEMS OF SOIL MECHANICS (Hauptprobleme der Bodenmechanik), Springer Verlag, Berlin, Germany, pp. 243–246. (11)

Briske, 1968
MEASUREMENTS ON THE STRESSES IN THE STRUTTED EXCAVATION DURING CONSTRUCTION OF THE SUBWAY IN KÖLN (in German), *Die Bautechnik*, Vol. 9. (11)

Brodeur, J. C., 1971
INFORMATION ON PILE PROJECTS, A. Johnson Co., Ltd., Montreal, Canada, private correspondence. (11)

Broms, B. B., 1964a

LATERAL RESISTANCE OF PILES IN COHESIVE SOILS, *Journal of the Soil Mechanics and Foundations Division*, ASCE, Vol. 90, No. SM2, Proc. Paper 3825, pp. 27–63. (11)

Broms, B. B., 1964b
LATERAL RESISTANCE OF PILES IN COHESIONLESS SOILS, *Journal of the Soil Mechanics and Foundations Division*, ASCE, Vol. 90, No. SM3, Proc. Paper 3909, pp. 123–156. (11)

Broms, B. B., 1965
DESIGN OF LATERALLY LOADED PILES, *Journal of the Soil Mechanics and Foundations Division*, ASCE, Vol. 91, No. SM3, Proc. Paper 4342, pp. 79–99. (11)

Broms, B. B., 1966
METHODS OF CALCULATING THE ULTIMATE BEADING CAPACITY OF PILES, A SUMMARY, *Sols-Soils*, No. 18, pp. 1–11. (11)

Broms, B. B., 1971
DESIGN OF PILE GROUPS WITH RESPECT TO NEGATIVE SKIN FRICTION, Report and Preliminary Report, Swedish Geotechnical Institute, Stockholm, Sweden, No. 42. (11)

Broms, B. B. and Hellman, L., 1968
END BEARING AND SKIN FRICTION OF PILES, Journal of the Soil Mechanics and Foundations Division, ASCE, Vol. 94, No. SM2, Proc. Paper 5846, pp. 421–429. (11)

Broms, B. B. and Hellman, L., 1970
METHODS USED IN SWEDEN TO EVALUATE THE BEARING CAPACITY OF END-BEARING PRECAST CONCRETE PILES, Proceedings of Conference on Behavior of Piles, Institution of Civil Engineers, London, England, pp. 27–20. (11)

Brotchie, J. F., Lewis, R. E. and Martin, K. G., 1972
AN OPTIMIZATION APPROACH TO VISCOUS DAMPING OF STRUCTURES, Division of Building Research Technical Paper No. 30, Commonwealth Scientific and Industrial Research Organization, Australia. (3)

Bruna, B., 1973
STRUCTURES OF TALL BUILDINGS USING PRECAST CONCRETE SKELETON DEVELOPED BY THE COMPANY KONSTRUKTIVA, Proceedings of the National Conference on Tall Buildings (Bratislava, Czechloslovakia, April) Lehigh University, Bethlehem, Pa. (3, 4)

Brungraber, R. J., 1973
THE USE OF LIGHTWEIGHT ALLOYS IN TALL BUILDINGS, Planning and Design of Tall Buildings, Proceedings of te 1972 ASCE-IABSE International Conference, ASCE, New York, Vol. 1a, No. 3-D2. (3)

Budzianowski, Z., 1965
BENDING OF LOW BUILDINGS ON THE MINING BASIN SLOPE, *Inzyniera i Budownictwo*, Warsaw, Poland, No. 7 (in Polish). (11)

Budzianowski, Z. and Krol, W., 1972
DESIGN OF TALL BUILDINGS IN MINING SUBSIDENCE AREAS, Proceedings, Regional Conference on the Planning and Design of Tall Buildings (Warsaw, Poland, November), Warsaw Technical University, Polish Group of IABSE, Warsaw, Poland, pp. 215–226. (11)

Building, 1970
TWIN TOWERS WILL DOMINATE THE SYDNEY SKYLINE, *Building*, February. (12A)

Building, 1972
EXTERNAL WALLS: MULTI-STOREY: BUILDING CONSTRUCTION DETAILS, *Building*, January. (12A)

Building Materials, 1973
FRAMING WITH STEEL AND CONCRETE MULTIBUILD SYSTEM, *Building Materials*, November/December. (3)

Building Materials, 1974
DIAMOND-SHAPED TOWER DONS A SPECIAL CLADDING, *Building Materials*, Vol. 16, No. 6. (3, 12A)

Building Materials, 1975
NEW TYPE SANDWICH PANELS MAKE UP A BUILDING'S FACE, *Building Materials*, Vol. 17, No. 5 (AMP Building, Perth, Australia). (3, 12A)

Building Practice, 1971

CONCRETE MATERIALS—WHAT DOES THE FUTURE HOLD? *Building Practice*, Bombay, India, March (translated into Italian and published in *Il Calcestruzzo Preconfenzionato*, No. 28, October/December, 1973). (3)
Building with Steel, 1972
FRAMES FOR TALL BUILDINGS, *Building with Steel*, Vol. 12, November. (3)
Bureau of Yards and Docks, 1962
SOIL MECHANICS, FOUNDATIONS AND EARTH STRUCTURES, DESIGN MANUAL NAVDOCKS DM-7, U.S. Navy, February. (11)
Button, D. A., 1975
CONSIDERATIONS OF ENERGY, ENVIRONMENT AND STRUCTURE IN WINDOW DESIGN, Proceedings of South African Conference (Johannesburg, South Africa, November) Horters Printers, Johannesburg, South Africa. (12A)
Byrd, T., 1973
WOOLWICH TOWER BLOCKS BEGIN TO SUFFER AFTER TEN YEARS STRESS, *Construction News*, August 16. (3)

CSA Standard B44, 1971
SAFETY CODE FOR ELEVATORS, DUMBWAITERS, ESCALATORS AND MOVING WALKS, Canadian Standards Association, Rexdale, Ontario, Canada. (2A)
CIMUR, 1965
FRENCH LIGHT FACADE TECHNIQUES: CURTAIN WALLS AND FACADE PANELS (Techniques Françaises des Façades Legeres: Murs-rideaux et panneaux de façade), Information Committee for the Development of Facade Panels and Curtain Walls, Editions Eyrolles, Paris, France. (12A)
Callender, J. H., ed., 1974
TIME-SAVER STANDARDS FOR ARCHITECTURAL DESIGN DATA, McGraw-Hill Book Co., Inc., New York. (12A)
Calzon, J. and Herrera, J. O., 1973
APPROXIMATE STRUCTURAL ANALYSIS OF HIGH-RISE BUILDINGS (Analysis Estructural Aproximado de Edificios de Gran Altura por Medio de Microordenadores), Proceedings of Region Conference on Tall Buildings (Madrid, Spain, September), Tipografia Artistica, Madrid, Spain (two editions: English and Spanish), pp. 3–10. (12B)
Camellerie, J. F., 1973
HYBRID FRAME CONSTRUCTION (STEEL AND CONCRETE), Planning and Design of Tall Buildings, Proceedings of the 1972 ASCE-IABSE International Conference, ASCE, New York, Vol. 1a, No. 4-7. (4)
Capatu, C., Ciubotaru, V. and Grecu, V., 1975
THE DIRECT FOUNDATION OF A TALL BUILDING ON WEAK SOILS WITH PARTIAL PREVENTION OF SETTLEMENT (Fundarea Directa a Unei Constructü Inalte pe Terenuri Slabe, Cu Impiedicarea Partiala a Refularü Acestora), Reinforced Concrete Tall Buildings, Porceedings of Conference (Iasi, Romania, October), Consiliul National al Inginerilor si Tehnicienilor, Iasi, Romania. (11)
Carrier, W. D., III and Christian, J. T., 1973
RIGID CIRCULAR PLATE RESTING ON A NON-HOMOGENEOUS ELASTIC HALF SPACE, *Geotechnique*, Vol. 23, March, pp. 67–84. (11)
Casagrande, A. and Fadum, R. E., 1944
APPLICATION OF SOIL MECHANICS IN DESIGNING BUILDING FOUNDATIONS, *Transactions*, ASCE, Vol. 109, pp. 383. (11)
Caspe, M. S., 1970
EARTHQUAKE ISOLATION OF MULTISTORY CONCRETE STRUCTURES, *American Concrete Institute Journal*, November. (3)
Cassinello, F., 1973
WALLS IN TALL BUILDINGS (Muros y Forjados en Edificios de Altura), Proceedings, Regional Conference on Tall Buildings (Madrid, Spain, September), Tipografia Artistica, Madrid, Spain (two editions: English and Spanish), pp. 1–6. (12B)
Castiglioni, A. and Urbano, C., 1971
ISOLATION OF MULTISTOREY BUILDINGS FROM GROUND-BORNE VIBRATIONS (Sull' Isolamento delle Vibrazioni in Edifici Multipiani), Instituto Lombardo di Scienze e Lettere, Vol. 105. (3)
Cederwall, K., 1962

SIX FACTORS THAT MAKE PILING HIGH QUALITY WORK, *Byggnadsindustrin*, Stockholm, Sweden. (11)

Chamecki, S., 1956
STRUCTURAL RIGIDITY IN CALCULATING SETTLEMENTS, *Proceedings*, ASCE, Vol. 82, Proc. Sep. No. 865. (11)

Chamecki, S., 1957
DISCUSSION ON FOUNDATION OF STRUCTURES, Proceedings, 4th International Conference on Soil Mechanics and Foundation Engineering (London, England), Vol. 3, pp. 162. (11)

Chamecki, S., 1969
CALCULATION OF PROGRESSIVE SETTLEMENTS OF FOUNDATIONS, *Annales de l'Institut Technique du Bâtiment et des Travaux Publics*, Paris, France, No. 261, September (in French). (11)

Chellis, R. D., 1961
PILE FOUNDATIONS, 2nd ed., McGraw-Hill Book Co., Inc., New York. (4, 11)

Chow, P. Y., Lu, H. K. and Lindsay, R., 1974
POUR-IN-PLACE PRESTRESSED CONCRETE CONSTRUCTION FOR HIGH RISE BUILDINGS IN SOUTH-EAST ASIA, Proceedings of the National Conference on Tall Buildings (Bangkok, Thailand, January), Asian Institute of Technology, Bangkok, Thailand. (4)

Christian, J. T., 1973
SOIL-STRUCTURE INTERACTION FOR TALL BUILDINGS, Planning and Design of Tall Buildings, Proceedings of the 1972 ASCE-IABSE International Conference, Vol. 1a, ASCE, New York. (11)

Christian, J. T., 1975
CHOICES AMONG PROCEDURES FOR DYNAMIC FINITE ELEMENT ANALYSIS, presented at ASCE National Convention (Denver, Colo.). (11)

Christiansen, J. V., 1973
CAST IN PLACE, REINFORCED CONCRETE SYSTEMS, Planning and Design of Tall Buildings, Proceedings of the 1972 ASCE-IABSE International Conference, ASCE, New York, Vol. 1a, No. 3-2. (3)

Chye, L. E. and Parmar, H. S., 1974
THE CONSTRUCTIONAL ASPECTS OF A TALL BUILDING, Proceedings of the National Conference on Tall Buildings (Kuala Lumpur, Malaysia, December), Institution of Engineers, Kuala Lumpur, Malaysia. (4)

Ciesielski, R. and Kawecki, J., 1973
DYNAMIC INFLUENCES ON FOUNDATION STRUCTURES FOR TOWER SHAPED STRUCTURES, Planning and Design of Tall Buildings, Porceedings of the 1972 ASCE-IABSE International Conference, Vol. 1a, ASCE, New York. (11)

Ciongradi, I., Missir, I. and Ungureanu, N., 1975
SOIL-FOUNDATION-STRUCTURE INTERACTION AT REINFORCED CONCRETE TALL BUILDINGS (Conlucrarea Spatiala Structura-Substructura-Teren la Cladiri Inalte de Beton Armat), Reinforced Concrete Tall Buildings, Proceedings of Conference (Iasi, Romania, October), Consiliul National al Inginerilor si Tehnicienilor, Iasi, Romania. (11)

Clark, J. I., Semchuk, W. and Goodman, K. S., 1966
EVALUATION OF PILE CAPACITY AND THE EFFECT OF NEGATIVE FRICTION, Proceedings of the Convention of the Canadian Good Road Association. (11)

Cleminson, C. A. and Rogers, R. L., 1974
ELEVATOR POWER (ENERGY) CONSUMPTION, *Elevator World*, Vol. XXII, No. 3. (2A)

Clough, G. W. and Tsui, Y., 1974
PERFORMANCE OF TIED-BACK WALLS IN CLAY, *Journal of the Geotechnical Engineering Division*, ASCE, Vol. 100, No. GT12, Proc. Paper 11028, pp. 1259–1274. (11)

Clough, R. H., 1972
CONSTRUCTION PROJECT MANAGEMENT, Wiley-Interscience, New York. (4)

Clough, R. H., 1975
CONSTRUCTION CONTRACTING, 3rd ed., John Wiley and Sons, Inc., New York. (4)

Colaco, J. P. and Banavalkar, P. V., 1974
PENNZOIL PLACE—A NEW SLANT IN STUCTURAL SYSTEMS, Proceedings of the

National Conference on Tall Buildings (Bangkok, Thailand, January), Asian Institute of Technology, Bangkok, Thailand. (3)

Cole, C. J. R., 1975
A REVIEW OF RESEARCH INTO LEARNING CURVES AND THEIR APPLICA-TION TO MULTI-STOREY CONSTRUCTION WORK, *Building Economist*, Vol. 13, No. 4. (4)

Concrete, 1970
STRENGTHENING TOWER BLOCKS OF LARGE PANEL CONSTRUCTION, *Concrete*, Vol. 4, No. 4. (3)

Construction Methods and Equipment, 1975
CONSTRUCTION SAFETY HANDBOOK, *Construction Methods and Equipment*, 116 p. (4)

Constructional Review, 1973
NO. 1, YORK STREET, SYDNEY, *Constructional Review*, Vol. 46, No. 2. (3)

Constructional Review, 1974a
MLC PROJECT, SYDNEY, *Constructional Review*, Vol. 47, No. 1. (3, 4)

Constructional Review, 1974b
T & G BUILDING, MELBOURNE, *Constructional Review*, Vol. 47, No. 1. (3)

Constructional Review, 1974c
444 ST. KILDA ROAD, MELBOURNE, *Constructional Review*, Vol. 47, No. 1. (3)

Constructional Review, 1974d
390 ST. KILDA ROAD, MELBOURNE, *Constructional Review*, Vol. 47, No. 4. (3, 4)

Constructional Review, 1975
TOWN HALL HOUSE, *Constructional Review*, Vol. 48, No. 4. (3)

Consulting Engineer, 1970
GROUND ANCHORS, *Consulting Engineer*, pp. 1–39. (4)

Consulting Engineer, 1975
BRUTE FORCE WITHOUT IGNORANCE, *Consulting Engineer*, Vol. 39, No. 2, February, pp. 39, 41. (4)

Contract Journal, 1971
HIGH RISE HOSPITAL GOES LIGHTWEIGHT, *Contract Journal*, Vol. 244, November 25. (3)

Cooke, R. W., 1974
THE SETTLEMENT OF FRICTION PILE FOUNDATIONS, Proceedings, Conference on Tall Buildings (Kuala Lumpur, Malaysia, December), Institution of Engineers, Kuala Lumpur, Malaysia. (11)

Cornfield, G. M., 1973
DEEP FOUNDATIONS—PILES AND CAISSONS, Planning and Design of Tall Buildings, Proceedings of the 1972 ASCE-IABSE International Conference, ASCE, New York, Vol. 1a, pp. 77–92. (11)

Correa, J. J., 1969
A TELESCOPIC TYPE OF PILE FOR SUBSIDENCE CONOITIONS, Proceedings of the Specialty Conference on Negative Skin Friction at the 7th International Conference on Soil Mechanics and Foundations Engineering (Mexico City, Mexico), Paper No. 11. (11)

Cosovliu, O., Mohor, I. and Rusu, A., 1975
INTERACTION PROBLEMS AT TALL BUILDINGS CONSTRUCTED ON MOIS-TURE SENSITIVE SOILS AND IN AREAS OF MACROSEISMIC INTENSITY (Probleme de Interactiune la Cladiri Inalte pe Terenuri Sensibile la Umezire si Zone de Intensitate Macroseismica), Reinforced Concrete Tall Buildings, Proceedings of Conference (Iasi, Romania, October), Consiliul National al Inginerilor si Tehnicienilor, Iasi, Romania. (11)

Crabtree, P. R., 1975
PLUMBING AND DRAINAGE IN TALL BUILDINGS, South African Conference on Tall Buildings (Johannesburg, South Africa, November), Hortors Printers, Johannesburg, South Africa. (2B)

Cuevas, J. A., 1936
THE FLOATING FOUNDATION OF THE NEW BUILDING OF THE NATIONAL LOTTERY OF MEXICO, Proceedings of the 1st International Conference on Soil Mechanics and Foundations Engineering (Cambridge), Vol. 1, pp. 294. (11)

Cunningham, J. A. and Robbins, J. P., 1974

ROCK CAISSONS FOR THE NORTHERN BUILDING IN CHICAGO'S LOOP,
Proceedings of the National Conference on Tall Buildings (Bangkok, Thailand, January),
Asian Institute of Technology, Bangkok, Thailand. (4, 11)

Cunningham, K. D., 1973
STEEL CONSTRUCTION, Planning and Design of Tall Buildings, Proceedings of the 1972
ASCE-IABSE International Conference, ASCE, New York, Vol. 1a, No. 4-5A. (4)

DIN, 1978 (draft)
ARTIFICIAL LIGHTING OF INTERIORS RECOMMENDATIONS, DIN 5035,
Deutsches Institut für Normung, Berlin, German Federal Republic. (2C)

Da Costa, A., 1973
CALCULATION OF HIGH BUIILDINGS FOR LOADS DURING THE CONSTRUC-
TION, Proceedings of the National Conference on Tall Buildings (Madrid, Spain,
September), Typografia Artistica, Alameda 12, Madrid, Spain. (4)

D'Appolonia, D. J., 1971
EFFECTS OF FOUNDATION CONSTRUCTION ON NEARBY STRUCTURES, 4th
Pan-American Conference on Soil Mechanics and Foundations Engineering (Puerto
Rico), State-of-the-Art Report. (11)

Daryanani, S., 1972
HEATING, VENTILATING AND AIR CONDITIONING, 6th Regional Conference
Proceedings (Delft, The Netherlands, May), Lehigh University, Bethlehem, Pa., p. 27.
(2B)

Daryanani, S. 1973
HEATING, VENTILATING AND AIR CONDITIONING (HVAC), Planning and
Design of Tall Buildings, Proceedings of the 1972 ASCE-IABSE International Confer-
ence, Vol. 1a, ASCE, New York, pp. 319–325. (2B)

Davisson, M. T., 1970
STATIC MEASUREMENTS OF PILE BEHAVIOUR, Design and Installation of Pile
Foundations, H. Y. Fang, ed., Envo Publishing Co., Inc, pp. 159–164. (11)

Davisson, M. T. and Gill, H. L., 1963
LATERALLY LOADED PILES IN A LAYERED SOIL SYSTEM *Journal of the Soil
Mechanics and Foundations Division*, ASCE, Vol. 89, No. SM3, Proc. Paper 3509, pp.
63–94. (11)

Davisson, M. T. and McDonald, V. J., 1969
ENERGY MEASUREMENTS FOR A DIESEL HAMMER, ASTM Symposium on Deep
Foundations, ASTM STP 44, Philadelphia, Pa., pp. 295–327. (11)

D'Cruz, A. M., 1974
EFFECT OF TALL BUILDINGS ON TELE-COMMUNICATIONS RADIO LINK,
Proceedings, Conference on Tall Buildings (Kuala Lumpur, Malaysia, December),
Institution of Engineers, Kuala Lumpur, Malaysia, pp. 5–39—5–40. (2C)

De Beer, E., 1948
CALCULATION OF BEAMS RESTING ON THE SOIL, THE COEFFICIENT K OF
THE SOIL (Calcul de poutres reposant sur le sol, le coefficient de raideur K du sol),
Annales des Travaux Publics de Belgique, June, August, October, December. (11)

De Beer, E., 1957
THE INFLUENCE OF THE WIDTH OF A FOUNDATION RAFT ON THE LON-
GITUDINAL DISTRIBUTION OF THE SOIL REACTIONS, 4th International
Conference on Soil Mechanics and Foundations Engineering (London, England), Vol. 1,
pp. 269. (11)

De Beer, E., 1963
BEARING CAPACITY CALCULATION FOR SHALLOW FOUNDATION WITH
INCLINED AND ECCENTRIC LOADS (Grundbruchberechnungen schrag und
ausmittig belasteter Flachgrundungen), *Verein Deutscher Ingenieure*, Band 105. (11)

De Beer, E., 1970a
SOIL MECHANICS, Standard Wetenschappelijke Uitgeverij, Antwerp, Belgium, 8e druk.
(11)

DeBeer, E., 1970b
EXPERIMENTAL DETERMINATION OF THE SHAPE FACTORS AND BEARING
CAPACITY FACTORS OF SAND, *Geotechnique*, London, England, pp. 387–411. (11)

De Beer, E., 1971

PROBLEMS PRESENTED BY THE CONSTRUCTION OF THE TUNNEL UNDER THE SCHELDT AT ANTWERP (Problèmes posés par la construction du tunnel sous l'Escaut à Anvers), *Annales de l'Institut Technique du Bâtiment et des Travaux Publics*, No. 286, Paris, France, October. (11)

De Beer, E., 1972
METHODS OF DETERMINING THE BEARING CAPACITY OF A TILE ON THE BASIS OF THE RESULTS OF PENETRATION TESTS (Méthodes de déduction de la capacité portante d'un pieu a partir des resultats des essais de penetration), *Annales des Travaux Publics de Belgique*. (11)

De Beer, E., 1973
SUMMARY REPORT: FOUNDATION DESIGN, Planning and Design of Tall Buildings, Proceedings of the 1972 ASCE-IABSE International Conference, Vol. 1a, ASCE, New York. (11)

Delgado-Vargas, M., 1975
LARGE DIAMETER FOUNDATION PIERS IN COLOMBIA, unpublished communication to the Council. (11)

De Mello, V. F. B., 1969
FOUNDATIONS OF BUILDINGS IN CLAY, 7th International Conference on Soil Mechanics and Foundation Engineering (Mexico City, Mexico), State-of-the-Art Report, State-of-the-Art Volume, pp. 49–136. (11)

Deshpande, R. L., 1973
LIFT SERVICE IN HIGH-RISE BUILDINGS, Proceedings of the National Conference on Tall Buildings (New Delhi, India, January), Indian National Group of the IABSE, New Delhi, India, pp. IV39–IV46. (2A)

DeSimone, S. V., 1973
DISTRIBUTION OF WIND LOADS TO SOIL, Planning and Design of Tall Buildings, Proceedings of the 1972 ASCE-IABSE International Conference, Vol. 1a, ASCE, New York. (11)

Despeyroux, J., 1975
CONSTRUCTION OF PREFABRICATED PANELS IN TALL BUILDINGS, Proceedings of the National Conference on Tall Buildings (Athens, Greece, October), Technical Chamber of Greece, Athens, Greece. (4)

de Stivolinski, L. W., 1969a
OCCUPATIONAL HEALTH IN THE CONSTRUCTION INDUSTRY, Technical Report No. 105, Department of Civil Engineering, Stanford University, Stanford, Calif. (4)

de Stivolinski, L. W., 1969b
A SURVEY OF THE SAFETY ENVIRONMENT OF THE CONSTRUCTION INDUSTRY, Technical Report No. 114, Department of Civil Engineering, Stanford University, Stanford, Calif. (4)

Devaty, F., Horina, B. and Reichel, V., 1973
FIREPROOF FLOORS WITH METAL PANELS, Tenth Regional Conference Proceedings (Bratislava, Czechoslovakia, April), Vol. I & II, CSVTA—Czechoslovak Scientific and Technical Association, Bratislava, Czechoslovakia (two editions: English and Czech), pp. 323–325. (12B)

De Viaris, G., 1973
PASSENGER ELEVATORS IN HIGH-RISE OFFICE BUILDINGS (Transporte Vertical De Passageiros Em Edificios De Escritorio De Grande Altura), Proceedings of the South American Regional Conference on Tall Buildings (Porto Alegre, Brazil, December), Vol. I and II, Sociedade de Engenharia do Rio Grande do Sul, Porto Alegre, Brazil, pp. 1–32. (2A)

Diaz-Caneja, F., 1973
THE PREFLEX SYSTEM IN THE STRUCTURES OF HIGH BUILDINGS THE "TOUR DE MIDI," Proceedings of the National Conference on Tall Buildings (Madrid, Spain, September), Typografia Artistica, Alameda 12, Madrid, Spain. (4)

Dimitrios, N., 1975
HORIZONTAL AND VERTICAL POWER DISTRIBUTION IN LARGE AND TALL BUILDINGS, Proceedings of Hellenic Conference on Tall Buildings (Athens, Greece, October), Technical Chamber of Greece, Athens, Greece. (2C)

Dismuke, T. D., 1973
  EXCAVATIONS AND DEEP FOUNDATIONS, Planning and Design of Tall Buildings, Proceedings of the 1972 ASCE-IABSE International Conference, Vol. 1a, ASCE, New York. (11)
Disque, R. O., 1973
  MASS PRODUCED STEEL SYSTEMS, Planning and Design of Tall Buildings, Proceedings of the 1972 ASCE-IABSE International Conference, ASCE, New York, Vol. 1a, No. 3-4. (3)
Dori, G., 1969
  STRUCTURAL STEELWORK OF OFFICE BUILDINGS, ROME, *Acier-Stahl-Steel*, Brussels, Belgium, November. (3)
Dowrick, E. J., 1977
  EARTHQUAKE RESISTENT DESIGN—A MANUAL FOR ENGINEERS AND ARCHITECTS, John Wiley and Sons, Inc., New York. (2A)
Drakatos, P. A., 1975
  THE INFLUENCE OF MECHANICAL VIBRATIONS ON THE CONSTRUCTION OF TALL BUILDINGS, Proceedings of the National Conference on Tall Buildings (Athens, Greece, October), Technical Chamber of Greece, Athens, Greece. (4)
Duncan, J. M. and Clough, G. W., 1971
  FINITE ELEMENT ANALYSES OF PORT ALLEN LOCK, *Journal of the Soil Mechanics and Foundations Division*, ASCE, Vol. 97, No. SM8, Proc. Paper 8317, pp. 1053–1068. (11)
Duncan, P. and Martin, J., 1970
  REBUILDING OF THE STOCK EXCHANGE: 1ST PHASE, *Structural Engineer*, Vol. 48, January. (4)
Dziewolski, R., 1973
  PRESTRESSED COMPOSITE STRUCTURES AND SPACE STRUCTURES IN THE CONSTRUCTION OF TALL BUILDINGS, Planning and Design of Tall Buildings, Proceedings of the 1972 ASCE-IABSE International Conference, ASCE, New York, Vol. 1a, No. 3-D1. (3)

EEI, 1978
  GLOSSARY OF ELECTRIC UTILITY TERMS, Statistical Committee, Edison Electric Institute, Washington, D.C. (2C)
Engineering, 1966
  BUILDING HIGH, *Engineering*, London, England, May 13, pp. 903–908. (3)
Engineering News-Record, 1961
  TIEBACKS—REMOVE CLUTTER IN EXCAVATION, *Engineering News-Record*, New York. Vol. 166, No. 23, June 8. (4)
Engineers Handbook, 1975
  SUBSIDENCE, *Engineers Handbook*, National Coal Board, London, England. (11)
Englert, A., 1975
  ELEVATOR PLANNING IN OFFICE BUILDINGS, Proceedings of the Hellenic Conference on Tall Buildings (Athens, Greece, October), Technical Chamber of Greece, Athens, Greece. (2A)
Environmental Advisory Service, 1976
  ENERGY CONSERVATION IN COMMERCIAL BUILDINGS, Pilkington Brothers Ltd., St. Helens, Lancs., England. (12A)
Essunger, G., 1973
  SUMMARY REPORT, Planning and Design of Tall Buildings, Proceedings of the 1972 ASCE-IABSE International Conference, Vol. 1a, ASCE, New York, pp. 1163–1169. (12A, 12B)
European Committee for Standardization, 1977
  SAFETY RULES FOR THE CONSTRUCTION AND INSTALLATION FOR LIFTS AND SERVICE LIFTS, CEN 81-1, European Committee for Standardization, Central Secretariat, Brussels, Belgium, October (Revised August 1978). (2A)

Fadum, R. E., 1948
  INFLUENCE VALUES FOR ESTIMATING STRESSES IN ELASTIC FOUNDATIONS, Proceedings of the 2nd International Conference on Soil Mechanics and Foundation Engineering, Vol. 3, pp. 77–84. (11)

Fang, H. Y., 1973
　　LANDSLIDES AND FOUNDATION DESIGN, Planning and Design of Tall Buildings, Proceedings of the 1972 ASCE-IABSE International Conference, Vol. 1a, ASCE, New York. (11)
Fang, H. Y., 1975
　　BASIC CONSIDERATION OF DESIGN, CONSTRUCTION AND MAINTENANCE OF TALL BUILDING FOUNDATIONS, Proceedings of the Pan-Pacific Conference on Tall Buildings (Honolulu, Hawaii, January), Arthur Chiu, University of Hawaii, Honolulu, Hawaii. (4, 11)
Fang, H. Y. and Cheng, H. K., 1974
　　LANDSLIDE AND TALL BUILDING FOUNDATION DESIGN, Proceedings of the Regional Conference on Tall Buildings (Bangkok, Thailand, January), Asian Institute of Technology, Bangkok, Thailand, pp. 781–795. (11)
Fang, H. Y., Dismuke, T. D. and Lim, H. P., 1975
　　TALL BUILDING FOUNDATION PROBLEMS IN LIMESTONE REGIONS, Proceedings of Hellenic Conference on Tall Buildings (Athens, Greece, October), Technical Chamber of Greece, Athens, Greece. (11)
Feagin, L. B., 1953
　　LATERAL LOAD TESTS ON GROUPS OF BATTERED AND VERTICAL PILES, Special Technical Publication No. 154, ASTM, Philadelphia, Pa. (11)
Feld, J., 1974
　　BUILDING FAILURES: FLOOR SUPPORT SHORING IN MULTI-STOREY CONSTRUCTION, Building Research and Practice, Vol. 2, No. 3. (4)
Felder, R., 1973
　　ELECTRICAL INSTALLATIONS (Elektrische Intallationen), Report 1—Tall Buildings (Berichte 1 Hochhaüser), Proceedings of Conference (Zurich, Switzerland, October), SIA-Fachgruppen für Architektur (FGA), Zurich, Switzerland, pp. 179–183. (2C)
Fellenius, B. H., 1963
　　DRIVING TESTS WITH ROCK-SHOES EQUIPPED WITH ROCK TIPS (in Swedish), Royal Swedish Academy of Engineering Sciences, Commission on Pile Research, Bulletin No. 1, Stockholm, Sweden. (11)
Fellenius, B. H., 1969a
　　NEGATIVE SKIN FRICTION ON PILES IN CLAY, A LITERATURE REVIEW, Report and Preliminary Report, Commission on Pile Research, Royal Swedish Academy of Engineering Sciences, No. 21, Stockholm, Sweden. (11)
Fellenius, B. H., 1969b
　　MODULUS OF ELASTICITY FOR PRECAST PILES (in Swedish), Vagoch Vattenbyggaren, Stockholm, Sweden, p. 33. (11)
Fellenius, B. H., 1971a
　　BENDING OF PILES DETERMINED BY INCLINOMETER MEASUREMENTS, presented to the 24th Annual Geotechnical Conference, held in Halifax, England. (11)
Fellenius, B. H., 1971b
　　NEGATIVE SKIN FRICTION ON LONG PILES DRIVEN IN CLAY, I: RESULTS OF A FULL-SCALE INVESTIGATION; II: GENERAL VIEWS AND DESIGN RECOMMENDATIONS, Swedish Geotechnical Institute, Proceedings No. 25, Stockholm, Sweden. (11)
Fellenius, B. H., 1971c
　　INFLUENCE OF PILE DRIVING ON SOIL COMPACTION, SOIL MOVEMENT AND BEARING CAPACTIY OF ADJACENT PILES, Proceedings of Conference on Pile Behavior, Discussion on Installation Procedures and Effects, Institution of Civil Engineers, London, England, pp. 144–145. (11)
Fellenius, B. H., 1973
　　PRECAST CONCRETE PILES, Planning and Design of Tall Buildings, Proceedings of the 1972 ASCE-IABSE International Conference, ASCE, New York, Vol. 1a, pp. 95–119. (11)
Fellenius, B. H. and Broms, B. B., 1969
　　NEGATIVE SKIN FRICTION FOR LONG PILES DDIVEN IN CLAY, Proceedings of the 7th Conference on Soil Mechanics and Foundation Engineering (Mexico City, Mexico), Vol. 2, pp. 93–98. (11)
Fellenius, B. H. and Haagen, T., 1969
　　A NEW PILE FORCE GAUGE FOR ACCURATE MEASUREMENT OF PILE

BEHAVIOUR, *Canadian Geotechnical Journal*, Vol. 6, No. 3, pp. 356–362. (11)

Fenoux, F., 1971
EXCAVATIONS IN CONGESTED URBAN AREAS (in French), *Annales de l'Institut Technique du Bâtiment et des Travaux Publics*, Paris, France, September. (11)

Finks, D. G. and Carroll, J. M., 1978
STANDARD HANDBOOK FOR ELECTRICAL ENGINEERS, 11th edition, McGraw-Hill Book Co., Inc., New York. (2C)

Fintel, M., 1968
STAGGERED WALL BEAMS FOR THE MULTISTORY BUILDINGS, *Civil Engineering*, ASCE, Vol. 38, No. 8, pp. 56–59. (3)

Fintel, M., 1971
RESPONSE OF BULIDINGS TO LATERAL FORCES, see ACI Committee 442. (3)

Fintel, M., 1974
HANDBOOK OF CONCRETE ENGINEERING, Van Nostrand Reinhold, New York. (4)

Finzi, L., 1968
LIGHT-GAGE FLOOR SYSTEMS PROVIDED TO INCLUDE UTILITIES, PROPOSALS AND EXPERIMENTS, Extrait du Rapport Final Huitième Congrès (New York, September), Association International des Ponts et Charpentes. (3)

Finzi, L., 1973
THE STRUCTURAL DESIGN OF TALL STEEL BUILDINGS, Proceedings of the National Conference on Tall Buildings (Sorrento, Italy, October), Collegio dei Tecnici Dell Acciaio, Milano, Italy. (3, 4)

Fiorato, A. E., Sozen, M. and Gamble, W. L., 1970
AN INVESTIGATION OF THE INTERACTION OF REINFORCED CONCRETE FRAMES WITH MASONRY FILLER WALLS, University of Illinois Civil Engineering Studies Report No. VILU-ENG-70-100, University of Illinois, Urbana, Ill. (12B)

Fleming, J. F., 1974
LATERAL TRUSS SYSTEMS IN HIGHRISE BUILDINGS, Proceedings of the National Conference on Tall Buildings (Bangkok, Thailand, January), Asian Institute of Technology, Bangkok, Thailand. (3)

Focht, J. A., 1964
OBSERVED HEAVE OF THREE EXCAVATIONS IN HOUSTON, TEXAS, presented at the ASCE Specialty Conference, held in Evanston, Ill., June. (11)

Focht, J. A., Jr., 1973
SOIL-STRUCTURE INTERACTION FOR TALL BUILDINGS, Planning and Design of Tall Buildings, Proceedings of the 1972 ASCE-IABSE International Conference, Vol. 1a, ASCE, New York. (11)

Focht, J. A., Khan, F. R. and Gemeinhardt, J. P., 1971
PERFORMANCE OF DEEP MAT FOUNDATION OF 52-STORY ONE SHELL PLAZA BUILDING, presented at ASCE Annual and National Environmental Engineering Meeting (St. Louis, Mo., October). (11)

Focht, J. A., Jr., Khan, F. R. and Gemeinhardt, J. P., 1974
PERFORMANCE OF DEEP MAT FOUNDATION OF 52-STORY ONE SHELL PLAZA BUILDING, Proceedings of the Regional Conference on Tall Buildings (Bangkok, Thailand, January), Asian Institute of Technology, Bangkok, Thailand. (11)

Forwood, B. S., 1974
THE DEVELOPMENT OF A DATA HANDLING FACILITY FOR A COMPUTER MODEL OF THE THERMAL ENVIRONMENT IN BUILDINGS, Department of Architectural Science, Report CR24, University of Sydney, N.S.W., Australia. (2B)

Fowler, J. R., 1973
BHP HOUSE, MELBOURNE, Proceedings of the National Conference on Tall Buildings (Sydney, Australia, August), Lehigh University, Bethlehem, Pa. (3)

Foxall, W. B., 1971
PROFESSIONAL CONSTRUCTION MANAGEMENT AND PROJECT ADMINISTRATION, *Architectural Record*, Vol. 149, No. 6, June, pp. 69–90. (4)

Freedom, B. G., 1973
HORIZONTAL TRANSPORTATION SYSTEMS, Joint Committee Report No. 9A, Lehigh University, Bethlehem, Pa. (2A)

Frohlich, O. K., 1953
ON THE SETTLING OF BUILDINGS COMBINED WITH DEVIATION FROM

THEIR ORIGINALLY VERTICAL POSITION, Proceedings of the 3rd International Conference on Soil Mechanics and Foundation Engineering (Zurich, Switzerland). (11)

Fruin, John J., 1970
PEDESTRIAN PLANNING AND DESIGN, Library of Congress, Catalogue No. 70-159312, Metropolitan Association of Urban Designers and Environmental Planners, Inc., New York. (2A)

Fuller, F. M., 1970
METHODS AND EQUIPMENT FOR THE INSTALLATION OF PILES IN FOREIGN COUNTRIES, *Design and Installation of Pile Foundations and Cellular Structures*, H. Y. Fang, ed., Envo Publishing Co., pp. 109–144. (11)

Garnett, M. W., 1973
THE AMP CENTER, SYDNEY, Proceedings of the National Conference on Tall Buildings (Sydney, Australia, August), Lehigh University, Bethlehem, Pa. (3, 4)

Gero, J. S. and Forwood, B. S., 1970
INTERACTIVE LIFT DESIGN-ANALYSIS, Report CR10, Department of Architectural Science, University of Sydney, N.S.W., Australia. (2A)

Gerwick, B. C., 1967
SLURRY-TRENCH TECHNIQUES FOR DIAPHRAGM WALLS IN DEEP FOUNDATION CONSTRUCTION, *Civil Engineering*, ASCE, Vol. 37, No. 12, pp. 70–72. (4)

Gerwick, B. C., 1973
HIGH CAPACITY PRESTRESSED CONCRETE PILING, Planning and Design of Tall Buildings, Proceedings of the 1972 ASCE-IABSE International Conference, ASCE, New York, Vol. 1a. (11)

Giangreco, E., 1969
TRENDS IN DESIGN OF STEEL CONSTRUCTIONS IN SEISMIC AREA (Orientamenti sulla Progettazione di Costruzioni in Acciaio in Zona Sismica), *Costruzioni Metalliche*, No. 6. (3)

Giangreco, E., 1971
PRESENT TRENDS IN THE ASEISMIC DESIGN OF METAL CONSTRUCTIONS (Tendances Actuelles dans le Calcul Antisismique des Constructions Métalliques), *Construction Métallique*, Paris, France, No. 3. (3)

Giangreco, E., 1973
GENERAL REPORT ON ITALIAN CONTRIBUTION TO TALL BUILDINGS, Proceedings of the National Conference on Tall Buildings (Sorrento, Italy, October), Collegio dei Tecnici dell'Acciaio, Milano, Italy. (4)

Gibson, R. E., 1967
SOME RESULTS CONCERNING DISPLACEMENTS AND STRESSES IN A NON-HOMOGENEOUS ELASTIC HALF SPACE, *Geotechnique*, London, England, Vol. 17, No. 1, pp. 58–67. (11)

Girault, P., 1964
A NEW TYPE OF PILE FOUNDATIONS, Proceedings of the Conference on Deep Foundations (Mexico City, Mexico), December. (11)

Glick, G. W., 1936
FOUNDATIONS OF THE NEW TELEPHONE BUILDING AT ALBANY, Proceedings of the 1st International Conference on Soil Mechanics and Foundation Engineering (Cambridge), Vol. I, p. 278. (11)

Goble, G. G., Moses, F. and Rausche, F., 1970
PREDICTION OF PILE BEHAVIOUR FROM DYNAMIC MEASUREMENTS, *Design and Installation of Pile Foundations and Cellular Structures*, H. Y. Fang, ed., Envo Publishing Co., pp. 281–296. (11)

Goble, G. G., Moses, F. and Rausche, F., 1971
A NEW TESTING PROCEDURE FOR AXIAL PILE STRENGTH, Offshore Technology Conference (Houston, Tex.), Paper OTC 1481. (11)

Godfrey, G. B., 1970
EXPOSED STEELWORK FOR MULTI-STOREY BUILDINGS, *Building Maintenance*, January, pp. 38–40. (12A)

Golder, H. Q., 1963
FLOATING FOUNDATIONS FOR A FACTORY BUILDING, *The Canadian Consulting Engineer*, Toronto, Canada, Vol. 5, No. 10, p. 65. (11)

Golder, H. Q., 1965
   STATE-OF-THE-ART OF FLOATING FOUNDATIONS, *Journal of the Soil Mechanics and Foundations Division*, ASCE, Vol. 91, No. SM2, Proc. Paper 4278, pp. 81–88. (11)
Golder, H. Q., 1971
   THE ALLOWABLE SETTLEMENT OF STRUCTURES, Proceedings of the 4th Pan-American Conference on Soil Mechanics and Foundation Engineering (San Juan, Puerto Rico). (11)
Goschy, B., 1975
   STRUCTURAL SYSTEMS (Tartoszerkezeti Kerdesek), Proceedings of the National Conference on Tall Buildings (Budapest, Hungary, May), Lehigh University, Bethlehem, Pa. (3)
Gould, J. P., 1970
   LATERAL PRESSURES ON RIGID PERMANENT STRUCTURES, presented at the June ASCE Specialty Conference on Lateral Stresses and Design of Earth Retaining Structures, held at Cornell University, Ithaca, N.Y. (11)
Grabowski, Z. and Zielinski, J., 1972
   INTERACTION OF SUBSOIL AND STRUCTURE OF TALL BUILDINGS, Proceedings of the Regional Conference on the Planning and Design of Tall Buildings (Warsaw, Poland, November), Warsaw Technical University, Polish Group of IABSE, Warsaw, Poland. (11).
Grabowski, Z. and Zielinski, J., 1973
   THE INFLUENCE OF VARYING OF SUBSOIL DEFORMABILITY MODULI FOR ESTIMATING SETTLEMENT AND FORCES IN TALL BUILDINGS, South American Regional Conference on Tall Buildings (Porto Alegre, Brazil, December), Sociedade de Engenharia do Rio Grande do Sul. (11)
Grainger, W. E. and Hancock, T. C., 1971
   WHITGIFT CENTRE, CROYDON, *Structural Engineer*, Vol. 49, February. (3)
Granholm, H., 1967
   THE BEARING CAPACITY OF REINFORCED CONCRETE PILES DRIVEN TO BED ROCK (in Swedish), Royal Swedish Academy of Engineering Science, Commission on Pile Research, Bulletin No. 10, Stockholm, Sweden, p. 58. (11)
Grant, R., Christian, J. T. and Vanmarcke, E. H., 1974
   DIFFERENTIAL SETTLEMENT OF BUILDINGS, *Journal of the Geotechnical Engineering Division*, ASCE, Vol. 100, No. GT9, Proc. Paper 10802, pp. 973–991. (11)
Grasshof, H., 1957
   INFLUENCE OF FLEXURAL RIGIDITY OF SUPERSTRUCTURE ON THE DISTRIBUTION OF CONTACT PRESSURE AND BENDING MOMENTS ON AN ELASTIC COMBINED FOOTING, Proceedings of the 4th International Conference on Soil Mechanics and Foundation Engineering (London, England), Vol. I, p. 300. (11)
Gunnar Birkerts and Associates, Architects, 1973
   SUSPENDED BANK BUILDING: FEDERAL RESERVE BANK AT MINNEAPOLIS, *Acier-Stahl-Steel*, Brussels, Belgium, June, pp. 250–251. (3)

HUD, 1969
   TOMORROW'S TRANSPORTATION—NEW SYSTEMS FOR THE URBAN FUTURE, Library of Congress Catalogue No. 68-61300, U.S. Government Printing Office, U.S. Department of Housing and Urban Development, Washington, D.C. (2A)
Habib, P. and Puyo, A., 1970
   STABILITY OF FONDATIONS OF STRUCTURES OF GREAT HEIGHT (in French), *Annales de l'Institut Technique du Bâtiment et des Travaux Publics*, Paris, France, No. 275, November. (11)
Halpern, R. C., 1973
   CONTROL OF THE CONSTRUCTION PROCESS, Planning of Tall Buildings, Proceedings of the 1972 ASCE-IABSE International Conference, ASCE, New York, Vol. 1a, No. 4-2. (4)
Hanna, T. H., 1968
   THE BENDING OF LONG H-SECTION PILES, *Canadian Geotechnical Journal*, Vol. 5, No. 3, pp. 150–172. (11)
Hanna, T. H., 1971
   THE DISTRIBUTION OF LOAD IN LONG PILES, *Sols-Soils*, No. 22-23, pp. 5–13. (11)

Hardin, B. O. and Drnevich, V., 1970
SHEAR MODULUS AND DAMPING IN SOILS: I, MEASUREMENT AND PA-
RAMETER EFFECTS; II, DESIGN EQUATIONS AND CURVES, Technical Report
UK4 27-70-CE 2 and 3, College of Engineering, University of Kentucky, Lexington, Ky.
(11)

Hellers, B. G. and Sahlin, S., 1971
STRESSES, CRACKS AND MATERIAL FATIGUE WHEN DRIVING REINFORCED
MODEL CONCRETE PILES (in Swedish), Royal Swedish Academy of Engineering
Sciences, Commission on Pile Research, Bulletin No. 14, Stockholm, Sweden, p. 109. (11)

Hellman, L., 1967
ON DRIVING END BEARING PILES TO REFUSAL (in Swedish), *Byggnadskonst* 8,
Stockholm, Sweden. (11)

Hellman, L., 1971
INVESTIGATION ON PILES FOR NORRKOPING KRAFTVARMEVERK, private
corresepondence. (11)

Helmfrid, H. P., 1971
AUTOMATIC PILE DRIVING, TESTING OF EQUIPMENT AND A COMPARISON
OF AUTOMATIC AND CONVENTIONAL PILE DRIVING (in Swedish), Report C
737, National Swedish Council for Building Research, Stockholm, Sweden. (11)

Hesselberg, E. H., 1974
MAJOR HOSPITAL TRANSPORT, *Elevator World*, Vol. XXII, No. 10. (2A)

Hetenyi, M., 1946
BEAMS ON ELASTIC FOUNDATION, The University of Michigan Press, Ann Arbor,
Mich. (11)

Higgins, L. R., 1973
DEMOLITION: NEWEST DIMENSION OF MODERN BLASTING, *Construction
Methods and Equipment*, Vol. 55, No. 1, pp. 58–65. (4)

Hiramoto, T., Mitsui, T. and Imamaka, M., 1974
SPEED UP OF HIGH-RISE ESCALATORS, *Elevator World*, Vol. XXII, No. 5. (2A)

Hisatoku, T. and Nishikawa, F., 1973
MIXED AND COMPOSITE CONCRETE AND STEEL SYSTEMS, Planning and Design
of Tall Buildings, Proceedings of the 1972 ASCE-IABSE International Conference,
ASCE, New York, Vol. 1a, No. 3-6. (3)

Ho, C., 1974
HYDRAULIC SERVICES IN A HIGH RISE BUILDING, Proceedings, Conference on
Tall Buildings (Kuala Lumpur, Malaysia, December), Institution of Engineers, Kuala
Lumpur, Malaysia, pp. 5–34—5–38. (2B)

Horvat, E., 1972
FOUNDATION DESIGN, 6th Regional Conference Proceedings (Delft, The Netherlands,
May), Lehigh University, Bethlehem, Pa. (11)

Horvat, E. and van der Veen, C., 1973
EFFECTS OF FOUNDATIONS ON ADJACENT STRUCTURES, Planning and Design
of Tall Buildings, Proceedings of the 1972 ASCE-IABSE International Conference, Vol.
1a, ASCE, New York. (11)

Hrennikoff, A., 1950
ANALYSIS OF PILE FOUNDATIONS WITH BATTER PILES, *Transactions*, ASCE,
Vol. 115, pp. 351–381. (11)

Hui, T. W. and Ladchumanan, K., 1974
FOUNDATION OF A 17-STOREY BUILDING ON A PINNACLED LIMESTONE
FORMATION IN KUALA LUMPUR, Proceedings, Conference on Tall Buildings
(Kuala Lumpur, Malaysia, December), Institution of Engineers, Kuala Lumpur,
Malaysia. (11)

Hunt, C. L. and Jaso, J., 1970
SKYSCRAPER FRAME WELDED BY A SEMI-AUTOMATIC PROCESS, *Metal
Construction*, Vol. 2, July. (4)

Huntington, W. C., 1957
EARTH PRESSURES AND RETAINING WALLS, John Wiley and Sons, Inc., New
York. (11)

Hurd, M. K., 1973
FORMWORK FOR CONCRETE, 3rd ed., American Concrete Institute, Detroit, Mich. (4)

Hutcheon, N. B. and Shorter, G. W., 1968
SMOKE PROBLEMS IN HIGH-RISE BUILDINGS, *ASHRAE Journal*, Vol. 10, No. 9, pp. 57–61. (2B)

Hye, T. E., 1974
PLANNING OF TELECOMS SERVICES FOR TALL BUILDINGS, Proceedings, Conference on Tall Buildings (Kuala Lumpur, Malaysia, December), Institution of Engineers, Kuala Lumpur, Malaysia, pp. 5–41—5–44. (2C)

IEEE, 1944
RECOMMENDED PRACTICE FOR ELECTRICAL POWER SYSTEMS IN COMMERCIAL BUILDINGS, STD-241-1944, Institute of Electrical and Electronic Engineers, New York. (2C)

IEEE, 1974
RECOMMENDED PRACTICE FOR ELECTRICAL POWER SYSTEMS IN COMMERCIAL BUILDINGS, STD-241-1974, Institute of Electrical and Electronic Engineers, New York. (2C)

Ikeda, T., 1974
CONSTRUCTION METHODS FOR HIGH-RISE BUILDINGS, Proceedings of the National Conference on Tall Buildings (Tokyo, Japan, August), Architectural Institute of Japan, Tokyo, Japan. (4)

Inouye, U., ed., 1964
PLANNING OF BUILDING SERVICE SYSTEMS FOR THE HIGH RISE BUILDINGS (Cho koso Kentiku no Setsubi Keikaku), Shokokusha Co., Tokyo, Japan, October. (2B)

Inouye, U., ed., 1971
SYSTEM DESIGN OF THE BUILDING SERVICE SYSTEMS FOR THE HIGH RISE BUILDING (Cho koso Kentiku Setsubi no Sisutemu Desain), Chugai Shuppan Co., Tokyo, Japan, September. (2B)

Inouye, U., 1974
HVAC AND PLUMBING SYSTEM OF JAPANESE HIGH RISE BUILDINGS, *Journal of SHASE*, Vol. 48, No. 6 (in Japanese). (2B)

Institution of Civil Engineers, 1966
LARGE BORED PILES, Proceedings of the Symposium of the Institution of Civil Engineers, London, England. (4).

Institution of Civil Engineers, 1969
SAFETY ON CONSTRUCTION SITES, Proceedings of a conference organized by the Institution of Civil Engineers under the auspices of the Council of Engineering Institutions, Institution of Civil Engineers, London, England, March. (4)

International Organization for Standardization, 1976
MECHANICAL TRANSPORTING SYSTEMS FOR BUILDING CONSTRUCTION, Association Française de Normalization Pour Europe, ISO/TC 59/SC-12, Paris, France, November. (2A)

Ionescu, I. and Ungureanu N., 1975
CONSIDERATIONS OF THE ANALYSIS OF SILOS AND TOWER CONSTRUCTION ON RAFT FOUNDATION (Consideratii Privind Calculul Silozurilor si Constructiilor Informa de Tern, Fundate pe Radier General), Reinforced Concrete Tall Buildings, Proceedings of Conference (Iasi, Romania, October), Consiliul National al Inginerilor si Tehnicienilor, Iasi, Romania. (11)

Irwin, A. W. and Bain, W. R. L., 1974
PLANNED OBSOLESCENCE AND DEMOLITION OF TALL BUILDINGS, *Build International*, Vol. 7, No. 6, pp. 549–561. (4)

Ishizaki, H., 1974
ON THE WIND RESISTANT DESIGN OF EXTERIOR CLADDING, Proceedings of the National Conference on Tall Buildings (Tokyo, Japan, August), Architectural Institute of Japan, Tokyo, Japan, pp. 85–86. (12A)

Ito, T., 1971
STRUCTURAL SYSTEM COMPOSED OF STEEL FRAME AND SHEAR WALLS, Proceedings, 3rd Regional Conference on Planning and Design of Tall Buildings (Tokyo, Japan, September), pp. 25–35. (3)

Iyengar, S. H., 1973

STRUCTURAL SYSTEMS FOR TWO ULTRA HIGH-RISE STRUCTURES, Proceedings, Australian and New Zealand Conference on the Planning and Design of Tall Buildings (Sydney, Australia, August), Section 10, pp. 528–543. (3)

JIS A 4301, 1970
SIZE OF CAR AND HOISTWAY OF ELEVATORS, Japanese Industrial Standard, Japanese Standards Association, Tokyo, Japan. (2A)

Jackson, N., 1974
CONCRETE QUALITY CONTROL, Proceedings of the National Conference on Tall Buildings (Bangkok, Thailand, January), Asian Institute of Technology, Bangkok, Thailand. (4)

Jackson, W. T., Perez, J. Y. and Lacroix, Y., 1974
FOUNDATION, CONSTRUCTION AND PERFORMANCE FOR A 34-STOREY BUILDING IN ST. LOUIS, Geotechnique, London, England, Vol. 24, No. 1. (4)

Jain, O. P. and Palaniswamy, S. P., 1973
EFFECT OF CONSTRUCTION STAGES ON THE STRESSES IN MULTI-STORIED FRAMES, Proceedings of the National Conference on Tall Buildings (New Delhi, India, January), Indian National Group of IABSE, New Delhi, India. (4)

Jaros, Baum, and Bolles (staff), 1978
THE PERFECT OFFICE BUILDING, Specifying Engineer, Vol. 39, No. 2, pp. 67–87. (2A, 2B)

Jendele, M., 1971
HIGH BUILDINGS WITH A CONCRETE BEARING SYSTEM IN CZECHOSLOVAKIA, Proceedings of the National Conference on Tall Buildings (Prague, Czechoslovakia, September), Lehigh University, Bethlehem, Pa. (3, 4)

Jendele, M., 1973
STRUCTURAL SYSTEMS OF TALL REINFORCED CONCRETE BUILDINGS, Proceedings of the National Conference on Tall Buildings (Bratislava, Czechoslovakia, April, 1971), Lehigh University, Bethlehem, Pa. (3)

Jernstedt, G. W., 1975
IMPLEMENTING URBAN CENTER REDEVELOPMENT BY EVOLUTION WITH THE HORIZONTAL BUILDING CONCEPT, unpublished communication to the Joint Committee, October. (2A)

Jerus, G. R., 1972a
FIRE SAFETY IN TALL BUILDINGS, 6th Regional Conference Proceedings (Delft, The Netherlands, May), Lehigh University, Pa., p. 27. (2B)

Jerus, G. R., 1972b
PLUMBING, 6th Regional Conference Proceedings (Delft, The Netherlands, May), Lehigh University, Pa., p. 28. (2B)

Jerus, G. R., 1973
PLUMBING AND FIRE PROTECTION, Planning and Design of Tall Buildings, Proceedings of the 1972 ASCE-IABSE International Conference, Vol. 1a, ASCE, New York, pp. 327–339. (2B)

Johannessen, I. J. and Bjerrum, L., 1965
MEASUREMENT OF THE COMPRESSION OF A STEEL PILE TO ROCK DUE TO SETTLEMENT OF THE SURROUNDING CLAY, Proceedings of the 7th International Conference on Soil Mechanics and Foundation Engineering, Vol. 2, pp. 261–264. (11)

Johnson, J. A., 1971
A TECHNIQUE FOR THE SETTLEMENT AND STRESS ANALYSIS OF MAT FOUNDATIONS USING THE FINITE ELEMENT METHOD, thesis presented to Vanderbilt University at Nashville, Tenn., in December, in partial fulfillment of the requirements for the degree of Doctor of Philosophy. (11)

Johnson, R. P., 1975
COMPOSITE STRUCTURES OF STEEL AND CONCRETE, VOL. 1, Beams, Columns, Frames and Applications in Building, Crosby Lockwood Staples, London, England, October. (3)

Jorg, S., 1975
THE WEST GERMAN STATE OF ART OF TALL BUILDINGS, QUESTIONS CONCERNING UNUSUAL AND OUTSTANDING ASPECTS OF TALL MULTI-

STOREY BUILDINGS (Maga es Kozepmagas Epitmenyek Kulonleges Tervezesi es Kivitelezesi Kerdesei), Proceedings of the National Conference on Tall Buildings (Budapest, Hungary, May). (4)

Jossa, P., 1975
INTRODUCTION TO THE STUDY OF TALL BUILDINGS (Introduzione allo Studio degli Edifici Alti), Editore Liguori, Napoli, Italy. (3)

Joustra, K., 1971
PRECAST PILES IN HOLLAND, private communication to B. H. Fellenius, Montrél, Canada. (11)

Kajfasz, S., 1973
INTERACTION APPROACH IN POLAND, Planning and Design of Tall Buildings, Proceedings of the 1972 ASCE-IABSE International Conference, Vol. 1a, ASCE, New York, pp. 1149–1151. (12A, 12B)

Kajitani, H., Komuro, H., Sudo, S. and Ishii, H., 1973
NIPPON STEEL BUILDING AT URBAN RENEWAL OF TOKIWABASHI DISTRICT (COMPLEX), Proceedings of the National Conference on Tall Buildings (Tokyo, Japan, August), Architectural Institute of Japan, Tokyo, Japan. (3)

Kang, M., 1959
ANALYSIS OF SHALLOW FOUNDATIONS (Berechnung von Flachgrundungen), Wilhelm Ernst und Sohn, Berlin, Germany. (11)

Kanjanavanit, R., 1974
INVESTIGATION OF THE SETTLEMENT OF KIAN GWAN BUILDING AND THE UNDERPINNING OF THE FOUNDATION, Proceedings of the Regional Conference on Tall Buildings (Bangkok, Thailand, January), Asian Institute of Technology, Bangkok, Thailand. (11)

Katz, A. R., 1974
GENERAL DESIGN CRITERIA FOR ELEVATOR SYSTEMS, Elevator World, Vol. XXII, No. 10. (2A)

Kauffman, J. E. and Christensen, J. F., 1972
LIGHTING HANDBOOK, 5th edition, Illuminating Engineering Society, New York. (2C)

Kausel, E. M. and Roesset, J. M., 1974
SOIL-STRUCTURE INTERACTION PROBLEMS FOR NUCLEAR CONTAINMENT STRUCTURES, presented to the ASCE Power Division Specialty Conference, held in Boulder, Colo. (11)

Kausel, E. M. and Roesset, J. M., 1975
DYNAMIC STIFFNESS OF CIRCULAR FOUNDATIONS, Journal of the Engineering Mechanics Division, ASCE, Vol. 101, No. EM6, Proc. Paper 11800, pp. 771–785. (11)

Kausel, E. M., Roesset, J. M. and Christian, J. T., 1976
NONLINEAR BEHAVIOR IN SOIL-STRUCTURE INTERACTION, Journal of the Geotechnical Engineering Division, ASCE, Vol. 102, No. GT11, Proc. Paper 12579, pp. 1159–1170. (11)

Kausel, E. M., Roesset, J. M. and Wass, G., 1975
DYNAMIC ANALYSIS OF FOOTINGS ON LAYERED MEDIA, Journal of the Engineering Mechanics Division, ASCE, Vol. 101, No. EM5, Proc. Paper 11652, pp. 679–693. (11)

Kavanagh, T. C., 1971
ARCHITECTURAL STRUCTURAL INTERACTION, 5th Regional Conference Proceedings (Prague, Czechoslovakia, September), Lehigh University, Bethlehem, Pa., p. 37. (12A, 12B)

Kavyrchine, M., 1973
REINFORCED, PRECAST AND PRESTRESSED CONCRETE, Planning and Design of Tall Buildings, Proceedings of the 1972 ASCE-IABSE International Conference, ASCE, New York, Vol. 1a, No. 3-1. (3)

Kawasaki, N. and Rahulan, G., 1974
CONSTRUCTION OF THE D.B.S. BUILDING, SINGAPORE, Proceedings of the National Conference on Tall Buildings (Kuala Lumpur, Malaysia, December), Institution of Engineers, Kuala Lumpur, Malaysia. (4)

Kebo, V., 1973
SOME EXPERIENCE ACQUIRED BY ASSEMBLY OF STEEL STRUCTURES OF MULTISTOREY BUILDINGS, Proceedings of the National Conference on Tall Buildings (Bratislava, Czechoslovakia, April), Lehigh University, Bethlehem, Pa. (4)

Kee, C. F., 1974

THE BEHAVIOR OF RAFT FOUNDATIONS IN LATERITIC SOILS, Proceedings, Conference on Tall Buildings (Kuala Lumpur, Malaysia, December), Institution of Engineers, Kuala Lumpur, Malaysia. (11)
Khan, F., 1969
TALL STEEL STRUCTURES, THE LATEST TRENDS, *Construction News*, December 11. (3)
Khan, F., 1971
LIGHTWEIGHT CONCRETE FOR TOTAL DESIGN OF ONE SHELL PLAZA, Paper SP 29-1, American Concrete Institute, pp. 1–14. (3)
Khan, F., 1973
NEWER STRUCTURAL SYSTEMS AND THEIR EFFECT ON THE CHANGING SCALE OF CITIES, Proceedings of the National Conference on Tall Buildings (Zurich, Switzerland, October), SIA-Fachgruppen Fur Bruckenbau Und Hochbau (FBH) Und Fur Architektur (FGA), Zurich, Switzerland. (3)
Khan, F., 1974
A CRISIS IN DESIGN—THE NEW ROLE OF THE STRUCTURAL ENGINEER, Proceedings of the Conference on Tall Buildings (Kuala Lumpur, Malaysia, December), Institution of Civil Engineers, Kuala Lumpur, Malaysia. (3)
Khan, F., 1975
TALL BUILDINGS—RECENT DEVELOPMENTS IN STRUCTURAL SYSTEMS AND ARCHITECTURAL EXPRESSIONS, Proceedings of the National Conference on Tall Buildings (Athens, Greece, October), Technical Chamber of Commerce, Athens, Greece. (3)
Khan, F. and Amin, N. R., 1973
ANALYSIS AND DESIGN OF FRAMED TUBE STRUCTURES FOR TALL CONCRETE BUILDINGS, *Structural Engineer*, Vol. 51, March. (3)
Khan, F. R. and Fintel, M., 1968a
EFFECTS OF COLUMN EXPOSURE IN TALL STRUCTURES—DESIGN CONSIDERATION AND FIELD OBSERVATIONS OF BUILDINGS, *ACI Journal*, American Concrete Institute, Vol. 65, No. 65-8, February, pp. 99–110. (12B)
Khan, F. R. and Fintel, M., 1968b
EFFECT OF COLUMN TEMPERATURE, CREEP, AND SHRINKAGE IN TALL STRUCTURES, Final Report, 8th Congress IABSE, New York, September, pp. 1015–1017. (12B)
Khan, F. R. and Nassetta, A. F., 1970
TEMPERATURE EFFECTS IN TALL STEEL FRAMED BUILDINGS, Part 3—Design Considerations, *Engineering Journal*, AISC, October, pp. 121–131. (12B)
Kheong, W. W., 1974
ELECTRICITY SUPPLY TO TALL BUILDINGS IN KUALA LUMPUR, Proceedings, Conference on Tall Buildings (Kuala Lumpur, Malaysia, December), Institution of Engineers, Kuala Lumpur, Malaysia, pp. 5–17—5–28. (2C)
Kittides, C. P., 1974
CONSTRUCTION MANAGEMENT: STATE OF THE ART IN 1974, *P. E. Professional Engineer*, Vol. 44, No. 6, June, pp. 22–26. (4)
Knill, B., 1976
1976—THE REAL WORLD MATCHES OLD PREDICTIONS, Materials Handling Engineering Industrial Publishing Co., Cleveland, Ohio, January. (2A)
Knowles, P. R., 1973
COMPOSITE STEEL AND CONCRETE CONSTRUCTION, John Wiley and Sons, Inc., New York. (4)
Komendant, A. E., 1972
CONTEMPORARY CONCRETE STRUCTURES, McGraw-Hill Book Co., Inc., New York. (4)
Konig, G., 1973
CAST-IN-PLACE REINFORCED CONCRETE SYSTEMS, Planning and Design of Tall Buildings, Proceedings of the 1972 ASCE-IABSE International Conference, ASCE, New York, Vol. 1a, No. 3-7. (3)
Konig, G., 1975
TALL REINFORCED CONCRETE BUILDINGS (Hochhaüser aus Stahl-Beton), Beton-Kalender, Wilhelm Ernst & Sohn, Berlin, Germany. (3)

Kort, C. L., 1972
VERTICAL TRANSPORTATION, 6th Regional Conference Proceedings (Delft, The Netherlands, May), Lehigh University, Bethlehem, Pa., p. 28. (2A)

Kort, C. L., 1973
VERTICAL TRANSPORTATION, Planning and Design of Tall Buildings, Proceedings of the 1972 ASCE-IABSE International Conference, Vol. 1a, ASCE, New York, pp. 341–348. (2A)

Kort, C. L., 1974
SKYSCRAPER TRANSPORT TRENDS, Elevator World, Vol. XXII, No. 10. (2A)

Kostem, C. N., 1970
THE STRESSES IN FOLDED PLATE ROOF TRAVERSES, Proceedings of Symposium, International Association for Shell and Spatial Structures (Vienna, Austria), Vol. 2. (3)

Kostem, C. N., 1973
OPTIMUM SHAPED PNEUMATIC ROOFS, Proceedings of the International Symposium on Industrialized Spatial and Shell Structures (Kielce, Poland). (3)

Kozak, J., 1973a
STRUCTURAL SYSTEMS OF TALL BUILDINGS IN STEEL OR COMBINED STEEL AND CONCRETE, Proceedings, 10th Regional Conference on Planning and Design of Tall Buildings (Bratislava, Czechoslovakia, April) pp. 118–134. (3)

Kozak, J., 1973b
STRUCTURAL SYSTEMS OF TALL BUILDINGS WITH CORE STRUCTURES, Planning and Design of Tall Buildings, Proceedings of the 1972 ASCE-IABSE International Conference, ASCE, New York, Vol. 1a, No. 3-8. (3)

Krishnamurthy, V. A., 1973
ELECTRICAL AND MECHANICAL SERVICES IN TALL BUILDINGS, Proceedings of National Conference on Tall Buildings (Delhi, India, January), Indian National Group of IABSE, New Delhi, India, pp. V17–V34. (2B, 2C)

Krol, W., 1964
STATICS OF REINFORCED CONCRETE FOUNDATIONS WITH CONSIDERATION OF THE RIGIDITY OF THE SUPERSTRUCTURE (Statyka Fundamentow Zelbetowych z Uwzglednieniem Sztywnosci Nadbudowy), Arkady, Warszawa; (Die Statik der Stahlbeton-fundamente unter Berucksichtung der Steifigkeit des Uberbaues), Wilhelm Ernst und Sohn, Berlin-München-Dusseldorf; (Statique des foundations en beton armé, compte tenu de la rigidité de la superstructure), Dunod, Paris. (11)

Krol, W., 1966
ON PILING IN MINING SUBSIDENCE AREAS (in Polish), Inzynieria i Budownictwo, No. 2. (11)

Krol, W. 1970
PROTECTION OF BUILDINGS AGAINST DESTRUCTION DUE TO MINING (in Polish), Budownictwo Betonowe, Vol. XII, Part 1, pp. 558–603. (11)

Krol, W. and Przybyla, H., 1974
DESIGN OF TALL BUILDINGS IN MINING SUBSIDENCE AREAS IN POLAND, unpublished communication to the Council. (11)

Krol, W., Badora, T. and Kawulok, M., 1973
ON THE PREFABRICATED BASEMENTS OF BUILDINGS IN MINING SUBSIDENCE AREAS (in Polish), Ochrona Terenow Gorniczych, No. 24. (11)

Krsmanovic, D., 1965
FOUNDATION BEAMS RESTING ON HOMOGENEOUS AND ISOTROPIC SOIL (Poutres de foundation reposant sur le sol homogène et isotrope), Société Savante de Bosnie-Herzegovine, Sarajevo, Yugoslavia. (11)

Kshirsagar, S. R. and Raman, V., 1973
PUBLIC HEALTH SERVICES IN TALL BUILDINGS, National Conference on Tall Buildings (New Delhi, India, January), Indian National Group of IABSE, New Delhi, India, pp. IV11–IV29. (2B)

Kubo, Y., Kanno, H., Mori, S., Uchino, M. and Funahashi, I., 1974
A TALL BUILDING ON DEEP AND INCLINED BEARING STRATUM, Proceedings of the National Conference on Tall Buildings (Tokyo, Japan, August), Architectural Institute of Japan, Tokyo, Japan. (11)

Larm, S., 1975

A SYSTEM OF COMPUTER PROGRAMS FOR DESIGNING, SELECTING AND ANALYSING AIR CONDITIONING SYSTEMS, Hellenic Conference on Tall Buildings (Athens, Greece, October), Technical Chamber of Greece, Athens, Greece. (2B)

Lenke, R. E., 1971
ARCHITECTURAL-STRUCTURAL INTERACTION, 2nd Regional Conference Proceedings (Bled, Yugoslavia, May), Lehigh University, Bethlehem, Pa., pp. 111–118. (12A)

Lenke, R. E., 1971
ARCHITECTURAL-STRUCTURAL INTERACTION, 2nd Regional Conference Proceedings (Bled, Yugoslavia, May), Lehigh University, Bethlehem, Pa., pp. 33–34. (12B)

Lenke, R. E., 1973
THEME REPORT, Planning and Design of Tall Buildings, Proceedings of the 1972 ASCE-IABSE International Conference, Vol. 1a, ASCE, New York, pp. 1057–1067. (12A, 12B)

Lerch, C. W., 1974
PERSONAL RAPID TRANSIT, Elevator World, Vol. XXII, No. 10. (2A)

Levitt, R. E., 1969
EFFECT OF TOP MANAGEMENT ON SAFETY CONSTRUCTION, Technical Report No. 196, Department of Civil Engineering, Stanford University, Stanford, Calif. (4)

Lewicki, B. and Cholewicki, A., 1972
STRUCTURAL DESIGN OF TALL CONCRETE BUILDINGS, Proceedings of the National Conference on Tall Buildings (Warsaw, Poland, November), Warsaw Technical University, Warsaw, Poland. (3)

Lewicki, G., Denar, K. and Kapron, M., 1975
ANALYSIS OF WORK OF SECONDARY STRUCTURAL SYSTEM IN BUILDING CORNER, Symposium on Bearing Walls (II Sympozjum CIB W23A). (3)

Lewis, W. S., 1974
INTEGRATED INDUSTRIAL TRANSPORT, Elevator World, Vol. XXII, No. 10. (2A)

Lewis, W. S., 1976
OSCILLATION OF ELEVATOR CABLES, unpublished communication to the Council. (2A)

Liauw, T. C., 1974
EVOLUTION OF NEW STRUCTURAL SYSTEMS FOR TALL BUILDINGS, Proceedings of the National Conference on Tall Buildings (Bangkok, Thailand, January), Asian Institute of Technology, Bangkok, Thailand. (3)

Libbey, R. M., 1975
DESIGN AND CONSTRUCTION OF THE PACIFIC TRADE CENTER BUILDING, Proceedings of the National Conference on Tall Buildings (Honolulu, Hawaii, January), Arthur Chiu, University of Hawaii, Honolulu, Hawaii. (4)

Lie, T. T. and McGuire, J. H., 1975
CONTROL OF SMOKE IN HIGH-RISE BUILDINGS, Fire Technology, Vol. 11, No. 1, February, pp. 15–22. (2B)

Lloyd, D. O., 1974
SOLID WASTE DISPOSAL FROM TALL BUILDINGS, Proceedings, Conference on Tall Buildings (Kuala Lumpur, Malaysia, December), Institution of Engineers, Kuala Lumpur, Malaysia, pp. 5–9 to 5–16. (2B)

Lo, M., 1975
SUBSURFACE INVESTIGATION—HONOLULU MUNICIPAL BUILDING, Pan-Pacific Tall Buildings Conference (Honolulu, Hawaii, January), University of Hawaii, Honolulu, Hawaii. (11)

Lohmann, S., 1973
FACADE WALL DESIGN ON THE TALL BUILDING (Fassadentechnik am Hochhaus), Report 1—Tall Buildings (Berichte 1 Hochhaüser), Proceedings of Conference (Zurich, Switzerland, October), SIA-Fachgruppen für Bruckenbau und Hochbau (FBH) und für Architektur (FGA), Zurich, Switzerland, p. 76. (12A)

Lousberg, E., 1957
CALCULATION OF THE DISTRIBUTION OF SOIL REACTIONS UNDERNEATH ECCENTRICALLY LOADED FOOTINGS, Proceedings of the 4th International Conference on Soil Mechanics and Foundations Engineering (London, England), p. 355. (11)

Lowery, L. L., Hirsch, T. J., Eduanus, T. C., Coyle, H. M. and Samson, C. H., 1969

PILE DRIVING ANALYSIS—STATE-OF-THE-ART, Research Report 33-13, Texas Transportation Institute, Texas A and M University, College Station, Tex. (11)

Lubinski, M. and Kwiatkowski, J., 1972
STATICAL AND STRUCTURAL SYSTEMS OF TALL STEEL BUILDINGS, Proceedings, Regional Conference on Planning and Design of Tall Buildings (Warsaw, Poland, November), Vol. 1, pp. 141–165. (3)

Lysmer, J. and Waas, G., 1972
SHEAR WAVES IN PLANE INFINITE STRUCTURES, Journal of the Engineering Mechanics Division, ASCE, Vol. 98, No. EM1, Proc. Paper 8716, pp. 85–105. (11)

Mansur, C. I., Hunter, A. H. and Davisson, M. T., 1964
PILE DRIVING AND LOADING TESTS AT LOCK AND DAM NO. 4, ARKANSAS RIVER AND TRIBUTARIES, U.S. Army Engineer District, Little Rock, Ark. (11)

Manu, G. and Sandor, Z., 1975
RETICULAR TALL BUILDINGS IN THE PRAHOVA DISTRICT (Constructii Inalte Reticulare in Judetul Prahova), Proceedings of the National Conference on Tall Buildings (Iasi, Romania, October), Vol. 1, Consiliul National al Inginerilor si Tehnicienilor, Iasi, Romania. (3)

Marais, G. H., 1975
AIR-CONDITIONING IN HIGH-RISE BUILDINGS, South African Conference on Tall Buildings (Johannesburg, South Africa, November), Hortors Printers, Johannesburg, South Africa. (2B)

Marcuson, W. F., III and Wahls, H. E., 1972
TIME EFFECTS ON DYNAMIC SHEAR MODULUS OF CLAYS, Journal of the Soil Mechanics and Foundations Division, ASCE, Vol. 98, No. SM12, Proc. Paper 9442, pp. 1359–1373. (11)

Marmot, A. and Gero, J. S., 1972
TOWARDS THE DEVELOPMENT OF AN EMPIRICAL MODEL FOR ELEVATOR LOBBIES, Report CR17, Department of Architectural Science, University of Sydney, N.S.W., Australia. (2A)

Marwah, H., 1973
CONSTRUCTION PROBLEMS OF FOUNDATIONS OF TALL BUILDINGS, Proceedings of National Conference on Tall Buildings (New Delhi, India, January), Indian National Group of IABSE, New Delhi, India. (11)

Masopust, R., 1973
PROBLEMS OF THE CALCULATION OF FOOTING SLABS ON A DEFORMABLE SOIL FOUNDATION FOR TALL BUILDINGS AND TALL STRUCTURES, 10th Regional Conference Proceedings (Bratislava, Czechoslovakia, April), CSTVA-Czechoslovak Scientific and Technical Association, Bratislava, Czechoslovakia. (11)

Matallana, A. and Gustavo, A., 1973
FOUNDATION WITHIN THE URBAN PERIMETER (Estructuras Para Cimentaciones Profundas Dentro Del Perimetro Urbano), Proceedings of the National Conference on Tall Buildings (Bogotá, Colombia, September), Colombia School of Engineering, Bogotá, Colombia. (11)

Matsushita, K. and Uchida, Y., 1973
HIGH-RISE BUILDING CONSTRUCTION DESIGN IN JAPAN AND ASIA, Planning and Design of Tall Buildings, Proceedings of the 1972 ASCE-IABSE International Conference, Vol. 1a, ASCE, New York, pp. 1067–1079. (12A, 12B)

Maurer, A. H., 1974
THE TRANSPORT SYSTEMS DIVISION, Elevator World, Vol. XXII, No. 10. (2A)

Mazzolani, F. M., 1974
DEVELOPMENT OF STRUCTURAL SCHEMES IN THE FIELD OF TALL BUILDINGS: SKYSCRAPER OR MEGA-STRUCTURE? (Evoluzione degli Schemi Strutturali nel Campo degli Edifici a Molti Piani: Grattacielo o Macro-Struttura), Ingegneri, Milan, Italy. (3)

Mazzolani, F. M. and Ramasco, R., 1971
STATICS OF FRAMED SPACE SYSTEMS WITH WALLS VARIOUSLY SHAPED (Statica dei Sistemi Intelaiati Spaziali con Irridimenti di Forma Qualsiasi), Giornale del Genio Civile, No. 3. (3)

McCue, G. M. and Kost, G., 1976

THE INTERACTION OF BUILDING COMPONENTS DURING EARTHQUAKES, National Technical Information Service, NSFIRA 7423153-MBT PB 258 326, Springfield, Va. (12B)

McGrath, W. L., 1974
COMFORT AND CONSERVATION IN LARGE BUILDING ENVIRONMENTAL CONTROL, Proceedings, Conference on Tall Buildings (Kuala Lumpur, Malaysia, December), Institution of Engineers, Kuala Lumpur, Malaysia, pp. 5-1—5-8. (2B, 2C)

McGuire, J. H. and Tamura, G. T., 1971
SMOKE CONTROL IN HIGH-BUILDINGS, Canadian Building Digest, CBD 134, Division of Building Research, Ottawa, Canada, February, p. 4. (2B)

McGuire, J. H. and Tamura, G. T., 1975
SIMPLE ANALYSIS OF SMOKE-FLOW PROBLEMS IN HIGH BUILDINGS, Fire Technology, Vol. 11, No. 1, February, pp. 15–22. (12B)

McGuire, J. H., Tamura, G. T. and Wilson, A. G., 1970
FACTORS IN CONTROLLING SMOKE IN HIGH BUILDINGS, American Society of Heating, Refrigerating, and Air-Conditioning Engineers, Symposium Bulletin Fire Hazards in Buildings (San Francisco, Calif., January), pp. 14–19. (2B)

McMillan, C. M., 1975a
AFRICAN EAGLE LIFE CENTRE—A HIGH-RISE PRECAST LOAD BEARING FACADE, Proceedings of the National Conference on Tall Buildings (Honolulu, Hawaii, January), University of Hawaii, Honolulu, Hawaii. (3)

McMillan, C. M., 1975b
OPTIMUM DESIGN OF HIGH-RISE BUILDINGS—A MULTI-DISCIPLINARY ENGINEERING APPROACH, Proceedings of the National Conference on Tall Buildings (Honolulu, Hawaii, January), University of Hawaii, Honolulu, Hawaii. (4)

Meyerhof, G. G., 1947
THE SETTLEMENT ANALYSIS OF BUILDING FRAMES, The Structural Engineer, London, England, September. (11)

Meyerhof, G. G., 1951
THE ULTIMATE BEARING CAPACITY OF FOUNDATIONS, Geotechnique, London, England, Vol. 2, p. 301. (11)

Meyerhof, G. G., 1960
THE DESIGN OF FRANKI PILES WITH SPECIAL REFERENCE TO GROUPS IN SAND, Proceedings of the Sixth International Congress on Bridges and Structural Engineering (Stockholm, Sweden). (11)

Mikos, J., Zarebski, W. and Kajrunajtys, J., 1972
STRUCTURAL, PHYSICAL AND TECHNOLOGICAL UNITY OF ERECTION OF MONOLITHIC MULTI-STOREY RESIDENTIAL BUILDINGS MADE OF PO-ROUS-AGGREGATE CONCRETES, Proceedings of the National Conference on Tall Buildings (Warsaw, Poland, November), Vol. II, Warsaw Technical University, Warsaw, Poland. (4)

Miller, P. O., 1972
MODEL ANALYSIS OF THE QANTAS CENTRE, Conference on Structural Models (Sydney, Australia); Cement and Concrete Association of Australia in conjunction with the Department of Architectural Science, University of Sydney, and Institution of Engineers, N.S.W. Division, Australia. (3)

Miller, P. O., 1973
QANTAS CENTER, SYDNEY, DESIGN AND CONSTRUCTION PLANNING, Proceedings of the National Conference on Tall Buildings (Sydney, Australia, August), Lehigh University, Bethlehem, Pa. (3, 4)

Mitsui, N. and Nava, T., 1973
ANALYSIS OF LATERAL QUAKING OF HIGH SPEED ELEVATORS, Elevator World, Vol. XXI, No. 3. (2A)

Moller, P., 1968
PILING AND PILE DESIGN, Cement och Betong, Malmö, Sweden, pp 78–83 (in Swedish). (11)

Moore, W. P., Jr., 1973
SUMMARY—PART I: STRUCTURAL SYSTEMS, Planning and Design of Tall Buildings, Proceedings of the 1972 ASCE-IABSE International Conference, ASCE, New York, Vol. 1a, No. TC-3. (3)

Moretto, 1971
DEEP FOUNDATIONS—SELECTED SYNTHESIS OF THE PRESENT STATE OF THE KNOWLEDGE ABOUT SOIL INTERACTION, *Revista Latino Americana de Geotechnia*, Caracas, Venezuela, Vol. I, No. 2, p. 142. (11)

Morgenstern, N. R. and Eisenstein, Z., 1970
METHODS OF ESTIMATING LATERAL LOADS AND DEFORMATIONS, ASCE Specialty Conference on Lateral Stresses and Design of Earth Retaining Structures (Cornell University, Ithaca, N.Y., June). (11)

Muench, W. F. and Ajimine, W. S., 1975
HIGH VOLTAGE VERTICAL DISTRIBUTION SYSTEM FOR HIGH-RISE RESIDENTIAL BUILDINGS, Proceedings of Pan-Pacific Tall Buildings Conference (Honolulu, Hawaii, January), University of Hawaii, Honolulu, Hawaii, pp. 151–160. (2C)

Mukland, J. and Padmanabhan, P., 1973
ECONOMY IN THE DESIGN OF TALL BUILDINGS—STRUCTURAL, Proceedings of the National Conference on Tall Buildings (New Delhi, India), Indian National Group of IABSE, New Delhi, India. (3)

Mukherjee, A. K., 1974
INTEGRATED FRAME-WALL SYSTEMS IN TALL BUILDINGS, Proceedings of the National Conference on Tall Buildings (Kuala Lumpur, Malaysia, December), Institution of Engineers, Kuala Lumpur, Malaysia. (3)

Munoz, J., 1973
BEHAVIOR OF TUBULAR STRUCTURES (Comportamiento de Estructuras Tubulares), Proceedings of the National Conference on Tall Buildings (Bogotá, Colombia, September), Escuela Colombiana de Ingenieria, Bogotá, Colombia. (3)

Murray, G. T., 1975
A SANITARY ENGINEER'S VIEWPOINT ON THE DESIGN, INSTALLATION, MAINTENANCE AND COST OF PLUMBING AND DRAINAGE SYSTEMS IN TALL BUILDINGS, South African Conference on Tall Buildings, (Johannesburg, South Africa, November), Hortors Printers, Johannesburg, South Africa. (2B)

Murray, T. M., 1975
DESIGN TO PREVENT FLOOR VIBRATIONS, *Engineering Journal*, American Institute of Steel Construction, Third Quarter. (3)

Muszynski, W. and Ruppert, J., 1972
A LIGHT-WEIGHT CURTAIN WALL, Proceedings of the Regional Conference on the Planning and Design of Tall Buildings (Warsaw, Poland, November), Vols. I & II, Warsaw Technical University, Polish Group of IABSE, Warsaw, Poland, pp. 295–301. (12A)

Muto, K., 1971
FLUTTERING DESIGN OF KEIO PLAZA HOTEL, Proceedings, 3rd Regional Conference on Planning and Design of Tall Buildings (Tokyo, Japan, September), pp. 107–110. (3)

Muto, K. and Nagata, M., 1974
THE EARTHQUAKE RESISTANT INSTALLING METHOD OF TELECOMMUNICATION INSTRUMENTS IN HIGH-RISE BUILDING, Proceedings of the National Conference on Tall Buildings (Tokyo, Japan, August), Architectural Institute of Japan, Tokyo, Japan, pp. 83–84. (2C)

NFPA, 1969
STANDARD PIPE AND HOSE SYSTEMS, Pamphlet No. 14, No. 10 Series, National Fire Protection Association, Boston, Mass. (2B)

NFPA, 1976a
STANDARD FOR THE INSTALLATION OF AIR CONDITIONING AND VENTILATING SYSTEMS, Standard 90A, National Fire Protection Association, Boston, Mass. (2B, 2C)

NFPA, 1976b
CODE FOR SAFETY TO LIFE FROM FIRE IN BUILDINGS AND STRUCTURES, Standard 101, National Fire Protection Association, Boston, Mass. (2B)

NFPA, 1978
STANDARD FOR INSTALLATION OF STANDPIPE AND HOSE SYSTEMS, NFPA-14, National Fire Protection Association, Boston, Mass. (2B)

NFPA, 1978
U.S. NATIONAL ELECTRICAL CODE, National Fire Protection Association, Boston, Mass. (2C)

NRCC #15764, 1977
MEASURES FOR FIRE SAFETY IN HIGH BUILDINGS, Associate Committee of National Building Code, National Research Council of Canada, Ontario, Canada. (2B)

Naka, T., 1973
STEEL REINFORCED CONCRETE—STRUCTURAL SYSTEM AND DESIGN SPEC-IFICATION, Proceedings of the National Conference on Tall Buildings (Tokyo, Japan, August), Section 3, Architectural Institute of Japan, Tokyo, Japan, pp. 9–22. (3)

Nakagawa, K., Takeda, T., Kida, Y. and Takagi, M., 1974
DESIGN AND EXPERIMENT ON OSAKA OHBAYASHI BUILDING, Proceedings of the National Conference on Tall Buildings (Tokyo, Japan, August), Architectural Institute of Japan, Tokyo, Japan. (3)

Nakamura, N., 1974
PRESENT PROBLEMS OVER HPC METHOD, Proceedings of the National Conference on Tall Buildings (Tokyo, Japan, August, 1973), Architectural Institute of Japan, Tokyo, Japan. (4)

Narita, H. and Yokoyama, F., 1974
THE STRUCTURAL DESIGN OF KAIJO BUILDING (TOKYO MARINE AND FIRE INSURANCE BUILDING), Proceedings of the National Conference on Tall Buildings (Tokyo, Japan, August), Architectural Institute of Japan, Tokyo, Japan. (3)

Nasser, J., 1973
USE OF THIN SHELLS FOR TALL BUILDINGS, Planning and Design of Tall Buildings, Proceedings of the 1972 ASCE-IABSE International Conference on Tall Buildings, ASCE, New York, Vol. 1a, No. 3-D6. (3)

Nassetta, A. F., 1973
STRUCTURAL STEEL TIERED BUILDING FRAMES, Planning and Design of Tall Buildings, Proceedings of the 1972 ASCE-IABSE International Conference on Tall Buildings, ASCE, New York, Vol. 1a, No. 3-3. (3)

National Building Code of Canada, 1970
NATIONAL BUILDING CODE OF CANADA, SECTION 4 2.5 FOUNDATIONS, NRC No. 11246, National Research Council of Canada, Ottawa, Canada. (11)

Navodariu, M., 1975
THE ACTUAL STAGE AND NEW TENDENCY IN THE CONSTRUCTION OF FLAT-STALL BUILDINGS (Stadiul Actual Si Noile Tendinte In Realizarea Cladirilor Inalte Pentru Locuinte), Proceedings of the National Conference on Tall Buildings (Iasi, Romania, October), Consiliul National Al Inginerilor si Technicienlor, Iasi, Romania. (4)

Nejman, T. and Radwanowski, L., 1973
HOMEOSTASE IN TALL BUILDINGS, Proceedings of the National Conference on Tall Buildings (Bratislava, Czechoslovakia, April), Lehigh University, Bethlehem, Pa. (3)

Nelson, F. C., 1968
THE USE OF VISCOELASTIC MATERIAL TO DAMP VIBRATIONS IN BUILDINGS AND LARGE STRUCTURES, Engineering Journal, AISC, April, pp. 72–78. (3)

New Civil Engineer, 1974a
HALF FLEXIBLE, HALF RIGID APPROACH FOR FRANKFURT'S GIANT NEW BUILDING, New Civil Engineer, July 18, pp. 32–33. (3)

New Civil Engineer, 1974b
NAT-WEST BANKS ON CLOVER-LEAF CANTILEVERS, New Civil Engineer, December 5. (3)

Newby, F., 1973
STIFFNESS RELATED TO NONSTRUCTURAL ELEMENTS, Planning and Design of Tall Buildings, Proceedings of the 1972 ASCE-IABSE International Conference, Vol. 1a, ASCE, New York, pp. 1141–1143. (12A)

Newby, F., 1973
STIFFNESS RELATED TO NONSTRUCTURAL ELEMENTS, Planning and Design of Tall Buildings, Proceedings of the 1972 ASCE-IABSE International Conference, Vol. 1a, ASCE, New York, pp. 1143–1149. (12B)

Newman, R. B. and staff of Bolt Beranek Newman, Inc., 1974
ACOUSTICS, Time-Saver Standards for Architectural Design Data, J. H. Callender, ed., McGraw-Hill Book Co., Inc., New York. (12A)

Newmark, N. M., 1947
INFLUENCE CHARTS FOR COMPUTATION OF VERTICAL DISPLACEMENTS IN ELASTIC FOUNDATIONS, *Bulletin of the Engineering Experiment Station*, University of Illinois, No. 367. (11)

Ng, P. K., Chong, S. C. and Rahulan, G., 1974
STRUCTURAL SYSTEMS OF SOME OF THE TALL BUILDINGS IN SINGAPORE AND KUALA LUMPUR, Proceedings of the National Conference on Tall Buildings (Bangkok, Thailand, January), Asian Institute of Technology, Bangkok, Thailand. (3)

Nisbet, R. F., 1973
WHICKHAM TOWER BLOCK: THE DESIGN AND CONSTRUCTION OF A 30-STOREY BLOCK OF FLATS, *Structural Engineer*, Vol. 51, July. (3, 4)

Noggaret, R., 1973
HAVAS BUILDING AT NEUILLY: A SCULPTURED BUILDING IN EXPOSED STEEL, *Acier-Stahl-Steel*, Brussels, Belgium, November. (3)

Norman, H. D., 1973
SERVICE SYSTEMS, Planning and Design of Tall Buildings, Proceedings of Conference (Sydney, Australia, August), Lehigh University, Bethlehem, Pa., pp. 499–512. (2A, 2B, 2C)

Norwegian Geotechnical Institute, 1962–1966
MEASUREMENTS OF A STRUTTED EXCAVATION, Technical Reports Nos. 1–8. (11)

O'Brien, J. J. and Zilley, R. G., 1971
CONTRACTORS MANAGEMENT HANDBOOK, McGraw-Hill Book Co., Inc., New York. (4)

Ohsaki, Y., 1969
EFFECT OF LOCAL SOIL CONDITIONS UPON EARTHQUAKE DAMAGE, Proceedings of the 7th International Conference on Soil Mechanics and Foundation Engineering (Mexico City, Mexico), Specialty Session 2, pp. 3–32. (11)

Ohta, S., Hisatomi, Y., Kaneko, M. and Yamahara, H., 1974
RESEARCH AND DEVELOPMENT OF A HPC TALL BUILDING SYSTEM, Proceedings of the National Conference on Tall Buildings (Tokyo, Japan, August), Architectural Institute of Japan, Tokyo, Japan. (3, 4)

Okell, J. C. and Robinson, R. A., 1975
ELECTRICAL RETICULATION SYSTEMS IN TALL BUILDINGS, Proceedings of South African Conference on Tall Buildings (Johannesburg, South Africa, November), Hortors Printers, Johannesburg, South Africa. (2C)

Opatril, J., 1973
ARCHITECTURAL STRUCTURES IN TALL BUILDINGS, 10th Regional Conference Proceedings (Bratislava, Czechoslovakia, April), Vols. I & II, CSTVA-Czechoslovak Scientific and Technical Association, Bratislava, Czechoslovakia (two editions: English and Czech), pp. 240–246. (12B)

Oravetz, B., 1975
SERVICE SYSTEMS IN HIGH AND MEDIUM-HIGH BUILDINGS (Mega es Kozepmagas Epuletek Epuletgepeszeti Kerdesei), Questions Concerning Unusual and Outstanding Aspects of Tall, Multi-Story Buildings (Magas es Kozepmegas Epitmenyek Kulongeles Tervezesi es Kivitelezesi Kerdsei), Proceedings of Conference (Budapest, Hungary, May), Dr. Gabos Gyorgy, 200 Interjedelem 20, 25/A/5IV, Budapest, Hungary, pp. 39–52. (2A, 2B, 2C)

Orczykowski, A., Korycki, S., Kwiecinski, B., Rymkiewicz, A. and Wadowski, A., 1972
THE PROBLEMS OF TALL CONCRETE BUILDINGS REALIZATION, Proceedings of the National Conference on Tall Buildings (Warsaw, Poland, November), Warsaw Technical University, Warsaw, Poland. (4)

Orme, D. H. and Thorburn, S., 1970
SYSTEM BUILT FLATS ON A DEEP BURIED QUARRY, *Structural Engineer*, Vol. 48, January, pp. 5–16. (3)

Ortmanns, G., 1978
THE INFLUENCE OF GLASS PANELS ON THE ENERGY BALANCE OF A BUILDING (Der Einfluss von Flachglas auf die Energiebilanz Eines Gebaudes), *Glasforum*, No. 6, June, p. 21–24. (12A)

Osborne, A., 1975
PRECAST PANELS FOR CENTRE RISING SIXTY LEVELS, *Building Materials*, Vol. 17, No. 6. (3, 4)

Ouyang, L., 1973
STRUCTURAL AND FOUNDATION DESIGN IN HONG KONG, Proceedings of the Regional Conference on Tall Buildings (Hong Kong, August), Lehigh University, Bethlehem, Pa. (11)

Paez, A., 1973
FOUNDATIONS (Los Problemas de Cimentacion Para Los Grandes Edificios), Proceedings of the National Conference on Tall Buildings (Bogotá, Colombia, September), Colombia School of Engineering, Bogotá, Colombia. (11)

Pagano, M., 1963
STRUCTURES (Strutture), Liguori, Vol. 1, No. 2, Napoli, Italy. (3)

Pagano, M. and Mazzolani, F. M., 1966a
EXPERIMENTAL FULL-SCALE INVESTIGATION ON ELASTIC-PLASTIC INSTABILITY OF TWO MULTI-STOREY STEEL FRAMES: PLANNING OF TESTS (Indagine Sperimentale al Vero sull' Instabilita' Elasto-Plastica di Due Telai Multipiani in Acciaio: Impostazione dello Studio Sperimentale), Construzioni Metalliche, No. 4. (3)

Pagano, M. and Mazzolani, F. M., 1966b
EXPERIMENTAL FULL-SCALE INVESTIGATION ON ELASTIC-PLASTIC INSTABILITY OF TWO MULTI-STOREY STEEL FRAMES: TESTING RESULTS (Indagine Sperimentale al Vero sull' Instabilita' Elasto-Plastica di Due Telai Multipiani in Acciaio: Risultati Sperimentali), Costruzioni Metalliche, No. 5. (3)

Pagano, M. and Mazzolani, F. M., 1966c
EXPERIMENTAL FULL-SCALE INVESTIGATION ON ELASTIC-PLASTIC INSTABILITY OF TWO MULTI-STOREY FRAMES: COMPARISON BETWEEN EXPERIMENTAL AND THEORETICAL RESULTS (Indagine Sperimentale al Vero sull' Instabilita' Elasto-Plastica di Due Telai Multipiani in Acciaio: Confronto frai Risultati Sperimentali e Teorici), Costruzioni Metalliche, No. 6. (3)

Pancewicz, Z. and Kwiatkowski, J., 1972
REVIEW OF BASIC PROBLEMS IN TALL STEEL BUILDINGS, Proceedings of the National Conference on Tall Buildings (Warsaw, Poland, November), Vol. 1, Warsaw Technical University, Warsaw, Poland. (3)

Pancewicz, Z., Kwiatkowski, J. and Ostrowski, B., 1972
STEEL PIN-JOINTED STRUCTURES WITH HEXAGONAL COLUMN ARRANGEMENT, Proceedings of the National Conference on Tall Buildings (Warsaw, Poland, November), Vol. II, Warsaw Technical University, Warsaw, Poland. (4)

Papadopoulos, M., 1975
SUN PROTECTION IN HOUSING, REGARDING THE GREEK CLIMATIC CONDITIONS (Sonnenschutz im Wohnungsbau, unter besonderer Berücksichtigung der speziellen klimatischen Bedingungen Griechenlands), dissertation presented to the Rheinisch-Wastfälische Technische Hochschule at Aachen, Federal Republic of Germany. (12A)

Paparoni, M., Holoma, S. and Dubac, H., 1973
CENTRAL PARK TOWERS, A SYSTEM OF SEGMENTAL TUBES (Torres del Parque Central, un Sistema Estructural de Tubo Segmentado), Proceedings of the National Conference on Tall Buildings (Porto Alegre, Brazil, December), Vol. 1, Sociedade de Engenharia do Rio Grande do Sul. (3)

Parmar, H. S. and Rahulan, G., 1974
TUNAS BUILDING—STRUCTURAL DESIGN OF A SLENDER BUILDING, Proceedings of the National Conference on Tall Buildings (Kuala Lumpur, Malaysia, December), Institution of Engineers, Kuala Lumpur, Malaysia. (3)

Pasternak, H., 1971
DOUBLE-DECK ELEVATORING, Progressive Architecture, Vol. 52, No. 12, pp. 70–73. (2A)

Pasternak, H., 1974
THE COMPLEX COMPLEX-PROJECT, Elevator World, Vol. XXII, No. 10. (2A)

Pawlowski, A., 1976
TRENDS IN SUSPENDED BUILDING CONSTRUCTION, unpublished communication to the Council. (3)

Peck, R. B., 1943
EARTH PRESSURES MEASUREMENTS IN DEEPER CUTS, Transactions, ASCE, Vol. 108, Paper No. 2200, pp. 1008–1036. (4)

Peck, R. B., 1969
DEEP EXCAVATIONS AND TUNNELING IN SOFT GROUND—STATE OF THE ART, Proceedings of the 7th International Conference on Soil Mechanics and Foundation Engineering (Mexico City, Mexico), pp. 259–281. (4, 11)

Peck, R. B., Hanson, W. E. and Thornburn, T. H., 1953
FOUNDATION ENGINEERING, John Wiley and Sons, Inc., New York. (11)

Pellegrini, S. E., 1973
CONSTRUCTION IN SOUTH AMERICA, Planning and Design of Tall Buildings, Proceedings of the 1972 ASCE-IABSE International Conference, Vol. 1a, ASCE, New York, pp. 1135–1141. (12A, 12B)

Penn, H., 1974
VERTICAL MOVEMENT OF MATERIALS IN HIGHRISE BUILDINGS, *Building Technology and Management*, Vol. 12, No. 4. (4)

Penzien, J., Sheffey, C. F. and Parmelee, R. A., 1964
SEISMIC ANALYSIS OF BRIDGES ON LONG PILES, *Journal of the Engineering Mechanics Division*, Proc. Paper 3953, pp. 223–254. (11)

Peter, J., 1964
DESIGN WITH GLASS, Materials in Modern Architecture Series, Vol. 1, Reinhold Publishing Corp., New York, N.Y. (12A)

Peyton, J. J., 1973
COLLINS PLACE PROJECT, MELBOURNE, Proceedings of the National Conference on Tall Buildings (Sydney, Australia, August), Lehigh University, Bethlehem, Pa. (3)

Peyton, J. J., 1974
COLLINS-WALES PROJECT—A 500 FT. TOWER IN SIMPLE HYBRID CONSTRUCTION, Proceedings of the National Conference on Tall Buildings (Kuala Lumpur, Malaysia, December), Institution of Engineers, Kuala Lumpur, Malaysia. (3, 4)

Picardi, E. A., 1973
STRUCTURAL SYSTEM—STANDARD OIL OF INDIANA BUILDING, *Journal of the Structural Division*, ASCE, Vol. 99, No. ST4, Proc. Paper 9642, pp. 605–620. (3)

Plantema, G. and Nolet, C. A., 1967
INFLUENCE OF PILE DRIVING ON THE CONE RESISTANCE IN A DEEP SAND LAYER, Proceedings of the 4th International Conference on Soil Mechanics and Foundation Engineering (London, England). (11)

Polack, J. H., 1973
ARCHITECTURAL ELEMENTS IN EUROPEAN PRACTICE, Planning and Design of Tall Buildings, Proceedings of the 1972 ASCE-IABSE International Conference, Vol. 1a, ASCE, New York, pp. 1079–1095. (12A, 12B)

Popov, E. P., 1950
SUCCESSIVE APPROXIMATIONS FOR BEAMS ON AN ELASTIC FOUNDATION, *Transactions*, Paper NO. 2457, May. (11)

Poulos, H. G. and Davis, E. H., 1974
ELASTIC SOLUTIONS FOR SOIL AND ROCK MECHANICS, John Wiley and Sons, Inc., New York. (11)

Pozzi, A., 1975
PLANNING OF STRUCTURES AND ITS RELATIONSHIP WITH CONSTRUCTION METHODS (Einfluss der Barmethoden auf den Entwurf von Tragwerken), Insbesondere die Gegenseitige Abhangigkeit von Engturf, Ausfuhrung und Nutzung bei der Gestaltung von Tragwerken, Einfuhrungsbericht zum Kongress in Tokio, IVBH, Zurich, Switzerland. (3, 4)

Prakash, S., 1962
BEHAVIOR OF PILE GROUPS SUBJECT TO LATERAL LOAD, thesis presented to the University of Illinois at Urbana, Ill., in partial fulfillment of the requirements for the degree of Doctor of Philosophy. (11)

Prentis, E. A. and White, L., 1950
UNDERPINNING, 2nd ed., Columbia University Press, New York. (4)

Price, R. G., 1972
DEMOLITION: THE ART OF SCIENCE, *Civil Engineering and Public Works Review*, Vol. 67, No. 789, pp. 383–385. (4)

Przybyla, H., 1973
STATIC CALCULATIONS OF BUILDINGS SUBJECTED TO UNDERMINING INFLUENCES (in Polish), Bulletin No. 3, Instytut Techniki Budowlanej. (11)

Przybyla, H., 1974a
CHARACTERISTICS OF TECHNICAL CONDITIONS CONCERNING PLANNING AND DESIGN OF BUIDINGS OF PUBLIC USE ON AREAS SUBJECTED TO MINING INFLUENCES (in Polish), *Ochrona Terenow Gorniczych*, Katowice, Poland, No. 27. (11)

Przybyla, H., 1974b
SAFETY EVALUATION OF STRUCTURE OF A BUILDING SUBJECTED TO MINING INFLUENCES (in Polish), Bulletin No. 1, Instytut Techniki Budowlanej. (11)

Przybyla, H. and Gubrynowicz, A., 1973
PASSENGER LIFTS IN MIDDLE-HEIGHT HOUSE IN MINING SUBSIDENCE AREAS (in Polish), *Ochrona Terenow Gorniczych*, Katowice, Poland, No. 26. (11)

Pun, P., 1974
A PRE-FABRICATED BUILDING SYSTEM DEVELOPED FOR MULTI-STORY INDUSTRIAL BUILDINGS IN HONG KONG, unpubished communication to the Council. (3)

Rafeiner, F., 1973
ARCHITECTURAL CRITERIA OF TALL BUILDINGS IN GERMANY AND EUROPE, Planning and Design of Tall Buildings, Proceedings of the 1972 ASCE-IABSE International Conference, Vol. 1a, ASCE, New York, pp. 1095–1115. (12A, 12B)

Rafeiner, F., 1975
THE DEVELOPMENT OF THE STRUCTURE OF TALL BUILDINGS FROM SINGLE EXPLOITATION TO NEUTRAL EXPLOITATION (Die Entwicklung der Hochhausstruktur von der Mononutzung zur Nutzungsneutralität), unpublished communication to the Joint Committee (in German). (12B)

Rainer, R. K. and Moon, P. F., 1973
SAFETY PRACTICES, Planning and Design of Tall Buildings, Proceedings of the 1972 ASCE-IABSE International Conference, ASCE, New York, Vol. 1a, No. 4-3. (4)

Ramesh, C. K., Nori, V. V. and Swaminathan, T. R., 1973
TALL BUILDINGS WITH SHEAR-WALL SYSTEMS—A STATUS REPORT, Proceedings of the National Conference on Tall Buildings (New Delhi, India, January), Indian National Group of the IABSE, New Delhi, India. (3)

Ranada, B., 1975
DESIGN AND CONSTRUCTION OF THE HONOLULU MUNICIPAL BUILDING, Proceedings of the National Conference on Tall Buildings (Honolulu, Hawaii, January), Arthur Chiu, University of Hawaii, Honolulu, Hawaii. (4)

Rane, V. S., 1973
WATER SUPPLY AND SANITARY SERVICES IN HIGH RISE BUILDINGS, National Conference on Tall Buildings (New Delhi, India, January), Indian National Group of IABSE, New Delhi, India, pp. IV31–IV37. (2B)

Rao, V. V. S. and Srivastava, O. S., 1974
STABILITY OF FOUNDATIONS OF TALL STRUCTURES UNDER EARTH-QUAKES—A CASE STUDY, Proceedings of the Regional Conference on Tall Buildings (Bangkok, Thailand, January), Asian Institute of Technology, Bangkok, Thailand. (11)

Reed, L. D., 1974
NOISE: ITS MEANING AND MEASUREMENT, *Elevator World*, Vol. XXII, No. 7. (2A)

Reese, L. C. and Matlock, H., 1956
NON-DIMENSIONAL SOLUTIONS AND LATERALLY LOADED PILES WITH SOIL MODULUS ASSUMED PROPORTIONAL TO DEPTH, Proceedings of the 8th Texas Conference on Soil Mechanics and Foundation Engineering (Austin, Tex.). (11)

Rehnman, S. E., 1968
THE BEARING CAPACITY OF SLOPING ROCK SURFACE LOADED STATISTICALLY BY A ROCK TIP, RESULTS OF MODEL TESTS (in Swedish), Royal Swedish Academy of Engineering Sciences, Commission on Pile Research, Bulletin No. 15, Stockholm, Sweden. (11)

Rehnman, S. E., 1970
THE STRENGTH OF ROCK TIPS, RESULTS FROM STATICAL LOAD TESTS (in Swedish), Royal Swedish Academy of Engineering Sciences, Commission on Pile Research, Bulletin No. 17, Stockholm, Sweden, 40 pp. (11)

Rehnman, S. E. and Broms, B. B., 1971

BEARING CAPACITY OF PILES DRIVEN INTO ROCK, *Canadian Geotechnical Journal*, Vol. 8, No. 2, pp. 151–162. (11)

Reiner, L. E., 1972
HANDBOOK OF CONSTRUCTION MANAGEMENT, Prentice-Hall, Inc., Englewood Cliffs, N.J. (4)

Reinitzhuber, F. K., 1973
SUMMARY REPORT—PART 2: STRUCTURAL SYSTEMS, Planning and Design of Tall Buildings, Proceedings of the 1972 ASCE-IABSE International Conference, ASCE, New York, Vol. 1a, No. TC-3. (3)

Reuter, F., 1972
CLEANING AND WASTE DISPOSAL, 6th Regional Conference Proceedings (Delft, The Netherlands, May), Lehigh University, Bethlehem, Pa., pp. 28–29. (2B)

Reuter, F., 1973
CLEANING AND WASTE DISPOSAL, Planning and Design of Tall Buildings, Proceedings of the 1972 ASCE-IABSE International Conference, Vol. 1a, ASCE, New York, pp. 363–374. (2B)

Richardson, P., 1973
SUMMARY REPORT, Planning and Design of Tall Buildings, Proceedings of the 1972 ASCE-IABSE International Conference, Vol. 1a, ASCE, New York, pp. 389–398. (2C)

Richart, F. E., Hall, J. R., Jr. and Woods, R. D., 1970
VIBRATIONS OF SOILS AND FOUNDATIONS, Prentice-Hall, Inc., Englewood Cliffs, N.J. (11)

Robertson, L., 1973
DESIGN OPPORTUNITIES IN CONSTRUCTION SAFETY, Proceedings of the National Conference on Tall Buildings (Hong Kong, August), Lehigh University, Bethlehem, Pa. (4)

Robertson, L. E., 1973
THEME REPORT: STRUCTURAL SYSTEMS, Planning and Design of Tall Buildings, Proceedings of the 1972 ASCE-IABSE International Conference, ASCE, New York, Vol. 1a, No. TC-3. (3)

Rocha, P. F., 1974
SETTLEMENT OF HIGH RISE BUILDINGS DUE TO THE CONSTRUCTION OF A SUBWAY ADJACENT TO THEIR FOUNDATIONS, unpublished communication to the Council. (11)

Rocha, P. F., Silveria, E. B. S. and Gaito, N., 1970
GEOTECHNICAL ASPECTS OF THE PROJECT OF SECTION 3 OF THE METRO OF SÃO PAULO (Aspectos geotecnicos do projet do trecho 3 do Metro de São Paulo), IV Congresso Brasileiro de Mecanica dos Solos e Engenharia de Fundacoes, August. (11)

Rodriguez Lamus, L. R., 1974
URBAN ASPECT OF THE CONSTRUCTION OF TALL BUILDINGS (Edificios Altos Aspectos Urbanisticos), Proceedings of the National Conference on Tall Buildings (Memorias del Seminario Nacional Sobre Edificios de Gran Altura) (Bogotá, Colombia, September 24–29, 1973), Colombia School of Engineering, Bogotá, Colombia, pp. 175–187. (2C)

Roesset, J. M. and Kausel, E. M., 1976
DYNAMIC SOIL STRUCTURE INTERACTION, 2nd International Conference on Numerical Methods in Geomechanics, Blacksburg, Va., Vol. I, pp. 3–19. (11)

Rohatyn, F. S., 1973
AUTOMATIC VOLTAGE DROP COMPENSATION FOR TALL BUILDINGS, Planning and Design of Tall Buildings, Proceedings of the 1972 ASCE-IABSE International Conference, Vol. 1a, ASCE, New York, pp. 382–389. (2C)

Romana, M., 1973
A SEMICOMPENSATED FOUNDATION FOR THE NEW SOCIAL SECURITY HOSPITAL IN BARCELONA, Proceedings of Regional Conference on Tall Buildings (Madrid, Spain, September), Typografia Artistica, Madrid, Spain. (11)

Romanoff, M., 1962
CORROSION OF STEEL PILING IN SOIL, Monograph 58, National Bureau of Standards, Gaithersburg, Md. (11)

Rooley, G. A. and Hadley, L. G., 1974
NON-ENVIRONMENTAL ENGINEERING SERVICES, Tall Buildings and People?

Proceedings of Conference held in Great Britain, September 17–19, The Institution of Structural Engineers, London, England, pp. 66–72. (2B)

Roret, J. A., 1973a
HIGH RISE CONSTRUCTION IN FRANCE, Planning and Design of Tall Buildings, Proceedings of the ASCE-IABSE International Conference, ASCE, New York, Vol. 1a, No. 4-4B. (4)

Roret, J. A., 1973b
TALL BUILDINGS IN STEEL (Bâtiments Elevés en Acier), Proceedings of the National Conference on Tall Buildings (Zurich, Switzerland, October), SIA-Fachgruppen für Bruckenbau und Hochbau (FBH) und für Architektur (FGA), Zurich, Switzerland. (3)

Rosiak, B., 1972
SYSTEM OF NATURAL VENTILATION IN TALL BUILDINGS, Proceedings of the Regional Conference on the Planning and Design of Tall Buildings (Warsaw, Poland, November), Warsaw Technical University, Polish Group of IABSE, Warsaw, Poland, pp. 27–34. (2B)

Rousseau, P. E., 1973
EVOLUTION OF CONCEPTION OF CURTAIN WALLS IN RELATION WITH FLEXIBILITY OF STRUCTURES, Planning and Design of Tall Buildings, Proceedings of the 1972 ASCE-IABSE International Conference, Vol. 1a, ASCE, New York, pp. 1153–1155. (12A, 12B)

Rush, R., 1978
INTERNAL DISTRIBUTION SYSTEMS, *Progressive Architecture*, Vol. 59, No. 7, pp. 86–91. (2A)

Ruzicka, G. C. and Robinson, A. R., 1977
DYNAMICS OF TUNED SECONDARY SYSTEMS, *Advances in Civil Engineering Through Engineering Mechanics*, Proceedings of 2nd Annual ASCE Engineering Mechanics Division Specialty Conference (Raleigh, N.C., May 23–25), pp. 188–191. (2A)

SAA, 1972
PREFERRED SIZES OF BUILDING COMPONENTS (METRIC UNITS), AS1224, Standards Association of Australia, Sydney, Australia. (12A)

SAA, 1973
CODE OF PRACTICE FOR INSTALLATION OF GLASS IN BUILDINGS, AS1288, Standards Association of Australia, Sydney, Australia. (12A)

SAA, 1974a
RULES FOR AUTOMATIC FIRE ALARM INSTALLATIONS (known as the SAA Code for Automatic Fire Alarm Installations), AS1670, Standards Association of Australia, Sydney, Australia. (2B)

SAA, 1974b
RULES FOR THE USE OF MECHANICAL VENTILATION AND AIR CONDITIONING IN BUILDINGS (known as the SAA Mechanical Ventilation and Air Conditioning Code), AS1668, Standards Association of Australia, Sydney, Australia. (2B)

SAA, 1975
RULES FOR THE DESIGN, INSTALLATION, TESTING AND OPERATION OF LIFTS, ESCALATORS AND MOVING WALKS (known as the SAA Life Code), AS1735, Standards Association of Australia, Sydney, Australia. (2A)

SEAOC, 1974
RECOMMENDED LATERAL FORCE REQUIREMENTS AND COMMENTARY, Seismology Committee, Structural Engineers Association of California, San Francisco, Calif. (12A, 12B)

SSPC, 1954
STEEL STRUCTURES PAINTING MANUAL, Vol. 1, Steel Structures Painting Council. (4)

SSPC, 1964
STEEL STRUCTURES PAINTING MANUAL, Vol. 2 (with 1964 supplement), Steel Structures Painting Council. (4)

Sabnis, G. M., 1972
USE OF PAPER HONEYCOMBED PANELS IN HOUSING CONSTRUCTION, Proceedings, Symposium on Panelized Structural Assemblies, Sir George Williams University, Montréal, Canada, May. (3)

Sander, D. M. and Tamura, G. T., 1973
   A FORTRAN IV PROGRAM TO SIMULATE AIR MOVEMENT IN MULTI-STOREY
   BUILDINGS, DBR Computer Program 170 35, National Research Council of Canada,
   Division of Building Research, Ottawa, Canada. (2B, 12B)
Sanglerat, G., 1972
   THE PENETROMETER AND SOIL EXPLORATION, Elsevier, Amsterdam, London,
   and New York. (11)
Sarrazin, M. A., 1970
   SOIL-STRUCTURE INTERACTION IN EARTHQUAKE RESISTANT DESIGN,
   Report R 70-59, Dept. of Civil Engineering, Massachusetts Institute of Technology,
   Cambridge, Mass. (11)
Schachinger, E. A., 1975
   EVALUATING MATERIALS HANDLING SYSTEMS FOR HOSPITALS, *Architectural
   Record*, Vol. 158, McGraw-Hill Book Co., Inc., New York, September. (2A)
Schall, R., 1962
   CURTAIN WALLS, Design Manual, Reinhold Publishing Corp., New York, N.Y. (12A)
Schaupp, W., 1965
   EXTERIOR WALLS, CLADDING, THERMAL INSULATION AND HUMIDITY
   PROTECTION (Die Aussenwand, Bekleidung Wärmedämmung Feutigkeitsschutz),
   Verlag Georg D. W. Callwey, Munich, German Federal Republic. (12A)
Schmidbauer, 1970
   DRYING OF DEEP EXCAVATIONS BENEATH THE GROUNDWATER LEVEL BY
   TEMPORARY DEWATERING (Trockenhaltung tiefer Bauwerke unter dem Grund-
   wasserspiegel durch Dauerabsenkung), *Vorträge der Baugrundtagung 1970* (Düsseldorf,
   Germany). (11)
Schmidt, W., 1966
   HIGH RISE BUILDINGS OF REINFORCED CONCRETE—WHAT ARE THE LIM-
   ITATIONS, *Journal of the American Concrete Institute*, December, pp. 1393–1400. (3)
Scott, R. F. and Schoustra, J. J., 1970
   SOIL MECHANICS AND ENGINEERING, McGraw-Hill Book Co., Inc., New York.
   (11)
Seed, H. B., 1969
   INFLUENCE OF LOCAL SOIL CONDITIONS ON EARTHQUAKE DAMAGE,
   Proceedings of the 7th International Conference on Soil Mechanics and Foundations
   Engineering (Mexico City, Mexico), pp. 33–66. (11)
Seed, H. B. and Idriss, I. M., 1967
   ANALYSIS OF SOIL LIQUEFACTION: NIIGITA EARTHQUAKE, *Journal of the Soil
   Mechanics and Foundations Division*, ASCE, Vol. 93, No. SM3, Proc. Paper 5233, pp.
   83–108. (11)
Seed, H. B. and Idriss, I. M., 1970
   SOIL MODULI AND DAMPING FACTORS FOR DYNAMIC RESPONSE ANAL-
   YSES, Report EERC-70-10, University of California. (11)
Seed, H. B. and Wilson, S. D., 1967
   THE TURNAGAIN HEIGHTS LANDSLIDE, ANCHORAGE, ALASKA, *Journal of the
   Soil Mechanics and Foundations Division*, ASCE, Vol. 93, No. SM4, Proc. Paper 5320, pp.
   325–353. (11)
Seed, H. B., Idriss, I. M. and Dezfulian, H., 1970
   RELATIONSHIPS BETWEEN SOIL CONDITIONS AND BUILDING DAMAGE IN
   THE CARACAS EARTHQUAKE OF 1967, Report EERC-70-2, University of Cali-
   fornia. (11)
Seed, H. B., Lysmer, J. and Hwang, R., 1975
   SOIL-STRUCTURE INTERACTION ANALYSES FOR SEISMIC RESPONSE, *Journal
   of the Geotechnical Engineering Division*, ASCE, Vol. 101, No. GT5, pp. 439–457. (11)
Selvaraj, S. and Sharma, S. P., 1974
   INFLUENCE OF CONSTRUCTION SEQUENCE ON THE STRESSES IN TALL
   BUILDING FRAMES, Proceedings of the National Conference on Tall Buildings
   (Bangkok, Thailand, January), Asian Institute of Technology, Bangkok, Thailand. (4)
Severinsson, S., 1965
   PRACTICAL EXPERIENCE FROM DRIVING HIGH QUALITY PRECAST CON-
   CRETE END-BEARING PILES, *Tidning for Byggnadskonst*, Vol. 57, No. 12, pp. 561–566
   (in Swedish). (11)

Sharma, J. S. and Sharma, S. K., 1973
  RECENT DEVELOPMENT OF NEW PLUMBING SYSTEMS FOR HIGH RISE
  BUILDINGS, National Conference on Tall Buildings (New Delhi, India, January),
  Indian National Group of IABSE, New Delhi, India, pp. VI1–VI9. (2B)
Sharpe, R. L., 1973
  SEISMIC DESIGN OF NONSTRUCTURAL ELEMENTS, Planning and Design of Tall
  Buildings, Proceedings of the 1972 ASCE-IABSE International Conference, Vol. 1a,
  ASCE, New York, pp. 1143–1149. (12A, 12B)
Shaw, C. Y., Sander, D. M. and Tamura, G. T., 1973
  AIR LEAKAGE MEASUREMENTS OF THE EXTERIOR WALLS OF TALL BUILD-
  INGS, Transactions, American Society of Heating, Refrigerating, and Air-Conditioning
  Engineers, New York, Vol. 79, Part 2, pp. 40–48. (2B, 12A)
Simon, L. U., 1973
  TALL BUILDINGS IN AUSTRALIA—CONSTRUCTION TRENDS, Planning and
  Design of Tall Buildings, Proceedings of the 1972 ASCE-IABSE International Confer-
  ence, ASCE, New York, Vol. 1a, No. 4-D1. (4)
Skempton, A. W. and MacDonald, D. H., 1956
  THE ALLOWABLE SETTLEMENTS OF BUILDINGS, Proceedings, Institution of Civil
  Engineers, London, England, Vol. 5, No. 3, p. 727. (11)
Skinner, W. E. A., 1971
  50 STOREY OFFICE TOWER IN HONG KONG, Civil Engineering and Public Works
  Review, January. (4)
Skinner, W. E. A., 1972
  THE CONNAUGHT CENTRE, HONG KONG, Structural Engineer, Vol. 50, November.
  (3)
Smith, E. A. L., 1960
  PILE DRIVING ANALYSIS BY THE WAVE EQUATION, Journal of the Soil Mechanics
  and Foundations Division, ASCE, Vol. 80, No. SM4, Proc. Paper 2574, pp. 35–61. (11)
Smith, G. C. K., 1973
  CONSTRUCTION PRACTICES IN THE UNITED KINGDOM, Planning and Design of
  Tall Buildings, Proceedings of the 1972 ASCE-IABSE International Conference, ASCE,
  New York, Vol. 1a, No. 4-D4. (4)
Smith, I. C., 1973
  THE BANK OF NEW ZEALAND, CONCEPT AND DESIGN, Proceedings of the
  National Conference on Tall Buildings (Sydney, Australia, August), Lehigh University,
  Bethlehem, Pa. (4)
Sofronie, R., 1973
  TALL BUILDINGS ELASTICALLY COUPLED, Planning and Design of Tall Buildings,
  Proceedings of the 1972 ASCE-IABSE International Conference, ASCE, New York, Vol.
  1a, No. 3-D5. (3)
Sofronie, R., 1974
  ON THE BRIDGING OF TALL BUILDINGS, Institute of Civil Engineers, Bucarest,
  Romania. (3)
Sofronie, R., 1975
  ON THE BRIDGING OF TALL BUILDINGS, Mec. Appl., Bucarest, Romania, Vol. 20,
  No. 1. (3)
Sofronie, R., 1976
  ON THE DYNAMICS OF BRIDGED STRUCTURES, Mec. Appl., Bucarest, Romania,
  Vol. 21, No. 3. (3)
Sokolov, A. G., 1973
  WEIGHT ANALYSIS OF BRACED FRAMES FOR PRISMATIC TALL BUILDINGS,
  Planning and Design of Tall Buildings, Proceedings of the 1972 ASCE-IABSE Inter-
  national Conference, ASCE, New York, Vol. 1a, No. 3-11. (3)
Sontag, H., 1970
  STEEL MULTI-STOREY GARAGES, Acier-Stahl-Steel, Brussels, Belgium, November. (3)
Sontag, H., 1973
  PRECAST COMPOSITE FLOORING, Planning and Design of Tall Buildings, Proceed-
  ings of the 1972 ASCE-IABSE International Conference on Tall Buildings, ASCE, New
  York, Vol. 1a, No. 3-10. (3)
Sorenson, C. P. and Tasker, H. E., 1965

CRACKING IN BRICK AND BLOCK MASONRY, Technical Study No. 43, Experimental Building Station, Sydney, Australia. (12B)

Souto Silveira, E. B. and Gaioto, N., 1969
WRITTEN CONTRIBUTION TO THE VII INTERNATIONAL CONFERENCE ON SOIL MECHANICS AND FOUNDATION ENGINEERING, Volume III, p. 367. (11)

Sowers, G. F., 1975
FAILURES IN LIMESTONES OF HUMID SUBTROPICS, *Journal of the Geotechnical Engineering Division*, ASCE, Vol. 101, No. GT8, Proc. Paper 11521, pp. 771–787. (11)

Spencer, J. W. and Anson, M., 1973
THE EFFECT OF BUILDING DESIGN VARIATIONS ON AIR-CONDITIONING LOADS, *Architectural Science Review*, Vol. 16, No. 2, June. (2B)

Steinbach, J. and Vey, E., 1975
CAISSON EVALUATION BY STRESS WAVE PROPAGATION METHOD, *Journal of the Geotechnical Engineering Division*, ASCE, Vol. 101, No. GT4, Proc. Paper 11245, pp. 361–378. (11)

Steinmann, G. A., 1973
TALL BUILDINGS IN CONCRETE (Bâtiments Elevés en Beton), Proceedings of the National Conference on Tall Buildings (Zurich, Switzerland, October), SIA-Fachgruppen fur Bruckenbau und Hochbau (FBH) und fur Architektur (FGA), Zurich, Switzerland. (3)

Stermac, A. C., Devata, M. and Selby, K. G., 1968
UNUSUAL MOVEMENTS OF ABUTMENTS SUPPORTED ON END-BEARING PILES, *Canadian Geotechnical Journal*, Vol. 5, No. 2, pp. 69–79. (11)

Strakosch, G. R., 1967
VERTICAL TRANSPORTATION: ELEVATORS AND ESCALATORS, John Wiley & Sons, Inc., New York. (2A)

Strakosch, G. R., 1973
HORIZONTAL VS. VERTICAL TRANSPORTATION, Planning and Design of Tall Buildings, Proceedings of the 1972 ASCE-IABSE International Conference, Vol. 1a, ASCE, New York, pp. 375–381. (2A)

Strunk, J., 1972
ELECTRICAL SYSTEMS, 6th Regional Conference Proceedings (Delft, The Netherlands, May), Lehigh University, Bethlehem, Pa., p. 28. (2C)

Strunk, J., 1973
ELECTRICAL SYSTEMS IN TALL BUILDINGS, Planning and Design of Tall Buildings, Proceedings of the 1972 ASCE-IABSE International Conference, Vol. 1a, ASCE, New York, pp. 349–363. (2C)

Sturgeon, W. C., ed., 1967
MEN AND MACHINES AGAINST THE MOUNTAIN, *Elevator World*, Annual Issue, Vol. XV, No. 10. (2A)

Sturgeon, W. C., ed., 1972
EARTHQUAKES AND ELEVATORS, *Elevator World*, Annual Issue, Vol. XX, No. 10. (2A)

Sturgeon, W. C., ed., 1974a
THE WORLD OF ELEVATOR CONSULTANTS, *Elevator World*, Annual Issue, Vol. XXII, No. 10. (2A)

Sturgeon, W. C., 1974b
ELEVATOR/ESCALATOR ENERGY ECONOMY, *Elevator World*, Vol. XXII, No. 11. (2A)

Sturt, R. J., 1974
MINERAL INSULATED CABLES, Proceedings, Conference on Tall Buildings (Kuala Lumpur, Malaysia, December), Institution of Engineers, Kuala Lumpur, Malaysia, pp. 5–29—5–33. (2C)

Subcommittee on the State-of-the-Art Survey of the Task Committee on Composite Construction of the Committee on Metals of the Structural Division, 1974
COMPOSITE STEEL CONCRETE CONSTRUCTION, *Journal of the Structural Division*, ASCE, Vol. 100, No. ST5, Proc. Paper 10561, pp. 1085–1139. (4)

Sundberg, G., 1968
ROUND PRETENSIONAL PILES, *Cement och Betong*, Malmö, Sweden, pp. 73–77 (in Swedish). (11)

Sung, M. A. M., 1974

A TRANSFER BOWL FOR A 20-STOREY TOWER BLOCK, Proceedings of the National Conference on Tall Buildings (Kuala Lumpur, Malaysia, December), Institution of Engineers, Kuala Lumpur, Malaysia. (3)

Swartz, W., 1972
PRE-ENGINEERING ELEVATORING, *Progressive Architecture*, Vol. 53, No. 12, pp. 66–67. (2A)

Swedish Building Code, 1967
PILE FOUNDATIONS: REQUIREMENTS, ADVICE AND RECOMMENDATIONS, Publ. No. 11, Swedish Board of Urban Planning, Stockholm, Sweden (in Swedish). (11)

Swedish Pile Commission, 1964
DRIVING AND TEST LOADINGS OF LONG CONCRETE PILES, TESTS AT GUBBERO, GOTHENBURG, Report 99, National Swedish Council for Building Research, Stockholm, Sweden (in Swedish). (11)

Swedish Pile Commission, 1970
RECOMMENDATION FOR PILE DRIVING TEST AND ROUTINE LOAD TESTING OF PILES, Rep. and Prel. Reports No. 11, Commission on Pile Research, Royal Swedish Academy of Engineering Sciences, Stockholm, Sweden, (11)

Swedish Pile Commssion, 1971
STATISTICS OF PILES DRIVEN IN SWEDEN 1962, 1966, 1968 AND 1970, Rep. and Prel. Reports No. 30, Commission on Pile Research, Royal Swedish Academy of Engineering Sciences, Stockholm, Sweden (in Swedish). (11)

Swiger, W. F., 1971
FOUNDATIONS, 2nd Regional Conference Proceedings (Bled, Yugoslavia, May), Lehigh University, Bethlehem, Pa. (11)

Swiger, W. F., 1973
THEME REPORT: FOUNDATION DESIGN, Planning and Design of Tall Buildings, Proceedings of the 1972 ASCE-IABSE International Conference, Vol. 1a, ASCE, New York. (11)

Swiger, W. F. and Fang, H. Y., 1971
FOUNDATIONS OF TALL BUILDINGS, 5th Regional Conference Proceedings (Chicago, Ill., November), Lehigh University, Bethlehem, Pa. (11)

Takenami, M., 1974
HOTEL NEW OTANI TOWER PROJECT, Proceedings of the National Conference on Tall Buildings (Tokyo, Japan, August, 1973), Architectural Institute of Japan, Tokyo, Japan. (3, 4)

Tamura, G. T., 1969
COMPUTER ANALYSIS OF SMOKE MOVEMENT IN TALL BUILDINGS, *Transactions*, American Society of Heating, Refrigerating, and Air-Conditioning Engineers, New York, Vol. 75, Part 2, pp. 81–92. (2B, 12B)

Tamura, G. T. and McGuire, J. H., 1971
SMOKE MOVEMENT IN HIGH-RISE BUILDINGS, Canadian Building Digest, CBD 133, National Research Council of Canada, Division of Building Research, Ottawa, Canada, January. (12B)

Tamura, G. T. and McGuire, J. H., 1973
THE PRESSURIZED BUILDING METHOD OF CONTROLLING SMOKE IN HIGH-RISE BUILDINGS, National Research Council of Canada, NRCC 13365, September. (2B)

Tamura, G. T. and Wilson, A. G., 1966
PRESSURE DIFFERENCE FOR A NINE-STORY BUILDING AS A RESULT OF CHIMNEY EFFECT AND VENTILATION SYSTEM OPERATION, *Transactions*, American Society of Heating, Refrigerating and Air-Conditioning Engineers, New York, Vol. 72, Part 1, pp. 180–189. (2B)

Tamura, G. T. and Wilson, A. G., 1967
PRESSURE DIFFERENCE FOR A NINE-STORY BUILDING AS A RESULT OF CHIMNEY EFFECT AND VENTILATION SYSTEM OPERATION, *Transactions*, American Society of Heating, Refrigerating and Air-Conditioning Engineers, New York, Vol. 73, Part 2. (2B)

Tamura, G. T. and Wilson, A. G., 1968
PRESSURE DIFFERENCES CAUSED BY WIND ON TWO TALL BUILDINGS, *Transactions*, American Society of Heating, Refrigerating, and Air-Conditioning Engineers, New York, Vol. 74, Part 2, pp. 182–188. (2B)

Tani, S., 1973
  STEEL-REINFORCED CONCRETE STRUCTURE-PREFABRICATED (HPC), Pro-
  ceedings of the National Conference on Tall Buildings (Tokyo, Japan, August),
  Architectural Institute of Japan, Tokyo, Japan. (4)
Taranath, B. S., 1975
  OPTIMUM BELT TRUSS LOCATIONS FOR HIGH-RISE STRUCTURES, *Structural
  Engineer*, Vol. 53, August. (3)
Tassios, T. P., 1974
  INVESTIGATIONS OF DIFFICULT SOILS IN SEISMIC REGIONS, Economic Com-
  mission for Europe (of UN), UN-ECE Seminar, Construction in Seismic Regions and in
  Regions with Difficult Ground Conditions (Bucharest, Romania, October). (11)
Taylor, D. C., 1973
  PARK TOWER, MELBOURNE, 30 STORY APARTMENT BUILDING, Proceedings of
  the National Conference on Tall Buildings (Sydney, Australia, August), Lehigh Univer-
  sity, Bethlehem, Pa. (3)
Taylor, E. E. F., 1973
  STEEL CONSTRUCTION, Planning and Design of Tall Buildings, Proceedings of the 1972
  ASCE-IABSE International Conference, ASCE, New York, Vol. 1a, No. 4-5B. (4)
Taylor, E. E. F., 1974
  JOINTS IN MULTI-STORY STEEL FRAMED BUILDINGS, Proceedings of the
  National Conference on Tall Buildings (Bangkok, Thailand, January), Asian Institute of
  Technology, Bangkok, Thailand. (4)
Tedesko, A., 1973
  UNUSUAL SOLUTIONS, Planning and Design of Tall Buildings, Proceedings of the 1972
  ASCE-IABSE International Conference, ASCE, New York, Vol. 1a, No. 4-D3. (3)
Teng, W. C., 1962
  FOUNDATION DESIGN, Prentice-Hall, Inc., Englewood Cliffs, N. J., Chapter 8. (11)
Terzaghi, K., 1934
  LARGE RETAINING WALL TESTS, *Engineering News-Record*, February 1, pp. 136–140.
  (11)
Terzaghi, K., 1936a
  A FUNDAMENTAL FALLACY IN EARTH PRESSURE COMPUTATIONS, *Journal of
  the Boston Society of Engineers*, April. (11)
Terzaghi, K., 1936b
  SETTLEMENT OF STRUCTURES, Proceedings, 1st International Conference on Soil
  Mechanics and Foundation Engineering, Vol. 3, p. 79. (11)
Terzaghi, K., 1943
  THEORETICAL SOIL MECHANICS, John Wiley & Sons, New York. (11)
Terzaghi, K., 1944
  Discussion of APPLICATION OF SOIL MECHANICS IN DESIGNING BUILDING
  FOUNDATIONS, by A. Casagrande and R. E. Fadum, *Transactions*, ASCE, Vol. 109, p.
  427. (11)
Terzaghi, K., 1955
  EVALUATION OF COEFFICIENTS OF SUBGRADE REACTION, *Geotechnique*, Vol.
  5, pp. 297–326. (11)
Terzaghi, K. and Peck, R. B., 1967
  SOIL MECHANICS IN ENGINEERING PRACTICE, 2nd ed., John Wiley and Sons,
  Inc., New York. (11)
Tettinek, W., 1953
  A CONTRIBUTION TO CALCULATING INCLINATION OF ECCENTRICALLY
  LOADED FOUNDATIONS, Proceedings of the 3rd International Conference on Soil
  Mechanics and Foundation Engineering (Zurich, Switzerland), Vol. 1, p. 461. (11)
The Building Centre of Israel Quarterly, 1971
  SYSTEMS BUILDING—METHODS, MATERIALS, MANAGEMENT, *The Building
  Centre of Israel Quarterly*, October-December. (3)
Thoma, R., 1972
  SERVICE SYSTEMS IN RELATION TO ARCHITECTURE, 6th Regional Conference
  Proceedings (Delft, The Netherlands, May), Lehigh University, Bethlehem, Pa., p. 27.
  (2B)
Thoma, R., 1973
  SERVICE SYSTEMS IN RELATION TO ARCHITECTURE, Planning and Design of

Tall Buildings, Proceedings of the 1972 ASCE-IABSE International Conference, Vol. 1a, ASCE, New York, pp. 307–317. (2B)

Thompson, P. J., 1973
OCBC CENTRE, SINGAPORE, Proceedings of the National Conference on Tall Buildings (Sydney, Australia, August), Lehigh University, Bethlehem, Pa. (3)

Thomson, A. G. and Williams, D. J., 1971
HEAD OFFICE FOR HEARTS OF OAK BENEFIT SOCIETY (LONDON), *Acier-Stahl-Steel*, Brussels, Belgium, February. (3)

Timoshenko, S. and Goodier, J. M., 1951
THEORY OF ELASTICITY, 2nd ed., McGraw-Hill Book Co., Inc., New York. (11)

Tombazis, A., Angelides, S., Argyropoulos, T. and Argyropoulos, I., 1975
KIFISSIA—APARTMENT PROJECT, PART II, Proceedings of the National Conference on Tall Buildings (Athens, Greece, October), Technical Chamber of Greece, Athens, Greece. (3)

Tomii, M., Matsui, C. and Sakino, K., 1974
CONCRETE FILLED STEEL TUBE STRUCTURES, Proceedings of the National Conference on Tall Buildings (Tokyo, Japan, August, 1973), Section 3, Architectural Institute of Japan, Tokyo, Japan, pp. 73–74. (3)

Tregenza, P. R., 1975
MOVEMENT OF PEOPLE WITHIN TALL BUILDINGS, Proceedings of Hellenic Conference on Tall Buildings (Athens, Greece, October), Technical Chamber of Greece, Athens, Greece. (2A)

Trow, W. A., 1967
ANALYSIS OF PILE LOAD TEST RESULTS, 48th Annual Convention of Canadian Good Roads Association (Vancouver, Canada). (11)

Trudeau, P. F., Whitman, R. V. and Christian, J. T., 1974
SHEAR WAVE VELOCITY AND MODULUS OF A MARINE CLAY, *Journal of the Boston Society of Civil Engineers*, Vol. 61, No. 1, pp. 12–25. (11)

Tschebotarioff, G. P., 1970
BRIDGE ABUTMENTS ON PLIES DRIVEN THROUGH PLASTIC CLAY, *Design and Installation of Pile Foundations and Cellular Structures*, H. Y. Fang, ed., Envo Publishing Co., pp. 225–238. (11)

Tschebotarioff, G. P. and Johnson, E. G., 1953
THE EFFECTS OF RESTRAINING BOUNDARIES ON THE POSSIBLE RESISTANCE OF SAND, Report submitted to the office of Naval Research, Project No. 081-117, Dept. of the Navy, Princeton University, Princeton, N.J., June 1. (11)

Tsytovich, N. A., 1961
FOUNDATION OF STRUCTURES, Proceedings of the 5th International Conference on Soil Mechanics and Foundation Engineering (Paris, France), Division 3/A, Vol. II, p. 824. (11)

Van der Veen, C., 1968
SOIL MECHANICS, 2nd ed., Kosmos Uitgeverij, Amsterdam, The Netherlands. (11)

Vanmarcke, E. H. and Chackravorty, M. K., 1973
PROBABILISTIC SEISMIC ANALYSIS OF EQUIPMENT WITHIN BUILDINGS, Proceedings of the 5th World Conference on Earthquake Engineering (Rome, Italy, July), Vol. 2. (2A)

Van Deusen, J., 1974
DOUBLE-DECK ELEVATORS, *Elevator World*, Mobile, Ala., October. (2A)

Van Weele, A. F., 1957
A METHOD OF SEPARATING THE BEARING CAPACITY OF A TEST PILE INTO SKIN FRICTION AND POINT RESISTANCE, Proceedings of the 4th International Conference on Soil Mechanics and Foundation Engineering (London, England), Vol. 2, pp. 76–80. (11)

Varga, L., 1973
FOUNDATIONS FOR TOWER-SHAPED STRUCTURES, 10th Regional Conference Proceedings (Bratislava, Czechoslovakia, April), CSVTA-Czechoslovak Scientific and Technical Association, Bratislava, Czechoslovakia. (11)

Vargas, M. and Silva, F., 1973
FOUNDATION PROBLEMS OF TALL BUILDINGS (O Problema das Fundacoes de

Edificios Altos), Proceedings, South American Regional Conference on Tall Buildings (Porto Alegre, Brazil, December), Sociedade de Engenharia do Rio Grande do Sul, Porto Alegre, Brazil. (11)

Vasiliev, A. P., Bychenkov, Y. D. and Matkov, N. G., 1973
PREFABRICATED REINFORCED CONCRETE MULTI-STORY FRAME BUILD-INGS IN THE U.S.S.R., Planning and Design of Tall Buildings, Proceedings of the 1972 ASCE-IABSE International Conference, ASCE, New York, Vol. 1a, No. 3-5. (3)

Vesic, A., 1961a
BEAMS ON ELASTIC SUBGRADE AND THE WINKLER'S HYPOTHESIS, Pro-ceedings of the 5th International Conference on Soil Mechanics and Foundation Engineering (Paris, France), Vol. I, pp. 845–850. (11)

Vesic, A., 1961b
BENDING OF BEAMS RESTING IN AN ELASTIC-ISOTROPIC SOLID, Journal of the Engineering Mechanics Division, ASCE, Vol. 87, No. EM2, Proc. Paper 2800, pp. 35–53. (11)

Vesic, A., 1967
A STUDY OF BEARING CAPACITY OF DEEP FOUNDATION, Georgia Institute of Technology, Engineering Experiment Station, Atlanta, Ga., March. (11)

Vesic, A., 1970
TESTS ON INSTRUMENTED PILES, OGEECHEE RIVER SITE, Journal of the Soil Mechanics and Foundation Division, ASCE, Vol. 96, No. SM2, Proc. Paper 7170, pp. 561–584. (11)

Vesic, A. S., Banks, D. C. and Woodard, J. M., 1965
AN EXPERIENTAL STUDY OF DYNAMIC BEARING CAPACITY OF FOOTINGS ON SAND, Proceedings of the 6th International Conference on Soil Mechanics and Foundation Engineering (Montréal, Canada), Vol. II, pp. 209–213. (11)

Veterans Administration, 1973
EARTHQUAKE RESISTANT DESIGN OF NON-STRUCTURAL ELEMENTS OF BUILDINGS, V. A. Construction Standard CD-55, Veterans Administration, Wash-ington, D.C. (2A)

Vetter, C. P., 1939
DESIGN OF PILE FOUNDATIONS, Transactions, ASCE, Vol. 104, pp. 758–778. (11)

von Döbeln, W., 1975
AIR CONDITIONING OF TALL BUILDINGS, Proceedings of Hellenic Conference on Tall Buildings (Athens, Greece, October), Technical Chamber of Greece, Athens, Greece. (2B)

Vorliček, M. and Holický, M., 1976
STATISTICAL DESIGN OF TOLERANCES OF ASSEMBLED STRUCTURES (Statistický Výpočet Toleranci Montovaných Konstrukcí), Academia, Prague, Czecho-slovakia. (3)

Waddell, J. J., 1974
CONCRETE CONSTRUCTION HANDBOOK, McGraw-Hill Book Co., Inc., New York. (4)

Wargon, A., 1973
CENTERPOINT PROJECT, SYDNEY, Proceedings of the National Conference on Tall Buildings (Sydney, Australia, August), Lehigh University, Bethlehem, Pa., (3, 4)

Warners, I. E., 1977
VERTICAL TRANSPORTATION—EUROPEAN CONCEPT, unpublished communica-tion to the Council. (2A)

Wasilkowski, F., 1951–1955
THE FULL PROTECTION OF BUILDINGS AGAINST DESTRUCTION DUE TO MINING (in Polish), Inzynieria i Budownictwo No. 7-8; No. 4; No. 3; No. 2. (11)

Wasilkowski, F., 1966
THE INFLUENCE OF GROUND CREEPING ON BUILDINGS FOUNDATIONS IN MINING SUBSIDENCE AREAS (in Polish), Inzynieria i Budownictow, Nos. 7 and 10. (11)

Wass, A., 1972
CONSTRUCTION MANAGEMENT AND CONTRACTING, Prentice-Hall, Inc., Engle-wood Cliffs, N.J. (4)

Weinhold, H., 1970
MACHINE-BORED CAISSONS FOR EARTH RETAINING SYSTEMS IN EUROPE, *Civil Engineering*, ASCE, Vol. 40, No. 7, pp. 64–67. (4)

Wells, F. R., 1974
STRUCTURAL SYSTEMS OF THREE SYDNEY HIGH RISE BUILDINGS, Proceedings of the National Conference on Tall Buildings (Kuala Lumpur, Malaysia, December), Institution of Engineers, Kuala Lumpur, Malaysia. (3)

Wheen, R. J., 1973
POSITIVE CONTROL OF CONSTRUCTION FLOOR LOADS IN MULTISTORY CONCRETE BUILDINGS, Proceedings of the National Conference on Tall Buildings (Madrid, Spain, September), Typografia Artistica, Alameda, Madrid, Spain. (4)

Wheen, R. J., 1974
PRACTICAL ASPECTS OF THE CONTROL OF CONSTRUCTION FLOOR LOADS IN TALL BUILDINGS, Proceedings of the National Conference on Tall Buildings (Bangkok, Thailand, January), Asian Institute of Technology, Bangkok, Thailand. (4)

White, E. E., 1958
DEEP FOUNDATIONS IN SOFT CHICAGO CLAY, *Civil Engineering*, ASCE, Vol. 28, No. 11, pp. 816–819. (4)

White, E. E., 1962
UNDERPINNING, *Foundation Engineering*, McGraw-Hill Book Co., Inc., New York, Chapter 9, pp. 826–964. (4)

White, E. E., 1964
DESIGN AND CONSTRUCTION OF BRACED CUTS, *Design of Structures to Resist Earth Pressures* (Soil Mechanics Lecture Series), ASCE Soil Mechanics and Foundations Division, Illinois Section and Department of Civil Engineering, Illinois Institute of Technology, Chicago, Ill., pp. 93–129. (4)

White, E. E., 1973
FOUNDATIONS, Planning and Design of Tall Buildings, Proceedings of the 1972 ASCE-IABSE International Conference, ASCE, New York, Vol. 1a, No. 4-4A. (4)

White, R. E., 1962
COFFERDAMS, *Foundation Engineering*, McGraw-Hill Book Co., Inc., New York, Chapter 10, pp. 894–964. (4)

Whitman, R. V., 1969a
EFFECT OF SOIL CONDITIONS UPON DAMAGE TO STRUCTURES, CARACAS EARTHQUAKE OF 29 JULY 1967, Study conducted for Presidential Commission for Study of the Earthquake, Massachusetts Institute of Technology, Cambridge, Mass. (11)

Whitman, R. V., 1969b
EQUIVALENT LUMPED SYSTEM FOR STRUCTURE FOUNDED UPON STRATUM OF SOIL, Proceedings of the Fourth World Conference on Earthquake Engineering (Santiago, Chile), Vol. II, A-6, pp. 133–142. (11)

Winkler, E., 1867
THE LAWS OF ELASTICITY AND STRENGTH (Die Lehre von der Elastizitaet und Festigkeit), H. Domenicus, Prague, Czechoslovakia, pp. 182–184. (11)

Wirthensohn, W., 1973
MECHANICAL INSTALLATIONS IN TALL BUILDINGS (Sanitar-Installationen), Report I—Tall Buildings (Berichte I, Hochhaüser), Proceedings of Conference (Zurich, Switzerland, October), SIA-Fachgruppen fur Bruckenbau und Hochbau (FBH) und fur Architektur (FGA), Zurich, Switzerland, pp. 175–177. (2B)

Wittman, F. H. and Birmoser, H., 1976
ON THE DAMPING OF SLENDER REINFORCED CONCRETE STRUCTURES (Zur Dampfung Schlanker Konstruktionen aus Stahlbeton), Proceedings of the 2nd Kolloquium Industrieaerodyn, FHS-Aachen, Germany. (3)

Wojnowski, W. and Mokrecki, R., 1972
LIGHT-WEIGHT METAL CURTAIN WALLS FOR TALL BUILDINGS, Proceedings of the Regional Conference on the Planning and Design of Tall Buildings (Warsaw, Poland, November), Vols. I & II, Warsaw Technical University, Polish Group of IABSE, Warsaw, Poland, pp. 253–260. (12A)

Wong, R. T. and Cooper, R. S., 1974
EVALUATION OF SETTLEMENT UNDER EARTHQUAKE LOADING CONDITIONS OF BUILDINGS FOUNDED IN GRANULAR SOILS, Proceedings of the

Regional Conference on Tall Buildings (Bangkok, Thailand, January), Asian Institute of Technology, Bangkok, Thailand. (11)

Wynne-Edwards, R., 1968
 CRACKS IN REINFORCED CONCRETE PILES, *Proceedings*, Institution of Civil Engineers, London, England, Vol. 39, pp. 133–134. (11)

Yano, K., 1974
 EFFECT OF CYCLIC LOADING ON BUILDINGS, Proceedings of the National Conference on Tall Buildings (Tokyo, Japan, August), Architectural Institute of Japan, Tokyo, Japan. (3)

Yano, K., Abe, K., Suitsu, H., Iida, Y. and Sumii, M., 1974
 DESIGN OF THE SHINGUKU-SUMITOMO BUILDING, Proceedings of the National Conference on Tall Buildings (Tokyo, Japan, August, 1973), Section 2, Architectural Institute of Japan, Tokyo, Japan, pp. 47–52. (3)

Yorkdale, A. H., 1973
 MASONRY BUILDING SYSTEMS, Planning and Design of Tall Buildings, Proceedings of the 1972 ASCE-IABSE International Conference, ASCE, New York, Vol. 1a, No. 3-9. (3)

Yuceoglu, U., Tedesco, J. W. and Driscoll, G. C., 1977
 CONNECTIONS BETWEEN EQUIPMENT AND STRUCTURES SUBJECT TO SEIS- MIC LOADS, Fritz Laboratory Report No. 424.2, Lehigh University, Bethlehem, Pa. (2A)

Zakic, B. D., 1965
 RESULTS OF THE LATERAL LOAD TEST OF THE PRESTRESSED CONCRETE STRUCTURE OF THE TALL BUILDING, PRECAST SYSTEM "TRUDBENIK," Report of Testing Construction Center, Institute for Testing Materials, SRS, Beograd, Yugoslavia, *Bul. Vojvode Misica* 43, No. 474/65. (3)

Zavelani, R. A., Binda, L. and Contro, R., 1974
 SPACE FRAME DESIGN WITH OPTIMAL CHOICE OF STANDARD COMPO- NENTS, Second Congresso Nazionale AIMETA (Naples, Italy, October). (3)

Zeevaert, L., 1944
 DISCUSSION OF "APPLICATION OF SOIL MECHANICS IN DESIGNING BUILD- ING FOUNDATIONS," by Casagrande A. and Fadum, R. E., *Transactions*, ASCE, Vol. 109, Paper No. 2213, pp. 419–426. (11)

Zeevaert, L., 1945a
 ELASTIC-PLASTIC EQUILIBRIUM IN THE SURFACE OF CONTACT OF RIGID PLATE AND A CLAY, *Congreso Matematicas*, December. (11)

Zeevaert, L., 1945b
 FUNDAMENTAL THEORIES AND EXPERIMENTS THAT APPLY TO THE DE- SIGN OF FOUNDATIONS IN SATURATED CLAYS, *Revista Ingenieria y Arqui- tectura*, p. 335 (in Spanish). (11)

Zeevaert, L., 1947
 THE OUTLINE OF A MAT FOUNDATION DESIGN ON MEXICO CITY CLAY, VII Texas Conference on Soil Mechanics and Foundations Engineering (January). (11)

Zeevaert, L., 1949
 PRESENT BUILDING FOUNDATION PROBLEMS IN MEXICO CITY, presented at the July ASCE meeting, held at Mexico City, Mexico. (11)

Zeevaert, L., 1950
 DISCUSSION OF "EFFECTS OF DRIVING PILES INTO SOFT CLAY," *Transactions*, ASCE, Vol. 115, Paper No. 2400, p. 286.

Zeevaert, L., 1952
 STRATIGRAPHY AND ENGINEERING PROBLEMS OF THE DEPOSITS OF LACUSTRINE CLAY OF THE CITY OF MEXICO, Congreso Cientifico Commemorativo del IV Centenario de la Universidad Nacional Autonoma, de Mexico (in Spanish). (11)

Zeevaert, L., 1953a
 OUTLINE OF THE STRATIGRAPHICAL AND MECHANICAL CHARACTERIS- TICS OF THE UNCONSOLIDATED SEDIMENTARY DEPOSITS IN THE BASIN OF THE VALLEY OF MEXICO, IV Congress INQUA (Rome, Italy, September). (11)

Zeevaert, L., 1953b
PORE PRESSURE MEASUREMENTS TO INVESTIGATE THE MAIN SOURCE OF SURFACE SUBSIDENCE IN MEXICO CITY, Proceedings of the 3rd International Conference on Soil Mechanics and Foundations Engineering (Zurich, Switzerland, August), Vol. II. (11)
Zeevaert, L., 1956
HEAVY AND TALL BUILDING PROBLEMS IN MEXICO CITY, *Journal of the Structural Division*, ASCE, Vol. 82, No. ST2, Proc. Paper 917, pp. 917-1—917-23. (11)
Zeevaert, L., 1957a
COMPENSATED FRICTION-PILE FOUNDATION TO REDUCE THE SETTLEMENT OF BUILDINGS ON THE HIGHLY COMPRESSIBLE VOLCANIC CLAY OF MEXICO CITY, Proceedings of the 4th International Conference on Soil Mechanics and Foundations Engineering (London, England). (11)
Zeevaert, L., 1957b
FOUNDATION DESIGN AND BEHAVIOR OF TOWER LATINO AMERICANA IN MEXICO CITY, *Geotechnique*, London, England, September. (11)
Zeevaert, L., 1957c
CONSOLIDATION OF MEXICO CITY VOLCANIC CLAY, Proceedings, Joint Meeting ASTM and SMMS, December, p. 28. (11)
Zeevaert, L., 1959a
COMPENSATED FOUNDATIONS, Proceedings of the I Pan-American Conference on Soil Mechanics and Foundations Engineering (Mexico), Vol. III, p. 1109. (11)
Zeevaert, L., 1959b
REDUCTION OF POINT-BEARING CAPACITY OF PILES BECAUSE OF NEGATIVE FRICTION, Proceedings of the I Pan-American Conference on Soil Mechanics and Foundations Engineering (Mexico), Vol. III, pp. 1145–1152. (11)
Zeevaert, L., 1960
BASE SHEAR IN TALL BUILDINGS DURING EARTHQUAKE OF JULY 28, 1957, IN MEXICO CITY, Proceedings of the 2nd World Conference on Earthquake Engineering (Tokyo, Japan, July). (11)
Zeevaert, L., 1961
LARGE COMPENSATED FOUNDATIONS ON VOLCANIC CLAY WITH HIGH COMPRESSIBILITY (in German), *Internationaler Baugrundkursus*, Essen, Germany, July. (11)
Zeevaert, L., 1962
FOUNDATION PROBLEMS RELATED TO GROUND SURFACE SUBSIDENCE IN MEXICO CITY, Special Technical Publication No. 322, American Society for Testing and Materials, Philadelphia, Pa. (11)
Zeevaert, L., 1963
THE EFFECT OF EARTHQUAKES IN SOFT SUBSOIL CONDITIONS, SEAOC Convention, Yosemite, Calif., October. (11)
Zeevaert, L., 1964a
STRONG GROUND MOTIONS RECORDED DURING EARTHQUAKES OF MAY 11 AND 19, 1962, IN MEXICO CITY, *Bulletin of the Seismological Society of America*, Vol. 54, No. 1, p. 209. (11)
Zeevaert, L., 1964b
STRUCTURAL STEEL BUILDING FRAMES IN EARTHQUAKE ENGINEERING, Steel Utilization Congress, Luxembourg, October. (11)
Zeevaert, L., 1964c
THE ENGINEERING OF LARGE STRUCTURES, McGraw-Hill Book Co., Inc., New York. (11)
Zeevaert, L., 1967a
CONSOLIDATION THEORY FOR MATERIALS SHOWING INTERGRANULAR VISCOSITY, III Pan-American Conference on Soil Mechanics and Foundation Engineering (Caracas, Venezuela), Vol. I, p. 89. (11)
Zeevaert, L., 1967b
FREE VIBRATION TORSION TESTS TO DETERMINE THE SHEAR MODULUS OF ELASTICITY OF SOILS, III Pan-American Conference on Soil Mechanics and Foundation Engineering (Caracas, Venezuela), Vol. I, p. 111. (11)
Zeevaert, L., 1973

DESIGN OF COMPENSATED FOUNDATIONS, Planning and Design of Tall Buildings, Proceedings of the 1972 ASCE-IABSE International Conference, Vol. 1a, ASCE, New York. (11)

Zunz, G. J., Michael, D. and Heydenrich, R. A., 1971
STANDARD BANK CENTRE, JOHANNESBURG, Proceedings of the Institution of Civil Engineers, Vol. 49, February. (3)

Contributors

The following list identifies those who have contributed material specifically for possible use in Volume SC. The names, affiliations, and countries are given, together with the chapter(s) to which a contribution was made. The committee chairmen and editors were given quite complete latitude in the use of material, and frequently length limitations prevented the inclusion of much valuable material. Thus, every contributor is listed, whether or not the material was used in the final version. The effort here is to recognize and acknowledge the contributions.

Some of the material came to headquarters directly, some came from the Proceedings of the first international conference, some were stimulated at the special sessions held at the regional conferences, and some came directly to the committee leaders. The bibliography contains all contributions, and most of the unpublished documents are in the Council data base.

Adendorff, K., University of Pretoria, Pretoria, ZA (4)
Adler, R., Otis Elevator Company, New York, USA (4)
Anderson, B., Lehigh University, Bethlehem, PA, USA (Appendix)
Arch, W. H., Redpath Dorman Long, Ltd., Bedford, GB (8)
Asrow, S. P., S. P. Asrow Associates, Chicago, IL, USA (8)

Au, L., Consulting Engineer, Downey, CA, USA (R)*
Aycardi, L. G., Aycardi Ingenieria, Bogotá, CO (R)
Aydinoglu, M. N., Lehigh University, Bethlehem, PA, USA (Appendix)
Bandel, H., Severud-Perrone-Sturn-Bandel, New York, NY, USA (1)
Batanero, J. G., Ciudad Universitaria, Madrid, E (R)

Baum, R. T., Jaros, Baum & Bolles, New York, NY, USA (2, 3, 4)
Beard, W., Harvey Wrecking Company, Chicago, IL, USA (8)
Beedle, L. S., Lehigh University, Bethlehem, PA, USA (Appendix)
Belloni, L., ELC-Electroconsult, Milano, I (7)
Bellows, Jr., W. S., W. S. Bellows Construction Corp., Houston, TX, USA (8)

Benazzi, R. V., Jaros, Baum & Bolles, New York, NY, USA (2)
Berry, O. R., affiliation not available, N. Hollywood, CA, USA (5, 6)
Blessman, J., RUA Gabriel Mascarello, Porto Alegre, BR (R)
Botha, J. P., University of Pretoria, Pretoria, ZA (4)
Botsai, E. E., Botsai, Overstreet & Associates, San Francisco, CA, USA (5, 6)

*Designates organizer of National/Regional Conference.

Bowen, F. M., information not available (8)
Brotchie, J. F., CSIRO, Highett, AUS (1)
Bruinette, K. E., Bruinette, Kruger, Stoffberg & Hugo, Pretoria, ZA (R)
Brungraber, R. J., Bucknell University, Lewisburg, PA, USA (1)
Bubnov, S. J., Yugoslav Association of Earthquake Engineering, Ljubljana, YU (R)

Button, D. A., Pilkington Brothers, Lancashire, GB (5)
Bychenkov, Yu. D., GOSSTROY, Moscow, SU (1)
Camellerie, J. F., Ebasco Services Incorporated, New York, NY, USA (8)
Cheng, H. K., H. K. Cheng & Associates, Hong Kong, HK (R)
Chiu, A., University of Hawaii at Manoa, Honolulu, HI, USA (R)

Cho, A., Skidmore, Owings & Merrill, Chicago, IL, USA (3)
Christian, J. T., Stone & Webster Engineering Corp., Boston, MA, USA (7)
Christiansen, J. W., Skilling, Helle, Christiansen, Robertson, Seattle, WA, USA (1)
Ciesielski, R., Technical University of Krakow, Krakow, PL (7)
Conway, D., UNESCO, Paris, F (R)

Cooke, R. W., Building Research Station, Garston, GB (7)
Cornfield, G. M. (Deceased), Consulting Engineer, Leatherhead, GB (7)
Coroneos, D., Hellenic Group of AIPC, Athens, GR (R)
Cowan, H. J., The University of Sydney, Sydney, AUS (6, R)
Crabtree, P. R., National Building Research Institute, Pretoria, ZA (2)

Cunningham, K. D., American Bridge Division, U.S. Steel, Pittsburgh, PA, USA (8)
Daryanani, S. L., Syska & Hennessy, Inc., New York, NY, USA (2)
De Beer, E., Rijksinstitut Voor Grondmechanik, Ghent, B (7)
Du Buen, O., National University of Mexico, Mexico City, MEX (R)
Delgado-Vargas, M., Universidad Nacional de Colombia, Bogotá, CO (7)

DeSimone, S. V., Mueser Rutledge, Wentworth & Johust, New York, NY, USA (7)
Dismuke, T. D., Bethlehem Steel Corp., Bethlehem, PA, USA (7)
Disque, R. O., American Institute of Steel Construction, New York, NY, USA (1)
Driscoll, G. C., Lehigh University, Bethlehem, PA, USA (Appendix)
Dziewolski, R., Consulting Engineer, Ceret, Boulogne, F (1)

Eberhart, H. D., University of California, Berkeley, CA, USA (5, 6)
El-Dermirdash, I. A., Cairo University, Giza, ET (R)
Erenyi, I., Civil Engineer, Budapest, H (1)
Essunger, G., Statens Planverk Building Division, Stockholm, S (5, 6)
Faltus, F., Technical University of Prague, Prague, CS (R)

Fang, H. Y., Lehigh University, Bethlehem, PA, USA (7)
Fellenius, B. H., Ottawa University, Ottawa, CDN (7)
Finzi, M., C. T. A., Milano, I (R)
Fisher, W. E., Department of the Army, Champaign, IL, USA (8)
Focht, Jr., J. A., McClelland Engineers, Inc., Houston, TX, USA (7)

Gerwick, Jr., B. C., Consulting Construction Engineer, San Francisco, CA, USA (7)
Goschy, E. B., Geotechnical Institute, Budapest, H (R)
Gramolin, I. V., GOSSTROY, Moscow, SU (R)
Halasz, O., Technical University, Budapest, H (R)
Halpern, R. C., Schal Associates, Inc., Chicago, IL, USA (8)

Healy, J., Department of the Army, Washington, D.C., USA (8)
Henderson, W., University of Edinburgh, Edinburgh, Scotland
Herbert, W. M., Jaros, Baum & Bolles, New York, NY, USA (3)
Hisatoku, T., Takenaku Komuten Co. Ltd., Osaka, J (1)
Hongladaromp, T., Petroleum Authority of Thailand, Bangkok, T (R)

Horvat, E., Gemeentewerken Rotterdam, Rotterdam, NL (7)
Jamiolkowski, M. B., Instituto Di Scienza Delle Construzioni, Torino, I (7)
Jernstedt, G. W., Cityscope & Mobility Company, Bolivar, PA, USA (4)
Jerus, G. R., Meyer, Strong & Jones, P. C., New York, NY, USA (2)
Kaddah, H. A., Hamed Kaddah & Partners, Cairo, ET (R)

Kajfasz, S., Polish Academy of Sciences, Warsaw, PL (5, 6)
Kartahardja, A., Directorate of Building Research, Bandung, RI (R)

Kavyrchine, M., CEBTP, Paris, F (1)
Kawecki, J., Technical University, Krakow, PL (7)
Kee, C. F., Messrs. Jurutera Konsultant Sdn, Kuala Lumpur, PTM (7)

Khan, F. R., Skidmore, Owings & Merrill, Chicago, IL, USA (3)
Klarich, A. B., Peddle, Thorp & Walker, Sydney Cove, AUS (5, 6)
Kokkinaki-Daniel, A., Aristotle University of Thessaloniki, Thessaloniki, GR (5)
König, G. F., König Und Heunisch, Frankfurt, BRD (1)
Kort, C. L., Consultant, Glen Rock, NJ, USA (4)

Kowalczyk, R. M., Polish Academy of Sciénces, Warsaw, PL (R)
Kozák, J., Vitkovice Design Office, Floglova, CS (1, R)
Krol, W. (Deceased), Politechnika Slaska In Gliwice, Gliwice, PL (7)
Kruger, P. S. B., University of Pretoria, Pretoria, ZA (4)
Ku, J., Institute of Structural Engineers, Hong Kong, HK (R)

Kwong, P. K., Skidmore, Owings & Merrill, Chicago, IL, USA (3)
Lee, S., University of Singapore, Singapore, SGP (R)
Lenke, R. E., Skidmore, Owings & Merrill, Chicago, IL, USA (5, 6)
Lewis, R. E., CSIRO, Highett, AUS (1)
Lewis, W. S., Jaros, Baum & Bolles, New York, NY, USA (4)

Lim, B., University of Singapore, Singapore, SGP (R)
Lloyd, D. O., D. Balfour & Sons, London, GB (2)
Lu, L. W., Lehigh University, Bethlehem, PA, USA (1, R)
Lubinski, M., Warsaw Technical University, Warsaw, PL (R)
Mackey, S., University of Hong Kong, Hong Kong, HK (R)

Marais, G. H., G. H. Marais & Vennote, Pretoria, ZA (2)
Marincek, M., University of Ljubljana, Ljubljana, YU (R)
Martin, K. G., CSIRO, Highett, AUS (1)
Masters, R. E., Jaros, Baum & Bolles, New York, NY, USA (2)
Matkov, N. G., GOSSTROY, Moscow, SU (1)

Matsushita, K., Tokyo Science University, Tokyo, J (5, 6)
Mazilu, P., Institute of Civil Engineers, Bucarest, R (R)
McCollam, G., McColl Construction, Chicago, IL, USA (8)
McQuire, J. H., National Research Council, Ottawa, CDN (2)
Moharram, A., Arab Consulting Engineers, Cairo, ET (R)

Moon, P. F., Auburn University, Auburn, AL, USA (8)
Moore, Jr., W. P., Walter P. Moore & Associates, Houston, TX, USA (5, 6)
Moyer, J. I., Lehigh University, Bethlehem, PA, USA
Murray, G. T., Alex, Murray Pty. Ltd., Durban, ZA (2)
Muto, E. K., Muto Institute of Structural Mechanics, Tokyo, J (R)

Naka, T., University of Tokyo, Tokyo, J (R)
Nassar, G. E., Arab Consulting Engineers, Cairo, ET (R)
Nasser, J., Consulting Engineer, Beirut, RL (1)
Nassetta, A. F., Weiskopf & Pickworth, New York, NY, USA (1)
Newby, F., Felix J. Samuely & Partners, London, GB (5, 6)

Nikai, S., Kajima Corporation, Tokyo, J (8)
Nishikawa, F., Takenaka Komuten Co., Ltd., Osaka, J (1)
Okell, J. C., Watson, Edwards & Van Der Spu, Johannesburg, ZA (3)
Pawlowski, Z., Warsaw Technical University, Warsaw, PL (1)
Pellegrini, S. E., affiliation not available, Porto Alegre, BR (5, 6)

Polak, J. H., Les Architectes Polak, Brussels, B (5, 6)
Przybyla, H., Institute of Building Technology, Gliwice, PL (7)
Pun, P., Peter Y. S. Pun & Associates, Hong Kong, HK (1)
Rafeiner, F., affiliation not available, Hamburg, BRD (5, 6)
Rahulan, G., Sepakat Setia Perunding, Kuala Lumpur, PTM (R)

Rainer, R. K., Auburn University, Auburn, AL, USA (8)
Rankine, J., Rankine & Hill Engineering Consultants, Sydney, AUS (3)
Reinitzhuber, F. K., Consulting Engineer, Duisburg-Rheinhausen, BRD (1, R)
Reuter, F., Schmidt-Reuter Ingenieurgesellschaft mblt & Co., Köln, BRD (2)

Richardson, P., Société d'Etude Progeco S A, Brussels, B (3)

Robertson, L. E., Skilling, Helle, Christiansen, Robertson, New York, NY, USA (1)
Robinson, R. A., Watson, Edwards & v.d. Spuy & Partners, Johannesburg, ZA (3)
Rocha, P. F., Promon Engenharis, São Paulo, BR (7)
Rohatyn, F. S., Queensboro Transformer & Machinery Corp., College Pt., NY, USA (3)
Roosseno, R., Professor, Jakarta, RI (R)

Roret, J. A., CFEM, Paris, F (8)
Rousseau, P. E., S. A. Chamebel, Vilvoorde, B (5, 6)
Rubanenko, B., Research & Design Institute for Dwelling, Moscow, SU (R)
Sadoff, L., Department of the Army, New York, NY, USA (8)
Sandberg, H. R., Alfred Benesch & Company, Chicago, IL, USA (R)

Schulz, G. W., Universität Innsbruck, Innsbruck, A (R)
Sfintesco, D., CTICM, Puteaux, F (R)
Shaffer, L. R., Department of the Army, Champaign, IL, USA (8)
Sharpe, R. L., Engineering Decision Analysis Co., Palo Alto, CA, USA (5, 6)
Shepherd, R., University of Auckland, Auckland, NZ (R)

Skubik, E., Skidmore, Owings & Merrill, Chicago, IL, USA (3)
Simon, L. U., University of Melbourne, Parkville, AUS (8)
Smith, G. G. K., GGK Smith Associates, Peterborough, GB (8)
Sofronie, R. A., Institute of Civil Engineering, Bucarest, R (1)
Sokolov, A. G., GOSSTROY, Moscow, SU (1)

Sontag, H. (Retired), Krupp Industrie-und Stahlbau, Berlin, BRD (1)
Stockdale, W. K., Washington Public Power, Richland, WA, USA (8)
Strakosch, G. R., Jaros, Baum & Bolles, New York, NY, USA (4)
Strunk, J., Strunk & Partner, Düsseldorf, BRD (3)
Subba Rao, T. N., Gammon India Ltd., Bombay, IND (8)

Swiger, W. F., Stone & Webster Engineering Corp., Boston, MA, USA (7)
Tamura, G. T., National Research Council, Ottawa, CDN (2)
Tassios, T., National Technical University of Athens, Athens, GR (7)
Taylor, E. E. F., Redpath Dorman Long, Ltd., Bedford, GB (8)
Tedesko, A., Consulting Engineer, Bronxville, NY, USA (8)

Thoma, R., Hentrich, Petschnigg & Partners, Düsseldorf, BRD (2, 3, 4)
Thomas, P., Ministry of Shipping & Transport, New Delhi, IND (R)
Thürlimann, B., Swiss Federal Institute of Technology, Zurich, CH (R)
Uchida, Y., University of Tokyo, Tokyo, J (5, 6)
van der Veen, C., Gemeentewaterleidingen, Sloterdijk, NL (7)

Van Douwen, A. A., Technical University of Delft, Delft, NL (R)
Vasiliev, A. P., GOSSTROY, Moscow, SU (1)
Vavaroutas, B. A., B. A. Vavaroutas Consulting Engineers, Athens, GR (R)
Wakabayashi, M., Kyoto University, Uji City, J (R)
Warners, E., Otis Liften BV, Amsterdam-Overamstel, NL (4)

Werden, R. G., Werden Associates, Jenkintown, PA, USA (4)
Wetherill, E. A., Bolt Beranek and Newman, Inc., Canoga Park, CA, USA (5)
White, E. E., Spencer, White & Prentis, Inc., Hackensack, NJ, USA (8)
Williams, G. M. J., Scott, Wilson, Kirkpatrick & Ptnrs., Hants, GB (5)
Williamson, Sr., G., information not available (8)
Yorkdale, A. H., Brick Institute of America, McLean, VA, USA (1)

Yuceoglu, U., Lehigh University, Bethlehem, PA, USA (1)
Zeevaert, L., Universidad Nacional Autonoma de Mexico, Mexico City, MEX (7)

Building Index

The following index enables the reader to identify the page number on which a particular building is mentioned. Numbers in italics designate page numbers for figures. Numbers in italics that follow cities refer to panoramic photographic views.

Name Index

The following list cites page numbers on which the indicated names are mentioned. The list includes the authors as well as other individuals or organizations named in the text.

Names followed by years refer to bibliographic citations that are included in the appendix entitled "References/Bibliography." When the name is followed by initials, the designated page shows membership in one of the committees of the Council.

Subject Index

floor slab soffit 253
floor space 389
floor space requirement 28
floor structure 6, 8, 9, 12, 14, 15, 20
floor system 4, 6, 9, 12, 16, 21, 49, 343, 404
floor to core connection 402
floor-by-floor 353
flooring 354
flow 88
flow demand 89
flow failure 267
flow net 273
flow net analysis 306
flow slide 334
flue 348
fluorescent fixture 107
fluorescent lamp 110, 118
fluorine 225
flying dust 411
flying form 396, 397
foam rubber jointing strip 253
fog horn 355
folded sheet plate 16
folding door 234
food display 116
food preparation kitchen 149
food serving 67
foot bridge 408
footcandle 107
footing 269, 284, 286, 324, 325, 326, 328, 334
force 192
foreign exchange 352
foreign material 387
forging equipment 386
fork truck loading and unloading 133
forklift 355
form 404, 408
form cleaning 394
form handling 406
form removal 396
form stripping schedule 397
forming cost 10
forming technique 396
formwork 15, 37, 351, 404
formwork stripping 15
fossil fuel 65
foundation 3, 6, 58, 66, 259, 260, 262, 265, 276, 280, 282, 284, 286, 291, 296, 300, 319, 323, 329, 333, 343, 406
foundation beam 272
foundation behavior 327
foundation condition 260, 261, 355
foundation construction 307, 355, 374

foundation construction method 364
foundation construction time 373
foundation contractor 411
foundation cost 398
foundation design 58, 292
foundation detail 284
foundation effect 279
foundation element 259, 284, 300
foundation engineer 261, 278, 281, 323, 326
foundation engineering 260, 275, 323, 327, 330
foundation excavation 302, 323
foundation grade elevation 273, 280
foundation investigation 261, 262, 265
foundation isolation 58
foundation item 343
foundation manual 330
foundation mat 270
foundation modulus 289, 290, 291
foundation performance 327
foundation practitioner 356
foundation pressure 276, 298, 300
foundation problem 259
foundation reaction slab 273
foundation size 326
foundation sketch 346
foundation slab 284
foundation soil 261, 324, 326, 328
foundation spring 328
foundation staging 351
foundation strata 328
foundation structure 273, 274, 275, 276, 279, 323
foundation study 260, 261
foundation support 293
foundation system 257, 259, 260, 344
foundation wall 283, 284, 344, 345, 346, 347, 411
foundation wall rotation 285
four-basement scheme 346
foyer 252
fracture 225, 233
fractured rock 359
frame 5, 27, 30, 38, 42, 55, 241
frame building 299
frame structure 193
frame-shear truss 5
frame-shear wall 5
framed girder 25
framed tube 5, 43
framed unit 194, 195
framework 300, 355
framing 197, 411
framing member 193, 196

material tower 352
material tower layout 351
materials and details 232
materials handling industry 156, 158
materials handling system 156
mathematical modeling 323
mathematical probability 143
mature occupancy 173
mature population density 146
mausoleum 132
maximum angular distortion 300
maximum building area 348
maximum car floor area 153
maximum demand 106
maximum drag load 316
maximum fabricated assembly piece 388
maximum horizontal acceleration 174
maximum moment 289, 297
maximum passenger transit time 140
maximum pour size 395
maximum pressure 76, 77, 89
maximum reliability 102
maximum speed 153
maximum speed for elevator 156
maximum static pressure 89
maximum stopping distance 135
maximum uniformity 21
maximum weight load 390
maximum wind 293
means of egress 136
measured deflection 289
measured response 330
measured settlement 300
mechanical air pressurization 242
mechanical device 86
mechanical element 248
mechanical equipment 95, 102, 138, 170
mechanical equipment area 82
mechanical equipment failure 165
mechanical equipment installation 170
mechanical equipment room 79, 81, 120, 149
mechanical excavating equipment 373
mechanical fan 242
mechanical fastener 225
mechanical fixing 216
mechanical floor 45, 352
mechanical installation 16
mechanical joint 212
mechanical lifting equipment 352
mechanical loss 172
mechanical opening 35
mechanical parking system 183
mechanical release 390
mechanical room 37, 42, 348

mechanical service 8
mechanical shaft 12
mechanical space 34
mechanical subcontractor 350
mechanical system 3, 19, 63, 65, 95, 121, 343
mechanical system control office 120, 121
mechanical trade 65, 350, 396
mechanical ventilating equipment 170
mechanical ventilation system 78
mechanical work 43, 399, 407, 408
mechanical-electrical equipment 70
mechanical-electrical system 10
medical test 355
meditation 118
medium soft clay 303
medium-height, long building 393
medium-rise structure 24, 193, 219
meeting hall 97
meeting room 132
megastructure 52
Melbourne, Australia 69, 85, 103, 109, 111
melting snow 89
member 33
member stress 372
men 381, 406, 411
merchandise 118
merchandising 48, 52
merchandising area 117
mercury lamp 110
message-tube techhnology 181
messenger 139
metal 193, 219, 223, 231, 232, 233
metal ceiling 251
metal channel wall furring 235
metal construction 196
metal crated diffuser 252
metal curtain wall 192, 193, 196, 197, 199, 231
metal deck 12, 16, 348
metal decking 253
metal exposure 253
metal frame 233
metal framework 193
metal halide lamp 110
metal material 197
metal mullion 211
metal pan 243, 251
metal pan stair 243
metal panel 211, 218, 234
metal panel frame 211
metal plastic laminate 234
metal raceway 108

submerged unit weight 293
subsequent loading 266
subsidence 306, 331, 332, 333, 358
subsidence area 332, 333
subsidence effect 333
subsidence wave 333
subsoil 272, 301, 304
subsoil material 272
subsoil stratigraphy 279
substantial length 35
substantial movement 283
subsurface condition 261
subsurface erosion 306
subsurface investigation 261
subsurface portion 265
subsurface stratification 260, 293, 296
subsystem analysis 67
suburban development 177
subway 259, 265, 283, 378
subway construction 304
suction box 202, 205, 206
suction pressure 75, 205
suction-box method 201
sudden failure 375
suitability 161
suitable car door 152
sulfate 312
sulfur 333
sump 305, 347
sun control 212
sun shading 212
super highrise building 47
superimposed load 198, 392
superimposed loading 204
superimposed weight 269
superpump 75
superstructure 259, 323
supertall building 46
supplementary fire protection 240
supplementary illumination 114
supply air 252
supply air riser 80
supply air system 79, 80
supply duct 79
supply fan 78, 120
supply system 79
support 304
support bracing 270
support condition 8
support system 344, 364, 378
supported excavation 305
supporting element 7
supporting service movement 139
supporting soil 286
supporting steel 170, 171

supporting structure 6
supporting wall 262
surcharge 302, 303, 315
surface area 315
surface condensation 210
surface finish 16, 250
surface flaking 236
surface footing 328
surface quality 387
surface seal 236, 250
surfacing material 193
surrounding building 398
surrounding soil 285, 319
suspended ceiling 236, 237, 250, 252, 253
suspended floor 402
suspended steel frame structure 400
suspended steelwork 388
suspended system 23
suspension 56
suspension grid work 253
suspension rod 234
suspension system 134, 251, 253, 255, 403, 404
swamp 411
sway system 406
sweating 89
Sweden 311, 312, 332, 377
Swedish turning penetrometer 262
sweep 387
swelling 281
swing 389
swing landing door 152
switch box 233
switching equipment 99
switchroom 240, 253
Switzerland 183
Sydney, Australia 12, 56, 67, 122, 123, 213, 214, 215
Sylmar earthquake (1971) 254
symmetrical building 246
systems 19
system approach 129, 134
system configuration 157
system cost 183
system pressure 85
system restraint 167
system riser 108
system selection 156, 343
system transformer 105
systems engineering tool 162

table form 406
tabulating 115
tack weld 16, 21
tack welded 384